Willem Floor is an independent scholar specialising i:
Safavid and modern ages. His recent publications include *A Fiscal History of Iran in the Safavid and Qajar Periods, 1500–1925*, *Safavid Government Institutions* and *Titles and Emoluments in Safavid Iran*.

Edmund Herzig is Masoumeh and Fereydoon Soudavar Professor of Persian Studies at the University of Oxford. He works on the history of Iran in the Safavid and contemporary periods and his research interests also include the history of the Caucasus and Central Asia. His recent publications include *Early Islamic Iran* (I.B.Tauris, co-edited with Sarah Stewart) and a special issue of *Central Asian Survey*, 'Tajikistan: The Sources of Statehood' (co-edited with John Heathershaw).

IRAN AND THE WORLD IN THE SAFAVID AGE

International Contact and Political
Development in Early Modern Persia

EDITED BY
WILLEM FLOOR AND EDMUND HERZIG

New paperback edition published in 2015 by I.B.Tauris & Co. Ltd
www.ibtauris.com

Distributed worldwide by I.B.Tauris & Co Ltd
Registered office: 6 Salem Road, London W2 4BU

First published in hardback in 2012 by I.B.Tauris & Co. Ltd

Copyright © 2012 Iran Heritage Foundation

All rights reserved. Except for brief quotations in a review, this book, or any part thereof, may not be reproduced, stored in or introduced into a retrieval system, or transmitted, in any form or by any means, electronic, mechanical, photocopying, recording or otherwise, without the prior written permission of the publisher.

ISBN: 978 1 78076 990 5 (PB)

A full CIP record for this book is available from the British Library
A full CIP record is available from the Library of Congress

Library of Congress Catalog Card Number: available

Typeset by Newgen Publishers, Chennai
Printed and bound by CPI Group (UK) Ltd, Croydon, CR0 4YY

Contents

List of Illustrations   ix
List of Contributors   xi

1   Introduction   1
    EDMUND HERZIG AND WILLEM FLOOR

PART I
THE SAFAVID EMPIRE IN THE EARLY MODERN WORLD

2   The Safavid Empire and the Sixteenth- and Seventeenth-Century Political and Strategic Balance of Power within the World System   17
    BERT FRAGNER

3   The Safavid Economy as Part of the World Economy   31
    RUDI MATTHEE

PART II
DIPLOMACY AND WAR

4   The Political Relations of Shah Esma'il I with the Mamluk Government (1501–16/907–22)   51
    RASOOL JAFARIAN

5   From Rhetoric of War to Realities of Peace: The Evolution of Ottoman-Iranian Diplomacy through the Safavid Era   81
    ERNEST TUCKER

6   The Battle of Sufiyan, 1605: A Symptom of Ottoman Military Decline?   91
    COLIN IMBER

7   An Infernal Triangle: The Contest between Mughals, Safavids and Portuguese, 1590–1605   103
    SANJAY SUBRAHMANYAM

8   The Shaybanid Uzbeks, Moghuls and Safavids in Eastern Iran   131
    BARAT DAHMARDEH

9   Safavid Persia and Its Diplomatic Relations with Venice   149
    GIORGIO ROTA

10   The Embassy of Don García de Silva y Figueroa to Shah 'Abbas I   161
    LUIS GIL

11 The Holy See, the Spanish Monarchy and Safavid Persia in the
    Sixteenth Century: Some Aspects of the Involvement
    of the Society of Jesus   181
    Enrique García Hernán

Part III
Commercial Connections

12 Arduous Travelling: The Qandahar-Isfahan Highway in the
    Seventeenth Century   207
    Willem Floor

13 Trade between the Ottomans and Safavids: The Acem
    Tüccarı and Others   237
    Suraiya Faroqhi

14 Sweden, Russia and the Safavid Empire: A Mercantile Perspective   253
    Stefan Troebst

15 The Armenian Colony in Amsterdam in the Seventeenth and
    Eighteenth Centuries: Armenian Merchants from Julfa before
    and after the Fall of the Safavid Empire   259
    René Arthur Bekius

16 Sarhad's Account-Book as a Source for Studying the Commercial
    Activities of New Julfa Merchants in the Eighteenth Century   285
    Shushanik Khachikyan

Part IV
Cross-Cultural Perceptions and Exchange

17 Mapping the *Regnum Sophorum*: Adam Olearius's Representation
    of the Safavid Empire (1647)   293
    Elio Brancaforte

18 The French Presence in Safavid Persia: A Preliminary Study   309
    Jean Calmard

19 The Presence of Ancient Secular and Religious Texts in Pietro
    della Valle's (1586–1652): Unpublished and Printed Writings   327
    Sonja Brentjes

20 The Image of the Safavids in English and French Literature (1500–1800) 347
    Parvin Loloi

21 Farang, Farangi and Farangestan: Safavid Historiography and the
    West (907–1148/1501–1736)   357
    Mansur Sefatgol

22	The Augustinians in Hormuz (1573–1622) CARLOS ALONSO VANES	365
23	European Catholic Missionary Propaganda among the Armenian Population of Safavid Iran KRISTINE KOSTIKYAN	371
24	The Safavid Presence in the Indian Ocean: A Reappraisal of the *Ship of Solayman*, a Seventeenth-Century Travel Account to Siam CHRISTOPH MARCINKOWSKI	379
25	The Safavid Potter at the Crossroad of Styles YOLANDE CROWE	407
26	European Religious Iconography in Safavid Iran: Decoration and Patronage of *Meydani* Bet'ghehem (Bethlehem of the Maydan) AMY S. LANDAU	425
27	Borrowed Terminology and Shared Techniques in New Julfa Armenian Commercial Documents EDMUND HERZIG	447

PART V
THE CAUCASUS: THE INTERNAL FRONTIER?

28	On the History of the Political Relations of Safavid Iran and Georgia: King Luarsab II and His Captivity in Iran GRIGOL BERADZE	459
29	Exploitation of the Frontier: The Caucasus Policy of Shah 'Abbas I HIROTAKE MAEDA	471
30	Iranian-Georgian Relations during the Reign of Rostom (1633–58) NANA GELASHVILI	491
Index		499

Illustrations

Tables

12.1	Halting stations and distances (in *farsakh*) between Qandahar and Gereshk	218
12.2	Halting stations and distances (in *farsakh*) between Gereshk and Delaram	219
12.3	Halting stations and distance (in *farsakh*) between Delaram and Farah	220
12.4	Halting stations and distance (in *farsakh*) between Farah and Berjand	222
12.5	Halting stations and distance (in *farsakh*) between Berjand and Tabas	223
12.6	Halting stations and distance (in *farsakh*) between Tabas and Biyabanak district	227
12.7	Halting stations and distance (in *farsakh*) between Tabas and Saghand	228
19.1	Texts and authors quoted by della Valle	330

Figures

17.1	Adam Olearius's map of Persia (*Nova Delineatio Persiæ et Confiniorum*, 1655) from the *Vermehrte, Newe Reysebeschreibung*	295
17.2	Title Cartouche; detail from Adam Olearius's *Nova Delineatio Persiæ et Confiniorum* (1655)	296
17.3	Persian costumes from the *Vermehrte, Newe Reysebeschreibung* (1656)	297
17.4	Frontispiece to Hans Weigel and Jost Amman's *Trachtenbuch* (1577)	298
17.5	Tatar warrior from Hans Weigel and Jost Amman's *Trachtenbuch* (1577)	299
17.6	Detail from National Geographic map 'Caspian Region: Promise and Peril' (1999)	300
17.7	Dedicatory cartouche and 'Candide Lector'; detail from the *Nova Delineatio Persiæ et Confiniorum* (1655)	301
17.8	Tabula Asiae VII of Ptolemy's *Geographia*, Sebastian Münster (ed.), (1540)	305
17.9	Map of Persia by Johann Baptist Homann (ca. 1720)	306
25.1	Posset pot, h. 16 cm, w. 23 cm, English 2002-65, by kind permission of the Ariana Museum, Geneva	409
25.2	Posset pot, h. 14.8 cm, V&A 882-1876, photograph by author	410
25.3	Posset pot, h. 14.8 cm, V&A 882-1876, photograph by author	410
25.4	Posset pot, h. 14 cm, English	411

25.5	Eggcup, h. 5.6 cm, V&A 605-1889, photograph by author	412
25.6	Eggcup, h. 5.5 cm, V&A 1143-1883, photograph by author	412
25.7	Candlestick, h. 6.3 cm, V&A 2472-1876, photograph by author	413
25.8	Jug, h. 15.2cm, V&A 639-1889, photograph by author	414
25.9	Shoes, V&A 1067b-1876, 2476b-1876, 1067c-1876, 442-1874, 443-1874	415
25.10	Two pairs of European shoes, l. 13 cm, 78 046.ab, 78 046.22ab, by kind permission of the Museum of the Rhode Island School of Design, Providence, USA	415
25.11	Bowl, w. 18.8 cm, h. 8.8 cm, G200 Pl. 240 a,b, Qandahar excavations	416
25.12	Aster dish, w. 22.5 cm, V&A 2715-1876, photograph by author	417
25.13	Pot, h. 11.5 cm, V&A 1248-1876, photograph by author	418
25.14	Ewer, h. 22.7 cm, V&A C.185-1977, photograph by author	420
25.15	Ewer, h. 22.7 cm, detail of neck and monogram	421
25.16	Dish, w. 23.1 cm, V&A 2714-1876, photograph by author	422
25.17	Bowl from Erivan	423
26.1	Panoramic view of Bethlehem Church	427
26.2	Christ Pantocrator	428
26.3	Baptism of Christ	429
26.4	Martyrdom of St Gregory the Illuminator	430
26.5	Deposition scene by Christoffel van Sichem	432
26.6	Deposition scene in the Bethlehem Church	433
26.7	Deposition scene by Hieronymous Wierix	435
26.8	Temptation scene in the Bethlehem Church	436
26.9	Temptation scene by Hieronymous Wierix	437
26.10	Temptation scene by Christoffel van Sichem	438
26.11	Storm at sea in the Bethlehem Church	439
26.12	Storm at sea by Adriaen Collaert	440
28.1	The seal of Luarsab II	464

Contributors

Father Carlos Alonso Vanes, O.S.A.
René Arthur Bekius, PhD student, University of Leiden
Grigol Beradze, Chief Consultant, G. Tsereteli Institute of Oriental Studies, Ilia State University, Tbilisi
Elio Brancaforte, Associate Professor of German, Tulane University, New Orleans, Louisiana
Sonja Brentjes, Researcher, Max Planck Institute for the History of Science, Berlin
Jean Calmard, Honorary Director of Research, CNRS, Paris
Yolande Crowe, independent scholar
Barat Dahmardeh, independent scholar
Suraiya Faroqhi, Professor Emerita, Ludwig Maximilian University of Munich
Willem Floor, independent scholar
Bert Fragner, Emeritus Professor, Institute for Iranian Studies, Austrian Academy of Sciences, Vienna
Nana Gelashvili, Associate Professor, Ivane Javakhishvili Tbilisi State University, Tbilisi
Luis Gil, Emeritus Professor, Complutense University, Madrid
Enrique García Hernán, Researcher, Institute of History, Centre for Humanities and Social Sciences, Spanish National Research Council, Madrid
Edmund Herzig, Masoumeh and Fereydoon Soudavar Professor of Persian Studies, University of Oxford
Colin Imber, Reader in Turkish (retired), University of Manchester
Rasool Jafarian, Associate Professor, Department of History, Faculty of Literature and Humanities, University of Tehran
Shushanik Khachikyan, Deputy Director, Matenadaran, Yerevan
Kristine Kostikyan, Senior Researcher, Institute of Oriental Studies, National Academy of Sciences, Yerevan
Amy S. Landau, Associate Curator of Islamic Art and Manuscripts, Walters Art Museum, Baltimore, Maryland
Parvin Loloi, independent scholar (affiliated to Swansea University)
Hirotake Maeda, Associate Professor, Faculty of Urban Liberal Arts, Tokyo Metropolitan University
Christoph Marcinkowski, Senior Political Analyst, Berlin
Rudi Matthee, Roshan Professor of Persian Studies, University of Maryland, College Park, Maryland
Giorgio Rota, Researcher, Institute for Iranian Studies, Austrian Academy of Sciences, Vienna

Mansur Sefatgol, Professor of History, University of Tehran
Sanjay Subrahmanyam, Professor and Doshi Chair of Indian History, UCLA, Los Angeles, California
Stefan Troebst, Professor of East European Cultural Studies, University of Leipzig
Ernest Tucker, Professor of Middle Eastern and Central Asian History, US Naval Academy, Annapolis, Maryland

1

Introduction

Edmund Herzig and Willem Floor

The chapters in this volume were selected from papers presented at the conference *Iran and the World in the Safavid Age* held in London at the School of Oriental and African Studies in September 2002. Collectively, these chapters provide a broad look at the international dimensions of Iran's history from the sixteenth to the early eighteenth centuries; they explore Iran's diplomatic, military and economic ties with neighbours and more distant countries; and reveal Iranian perceptions of other nations and cultures, as well how the Safavid Empire appeared to the foreign diplomats, merchants and travellers who visited it. The Safavid age has long been recognized as a period of special interest in the history of Iran in the Islamic era. A period of rare dynastic continuity and stability, military might, artistic brilliance and economic prosperity, the two centuries of Safavid rule were also important in laying the foundations for the emergence of the modern state of Iran.

The aim of the conference was to bring together scholars currently working on the international history of the Safavid Empire, and to identify the main lines of research and the ways in which contemporary interpretations build on, or break with, previous understandings. Throughout the twentieth century the dominant school in Iranian history writing (among both Iranian and international scholars) was the nationalist one. That approach emphasized the importance of the Safavid period in the emergence of modern Iran – some scholars going so far as to claim the Safavid Empire as an Iranian (proto-)nation state. Such an approach tended to stress the Safavids' conflicts with their immediate neighbours, establishing and defending the borders of what became modern Iran, and their growing cultural differentiation from the Turks, Arabs, Uzbeks and Indians around them. The establishment of Twelver Shi'ism as the state religion and a growing sense of a distinct, Iranian identity were seen as central to Iran becoming less a part of a wider continuum of Muslim states stretching from the Mediterranean to Central Asia and the Indian Ocean, and more a clearly demarcated and distinct entity, whose links with other Muslim powers were in decline (or of declining importance), while relations with the rising powers of Europe (Portugal, Spain, France, the Netherlands, England and Russia) developed, hinting at the shape of things to come. The shifting balance of world power, it was argued, reinforced these trends, as the opening of maritime trade between Europe and the East caused a rapid decline in the overland caravan trade on the silk road, leading in turn to an atrophy in cultural exchanges between the Muslim societies of the Levant, the Middle East, Central Asia and the Indian Subcontinent. The better survival of and easier access to European sources rather than Persian or Ottoman ones further encouraged the focus on relations with Europeans.

Recent research has challenged this perspective. A broader reaction against Orientalism and Eurocentrism in research into Middle Eastern history has shifted the attention of Safavid foreign relations from Western Europe to its neighbours, the Ottomans, Mughals, Shaybani Uzbeks and Russians. The belief that commercial and cultural exchange along the overland routes of Western and Central Asia declined following European maritime discoveries has been successfully challenged. New research has also demonstrated that the advent of European navigation and shipping in the East, though it may have diverted part of the European transit trade to the ocean route, far from undermining intra-Asian trade, lent a new lease of life to maritime exchange between the ports of the Indian Ocean and the Persian Gulf and an intensification of Safavid trade with all its neighbours. The Islamic Revolution of 1979 affected Safavid studies both in Iran and outside, refocusing attention on the religious aspects of the age. In terms of international history, the implications of the adoption of Shi'ism remain keenly debated. There is an unresolved argument over relations with other Shi'i communities: what was the level and significance of the migration of Shi'i Arab clerics to Iran?; how important was the religious factor in the Safavid alliance with the Shi'i states of the Deccan? In terms of relations with Sunni neighbours, doubt has been cast on the idea that the new sectarian frontier was a significant barrier to wider cultural exchange, while the importance of religion as a factor (rather than a polemical instrument) in political/diplomatic relations has also been called into question: how far, for example, did sectarian differences facilitate anti-Ottoman alliances with Christian powers? There has also been new research into Shi'i attitudes and behaviour towards non-Muslims in this period, both internal minorities (the Armenians, Jews and Zoroastrians), and the Europeans (including Catholic religious orders) with whom Iranians were coming into increasingly frequent contact.

The chapters presented here contribute to these debates and open some new lines of research: in particular in the emphasis on the history of the Safavid frontiers – viewing them as arenas of dynamic competition among imperial and local actors, rather than as blank pages on which the metropolitan powers drew and redrew their borders; and in several chapters on the Caucasus, which reveal the region's unique character as a kind of internal border region, where the religious frontier, as well as competition with the Ottomans and Russians, led to a unique pattern of relations which extended also to the Caucasians (Armenians and Georgians) serving the dynasty at the imperial centre.

The chapters have been grouped into five parts. Part I provides an overview and context for the detailed studies that follow. Bert Fragner's chapter on Safavid Iran and the strategic balance of power outlines the political and religio-ideological genesis of the Safavid Empire, arguing that while the coronation of Shah Isma'il, the first monarch of the dynasty, as Emperor of Iran (*padshah-e Iran*) was no more than a continuation of a tradition established since the time of the thirteenth-century Mongol Il-Khanid dynasty, in the longer term the Safavid Empire marked a real change in the strategic balance of the region. After a long period of intermittent division between competing Azerbaijani and Khorasani centres, the Safavids reunited the eastern and western parts of *Iranzamin* and, from the seventeenth century, ruled the whole territory from a capital (Isfahan) in the heart of the Iranian plateau and used all the symbolic trappings of a unified empire (a uniform coinage and a distinct dynastic chancery style, *inter alia*). Fragner also emphasizes the traumatic impact of the Safavids' Shi'ism, especially in the extremist early days of the new dynasty, and its long-term legacy of mental isolation, but recognizes that after two or three generations of consolidation, Safavid Iran was well embedded within an international structure also comprising the Ottomans, the Shaybani Uzbeks and the Mughals. He adopts Marshall Hodgson's phrase 'the Gunpowder Empires' to describe the regional international system of the age. By the seventeenth century, the Safavid state had changed from being a disruptive challenge to a cornerstone of the existing regional order, with the dynasty's greatest ruler, Shah 'Abbas I, consciously striving to match his Ottoman and Mughal rivals (for example, in maritime achievement) and to surpass the Uzbeks. Fragner sees the 'identity game' as a part of this inter-imperial rivalry and argues that the development of a distinct Twelver Shi'i Iranian identity was a conscious or unconscious element of the Safavids' international positioning. While recognizing that the period also saw an unprecedented intensification of contact with the West, prefiguring the later developments of the West's imperial age, Fragner suggests that Safavid Iran's international place was first and foremost embedded within the system of the Gunpowder Empires.

Rudi Matthee's chapter on the Safavid economy as part of the world economy is divided into two parts. First, he assesses the importance of Safavid Iran's contribution to worldwide economic activities of its day, suggesting that although the Safavid economy is entirely unmeasurable and to a large extent is unknowable, it is clear that in terms of population, consumption, production and exchange, Iran was a relatively minor economic power in this period. Nevertheless, because of its location at what was still a strategic crossroads of commercial exchange, Safavid Iran had a significance which belied its meagre quantitative contribution. Matthee cites recent research to prove Iran's global importance in the international trade in bullion, textiles (especially from South Asia), raw silk and several other commodities, for most of which the Safavid Empire was primarily a country of transit, rather than of origin or destination. The global reach of Safavid commerce is indicated both by commodities – for example, Chinese porcelain and their Iranian imitations – and by the cosmopolitan merchants reaching Iran's bazaars, ports and caravanserais from major commercial centres throughout the old world, just as Iran's merchants 'were at home from Thailand and Tibet to Sweden and England'. This high degree of interconnectedness with other centres of international trade does not, however, alter the fact that Iran's role in regional and global trade was largely because of factors over which it had no control – for example, the conquest of Hormuz by the Portuguese at the start of the sixteenth century and their efforts to promote Persian Gulf trade and to block Red Sea trade produced a trade bonanza for the Safavids – leading to volatility and periodic crisis. In the second part of the chapter, Matthee explores Iran's commercial linkages to regions throughout the eastern hemisphere. As he notes, South Asia was the regional economic powerhouse of the age, and in many ways Safavid Iran was its satellite, tied by dual overland (via Qandahar) and maritime (via Bandar Abbas) routes. Trade with the Levant and the much smaller trade with Russia were to a great extent branch lines of the trunk route to India – most of the goods exported from Iran to these destinations originated in South Asia, which was the eventual terminus for most of Iran's imports from North and West, in particular of the gold and silver that figured so prominently. Throughout the Safavid age, direct maritime trade with western Europe remained relatively unimportant, as was the role of the European maritime trading companies.

Both Fragner and Matthee emphasize Safavid Iran's interaction with and integration into the regional political, cultural and economic structures embodied in the Ottoman, Mughal, Shaybani Uzbek and Safavid Empires. While western Europeans were beginning to penetrate these structures, for the most part they remained marginal to the concerns of the Safavids and their subjects. If new contacts with Europeans at this time excited mutual curiosity and exposure to unfamiliar arts, sciences and ideas for a small elite, closer to home Iran's political, commercial and cultural interaction with other parts of the Muslim world took on a new intensity, stimulating the circulation of fabrics and fashions, artists and artefacts from Isfahan to Istanbul, from Delhi and beyond in a way that touched the lives of many more. These ties developed despite the growing religious differentiation of Twelver Shi'i Iran from the neighbouring Sunni empires.

The chapters in Part II deal with various aspects of Safavid diplomatic and military history. Rasool Jafarian provides a detailed discussion of the relations between Esma'il I Safavi and the Mamluks, Zu'l-Qadrs and Ottomans at the start of the sixteenth century. He uses Arabic as well as Persian sources to show the complex and fast-moving pattern of sectarian and political interests that shaped relations, as well as the considerable room for manoeuvre enjoyed by the smaller and local rulers by balancing – and shifting – their allegiances among the major powers. The chapter also brings out the marked differences in the versions of events and explanations of motivation presented in Safavid, Mamluk and Ottoman sources.

Ernest Tucker's chapter explores the record of Ottoman-Safavid diplomacy through embassies, correspondence and treaties to show the shifting balance between the rhetoric of hostile religious polemic and of amicable and peaceful co-existence. He notes that even in the early period, there were instances when the two sides emphasized the protection of trade and travellers, while conversely, trotting out accusations of Safavid heresy to justify Ottoman attacks, and into the eighteenth century.

It is well known that the general tenor of relations improved from the hostility of the early sixteenth century to the long peace of the later seventeenth century, but Tucker's other findings - of a generally more conciliatory rhetoric on the Safavid side than on the Ottoman, and of parallels with contemporary trends in European diplomacy - will be new to most students of the subject. Tucker emphasizes the importance of the 1639 treaty of Zuhab, with its emphasis on border delimitation and the protection of travellers, noting that it served as a pattern for future agreements between subsequent Ottoman and Iranian governments.

Continuing on the western frontier, Colin Imber discusses the significance for the Ottomans of their defeat by Abbas I at the Battle of Sufiyan in 1605, which is described in Turkish sources as a disaster. Imber considers whether the defeat was indicative of an Ottoman military decline relative to the Safavids (similar to the decline relative to the Europeans that had become apparent in their campaigns against the Austrians on the western front in the immediately preceding period). However, discussing Abbas' successes against the Ottomans in 1603-4, when the shah recaptured Tabriz, Nakhichevan and Yerevan, Imber dismisses Safavid siege warfare as archaic (compared with Ottoman practice) and attributes its success to several other factors. The Ottomans were fighting on three fronts (eastern, western and domestic - against the *jelalis*). Political circumstances (the unstable allegiances of Kurdish frontier chiefs) favoured the Safavids. Also, Abbas showed special qualities as a commander: he was decisive, capable of leading forced marches and rapid strikes to seize tactical advantage (Tabriz 1603), and was able to motivate and maintain his army in the field for lengthy siege operations (Yerevan 1604). Imber's discussion of the 1605 autumn campaign and the battle of Sufiyan leads him to similar conclusions. While Safavid sources attribute success largely to Abbas's genius and Ottoman accounts stress the failures of their general, both place emphasis on leadership rather than the superiority of the Safavid army. Indeed, the sources indicate that the Safavids treated the Ottoman army with considerable respect, avoiding direct confrontation until the enemy had been worn down through scorched earth tactics and skirmishes.

Sanjay Subrahmanyam's chapter discusses the balance of power in the 'infernal triangle' constituted by the three powers of Safavid Iran, Mughal India and the Portuguese *Estado da Índia* at the turn of the seventeenth century. The Mughal state only expanded to become a major empire, with access to the oceans in both Bengal and Gujarat, during the reign of Akbar in the 1570s. The following years marked a watershed in Portuguese relations with Indian powers, as the Shi'i rulers of the Deccan ceased to be viewed as the main threat to Goa and the Portuguese position on the Indian mainland and began to be seen as potential allies in the face of the ascendant Mughal power. Subrahmanyam explores the views of the rival powers as reflected in Portuguese and Mughal sources, noting the tendency of both to underestimate the growing strength of the Safavids under Shah 'Abbas I and, on the part of the Portuguese, a failure to identify the threat this posed to their possession of Hormuz (lost in 1622).

Barat Dahmardeh's chapter also discusses the eastern borders of the Safavid realm, providing a detailed account of the relations of the local dynasts of Sistan with the Safavids, Shaybani Uzbeks and Mughals. In a pattern that bears close comparison with the situation of the Zu'l-Qadr and Kurdish frontier lords in the west, he shows that the local elites were primarily interested in securing the continuation of their own position and authority, and were ready to accept the suzerainty of the Safavids or other major powers, provided they did not seek to impose a too close controls. The long period of Safavid weakness in the East, from the death of Tahmasb I in 1576 to around 1600, when Shah 'Abbas I succeeded in re-establishing control over the feuding qezelbash and could turn his attention to external enemies, saw Sistan suffering intensifying plunder and invasion by the Uzbeks, leading some of its elites to seek support or refuge with Akbar, the Mughal Emperor, or to accept Uzbek overlordship. After Shah 'Abbas I's victory over the Uzbeks, however, he was able to restore Safavid authority in Sistan, retaining the local dynasts as governors to achieve local acquiescence to Safavid rule.

Giorgio Rota's chapter on Safavid-Venetian relations covers the entire Safavid period, allowing him to place the evolution of relations in a broad historical context. This suggests that relations fall into two distinct periods (before and after the accession of Shah 'Abbas I). He notes the recurring theme of anti-Ottoman military alliance, but argues that the emphasis on, and expectation of, military cooperation diminished over time, as the prospects of effective coordination against the Ottomans remained as remote as ever, and as both parties found other ways to deal with the Turkish threat. While political-military relations are the focus of Rota's attention, he notes that from the reign of Shah 'Abbas I, commercial and religious issues seem to have been as or more important in exchanges between the Serenissima and the Safavid court. Rota also argues that Venice's failure to send full ambassadors to Iran, and its haphazard selection of envoys, suggests that relations with the Safavids were not the highest of priorities.

Luis Gil's contribution, in contrast with Rota's wide-ranging look at Venetian-Safavid relations, presents a detailed study of a single Spanish embassy to the court of Shah 'Abbas I – that of Don García de Silva y Figueroa (1614–24). The mission was beset by difficulties from the start, not least intense rivalries among various persons wishing to present themselves as representatives of either Persia or Spain in their diplomatic exchanges, obstruction from the Portuguese authorities in Goa (who considered Silva's embassy a threat to their own authority and positions), and competition between the Catholic orders (Augustinians and Carmelites) with missions in Persia. Also, the timing was inauspicious, as the embassy coincided with a determined drive towards the Persian Gulf and Hormuz on the part of Shah 'Abbas I, a drive which brought Persia and Spain into military confrontation culminating in the Safavid capture of Hormuz in 1622. Gil's discussion of the embassy demonstrates the futility of Silva's mission (of which the ambassador himself was well aware), which was conceived in Spain on the basis of unreliable information and a poor understanding or Shah 'Abbas I's priorities and intentions.

The journal left by Silva provides a detailed, if sometimes deliberately incomplete, account of the ambassador's travels and negotiations, providing a wealth of information on a wide range of subjects, including one of the first descriptions of the ruins of Persepolis.

Enrique García Hernán's chapter discusses the role of the Jesuits in Papal-Spanish-Persian relations, especially their contribution to Papal and Spanish interests in the formation of a military alliance with Persia. This became prominent during the Pontificate of Pius V, whose ambitions to revive Christendom and Catholicism led to an alliance with Muslim Persia to defeat the Ottoman enemy (in preference to seeking help from the hated Christian schismatics), and continued in subsequent decades, with several members of the Society of Jesus being energetic advocates of military cooperation with the Persians against the Turks.

Trade and economy are the focus in Part III which opens with Willem Floor's chapter on the route from Qandahar to Isfahan in the seventeenth century. Concentrating on one of the two main overland routes linking India and Iran, Floor discusses the thriving state of trade between Iran and India and the continuing importance of the overland route. Merchants' decisions about which route to take depended above all on two factors: security and costs (notably tolls and customs dues), neither of which could be predicted with certainty, but about which travellers tried hard to get information. Turning to the desert route between Qandahar and Isfahan via Tabas, Floor suggests that it was an important commercial artery in the seventeenth century, despite the formidable obstacles presented by the terrain and climate. In spite of its importance, it has not been the subject of serious study, so Floor devotes a majority of his chapter to identifying the line of march and the way stations mentioned in the several sources that give itineraries, thereby contributing to the study of Iran's historical geography, as well as to Safavid history.

Suraiya Faroqhi's chapter on the Acem *tüccarı* (Persian merchants) and Ottoman-Safavid trade discusses the balance of commercial and political/military considerations that shaped Ottoman policy towards the Safavid Empire. Sometimes, especially during periods of war and internal trouble from the Shi'a of Anatolia, fears of subversion and espionage by Safavid agents led to punitive policies against them. The complementary desires to reduce Safavid revenues, to deprive the shahs of coin, horses, arms and other strategic goods, and to respond to the complaints of Ottoman manufacturers about competition from Iran for metals and other raw materials also encouraged the sultans to discourage trade with Iran. However, the benefits of trade, the appeal to the Ottoman elite for silks and other luxury goods imported from Iran, and the interests of other classes of Ottoman subjects – merchants and silk manufacturers, and the officials who took a share of the proceeds of trade – in the continuation of trade pushed policy in the opposite direction. Over time, as the Ottomans ceased to consider the Safavids a threat, the balance tipped towards the promotion of trade. The import of Iranian raw silk to Bursa, Istanbul, Aleppo and Izmir remained at the heart of this trade in the years 1550 to 1650, and that trade was mainly in the hands of merchants from Safavid

Iran, probably mostly Armenian, but the Ottoman documents do not distinguish between Muslims and non-Muslims.

In his discussion of Swedish interest in trade with Iran, Stefan Troebst explores German and Swedish sources to shed light on the subject. Sweden's interest was originally in gaining control, or at least a share, of Russia's trade with western Europe, but in the seventeenth century it was clearly understood that goods from Iran constituted an essential component of that trade. As early as the second decade of the seventeenth century, Stockholm tried to interest Moscow in trading via Sweden's Baltic port of Narva, rather than via Archangel on the White Sea and such initiatives, sometimes in collaboration with other European states, continued intermittently throughout the seventeenth century, with occasional efforts to establish direct relations with the Safavid shahs. In the 1680s Ludvig Fabritius was able to negotiate permissions for merchants from Iran (principally Armenians) to trade via Novgorod and Narva, granting them privileges in Narva to encourage the trade. This proved effective and from the 1690s the route via Narva became one of the regular routes between Iran and Amsterdam. This fruition of nearly a century of efforts to give Sweden a share of the Iran trade proved short-lived, however, as the outbreak of the Great Northern War (1700), the foundation of St Petersburg (1703) and Russian conquest of Sweden's territories on the eastern shores of the Baltic undid Fabritius' work.

Armenian merchants on the westward trade routes are also the subject of René Bekius's chapter, which traces the history of their community in Amsterdam in the seventeenth and eighteenth centuries using surviving monuments and inscriptions, Armenian books published in Amsterdam, and surviving Armenian and Dutch records. His findings indicate a substantial community (he has been able to identify some 800 individuals) that was in close contact and cooperation (as well as competition) with their Dutch counterparts, while retaining a distinct identity and forming the congregation of an Armenian church in the city.

Shushanik Khachikyan's chapter provides a detailed account of the trade of Safavid Armenian merchants on the basis of a surviving account-book. Sarhad son of Shahveli is one of the Armenians who visited Amsterdam, as discussed by Bekius, and the trade that he and his family was involved in was typical of its era, centring on the export to western Europe of Iranian raw silk. Khachikyan mines Sarhad's account-book for detailed information about the commercial and financial practices of Safavid merchants, as well as about the business activities of a single individual, shedding light on a subject that remains only partially understood.

In Part IV of the volume the chapters address various aspects of cross-cultural perceptions and exchange. Elio Brancaforte presents a study of Adam Olearius's map of the Caspian Sea, which he sees as marking an important transition from medieval map-making to the enlightenment era, with its greater concern for accuracy and a scientific approach. In these terms, the famous German traveller's map marked a major step forward for European knowledge of the Caspian, partly because of Olearius's inquisitive use of Muslim sources. Brancaforte also makes use of the pictorial and textual elements of the map to illustrate the representation of the exotic East to a seventeenth-century North European audience and to demonstrate the assertion of the author's identity and presence in the work.

Jean Calmard's chapter offers a comprehensive overview of the French presence in Safavid Iran, discussing the several purposes that drew the French to Persia in this period – from hopes of political alliance, to commercial interests, to religious motives. Compared with the French community in the Ottoman Empire (where there was a resident French ambassador from the reign of Francis I onward), French residents in Safavid Persia were few in number, though a diverse group nonetheless, counting among their number members of religious orders, merchants, adventurers and craftsmen, and including Catholics and Huguenots. While relatively few of these French residents left written accounts, it is clear that they acted as a conduit for cultural and technical exchange, though intellectual traffic was constrained by language barriers and by the limited mutual interest between them and the Persians.

Sonja Brentje's chapter on the writings of early seventeenth-century traveller Pietro della Valle describes his treatment of Iran as a 'construction of censorship and academic aspirations'. In a close examination of the Italian's published and unpublished work, she identifies a marked difference between della Valle the active traveller, who sought to find out as much as possible about the contemporary country and people, and della Valle the armchair scholar back home, who reshaped his travel diaries into a work of erudition, energetically editing his original observations, especially in relation to 'the image of the Orient, the image of della Valle himself and the image of ancient secular and religious knowledge and values' to produce works which, the author supposed, would be more appropriate to the demands of a cultivated and scholarly audience, but which provide a less vivid and original picture of the subject and of della Valle himself than the raw originals.

The place of Persia and the Sophy (the Sufi – that is, the Safavid shah) in contemporary English and French literature is the subject of Parvin Loloi's chapter. She explores the development of Persian themes and images from the enriching exoticism of the sixteenth century, when Persia seemed very remote and appeared more or less a fantasy land of untold wealth and opportunities for adventure, to the seventeenth and eighteenth centuries, when, in English works, writing about Persia became a safe way of raising controversial political subjects with impunity, while in the work of the French *philosophers*, Persia is used to cast an unflattering comparative light on the evils of French society and politics.

Mansur Sefatgol, in contrast, discusses the place of Europe in Persian historiography of the Safavid period, noting that Safavid historians paid little attention to the 'Franks', largely because their focus was primarily dynastic, and also partly perhaps, because of a conviction of the superiority of their own culture and beliefs. Eskandar Bayg Monshi is a partial exception to this pattern, and there is evidence of at least some knowledge of the countries and rulers of Europe, from the reign of Shah 'Abbas I, when contacts intensified, but by and large Persian authors show little interest in or knowledge of Europe and Europeans, except perhaps in their religious beliefs and in the schism between Catholics and Protestants (though those terms are never used in Persian sources).

Carlos Alonso' Vanes chapter deals with the Augustinian mission on Hormuz, which was established in 1573, a few years after the Jesuits departed, and continued until the joint Anglo-Persian operation that captured the island in 1622. He discusses the various roles and activities of the Augustinians, which ranged from ministry to the Portuguese garrison and Catholics on passing vessels, to proselytizing and medical work. As he notes, Hormuz was a key point in the Portuguese empire in Asia, so the mission there witnessed and participated in a number of interesting episodes and hosted several important visitors, including a number of envoys between the Safavid and European courts.

Kristine Kostikyan's chapter discusses the activities of Catholic missionaries among Iran's Armenian community (since missionary work among Muslims was forbidden) in Azerbaijan and the Caucasian provinces, and in Isfahan/New Julfa. She notes the factors that assisted the missionaries in converting Armenian Gregorian Christians to Catholicism, laying emphasis on the lack of state protection for the Armenian church and the resources of the papacy, which allowed its missionaries to win people over with free education, medical treatment, and the like. During the seventeenth century the Armenian church became more effective at resisting the efforts of the Catholics, both through published and unpublished polemic, and by using their access at court to weaken the position of the Catholic missionary orders. The split between Catholic and Gregorian Armenians created many problems and antagonisms for the community, and made it a focus for international rivalry, especially in the eighteenth century, when Russia started to project itself as the protector of eastern Christians in the Caucasus and beyond.

In his discussion of the unique Persian travelogue, The *Ship of Solayman*, written by the secretary to an embassy from Shah Solayman to King Narai of Siam, Christoph Marcinkowski emphasises the work's evidence of the number and importance of Iranian and Indian Shi'is in Siam at that time and discusses the information about them given in the travelogue and other sources. He notes the author's 'haughty perspective of supposed cultural superiority', which makes him neglect or disparage much of what he witnesses of Thai culture and society. He also notes the author's often strange or surprising remarks regarding geography, natural history and the peoples and governments he discusses. Though large parts of the relation are implausible, prejudiced or quite fantastic, they are of exceptional interest in showing us the knowledge and understanding – and their sources – regarding the outside world of a well-educated official of the late Safavid period.

Yolande Crowe's chapter draws attention to the hitherto neglected and underrated blue and white pottery of the Safavid of the seventeenth and eighteenth centuries. Locating production 'at the crossroads of style', she explores the influences – from China to England – that can be traced in the work of the Safavid craftsmen and remarks on the elegance and artistic quality of their work, often surpassing that of the patterns from which it was derived. A number of surviving pieces bear

Armenian inscriptions, whose significance Crowe discusses, suggesting that they may have been manufactured to order for members of one of the Julfa merchant families. Similarities with wares produced by Armenian potters in Ottoman Kutahya indicate, Crowe argues, that patterns travelled along the overland as well as the maritime routes. The evidence of openness to foreign styles and forms in the pottery discussed by Crowe contrasts sharply with the closed-mindedness of the author of the *Ship of Solayman* discussed by Marcinkowski.

In her exploration of the decoration of the Holy Bethlehem Church, Amy Landau considers the reasons for the Armenians' adoption of a novel style for the churches in New Julfa and traces the sources and transmission process that brought the Europeanized wall painting and iconography to Safavid Iran. She demonstrates the importance of this church to our understanding of seventeenth-century Safavid painting and its relationship to foreign stimuli and argues that it shows that Safavid artists' adoption of the Europeanized style began in the first half of the seventeenth century, several decades earlier than previously recognized. She suggests that one of the painters of the church decorations should be identified with the Minas mentioned by the historian Arak'el Davrizhets'i as having trained with a European master in Aleppo, and challenges the view that the woodcuts of Christoffel van Sichem II were the model for the iconography of the Holy Bethlehem murals, pointing instead to an earlier source, the bible illustrations contained in the *Imagines* of the Jesuit Jerome Nadal, which were van Sichem's prototype, and whose several editions are known to have achieved global circulation in the late sixteenth and early seventeenth centuries. The chapter also suggests that the Julfans' adoption of European church decoration is indicative of a broader cultural assimilation between Armenians and Europeans in this age, arguing that the Gregorian Armenian clergy, and the Jesuits who may have introduced Armenians to Nadal's work, shared similar didactic intentions in their use of religious imagery.

Edmund Herzig discusses the borrowed terminology and techniques recorded in surviving Armenian commercial documents of the Safavid period. He argues that these borrowings present an interesting example of selective cross-cultural exchange, one that requires further study. From the point of view of Safavid history, he suggests, the most interesting and significant conclusion to be drawn concerns the cosmopolitanism of the merchants of Safavid Iran, arguing that the borrowed terminology and shared techniques indicate that, at least as far as long-distance trade is concerned, the Safavid world was fully integrated into a wider trading world whose principal axis ran from the Mediterranean to the Indian Ocean.

The chapters in Part V focus on the Safavids' northern Caucasus frontier and their relations with the Caucasian Georgians and Armenians, many of whom gained prominence as members of the Safavid military, political and commercial elite. Grigol Beradze's chapter discusses the tragic story of Luarsab II, king of Kartli and martyr. Luarsab was taken prisoner by Shah 'Abbas I during his Georgian campaign of 1614 and was murdered in captivity some eight years later by order of the shah, because of his steadfast refusal to follow other Georgian princes in renouncing

Christianity and adopting Islam in order to find favour and employment in the shah's service. The second part of the chapter discusses Luarsab's seal, noting that it differs in some important respects from the seals of other Georgian kings of the era. Its shape appears to reveal Ottoman influence, but most notably it omits from its inscription the usual statements of vassalage and subservience to the Safavids. Beradze's cautious conclusion regarding such 'dissident' characteristics is that, 'for the time being it is quite difficult to say whether the 14-year-old Luarsab, immediately after ascending the throne of Kartli, personally (or on somebody's advice) refused to include the political formula of submission to the shah in the legend of his seal, or whether the absence of such a formula on his seal was conditioned by some other circumstances'.

Hirotake Maeda's chapter on the Caucasus policy of Shah 'Abbas I is based on research into both Georgian and Persian sources, making particular use of the recently discovered third volume of the *Afzal al-tavarikh*. Fazli Isfahani, the author of the volume, was *vazir* to the Safavid governor of Barda and Kakheti in the Caucasus, so is an exceptionally well-informed source. On the basis of the evidence from all these sources, Maeda challenges the standard 'slave soldier' paradigm about the Safavid *gholams*, demonstrating that many of the prominent members of this elite group did not enter royal service as captives of war, nor did they sever ties with their roots in the Caucasus; many were members of elite families which continued to thrive 'back home' and with whom they maintained connections. He points to the political significance of the rise of Caucasians in the early years of Abbas's reign, a time when the Ottomans had conquered the Safavids' Caucasian provinces. Prior to his campaigns from 1603 onwards to regain control of these territories, Abbas prepared the ground by bringing Caucasian elites into positions of authority in royal service (including a succession of Georgian mayors of the royal capital), rewarding them with fiefdoms in Iran and forming marriage alliances with elite families. While noting parallels with Abbas's policies in relation to other frontier provinces, Maeda argues that there were distinctive elements in the Caucasus, notably the extensive use of forced migration to alter the demographic balance, rendering troublesome territories in the Caucasus more manageable through the introduction of *qezelbash* tribes, while relocating en masse – while retaining their distinct cultural and nation identity – 'useful' Caucasian populations (Georgian, Armenian, Muslim and Jewish) to other provinces. The evidence leads to the conclusion that the defining characteristic of the Safavid *gholam* phenomenon was the transformation of local elites into state elites (rather than the recruitment of slave soldiers), just as the forced migration policy was directed towards the transformation of potentially troublesome frontier communities into useful subjects.

Nana Gelashvili also deals with Georgian-Iranian relations, but focuses on the career of Rostom, who ruled Kartli from 1632 to 1658, and also Kakheti for much of that period. Gelashvili explores Rostom's early life, as Khosro Mirza, a convert to Islam at the Safavid court, where he attracted the attention of Shah 'Abbas I, and where he played a key role in securing the succession of Shah Safi, earning the latter's trust and favour. The chapter discusses the intra-Georgian rivalries among the royal *gholams,* and discusses Khosro/Rostom's period as king and *vali* of Kartli, noting that the Safavid policy towards Georgia in this period was one of compromise. Georgian rulers who were loyal to the Safavid court were allowed a high degree of autonomy. The strong bond between Rostom and Shah Safi allowed both to exploit the potential of Rostom's rule in Kartli to advance their own political ends. These included extending the authority of the ruler of Kartli over Kakheti, and strengthening his hand against Georgian rebels and rivals, but also consolidating Safavid control in Georgia and the surrounding territories, while discouraging possible Ottoman advances and overtures in the region. While Rostom's reign saw a degree of Persianization and Islamization of Georgia, Gelashvili concludes that the latter at least was a very limited phenomenon and that Georgian conversions to Islam were mostly limited to 'political' conversions among the elite to demonstrate their attachment to the Safavid court. She argues that the patronage of Christian art and religion under Rostom and his pious second wife Mariam gives us a truer reflection of Rostom's religious affiliation and that loyalty to his Iranian master in fact allowed Georgia to preserve its traditions and rebuild its economic and social life after the disastrous wars and devastation of the preceding decades.

Part I

The Safavid Empire in the Early Modern World

2

The Safavid Empire and the Sixteenth- and Seventeenth-Century Political and Strategic Balance of Power within the World System

Bert Fragner

Following the breakdown of the Sasanian Empire in AD 651, no other dynasty in the medieval and early modern history of Iran compared with the Safavid Empire in terms of power, territorial extent and longevity. The Safavid period in Iran should be dated from the aftermath of the battle against the last Aq Qoyunlu prince, Alvand, and the subsequent coronation in 1502 of Shah Esmail in Tabriz as the *padshah-e Iran* (Emperor of Iran). It extends to the dethronement in 1732 of Tahmasb II, a son of Shah Soltan Hosayn, by Tahmasb-Qoli, later known as Nader-Qoli and subsequently as Nader Shah Afshar. However, we may also date the end of the Safavid period to the widely accepted 1722, the year of the Afghan conquest of Isfahan and the dethronement of Shah Soltan Hosayn. Either way, the Safavid period lasted more than two centuries.

At the end of the fifteenth century, the last phase of Timurid power in Khorasan and Transoxiana in the East, western Iran was in the hands of Türkmen princes. Before 1467 it had been under the leadership of Jahanshah the Qara Qoyunlu tribal federation; thereafter, it was under the Aq Qoyunlu, Uzun Hasan. In both parts of Iran, Chinggisid geopolitical conceptions originating from the period of Mongol rule (thirteenth and fourteenth centuries) continued to hold sway. The Qara Qoyunlu and Aq Qoyunlu considered themselves the legitimate successors of the Chinggisid Il-Khans. Both groups followed Il-Khanid bureaucratic and fiscal administrative traditions and, above all, they maintained the territorial conceptions brought into existence by Il-Khanid rule. Following the pattern of Ghazan-Khan, they considered themselves as the *padshah-e Iran* when they conquered the once Il-Khanid metropolitan capital of Tabriz, the *dar-al-saltane* (capital) of Iran's Mongol rulers. The conquest of Azerbaijan and particularly of Tabriz instilled in them the conviction of their hereditary right to rule the territory which they called (as the Il-Khans had done) *Iran-zamin* (the land of Iran), which included Khorasan up to the banks of the Oxus River and, in the south-east, extended to the fortress of Qandahar. The area beyond the fortress was conceived to belong to the North Indian Delhi sultans (and, subsequently, to the Mughal emperors). This concept had been challenged by the Timurid geopolitical model, according to which Khorasan, together with Transoxiana, shaped the core of a territory which Timur and his successors had legally inherited from the early Khans of Chaghatay. Thus, in the early sixteenth century the political geography of Iran was still defined in terms of Chinggisid mental mapping and territorial thinking.

This was but one aspect of political thinking under the fifteenth-century Türkmens of eastern Anatolia, who in the course of the preceding centuries had twice attempted to remigrate eastward to Azerbaijan from Asia Minor, where their ancestors had settled following the Battle of Manzikert/Malazgirt (AD 1071). Their attempts to remigrate to the East were made for plausible reasons; the strategic leaders of the strong and vast Ottoman Empire, after successfully conquering significant parts of south-eastern Europe, had made Constantinople their capital in 1453. At the beginning of the sixteenth century, they were preparing to extend Ottoman rule into western Asia; that is, towards Syria, Egypt and the Arab lands. It was not until the second half of the fifteenth century that the Ottomans turned their strategic attention towards the eastern parts of Anatolia, after many years of firm rule on south-eastern European soil.

The Ottomans used their military and political power to exert increasing pressure against Türkmen tribal pastoralists in central, southern and eastern Anatolia. Therefore, to the Qara and Aq Qoyunlu princes, 'Go East!' meant two things: on the one hand, these Anatolian Türkmen aimed to militarily resist Ottoman pressure from the west; on the other, they increasingly responded to this pressure, not by surrendering to the powerful enemy, but by withdrawing gradually to the East – that is, to Azerbaijan. The Aq Qoyunlu ruler Uzun Hasan (r. 1453–78) provides an illustrative example; to him, fighting Qara Qoyunlu power in Anatolia meant gaining an opportunity to establish a new empire to challenge the awesome Ottomans in the west. From 1467 onwards, Uzan Hasan held a political position in Tabriz which referred semiotically to legitimizing the inheritance of the vanished Il-Khans (as Jahanshah had done before him), but his strategic aim was to maintain his position in order to compete with the Ottomans. One of the results of this development was that the Aq Qoyunlu rulers gradually began to present themselves, not only as 'Iranian kings', but also, increasingly, as mature and able enemies of the Ottomans. This drew them into the political 'great game' of the era, which necessitated forming alliances with other powers that were in competition or conflict with the Ottomans, such as Venice, Genoa, Vienna and even Poland – all of which were also fighting the Ottoman threat. Thus Uzun Hasan and his successors developed strong diplomatic relations with non-Muslim European powers.

By the end of the fifteenth century, Türkmen tribal rulers in eastern Anatolia and in Azerbaijan had gained knowledge of a transregional and European-styled world policy. At the same time, they elaborated a historicist view which imagined a post-Mongol and Iranian layout, thus impressing their tribal subjects and the local population in their territories.

The Aq Qoyunlus' efforts to establish a strong empire comparable to that of the Ottomans and to form alliances with European powers were ultimately stopped, not so much by the Ottomans as by an unforeseen internal development, the sectarian Safavid religious movement, which had successfully won the support of an increasing number of the Aq Qoyunlu's tribal subjects as well as of their tribal cousins in Ottoman Anatolia. The Safavids' magic formula was an extraordinary amalgamation of tribal concepts and extremist religious ideas. This combination created an ideology with a capacity for mass mobilization that proved highly attractive to their tribal and pastoral followers and provided the structural starting point for their rise as a political force. We have to keep in mind that the early Safavids' religious concepts were not at all the same as those of the Twelver (or Imami) Shi'ites; rather, they were a popular mixture of gnostic and strongly extremist Ismaili ideas, albeit with some loose, allusive connections to the Shi'ite mainstream. Over the next centuries, this religious creed gradually emerged as the basic ideology of what is called the Alevîs religious movement in present-day Turkey. In about 1500, the fanatic and militant followers of young Shah Esmail considered him an incarnation of God, an idea which was maintained in the collective belief in his divine invincibility until the crucial Battle of Chalderan in 1514. Following this disaster, in the first two decades of the sixteenth century, religious and political pragmatism enabled the Safavid political elites to effectively foster Twelver Shi'ism, replacing the early radical and extremist faith which had been an important precondition to Shah Esmail's takeover of power in 1502.

We may summarize the historical situation after 1500 in eastern Anatolia and in Iran as follows: Aq Qoyunlu rule had laid the foundations for the development of an imperial structure, ready to compete with and rival that of the Ottomans, which became increasingly involved in creating transregional globalizing structures that created new strategic links between Iran and the West. In comparison, Safavid power somewhat resembled a regressive rollback. As a tribal and sectarian movement, *prima vista* it was not at all prepared to enter into globalizing structures but was supported internally by a strong tribal identity and religious mass fanaticism in Anatolia and Azerbaijan – apparently not the stuff proto-modernist developments open to global views would be made of. The religious differences between the Safavids and their Muslim neighbours – the Ottomans in the west and the Shaybanids in the north-east – indicated strong and dangerous political tensions between these empires. Almost all the neighbours of the Safavids were mainstream Sunnis whilst the early Safavids were propagating fanatical anti-Sunnism based on their extremist Shi'ite faith.

Until the first years of the tenth century (hijri) – roughly AD 1500 – Shi'ism was by no means discredited in the Ottoman Empire or among mainstream Sunnis in the Islamic world, in general; rather, it was perceived and widely accepted as a different branch of Islamic thinking. Thus outspoken Sunnis, such as the divine and later fanatic enemy of the Safavids Fazlollah Ruzbehan Xunji, and even the Ottoman Sultan Selim Yavuz, Esmail's great counterpart at the Battle of Chalderan, wrote poems glorifying the Twelve Imams.

It was the hostility and fanatical hatred of Sunnism among Esmail's ultra-Shi'ite adherents that caused a long-lasting counter-reaction. In the decades following the showdown at Chalderan, Twelver Shi'ism gradually took hold, replacing that fanatical early Safavid ultra-Shi'ism. But the Sunnis' bad feelings towards the Shi'ites and Shi'ism in general remained undiminished and were eventually directed at Twelver Shi'ism. Thus the beginnings of the great polarization between Sunnism and Shi'ism (and Twelver Shi'ism in particular) date back to the early Safavid movement, which at the time practised strange, extremist customs such as *tabarra* (cursing the Rightly Guided Caliphs), which has remained a trauma in Sunni mentalities up to the present day.

In fact, at the start of the Safavid period Twelver Shi'ism was imported into Iran largely from Syria and Mount Lebanon, and to a much lesser extent from Hilla in Mesopotamia. Shah Esmail embraced Twelver Shi'i jurisprudence as a way to maintain public order and to organize his administration on an evidently non-Sunni basis. There is little to suggest that his initial concern was with ensuring that it gained public acceptance as the faith practised by ordinary believers. The long process of reducing the original theocratic character of early Safavid rule to a more or less shari'a-based legal system in Iran was accompanied by the gradual implementation of Twelver Shi'ism as the official religious practice in Iranian society.

It may have been for these reasons that Iranian Twelver Shi'ites became the object of Sunni prejudice originally held against the early Safavids. Such prejudices were held by Ottoman Sunnis, Uzbek Sunnis, and even by the Sunnis of Muslim India. That Twelver Shi'ite Iranians have suffered a certain mental isolation since Safavid rule in the view of their Sunni neighbours can hardly be denied.

Let us once more consider the implementation of Twelver Shi'ism in Iran, or, more precisely, the gradual shift from the popular and almost anarchic extreme Shi'ism practised by the tribal adherents of young Shah Esmail – the Qezelbash – to the dogmatically and juridically well-codified Twelver Shi'ism that held sway in Iran in the second century of Safavid rule. The disastrous breakdown of the Qezelbash troops, who had once seemed invincible, on the Chalderan battlefield (1514) caused a longer-lasting political crisis. The resulting about-turn from early-Safavid extreme Shi'ism to Twelver Shi'ism was but one important measure of the Safavid ability to maintain political power. Under Esmail's successors, the renunciation of the shah's divinity in favour of recognizing him as the powerful supporter of the Hidden Imam and a Seyyed descended from Muhammad, as well as the *padshah-e Iran* in the tradition of their Aq Qoyunlu forerunners, turned out to be a perfect way to re-establish political order. Still, until the end of Safavid rule in the early eighteenth century, the belief of the fighting Qezelbash tribes that Shah Esmail was their divine *morshed-e kamel* (spiritual leader) was the fundamental basis of their loyalty to him – a religious concept that had nothing to do with Twelver Shi'ism but perpetuated the early stage of radical Shi'ism that had developed within the mystical order of the Safavids prior to the reign of Shah Esmail. The fostering of Twelver Shi'ism in the Safavid state and in Iranian society under Safavid rule to a great extent paralleled Iran's re-entry onto the global stage, after an interruption of two decades.

At the time of Esmail's death in 1524, his successor, Tahmasb, was but a little boy, and it was about twelve years before he gained some actual power. The political situation in Iran at the time was characterized by the permanent and cruel internal wars among various Qezelbash tribes, though these tribes were also successful in defending Safavid territories between Azerbaijan and eastern Khorasan against Ottoman invaders in the west and annual disastrous Uzbek raids throughout Khorasan in the east. The peace treaty of Amasya (1566) between the Iranian shah and the Ottoman sultan marked the beginning of a fascinating new relationship. In Safavid Iran, Tahmasb ruled as a pious Twelver Shi'ite king, having officially renounced all his pretensions to being the God-like leader his ancestors had been for Safavid supporters in territories controlled by the Ottomans. Documentary evidence shows that Tahmasb secretly harboured intentions to maintain this kind of religious influence on the Anatolian Qezelbash Türkmens. But following the treaty of Amasya, this influence shrank, and contact between those Anatolians and the Safavid shahs gradually decreased. The increased isolation of Qezelbash Türkmens from the shah's court led to the formation of the Alevîs, a rather closed religious group in Anatolia, which to this day has maintained a liturgical devotion to the memory of Shah Esmail, his messages and his poetry. In general, however, the Anatolian Alevîs emerged as an independent religious group.

The rage that coloured Ottoman political language when they denounced their heretic neighbours using pejorative terms like 'the Qezelbash state' or simply calling them *rafezi* or *ravafiz* – heretics – decreased markedly after the Amasya treaty. In the East, however, for another 10 to 20 years the Shaybanid Khans continued to appeal for Ottoman support in their righteous war against the Iranian semi-unbelievers in Khorasan, but eventually, at the beginning of the rule of Shah 'Abbas I, they too were reconciled to the existence of the southern empire. It was the same with Akbar's Mughal empire in India. If we consider the end of the sixteenth century as a kind of turning point in the history of western and south-west Asia, we should take into account that it can be attributed not only to the genius of 'Abbas I, who led Safavid Iran towards its golden period, but also to a changed geopolitical situation, which meant that Iran's existence as a homogeneous territorial state was no longer challenged by any of her neighbours. After his coronation, it was, therefore, up to 'Abbas I to take advantage of this gradually developing structural situation and calming internal strife by taking internal rather than external measures. This is important when considering the structural reasons for Iran's rise to cultural, societal and political peaks in the seventeenth century under Safavid rule.

It took two to three generations for Safavid Iran to become embedded within an Islamicate structure surrounded by the Ottomans in the west and in the Fertile Crescent, the Uzbeks in Transoxiana and the Mughals in India. These were roughly the lands designated by Marshall G. Hodgson as the 'gunpowder empires' (see Hodgson, *The Venture of Islam*, 'The gunpowder empires and modern times', Volume Three, Chicago, 1974, particularly pp. 3–15: 'Prologue to Book Five'). Within this structure, Safavid Iran was not so much in the avant-garde but rather a link in the chain, a coping stone which ultimately brought the neighbouring empires closer together. European interest in Iran followed a similar pattern. In the beginning Iran was not of interest to Western powers for its own sake. As it had been under the Aq Qoyunlu princes, Iran was attractive as an additional ally against the Ottomans, while for European traders Iran offered a route to India. In other words, Iran's appeal to the West was as a means of getting at an important enemy, or getting to an important trading destination. The Iranian *hinterland* was not the first priority of the Portuguese who were establishing themselves in the Strait of Hormuz; they were mainly interested in gaining the strategic advantage of a good point of control over the northern part of the Indian Ocean. It was not until the end of Tahmasb's reign, and definitely in the period of 'Abbas's rule, that European merchants began to be attracted to the commercial opportunities offered by Iran itself, its export products and its markets, where European goods might be sold or exchanged. If we consider the period from 'Abbas I to Soleyman – that is, the seventeenth century – as the heyday of Safavid power and of Safavid Iran, we should appreciate that this apogee was mainly the consequence of the wider strategic and economic context in which Iran was now embedded. The ruling elite around 'Abbas understood this. Under 'Abbas, the Safavid state made many efforts to achieve a level of political control over economic resources, and to stimulate trade through investment in infrastructure and internal security, and incentives to greater productivity, which would put it on equal footing with both the Ottomans and the Mughals, and make it definitely superior to the Uzbeks in Transoxiana.

Iran's development of a strong seafaring position is a good example. Because of its location in the Persian Gulf, Iran had been a strong seafaring power under the Sasanians. But during the periods of Mongol, Timurid and Türkmen rule, Iran's rulers paid more attention to continental trade activities than to maritime ones. Therefore, in the early sixteenth century, maritime trade bases were far more developed in the Ottoman Empire and along the coasts of the Indian subcontinent. Understanding the advantages this gave his two important rivals, 'Abbas took a keen interest in maritime trade, attaching an importance to controlling the Persian Gulf and Caspian ports, encouraging overseas merchants to open trade relations with Iran, and taking measures to guarantee their safety on the roads from the coast to the capital. The Ottoman and Indian examples may have served as models for 'Abbas's maritime interests, which eventually resulted in the annihilation of Portugal's position in the Persian Gulf. 'Abbas also attempted to replace the Qezelbash tribal army with a standing army based on the employment of royal slaves; this, too, can be plausibly linked to the influence of the Ottoman military structure.

There were other factors that supported Iran's effectiveness in gaining a strong international embeddedness. These may have been taken into account less consciously, but they nevertheless resulted in great success. As part of a larger structure that included the Mughals and Ottomans, Iran had an urgent need to project a distinct political and cultural identity, similar to their neighbours' projection of 'Rum' and 'Hendustan'. To optimize the political and commercial effects of such a performance of imperial identity, elements and components of this 'identity-game' would have to be distinctive from those of the Mughals and Ottomans but compatible with them as well. In my view, Iran's cultural self-representation functioned strongly in both directions. Being officially Twelver Shi'ite, it was not difficult for Safavid representatives to present themselves as a distinct cultural and political unit in comparison to their western, northern and south-eastern neighbours, all of whom were Sunni. Linguistically, the Safavid elites – dynastic, military and even administrative – were unofficially strongly Turkicized and so were readily able to communicate in Turkish (including the Muslim military elites in Mughal India, who had many Turkic elements). Persian, the official language of the Safavid Empire, was also the first language of political and cultural performance throughout the Gunpowder Empires, which helped Iran to position itself as the cultural heartland of the whole region, notwithstanding the fact that she still was perceived as a centrally located heretic territory.

In considering Iran's linguistic advantage, we should also take into consideration that among the Ottomans, Ottoman Turkish was perceived as the official language of the state and society, whereas Persian was widely esteemed as a language of refined poetry, mysticism and unofficial elite culture. In neighbouring Khorazm (Khiva), the Turkish language Chaghatay held a similar position to Ottoman in the lands of 'Rum', Persian being even more prestigious and the official language of administration, court and public life in the rest of Transoxiana. Nowhere in Mughal India was Persian the mother tongue, but it was the official elite lingua franca all over India, among both Muslims and non-Muslims.

Iran's linguistic position relative to the Ottomans and the Mughals was slightly different. Persian was 'at home' in Iran as an official language since the Safavid territories included most of the lands where Persian and its dialects constituted the vernacular mother tongue, but it was also appreciated in a literary and aesthetic sense both within and outside Iran. Turkish, which was so highly appreciated among the Ottomans and also in parts of Central Asia, was well known but less esteemed in Iran. It is still easy to imagine that in the non-Iranian lands of the region, Iranians may have enjoyed high cultural prestige, and paradoxically, their distinct religious faith might even have added to that prestige. This contributed to a permanent brain-drain of intellectuals from Iran into Ottoman and Mughal lands from the beginning of Safavid rule over the next two centuries. This migration of Iranians into neighbouring countries was caused by political reasons in the early sixteenth century, when many Sunni Iranians fled the new Shi'i Safavid regime. Later on, Iranians were attracted by higher incomes and wages. Compared with its Ottoman and Mughal neighbours, Safavid Iran was not as productive economically, although culturally and politically they were much stronger.

Following their victorious siege of Tabriz in the year 1502, the Safavids had taken power from the Aq Qoyunlu princes in western Iran, thus eventually inheriting the legacy of the vanished empire of the Mongol Il-khans. About six years later, it was the Qezelbash troops that captured the great Timurid capital Herat, located in Khorasan, from the last Timurid prince Badi-al-zaman Mirza. Although he had been defeated two years earlier by Uzbek warriors under Shaybanid command, it was the Safavids who reaped the rewards. Most of the artists and craftsmen that had belonged to the Timurid court of Herat were more or less willing to move to the new court at Tabriz. They brought many of the Herati traditions with them, thus securing the continuity of Timurid courtly culture under Safavid rule. It is worth mentioning that a good number of them did not stay in Tabriz for long but continued migrating westward into the Ottoman Empire where they were able to find better and more secure employment. Others moved into northern India. Nevertheless, in many practical respects we find more continuation of the Herati Timurid culture among the Safavids than among their Timurid grandchildren in what emerged some decades later as Mughal India – despite the fact that the Mughals consciously cultivated the memory of their Timurid ancestors.

The Safavids had some consciousness of the significance of such matters, which suggests a more developed sense of identity than one may expect. The India-based geographer of Iranian origin and identity, Mohammad-e Mofid, who flourished in the late seventeenth century, ascribed two important historical accomplishments to the house of the Safavids: one, predictably enough, was maintaining and sheltering Twelver Shi'ite faith in an entirely Sunni Muslim world; the other was the unification of western Iran with the formerly Timurid country of Khorasan, which had been ruled by the Aq Qoyunlu princes before the Safavids. Therefore, Tabriz was graced with the official epithet *dar-al-saltane* which dated back to the Il-khans, who amalgamated the then obsolete titles *dar-al-salam* (Abode of Peace) or *dar-al-khelafe* (Abode of the Caliph) for Baghdad, and the less prestigious *dar-al-molk* (Abode of Dominion) for the seats of government of princes subordinate to the Caliph. Thus from 1508 onwards, Safavid Iran had two *dar-al-saltanes*: Tabriz and Herat. Under Tahmasb, Qazvin became the third *dar-al-saltane*, and by approximately 1600, after Shah 'Abbas I had made Isfahan the Safavid imperial capital, it boasted no fewer than four *dar-al-saltanes*. It was no surprise when two centuries later the Qajars decided to promote the status of their new capital Tehran by honouring it with the re-excavated epithet *dar-al-khelafe*, thus avoiding further inflation of titles and linking their new capital to the memory of the legendary fame of 'Abbasid Baghdad. 'Abbas's preference for Isfahan as the imperial capital over Tabriz, Herat or Qazvin might be understood as another indication of his intended amalgamation of a western Iran, inherited from the Türkmen princes, and the former Timurid Khorasan.

The solid and consciously constructed semiotic self-representation of the Safavid kings also influenced the design of Safavid royal fermans and coins, and of the monetary system in general. Under Shah Esmail, there were two types of early Safavid coinage: in western Iran, multiples of various silver dinars were struck, such as *dinar-e tabrizi, dinar-e 'eraqi*; simultaneously, in Timurid eastern Iran, and in western Iran and eastern Anatolia, coins of Timurid type – *tangehs* – were also struck, the most popular of them being the *shahrokhi*. It was the Safavids who unified these different types of coinage into standardized multiples of silver dinars. Even the local coinage of *laris* in Larestan, a coin of strange shape that had been very popular in Indian Ocean trade, was re-standardized under 'Abbas's rule according to Safavid coin weight.

It may have been their repeated encounters with Ottoman royal fermans that stimulated the Safavid taste for developing distinct designs or their own chancellery documents. In their royal documents we can see a somewhat similar unifying and integrating attitude, to that of coinage. Dating back to the reign of Timur himself, the Timurids cultivated a very distinctive pattern of inscribing royal titles in royal decrees. This may have been inspired by the rather pompous chancellery customs of the Ottomans, who decorated their fermans with the famous Ottoman *tughra*, a well-known figure containing the ruling sultan's full name. To use something of equal value but clearly distinct in shape, Timur had a pattern of intitulation created which bore, among others, the Turkish translation of the Mongol expression *üge manu'* (a word of Us) originally ascribed to Chinggis Khan himself. The Timurid equivalent was the Turkic word *sözümiz*. In due course, it was not only the Timurid scribes who used this particular wording of intitulation; the Qara Qoyunlu and the Aq Qoyunlu made use of the same semantic element. Under Shah Esmail and in the first twelve or thirteen years of Tahmasb's reign, the Safavid kings continued to use a specific version of the *sözümiz* intitulation. It was in the late 1630s that a new pattern for Safavid royal decrees was designed, along with some other chancellery reforms. If the contemporary understanding of the word modern is mainly orientated along functionality, then these new Safavid ferman patterns could have been called modern.

Various seals of distinct shapes crowned the document, depending on its type. The calligraphic style used for this new type of fermans was no longer *ta'liq* (which until then had been typical of fermans of the *sözümiz* style); it was replaced with the much more readable and easy-to-write style *nasta'liq*, which had become fashionable in Persophone areas, primarily during the fifteenth century. To authenticate the document, the tradition of including an elaborate *tughra* (calligraphic monogram) – a tradition which was maintained in Ottoman practice – was abandoned in favour of writing a more practical formula at the top of the texts. Common formulae included *farman-e homayun shod* (a royal decree has been promulgated) and, especially from the reign of Abbas I onwards, *hokm-e jahan-mota shod* (a decree which the whole world obeys has been promulgated'). The *mohrdar* (the Keeper of the Seal) then had to attach one print of the royal seal at the top of the decree.

This pattern of Safavid royal decrees was maintained until the end of Safavid rule, with modifications by Nader Shah and ultimately the Qajars until the early 1920s. It clearly marked all kinds of Iranian chancellery documents as distinctive, not only from Ottoman but also from Uzbek (the latter used to stick closely to the Timurid pattern) and Mughal patterns. The Mughals were of Timurid origin and very proud of their heritage, but eventually they stopped using their ancestor's customs in coinage and chancellery affairs and developed their own.

Around the year 1600, during the reign of 'Abbas I, the Safavid dynasty reached its apogee. At that time – and for several more decades – Safavid Iran was firmly embedded in, and well recognized by, the neighbouring Gunpowder Empires, which together formed an interrelated kind of world system. In the period of 'Abbas, the Safavid Empire reached its definitive structural shape; theocratic aspects, which had been so forceful in the early stage of the empire under Shah Esmail I, were more and more limited to those military affairs and activities that were still based on the tribal structure of the Qezelbash. In addition to the Qezelbash tribes, 'Abbas royal power relied heavily on forces recruited from Armenians, Georgians and other ethnic groups from the Caucasus, which were in principle Christians. The status of these troops under Islamic Law was 'royal slavery' (a variant of the *mamluk* system of Egypt and the Ottoman *devşirme*). This system of military slavery was extended to administration too, mainly among the officials of the royal household. The domains belonging directly to the royal household formed a second and somewhat parallel state within Safavid Iran. On the one hand there were the state provinces whose revenue was – at least in theory – calculated by the *divan* (the state administrative institution), and used to support the Qezelbash troops and/or tribes within these provinces. On the other hand, there were the royal domains administered directly by royal agents, who were, like the 'slave' troops, directly subordinate to the king himself.

The mystical theocracy of Esmail I in the early years, and the later absolutist centralism associated especially with the reign of 'Abbas I, were the two pillars the Safavid Empire was built on. It was the absolutist centralism that enabled the rise of Twelver Shi'ism in Iranian society. For almost two generations, this system proved to be superficially very successful. At the same time, contradictory currents became increasingly visible. For example, the military loyalty of the Qezelbash depended on the king's charisma. But the Qezelbash tribes' territorial interests in the state-provinces assigned to their leaders, coupled with diminishing attention paid to them by the later shahs, meant that the shah's influence on them eventually diminished, and the Qezelbash transferred their loyalty from the shah to their own tribal federations and their provincial territories.

Similarly, the royal domains system, which for the first two generations after 'Abbas I proved a productive and effective system for generating capital for investment, fell victim to corruption and over-extraction of resources, setting the stage for the crisis for Safavid rule after 1700. It created a situation where a rather non-spectacular, maybe even ephemeral, military event in the shape of Afghan aggression against the central areas of Iran c.1720 dramatically endangered the existence of the whole empire. There were few left willing to defend the imperial rulers: the Qezelbash troops no longer believed in the king's divine character and charismatic power; royal slave troops lacked motivation because the system could no longer be relied on to pay their wages.

Let us again consider the Gunpowder Empires perspective; that is, compare Safavid power with that of its neighbouring empires. The breakdown of the Safavids roughly coincided with a similar crisis in the Mughal empire and the beginning of an era of continuous decline among the Ottomans, which set in after their failure at Vienna in 1683. Mughal reign eventually fell victim to British colonialism. The Ottoman Empire gradually started shrinking and was soon transformed into Atlantic Europe's 'semi-periphery', according to historians Immanuel Wallerstein and Ömer Lütfı Barkan. Safavid Persia had relied heavily on its own internal structures, and during the enduring crisis which struck the whole embedding superstructure of the Gunpowder Empires at the end of the seventeenth century, the Safavids had no means of resisting this general trend.

Still, there was no period in Iran's history when European travellers, ambassadors and envoys visited its lands as frequently as in the Safavid period. Commercial and diplomatic relations between Isfahan and the metropoles of the western world strengthened, and there was – and is – a lot of speculation about whether Iran was incorporated into the modern world system under the Safavids.

I doubt that it was. Within the system of the Gunpowder Empires, Iran not only held a top-ranking position in economic and political terms, but was also well-embedded, achieving a near cultural hegemony with the Ottomans, Uzbeks and Indians. Moreover, Safavid Iran was strongly based on her own structural resources and lacked the potential to expand that the Ottomans and the Indian Mughals had. Iran was the meeting point for regional commercial relations and communications within the Gunpowder system. What was – and still is – extremely important is the fact that the Safavids succeeded convincingly in establishing early semiotic markers of political and cultural self-identity: consciousness of territorial consistency; distinct religious consciousness; linguistic awareness of the intraregional importance and role of the Persian language; the conviction of being different to all neighbours in manners and behaviour, currency, representation of power, religion, and even architecture. The Safavids were able to present themselves successfully as the natural inheritors of vanished Timurid princely splendour.

This might be the reason for an interesting and, until then, rather rare and unexpected effect, namely the long-lasting collective 'nostalgic feeling for the Safavid period' after their rule had come to an end. Even two or three generations after the fall of the Safavids, princes pretending to be the legal heirs to Safavid power were able to find a political echo among the public. Karim Khan Zand found much popular support by pretending to reign as a *vakil* (regent) on behalf of Safavid power. On the other hand, Nader Shah accepted the crown (or, more precisely, the *jigheh*, the royal brooch of feathers) only on condition that the Qezelbash chiefs promised not to venerate the signs and symbols of the Safavid house any longer. In the nineteenth century Mohammad Hashem Rostam-al-hokama, an intellectual, bureaucrat and historiographer, tried to convince his ruler, Fath Ali Shah, that he should stake his claim not only on the strength of his Qajar inheritance but also because he represented the maintenance of a Timurid-Safavid-Qajar dynastic continuity. Recognition of the strength of the Safavid myth can be observed also in the actions of the Qajar prince and temporary governor of Isfahan, Mas'ud Mirza Zell-al-Soltan, who sought to combat the Safavids' hold on the public by painting over the tiles of some of their architectural remnants and by cutting down old poplars along the Chahar-Bagh Avenue in Isfahan.

The Safavid structures of power and political culture emerged creatively from an indigenous system. The Safavids optimized their achievements within the World System of the Gunpowder Empires, and the Safavids vanished when this system entered a period of collective crisis. Unlike Mughal India and the Ottoman Empire, Safavid Iran did not immediately become a peripheral or semi-peripheral entity within the Western modern world system, however. It was not until the nineteenth century that Iran experienced that destiny.

This may suggest a plausible reason for Iran's representative and collective cultural performance until today: whilst other countries within this system soon entered colonial or semi-colonial relations with Western powers, Iran remained unabashedly pre-modern until the end of the eighteenth century and was still well established within traditional and pre-colonial parameters. Maybe a bit more old-fashioned than her neighbours but with a sound collective feeling of cultural self-consciousness and pride – an attitude that can still be seen in many Iranians today. We – the Aniran people in the huge, scholarly community of researchers on Iranian culture and history – may sometimes complain about this attitude, but basically and deep in our hearts we admire and love it.

3

The Safavid Economy as Part of the World Economy

Rudi Matthee

In recent years a number of book length studies, articles and dissertations have examined various aspects of the Safavid economy. With the publication of Willem Floor's *The Economy of Safavid Persia*, we even have a detailed and comprehensive overview of economic activities, trade, agriculture and industry, import and export goods, in the Safavid period.[1] This chapter is not meant to duplicate any of this, much less to offer substantial new quantitative data on the subject. It merely seeks to tie various strands together in a synthetic exercise. Its objective is to examine the scope and significance of the Safavid economy, or at least its commercial sector, by placing it in the context of the world economy of the sixteenth and seventeenth centuries.

The first part of the chapter argues that, while Iran's economic output is unknown and probably unknowable, it is clear that its contribution to worldwide economic activities was relatively slight.

The second part, making the point that slight does not equal uninteresting or even insignificant, will examine and compare the many linkages that connected Safavid Iran to regions throughout the eastern hemisphere, from Japan and the East Indies to India, from Central Asia to Russia and Scandinavia via the Volga route, and from the Arabian peninsula to Anatolia and western Europe via the Mediterranean as well as the Cape route. I will attempt to assess the relative importance of these connections and how, over time, they were affected by economic and political change. It will be seen that, in terms of economic output Iran, with its small population and limited resources, lagged far behind the more populous areas of south and west Asia. Yet within these parameters, and given the fact that the country was home to less than 10 million people, Iran still made an important contribution to global economic activity, precisely because of its location at the crossroads of several commercial routes and its attendant function as a crucial entrepôt for a number of commodities. Iran exported a substantial amount of raw silk to the West, but even more important was the role the country played in the regional and transregional overland and maritime transit trade of consumer goods such as spices, sugar and textiles, which originated in India and the East Indies and moved westward to satisfy the markets of west Asia (including that of Iran). Of similar importance was the flow of precious metals going in the opposite direction. Safavid Iran furnished the Indian subcontinent with a considerable volume of gold and silver specie and bullion.

Nature, size and significance

The Safavid economy remains an elusive concept, alternately overrated in its output and global importance, and downplayed or even ignored as being insignificant compared with that of neighbouring India or the Ottoman Empire. At the outset a number of caveats are in order. Part of its elusiveness is related to the fact that in a country as large, diverse, difficult to access, and unevenly endowed with natural resources as Safavid Iran it is hardly possible to speak of one overarching economy. In the late nineteenth century one English observer noted that the people of Baluchistan spoke of Kerman the way the English peasant spoke of London.[2] The country is likely to have been even more fragmented and the isolation of outlying areas greater two centuries earlier. As various scholars have pointed out recently, the Safavid economy really consisted of a series of regional economies, each centring on a provincial town. In the seventeenth century Isfahan, with a population that at its peak may have reached a half million, functioned as the country's principal urban centre, the fount of political power as long as the shah was in town and, as the most populous city and a nodal point where many commercial links converged, the realm's most important trading centre.[3] Tabriz, with anywhere between 100,000 and 300,000 inhabitants in the mid-1600s, played a similar role for the north-western part of the country inasmuch as it was a crucial waypoint for trade with the Ottoman Empire and the Caucasus.[4] Shiraz was the most important city in the south, and in the early Safavid period perhaps the most important city of the country. Under Shah Esmaʻil (r. 1501–24) it may have had a population of 75,000, a number that seems to have changed little until the city's decline in the second half of the seventeenth century.[5] Little is known about the economic significance of Mashhad, the main centre of Khurasan. While the city is not likely to have been on a par with Tabriz, its position as the gateway to Central Asia and its location on one of the commercial routes to India made it the most important entrepôt for trade with the lands lying to the east and the north-east.

There were also commodities that spanned the entire economic realm. Silk was one. Cultivated in areas as diverse as the Caspian provinces and Shirvan, Yazd and Khurasan, it was exported in raw form via the overland route across Anatolia or Mesopotamia to the ports of the Levant, via the Persian Gulf around the Cape of Good Hope, and along the Volga route to Moscow, and on to Europe via the White Sea or the Baltic Sea. No other export commodity had such a wide geographical range, even though as an export product silk was a distant second to bullion in terms of volume and value. Textiles, too, covered all of Iran, entering and leaving the country at numerous points, but domestic output was very limited so that the bulk of them were imported. As import goods, textiles in fact matched bullion as an export commodity in volume and value.

The other dimension of the elusiveness lies in the limitation of our purview. When we analyse and try to make quantitative statements about the Safavid economy, we really address little more than the commercial sector. Trade, after all, is the only activity for which we have any real data – and at times the only activity for which we have any documentation. Floor argues that agriculture and related activities combined contributed at least 70 per cent of the country's GNP.[6] Whether or not we accept that figure, it is clear that an analysis of Safavid trade can never substitute for a discussion of the Safavid economy.

Of course, the overall lack of data involves commercial activity as well. We have little idea of the volume of trade flowing within the country, and our figures on import and export goods are virtually limited to the seventeenth century and only concern the merchandise handled by the maritime companies. Since we do not know their share of the total market, their numbers – which are anyhow incomplete because of the unreported private trading – may look impressive when tallied up but tell us little about the total movement of goods. For one, almost all information about imports and exports concerns Bandar 'Abbas. We have almost no figures for Kung, the other major port that at various times in the seventeenth century played a role just barely inferior to that of Bandar 'Abbas. Finally, a large proportion of imports and exports – including that of bullion – consisted of transit goods, and it is simply impossible to disentangle the two.

For all the deficiency in our quantitative knowledge, there is no question that, as a productive and consumer market, Safavid Iran was of modest size. According to the most plausible estimate, the total Iranian population at the height of the dynasty – in the early to mid-seventeenth century – numbered approximately 7 to 8 million people, perhaps less. India at the same time had a population of between 60 and 100 million, while the highest (and probably exaggerated) figure given for the Ottoman Empire at the turn of the seventeenth century was 30 to 35 million inhabitants.[7] In terms of sheer numbers Iran therefore compares with Central Asia, another humble economic player in the region.[8] About a quarter of Iran's inhabitants, moreover, were pastoralists, nomads who, eking out lives of subsistence or near-subsistence, made only a modest contribution to the country's economic life. Although the silk trade was fully monetized, cash played a minor role in many parts of the country. The income of the Safavid government in the seventeenth century tells the story. Combined state (*mamalik*) and crown (*khassah*) revenue is generally given as somewhere around 700,000 tumans, or no more than one-tenth of a tuman per inhabitant. Less than 200,000 tumans of this was crown revenue.[9] It is instructive to compare this figure with the income of the royal house in France, a country that, with slightly less than 20 million inhabitants, was a little more than twice as large as Iran. In the years from 1620 to 1630, a period of peace, the annual income of the French crown was approximately 40 million livres tournois, the approximate equivalent of 1 million tumans.[10] Observations by foreign traders are equally as suggestive. In a much quoted observation, the English in 1618, disappointed at their initial sales, called Iran 'miserably poor of money with little trade in itself'.[11] Later assessments by foreign merchants active in Safavid territory tend to echo this verdict, and especially the jeremiad about the scarcity of current coin among those who traded with Iran can be heard even at times when the economy was not obviously in crisis.

The volume of export products was equally as limited. If we disregard bullion, silk was the country's largest export commodity. In a good year, Iran may have exported 5,000 (perhaps 6,000) bales of silk. The second most important export commodity, that of Kirman wool, for some time in the later seventeenth century whetted the appetite of Western maritime companies desperate for an alternative to problematic silk, but it never fulfilled their hopes for neither the Dutch nor the English ever exported more than an annual volume of some 500 bales, and in most years they shipped much less.[12]

The arrival in the Ottoman town of Bursa, in 1511, of a merchant who had come from China via Iran speaks to the fact that Iran's economy was part of the world economy.[13] The Iranian-Armenians operating out of New Julfa had agents from London to the shores and islands of East and Southeast Asia. The resident Indian merchants, moneychangers and brokers who were active in all Iranian cities interacted with their kin in south and Central Asia and Russia. Iranian silk was carried to north-western Europe via Archangelsk on the White Sea and around the tip of southern Africa. Iran's Persian Gulf ports communicated with far-flung entrepôts around the Indian Ocean basin. Ceramics are perhaps the best example of Iran's hemispheric ambit. Safavid Iran was a consumer of fine white and blue Chinese porcelain until the collapse of the Ming dynasty in the 1640s, when production and export were halted. The ceramics factories of Kirman picked up the slack and began to provide Iran as well as Europe with imitations of chinaware.[14]

As Willem Floor argued, the importance of Safavid commerce lies in the fact that it was essentially a transit trade, because of Iran's strategic location between what was perhaps the world's most productive region, India, and what was rapidly becoming the world's most voracious consumer, western Europe.[15] India offered spices, textiles and, being largely self-sufficient, demanded bullion in return. Europe craved spices, textiles and raw silk, and had as yet little to offer other than silver and gold, both of which were abundantly available through the influx from the New World. This does not mean that merchandise just flowed through Iran without leaving a trace or that the country did not consume any of the imports – many of the spices and virtually all of the enormous amounts of sugar that were brought in remained in the country. It is clear, however, that Iran's role in all this was proportionally much larger than its population and its level of consumption warranted. Iran shared this feature with Russia and, to a lesser extent, the Ottoman

Empire, both of which saw a strong transit trade use their territory on its way to European markets.

The part Iran played as a transit and distribution centre explains the commercial activity even at a time when the region was no longer at the fulcrum of global developments. Braudel's choice of the period 1578-83, 'when the war of Portugal opened the great battle for control of the Atlantic and world domination', remains as good a date as any for the fundamental changes that would soon show up in the form of Western political and economic world hegemony.[16] Yet regardless of where we choose to situate the turning point, we now know that there was no immediate decline of the overland trade as a result of the expansion of the maritime link around the Cape of Good Hope. The traditional routes to the Levant via Anatolia and Mesopotamia continued well into the eighteenth century, and in the late 1600s the Volga route between Astrakhan and Moscow actually emerged as a modest alternative trajectory for merchandise carried between Iran to northwestern Europe. There is no question, though, that the new developments were taking place elsewhere. While the Europeans were integral, and not always the most successful, players in the Indian Ocean commerce, their trade was growing into a global network, and they alone were in a position to make efforts to acquire a commodity only if it was cost-effective and radically turn elsewhere if it no longer served their purposes. Iranian silk is a good example. Relatively expense, uneven in quality, difficult to procure given the distances involved, it was unreliable and, as such, simply could not compete with silk from Bengal. This circumstance also explains the inherent instability of the market. What the Dutch said about Indian cloth – that its market was unstable and showed wild fluctuation – is true for all goods brought to a market that itself had little absorption capacity and hence was quickly saturated.[17] Time and again in the seventeenth century merchants complained that Isfahan had been oversupplied with a commodity like broadcloth, which could no longer be sold at any profit. The combination of all these factors explains Iran's economic vulnerability. Unable to control either the origin or the terminus of the flow and short on extractable precious metal, the country was at the mercy of international developments, crises caused by war and political turmoil in nearby and distant lands.

In light of all this, it is inevitable to regard the Safavid economy as unknowable as well as tempting to dismiss it as unimportant. It would be mistake to give in to the latter inclination, however. For one, with the establishment of the Safavids, Iran seems to have witnessed a remarkable expansion of economic activity. The tribute the rulers of Hormuz paid to the Portuguese went up from 15,000 ashrafis in 1507 to 25,000 in 1517. In 1523 they paid 60,000 and in 1529 the sum had gone up to 100,000.[18] Second, precisely the fact that Iranian trade was for the most part a transit trade makes it fascinating to put it in a wider regional and transregional context. Merchants from all over Asia and Europe could be found in the main entrepôts and distribution centres, and Iranian merchants, Armenian, Jewish and Muslim, were at home from Thailand and Tibet to Sweden and England. Members of the Indian merchant diaspora were extremely well represented in Iran, and thus contributed to the integration of the country into a regional network that had South Asia as its engine and that stretched far and wide into the Asian continent and the seas around it, encompassing the Indian Ocean basin as far as al-Mukha in the Red Sea and Basra in the Persian Gulf, all of Central Asia, and Russia as far as Moscow. In this, South Asia was clearly the regional 'world economy', serving as the source of manpower and the industrial centre, manufacturing goods that were coveted by people all over west Asia and beyond, while the inhabitants of Europe, and to a lesser extent of the Ottoman Empire, Central Asia and Russia, functioned as consumers who were generally forced to pay for their habits with hard cash.

All of this does not mean that we cannot say or surmise anything about the Safavid economy with any degree of certitude. It just serves as a reminder that most statements will be qualitative and comparative rather than quantitative, and that the hard data that do exist must be handled with care and caution because they are so scattered and incomplete.

With these caveats in mind, I shall next try to summarize our knowledge of Iran's place in the world economy by considering the routes that linked Iran to India, the Ottoman Empire, Russia and Europe via the Cape of Good Hope. Central Asia will be left out for being a less significant connection. Despite recent attempts to rehabilitate Central Asia as a commercial powerhouse, the fact remains that it was a sparsely populated region that had little to offer the outside world other than horses, most of which were exported to India.[19] The trade between Turan and Iran is as poorly documented as any, but it is clear that, aside from some volume of fruit, lapis lazuli and Chinese rhubarb going from north to south, and Iranian horses and modest quantities of silk products being exported the other way, commercial traffic was limited, indeed could not be but limited given the small size of the respective resources and population of both regions.[20]

The trade with India

It is a truism to say that India's economy was altogether more vibrant than Iran's. This was mostly a function of a far larger population combined with climatic, physical and environmental circumstances – having to do with fertile soil, abundant rainfall, navigable rivers and accessible terrain – that gave the subcontinent a tremendous agricultural and industrial surplus. The country, moreover, had the good fortune that people in nearby and distant lands, ranging from Iran and Central Asia to western Europe, coveted many of the goods that it grew and manufactured. A useful general indicator of the relative strength of the Indian vis-à-vis the Iranian economy is found in the difference in the availability of capital and the circulation of currency as reflected in the difference in commercial interest rates. In India, in places as varied as Surat, Ahmedabad and Agra, interest rates fell from 12 per cent to 6–9 per cent per annum between the 1620s and the 1680s.[21]

In 1697, an annual minimum of 6 per cent was charged in Surat.²² In Iran, in contrast, commercial loans around 1640 carried an annual interest of 15 to 20 per cent, while Banyan moneylenders in Isfahan charged up to 18 per cent in the mid-seventeenth century.²³ Inasmuch as credit depended on the availability of cash in both countries, the interest differential suggests the disadvantageous position of Iran, a country of low capital accumulation.

It is well known that the trade between India and Iran followed either the maritime run between Surat and Hormuz, and later Bandar ʿAbbas, or the overland route from Lahore to Iran via Qandahar and Farah. The former route served in part as a transshipment vehicle for goods destined for Basra and further on to the Ottoman cities and Mediterranean ports. In the sixteenth century, for instance, drugs and spices were carried to Tripoli and Damascus via Hormuz and Basra.²⁴

We know little about the land route, but enough to be aware of its significance, especially at a time when the sea route was blocked. In fact, something of a complementary or see-saw relationship seems to have existed between the two trajectories. The Qandahar trade was important and lively, with interruptions only occurring at times of turmoil and war, when it was said to be less costly than the maritime route.²⁵ Thus in the first decade of the seventeenth century, when the ruler of Shiraz, a 'vassal of the Persians', disturbed Hormuz and banned caravans coming from the coast from going to Iran, the overland connection is said to have carried a far greater volume of goods than the maritime route.²⁶ This must have changed before 1618, though, for in that year the English noted that formerly – that is, before the fall of Hormuz to the Safavids and the closure of the port – only some 3,000 camels would travel between Lahore and Isfahan, but that at present the number had gone up to 12,000 to 14,000.²⁷ The Dutch in 1639 estimated that 25,000 to 30,000 camels laden with Indian cloth travelled overland, destined for Iran, the Ottoman Empire and Arabia.²⁸ In 1644, Isfahan experienced a glut of Indian cloth, with 5,000 to 6,000 camels carrying textiles having arrived from Agra within a period of eight months.²⁹ Aside from cloth, India exported large amounts of indigo to Iran via the Qandahar route. Sugar from Agra was an important part of the goods as well.³⁰ In the last decade of the seventeenth century the English claimed that the trade of Mashhad relied mostly on India, 'from whence comes all sorts of cloth, chints, shauls, indigo'.³¹ The road was occasionally blocked due to war between the Safavids and the Mughals, or Afghan or Uzbeg unrest and banditry, such as happened at various times in the 1630s and 1640s and again in the late 1690s.

The volume of the sea-borne trade tended to exceed that of the overland traffic except when shipping lanes were closed due to excessive piracy or war. We lack solid figures on the value of the maritime trade, but we have quite a few figures concerning the customs income of Hormuz from the moment in 1515 that the Portuguese took control of the tollhouse of Hormuz and the island became a Portuguese protectorate, and some educated guesses with regard to the magnitude of the movement of bullion from Iran to India. The Portuguese took over Hormuz, not with the idea of blocking its trade, but rather to tap into its riches and to further develop its commercial activity. They succeeded in this endeavour, so that Hormuz, assisted by a Portuguese blockade of the Red Sea, rose to become the main entrepôt of the Persian Gulf, accommodating more than 150 vessels in 1514.[32] The port's customs income shows typical annual revenue of some 100,000 serafin – a gold currency of 2.56–2.57 grammes each – for the period between 1515 and 1551, with one upward extreme of 135,000 (in 1550), and more modest figures in the lower 60,000 serafin range for some years. For the period between 1551 and 1573 no figures have been preserved. As of 1574 the average revenue almost doubled as compared with the earlier years, to 170,000, 180,000 and 192,000 serafin for 1574, 1588 and 1605, respectively. In 1610 tolls still brought in 153,000 serafin, but as the Iranians began to make life difficult for the Portuguese, the income seems to have fallen.[33]

Bullion exports exhibit a similar pattern. Haider quotes Godinho's claim according to which in 1602 the annual export of bullion from Hormuz amounted to 41.74 metric tons of silver. Between 1610 and 1622, the years the Iranians ousted the Portuguese from Hormuz and took control of the port, trade slumped and, as noted earlier, the caravan trade witnessed a fourfold increase. By 1630 the maritime connection resumed its dominance, and soon the volume of bullion exports may have reached the 25 metric tons suggested by Haider.[34]

In the words of Scott Levi, 'it is a defining feature of early modern Asian trade that markets around the world were stocked with India's textile surplus'.[35] Cloth indeed was by far the dominant Indian article exported to Iran. The colourful and expensive Indian textiles, foremost chits (chintzes), block-printed textiles from Coromandel, had a reputation, but it was actually rather coarse and cheap cotton cloth, salempuris, dongries (dungarees) and many other varieties, that formed the bulk of Indian textile exports to Iran.[36] Iran had its own textile-manufacturing industry but could not compete on price with these Indian calicoes, so that huge quantities of these textiles were shipped to the Persian Gulf.[37] In the 1659–60 trading season, the Dutch East India Company (Verenigde Oostindische Compagnie or VOC) sold a total of 80,197 pieces of Indian cloth in Bandar 'Abbas.[38] In 1662–3 the Dutch exported 33,600 pieces from Coromandel alone, the most in any year.[39] And in the 1708–9 trading season they imported 46,100 pieces of Indian cloth, at a value of some Dfl. (Dutch florins) 240,345.[40]

It is hard to tell how much of these and other textiles were destined for the Iranian market, for after arriving in Bandar 'Abbas much of the cargo was transshipped, carried on to Kung and especially to Basra and Mesopotamia, where dark cloth from which the local *abayas* were woven was extremely popular and always found a good market.

Yet the import of Indian textiles appears to have grown throughout the seventeenth century and at the turn of the eighteenth century reached enormous proportions, in terms of value on a par with highly prized spices such as cloves, pepper and sugar.

Sugar was another important item in the trade with India. Little of it was carried overland, but the volume shipped via the Persian Gulf, originating either in India or in Oman, a substantial sugar producer in its own right, was impressive. Rüdiger

Klein estimates the total volume of sugar around 1670 to have been approximately 3 million pounds.[41] Since hardly any sugar seems to have been carried in transit, this figure, if true, would have meant half a pound for each Iranian.

As is well known, the volume and value of the goods Iran exported to India paled in comparison to what the country received from the subcontinent. These goods consisted of pearls, rosewater, some wine, pistachio nuts, almonds, carpets, velvets, and modest numbers of horses. None of these amounted to any substantial volume, though – in 1634, for instance – the Dutch estimated the annual pearl exports from the Persian Gulf to be one camel load.[42]

Owing mostly to Iran's lack of viable export goods beyond silk, the country's main export to the subcontinent consisted of bullion and specie, both gold and silver. The capital flight this represented also derived from a related phenomenon, the aforementioned high cost of borrowing capital in Iran. This, as well as a desire to maximize the investment in Indian commodities made the VOC directors urge their agents in the Persian Gulf to minimize silk purchases and switch to bullion and specie exports. Even though the Dutch often lost on the export of specie (especially silver) from Iran, they continued to pursue this policy for lack of alternative options. The volume was enormous, and the proportion to goods, estimated by Om Prakash at 79.4 to 20.6 per cent in the case of the English and 87.5 to 12.5 per cent in the case of the Dutch between 1660 and 1720, reflects the importance of the phenomenon.[43] It has been estimated that between 1643 and 1683, average Dutch gold and silver exports from Iran to India easily amounted to Dfl. 500,000 a year, with some years showing a figure of above one million.[44] In the 1690s Iran was the single most important source of treasure for the Dutch Company.[45] Between 1701 and 1712, years when the Safavid economy had lost most of its former lustre, the VOC shipped 1,764,600 ducats from Bandar 'Abbas. V. B. Gupta estimates that between 1643 and 1687, the share of the Europeans in the bullion imports into Surat in most years was roughly equal to that of the Indian merchants.[46] If we accept this, with the caveat that Armenian merchants are not included and that no distinction is made between the flow coming from the Red Sea and that originating in the Persian Gulf, we still get an idea of the magnitude of the traffic.

Overall, it is clear that, despite the advent of the European maritime companies and the attendant highly visible trade connection that developed between Iran and Europe in the seventeenth century, the volume and frequency of Iran's trade with the Indian subcontinent continued to far exceed commerce with the West.

The Levant connection

While we have a good idea of the type of goods carried between Iran and the ports of the Levant in the Safavid period, precious little is known about the volume of trade. A Dutch consul in Istanbul in 1663 noted that about 20 caravans arrived from Iran each year, calling this a drop-off from previous years.[47] Each caravan consisted of some 300 to 400 camels, so that in slack times between 6,000 and 8,000 camels would annually have carried as many loads, amounting to between 1,200,000 kg and 1,600,000 kg of merchandise, to the ports of the Levant.[48] About half, or somewhat less than half, is likely to have consisted of silk. The exact volume of silk carried to Aleppo and Izmir is a matter of some dispute and anyhow varied considerably from year to year, but a reasonable estimate would be that in a good year 4,000 bales were taken to those Ottoman ports.[49] In the early eighteenth century, when Iran suffered outside attack and internal turmoil, caravans arriving from Iran still annually carried some 2,000 bales through Anatolia.[50]

But other goods, among them textiles, were part of the repertoire as well. It appears that many of the Indian textiles that entered Iran in myriad varieties were in fact destined for the Ottoman market.[51] A large volume of cattle, too, was transported to Ottoman territory. In addition, Iran exported varying quantities of cotton, madder, gallnuts, goat hair and drugs to the Ottoman Empire.[52] At the turn of the eighteenth century, the amount of goat hair is estimated to have been 400 to 500 bales per year.[53]

A variety of goods was carried to Iran from the Levant in exchange for the commodities heading for Ottoman territory. Textiles counted as by far the most important. While refined and valuable Indian ones went West, coarse cloth originating in Europe made its way East. In the mid-sixteenth century the English reported that the Armenian merchants annually brought 4,000 to 6,000 pieces of kersies from Aleppo to Iran.[54] Almost a century and a half later, the English still shipped large amounts of broadcloth to the Levant to be transported to Iran, where they were exchanged for silk, or even carried on to India.[55] The volume of broadcloth that reached Safavid territory via this route was quite substantial and most of it seems to have been consumed in Iran itself.[56] In 1696, the English surmised that each year about 10,000 pieces of cloth made their way to Iran from the Ottoman Empire.[57] The figure for the 1680s was probably higher, for in 1680 the English Levant Company exported a total of 28,771 pieces to the Levant, half of which may have ended up in Iran. The average annual shipment in the period 1671–83 was 19,863 pieces.[58]

None of this covered the value of Iran's exports, however, so that bullion had to be brought into the country to even out the balance. For the bullion trade between the Ottoman Empire and Iran we have no figures at all. We only get a vague sense of proportion and magnitude through the following two observations. One early eighteenth-century source claims that the merchants coming from the Ottoman Empire sometimes came with more silver than merchandise.[59] Another alleges that the Armenians – by far the most active merchants between Iran and the Levant – would bring 200,000 gold ducats with them with each caravan.[60]

The Russian connection

Armenian merchants from Iran traded with Russia long before Russia controlled the Caspian route.[61] Trade between Iran and Russia long remained insignificant, however. From the moment that the expanding city state of Muscovy extended its range to include Islamic west Asia in the sixteenth century, most commerce initially seems to have consisted of so-called embassy trade. This continued to be an important vehicle throughout the Safavid period. But as of the late sixteenth century, Persian, Russian and increasingly Armenian-Iranian merchants began to conduct a private trade of some significance. The upswing of trade was connected to the growth of re-export possibilities to western Europe – Russia, too, was mostly a transit country – and soon led to the establishment of a small and fluctuating Russian merchant colony in a place like Shamakhi, the gateway into Iran in the Caucasus.[62] It is estimated that more than 70 per cent of the value of Iranian exports to Russia in this period consisted of textiles. Of the goods carried by Butak Bayg, who in 1597 travelled to Moscow on an embassy trade mission, 90 per cent consisted of silk cloth.[63] Given the presence of a sizeable Indian merchant community in various towns in Azerbaijan in the seventeenth century, one suspects that, as in the case of the Ottoman Empire, most of this was in the form of Indian cloth, with a minor percentage consisting of precious textiles manufactured in Iran, velvets, satins and taffetas.[64] In fact, much of the cloth sold in Isfahan and Gilan had Russia as its destination, and Dutch reports indicate that the presence or absence of Russian and Polish merchants purchasing Indian cloth in Iran had an important effect on the market.[65] These precious textiles, manufactured in towns such as Ardabil, Tabriz, Qazvin and Kashan, continued to be among the goods exported to Russia until the last days of Safavid rule.[66] Carpets, morocco, saffron, dyes, precious stones and steel arms completed the assortment of goods carried from Iran to Russia, all in small volumes.[67]

Russia, in turn, exported modest quantities of furs, leather skins, wax, arms, sabres, spears, helmets and armour. Metal wares, axes, nails, and especially knives, were popular items too.[68] Even cloth of unclear provenance was carried from Russia to Iran via the Caspian Sea, and in 1644 it was noted that the supply of cloth from Muscovy and Aleppo had made the sale of cloth imported by the Dutch difficult.[69] The aggregate value of these exports did not equal that of imports from Iran, so that the Russians, too, had to make up their trade deficit by exporting bullion and specie. Figures about this are sparse. One observer noted in 1663 that silver accounted for 9 per cent, copper 5 per cent and gold 4 per cent of all Russian exports to Iran.[70] If these figures are at all representative, they suggest that Russia's deficit with Iran was much smaller than Iran's with India.

The assortment of wares itself did not undergo any significant change until the early eighteenth century.[71] Over time, the proportion of Iranian exports seems to have shifted to silk, though. Still, silk imports long remained rather small in volume, part of a trade that continued to be incidental, often part of the embassy trade, rather than regular and sustained. One observer from the mid-seventeenth century estimated the total volume of Iranian silk annually transshipped through Archangelsk – the main port until the end of the century – to be no more than 120 to 150 bales.[72]

It is only in the later seventeenth century that the silk trade turned into a substantial export commodity and not until after 1676, the year Moscow reinstated a treaty with the Armenian merchants that it had concluded in 1673, did silk exports take off. By the late seventeenth century, some 50 per cent of Iran's exports to Russia may have been in silk.[73] If we combine this with Kukanova's data, according to which on average some 400 bales of raw Iranian silk were transported through Russia in the late seventeenth century, we get a picture of the continuing modest volume of goods carried via the Volga route.[74] One modern author claims that Iran was the most important basis for almost all of Moscow's trade in the seventeenth century.[75] However that may be, the conclusion is still inescapable that, even in its heyday – that is, at the turn of the eighteenth century – the value of the goods carried via the Russian trade link did not exceed one-tenth of that of the Levant connection in its best years.

The maritime connection to Europe

We can be brief about Iran's role in the trade connection opened up by the Europeans via the Cape of Good Hope at the turn of the sixteenth century. As far as Iran is concerned, the significance of this initiative was rather modest. Even Steensgaard, who set out to examine the extent to which the maritime trade had undermined the overland trade, concluded that the diversion had been partial at best. If anything, later inquiries have further tilted the balance to the land trade.[76] The volume of trade taken to western Europe around the Cape of Good Hope in the 1620s is relatively well known (though it is often impossible to separate goods destined for Iran from those carried for other Asian destinations), but it is hardly impressive. Aside from silk, of which in most years no more than 500 bales was exported – only in three years did the combined exports of the VOC and the East India Company (EIC) exceed 1,000 bales – and in the second half of the seventeenth century a few hundred bales of Kirman goats' wool per annum. Little else made its way to Europe from Iran along this route.

Conclusion

Endowed with a small population and devoid of significant internal resources, Safavid Iran could not but be a modest economic player in terms of its productive capacity and the level of its domestic consumption. That the country nevertheless played a rather important role in the global commercial economy of the sixteenth and seventeenth centuries was due for the most part to its location astride some of the most active trade routes of west Asia. It is as a transit country for a variety of commodities, among them precious metals, that Safavid Iran made its mark on the world economy of the time. Similar to what Claude Cahen said of trade passing through Mongol territory, much merchandise 'went though the country, but didn't belong to it'.[77] Raphaël du Mans's well-known phrase that Iran was like a caravanserai, with goods coming in on one end and flowing out at the other, disregards the sizeable percentage of goods that remained and were consumed in the country, but nonetheless pithily captures this truth. Indeed, the intensification and acceleration of its interaction with the world and the part commercial traffic played in this development stand out as one of the defining features of the Safavid period.

After all the work that has been done in the last decade, it is hardly necessary to restate two additional, related conclusions. The first is that, at all times, the volume of trade handled by indigenous merchants, even those engaged in the maritime trade, far exceeded that carried by the maritime companies. The latter gained an important role in the movement of spices, textiles and bullion, but even by their own admission were no match for the Armenian and Indian merchants who plied their trade between India and Iran. The second is that the overland trade through Iran was but little affected by the advent of the Europeans and continued right up to the last decade of the reign of the Safavids, when a breakdown in security and increased political turmoil led to a severe disruption of the links with the Ottoman Empire.

Notes

Author's note: The research and writing of this article was made possible by a National Endowment for the Humanities fellowship at the Institute for Advanced Study in Princeton. Any views, findings, conclusions or recommendation expressed here do not necessarily reflect those of the National Endowment of the Humanities.

1. Willem Floor, *The Economy of Safavid Persia* (Wiesbaden, 2000).
2. E. A. Floyer, 'Journal of a route from Jask to Bampur', *Journal of the Royal Geographic Society* 47 (1877), p. 194.
3. See the discussion by John Emerson, 'Ex Occidente Lux: Some European sources on the economic structure of Persia between about 1630 and 1690' (Ph.D. dissertation, University of Cambridge, 1969), pp. 239–40, who concludes that the oft-quoted figure of 600,000 and more for Isfahan given by Chardin is exaggerated and that the true number may have been no more than 225,000. That number seems too low, unless it pertains to the city proper, as opposed to the entire oasis.
4. Don Juan of Persia gives a population of 360,000, a number that seems too high for the turn of the seventeenth century. See *Don Juan of Persia a Shi'ah Catholic*, trans. and ed. G. Le Strange (London, 1926), p. 39. Chardin's estimate of 500,000 for the mid-1660s is even more off the mark. See Jean Chardin, *Voyages du chevalier Chardin, en Perse, et autres lieux de l'Orient*, ed. L. Langlès, 10 vols and atlas (Paris, 1810–11), 2, p. 327. The total population may not have been much less than 300,000, though. The Safavid chronicler Junabadi claims that in circa. 1580 Tabriz counted 60,000 houses. See Mirza Bayg ibn Hasan Junabadi, *Rawzat al-Safaviyah*, ed. Ghulamriza Tabataba'i Majd (Tehran, 1378/1999), p. 629. Evliya Celebi in the mid-1600s and Villotte at the turn of the eighteenth century estimated a population of some 300,000. See Evliya Efendi, *Narrative of Travels in Europe, Asia and Africa in the Seventeenth Century*, ed. and trans. Joseph von Hammer, 2 vols (London, 1834; repr. New York and London, 1968), 2, pp. 33–41; and [P. Villotte], *Voyages d'un missionnaire de la Compagnie de Jésus en Turquie, en Perse, en Arménie, en Arabie et en Barbarie* (Paris, 1730), p. 175.

5. See Ronald Bishop Smith, ed., *The First Age of the Portuguese Embassies, Navigations and Peregrinations in Persia (1507-1524)* (Bethesda, 1970), p. 27. The figure of 200,000 for 1514, given in Gugliemo Berchet, ed., *La repubblica di Venezia e la Persia* (Turin, 1865, repr. Tehran, 1976), p. 275, is no doubt wildly exaggerated. Chardin, *Voyages*, 8, p. 435, gave Shiraz 12,000 households or perhaps 60,000 inhabitants in the mid-seventeenth century, and claimed that the number of households had fallen to 4,000 after a terrible flood in 1668. The Venetian traveller Bembo in 1674 reported 40,000 households, but he is likely inadvertently to have added a zero to the real number. See Ambrosio Bembo, 'Viaggio e giornale per parte dell'Asia di quattro anni incirc fatto da me Ambrosio Bembo Nob. Veneto', fo. 214, Ms. in the James Ford Library, University of Minnesota, Minneapolis.
6. Floor, *The Economy of Safavid Persia*, p. 28.
7. The figures for India and Iran appear in Stephen Frederic Dale, *Indian Merchants and Eurasian Trade, 1600-1750* (Cambridge, 1994), pp. 15-19; the number for the Ottoman Empire is from Ö. L. Barkan, 'Essai sur les données statistiques des registres de recensement dans l'Empire Ottoman au XVe et XVIe siècles', *Journal of the Social and Economic History of the Orient* 1 (1957), p. 26, and is discussed in Halil Inalcik and Donald Quataert, eds, *An Economic and Social History of the Ottoman Empire*, 2 vols (Cambridge, 1994), 2, p. 25.
8. The population of Central Asia in the seventeenth century has been estimated as approximately 5 million. See Dale, *Indian Merchants*, p. 21.
9. See the discussion in *Tadhkirat al-Muluk: A Manual of Safavid Administration*, ed. and trans. V. Minorsky (Cambridge, 1947; repr. 1980), pp. 173-82.
10. Pierre Goubert, *Mazarin* (Paris: Fayard, 1990), p. 186. For more detailed information on the issue, see Françoise Bayard, *Le monde des financiers au XVII siècle* (Paris, 1988), 22ff.
11. W. Noel Sainsbury, ed., *Calendar of State Papers, Colonial Series, East Indies, China and Japan, 1617-1621* (London, 1870; repr. Vaduz, 1964), p. 199.
12. See Rudi Matthee, 'The East India Company trade in Kerman wool, 1658-1730', in Jean Calmard, ed., *Etudes Safavides* (Paris and Tehran, 1993), pp. 367-9.
13. See Jean-Louis Bacqué-Grammont, 'Les événements d'Asie Centrale en 1510 d'après un document ottoman', *Cahiers du Monde Russe et Soviétique* 12 (1971), pp. 189-207.
14. For this, see T. Volker, *Porcelain and the Dutch East India Company as Recorded in the Dagh-Registers of Batavia Castle, Those of Hirado and Deshima and Other Contemporary Papers 1602-1682* (Leiden, 1971); and, more recently, the excellent study of Yolande Crowe, *Persia and China: Safavid Blue and White Ceramics in the Victoria and Albert Museum 1501-1738* (Geneva, 2002).
15. Floor, *The Economy of Safavid Persia*, p. 197.
16. Fernand Braudel, *The Mediterranean and the Mediterranean World in the Age of Philip II*, trans. Siyân Renolds, 2 vols (Berkeley, 1973), 2, p. 1176.
17. H. Dunlop, ed., *De geschiedenis der Oost-Indische Compagnie in Perzië, 1630-1639* (The Hague, 1930), pp. 565-6.
18. Georg Schurhammer, SJ, *Franz Xavier, sein Leben und seine Zeit*, Bd. II/1, Asien: Indien und Indonesien (1541-1547) (Freiburg-Basel-Vienna, 1963), pp. 141, 245.
19. See especially Scott C. Levi, *The Indian Diaspora in Central Asia and Its Trade* (Leiden, 2002).
20. For the various commodities exchanged between Iran and Turan, see Levi, *The Indian Diaspora*, and Audrey Burton, *Bukharan Trade 1558-1718* (Bloomington, 1993), p. 25.
21. See Irfan Habib, 'Merchant communities in precolonial India', in James D. Tracy, ed., *The Rise of Merchant Empires: Long-Distance Trade in the Early Modern World 1350-1750* (Cambridge, 1990), p. 393; and H. W. van Santen, 'De Verenigde Oost-Indische Compagnie in Gujarat en Hindustan, 1620-1660' (Ph.D. dissertation, University of Leiden 1982), p. 120.
22. India Office Records (London), E/3/93, Company to Doud, 10 March 1698, fo. 35.
23. Nationaal Archief (NA) (Dutch National Archives), The Hague, Coll. Geleynssen de Jongh 157, Gel. De Jongh, Gamron to Batavia, 31 May 1641, fol. unfol; Jean-Baptiste Tavernier, *Les six voyages de J.-B. Tavernier* (Paris, 1676), p. 528.

24. Sanjay Subrahmanyam, *The Portuguese Empire in Asia 1500-1700: A Political and Economic History* (London and New York, 1993), p. 76.
25. Warnerus, letter 22 February 1663, in K. Heeringa, ed., *Bronnen tot de geschiedenis van den Levantschen handel*, 2 vols (The Hague, 1910-17), 2, pp. 163-4.
26. Antonio de Gouvea, 'Memorial para el Consejo de Estado sobre la conservación de la paz y amistad entre Su Magestad y el rey de Persia', in Carlos Alonso, ed., 'La embajada persa de Denguiz Beg y Antonio de Gouvea, osa, a la luz de nuevos documentos', *Archivo Agustiniano* 64 (1980), p. 57.
27. In Samuel Purchas, *Hakluytus Posthumus or Purchas His Pilgrimes*, 12 vols (Glasgow, 1905-07), 3, p. 268.
28. W. Ph. Coolhaas, ed., *Generale missiven van gouverneurs-generaal en raden aan Heren XVII der Verenigde Oostindische Compagnie*, vol. 2, 1639-55 (The Hague, 1964), pp. 32-3.
29. NA, VOC 1146, Constant, Gamron to Batavia, 24 May 1644, fo. 928v.
30. NA, VOC 1135, Van Oostende, Isfahan to Geleynssen de Jongh, Gamron, 12 February 1641, fo. 672v; IOR, G/36/104, 24 February 1666.
31. IOR E/3/52/6285, Lee, Mashhad to Owen, Gombroon, 9 October 1696, unfol.
32. Vitorino Magalhães Godinho, *L'Economie de l'empire portugais aux XVe et XVIe siècles* (Paris, 1969), p. 768.
33. Vitorino Magalhães Godinho, *Les finances de l'état portugais des Indes Orientales (1517-1635)* (Paris, 1982), pp. 45-9.
34. Najaf Haider, 'Precious metal flows and currency circulation in the Mughal Empire', *Journal of the Economic and Social History of the Orient* 39 (1996), pp. 305-7.
35. Levi, *The Indian Diaspora*, p. 46.
36. For these terms, see *Hobson Jobson* (Delhi, 3d edn, 1994). A good discussion of the complexity presented by the bewildering variety in Indian textiles exported to the Middle East and beyond in this period, including the difficulty of understanding the terminology involved, can be found in C. G. Brouwer, 'White, silk, striped commerbands with silver heads: Textiles in the tollhouse of seventeenth-century al-Mukha, listed by Dutch traders', *Khil'a. Journal for Dress and Textiles in the Islamic World* 1 (2005), pp. 15-67.
37. For this, see Willem Floor, *The Persian Textile Industry in Historical Perspective 1500-1925* (Paris, 1999), pp. 144-5.
38. NA, VOC 1232, trade figures, 1 May 1659 to 30 April 1660, fos. 679v-80.
39. Rüdiger Klein, 'Trade in the Safavid port city of Bandar 'Abbas and the Persian Gulf Area (ca. 1600-1680. A study of selected aspects)' (Ph.D. dissertation, University of London, 1993-94), p. 335, and table on p. 336. This is the only study which provides figures on Indian textile imports into Iran in the seventeenth century. For an overview of the topic without any quantitative analysis, see Linda Hansen, 'Indiaas textiel voor Perzië, Ruilmiddel voor de VOC', *Jaarboek Stichting Textielcommissie Nederland* (2002), pp. 144-65.
40. NA, VOC 1798, List imports Gamron, 1 September 1708-31 August 1709, fos. 50-53.
41. Klein, 'Trade in the Safavid port city of Bandar 'Abbas', p. 391.
42. Dunlop, *Bronnen*, p. 481.
43. Om Prakash, 'Foreign merchants and Indian mints', in John F. Richards, ed., *The Imperial Monetary System of Mughal India* (Delhi, 1987), p. 172.
44. Willem Floor and Patrick Clawson, 'Safavid Iran's search for silver and gold', *International Journal of Middle East Studies* 32 (2000), p. 350.
45. F. S. Gaastra, 'The export of precious metal from Europe to Asia', in J. F. Richards, ed., *Precious Metals in the Later Medieval and Early Modern Worlds* (Durham, NC, 1983), p. 465.
46. V. B. Gupta, 'Imports of treasure and Surat's trade in the 17th century', in H. G. van Cauwenberghe, ed., *Money, Coins and Commerce: Essays in the Monetary History of Asia and Europe* (Leuven, 1991), p. 470.
47. Warnerus, letter 22 February 1663, in Heeringa, ed., *Bronnen*, 2, p. 163.

48. The figure of 300 to 400 camels is given in a 1682 French estimate. See Katsumi Fukasawa, *Toilerie et commerce du Levant d'Alep à Marseille* (Paris, 1987), p. 40.
49. See the discussion in Rudolph P. Matthee, *The Politics of Trade in Safavid Iran: Silk for Silver 1600-1730* (Cambridge, 1999), p. 42.
50. Neşe Erim, 'Trade, traders and the state in eighteenth-century Erzurum', *New Perspectives on Turkey* 5–6 (1991), p. 129.
51. Warnerus, letter 22 February 1663, in Heeringa, *Bronnen*, 2, pp. 163–4; Francis Richard, ed., *Raphaël du Mans missionnaire en Perse au XVIIe s*, 2 vols (Paris, 1995), 1, p. 138.
52. Chardin, *Voyages*, 3, p. 380; 4, pp. 165–6.
53. Jacques Savary, *Le parfait négociant ou instruction génerale pour ce qui regarde le commerce des merchandises de France, & des pays étrangers*, 2 vols, 7th edn (Paris, 1713), 1, p. 721.
54. Morgan, ed., *Early Voyages*, 2, p. 397, Edwards from Shamakhi, 8 August 1566.
55. IOR, E/3/52/6289, Major, Tabriz to London, 14 October 1696, unfol.
56. IOR, E/3/50 Company, London to Surat, 3 January 1694, fo. 165v.
57. IOR, E/3/52/6289, Major, Tabriz to London, 14 October 1696, unfol.
58. Alfred C. Wood, *A History of the Levant Company* (London, 1935), pp. 108, 116.
59. P. P. Bushev, *Posol'stvo Artemiia Volynskogo v Iran v 1715-1718 gg.* (Moscow, 1978), p. 255.
60. Vahan Bayburdyan, *Naqsh-i Aramanah-i Irani dar tijarat-i bayn al-milali ta payan-i sadah-i 17 miladi* (Tehran, 1375/1996), p. 113.
61. In 1544 the beglerbeg (governor) of Shirvan asked Tsar Ivan IV to renew the privileges enjoyed by Armenian merchants for trade with Moscow. See P. P. Bushev, *Istoriia posol'stv i diplomaticheskikh otnoshenii russkogo i iranskogo gosudarstv v 1586-1612 gg.* (Moscow, 1976), p. 40.
62. M. V. Fekhner, *Torgovlia russkogo gosudarstva so strananmi vostoka v XVI veke* (Moscow, 1956), p. 80.
63. Ibid., pp. 66–7.
64. A. A. Rakhmani, *Azerbaidzhan v kontse XVI i XVII vekov* (Baku, 1981), p. 181.
65. NA, VOC 889, Uitgaande brieven, 13 September 1665, fo. 514. In 1680 the Dutch complained that various Indian textiles were left unsold in Isfahan because the Polish, Russian and Uzbeg merchants were not showing up. See NA, VOC 1343, Casembroot, Gamron to Heren XVII, 2 July 1680, fo. 607.
66. V. P. Lystsov, *Persidskii pokhod Petra I 1722-1723* (Moscow, 1951), pp. 35–6.
67. Fekhner, *Torgovlia*, 52ff, pp. 79–80; I. G. Kukanova, 'Rol' armianskogo kupechestva v razvitii russko-iranskoi torgovli v poslednei treti XVII v.', *Kratkie Soobsheniia Instituta Narodov Azii* 30 (1961), p. 28.
68. Fekhner, *Torgovlia*, pp. 53, 55.
69. NA, VOC 1146, Constant, Isfahan to Heren XVII, 13 July 1644; and VOC 1152, Constant, Gamron to Batavia, 11 March 1645, fo. 83.
70. M. Kh. Geidarov, *Remeslennoe proizvodstvo v gorodakh Azerbaidzhana v XVII v.* (Baku, 1967), p. 77.
71. I. G. Kukanova, *Ocherki po istorii russko-iranskikh torgovykh otnoshenii v XVII-pervoi poloviniie XIX veka* (Saransk, 1977), p. 55; and Archives du Ministère de Affaires Etrangères, Paris, Perse, A.E. Perse 5, Padery, 'Memorandum on foreign trade in Iran, 1718', fo. 188.
72. 'Beskrivning av handelsförhållandena i Ryssland, avfattad av Johan de Rodes', doc. 19 in Artur Attman et al., eds, *Ekonomiska förbindelser mellan Sverige och Ryssland under 1600-talet. Dokument ur svenska archiv* (Stockholm, 1978), p. 114.
73. Wolfgang Sartor, 'Die Wolga als internationaler Handelsweg für persische Rohseide: Ein Beitrag zur Handelsgeschichte Russlands im 17. und 18. Jahrhundert' (Ph.D. dissertation, Free University, Berlin, 1992), p. 194.
74. Stefan Troebst, 'Isfahan-Moskau-Amsterdam. Zur Entstehungsgeschichte des moskauischen Transitprivilegs für die Armenische Handelskompagnie in Persien (1666–1676)', 208, quoting Kukanova, *Ocherki*, table 2, pp. 91–9.

75. O. P. Markova, 'Russko-iranskaia torgovlia v poslednie desiateletiia XVIII veka', *Uchenye Zapiski Institut Vostokvednenia A.N. Azerb. SSR* 1 (1959), p. 103.
76. See, for instance, Matthee, *The Politics of Trade in Safavid Iran*.
77. Claude Cahen, 'Quelques mots sur le déclin commercial du monde musulman à la fin du moyen age', in Michael Cook, ed., *Studies in the Economic History of the Middle East from the Rise of Islam to the Present Day* (London, 1970), p. 36.

Part II

Diplomacy and War

4

The Political Relations of Shah Esmaʻil I with the Mamluk Government (1501–16/907–22)

Rasool Jafarian

In the late ninth century AH/fifteenth century AD, three powerful governments ruled the territory between Anatolia, Egypt-Damascus and Iran.

The first was the Mamluks (648–923/1250–1517), an ancient government that had been ruling the rich land of Egypt and Damascus since the fourth decade of the seventh century AH onwards. After resisting the Mongols, and defeating them in ʻAyn Jalut (16 Ramadan 658/3 September 1260), the Mamluks transferred the ʻAbbasid caliphate to Cairo as the capital. From its establishment by Shajarat-al-durr in 648/1250 to its fall in 922/1516, when Qansawh-al-Ghuri[1] (906–22/1501–16) was killed by Sultan Selim, it proved to be one of the most powerful and enduring Islamic governments.

The second government was the Ottoman Empire, which by the sixteenth century had ambitions to replace the Mamluks and establish its authority over the two sacred sanctuaries of Mecca and Medina. The third one was Aq Qoyunlu which, after overthrowing Qara Qoyunlu, occupied eastern Asia minor during the reign of its most powerful monarch Uzun Hasan (857–82/1453–78). It gained possession of Iran (as far as Yazd, Shiraz and Isfahan) from the Timurids after defeating and killing Sultan Abu Saʻid in Azerbaijan in 873/1468–9. Though it was militarily weaker, this government's power was based on a tribal confederacy that made it strong enough to be a potential problem for both the Ottoman and Mamluk governments. At first, the Aq Qoyunlu government was not a threat to the Ottomans. It strived to penetrate into the Turkoman-inhabited area of Anatolia that separated Ottoman and Mamluk territory and was close to the Aq Qoyunlu capital in Tabriz. This made the Turkoman confrontation with the Ottomans more serious. At the same time, the Europeans fighting the Ottomans also tried to stir Uzun Hasan against the Ottomans. The result was a battle between Uzun Hasan and the Ottoman sultan in Konya in 876/1471–2. The Aq Qoyunlu army was defeated and had to be satisfied with the areas already seized. Meanwhile, the Mamluks had good relations with the Ottomans and felt the danger from Uzun Hasan in the northern Euphrates valley and hence preferred to support the Ottoman government. Earlier, Uzun Hasan's constant attacks on Aleppo had resulted in war between the Aq Qoyunlu and the Mamluks. Uzun Hasan hoped to reach a compromise with the Mamluks but due to the coalition of Mamluks and Ottomans against the Turkomans he could not achieve one.[2]

Although Uzun Hasan passed away in 882, the Aq Qoyunlu, led by Sultan Ya'qub, remained in power in Tabriz, Fars and Iraq. During Ya'qub's reign another conflict with the Mamluks arose when Amir Sayf, one of the emirs in northern Damascus, revolted against Qaitbay, the Mamluk sultan, in 885/1480. He was defeated by Yishbak, a well-known Mamluk commander, and had to flee to Ruha in the realm of Aq Qoyunlu. Yishbak tried to occupy the city, was defeated and then killed. Qaitbay, the Mamluk sultan, dispatched another army but after Sultan Ya'qub's apology and negotiations, peace was established between them.[3]

When, in 906 and 907, Fars, Iraq and a part of eastern Anatolia were conquered by Shah Esma'il, the Safavids replaced the Aq Qoyunlu as the third powerful government.

Ottoman and Mamluk ties until Selim I

There was a long history of friendly ties between the Ottomans and Mamluks. Since Mamluk sultans had the 'Abbasid caliphates as a legitimizing element of power and ruled the two sacred sanctuaries, they were much respected by Sunnite Muslims, especially the Ottomans. Ever since the Ottomans formed an emirate on the boundary separating Islam from non-Islam in Anatolia right up to its conquest of Constantinople (857/1453), the rationale behind Ottoman conquests had not been to establish an empire but to spread Islam. The final defeat of the Byzantines fulfilled a centuries-old Muslim ambition.[4] Therefore, until the late fifteenth century, the Ottomans did not face any border problems from either the Mamluk or the Aq Qoyunlu. There were several reasons for this. One was racial competition between these governments of Turkish origin, which paved the way for them to compete psychologically. At the same time, the Europeans were not passive either. They tried to stimulate the enemies of the Ottomans into creating problems on the eastern borders in order to divert them from the west. Another reason was the emergence of Turkoman tribes between Aleppo and Anatolia and their attempt to gain either Mamluk or Ottoman support against their rivals. One of these was the Zu'l-Qadr[5] Turkoman tribe, which had ruled over the area bearing its name for nearly two centuries (738–928/1337–1522). During the latter years of the reign of the emir, Sayf-al-Din Malik Aslan, one of the Zu'l-Qadr leaders ruling over Albistan, the provincial capital on the Mamluk side, was assassinated in Cairo in 870/1465–6. The Mamluk sultan appointed his brother, Shah

Budaq, as his successor, but after a while another brother, Shah Savar, revolted against Shah Budaq with the support and stimulation of the Ottomans and seized power. In order to support Budaq, Khush Qadam, the Mamluk sultan, deployed troops to suppress Shah Savar. Despite his efforts, Shah Savar remained in power and resisted attempts to overthrow him. However, after Qaytbay assumed power in 872/1467-8 and deployed more troops in 876/1471-2, Shah Savar was not only defeated by Mamluk forces but also captured and then killed in Cairo in 877. Shah Budaq was reinstalled to power in the Zu'l-Qadr area by 884/1479, but a third brother, 'Ala' al-Dawle, defeated him and remained in power until he was murdered by Sultan Selim in 921/1515. The Zu'l-Qadr government was traditionally dependent upon the Mamluks although it was more autonomous during 'Ala' al-Dawle's time. In 886/1481 Sultan Mehmet II passed away and Sultan Bayezid succeeded him. Later on, peace between the Ottomans and Mamluks was replaced by dispute. One dispute was related to the frontier area separating the two governments. To conserve his autonomous government, 'Ala' al-Dawle had a two-fold policy towards the Ottoman and Mamluk governments. In spite of his traditional dependence upon the Mamluks, he was supported by the Ottomans for a while. He attacked areas within Mamluk[6] territory turning the Mamluks against the Ottomans, whom they considered the main instigators.[7]

In a separate development, the Mamluk governor of Jeddah arrested the Deccani Bahmanshahid first minister who was carrying a lot of presents for the Ottoman sultan and sent them instead to Qaytbay in Egypt.[8] Furthermore, Sultan Qaytbay's harbouring of a refugee – Cem Sultan, Bayezid's rebellious brother – created a number of problems for government ties[9] causing a deterioration in the longstanding cordial relations between Mamluks and Ottomans.[10]

The biggest problem, however, was 'Ala' al-Dawle,[11] whose attacks made the Mamluk sultan dispatch Amir Tamraz against him in 889/1484. During the conflict, 'Ala' al-Dawle was defeated and had to flee to the Ottomans. A number of Ottoman soldiers were found among the captives and Ottoman attacks on some cities, such as Tarsus, Adina, Kulak and Masisa, within the Mamluk realm intensified the Mamluk sultan's anger.[12] Therefore, he started recruiting soldiers to attack the Ottomans. 'Ala' al-Dawle now changed sides and joined the Mamluks, whereas his brother, Shah Budaq, joined the Ottomans. In a battle in late 891/1486, the Mamluk army overcame the Ottomans.[13] Clashes continued until the Ottomans were defeated in a battle in Adina.[14] The Mamluks maintained their military morale against the Ottomans and went on recruiting forces until the Ottoman sultan, Bayezid II, sent a message of compromise and returned the occupied fortresses to the Mamluks in early 897/1491-2. The Ottomans and Mamluks reached a compromise and released those taken captive during the conflict.[15] Yet, the dispute between the two governments was not about occupying each other's territory but about the Turkoman area separating them. After that, the Ottomans ceased their limited interference in the border areas with the Mamluks. Instead they began to concentrate on containing the Aq Qoyunlu government[16] and on Europe, allowing a resumption of peaceful relations with the Mamluks until the end of Bayezid's reign and even in the early years of Selim's sultanate.[17] In this period, ambassadors were exchanged and the Ottomans even replied in the affirmative to Sultan Qansuh-al-Ghawri's request for wood to equip his battleships against the Europeans.[18] However, a few years after his coronation Selim turned his attention to the East. It was then that the Safavid government sustained a heavy defeat in Chalderan, 9 Rajab II 920 (23 August 1514), and the Mamluk government collapsed.

The establishment of the Safavids and 'Ala' al-Dawle Zu'l-Qadr

Prior to Selim I not only did the ties between Ottoman and Mamluk governments improve, but they also led to new changes in the Islamic east. The Aq Qoyunlu, who had ruled over the area connecting Central Iran from Isfahan to Tabriz, southern Turkey and Iraq, were replaced by the new Safavid government, established by Shah Esma'il Safavi in 907/1501-2 with its capital in Tabriz. Shah Esma'il's constant conquests of vast areas and removal of locally autonomous governments were done so fast that they surprised the other governments. The news of the establishment of Safavid power, which preceded the wiping out of all local rivals and the remainder of Aq Qoyunlu, soon reached Damascus. The Shi'ism of Shah Esma'il's government distinguished it from previous governments and caused shock in the Sunni capitals of Cairo, Damascus and Istanbul. Although the people of Damascus were acquainted with Shi'ism and had observed Shi'ite mourning groups in the city,[19] the news of the coming to power of Esma'il, who was known as a rebel Sufi, or Sufi Khareji,[20] and his territorial expansion to the East was greeted with concern in Damascus in 907.[21]

The sectarian tendency of the new government was intolerable to both the Mamluks and the Ottomans. They heard exaggerated accounts of the massacre of Iranian Sunnis. However, we should not suppose that the threat posed by Shah Esma'il was sufficient to bring about a coalition of the Ottomans and Mamluks against the Safavids. On the contrary, Mamluk policy entailed not only that it take advantage of the newly established government through its clandestine competition with the Ottomans, particularly over eastern Anatolia where the Safavid removal of the Aq Qoyunlu was a benefit in itself, but also that it put the Ottoman government under pressure. The time was not ripe, however, for the Mamluks to develop close ties with the Safavid.

We will return now to our main focus on the central area separating the three governments of the Ottomans, Mamluks and Turkomans. Those parts of eastern south and central Asia Minor that were outside Ottoman control had so far been ruled by the Zu'l-Qadr, though there were other tribes living in different areas like Konya, Diyarbakr and so on. When 'Ala' al-Dawle Zu'l-Qadr assumed power in this area, he intended to consolidate his position by taking advantage of the competition between the Mamluk and Ottoman governments. He allied with either the Ottomans or the Mamluks depending upon the circumstances.[22] To the east of the Zu'l-Qadr's autonomous government, the new Safavid government emerged claiming the authority and realm of both the Aq Qoyunlu and Timurids. It enjoyed support among the Turkoman tribes in central Asia Minor. Having realized the threat posed by Shah Esma'il, 'Ala' al-Dawle attempted to support the remnants of the Aq Qoyunlu government still ruling in Baghdad, namely Sultan Murad, the son of Sultan Ya'qub and grandson of Uzun Hasan. Sultan Murad, who had already fled from Baghdad towards 'Ala' al-Dawle, married the latter's daughter.[23] It was natural for Shah Esma'il to become more conscious and sensitive as soon as he realized the threat from the western side.

In 1504–5/910 'Ala' al-Dawle had liberated the fortress in Diyarbakr from Amir Bayg Musillu's possession and entrusted it to Sultan Murad. A local emir still a supporter of Shaykh Safi's lineage, Amir Bayg, approached Shah Esma'il and became his seal-bearer and encouraged Shah Esma'il in 1507/913 to set off for Diyarbakr and take it back from 'Ala' al-Dawle. Shah Esma'il crossed Qaysariyya, Sultan Bayezid's realm, trying not to harm the Bayezid's sovereignty. It is said that he simultaneously sent an envoy called Zakariya Bayg towards Qansu and one called Quli Bayg towards Bayezid to assure them that his actions were merely for the security of his own borders.[24] He then advanced into Albistan, 'Ala' al-Dawle's base, forcing the latter to flee from the Qezelbash army. Despite sporadic fighting, there was no battle between the shah and 'Ala' al-Dawle.[25] Returning to Khoy, the shah appointed Khan Muhammad Ostajlu, Mirza Bayg's son and Shah Esma'il's sister's husband, as the governor of Diyarbakr. Ostajlu's 2,000-strong Qezelbash force was compelled to fight a 10,000-strong army commanded by 'Ala' al-Dawle's son, Qasim (known as Saruqaplan), who was a veteran commander. In the battle, Saruqaplan was captured and killed, giving the Safavids possession of Diyarbakr. 'Upon hearing the sorrowful news, 'Ala' al-Dawle shed tears like drops of blood down his countenance.'[26] It was evident that this would not be the last battle between the Zu'l-Qadr and the Qezelbash.

In 914 'Ala' al-Dawle once again dispatched an army against Khan Muhammad Ostajlu, this time commanded by two other sons, Kur Shahrukh and Ahmad Bayg. Again the much larger Zu'l-Qadr army was defeated by Khan Muhammad Khan. Sustaining heavy casualties, the army had to flee and both commanders were captured and killed by Muhammad Khan. 'Ala' al-Dawle again 'upon hearing the news wept hard, dressed in black and his agents also began mourning in an unprecedented way.' 'Ala' al-Dawle's persistence bore no fruit. As Rumlu puts it, 'his covetousness for the governorship of Diyarbakr' was akin to 'flogging a dead horse'.[27] Shah Esma'il who had heard how his troops gained the victory in Diyarbakr set out for Hamadan and Baghdad, adding Arab Iraq to his conquests in 914. As noted above, Baghdad had earlier been in Sultan Murad's possession, but later was independently ruled by Barik Bayg Parnak. He fled the Safavid advance leaving them in possession of Baghdad with no bloodshed.[28]

Mamluks and Safavids: The first ties

Here we have to refer back and review Shah Esmaʻil's relations with the Mamluk sultan, Qansu al-Ghuri, who had been in power in Egypt since 906/1500. The relationship gave Sultan Selim the pretext for a military expedition to Egypt to overthrow the Mamluk government.[29] Iran was by now unified under the banner of the Safavids and had a long border with the Mamluks following the course of the Euphrates. In Asia Minor there was an area separating the Safavid-Mamluk governments, and near northern Iraq and Damascus another area where the territories of all three governments of the Ottomans, Mamluks and Safavids converged.

At this time, Qansu al-Ghuri introduced himself as the protector of the two sacred sanctuaries (Mecca and Medina) and the supporter of Sunnism, particularly since he had the ʻAbbasid caliph at hand. It seems that after Shah Esmaʻil came into power, many Sunnites escaped to Damascus and from there moved to the two sacred sanctuaries or other places. They must have made some effort to keep the Mamluk emirs abreast of events in Iran and must have stressed the threat posed by Shah Esmaʻil. Since Shah Esmaʻil came to power in 907, both Bayezid and Qansu were keen to be informed about the events taking place in Iran.

In Safar 908, news spread to Cairo from Aleppo saying that a foreigner called Shah Esmaʻil Safavi had come into power. It caused worry in Cairo. All the emirs gathered at the Mamluk sultan's behest to consult about affairs related to the Safavids.[30] Some measures were even adopted for deploying troops to Aleppo.[31] After a couple of days there was a rumour of Shah Esmaʻil's murder by Amir Qasem Bayg; it was immediately denied.[32] Bayezid, in a letter to Rustam Bayg Kord, governor of Chashmkazak in Kurdistan, in Rabiʻ-al-thani 908 tried to get some information about Shah Esmaʻil. Rustam Bayg wrote:

> what was reported about the Qezelbash, may Allah curse them, was that the intention of such a rebellious tribe was to harm Alvand Khan, and to set out for Iraq to defeat Murad Khan to deal with the Purnakids' affairs in Iraq; and to unite and come to an agreement with the Egyptian Charakisa and then go to Diyarbakr and Marʻash.[33]

Qansu al-Ghuri, on the other hand, who was conscious of the threat of Shah Esmaʻil, wrote a letter to Bayezid (that letter is no longer traceable), but Bayezid's answer (Rabiʻ-al-awwal 910/1504) shows that Qansu had referred in his letter to the emergence of a man in the East who had defeated the governors of the area. In his next letter to Bayezid, Qansu used bitter language about Shah Esmaʻil and the new Shiʼi dispensation to the East and stressed the necessity of confronting him.[34] Qansu's religious position against the Qezelbash in his letter is based on the impression that the Sunni fugitives fleeing to Damascus had given him. His view of Shiʼism as a dangerous heresy (*rafd*) mirrored that of the Sunni residents of Damascus.

No more information about Qansu and Bayezid's next measure is available. In 910 there was a rumour that the 'Khareji Haydar Sufi', implying Esmaʻil, Haydar Sufi's son, had attacked the territory ruled by ʻAlaʻ al-Dawle and had advanced towards

Aleppo.³⁵ Yet this is not mentioned in Safavid sources. Another piece of news reported on 17 Sha'ban 911/November 1505 was that someone had emerged in Sa' id's realm and claimed that he was a Sufi Caliph (of Shah Esma'il). According to Ibn Tulun he had talked blasphemously about the Qur'an and Hadith. He was taken to Egypt and beheaded along with two other persons by legal decision of Shaykh Shams-al-din, the Hanafi Egyptian Mufti.

In 913/1507, Shah Esma'il began to clash with 'Ala' al-Dawle in Diyarbakr. It was of significance for Qansu that 'Ala' al-Dawle remained in his position as an obstacle against Ottoman or Safavid advances on the Mamluk realm. Although Shah Esma'il's clash with 'Ala' al-Dawle resulted in the Safavid's gaining Diyarbakr, it did not cause 'Ala' al-Dawle to succumb.

The news of Shah Esma'il's victories in 913 reached Cairo via Aleppo.³⁶ It was reported that the vanguard of the Qezelbash army had reached as far as Malatya. Some obscene acts were attributed to Shah Esma'il as well. Upon hearing the news, the sultan summoned his emirs for a consultation. They decided to send an army. The sultan reviewed the army in the presence of the Ottoman sultan's representative and made preparations to dispatch it, along with a number of emirs. Word was sent to Aleppo to expect the army and to encourage the Aleppo officials to recruit soldiers and collect information.³⁷ Then another piece of news reached Cairo, stating that the Sufi army had crossed the Euphrates and had come closer to the sultan's realm and that 'Ala' al-Dawle³⁸ was leading a Turkoman force against him. This news filled Cairo with anxiety and preparations to dispatch the army were suspended.³⁹

On Tuesday 9 Jamadi al-thani 913, an envoy from 'Ala' al-Dawle arrived in Cairo bearing a report of victory against the Safavid. He presented a number of heads wearing the distinctive red hats of the Safavid Qezelbash, claiming they were the heads of some emirs. The sultan was very pleased and commanded that they hang the heads from the gate of Zuwayla. When the reported news was confirmed, preparations to dispatch an army ceased.⁴⁰

In Sha'ban 913, an envoy from Shah Esma'il arrived in Cairo. He had a letter in which the shah had written that he had not been aware that his troops had penetrated Mamluk territory and sent his apologies. Qansu treated the envoy with respect. Ibn Ayas adds that they wore red hats (*taratir humr*).⁴¹

When Shah Esma'il seized Baghdad in 914/1508, Sultan Murad tried to take Baghdad back by asking Ottoman and Mamluk forces to help. For this reason in Ramadan 914 Sultan Murad's envoy came to Cairo to ask Sultan Qansu for help. The sultan welcomed him and, according to his usual practice, invited him to be present at a ceremony held on the Maydan (open area).⁴² But if he expected the sultan to provide him with troops, he was disappointed.⁴³

In the following days, rumours spread round Cairo that Shah Esma'il had attacked the sultan's territory, but were denied immediately.⁴⁴ Similar rumours circulated in 916/1510 that Shah Esma'il's army had attacked Aleppo, but these rumours also were quickly suppressed.⁴⁵

In Rabi' al-awwal 916, Sultan Qansu sent a representative, Amir Tamurbay Hindi (Sudun al-Hindi), to Esma'il.[46] In Jamadi al-thani of the same year, news reached Cairo that the governor of Bira had arrested a number of Sufi adherents of Shah Esma'il who were carrying letters for the *farangi* (European) shahs requesting them to attack the Egyptian sultan by sea while Esma'il attacked by land. The governor who had arrested them sent them to the sultan.[47] In Dhi'l-qa'da of the same year, Qansu al-Ghuri summoned the European consuls in Alexandria, Damascus and Tripoli to Cairo and reprimanded them. While there is no other evidence to support this report, we know that on other occasions Shah Esma'il wrote letters to encourage the European powers to coordinate their attacks on the Egyptian and Ottoman sultans,[48] even though only one such letter, dated 9 Shawwal 924[49]/October 1517, survives. That letter was written to Charles IV, the Holy Roman Emperor, but the response reached the Safavid court only after Shah Esma'il's demise.[50] The letter contained a proposal for a two-sided attack from west and east, but on the Ottoman, rather than the Mamluk, sultan.

In late 916/1511 news of Yishbak Khan's murder reached Cairo. According to Ibn Ayas, news came from Aleppo of Esma'il's 915/1510 defeat of Mohammad Shaybani Khan Uzbak, the founder of the Shaybani dynasty to the north-east of the Safavid realm, and that he had killed and beheaded him. Sultan Qansuh, with whom the emirs stayed until noon, had been extremely disturbed. After hearing about Shaybani Khan's defeat and death, the sultan feared an attack by Esma'il.[51] This utterance, in addition to expressing Ibn Ayas's feeling for Uzbak Khan against Shah Esma'il, does indicate that Shiybak Khan seemed to have been fighting Esma'il in defence of Egyptian and Roman sultans, Sunnism in fact. Furthermore, the Egyptian sultan was very concerned about the eastern borders of the country on the banks of Euphrates because of the advancing Qezelbash forces.

Shah Esma'il's envoy to Damascus and Cairo and its consequences

The first news of the arrival of an envoy of Shah Esma'il in Damascus concerns the one who brought Shaybak (Shaybani) Khan's head to demonstrate Shah Esma'il's victory over the Uzbaks. Shah Esma'il's letter to Qansu al-Ghuri has survived and there is also considerable information in Mamluk sources.[52]

According to al-Ansari, Shah Esma'il's envoy arrived in Damascus on Monday 11 Safar 917/March 1511. Sibay, the emir of Damascus, commanded that local nobles attend formally and welcome him. There was a firework display and soldiers lined the route from the Mastaba of the sultan to Ablaq's palace near the fortress. Meanwhile Yakhshabay, the Grand Chamberlain (Hajib al-hujjab) and Amir Kabir Qalaj were in attendance. The emir himself, however, remained in the Dar-al-sa'da when the envoy arrived, welcoming him there before his departure for Cairo. In the Dar al-sa'ada, the envoy sat next to Sayyid Kamal al-Din, the Shi'i jurist of Dar al-'Adl and submitted Esma'il's letter, in Persian, to the emir. The Naqib al-Ashraf, an Iranian, was called to translate it into Arabic. It opened with the *bismillah,* under which was written 'O 'Ali', and continued, 'a letter from Shah Esma'il, sultan of Iran and the two Iraqs. We have sent our envoy to the governors of Aleppo, Damascus and Egypt to give the glad tidings of our victory over Uzbak Khan, the ruler of Khurasan. We have beheaded him and occupied all his lands.' Al-Ansari adds that the letter also implied a threat towards the Damascus and Aleppo governments. It noted that the shah had also sent his envoys to the Ottoman sultan.[53] Touching briefly upon the arrival of Esma'il's envoys, Ibn Tulun wrote that they had the heads of some Muslims with them (*wa-ma'hum ra's ba'd al-muslimin*).[54]

The envoy arrived in Cairo in Rabi' al-awwal 917. According to al-Ansari, the army stood in line from the house of dervishes to the fortress. The envoy's reception was exceptional due to the large number of people, as well as the presence of officials.

The envoy paid a visit to Qansu al-Ghuri and submitted Shaybak Khan's head to him saying, '*hadha ra's 'aduwwika ya mawlana*'. Qansu covered the head and buried it. Then, the envoy presented him with a prayer carpet, a Qur'an and a bow saying that no one could ever bend this bow. Qansu later invited the envoy as a guest and commanded that he should be well-entertained. People asked the envoy, 'Are you satisfied with Abu Bakr?', implying that he was a heretic and causing him embarrassment. The sultan ordered the people to avoid such talk as he was afraid of a curse on the Prophet's successors in return.[55]

Ibn Ayas describes the envoy's arrival in Egypt in detail. As soon as the envoy noticed the sultan, he kissed the floor and then the sultan's foot. Then he read the Shah's letter out and presented a Qur'an, a prayer carpet and a bow. He claimed that no one could bend the bow. The sultan commanded one of his agents called Zardkash II to break it and he did. Ibn Ayas has emphasized the glory and greatness of the reception ceremony with the following sentence: '*wa-kana dhalika al-mawkib min al-mawakib al-mashhuda*'.[56]

Ibn Ayas has also referred to the entertainment the Egyptian sultan had arranged for Shah Esma'il's envoy on Tuesday 28 Rabi' al-awwal 917. The sultan took him to the Maydan and after firing some cannons, *darb al-kurra*, he sat beside a small pool, *al-bahra*, built in the Maydan. After the Sufi (i.e. Safavid) envoy was brought in, he was not only entertained extremely well, but also received gifts. He was then taken back to his residence. The sultan had appointed some of his special servants, *khasikiyya*, to be with him and not to allow people to meet him. Moreover, none of the Sufi members of the delegation were permitted to go shopping or meet people. Only once they went out with Azdmar, an attendant, to pay homage to the grave of Imam Shafi'i and Imam Layth and then were brought back to their residence. Referring to the man called Sharif Husayn, an Iranian, who translated Esma'il's letter, Ibn Ayas pointed out two versus of a poem Shah Esma'il had written at the bottom of his letter:

nahnu unas qad ghada sha'nuna	*hubb 'Ali -bn Abi Talib*
ya'ibuna al-nas 'ala hubbihi	*fa-la'nat Allah 'ala al-'a'ib*

He also added that Esmaʿil had sent a letter to Sultan Selim with two verses.[57] Sultan Selim wrote the following verses in response,

> ma ʿaybukum hadha wa-lakinnahu   bi-ghadd alladhi luqiba bi-l-sahib
> kadhabtumu ʿanhu wa-ʿan ibnatihi   fa-laʿnat Allah ʿala al-kadhib[58]

Since Esmaʿil's letter to Qansu is still available, it is easy to find out how falsely Ibn Ayas had voiced his opinion about the verses of poem composed by Esmaʿil. As a matter of fact, there were some verses of Persian poetry in the letter as opening sentences, unless another letter existed.[59] Meanwhile, the couplet we will see later had been within the letter, reflecting their literal aspect.

While Ibn Ayas was reporting on the presence of Shah Esmaʿil's envoy in Cairo, he added that after killing Uzbak Khan, Esmaʿil threatened the Egyptian people with the following two verses:

> al-sayf wa-l-khanjar rayhanuna   uff ʿala al-narjis wa-l-as
> mudamuna min dam aʿdaʾina   wa-kaʾsuna jamjamat al-raʾs

He also reiterated that after Esmaʿil beheaded Uzbak Khan, he used his skull as a bowl for wine.

In this last poem, wherein 'sword' was preferred to 'daffodil', had created fear that it was a threat against the Egyptian sultan. The story is, the Mamluk sultan had built an open place known as the Maydan in Cairo for holding celebrations, reception ceremonies and amusements and had planted trees, flowers such as daffodils, and so on. The two Arabic verses written in Esmaʿil's letter that asserted the superiority of the sword over the flower were mistakenly interpreted as an intention to threaten the Egyptian sultan. Shah Esmaʿil's sudden emergence, his conquests, as well as his spreading the news in Egypt, seemed to confirm the point. This matter is referred to by Ibn Ayas as well. Furthermore, Shah Esmaʿil had boldly said that the enemies' blood would be the wine and their skulls would be the bowls.[60]

These two points stimulated the Egyptian poets and men of letters to react. Ibn Ayas included a large number of poems over several pages,[61] and composed the following verses himself:

> bi-l-sayf wa-l-khanjar nufni al-ʿadi   wa-kam lana fi al-harb min baʾs
> naslub bi-l-ruʿb ʿuqul al-wara   wa-ʿaqluna wafir fi al-raʾs

In the poems given by Ibn Ayas, polemic against the heretic Shiʾis and the Safavid army is prominent:

> wa-laysa shurb al-dam fi sharʿina   bi-jaʾiz wa-l-dhamm li-l-asa
> man yabghud al-sadiq aw sahbahu   fa-dhaka ashqa al-khalq fi al-nas

and

> ʿasakir al-sufi in farzanat   fa-rukhkhuhum makshuf li-l-nas
> wa-nafsuhum qad ujizat khifatan   min ʿazmina maʿ shiddat al-baʾs

Esma'il's drinking wine from Uzbak Khan's skull is reflected in the verses below, which suggest that this action – if taken – was an ironic statement in support of the Safavid government.

> *ya qa'ilan uff 'ala al-narjisi   uff 'ala al-baghi 'ala al-nas*
> *fa-inna khayr al-nas man la yari   shurb dam al-muslim fi al-ka's*

Sharbini, another poet, answered:

> *magharis al-sunna bustanuna   naqta' minhu hamat al-ra's*
> *wa-l-dam la yushrab fi shar'ina   lakin fina quwwat al-ba's*

Shaykh Jamal-al-Din Salamuni also reacted against the poem attributed to Esma'il:

> *uff 'ala uffika ya kharijan   hijaka muhtaj ila al-as*
> *ma anta illa ja'li 'ala   rafdika shamm al-ward wa-l-as*

Referring to Esma'il's action with Uzbak Khan's skull, he said:

> *in kana darb al-sayf rayhanakum   ka'sukum jamjamat al-ra's*
> *wa-shurbukum min dam a'da'ikum   uff 'alaykum ardhal al-nas*

Mahmud al-Khalili said:

> *al-'izz wa-l-satwa rayhanuna   la min shadha al-narjis wa-l-as*
> *sharabuna al-tawhid la min dam   yushrab min jamjamat al-ra's*

Ibn 'Aqil's poem was as follows:

> *tilawat al-Quran rayhanuna nanshaq minhu khayr anfasi*
> *sharabuna al-dhikr bihi yartawi   sana qalb ghafil qasi*
> *wa-l-'adl wa-l-insaf -bn da'bina   min ajl dha sudna 'ala al-nas*
> *thana'una bayn al-wara nashruhu   adhka min al-narjis wa-l-as*
> *wa-l-hamd li-llah 'ala annana   ahl al-'ula wa-l-ayd wa-l-ba's*
> *man azhara al-ghadr lana fa-l-jafa   manaluhu wa-l-sayf li-l-ra's*
> *wa-man atana mukhlisan wuddahu   lahu ladayna kull inas*

Ibn Ayas here compares Shah Esma'il with the Il-Khan conqueror and enemy of the Mamluks, Hulagu Khan, referring to the threatening poem, Hulagu wrote to the Egyptian sultan before he suffered defeat at his hands, before adding, '*fa-l-sufi bi-l-nisba ila Hulaku la shay*'.[62]

In another poem, Muhyi'l-Din Nu'aymi quotes the sultan as reacting against Esma'il's poem:

> *al-'ilm wa-l-hilm rayhanuna   wa-l-jud wa-l-ihsan li-l-nas*
> *shamsuna al-'adl li-kull al-wara   ma' shiddat al-quwwa wa-l-ba's*
> *sharabuna al-dhikr wa-ka's al-taqi   uff 'ala jamjamat al-ra's*[63]

The next events indicated that the enemy of Egypt, Damascus and the Mamluk government was not Shah Esmaʻil but the Ottoman sultan whom the Mamluk historians had so far been praising. Both Ibn Ayas's explanation and the grounds Esmaʻil had given by sending Uzbak Khan's head culminated in the Damascus Sunni Muslims bearing a grudge against Esmaʻil, so that after the Battle of Chalderan the Damascenes rejoiced.

After taking leave of Qansu, Esmaʻil's envoy left Cairo for Damascus on Monday 2 Jamadi al-awwal.[64] Ibn Tulun reports that, on returning to Damascus, he was welcomed by the governor.[65] Al-Ansari has referred to his return to Damascus, reception ceremony and his residence in al-Marja.[66] In al-Ansari's version, Shah Esmaʻil's envoy arrived in Damascus (Cairo) on 16 Jamadi al-awwal and was received by Qansu. The sultan granted him an *ʻaba* (men's loose sleeveless cloak open in front) and *qaba* (long garment open in front) as gifts and ordered Cairo emirs to entertain him as their guest. He also provided him with gold to cover the costs of the return journey.[67] Iranian sources mention that after Shah Esmaʻil gained victory in Khurasan, representatives of Bayezid and Qansu came to offer congratulations.[68]

In relation to the envoy's visit, several points stand out. First, it is said that the receptions given both by the governor of Damascus and by the Egyptian sultan were so glorious that historians have called them unique. The second is that Esmaʻil's handing of Shaybak Khan's head to the Egyptian sultan suggests that this was the head of a mutual enemy. Does it, perhaps, refer to the alliance between the Uzbaks and the Ottomans? Given the sound relations between the Ottoman and Mamluk governments, this does not appear likely. It probably alludes to Shah Esmaʻil's desire to keep himself close to the Mamluk sultan by presenting Uzbak Khan as a common foe. The third point of interest is that the Egyptian people's attention to the Shi'i beliefs of Esmaʻil and his envoy had the potential to damage relations. Therefore, the Egyptian sultan prevented people from playing jokes with Shah Esmaʻil's envoy.

Fourth, Esmaʻil's present for the Egyptian sultan was of three types: prayer carpet, Qur'an and a bow. The first two items were to emphasize that the Safavid government was Muslim and a performer of prayer. It was a denial of the accusations against the Safavids that were propagated in Ottoman lands and Damascus, accusations that originated with Sunni fugitives from Iran.[69]

The fifth point of interest is that sending Uzbak Khan's head incensed the Sunni people of Damascus. As discussed before, the report about Uzbak Khan's skull had drawn the attention of a number of men of letters in Damascus and Cairo and became a means of taunting the Safavid government. According to al-Ansari, on 1 Jamadi al-awwal 917/27 July 1511, it was reported in Damascus that the Ottoman army had been defeated. The story was that a group of people in Ottoman lands had baulked at obeying the Ottoman sultan and had followed Shah Esmaʻil. The sultan organized an army and asked for help from his representative in Aleppo. His request was granted, so they launched an attack; Esmaʻil's followers, however, overcame the army and refused to obey the sultan, openly giving their allegiance to the Sufi (Esma'il). This raised anxiety in Aleppo.[70]

Although we are not aware how the Mamluks analysed the reports, it is certain that Shah Esma'il's envoy was still in Damascus at the time, and was received and seen off respectfully. Al-Ansari has added that the Damascus pilgrimage caravan stopped its journey halfway at the news that 'al-'aduww al-Safi' intended to attack Damascus.[71] Discussing the events of the year 917, Ibn Tulun also refers to the stopping of the pilgrimage, justifying the decision by saying that the foreigner Esma'il wanted to perform the pilgrimage and hang the Ka'ba curtain himself:

la hawla wa-la quwwa illa bi-llah.[72]

A rumour spread early in 918 (Muharram/March 1512) that Esma'il's troops had arrived at Bira and that the vanguard had confronted a group of soldiers from that city. It frightened the Egyptian sultan, who was facing an Arab revolt at the same time. The news was so shocking that he turned back from moving towards the border area, near Alexandria.[73]

It is not clear how strong the rumours were. A number of groups that had some ties with the Safavid movement might have been active in Diyarbakr and the outskirts of Aleppo. Shah Esma'il was not at all aware of their activities, nor is any report of it recorded in the Safavid sources, as is also the case with Shah Qoli Baba's revolt in Qaraman. As discussed earlier, following the activities of a few Shi'i groups on the outskirts of Aleppo, Shah Esma'il sent an envoy to apologize to the Egyptian sultan.

On 18 Rabi' al-awwal, 918 the emir of Sis sent a number of heads with Qezelbashi red hats on to Cairo. It was guessed that they were members of the Safavid army who had raised a disturbance in the area. After arresting and beheading them all, the emir sent their heads to the sultan. The sultan commanded that the heads be put on spears and displayed around Cairo and then hung from the Bab al-nasr and Bab al-futuh gates. A rumour spread that Shah Esma'il had assumed power in that area and sent an envoy to the sultan.[74]

On Saturday 12 Rabi' al-awwal, 918 Emir Taymurbay Hindi, who had been sent to Shah Esma'il by Qansu, returned to Cairo after two years. He had had a difficult journey with numerous troubles. Many of his horses and a group of his servants and companions had died and Shah Esma'il had misbehaved and shown disrespect towards him. It is even said that he gave him audience only once and did not answer the sultan's letter. All he did he was to send an envoy to convey a message to the Egyptian sultan. On his arrival in Cairo, Taymurbay Hindi informed the sultan that Shah Esma'il's envoy accompanied by the Georgian (Kurj) king's envoy were on their way. The sultan commanded Zayni Barakat Muhtasab to meet them and provide facilities for them. Lodging was provided in Qani Bay Sulq's house for the envoy – and for the 100 Sufis who accompanied him! He was considered a bad-tempered man who had misbehaved to the governor of Aleppo. Two days later the sultan received

Esmaʻil's envoy in the fortress where his emirs and army were present. The envoy presented gifts, which amounted to 40 loads.

Ibn Ayas has enumerated them as follows: seven panthers, silver dishes, golden bowls, velvet and silk garments, Roman prayer carpet and many bows. As soon as the two envoys came up to the sultan, they kissed the ground and submitted Esmaʻil's letter. When they began reading it out the harsh words made the sultan so angry that fury appeared in his face. The day after the Georgian king's representative presented his gifts.[75]

Unfortunately, although Ibn Ayas lists the gifts, he does not say a word about Shah Esmaʻil's letter. It is clear that the writing style of the Persian letters of that time was very difficult and that translations did not help their readers understand them. By the phrase of *'alfaz yabasathu wa-kalam fajj'* concerning Esmaʻil's letter, Ibn Ayas may refer to the administrative prose of that time. By *'alfaz yabasathu'*, he may be referring to diplomatic disrespect.

On the 27th of the same month, the sultan received Shah Esmaʻil's envoy once again, took him to the Maydan where entertainments were provided that left the envoy amazed by their systematic organization.[76] On 8 Jamadi al-awwal 918 (22 July 1512) the sultan again received Esmaʻil's envoy and presented gifts to him and the accompanying delegation. In answer to Shah Esmaʻil's abusive letter, the sultan wrote a similar one back to Shah Esmaʻil. Ibn Ayas added:

> wa-hadha awwal ibtidaʾ wuquʻ al-wahsha bayn al-Sultan wa-bayn Shah Ismaʻil al-Sufi

Besides the sultan, his envoy had misbehaved towards Taymurbay Hindi.[77]

Despite the exchange of envoys, it is clear that the Egyptian sultan was not at all pleased with Shah Esmaʻil's coming into power. In Rabiʻ al-thani, 919 (June 1913) it was reported that in a battle with the king of the Tatars (i.e. the Uzbeks), Shah Esmaʻil sustained heavy defeat and lost nearly 30,000 of his troops. He himself was wounded and missing. The news was confirmed by seven representatives – that is, the governors of the cities around – and cheered the sultan up.[78]

Comparing this report with what occurred in Khurasan that year shows both the strength and the unreliability of the Egyptian rumours. In fact Shah Esmaʻil's military expedition to Khurasan in the above-mentioned year was a success. ʻUbayd Khan Uzbek was compelled to flee and abandon Khurasan wholly to Shah Esmaʻil without a fight.[79]

The coming to power of Sultan Selim I

The Safavid seizure of both Diyarbakr and Arab Iraq and the valour of Muhammad Khan Ostajlu enraged the Ottoman government. They were also concerned by the formation of a new dynasty that claimed the inheritance of both the Timurids and the Aq Qoyunlu and which was spreading its influence over many minor rulers and commanders. At this juncture Bayezid II was sultan, while the Black

Sea coast and the area to the north of Qaraman were under Selim I's control as governor of Trabzon. Since Selim was in the eastern parts of the Ottoman government and the aforesaid developments occurred in areas to the south, they aroused his enmity towards Shah Esma'il. In addition to his Sunni prejudices, Selim was jealous of a 20-year-old man with so many victories. History shows that Selim was a stubborn and bloodthirsty man, who did not mind massacring not only Shi'is but also Sunnis – as he did in Egypt and Damascus – in order to achieve his goals.[80]

At this time, the Mamluk statesmen considered the newly established Safavid government as one that could unify the Iranians and form a mighty power on which they could count in their conflict with the Ottomans. However, they still were sensitive regarding the border along the course of the Euphrates.

On the other hand, apart from the issues in the Du'l-Qadr region, several other factors infuriated Sultan Selim. First, Shah Esma'il not only insisted on the spread of Shi'ism in central Iran, displacing Sunni scholars and forcing them to flee,[81] but he also penetrated into Transoxiana and deposed his ally Shaybak Khan in 916. Moreover, in order to show off his might and humiliate the Ottoman caliph, who presented himself as a supporter of Sunnism and of the Uzbeks, and who had both overtly and covertly helped the latter, Shah Esma'il, 'ordered them to decapitate and skin him (Shaybak Khan) and like a blade of straw send him to Sultan Bayezid, the Roman sultan'.[82] Beyond any doubt this point, plus the incitement of the Sunni fugitives from Iran, caused Selim serious concern.[83]

Second, the Ottoman subjects in Qaraman revolted and took sides with Shah Esma'il. And even without Shah Esma'il's prompting, many Ottoman followers of Shaykh Safi's lineage decided to set out for Iran to join the Qezelbash army. Meanwhile, Shah Qoli Baba Takalu's revolt in 917 created many troubles for the Ottoman government.[84] It was not only the uprising itself, but the danger that if the Ottoman government failed to react promptly, eastern Anatolia would be captured by the newly established Safavid government.

In 918, Shah Esma'il sent Nur 'Ali, his Rumlu *khalife* (a title designating him as the head of the Safavi Sufi order and Esma'il's own representative in the Rumlu tribe), to Qarahisar, an area that was under Ottoman, control to recruit forces supportive of Shaykh Safi's Sufi order. He persuaded a great number of 'Safavid devotees' and did battle with Fa'iq Bayg, the Ottoman governor appointed by Sultan Selim. The Ottomans were defeated and sustained heavy casualties and 'the sermon was delivered for Khaqan Iskandar Nishan (i.e. Shah Esma'il – indicating that the Safavids had won the territory)'.[85] Other battles between the Ottomans and the Qezelbash also resulted in Ottoman defeat. It is clear that these events all provoked Selim, who was governor of Trabzon and on the threshold of a sultanate. Selim was displeased with his father Bayezid's lack of interest regarding the eastern provinces. Bayezid adopted no serious measures, although the Ottomans had been beaten several times by the Mamluks and most recently by the Safavids. According to Rumlu, during

Bayezid's term the Ottomans sustained heavy defeats, notably at the hands of the Egyptian army.[86]

As soon as Selim came to the throne in 918/1512, he decided to address the eastern problem. He had two major hurdles ahead, namely, Shah Esmaʿil and the Mamluks.[87] Concerning Iran, he was determined to neutralize the threats created for the Sunnis in this land and assist the Uzbaks in Transoxiana by destroying the Safavid government. Indeed, removing Esmaʿil was Selim's main foreign policy goal. If successful, he would be able to seize Iran wholly and unite the Ottoman and Uzbek Sunni territories. He had sufficient justification: first, he moved east towards Iran under the pretext of religious war and with the aim of territorial expansion and the glory of victory. Second, Muhammad Khan Ostajlu had gone to extremes in bad manners, conceit and threats in his letters to Sultan Selim. This seems to have been a crucial factor in Selim's motivation. The damage that Nur ʿAli had done spurred his resolve.[88]

These were the principal motivations behind Selim's determination to bring Shah Esmaʿil to battle. The battle took place at Chalderan on 2 Rajab 920/23 August 1514.[89] In the battle, Shah Esmaʿil, who like his governors had become too proud of himself, was defeated. The defeat stopped Safavid expansion, but it did not lead to the downfall of the dynasty, which continued to be a menace to the Ottoman government. After Selim overcame the Safavids, he turned against the Mamluks, revealing that 'religious war' with the Safavids had been nothing but a pretext and that he was equally ready to shed Sunni blood.

Shah Esmaʿil, a pretext for the Mamluk's fall after Chalderan

As far as this chapter is concerned, it was Qansu's stance and Selim's next actions that paved the way for the attack by the Ottoman army on Damascus and Cairo and the eradication of the Mamluk government as a consequence.

When Sultan Selim decided to attack Iran, he expected Qansu and independent governors like the Du'l-Qadr to assist him.[90] Therefore, he sent an envoy to Cairo in Rabiʿ al-awwal, 920 to inform Qansu of his decision to attack Iran and to ask him for help.[91] What was of great importance for Selim was the position of the Egyptian sultan regarding Esmaʿil. According to some Ottoman sources and on the basis of the accusations levelled against Qansu by Selim later, it seems that Qansu had allied with Shah Esmaʿil. However, there is no other evidence for an alliance between the Mamluks and Safavids, and it may well be the case that this accusation was fabricated to justify toppling the old Mamluk government and bringing the rich lands of Damascus and Egypt into the Ottoman fold. The dispatch of envoys between the Safavid and Mamluk governments, which certainly did take place, was quite normal and does not prove that there was an alliance between them.

Two further points should be taken into account in this respect. First, after Selim came to power, if the Mamluk government was informed of the Ottoman intentions, it is possible that it might have decided on a clandestine agreement with the Safavids. There are other examples of Mamluk rulers adopting this course of action for the sake of political expediency. Shah Esmaʻil might have viewed such an arrangement favourably in his confrontation with the Ottomans. At least it would prevent a Mamluk-Ottoman coalition against him. Such a scheme seems to have hatched after the Battle of Chalderan, when Selim was set to fight Shah Esmaʻil once again in 922/151, as we will see below.

Second, Qansu as the guardian of the two sacred sanctuaries, opposed Selim's war with the Safavids on the grounds of religious expediency for Sunni Muslims in Iran. Notwithstanding his opposition to the heretical Shi'is, he feared that war with the Safavids might be to the detriment of Iran's Sunnis, who might be targeted by Qezelbash's extremism in the aftermath of the war. If he advised Selim not to wage war against Esmaʻil, it could have been due to religious expediency rather than in alliance with the Safavids.

Mamluk sources reveal that Damascene and Egyptian scholars harboured hatred for Shah Esmaʻil, this contradicts the Ottoman sources, which are full of accusations against the Mamluk sultan for his alleged cooperation with Shah Esmaʻil. Muhammad Farid Bayg writes, 'Any son of Amir Ahmad, Selim's brother who was opposed to him, who sought refuge with Esmaʻil was protected by him.' Esmaʻil also sent an envoy to the Egyptian sultan calling on him to form an alliance against the Ottomans and not to allow the Ottomans to violate the boundaries. Esmaʻil realized that Sultan Selim was powerful enough to defeat each of them singly, but could not deal with a Safavid-Mamluk alliance.[92] The same writer in another passage describes Qansu as Shah Esmaʻil's follower and ally.[93]

Contrary to the suggestion that the Mamluks and Safavids were allies before the 1514 campaign, it seems that at that time the Mamluks were on the Ottoman side. On 7 Rajab, 920/28 August 1514 (five days after the Battle of Chalderan), when Selim was busy fighting the Iranians, Mamluk governors in Cairo were busy organizing an army to support Selim. Al-Ansari writes that a Mamluk army led by four commanders left Cairo with the aim of aiding Sultan Selim and establishing a debt of gratitude.

> wa-qasada al-Sultan bi-tilka, al-maniya (al-minna) ʻala Sultan al-Rum wa-in yuzhir bi-dhalika al-musaʻada, la-yadfaʻahu ʻan mamlakatahu, wa-an yasir lahu jamilatan ʻala Malik al-Rum.

The army arrived in Damascus on 13 Shaʻban.[94] The army must have stopped when informed of Shah Esmaʻil's defeat. Fifteen days after the Battle of Chalderan an envoy from Selim reached Damascus to announce the Ottoman victory over the Safavids. The news cheered people up.[95] When Qansu heard the first rumours of Selim's victory he was so delighted that he commanded the recitation of the Holy Qur'an from beginning to end.[96] During the following days rumours abounded of Esmaʻil's murder or capture by Selim until a more reliable report reached Cairo.[97] But the celebrations of Qansu and his emirs were short-lived, and were soon overshadowed by the fear that Selim would next turn on Qansu. They were pleased at the victory of a Sunni power over the newly established Shi'i government but not to the extent of playing trumpets or decorating cities. According to Ibn Ayas,

> fa-lam yarsum al-Sultan bi-daqq al-kusat li-hadha al-khabar, wa-kadhalika al-umara', akhadhu hadhrahum min Ibn 'Uthman wa-khashaw min satwatihi wa-shiddat ba'sihi li-ma yahduth minhu ba'd dhalika ila jihat al-Sultan

Selim's next actions, from the killing of 'Ala' al-Dawle up to the next military expedition to Iran in 922, made it clear to the Mamluk emirs that everything had changed. With winter over and the spring campaigning season at hand, Ottoman military operations resumed. There was a rumour that the Ottoman sultan's real intention was to advance on Damascus, contrary to the rumours he was spreading that his target was Iran. These reports reached Cairo in Safar 921 and were recorded by Ibn Ayas, who claims that the sultan sent someone to the area to get information.[99]

Selim's first action was to arrange for the murder of 'Ala' al-Dawle, one of the Mamluk's old allies. It is reported that when the Ottoman army was on its way to Iran, a group from the Zu'l-Qadr army attacked it from behind, killing and plundering.[100] In a letter to 'Ala' al-Dawle, Selim accuses the Zu'l-Qadr emirs of plundering some of the provisions he had prepared for the next year's campaign in Iran and burning the rest.[101] For this reason, and due to 'Ala' al-Dawle's former deception, and despite their common religion with the Ottomans, Selim sent an army to oust the Du'l-qadr government,[102] while the rest of his forces set out for Iran or Egypt.[103]

Could it be possible that 'Ala' al-Dawle was prompted by the Mamluk sultan to attack the Ottoman army from behind? In his reply to 'Ala' al-Dawle, who had written to complain that he did not know the sultan's justification for attacking his territory, Selim declared that he wanted to teach him not to receive Esma'il's envoys any more nor to promise him help against the Ottomans.[104] This indicates that Selim suppressed all his opponents by accusing them of cooperating with Shah Esma'il, even though the Safavid monarch was hated by all the Sunnis.

The news of 'Ala' al-Dawle's murder spurred the Mamluk emirs into action. In Rabi' al-awwal 921/April 1515, one of the Mamluk emirs fled to Istanbul, giving rise to a rumour that he was provoking Selim to occupy the lands of the Egyptian sultan.[105]

As Sultan Selim began to remove all local emirs, specially the Dhu l-qadrs in Diyarbakr, Sivas, Mar'ash, Malatiyya and other areas, the Mamluks became more conscious of the Ottoman threat. Removing the local governments that lay between the Ottoman and Mamluk lands and traditionally depended upon the Mamluks[106] prepared the ground for an Ottoman attack on Damascus and then Egypt.[107] Shah Esma'il's defeat the previous year paved the way for the Ottomans. This is what had frightened Qansu and his agents, who were partly aware of Sultan Selim's decisions and intentions. Therefore, they decided to cooperate with Esma'il, at least to prevent Selim from removing the Safavid government and changing the three way balance of power in the region.

Neither Iranian nor Mamluk sources contain any record of an alliance, confirming that this was a trumped up accusation. Qansu was afraid of being attacked by Selim and did his utmost to put the country out of danger, but at the same time he was afraid of a victory for Shah Esma'il, unlikely though that was. When the discussion was about Selim's second attack on Iran, Qansu said, 'I should stay in Aleppo and observe the war between Selim and Esma'il. Whichever side wins, it will attack our lands.'[108]

The historian Iraj Nawbakht suggests that Shah Esma'il, in a contact with the Mamluks, voiced the view that after him it would be Syria's turn to be dominated. He requested the Mamluk ruler not to remain neutral over war with the Ottomans. In order to build unity, the Mamluk sultan sent one of his jesters, named 'Ajmi Jinaqchi, to Esma'il and did not take any measures to stop the Ottomans moving against Esma'il. When Selim sent 'Ala' al-Dawle's head to the Egyptian sultan he was shocked and sent a message to Shah Esma'il to propose an alliance, promising him that after the removal of Selim, Anatolia (Rum) would be his. Pleased with the letter, Esma'il sent one of his famous commanders, Qarakhan, with a large army to the vicinity of Diyarbakr. Qarakhan, after initial successes against the Ottomans, was later defeated and killed.[109] Esma'il and the Mamluk sultan had agreed to deploy troops on their borders with the Ottomans. The Mamluk sultan set out for Aleppo, but, due to Qarakhan's murder, Shah Esma'il did nothing. Sultan Selim wrote to the Mamluk sultan that he intended to attack Shah Esma'il. He advised him to return to Cairo but the sultan answered, 'Here is mine. I go nowhere!' In an answer Selim wrote, 'With such intention you are a present enemy and Shah Esma'il an absent one! Your presence in Aleppo is not for any benefit. I am not able to move towards the absent enemy while I notice your enmity.' Then he diverted his course from Malatya to Aleppo.[110]

It is debatable how reliable this report is. It is clear that the Egyptian sultan did not support Selim's decision to eliminate Shah Esma'il and had sent an envoy to Iran for this reason. It is also definite that he had set out for Syria and Aleppo and deployed troops to the area. His action could be seen either as a precautionary measure to confront the Ottomans' probable attempt to occupy Syria or, less likely, as an action in defence of Shah Esma'il. The attack of the 60,000 or 100,000-strong army on Iran was also a menace to Syria and caused the Egyptian sultan to take cautious action. Even earlier, when Selim set out in 920 to fight Shah Esma'il, Qansu's governors advised him to go to Aleppo with an army and wait there to observe how the clashes between the Ottoman sultan and Esma'il went.[111] Therefore, it was most likely that leading an army to Aleppo was intended neither to fight Selim nor to ally with Shah Esma'il, but rather to make a show of strength to both. The fact that Selim crossed areas claimed by the Mamluks made the threat more tangible, although they were ruled by the autonomous Zu'l-Qadr government. The

Ottoman (and, based on them, recent Turkish) sources,[112] however, claim the existence of an alliance between Qansu and Esma'il and lay stress on a rumour that Qansu had joined forces with the heretical Safavids. According to one report, when Selim decided to cross Mar'ash and advance towards the Euphrates, the sultan was informed that, because of Selim's enmity to Esma'il, 'the Egyptian sultan has commanded his officers and borderguards to obstruct the Ottoman enemies or attack them in the back to kill them all'.[113] The truth is probably that a number of Mamluk borderguards warned the Ottoman army led by Sinan Pasha not to cross Mamluk territory.[114] Certainly, Qansu did not wish to clash with the Ottomans' massive army. He would never have taken such an incautious action since he was quite aware of the status of his army. Despite Uzuncharshili's report,[115] Qansu's movement to Aleppo was not to join forces with Shah Esma'il, otherwise there would surely have been some mention of this in Safavid sources.[116]

The rumour of Esma'il's unity with Qansu was even reflected in Anjulillu's itinerary. He writes, 'In 1516/922 when the Turk, Selim, was informed of the putative alliance between the Egyptian sultan and the Sufi and heard that the green-clad, Uzbak had put Esma'il in trouble, he decided to move with a massive army to attack the Egyptian sultan.'[117] Beyond any doubt the news reached the Italian from the Turks. Referring to the Ottoman advance into Albistan, which was Turkoman territory, he relates that upon hearing of this, the Sufi sent some envoys to the Mamluk sultan, Khafur, known as Ghuri, announcing that he himself would move towards Sinan Pasha from one side and Ghuri must do so from the other side to compel Sinan to succumb from both sides. Whatever the Sufi said, the sultan agreed and after recruiting armies, he left Cairo for Aleppo. As soon as Selim heard of this, he left Constantinople on 5 June 1516 (3 Jamadi al-thani 921) to join Sinan Pasha. On his way, he sent his envoys, the Qadi Lashkar and Zaki Pasha, to the Mamluk sultan to ask why he had unexpectedly gone to Aleppo. Nevertheless, the answer he received was not convincing at all, indicating that there was some secret agreement between the Sufi and the sultan. Meanwhile, Selim gathered all the religious jurists and scholars and asked them what God's demand was. They responded that the sultan's first responsibility was to remove that sharp thorn (i.e. the Mamluk sultan).[118] This narration reflects the Ottoman position exactly.

According to a number of sources, another influential factor in prompting Selim to fight the Mamluks was that the Aleppo governor, Khayr al-Din Pasha, who was ruling there with Qansu's permission, was so scared that he sent many eloquent envoys conveying petitions to Sultan Selim saying, 'what a surprise that his Majesty spends his time on Iranian trips with the Ottoman treasures and deprives himself of the bliss of serving the sacred premises of Mecca! If that dignified sultan pays heed to Aleppo, I will hereby submit the fortress to provide him with the opportunity of serving the two sacred sanctuaries this year ...' Receiving Khayr al-Din's message, Sultan Selim began to hope of conquering Saudi Arabia, lost interest in Iran and turned his attention to Aleppo.[119]

Most of the sources have alluded to the role of Sultan Selim's deception in misleading Sultan Qansu; indicating that his intention was always to conquer Syria and Egypt but he had pretended that he intended to go to Iran.[120] Such a trick would be in keeping with his spreading the rumour that Sultan Qansu had allied with Shah Esma'il against the Ottomans.

Earlier, when Qansu had tried to dissuade Selim from attacking Esma'il, Selim wrote to him, 'The Sultan is like my father. I have asked him to pray for me, so I expect him not to mediate between Shah Esma'il and me. I will never return as long as I do not eradicate Shah Esma'il.' According to Ibn Ayas, although Selim's target was Qansu, he pretended that it was Esma'il.[121]

While Qansu was trying to persuade Selim to reconcile with Shah Esma'il, Selim gathered the Sunni *'olama* to issue a decree against the Egyptian sultan. The question was, 'How lawful is it if we battle with a Muslim sultan who prevents us from attacking an atheist group?' Their judgement was that 'war against such a Muslim sultan is lawful'.[122]

It was said that Baba 'Ali had received authentic reports showing that Shah Esma'il had close relations with the Egyptian court and had offered them many gifts. Besides, there had been talks between Esma'il and the Egyptian sultan on the subject of encouraging the Egyptian sultan to persuade Selim to reconcile with Shah Esma'il and 'if he refused, he should fight him. And if he took Diyarbakr and Du'l-qadr lands away from the sultan, he should add them to Egyptian territory with no allegations. They signed the treaty and exchanged the documents.'[123]

Such false reports were rumours spread by the Ottoman court that transferred into the history books. Later on, reporting his victory over the Mamluks to Shirvanshah Shaykh Ebrahim, Selim emphasized the alliance between Qansu and Shah Esma'il as a justification for his attack on Egypt and Damascus. He referred to his decision to wage war against Esma'il in 922 as follows,

> ... with God's help at the birth of spring, accompanied by the Muslim armies, we set out for Iranian territory to announce Muslimdom and wipe the dualist Qezelbash off the face of the earth. When we arrived in the Du'l-qadr lands, we realized that the Egyptian sultan Qansu al-Ghuri, affected by the deception of the old and new Esma'ili atheists, was set to assist the atheists and had targeted the area with a massive army. Although he had the honour of serving the two sacred sanctuaries and supported the Islamic principles, he turned his back on all his vows and joined the enemies.[124]

In Jamadi al-thani 922/July 1516, when Selim left Üsküdar for the East, he sent a lengthy letter along with Qarakhan's head, one of Shah Esma'il's commanders, as a record of victory to Qansu. As an answer, Qansu expressed his satisfaction with the Ottoman army's recent victory over the 'atheist Qezelbash'. Saying that they had held special ceremonies for happiness, he sent an envoy with many presents to Selim to congratulate him.[125]

Selim's next letter, which was written deceptively, included some issues that were supposed to change Qansu's mind about Selim's probable attack on Syria. There were issues like the gifts of the Indian king, sending wood to Sultan Qansu, and so on.

Nonetheless, the Egyptian envoy in the Ottoman army had sensed the danger to the Mamluks and Shah Esma'il. As soon as he returned, Qansu, in a letter to Shah Esma'il, notified him of the sultan's hostile intention and asked for help. However, before the letter even reached Iran everything was over for the Mamluks.[126]

On the other hand, while Selim's ostensible intention was Iran, Qansu posed the issue of Ottoman-Safavid compromise in a long letter. Mentioning that he recognized that the sultan's purpose was war against the atheist Qezelbash, Qansu wrote, 'After consultation with our emirs, we have reached an agreement to set out for Aleppo and Damascus with an army and establish peace between you. Allah has praised compromising in the Qur'an owing to the fact that it eliminates all kinds of sedition and corruption.' Elsewhere in his letter, Qansu laid stress on this point,

> The area to which you are determined to go is one where the residents are mostly Sunnites and orthodox and have suffered for many years. We have heard from the pilgrims who come to the two sacred sanctuaries from that land that Shah Esma'il is no longer determined to confront you and intends to follow the same policy as Uzun Hasan. They have tasted your bitter swords and have lost their fortresses and lands, so they have no braveness remaining. Today we are the servants of the two sacred sanctuaries and we consider it expedient that you compromise for the public welfare. What is important for you is to conquer the island of Rhodes and wage war against the unbelievers. Our request is that you agree to compromise.[127]

Enraged by Qansu's request, Selim responded,

> My war with Ardabil Ughli (Shah Esma'il) is for religion not kingdom. If I intended to conquer territories, Europe (*farang*) would be nearer and better than ruined Iran. As long as Ardabil Ughli does not repent, change his atheistic ways... content himself with Bayazid and ignore other lands, I will never compromise.

Meanwhile, he was informed that Qansu was on his way to Aleppo with 50,000 soldiers on horseback and lots of military equipment. Qansu was of the opinion that he should stay in Aleppo and wait for the result of the war between Selim and Esma'il because the winner would attack his realm.[128]

Regarding Qansu's presence in Aleppo, Selim thought that if he went to Iran to attack Shah Esma'il, the Egyptian sultan would block his way back. Therefore he decided to attack the Mamluk first and then deal with Iran.[129] There were also other rumours, most of them manufactured by Selim's army. Among these was an alleged plot by a number of the Egyptian sultan's envoys to assassinate Selim. Although Sultan Selim spread this rumour, he also wrote a reprimanding letter to Qansu about it.[130] He repeatedly reiterated that he was informed of the fact that there existed correspondence between the Egyptian sultan and Shah Esma'il about forming a common front to fight the Ottomans.[131] The truth, however, is that occupation of Damascus and Egypt and the toppling of the Mamluk government was an important item on Selim's foreign policy agenda. There is no doubt that the removal of the 50,000-soldier Mamluk army was not sufficient grounds for Selim to advance to Damascus and then Cairo and wipe out the Sunni Mamluk government forever while leaving the Shi'ite Shah Esma'il in peace.[132] He stayed in Damascus for about two years, until he totally forgot Esma'il. On the other hand, Esma'il who had sustained a psychological defeat after Chalderan, now preferred not to participate in battles personally. It is said that he stated, 'It is dastardliness to attack and plunder his properties while he, Selim, is not in his territory. We will wait until he comes back!'[133]

As a conclusion, it is worth saying that it was important for Selim to present Qansu as being at fault because he was allied with Shah Esma'il. Consequently in the record of victory written to celebrate the toppling of the Mamluk government, he emphasized the fact that when they arrived in Du'l-qadr lands, 'We realized that the Egyptian Sultan, Qansu al-Ghuri, affected by the deceptions of the old and new Esma'ili atheists, was set to assist atheism and with a glorious army had targeted the area.'[134] By the same token, Shah Esma'il became a pretext for the Ottoman government to attack the Mamluks.

On 25 Rajab 922 (24 August 1516), a battle took place between the Ottoman and Mamluk armies in Marj Dabiq (Wabiq), north of Aleppo in which the Mamluk army was defeated and Qansu, very old, fell from his horse and died. Most of his commanders were killed as well. This defeat was an end to the 260-year-old Mamluk government and sealed Ottoman dominance over Damascus and Egypt.

Notes

1. The name appears as Qanasu al-Ghuri in Arabic sources. Its correct form is Qansawh al-Ghuri, its incorrect form Qansu al-Ghuri (see EI2. vol. IV, p. 552.) In Persian sources it is shown in different forms: Qanisa Ghuri (Qommi, Ahmad ebn Sharaf al-din Hosayn al-Hosayni, *Kholasat al-tavarikh*, ed. Ehsan Eshraqi (Tehran: Tehran University. 1359 H.Sh), p. 96); Qunisa (Modtar, Allah Dita, ed., *Jahangosha-ye Khaqan* (Islamabad: Persian Research Centre for Iran and Pakistan 1364 H.Sh), p. 126); Qani Sad (Montazar Saheb, Asghar, ed., *'Alam ara-ye Shah Esma'il* (Tehran: Bongah-e tarjome va nashr-e ketab 1349 H.Sh), p. 62.); Qanisaw and Qaynsa (Valeh Esfahani, Mohammad Yusof, *Khold-e Barin*, ed. Mirhaseim Mohaddes (Tehran: Bonyad-e Mawqufat-e Afshar 1372 H.Sh), pp. 165, 886); Qaldu Ghuri! (Rahimzade Safavi, Ali Asghar, *Zendegani-ye Shah Esma'il Safavi: sharh-e jangha va tarikh* (Tehran: Khayyam, 1341 H.Sh.). *Shah Esma'il*, p. 383, Nava'i, 'Abdol-Hosayn, *Shah Esma'il Safavi: Majmu'e-ye asnad va mokatebat-e tarikhi* (Tehran: Arghavan 1368 H.Sh), p. 88).
2. al-Sayyid al-Raqid, Muhammad, 'Abd al-Mu'nim. *Al-Ghazw al-'uthmani li Misr wa nata'iju 'ala'l-watan al-'arabi* (Cairo: Mu'assisat shabab al-jami'a 1972 M, pp. 97–8.
3. Ibid., p. 98.
4. The news of the conquest of Constantinople made people in Cairo cheerful. The Mamluk government sent envoys conveying congratulation messages to Sultan Mehmet the Conqueror. Yaghi, Esma'il Ahmad, *Dawlat-e 'Othmani az eqtedar ta enhelal*, trans. Rasul Jafariyan (Qum: Pazhuheshkade-ye Hawze va Daneshgah 1379 H.Sh), p. 54.
5. In Mamluk and Damascene historical sources, this area is called Dhu'l-Ghadir or Dulghadir (Dulqadir) and the present government is called Durlaghadiriyya. For the etymology of this term, see introduction to Ibn 'Aja, Muhammad Ibn Mahmud al-Halabi, *Al-'Araq bayn al-Mamalik wa l-'uthmaniyyin al-atrak*, ed. Muhammad Ahmad Dahman (Damascus: Dar al-fikr 1460 H.Q), pp. 23–4. For the list of the emirs in this government from 740 to 921 or 928 see, ibid., p. 29. Many members of the Zu'l-Qadr tribe joined the Safavids. Faruq Sumer, *Naqsh-e Torkan-e Anatoli dar tashkil va tawse'e-ye dawlat-e Safavi*, trans. Ehsan Eshraqi, Mohammad Taqi Emami (Tehran: Nashr-e Gostare 1371 H.Sh), pp. 214–15.

6. Ibn 'Aja, *Al-'Araq bayn al-mamalik*, pp. 33–61. Since the Ottoman sultan was not ready to face his Mamluk counterpart, he did not support Shah Savar. al-Sayyid al-Raqid, *Al-Ghazw al-'uthmani li Misr*, pp. 93–5, pp. 182–3.
7. Until 'Ala' al-Dawle was killed by Sultan Selim in 921, he had a double-standard policy towards the Ottoman and Mamluk governments. According to Rumlu he told the Ottoman envoys that he was a follower of the Ottoman sultan and hated the Egyptians. He followed the same policy with the envoys of the Egyptian sultan. He received a lot of gold and always said, 'I have two hens one of which lays golden eggs and the other, silver'. Rumlu, Hasan Bayg, *Ahsan al-tavarikh*, ed. Abdol-Hosayn Nava'i (Tehran: Babak 1357 H.Sh), p. 202; Qommi, *Kholasat*, vol. 1, p. 135. Elsewhere indicating that 'Ala' al-Dawle's father was chosen by Uzun Hasan as the greybeard among the Du'l-qadrs in the region, it is said that 'Ala' al-Dawle taught Satan how to deceive. He was so skillful that he received tribute from the Ottoman and Egyptian Sultans. *'Alam ara-ye Shah Esma'il*, pp. 62, 248. The same source gives further information about his double-standards towards the Ottoman and Egyptian Sultans. See also, *Jahangosha-ye Khaqan*, p. 278; Valeh Esfahani; *Khold-e Barin*, p. 251.
8. Ibn Ayas, Muhammad Ibn Ahmad, *Bada'i' al-zuhur fi waqayi' al-duhur*, ed. Muhammad Mustafa (Cairo: al-Hiy'at al-misriyyat al-'ammat li'l-kitab1984 M), vol. 3, p. 215.
9. See Yaghi, *Dawlat-e 'Othmani az eqtedar ta enhelal*, pp. 47–8.
10. Much information is available in historical sources regarding this, but it is not relevant in this context.
11. Rumlu, *Ahsan*, p. 203.
12. al-Ansari, *Hawadith al-zaman*, pp. 199, 206.
13. Ibid., p. 210; Ibn 'Aja, *Al-'Araq bayn al-mamalik*, pp. 185–6.
14. al-Ansari, *Hawadith al-zaman*, p. 214.
15. Ibid., pp. 225–6; Ibn 'Aja, *Al-'Araq bayn al-mamalik*, pp. 198–9.
16. Ibn 'Aja, *Al-'Araq bayn al-mamalik*, p. 199.
17. al-Sayyid al-Raqid, *Al-Ghazw al-'uthmani li Misr*, p. 106.
18. al-Ansari, *Hawadith al-zaman*, p. 448.
19. Ibn Tulun, Shams al-din al-salihi. *I'lam al-wara bi man walla na'iba min al-atrak bi Dimashq al-Sham al-kubra*, ed. Muhammad Ahmad Dahman (Damascus: al-Taba'at al-'ula 1383 H.Q), p. 139.
20. al-Ansari, *Hawadith al-zaman*, p. 517; Ibn Tulun, Shams al-din al-salihi. *Mufakihat al-khullan fi hawadith al-zaman*, Modtar, Allah Dita, ed., *Jahangosha-ye Khaqan* (Islamabad: Persian Research Centre for Iran and Pakistan 1364 H.Sh), vol. I, p. 161.
21. Ibn Tulun, *I'lam al-wara*, p. 145.
22. As an example Budaq Bayg Du'l-Qadr took refuge with the Ottomans and attacked the Du'l-qadrs. Later, in order to take revenge, 'Ala' al-Dawle fought Budaq Bayg, captured an Ottoman commander in the army and sent him to the Egyptian sultan, Qansu. See, Rumlu, *Ahsan*, p. 142.
23. *Jahangosha-ye Khaqan*, p. 186.
24. Hushang Mahdavi, 'Abdo'l-Reza. *Tarikh-e ravabet-e khareji-ye Iran* (5th ed.) (Tehran: Amir Kabir 1375 H.Sh), p. 13.
25. Rumlu, *Ahsan*, pp. 124–5.
26. Rumlu, *Ahsan*, pp. 127–8; Sultan Murad stayed with 'Ala' al-Dawle until 920 and later proceeded to Iran via Diyarbakr in the period immediately before Selim I's attack to recapture it from Durmish Khan, a Safavid governor, considering it his ancestor's property. He was killed in a battle with Durmish Khan on the last day of Ramadan, 920. Rumlu, *Ahsan*, p. 197; al-'Azzawi, 'Abbas, *Ta'rikh al-'Iraq bayn ihtilalayn* (Baghdad: al-Maktabat al-ahliyya 1939 M), vol. III, p. 313.
27. Rumlu, *Ahsan*, pp. 140–1.
28. Gholam Sarwar, *Tarikh-e Shah Esma'il Safavi*, trans. Mohammad Baqer Aram, 'Abbas Qoli Ghaffari-Fard (Tehran: Markaz-e nashr-e daneshgahi 1374 H.Sh), p. 67.
29. As if it were really a pretext. Sultan Selim, who was an ambitious man and tried to record his name as the greatest Ottoman conqueror, was seeking to expand the Ottoman geographical realm in the East. He became successful. He could expand Ottoman lands twice as much as his father did during

his eight-year sultanate. Selim, as a matter of fact, was only looking for an opportunity to conquer Egypt. The ties between Mamluk and Shah Esma'il could have been a pretext for him.

30. Ibn Ayas, *Bada'i' al-zuhur*, vol. IV, p. 39.
31. Ibn Tulun, *Mufakihat al-khullan*, vol. I, p. 261.
32. Ibn Tulun, *Mufakihat al-khullan*, vol. I, p. 262.
33. Firaydun Bayg, *Mansha'at al-salatin*, 2 vols. (Istanbul: Dar al-Tiba'at al-'Amire, 1256–74/1848–54), pp. 353–4.
34. The Arabic version of the letter is as follows: *ama qissat ghalbat farqi al-dala al-sharqiya, fa-innaha baliyya 'amma zaharat fi tilka al-nawahi; fa-daf'uhum lazim bal wajib 'ala al-adani wa-l-aqasi; fa-l-maqsud fi daf'ihim wa-istisalihim bi-'inayat al-Malik al-'allam al-muwafaqa wa-l-ihtimam li-annahum ahl al-bida' wa-l-dalala wa-ashab al-sharr wa-l-shaqawa, kulluhum rawafid wa-jammhum mala'in, laysa fi qulubihim al-radi'a ithr al-rahma wa-l-shafqa wa-la fi tinatihim al-khabitha 'ala'im al-hidaya wa-l-ra'fa, wa-innahum hataku 'ard al-mu'minin wa-l-mu'minat wa-qatalu 'ulama' al-din wa-l-sadat wa-agharu amwalahum wa-asaru sibyanahum wa-'amalu fi hadhihi al-mamlaka a'malan la yara mithlahu ahad min al-khuruj al-awlad al-jinkiziyya wa-la sami'a shibhahu udhun fi zuhur al-ahzab al-taymuriyya; awla'ika hum al-kafara al-fajara; allahuma dammarhum wa-qaharhum wa-farraq shamlahum wa-kassar a'naqahum wa-tahhar al-ardin 'an ha'ula' al-arjas al-anjas.* Ibid., pp. 354–7; Nava'i, *Shah Esma'il Safavi*, p. 91.
35. Ibn Tulun, *A'lam al-wara*, p. 188 refers to the efforts made against Haydar Sufi.
36. A largely fanciful Safavid history entitled *Alam ara-ye Safavi* refers to a meeting in which Shah Esma'il's valour was praised in the presence of Qansu. It also mentions that the sultan's Abyssinian servant boasted that he would bring Esma'il's head and set out for Aleppo and then Iran along with 300 people. He fought Murad Bayg, but was killed. As soon as the news reached the Egyptian sultan, he 'secretly turned into an enthusiast for the mighty sultan (i.e. Shah Esma'il) and said we should send a perceptive and well-spoken man to visit Shah Esma'il and express our affection and apologize to him for the army's misbehaviour. This dynasty is noble and great ... the envoy was sent.' *Alam ara-ye Safavi*, pp. 153–4; *Jahangosha-ye Khaqan*, pp. 480–1; Valeh Esfahani, *Khold-e Barin*, p. 232. (The two latter sources are more important.)
37. Ibn Ayas, *Bada'i' al-zuhur*, vol. IV, p. 118; Ibn Tulun, *Mufakihat al-khullan*, vol. I, pp. 316–18.
38. He is referred to as 'Ali Dulat in Mamluk sources. Ibn Ayas, *Bada'i' al-zuhur*, vol. IV, p. 121.
39. Ibid., vol. III, p. 121.
40. Ibid., vol. IV, p. 122.
41. Ibid., vol. IV, p. 123.
42. Ibid., vol. IV, pp. 143, 145.
43. Ibid., vol. IV, p. 146.
44. Ibid., vol. IV, p. 145.
45. Ibid., vol. IV, p. 184.
46. Ibn Tulun, *Mufakihat al-khullan*, vol. I, p. 342; Ibn Ayas, *Bada'i' al-zuhur*, vol. IV, p. 184.
47. Ibid., vol. IV, p. 191.
48. Ibid., vol. IV, p. 205; Ibn Tulun, *Mufakihat al-khullan*, vol. I, p. 343.
49. Gholam Sarvar refers to the date of the letter as 924 and adds that Charles V received it six years later (*Shah Esma'il*, p. 113), whereas a few years before him Nasrollah Falsafi, in *Tarikh-e ravabet-e khareji-ye Iran va Orupa dar dawre-ye Safaviye*, pp. 163–4 (translation from 'Moraselat-e Karl-e Panjom' and Nava'i, *Iran va jahan*, vol. I, pp. 153–4) had written that the letter had been written on 29 Shawwal 929. On that basis it was received by the Holy Roman Emperor only two years later.
50. The translation of this letter was published in *Kave* periodical (Iraj Afshar, p. 564) Gholam Sarvar, *Shah Esma'il*, pp. 112–13.
51. Ibn Ayas, *Bada'i' al-zuhur*, vol. IV, p. 207.
52. Nava'i, *Shah Esma'il Safavi*, pp. 93–5.
53. al-Ansari, *Hawadith al-zaman*, pp. 469–70.
54. Ibn Tulun, *Mufakihat al-khullan*, vol. I, p. 354.

55. al-Ansari, *Hawadith al-zaman*, p. 472.
56. Ibn Ayas, *Bada'i' al-zuhur*, vol. IV, pp. 219–20.
57. Rumlu (*Ahsan*, p. 161) wrote that the head was sent to Bayezid. At that time Selim was still in Tirabuzan, although he was abreast of Esma'il's acts.
58. Ibn Ayas, *Bada'i' al-zuhur*, vol. IV, pp. 2201.
59. Nava'i, 'Abdol Hosayn, ed., *Shah Esma'il Safavi, Asnad va Mokatebat-e Tarikhi* (Tehran: Bonyad-e Farhang-e Iran, 1347/1968), p. 95. The published text is erroneous. The correct version can be found in Mirza Ghulam Ahmad numbered 3455 in the Majles library (pp. 120–1).
60. Ibn Ayas, *Bada'i' al-zuhur*, vol. IV, pp. 220–1. According to Rumlu, they covered the skull with gold, made a bowl, filled it with wine and passed it around for all at a party. Rumlu, *Ahsan*, p. 161.
61. Ibn Ayas, *Bada'i' al-zuhur*, vol. IV, pp. 221–7.
62. Ibid., p. 228.
63. Ibn Tulun, *Mufakihat al-khullan*, vol. I, p. 357.
64. Ibn Ayas, *Bada'i' al-zuhur*, p. 230.
65. Ibn Tulun, *Mufakihat al-khullan*, vol. I, p. 357.
66. al-Ansari, *Hawadith al-zaman*, p. 484.
67. Ibid., pp. 473–4. al-Ansari reported it ambiguously. It is not definite whether he meant that the meeting with the sultan was in Cairo or Qansu was in Damascus then! Earlier he had discussed that Shah Esma'il's envoy visited the sultan in Cairo.
68. *Jahangosha-ye khaqan*, p. 404; Qommi, *Kholasat*, vol. I, p. 117; Shirazi, 'Abdi Bayg. *Takmilat al-akhbar*, ed. 'Abdol-Hosayn Nava'i (Tehran: Nay 1369 H.Sh), p. 51.
69. They sometimes took presents for the Ottoman sultan. For instance, in 923 when Selim conquered Egypt 'Qadi al-balad al-rumi Zayn al-abidin' who were rejected by Esma'il and became fugitives, sent some gifts for Selim. Ibn Tulun, *Mufakihat al-khullan*, vol. II, p. 58.
70. al-Ansari, *Hawadith al-zaman*, p. 473.
71. Ibid., pp. 744–78.
72. Ibn Tulun, *Mufakahat al-khillan*, vol. I, p. 362. Unfortunately one word of what Ibn Tulun has said is omitted. Its Arabic version is as follows: *li-kawnihi qila in al-khariji Isma'il al-sufi .... (al-)ka'ba thawban, wa-innahu baqi li-l-hajj wa-yulbisnahu iyyahu, wa-zada wuquf al-hal wa-la quwwa illa bi-llah.*
73. Ibn Ayas, *Bada'i' al-zuhur*, vol. IV, pp. 257–8.
74. Ibid., vol. IV, p. 262.
75. Ibid., vol. IV, pp. 265–6.
76. Ibid., vol. IV, p. 268.
77. Ibid., vol. IV, p. 271.
78. Ibid., vol. IV, p. 311.
79. Ibid., vol. IV, pp. 179–82.
80. Espenaqchi has written, 'It is definite that forty thousand in Haydariyya, fifty thousand in Egypt and thirty thousand of Jalileyan qorb were massacred by this cruel man. In these four wars and the wars among Hungary, Diyarbakr and Georgia particularly the war between Du'l-qadriyya and Mount Lebanon and Gaza (Ghazza), the ones who were killed from both sides affected by the difficulties of the journey were more than a hundred thousand. The total victims are recorded as two hundred and fifty thousand.' Espenaqchi, Pashazade, Mohammad, 'Aref. *Enqelab al-Islam bayn al-khavas va'l-'avam*, ed. Rasul Jafariyan (Qum: Dalil 1379 H.Sh), p. 265.
81. Concerning such scholars see Ja'fariyan, Rasul, *Safaviye dar 'arse-ye din, farhang va siyasat*, 3 volumes (Qum: Pezhuheshkade-ye Hawze va Daneshgah, i1379 H.Sh.) vol. I, pp. 78–107.
82. Rumlu, *Ahsan*, p. 161.
83. Reportedly, when Khalil Aqa, Shah Esma'il's envoy turned in the head to the Ottoman court, he was killed by Selim's stimulation who was not a sultan yet. *'Alam Aray Safavi*, p. 332.
84. Rumlu, *Ahsan*, pp. 165–6.
85. Ibid., p. 175.
86. Ibid., p. 177.

87. al-Sayyid al- Raqid, 'Abd al-Mu'nim. *Al-Ghazw al-'uthmani li Misr wa nata'iju 'ala'l-watan al-'arabi.*, p. 139.
88. Rumlu, *Ahsan*, pp. 187-8.
89. For the Arabic version of what Selim has written about the Chalderan war in detail, see Ibn Tulun, *Mufakihat al-khullan*, vol. II, pp. 44-57; Persian version in brief in Espenaqchi, *Enqelab*, pp. 113-15.
90. An example was the letter he wrote to Muhammad Bayg Aq Qoyunlu. Nava'i, *Shah Esma'il*, pp. 51-2.
91. Ibn Ayas, *Bada'i' al-zuhur*, vol. IV, p. 373.
92. Farid Bayg, Mohammad, *Ahsan al-tavarikh: Tarikh-e dawlat-e Osmani* (Tehran: Matba'e-ye Baqerzade, 1332 H.Q), p. 61.
93. Ibid., p. 63.
94. al-Ansari, *Hawadith al-zaman*, pp. 504-5.
95. Ibn Tulun, *A'lam al-wara*, p. 206.
96. Ibn Ayas, *Bada'i' al-zuhur*, vol. IV, p. 393.
97. Ibid., vol. IV, pp. 396, 400, 403.
98. Ibid., vol. IV, p. 398.
99. Ibid., vol. IV, p. 445.
100. Ibid., vol. IV, p. 452.
101. *'Alam ara-ye Shah Esma'il*, pp. 561-2; Shokre, Yadollah, ed., *'Alam ara-ye Safavi* (Tehran: Entesharat-e Ettila'at 1363 H.Sh), p. 542.
102. al-Ansari, *Hawadith al-zaman*, pp. 512-13; Rumlu, *Ahsan*, pp. 202-3.
103. Qommi, *Kholasat*, p. 135; *Jahangosha-ye khaqan*, p. 524; Valeh Esfahani, *Khold-e Barin*, p. 252.
104. *Safarname-ye Veniziyan dar Iran*, trans. Manuchehr Amiri (Tehran. Kharazmi 1349 H.Sh), p. 332.
105. Ibn Ayas, *Bada'i' al-zuhur*, vol. IV, p. 449.
106. Concerning 'Ala' al-Dawle's two-fold policy towards the Mamluk and Ottoman governments, see Rumlu, *Ahsan*, p. 202.
107. Selim's deceitful effort was to calm Mamluk fears of Ottoman attack and discourage preparations against it. After dealing with 'Ala' al-Dawle he wrote to Qansu that the main problem had been 'Ala' al-Dawle, so that now he could entrust his land to the Egyptian sultan. Uzuncharshili, Esma'il Haqqi (Uzunçarşılı, İsmail Hakkı), *Tarikh-e Osmani*, trans. Iraj Nawbakht (Tehran: Kayhan 1369 H.Sh), p. 301. In another report he sent Qadi 'Askar to Aleppo to try to change Qansu's mind, saying that they had carte blanche: 'kull hadha hiyal wa-khida' hatta yubtil himmat al-Sultan 'an al-qital'. Another of his plans was to request sugar and Halwa (confectionery) from Qansu, who sent him a hundred loads 'wa-kull dhalika hiyal minhu'. This was also a trick. Apart from the letter, he sent some precious gifts to the sultan. Ibn Ayas, *Bada'i' al-zuhur*, vol. IV, p. 60; Uzuncharshili, *Tarikh-e Osmani*, p. 303.
108. It is reported by Ibn Ayas (*Bada'i' al-zuhur*, vol. V, p. 35). He introduced his jester as 'Ajmi al-Shinqiji adding that he had been seemingly sent to the governors of Aleppo and Damascus, but when he was delayed, the rumor went round that he had been sent to Esma'il.
109. For the reports concerning Qara Khan, his clashes with the Romans, its causes and the seizure of Diyarbakr by the Ottomans see Qommi, *Kholasat*, p. 136. In this book there is no reference to Qara Khan's cooperation with the Egyptians. He was accused of clashing to take Mardin, Diyarbakr's capital, back without Shah Esma'il's permission.
110. Uzuncharshili, *Tarikh-e Osmani*, vol. II, p. 302; Iraj Nawbakht, *Tarikh-e Lutfi Pasha*, pp. 241-7.
111. Ibn Ayas, *Bada'i' al-zuhur*, vol. IV, pp. 376, 381.
112. Faruq Sumer, *Naqsh-e turkan-e Anatoli dar tashkil va tawse'e-ye dawlat-e Safavi* (p. 49) is an exception. Referring to the Safavids' long borders with the Mamluks and the fact that the majority of the Syrians and Egyptians were Sunnis, he mentions that the Mamluk government was indifferent to Shah Esma'il's activities and to the joining of many Turkomans with Esma'il. In his footnotes he points out the limited references to the Safavids in Mamluk sources.
113. Hamer Purgeshtal, (Josef von Hammer-Purgstall), *Tarikh-e Emperaturi-ye 'Otsmani*, trans. Mirza Zaki, ed. 'Aliabadi Jamshid Kiyanfar (Tehran: Zarrin 1367 H.Sh), vol. II, p. 879.

114. Uzuncharshili, *Tarikh-e Osmani*, p. 303.
115. Ibid.
116. As an example see Qommi, *Kholasat*, p. 137. In this book, written by using various sources of that time, nothing is discussed in this regard and Qansu's defeat is reported with no care. Also, *'Alam Ara-ye Shah Esma'il*, pp. 5637; Valeh Esfahani, *Khold-e Barin*, pp. 256–7.
117. *Safarname-ye Veniziyan dar Iran*, p. 335.
118. Ibid., pp. 334–5.
119. *Jahangosha-ye Khaqan*, pp. 535–6; Valeh Esfahani, *Khold-e Barin*, p. 256.
120. Uzuncharshili, *Tarikh-e Osmani*, vol. II, p. 303.
121. Ibn Ayas, *Bada'i' al-zuhur*, vol. V, p. 60; Uzuncharshili, *Tarikh-e Osmani*, p. 301.
122. Uzuncharshili, *Tarikh-e Osmani*, p. 303.
123. Espenaqchi, *Enqelab*, p. 173.
124. Ibid., p. 220.
125. Ibid., p. 178.
126. Ibid., pp. 180–1.
127. Ibid., pp. 182–3.
128. Ibn Ayas, *Bada'i' al-zuhur*, vol. V, p. 22.
129. Espenaqchi, *Enqelab*, p. 187.
130. Ibid., p. 188.
131. Ibn Tulun, *A'lam al-wara*, pp. 274–5.
132. Ibn Ayas has pointed out that Esma'il's envoy went to Selim in Rabi' al-thani, 923. When Selim read Esma'il's letter he became so angry that he wanted to kill the envoy. The envoy ran away and although they looked for him in all the houses of old Egypt, they could find him neither on land nor sea. Ibn Ayas, *Bada'i' al-zuhur*, vol. V, p. 180. In 924 when Selim had occupied all the Mamluk lands, a special envoy came to him from Esma'il's side and offered him lots of gifts in Damascus and requested him to come to an agreement with Iran. (Espenaqchi, *Enqelab*, pp. 152–3. Compare with Ibn Tulun, *Mufakihat al-khullan*, vol. II, p. 61.) At this time, Selim was not thinking of the Safavids' removal any more. Because he still needed time to digest the huge wealth of the occupied Mamluk lands, Selim never expected these envoys. According to Ibn Ayas they came in an informal manner not to be stopped. Upon arrival, they gave Selim their gifts and Esma'il's letter in which there were sentences about compromise. Enraged by the letter, Selim said: 'This is Esma'il's trick to change my mind about confrontation with him, which is exactly what I did about Qansu'. Ibn Ayas, *Bada'i' al-zuhur*, vol. V, pp. 247–8. More explanations about the letter can be found on p. 253.
133. Shamlu, Vali Qoli, *Qasas al-khaqani* (vol.1), ed. Sadat Naseri (Tehran 1371 H.Sh), vol. I; without a doubt, the Qezelbash army, although small, was dangerous for Selim. He himself was aware of it. he praised the valour of the Qezelbash, but criticized them for supporting an atheist person. Khaja Sa'd al-din, *Taj al-tavarikh*, p. 258 quoted from Sumer, Faruq, *Naqsh-e Torkan-e Anatoli*, pp. 51–2 (footnote).
134. Espenaqchi, *Enqelab*, p. 214.

References

al-Ansari, Ahmad Ibn Muhammad Ibn, 'Umar. *Hawadith al-zaman wa wafayat al-shuyukh wa al-aqran*, 'Abd al-'Aziz Fayyad Harfush (ed.) (Beirut: Dar al-nafa'is 2000 M/1421 H.Q).

al-'Azzawi, 'Abbas, *Ta'rikh al-'Iraq bayn ihtilalayn* (Baghdad: al-Maktabat al-ahliyya 1939 M).

Espenaqchi Pashazade, Mohammad, 'Aref. *Enqelab al-Islam bayn al-khavas va'l-'avam*. Rasul Jafariyan (ed.) (Qum: Dalil 1379 H.Sh).

Falsafi, Nasrollah, *Tarikh-e ravabet-e khareji-ye Iran dar dawre-ye Safaviye* (Tehran: Chapkhane-ye Iran. 1316 H.Sh).

Farid Bayg, Mohammad, *Ahsan al-tavarikh dar tarikh-e al-e Osman* (Tehran: Matba'e-ye Baqerzade. 1332 H.Q).

Firaydun Bayg, *Munsha'at al-Salatin*, 2 vols. (Istanbul: Dar al-Tiba'at al-'Amire, 1256–74/1848–54), pp. 353–4.

Hamer Purgeshtal (Josef von Hammer-Purgstall), *Tarikh-e Emperaturi-ye 'Otsmani*. Mirza Zaki 'Aliabadi (trans.), Jamshid Kiyanfar (ed.) (Tehran: Zarrin 1367 H.Sh.)

Hushang Mahdavi, 'Abdo'l-Reza. *Tarikh-e ravabet-e khareji-ye Iran* (5th ed.) (Tehran: Amir Kabir 1375 H.Sh).

Ibn 'Aja, Muhammad Ibn Mahmud al-Halabi, *Al-'Araq bayn al-Mamalik wa l-'uthmaniyyin al-atrak*, Muhammad Ahmad Dahman (ed.) (Damascus: Dar al-fikr 1460 H.Q).

Ibn Ayas, Muhammad Ibn Ahmad, *Bada'i' al-zuhur fi waqayi' al-duhur*, Muhammad Mustafa (ed.) (Cairo: al-Hiy'at al-misriyyat al-'ammat li'l-kitab1984 M).

Ibn Tulun, *Shams al-din al-salihi. I'lam al-wara bi man walla na'iba min al-atrak bi Dimashq al-Sham al-kubra*, Muhammad Ahmad Dahman (ed.) (Damascus: al-Taba'at al-'ula 1964 M/1383 H.Q).

—— *Mufakihat al-khullan fi hawadith al-zaman*, Modtar, Allah Dita (ed.), *Jahangosha-ye Khaqan* (Islamabad: Persian Research Centre for Iran and Pakistan 1364 H.Sh.).

Montazar Saheb, Asghar (ed.), *'Alam ara-ye Shah Esma'il* (Tehran: Bongah-e tarjome va nashr-e ketab 1349 H.Sh).

Muhammad Mustafa (ed.), 'Cairo: al-Mu'assisat al-misriyyat al-'amma 1962 M.

Nava'i, 'Abdol-Hosayn, *Iran va jahan: az Moghul ta Qajariye* (vol.1) (3rd ed.) (Tehran: Nashr-e Homa 1370 H.Sh).

—— *Shah Esma'il Safavi: Majmu'e-ye asnad va mokatebat-e tarikhi* (Tehran: Arghavan 1368 H.Sh).

Qommi, Ahmad ebn Sharaf al-din Hosayn al-Hosayni, *Kholasat al-tavarikh*, Ehsan Eshraqi (ed.) (Tehran: Tehran University. 1359 H.Sh).

Rumlu, Hasan Bayg, *Ahsan al-tavarikh* 'Abdol-Hosayn Nava'i (ed.) (Tehran: Babak 1357 H.Sh).

Safarname-ye Veniziyan dar Iran, Manuchehr Amiri (trans.) (Tehran. Kharazmi 1349 H.Sh).

Sarvar, Gholam (Sarwar, Ghulam), *Tarikh-e Shah Esma'il Safavi*, Mohammad Baqer Aram, 'Abbas Qoli Ghaffari-Fard (trans.) (Tehran: Markaz-e nashr-e daneshgahi 1374 H.Sh.).

al-Sayyid al-Raqid, Muhammad, 'Abd al-Mu'nim. *Al-Ghazw al-'uthmani li Misr wa nata'iju 'ala'l-watan al-'arabi* (Cairo: Mu'assisat shabab al-jami'a 1972 M).

Shamlu, Vali Qoli, *Qasas al-khaqani* (vol.1), Sadat Naseri (ed.) (Tehran 1371 H.Sh).

Shirazi, 'Abdi Bayg. *Takmilat al-akhbar*, 'Abdol-Hosayn Nava'i (ed.) (Tehran: Nay 1369 H.Sh).

Shokre, Yadollah (ed.), *'Alam ara-ye Safavi* (Tehran: Entesharat-e Ettila'at 1363 H.Sh).

Sumer, Faruq, *Naqsh-e Torkan-e Anatoli dar tashkil va tawse'e - ye dawlat-e Safavi*, Ehsan Eshraqi, Mohammad Taqi Emami (trans.) (Tehran: Nashr-e Gostare 1371 H.Sh).

Uzuncharshili, Esma'il Haqqi (Uzunçarşılı, İsmail Hakkı), *Tarikh-e Osmani*, Iraj Nawbakht (trans.) (Tehran: Kayhan 1369 H.Sh).

Valeh Esfahani, Mohammad Yusof, *Khold-e Barin*, Mirhaseim Mohaddes (ed.) (Tehran: Bonyad-e Mawqufat-e Afshar 1372 H.Sh).

Yaghi, Esma'il Ahmad, *Dawlat-e 'Othmani az eqtedar ta enhelal*, Rasul Jafariyan (trans.) (Qum: Pazhuheshkade-ye Hawze va Daneshgah 1379 H.Sh).

# 5

From Rhetoric of War to Realities of Peace: The Evolution of Ottoman-Iranian Diplomacy through the Safavid Era

Ernest Tucker

Introduction

When Ismail I became the first Safavid shah in 1501, an era of competition commenced between him and the Ottomans, who did not really accept his basic political and religious legitimacy. The Ottomans perceived him and his successors as heretics due to the Safavid belief that the shah possessed a special link to the Shi'i Imams. The Ottomans used this belief to legitimate military campaigns against the Safavids, particularly in the border zones of eastern Anatolia, the Caucasus and Iraq. Following the decisive Ottoman defeat of Ismail and his followers at Chalderan in 1514, though, the Ottoman-Safavid frontier settled down into a steady low-level confrontation that continued over the next century, escalating only a few times into open war. Such escalations generally occurred when the Ottomans were not on campaign against the Habsburgs in Europe and the Safavids were not fighting the Uzbeks in Central Asia. The most significant incursion of Safavid forces into Ottoman territory during this period was the 1623 conquest by Shah 'Abbas I (1587–1629) of Baghdad, subsequently occupied by Iran for the next 15 years.

Despite a persistent backdrop conflict between the two empires, their successive peace agreements gradually became less polemical exhortations and more diplomatic attempts to establish correct relations. This trend culminated in the 1639 treaty of Zuhab, which delineated borders and emphasized the need for both sides to protect merchants and pilgrims transiting those borders. Earlier Ottoman-Safavid agreements had partially discussed these points, but the 1639 Zuhab treaty proved more resilient than any other treaty of the Safavid era, remaining a point of departure for almost all subsequent diplomatic agreements between the two sides.

Historians examining the emergence of modern Iran as a nation-state in Safavid times have recalled the enduring qualities of this agreement and have portrayed it as ushering in an era of peace with the Ottomans for Iran following a long period of conflict.[1] The agreement's pragmatic dimensions had their origins as far back as the 1555 Ottoman-Safavid Amasya accord. The Zuhab treaty was the culmination of incrementally and successively more substantial agreements concluded in the eight decades following the Amasya accord. This long period of development helped create stable conditions for peace between these empires that actually did not formally require them to relinquish their mutual grievances. Therefore, despite deep intrinsic conflicts of political and religious legitimacy, Safavid Iran and the Ottoman Empire began building a framework early in their relationship for a *de facto* stable relationship, while always holding *de jure* justification for hostilities in reserve should the need ever arise. Despite the fact that they never really reached agreement on the precise delineation of their common border, the Ottoman and Safavid empires built, through several agreements, an enduring way for distinct Muslim nations to recognize one another apart from the constraints of competing universal religious worldviews.

The diplomatic process that led up to the treaty of Zuhab bears some resemblance to the way that international diplomacy evolved in Europe during the seventeenth century to allow nations with abiding religious and political conflicts to maintain relations. Similar to the process that led to the 1648 peace of Westphalia and marked the end of the Thirty Years' War in Europe, the emergence of a stable Ottoman-Safavid connection was driven by both sides' practical need to facilitate the transit of pilgrims and merchants across the frontier.

The ideological context of the Ottoman-Safavid relationship

The Safavid Empire that began to emerge after the conquest of Tabriz in 1501 immediately posed serious challenges to emerging Ottoman views of Islamic orthodoxy.[2] In describing the clash of the Iranian and Ottoman armies at Chalderan in 1514 as a struggle between religion and unbelief, Ottoman chroniclers began a long tradition of portraying the Safavids as *kuffar* (infidels).[3] In a letter from Sultan Selim to Shah Ismail before this battle, the imagery was cast in ancient terms, with the sultan becoming the 'Alexander of eminence' against the 'usurping Darius', 'the malevolent Zahhak', 'the peer of Cain', Ismail. Ismail was admonished:

> You no longer uphold the commandments and prohibitions of the Divine Law...you have incited your abominable Shi'i faction to unsanctified sexual union and to the shedding of innocent blood that like they 'Who listen to falsehood and consume the unlawful' [Quran V:42] you have given ear to idle, deceitful words and have eaten that which is forbidden... Indeed, as both the *fatwas* of distinguished *ulama* who base their opinion on reason and tradition alike

and the consensus of the Sunni community agree that the ancient obligation of extirpation, extermination, and expulsion of evil innovation must be the aim of our exalted aspiration, for 'Religious zeal is a victory for the Faith of God the Beneficent'; then, in accordance with the words of the Prophet (Peace be upon him!) 'Whosoever introduces evil innovation into our order must be expelled' and 'Whosoever does aught against our order must be expelled,' action has become necessary and exigent.[4]

This letter provides a good example of the parameters of the formal, rhetorical version of the Ottoman anti-Safavid view that could always be trotted out when useful.

Scholars have suggested that Ottoman concern about the popularity of Safavid ideas among various segments of the Ottoman population helped increase their hostility towards Iran through the middle of the sixteenth century. Anti-Iranian Ottoman *fatwas* of the sixteenth century continued to reflect such anxieties and were targeted against the Qezelbash in particular. The famed Ottoman *Shaykh al-Islam* Ebussuud Efendi (who served 1545–74) presented arguments that would recur in subsequent *fatwas*, calling the Qezelbash infidels because they practised *sabb* (the cursing of Abu Bakr and other companions of the Prophet).[5] Ebussuud went as far as to proclaim that 'killing this group is more important than killing other groups', because they sowed corruption and discord among Muslims just like the false prophet Musaylima. He noted that some Muslim scholars, such as Ahmad ibn Hanbal, allowed those who cursed the companions of the Prophet to be killed even if they had repented of their infidelities.[6] Ebussuud compared the Qezelbash with the first Muslim apostates who turned against Muhammad and his companions in the early years of the Islamic *umma* after having converted to Islam.

When another round of Ottoman-Safavid conflict broke out between 1578 and 1590, further anti-Qezelbash polemics built upon Ebussuud's work. One chapter of the 1581 *Mushtamil al-Aqawil* of Şeyh Seyyid Mutahhar began, 'as for this group who are called Qezelbash, may God eradicate them and ruin them', and went on to justify killing them for their offences.[7] This work also warned against marriages between Qezelbash and Sunni Muslims. At the beginning of the seventeenth century, during yet another round of conflict with Shah 'Abbas I, then Ottoman *Shaykh al-Islam* Esad Efendi produced a polemic that repeated the objections against cursing of the companions, but offered a more detailed critique of Shi'i ritual practices, accusing Iranians of drinking wine and of unlawfully enslaving and killing Sunni Muslims.[8]

The sectarian hatred that coloured these polemics and *fatwas* was most obviously unveiled during wartime, when there was a need to justify and set rules for conflict with Iran. Nevertheless, these documents reflected a persistent religious animosity that did not cease even when hostilities subsided. Ottoman chronicles and documents revealed an ambient dislike of the Safavids through liberal use of such epithets for Iranians as '*kızılbaş-ı dinharaş-ı dalaletmaaş*' ('Qezelbash religion-destroyers who have gone astray') and 'Şah-i gümrah' ('heretical or misguided shah'), which by the eighteenth century had become almost stock terms of reference for Iranian soldiers and their monarchs.[9] It is interesting to note, in contrast, that the Safavid chronicles treated the Ottomans with much greater respect and virtually never raised religious issues, preferring to portray the Ottomans as worthy adversaries in battle, but more importantly, as victorious warriors of Islam against the Europeans. An example of this approach can be found in Eskandar Bayg Munshi's laudatory account of the 1596 battle of Haçova where the Ottomans defeated a coalition of European forces.[10]

Early Ottoman-Safavid peace agreements

However, this enmity was merely one component of the relationship between the two countries during this period. Inter-dynastic relations between the Ottomans and Safavids were marked by numerous congratulatory letters, embassies, and gift exchanges, particularly upon the enthronement of new monarchs. There were 22 Ottoman embassies to the Persians and 61 Persian embassies to the Ottomans during the period 1500–1750, many of which were dispatched to exchange gifts and congratulate new monarchs.[11] In addition, a remarkable expansion of trade routes between Iran and the market centres of western Anatolia, such as Bursa, occurred through the sixteenth century. In the seventeenth century, the Safavids maintained a quasi-diplomatic representative in Bursa known as the *shahbandar-i A'jam* to look after the interests of Iranian merchants there.[12] The Safavids, of course, maintained continued interest in the key Shi'i pilgrimage sites of Ottoman Iraq: Najaf and Karbala. Suraiya Faroqhi notes that, even if they had wanted to, it would have been difficult for the Ottomans to bar Iranian pilgrims from visiting Karbala and Najaf. She records that despite Ottoman attempts to clamp down on Iranian connections with Iraq, pilgrims from Iran were able to visit Iraq and that the shah even posted representatives there on a somewhat regular basis.[13]

Early Ottoman-Safavid peace agreements tried to satisfy contradictory visions of religious relations between the two empires: they called for the elimination of particularly Shi'i Iranian practices such as *sabb*, to which the Ottomans objected, but reaffirmed strong support for the rights of all Muslims to make the *hajj*. The first important peace between the Ottomans and Safavids, the Amasya agreement of 1555, took the form of an imperial decree that, in a more polite way, echoed the religious polemic of the *fatwas* mentioned above. It began with a long exhortation that Iranians should respect not only Ali but the other three rightly guided caliphs as well. However, the document then proceeded to affirm that the Ottoman sultan regarded the protection of all pilgrims to Mecca and Medina from among the Muslim masses ('*umum-i Muslimin*) as a sacred duty and to warn Ottoman officials that they were not to interfere with travellers coming from the direction of Iran.[14] Although the decree contained no specific language recognizing any official status for Iranians in particular, its wording confirmed in a general sense the sultan's view of his status as protector of all Muslims.

Ottoman-Safavid agreements concluded during the reign of Shah 'Abbas I contained provisions designed to promote stable and peaceful relations between the two countries. In the treaty of 1590, Iranians again were enjoined to stop cursing the first three caliphs, while borders that had been established after the campaigns of the previous decade were confirmed and each side pledged not to harbour rebels and refugees from the other. There was no mention made of pilgrims at all.[15] The inconclusive agreements of 1613 and 1619 that were negotiated during a period of renewed Ottoman-Safavid clashes in the Caucasus pursued the same goals: establishing a stable border and eradicating the primary formal cause of religious enmity – the cursing of companions of the Prophet, especially the first three caliphs.

The text of the 1619 agreement mentioned pilgrims again. It decreed that *hajj* visitors from Iran would be permitted to travel via Aleppo and Damascus, but not via Baghdad and Basra, due to the insecurity of the roads there. It stated that, 'those pilgrims wishing to make the *hajj* who come from [or 'via'] your province [*vilayetinizden*] will travel via Aleppo and Syria and, because the safety of the Baghdad and Basra routes cannot be assured ... will not be permitted to pass [that way].'[16] Although this treaty offered protection to pilgrims coming from Iran, it preserved a certain ambiguity because it could have been interpreted as referring to all those coming either 'from' or 'via' Iran, which could include Sunni Muslims from India or Central Asia. However, the specific ban on travel by way of Baghdad and Basra on safety grounds implied that Shi'i pilgrims' rights to visit shrines in Iraq near those cities would be curtailed.

Problems caused by Iranian pilgrims vexed the Ottomans for centuries. Iranian pilgrims were often forbidden from travelling to Mecca via the eastern route through Baghdad, Basra and al-Hasa, ostensibly for security reasons, but probably also to prevent fraternization between the Shi'is of Iran and the Shi'i community in al-Hasa, which had been loosely incorporated into Ottoman domains by the middle of the sixteenth century.[17] The language of the 1619 *hajj* clause signalled a general Ottoman policy of that time to control the time and place of Iranian pilgrimages very carefully. The question of Iranian access to Najaf and Karbala proved a continuing dilemma. In the end, the Ottoman approach to pilgrims was characterized by a pragmatic approach through language that skirted around issues of religious sensitivity such as Shi'i shrine visits while facilitating the *hajj* traffic on a broad scale.

The treaty of Zuhab

This pragmatism was finally to be codified in the 1639 treaty of Zuhab, the lasting agreement between the Ottomans and the Safavids whose parameters endured for several centuries even beyond the tenure of the original signatories. It was concluded after the Ottoman recapture of Baghdad from the Safavids, who had held it for the 15 years since its conquest by Shah 'Abbas I. The two sides came to terms in 1639 because of looming threats to the Ottomans in Europe from the Holy Roman Empire and the Holy League, as well as the establishment of relative border stability between Iran and the Ottoman Empire after many decades of sporadic, inconclusive conflict. In such circumstances, this treaty focused on establishing the boundary between the Ottoman Empire and Iran to the exclusion of virtually all other issues, although it did repeat the injunction against cursing companions of the Prophet and generally called for the security of travellers between the two countries.[18]

The delineation of a formal diplomatic relationship through this agreement resulted in an equilibrium between the two empires that would not be disturbed for over 75 years. Subsequent dynasties and regimes would address more details of this formal, legal relationship between the two countries, but the power of the relationship that the agreement established is shown by how much trouble the Ottomans took to preserve its conditions even following the collapse of Safavid rule in the 1720s.

At that time, the Ottomans became involved in Iran and the Caucasus in contradictory and complex ways. Following the Afghan seizure of Isfahan in 1722, they attacked the retreating Safavids in order to seize territory in Azerbaijan and the Caucasus, using the old pretext of declaring them *kuffar*. Soon after this, though, the Ottomans paradoxically joined the Russians in an attempt to restore the Safavids to the Iranian throne – creating the unusual situation of a Sunni power (the Ottoman Empire) allying with an Orthodox Christian power (Russia) to support a Shi'i Muslim power (Iran), against the staunchly Sunni Muslim Afghan invaders. In the end, after the Afghans had secured control over Iran, the Ottomans signed a treaty with them in 1727 that essentially recapitulated the terms of the Zuhab agreement.

The main new clause that it introduced was a provision calling for the regular exchange of ambassadors, an increasingly common component of diplomacy in early modern Europe as well. Also, this treaty called for the peaceful exchange of visitors and goods between the two countries, maintaining momentum towards subsequent improved economic and social relations beyond the mere clarification of frontiers.[19]

In light of later agreements, the Zuhab treaty thus can be viewed as the culmination of a process of normalization that had begun with the treaty of Amasya. The Zuhab treaty's particular characteristics of border delineation and traveller protection also resemble European treaties of the early modern era. In European history, the 1648 treaty of Westphalia began to establish a framework for international relations that evolved over subsequent centuries.[20] It is true that the agreements of Westphalia and Zuhab occurred in such radically different contexts that specific comparisons between them are limited. Nonetheless, the treaty of Zuhab has similar significance in the general history of Middle Eastern diplomacy as an important stage in the evolution of international Muslim relations – a process that continues along the Iran-Iraq border today.

The Safavid-Ottoman diplomatic relationship in its contemporary context

The proximity in time between the signing of the 1639 treaty of Zuhab and the 1648 treaty of Westphalia might not be wholly coincidental, either. It has become generally accepted that the rise of Italian city-state diplomacy in Renaissance Europe presaged the development of modern international relations because diplomacy was transformed from agreements drawn up as personal commitments between rulers into written contracts between states.[21] Due to their presence in south-eastern Europe and the Mediterranean, the Ottomans were unavoidably drawn into the matrix of nation-state diplomacy that was developing in early modern Europe.[22] With the expanding impact of the Reformation, a diplomacy not rooted in religious or feudal affinities became the key to maintaining stability in Europe. Diplomacy now relied on a new concept of a 'law of nations' that modern theorists like the seventeenth-century Dutch theorist Grotius based on revived and reconceived versions of classical ideas on 'natural law'. Grotius established the parameters of what is considered the modern law of nations in the early seventeenth century with his idea that certain 'laws of nature' applied to interstate relations.

For Grotius, this only applied to the Christian world, since he advocated a Christian common cause against 'enemies of the faith'. However, he apparently saw fit to recognize agreements between European and non-Christian powers as still being derived from 'natural law'; Grotius' criterion for valid international treaties.[23] Of course, no government of that time in the Middle East recognized an abstract 'natural law' as a basis for anything – all law derived from recognized Islamic sources. However, the evolution of the Safavid-Ottoman diplomatic relationship indicates that the *de facto* acceptance of a formal, regular diplomatic relationship had the power to endure despite its uneasy existence against a constant background of *de jure* hostility. The real *de facto* power of the dimensions of the Zuhab agreement is reflected in how nearly all subsequent treaties between the Ottomans, Safavids and their successors maintained the borders delineated in 1639. As noted above, even the Afghans, who challenged Ottoman assumptions about relations with Iran for almost a decade in the 1720s, finally reaffirmed the framework set down by their Safavid predecessors whose country they had invaded and whose rule they had overthrown.

Despite the profound dislocations experienced in Iran over the course of the eighteenth century in the chaotic reign of Nadir Shah, the peaceful but fleeting Zand interlude, and the establishment of Qajar rule, the diplomatic framework established at Zuhab had become well established by the mid-nineteenth century.

The most serious conflict over the borders that it had defined took place over control of the Shatt al-Arab during the nineteenth and twentieth centuries, long after the original signatories of Zuhab had passed into history. These disputes though, the most recent of which ended with the 1990 peace agreement between Iraq and Iran, still took place within the parameters of a relationship first established during the Safavid period between that dynasty and the Ottomans. This relationship was based on a *de facto* acceptance of a border and the recognition of the rights of travellers to move across it, despite continuous religious and political friction.

Notes

1. For example, see H. R. Roemer, 'Safavid Iran', in Peter Jackson and Laurence Lockhart (eds), *Cambridge History of Iran*, vol. 6 (Cambridge, Cambridge University Press, 1986), p. 285, and Roger Savory, *Iran under the Safavids* (Cambridge: Cambridge University Press, 1980), p. 202.
2. For an account of the beginning of the Ottoman-Safavid relationship, see Adel Allouche, *The Origins and Development of the Ottoman-Safavid Conflict (906-962/1500-1555)* (Berlin: Klaus Schwarz, 1983).
3. Ibid., 110-12. For a discussion of how this polemic developed, see J. R. Walsh, 'Ottoman-Safavid Historiography', *Historians of the Middle East*, edited by Bernard Lewis and P. M. Holt (London: Oxford University Press, 1962), pp. 197-211.
4. 'Selim to Isma'il' in William McNeill and Marilyn Waldman (eds), *The Islamic World* (Chicago: University of Chicago Press, 1973), pp. 339-40.
5. M. Ertuğrul Düzdağ, *Şeyhülislam Ebussuud Efendi Işığında 16. Asır Türk Hayatı* (Istanbul: Enderun Kitabevi, 1972), pp. 109-11.
6. Ibid., p. 111.
7. A partial edition of this text and detailed discussion of the religious content of sixteenth-century Ottoman anti-Safavid polemics can be found in Elke Eberhard, *Osmanische Polemik gegen die Safawiden im 16. Jahrhundert nach arabischen Handschriften* (Freiburg: Klaus Schwarz, 1970).
8. J. H. Mordtmann, 'Sunnitisch-schiitische Polemik im 17. Jahrhundert', *Mitteilungen des Seminars für Orientalische Sprachen* 29 (1926), pp. 116-19.
9. Celalzade Mustafa, *Geschichte Sultan Süleyman Kanunis von 1520 bis 1557*, ed. Petra Kappert (Wiesbaden: Franz Steiner, 1981), p. 19b, and Mustafa Naima, *Tarih-i Naima*, 6 vols (Istanbul: Tabhane-yi Amire, 1863), 1, pp. 344, 346.
10. Eskandar Bayg Monshi, *History of Shah 'Abbas the Great*, 3 vols, trans. Roger Savory (Boulder: Westview, 1978), 2, pp. 688-9.
11. Faik Reşit Unat, *Osmanlı Sefirleri ve Sefaretnameleri* (Istanbul: Türk Tarih Kurumu, 1987), pp. 241-6.
12. Haim Gerber, *Economy and Society in an Ottoman City: Bursa, 1600-1700* (Jerusalem: Hebrew University, 1988), p. 116.
13. Suraiya Faroqhi, *Pilgrims and Sultans: The Hajj under the Ottomans* (London: I.B.Tauris, 1994), pp. 137-8.
14. Celalzade Mustafa, *Geschichte*, pp. 496a-97a.
15. Bekir Kütükoğlu, *Osmanlı-İran Siyasi Münasebetleri* (Istanbul: Edebiyat Fakültesi, 1962), pp. 195-6.
16. Feridun Bey, *Mecmua-i Münşeat-i Selatin*, 2 vols (Istanbul: Darütteba Ulamire, 1858), 2, p. 261.
17. Faroqhi, *Pilgrims and Sultans*, pp. 135-6.
18. For the Ottoman text of the treaty see *Muahedat Mecmuası*, 5 vols (Istanbul: Hakikat Matbaası, 1878-1882) 2, pp. 308-12.
19. For an Ottoman version of the text of this treaty, see *Muahedat Mecmuası*, 2, pp. 312-15.

20. For a recent discussion of the peace of Westphalia, see Derek Croxton, *Peacemaking in Early Modern Europe: Cardinal Mazarin and the Congress of Westphalia, 1643-1648* (London: Associated University Presses, 1999).
21. See Garrett Mattingly, *Renaissance Diplomacy* (Boston: Houghton Mifflin, 1955).
22. See Rifa'at Abou-el-Haj, 'Ottoman attitudes toward peace making: The Karlowitz case', *Der Islam* 51 (1974), pp. 131-7.
23. See Majid Khadduri, *War and Peace in the Law of Islam* (Baltimore: Johns Hopkins Press, 1955), p. 276.

6

The Battle of Sufiyan, 1605: A Symptom of Ottoman Military Decline?

Colin Imber

A three-front war and the loss of Ottoman military supremacy

The Ottoman chronicler Ibrahim Peçevi ends his account of Shah 'Abbas's victory over an Ottoman army at Sufiyan in 1605 with the words: 'In short, it was a shameful defeat such as the Ottoman Empire had never seen. May God Most High never let it happen again! Amen.'[1] The comment is significant, since Peçevi was an experienced soldier who took a close interest in military affairs. In particular, he was a veteran of the Ottoman war with Austria of 1593–1606, during the course of which it became evident that the Austrian forces, at least in field warfare, were superior to the Ottoman. Even the great Ottoman victories at Mezö-Keresztes in 1596 and Kanizsa in 1600 were the products of chance. At Mezö-Kerezstes, the Ottoman cavalry was unable even to approach the Austrian line, and then, when the Austrians counter-attacked, they advanced almost without resistance to the Ottoman camp. It was an attack by the orderlies in the camp when the Austrian troops had dropped their weapons and set about plundering that encouraged the defeated Ottoman soldiers to return and slaughter the plunderers. At Kanizsa, when an Austrian army arrived to relieve the besieged fortress, the Ottoman troops refused to attack the Austrian line and fled. Unable to see in the thick mist, the Austrians believed that the troops had withdrawn in order to lure them into a trap, as had happened – or so they believed – at Mezö-Keresztes. After several days, they withdrew, leaving the Ottomans to complete the reduction of the fortress. Other encounters in the field had a less happy outcome for the Ottoman army.[2]

In Hungary, Austrian superiority in field warfare was very clearly the result of new tactics and weapons which the Ottomans were encountering for the first time. Their predominantly cavalry army was unable to withstand the lethal combination of pike and shot, and volley fire from entrenched positions.[3] In the end, their continuing expertise in siege warfare, their ability to maintain and supply armies in the field,[4] failures in the Austrian command and the anti-Habsburg rebellion in Transylvania in 1605 allowed the Ottomans to maintain their position in Hungary. The war ended in stalemate in 1606.[5] This contrasts with the situation on the eastern front where, in only four years between 1603 and 1607, the Ottomans lost all the territories in the Caucasus and Azerbaijan that they had won from the Safavids between 1578 and 1590. This was a far greater setback than anything that had happened in Hungary, and raises the question of whether the Safavids, like the Austrians, had developed military tactics and technology that had rendered Ottoman warfare obsolescent.

The military capabilities of the two sides were not, however, the only factors in the war. It is important first of all to consider the moment that Shah 'Abbas chose to launch his attack on Tabriz which began the hostilities. In 1603, the Ottomans were already fighting on two fronts, in Hungary against the Habsburgs and in Anatolia against the *jelali* rebels,[6] and lacked the resources to fight on a third. It might be possible, therefore, to view 'Abbas's success in re-capturing Tabriz and Nakhichevan in 1603 and Yerevan in 1604 simply as the result of his having larger forces at his disposal. Next, it is important to consider the political aspect of the war. Even if the Ottoman-Safavid border was in principle clearly defined, in reality it was not, and the security of both empires in this region was dependent upon gaining the allegiance of local lords, in particular of the Kurdish emirs. This is a point which Eskandar Bayg Monshi stresses when, in describing the desertion of Suleyman Bey of Khoshab to Shah 'Abbas, he adds the comment that the Kurds 'offer their allegiance to whichever party is in the ascendant'.[7] It was in fact the departure of much of the Ottoman garrison to besiege the rebel Kurdish lord Alaeddin Bey in 1603 that had given Shah 'Abbas the opportunity to reconquer Tabriz.[8] Local politics could therefore be as decisive as military tactics in determining who won or lost. At Sufiyan, however, Shah 'Abbas defeated a full-scale Ottoman army in the field, suggesting that by this time the Safavids enjoyed a military superiority over the Ottomans.

Accounts of engagements before Sufiyan do not, however, support this view. Eskandar Bayg Monshi's account of the Safavid commander Emir Guna Khan's successful field battle against an Ottoman counterpart, Tekkeli Mehmed, near Nakhichevan suggests that the encounter was a straightforward cavalry skirmish, with luck rather than tactics determining the outcome.[9] Furthermore, in the conduct of sieges the Safavids clearly lacked the skills of the Ottomans. Tabriz fell during the absence of a part of the garrison, and Nakhichevan when the garrison deserted to 'Abbas after Şerif Pasha had taken the decision to destroy the fortress and withdraw.[10] The Safavids met with strong resistance only at Yerevan, where the double fortress fell in June 1604, after a siege lasting more than nine months. This prolonged operation contrasts with the Ottoman conquest, within a single month, of the complex of modern fortresses at Esztergom in Hungary in 1605. A feature of the Safavid siege, which both Eskandar Bayg Monshi and the Ottoman sources emphasize, is the size of the Safavid artillery. Peçevi refers to 'five large cannon casting stones of ninety *okkas*',[11] adding that the besiegers also cast new ones. Eskandar Bayg Monshi refers to 'two huge siege guns firing shots weighing thirty Tabriz *mann*'.[12] Impressive though these guns evidently were, this form of siege warfare was already obsolete. The use of very large siege cannon and the practice of casting artillery in the field had been typical of Ottoman warfare in the late fifteenth century. In the early sixteenth century, the Ottomans had adopted the practice, introduced by the French king Charles VIII during his Italian campaign of 1494-5, of using batteries of smaller guns which were more manoeuvrable and could fire more rapidly.[13] At Esztergom it was continuous fire rather than monster guns that the Ottoman commander Lala Mehmed Pasha used to reduce the fortresses. In short, Safavid siege artillery was obsolete.

Before Sufiyan, therefore, the Safavids do not seem to have enjoyed any technical advantage over the Ottoman forces. One point which does, however, emerge is Shah 'Abbas's skill as a commander. Safavid techniques of siege warfare may have been relatively crude, but the fact that Eskandar Bayg Monshi comments specifically on the Ottoman practice of building fortresses to control and protect conquered lands, and feels the need to explain why 'Abbas reconstructed the Ottoman fortress at Tabriz,[14] suggests that, for the Safavids, systematic fortress warfare was an innovation of 'Abbas's time. It seems, therefore, that the shah was quick to learn from the practice of his enemies. Another characteristic of the shah's command was his ability to make forced marches. This is something which Eskandar Bayg Monshi highlights,[15] as does Peçevi, when he recalls how, on hearing of the absence of the Ottoman garrison from Tabriz in 1603, "Abbas was able to recapture the city after completing the one month's march from Isfahan in little over a week. It was, above all, this rapid advance that gave him the victory.'[16] Most importantly, however, the fact that at Yerevan 'Abbas was able to keep an army in the field throughout the winter and for nine months altogether, suggests that he had an unusual ability to discipline and motivate his troops. Shah 'Abbas appears therefore as a military commander who was adept at learning lessons from the enemy, exploiting opportunities and maintaining the morale of his men. Before 1604/5, however, he had never engaged an Ottoman army in full strength.

The campaigns of 1604-5 and the battle of Sufiyan

In 1604 the Ottoman commander Cigalazade Sinan Pasha left Istanbul for Erzurum on a campaign to suppress rebels in Anatolia and to recover the Ottoman fortresses and territories lost to Shah 'Abbas. He evidently tried to achieve the first of these tasks not by attacking the *jelali* rebels, but by recruiting them into his army. The campaign against the Safavids began with a march via Yerevan in the direction of Shirvan, where his son Mahmud Pasha was governor. Shah 'Abbas, Eskandar tells us, had anticipated his passage and had destroyed crops in the district of Kars, and harried the land between Kars and Erzurum in order to deny supplies to Cigalazade. In early November, expecting Cigalazade to turn back, he disbanded most of his army. However, despite the lateness of the season, the Ottomans continued their progress beyond Yerevan. Even if he had wished to do so, the shah, with much of his army dispersed, was in no position for a battle. Instead he systematically depopulated the countryside in the line of Cigalazade's march, planning, according to Eskandar, to attack the Ottomans in a narrow defile beyond the Aras, evidently at a spot where the terrain would compensate for his lack of manpower. By now, however, he had observed from the thinness of the captured horses that his patrols brought in, that the Ottoman army was short of fodder. This was evidence that his strategy was working. Shortly afterwards he heard that the Ottomans had retreated.[17]

Eskandar Bayg Monshi agrees with the Ottoman narratives that this was the result of a mutiny. According to Eskandar, the troops – especially Janissaries – pulled down the commander's tent in protest at his insistence on continuing the campaign beyond Kars when the season was so advanced.[18] Peçevi, reporting the same incident, dwells on the troops' complaints about the direction of the campaign towards Shirvan, quoting them as taunting Cigalazade, with a reference to his Italian origin and former office as admiral: 'If you campaign on the sea you go to visit your father; if you campaign on land you think to visit your son.'[19] Kâtib Çelebi, who summarizes the Ottoman narratives adds to this the troops' objection that it was impossible to pursue the highly mobile shah with a heavily laden army, and their refusal to accept the commander's plan to spend the winter in Gäncä or Karabagh.[20] There seems, in addition, to have been uncertainty about the immediate goal of the campaign. According to Kâtib Çelebi, Cigalazade aimed to capture the shah. He refused, however, the request of Köse Sefer Pasha of Erzurum, Ahmed Pasha of Sivas and Alaca Atlu Pasha to pursue the shah with 10,000 *jelali* troops. In his version of their speech, Peçevi makes the commanders remind Cigalazade that one of his duties is also to defeat the rebels: 'If we conquer the Shah and plunder his men, the fortune and glory will be yours, and the honour will be the Padishah's. But if the Shah defeats and destroys us, it will bring good fortune to the Padishah. All these *jelalis* will have been destroyed, and the snake crushed by the hand of the enemy.'[21] Instead, however, the army turned in the direction of Tabriz and then to Van, where Cigalazade proposed to spend the winter.

In contrast to this confusion in planning, Shah 'Abbas followed the very clear strategy of retreating before the Ottoman advance, and depriving their army of food by harrying their foragers and stripping the countryside of both people and supplies. It was the same tactic that Shah Tahmasp had used very effectively against the armies of Süleyman the Magnificent in the previous century.

Kâtib Çelebi, in particular, emphasizes Cigalazade's folly in going to Van. In his version of events, experienced commanders advised Cigalazade to go to Amid or Aleppo, as no commander had ever exposed himself to the danger of spending winter on the frontier.[22] Cigalazade ignored the advice, 'arrogantly', as Eskandar puts it, 'holding the Qezelbash army in low esteem.'[23] His apparent insouciance may indeed reflect contempt for Safavid military capabilities, arising from his experience as the Ottoman commander who, in 1588, had conquered Nihavend. However, Cigalazade did recognize the importance of Ottoman alliances with the Kurdish emirs in the region of the frontier. He summoned them to Van, 'enticing them', according to Peçevi, 'with promises and favours'. 'He was', Peçevi continues, 'especially solicitous towards the Kurdish lords of Diyabekir and especially towards Mir Sheref, the governor of Cizre.'[24] Eskandar, however, comments that the Kurds were merely 'following their usual blameworthy habit of keeping in with both sides'.[25] Cigalazade also, it seems, kept in mind his brief to suppress the *jelalis*, appointing a former rebel, Ahmed Pasha, as governor of Van and then because, in Peçevi's words, 'Ahmed Pasha's health was not good, sending to him his own chief physician, as though making to cure him. He saw to the matter within a few days. That is to say, he poisoned him.' He appointed Zincirkıran Ali Pasha in the rebel's place.[26]

Cigalazade's folly in remaining on the frontier when the majority of his army had dispersed became evident in the spring. In May, recognizing the opportunity, Shah 'Abbas sent Allahverdi Khan from Tabriz to besiege Van, and such, according to Eskandar Bayg Monshi, was Cigalazade's neglect of 'normal military precautions' that he was unaware of the Safavid approach until the army was within a day's march of Van. 'In fact', Eskandar continues, 'Zu'l-Faqar Khan and his men, who were in the Safavid van, captured a number of Ottoman stableboys, and seized some of their horses which were grazing in the meadows along the road.' Eskandar adds that Allahverdi Khan was at this point joined by a Kurdish emir Shirazi Sultan Mahmudî and some of his relatives, but adds that the rest of the emirs 'as usual delayed, and simply sent messages to the Safavid commander'. In the first engagement outside the walls of Van, the Safavids drove the Ottoman forces back to the ditch surrounding the fortress, taking prisoners including a high-ranking official, the *müteferrikabaşı* Handan Ağa. As Allahverdi Khan surrounded the town, he received news that Mehmed Pasha was bringing reinforcements to Van from Erzurum, and sent his commander Qarchaqay Bayg to intercept this force. Qarchaqay's departure encouraged a second Ottoman sortie from the fortress. This too was a failure, and at about the same time Cigalazade must have heard of Qarchaqay Bayg's victory over Mehmed Pasha.[27] In his account of the defence of Van, Peçevi confines himself to the contemptuous comment that 'all the commander did was to fire a few shots from the castle at the Qezelbash'.[28]

Realizing the danger of his position, Cigalazade left Van by boat for Adilcevaz, leaving Şems Bey in command of the fortress. At Adilcevaz he commandeered the pack animals belonging to the sanjak (district) governor Mir Şah Bey and set out for Hasankale in the direction of Erzurum.[29] On hearing of Cigalazade's departure, Allahverdi Khan departed for Adilcevaz and Erciş but, finding that Cigalazade had already left, abandoned both the pursuit of the commander and the siege of Van and returned to the shah near Khoy.[30]

Cigalazade's humiliations did not remove the danger to Shah 'Abbas of an Ottoman invasion. The Ottoman commander spent the time between his arrival at Hasankale and the autumn of 1605 mustering an army, which included the contingents of Mir Sheref and other Kurdish chiefs, presumably those whom he had called to Van in the previous winter. In November the army departed, following the Tasuj road in the direction of Tabriz. The commander's intention, Eskandar tells us, was to occupy Ardabil and to spend the winter at Kızılağaç near Shirvan.[31]

The shah clearly considered it too dangerous to launch a direct attack on Cigalazade's army. Instead he shadowed it in the mountains, following a parallel route from Khoy to Marand, observing the Ottoman advance, but remaining as far as possible unobserved. As in the previous autumn, he followed Shah Tahmasp's tactics, ordering the governor of Tabriz to remove all the population and all food supplies from the Ottoman line of march. His plan, Eskandar reports from 'officers close to the Shah', was not to attack the Ottomans in force, but to wear the army down by attrition. Then, if Cigalazade besieged the fort at Tabriz, he planned to block the Ottoman retreat and, when winter and lack of food had taken their toll on the besiegers, to launch simultaneous attacks from the fortress and from the rear.[32]

The shah did not intend to start a battle. Nevertheless, before he reached Sufiyan he had, according to Eskandar, organized his army to fight, with himself in the centre, with the vanguard, left and right wings each under different commanders, and Allahverdi Khan leading a squadron detached from the main body of the army. All the commanders received orders to act with extreme caution. When, on 6 November 1605, the armies came close to each other at Sufiyan, Qarchaqay Bayg and his men became visible to the Ottomans as they reached the top of rising ground. It was this, according to Eskandar, that precipitated the battle. Remembering the shah's orders to avoid a major confrontation, Qarchaqay Bayg retreated out of sight and, taking this as a sign of weakness, the Ottomans immediately attacked.[33]

The Ottoman accounts also suggest a sudden and unexpected opening to the battle. Peçevi and, after him, Kâtib Çelebi report that when the Ottoman army had alighted in the valley of Tabriz, 'before even the tents had been pitched or tactics discussed', the governor-general of Erzurum Köse Sefer persuaded a number of other commanders, 'altogether sixteen with the title of governor-general, and twenty sanjak governors, some in and some out of office' to set off in pursuit of the shah.[34] It was presumably Qarchaqay Bayg's appearance that had precipitated this action.

Kâtib Çelebi presents the initial Ottoman attack as throwing the enemy into confusion, and driving them back into the shah's ranks.[35] Eskandar's account is probably more accurate, describing the Ottoman assault as creating confusion in the Safavid vanguard, until the shah sent reinforcements after receiving a report of the engagement.[36] What, however, was decisive was the shah's awareness that the attackers had become separated from the camp: Peçevi presents him at this point as saying 'This is our opportunity!'[37] In order, Eskandar reports, to prevent the Ottomans breaking through at the point of their attack, he sent a force to cause a diversion in the direction of the Ottoman camp. The effect was to draw the Ottoman troops away from the assault to the assistance of their fellows, but as they moved, they found themselves ambushed from all sides.[38] With fresh Safavid troops now between the camp and the Ottoman army, very few of the Ottoman attackers returned. Peçevi reports that, of the commanders, only Tekkeli Mehmed Pasha, the *jelali* Karakaş Pasha and Kaçar Mehmed Pasha were able to fight their way through the Safavid ranks to the safety of the camp.[39] Köse Sefer Pasha who had started the action was captured and executed.[40]

The Ottoman defeat on the first day of the battle was serious but not total. Cigalazade had not sent all his troops into battle, caution had prevented the Safavids from attacking the fortified camp, and the governor of Aleppo, Canbuladoğlu Hüseyn, was approaching with reinforcements. The next phase in the Ottoman rout occurred during the night. 'That night', Peçevi tells us, 'the Kurdish lords came to the shameless commander at the time of the evening prayer to discuss what would be the outcome of all this, and tried to have a meeting with him. [The guards], however, did not allow access on the grounds that the great man was resting...Some of the people who came there said that the commander had fled; others spoke whatever thousand words came into their heads. Everybody gave whatever explanation they fancied.' In the face of Cigalazade's refusal to speak to them, the Kurdish lords departed with their followers. To compound the disaster, the fugitives encountered Canbuladoğlu Hüseyn with 'more than 12,000 troops' and Rizaeddin Khan of Bitlis with several thousand Kurdish soldiers. When they heard from the Kurdish lords that the Safavids had routed the Ottoman army, they too turned back. Canbuladoğlu Hüseyn, however, remained to meet Cigalazade on his return.[41]

Peçevi attributes the desertion of the Kurds entirely to Cigalazade's refusal to meet with their lords, and gives an explanation for Cigalazade's behaviour. 'In fact', he writes, 'Cigalazade was a brave, experienced and very capable warrior, but he was addicted to "pleasure". On this occasion he was in a state of relaxed intoxication, and they would not wake him. It was this that led to such a disastrous defeat.'[42] Since he knew Cigalazade from that commander's time on the Hungarian front, Peçevi may well be right. Eskandar, however, suggests that this was not the only cause of the Kurds' desertion. In his narrative, on the day after the battle, the shah sent a message to Mir Sheref of Bitlis via one of his retainers whom the Safavids had captured. In it, he proposed to Mir Sheref that if he wished no harm to come to himself or his men, he should either join the Safavid army or withdraw. Mir Sheref chose to withdraw, leaving his baggage.[43] Peçevi, too, notes that the departing Kurds abandoned their tents.[44]

On the day after the battle, Cigalazade attempted to raise the morale of the remaining troops, 'but', says Peçevi, 'did not move beyond the edge of the camp, where he stood keeping his ears open and eyes fixed in the direction of the enemy. He saw absolutely no movement on the enemy side.' In Peçevi's story, the final stage of the defeat came after midday, when Kaçar Mehmed Pasha and his men began to load clothes and provisions onto their horses, trying to hide what they were doing by concealing the horses in their tents. Then, in the late afternoon, someone shouted: 'What are you waiting for! The Qezelbash are just outside the camp and have seized the guns!' The rumour, it seems, was false, but it precipitated a general flight. 'The commander', Peçevi continues, 'was left in the field. Mounting the Janissaries, together with 2,000 *kapıkulu*s and the honourable among the troops onto the camels which the soldiers had left, and leaving the treasury and the encampment as it was, he followed the fugitives and made hurriedly for Van.' Peçevi emphasizes the caution of the Safavids in approaching the Ottoman camp after they had become aware of the Ottoman flight: 'fearing an Ottoman trick, they did not come immediately, but rather came on the following day, searching carefully on all sides.'[45] Eskandar, in contrast, leaves the impression that the Safavid plundering began at midnight, as soon as the news of the Ottoman flight became known. Both, however, emphasize the value of the booty. In Eskandar's words, 'Those who had penetrated furthest into the Ottoman camp reported that they had found tents still fully carpeted, with treasure chests still in place, camels still lying in front of the tents, and horses in the stables.'[46]

Shah 'Abbas's victory at Sufiyan had important consequences. The purpose of the Ottoman campaign had been to recover the territories in Azerbaijan and the Caucasus lost since 1603. The Ottoman defeat ensured that the conquered places remained in Safavid possession, and, by 1607, enabled the shah to reconquer the remainder of the lands lost to the Ottomans in the war of 1578–90. For the Ottomans, the campaign produced a further disaster. When Cigalazade Sinan Pasha met Canbuladoğlu Hüseyn at Van on his return from Sufiyan, he executed him for his failure to join the campaign. His death was the pretext for the rebellion of his nephew Canbuladoğlu Ali of Aleppo, a revolt which for a while seemed to herald the dismemberment of the empire.[47]

Conclusion

For the Ottomans the battle of Sufiyan was a greater disaster than anything that they had experienced in Hungary, where the war which had begun in 1593 had revealed Ottoman military deficiencies in the face of new European weapons and tactics. At Sufiyan, however, as in other Ottoman-Safavid encounters since 1603, there is nothing to suggest that the Safavids enjoyed a systemic advantage in weapons or ways of fighting. Indeed, 'Abbas's extreme caution in the campaign suggests that he was doubtful about his abilities to defeat a full-scale Ottoman army. During Cigalazade's advance beyond Yerevan in 1604 and his advance to Sufiyan in the following year, 'Abbas adopted the same tactic as his ancestor Shah Tahmasp: he remained out of sight, while harrying Cigalazade's army and depriving him of supplies. He clearly did not want to risk a full-scale engagement. The fighting itself seems from all accounts to have been primarily a cavalry engagement, supported by arquebus fire, a form of warfare with which the Ottomans were perfectly familiar. Both Peçevi and Eskandar also emphasize 'Abbas's extreme caution, following his victory in the field, in approaching the Ottoman camp, 'protected as it was by gun-carriages and arquebusiers'.⁴⁸ Unless it was simply that 'Abbas feared the approach of Canbuladoğlu's contingent, this caution perhaps indicates that Safavid field-artillery was either non-existent or else too weak to overwhelm the camp.

The victory was not, therefore, the product of superior Safavid weapons or new fighting techniques. For Eskandar, as one might expect, the cause of victory was – apart from divine favour – the genius of the shah. Peçevi on the other hand attributes the Ottoman rout almost solely to the deficiencies of Cigalazade Sinan Pasha as a commander, and structures his narrative around this judgement. To his description of Cigalazade's refusal to speak to the Kurdish lords, he adds the comment: 'When the decree of God, the Praised, the Exalted, runs counter to an undertaking, it is men like this who become commanders of the troops of Islam!'⁴⁹ Peçevi, as one would expect, does not directly praise the shah. Nevertheless, he does so obliquely, when he credits him with immediately exploiting the opportunity presented by the separation of the attacking Ottoman troops from the camp.

The course of the campaign suggests that both authors are correct, even if their views seem to sit too comfortably with literary convention. The events of Cigalazade's advance in the autumn of 1604 suggest an inability to gain the confidence of his troops and uncertainty as to the goal of the campaign, whether it was to reconquer lost territory or to capture the shah. Second, Cigalazade's decision, after his troops had forced him to retreat, to spend the winter at Van was clearly a mistake, compounded by his carelessness in failing to take precautions against a possible Safavid attack. At Sufiyan itself, his failure to restore the confidence of his men after 'Abbas's victory led to their desertion and to the complete humiliation of Ottoman arms. 'Abbas, on the other hand, seems to have had well formulated plans to wear down the Ottoman army by attrition: it must in part at least have been this tactic that forced Cigalazade's retreat in 1604. Equally important, however, he was able to seize opportunities as they arose. In the spring of 1605, Cigalazade's presence at Van with much reduced forces presented him with the opportunity to humiliate the Ottoman commander. At Sufiyan, when the Ottoman attack forced him to give battle against his wishes, he immediately saw the opportunity which the gap in the Ottoman army presented. If we follow Eskandar's narrative, he augmented this advantage by maintaining control over the actions of his troops throughout the battle, catching the Ottomans in an ambush and preventing their defeated troops returning to the safety of the armed camp. He also seems to have maintained the morale of his own men, persuading the remnants of the Safavid vanguard to stand firm until reinforcements arrived, following their initial rout in the face of the Ottoman assault.⁵⁰ In addition, if we are to believe Eskandar, he knew the political composition of the Ottoman army well enough to engineer the desertion of Mir Sheref and his contingent.

There was, however, an important factor in the Ottoman defeat which perhaps reflects more than the relative capabilities of the commanders. The battle began, against the wishes of either Shah 'Abbas or Cigalazade Sinan, when Köse Sefer and a group of commanders launched an unauthorized attack, an action which opened the gap the shah was able to exploit. This act contrasted with the tight control which 'Abbas seems to have exercised over his own men. This indiscipline quite possibly reflects the nature of Ottoman armies in the early seventeenth century, for which the *jelali* rebels in Anatolia were a source of recruitment. While skilled in arms, the *jelalis* were essentially freebooters, and more used to fighting against officers of the sultan than to obeying their orders. Their tendency to act independently had already caused disasters on the Hungarian front, notably the failed Ottoman attempt to regain the Danubian island of Csepel near Buda in 1603.[51] It was perhaps in the same independent spirit that Köse Sefer and his followers made the unauthorized attack that was ultimately to give Shah 'Abbas the victory. If this is so, it might be possible to consider the widespread anarchy in Anatolia as another ingredient in the Ottoman defeat. What Sufiyan does not prove, however, is an absolute decline in Ottoman military capabilities.

Notes

1. Ibrahim Peçevi, *Tarih-i Peçevi* (Istanbul, 1980). Reprint, with introduction and index by F. Ç. Derin and V. Çabuk, of *Tarih-i Peçevi* (Istanbul, 1866).
2. See Colin Imber, 'Ibrahim Peçevi on war: A note on the European "military revolution"', in Colin Imber and Keiko Kiyotaki (eds.), *Frontiers of Ottoman Studies: State, Province, and the West*, 2 volumes (London and New York: I.B.Tauris 2005), v. 2, pp. 7–22.
3. On these military innovations, see Geoffrey Parker, *The Military Revolution* (Cambridge, 1988); Thomas F. Arnold, 'War in sixteenth-century Europe: Revolution and renaissance', in Jeremy Black (ed.), *European Warfare, 1453-1815* (Basingstoke, 1999).
4. See Caroline Finkel, *The Administration of Warfare: The Ottoman Military Campaigns in Hungary* (Vienna, 1988).
5. On the war of 1593–1606, see Jan Paul Niederkorn, *Die europäischen Mächte und der 'Lange Türkenkrieg' Kaiser Rudolfs II.* (Vienna, 1993).
6. On the *jelali* rebellions and the Ottoman-Safavid wars in this context, see William J. Griswold, *The Great Anatolian Rebellion, 1000-1020/1591-1611* (Berlin, 1983). For the campaigns of Cigalazade Sinan Pasha and the battle of Sufiyan, see pp. 99–109.
7. Eskandar Bayg Monshi (trans. R. M. Savory), *History of Shah 'Abbas the Great (Tarikh-e 'Alamara-ye 'Abbasi)* (Boulder, CO, 1978), 2.856.
8. Peçevi, *Tarih-i Peçevi*, 2.258.
9. Eskandar Bayg Monshi, *History of Shah 'Abbas*, 2.867–8.
10. Peçevi, *Tarih-i Peçevi*, 2.260.
11. Ibid., 2.260.
12. Eskandar Bayg Monshi, *History of Shah 'Abbas*, 2.843.
13. On developments in Ottoman artillery, see Gabor Ágoston, 'Ottoman artillery and European military technology in the fifteenth and seventeenth centuries', *Acta Orientalia* (Budapest), 47 (1994), pp. 15–48.
14. Eskandar Bayg Monshi, *History of Shah 'Abbas*, 2.872–3.
15. Ibid., 2.868.
16. Peçevi, *Tarih-i Peçevi*, 2.258.
17. Eskandar Bayg Monshi, *History of Shah 'Abbas*, 2.858–60.
18. Ibid., 2.860.
19. Peçevi, *Tarih-i Peçevi*, 2.261.

20. Kâtib Çelebi, *Fezleke*, vol. 2, Istanbul: 1287/1870.
21. Peçevi, *Tarih-i Peçevi*, 2.262; Kâtib Çelebi, 2.244-5.
22. Kâtib Çelebi, 2.245.
23. Eskandar Bayg Monshi, *History of Shah 'Abbas*, 2.861.
24. Peçevi, *Tarih-i Peçevi*, 2.262.
25. Eskandar Bayg Monshi, *History of Shah 'Abbas*, 2.860.
26. Peçevi, *Tarih-i Peçevi*, 2.262.
27. Eskandar Bayg Monshi, *History of Shah 'Abbas*, 2.874-6.
28. Peçevi, *Tarih-i Peçevi*, 2.263.
29. Ibid., 2.263.
30. Eskandar Bayg Monshi, *History of Shah 'Abbas*, 2.876.
31. Eskandar Bayg Monshi, *History of Shah 'Abbas*, 2.886-7.
32. Eskandar Bayg Monshi, *History of Shah 'Abbas*, 2.889.
33. Eskandar Bayg Monshi, *History of Shah 'Abbas*, 2.888-9.
34. Peçevi, *Tarih-i Peçevi*, 2.263-4; Kâtib Çelebi, 2.265.
35. Kâtib Çelebi, 2.265.
36. Eskandar Bayg Monshi, *History of Shah 'Abbas*, 2.890.
37. Peçevi, *Tarih-i Peçevi*, 2.264.
38. Eskandar Bayg Monshi, *History of Shah 'Abbas*, 2.890-1.
39. Peçevi, *Tarih-i Peçevi*, 2.264.
40. Eskandar Bayg Monshi, *History of Shah 'Abbas*, 2.891.
41. Peçevi, *Tarih-i Peçevi*, 2.264-5.
42. Ibid., 2.266.
43. Eskandar Bayg Monshi, *History of Shah 'Abbas*, 2.894.
44. Peçevi, *Tarih-i Peçevi*, 2.265.
45. Ibid., 2.265-6.
46. Eskandar Bayg Monshi, *History of Shah 'Abbas*, 2.896-7.
47. Peçevi, *Tarih-i Peçevi*, 2.266; William J. Griswold, *The Great Anatolian Rebellion*, 107ff.
48. Eskandar Bayg Monshi, *History of Shah 'Abbas*, 2.894.
49. Peçevi, *Tarih-i Peçevi*, 2.266.
50. Eskandar Bayg Monshi, *History of Shah 'Abbas*, 2.890.
51. Peçevi, *Tarih-i Peçevi*, 2.271-2.

7

An Infernal Triangle: The Contest between Mughals, Safavids and Portuguese, 1590–1605

Sanjay Subrahmanyam

Introduction

In the closing years of the sixteenth century, the Portuguese administration in Goa watched anxiously, as a complex triangular war seemed to be on the point of breaking out, involving the Safavid state of Shah 'Abbas I, the Mughal empire of Jalal-al-Din Muhammad Akbar, and the Shaybanid state under 'Abdullah Khan. The letters of the Portuguese viceroy, Dom Francisco da Gama, fourth Count of Vidigueira and direct descendant of Vasco da Gama, in late 1599 are full of mentions of this shifting balance, in which Safavid power seemed to be on the ascendant, and that of the Mughals in check; in the viceroy's view, 'at this time (...) the Mogor is greatly troubled by fear of the Xaa ['Abbas]'.[1] Interestingly, the same viceroy had spelt out a rather different perception of threat in a letter to the Habsburg Crown just a year earlier, that is dated December 1598. He wrote:

> On the 9th of September, Jerónimo Xavier, a religious of the Company of Jesus who resides in the court of Equebar [Akbar], advised me that in some rivers that enter deep into the interior, he is making ready a great number of foists, and three large *naos*, and that it is imagined that his intention is to attack the fortress of Ormus or that of Diu. And even though in the judgement of those who understand these matters well, there are many difficulties that stand in the way of the Mogor achieving this intent, I have fostered all of them [the difficulties], to keep myself on guard as soon as it was heard that the enemy was ready, advising the Captain of Ormus of what was required and supplying him with the necessary, and that of Diu too in the same way.[2]

The fiscal superintendent (*provedor da fazenda*) of the northern sector, a certain Luís Álvares Camelo, was sent out with gunpowder and other supplies to take care of the

Portuguese fortresses in Gujarat and the Persian Gulf, and Vidigueira activated his network of spies in the neighbouring courts. However, he then heard from the Jesuits that the Mughal preparations had lost momentum, since the pressing priority was now their impending war with the Shaybanids. These rumours that the Portuguese viceroy gathered paralleled in a rather curious fashion earlier rumours among the Mughals (in 1592-3), that the 'Firangi soldiers from Hormuz' planned an attack on Sind in support of the former ruler there, Mirza Jani Bayg.[3] Neither set of rumours appears to have been founded, but the perceptions they embody are interesting, as we see from another letter written by the same Portuguese viceroy, this one written in late December 1599.

> The king Equebar is now a little less than sixty years old, and while at his court in Laor retreated in a dissimulating manner, for he feared the king of Persia, who was approaching very close to him through the kingdom of the Uzbeques into which he had entered; now he is in Agraa, [and] he is a great, clever and devious captain. He does not trust his oldest son, for fear that he might kill him with poison. And he has called for his other son, whom he had accommodated in the part of his domains that borders Bengal. The desire that he has to approach this island [Goa] is insatiable, but from the winter [monsoon] until now, the war that he was making against the kingdom of the Melique [Ahmadnagar] has been suspended (...).[4]

Vidigueira was not always the most sound tactician himself, but there is little doubt about the extent of his network and the quality of his information. This information extended to all the major diplomatic activity in and around the western Indian Ocean at that time, and included any movements between the Safavids and the Mughals that involved the Persian Gulf. He thus writes, in another letter of the same time, in the context of trading fleets (*cáfilas*) from Hormuz to Goa:

> [I]n my time, one [*cáfila*] was diverted, for it came with an ambassador of the Xaa to the Mogor in the company of another who had been sent to him ['Abbas], and he brought with him around five thousand persons and he wished that Dom António de Lima embark him in the fortress of Ormuz. [C]ouncil was held on this, in which it was decided that if they wished to embark themselves and with their servitors (for there was place for no more) there, they could do so, but otherwise they could not enter and I approved this resolution, for given the intentions of these people [to capture Hormuz] it was not a bad occasion to implement them, and with this reply which they did not accept they took the land route, passing through very difficult regions for fear of Abdulacão, King of the Usbeques, whom, had he not died at that time, none of them would have escaped on account of the great differences there were between him and Equebar, for whom his death was a great good fortune, for there was much trouble between them. [T]he Xaa has captured most of his kingdoms, approaching

through those regions so close to Equebar that he forced him to retreat from Laor, and they are today not as great friends as they used to be for they have clashed in that ambition.[5]

The reference is probably to the Safavid embassy to the Mughals, led by Mirza 'Ali Bayg Qurchi, which arrived at Agra in early 1599, in order to verify Akbar's intentions about 'Abdullah Khan's erstwhile territories. In late 1594, a series of ambassadorial exchanges had been set in motion, when the Safavid representative Yadgar Sultan Rumlu was permitted to return to Iran. Along with him, Akbar sent Mirza Ziya-al-Din (accompanied by Khwaja Abu Nasir) to Iran as his ambassador, with the idea that they should go from Lahore to Lahori Bandar and then to Hormuz. Then in 1598, a certain Minuchihr Bayg was sent back by 'Abbas as his ambassador, with rich presents, and eventually in 1599 another embassy also comprising Mirza 'Ali Bayg Qurchi (Karamilu).[6] The Portuguese evidently kept close track of these exchanges, in particular because they so often passed through Hormuz. Vidigueira's calculation evidently was that the Safavid front would preoccupy Akbar, and that – in the specific context of the death of 'Abdullah Khan in 1598 – would suffice to take the pressure off Goa and the Deccan.

This chapter is conceived of as a modest contribution to the history of the complex triangular relationship that existed in the late sixteenth and early seventeenth centuries between a set of rather unequal powers: first, the expanding Mughal empire in northern India, that carried all before it in the decades after about 1560; second, the Portuguese *Estado da Índia*, with its political heart at Goa, and subsidiary centres at Daman, Diu and the *Província do Norte*; and finally, the Safavid state in Iran that from its very inception in about 1500 had also maintained privileged relations with the Muslim sovereigns of the Deccan.[7] Of these political entities, two had coincidentally been founded at practically the same moment, in the very beginning of the sixteenth century. The Portuguese had arrived in the western Indian Ocean in 1497, and declared the *Estado da Índia* to be a stable political entity (rather than deriving simply from a succession of fleets sent out from Portugal) from the time of the initial viceroyalty of Dom Francisco de Almeida (1505–09), seizing Goa from the control of the Bijapur rulers in 1510. The Safavids, a Sufi order that had long nurtured political ambitions from its base at Ardabil, erupted onto the Iranian political scene at much the same time as the first Portuguese fleets arrived off the west coast of India, and rapidly consolidated power under the charismatic figure of Shah Isma'il I, whose aura of total invincibility began to wear thin only after the defeat he suffered at the hands of the Ottomans in the Battle of Chalderan in 1514.[8]

The relative latecomers amongst the three were the Mughals, a dynasty that derived from the great Central Asian conqueror, Amir Timur (d. 1405), and also in a more distant way from Chinggis Khan. This prestigious lineage was, however, not enough to guarantee success and the founder of the Mughal dynasty in India, Zahir-al-Din Muhammad Babur, had to spend long years as a peripatetic prince before he eventually managed to gain control over northern India in the 1520s. His son and successor, Humayun, was to have a chequered career. The first of the Indian Mughals to have direct diplomatic contacts with the Portuguese, he seems to have nurtured ambitions in the 1530s in the direction of the two major maritime provinces – Gujarat to the west, and Bengal to the east. His ambitions in neither case quite came to fruition, although he did make successful inroads for a time in both directions. Eventually, in the latter half of the 1530s, Humayun's own expansionary ambitions came undone, as he himself was exiled on account of the rising power of the Afghans in northern India under Sher Shah Suri. Forced into retreat first via Sind, and then Afghanistan, Humayun found refuge for a time in Iran, under the rule of Shah Tahmasp, son of the Safavid dynasty's charismatic founder. He accepted the difficult conditions that Tahmasp laid down for his support, and eventually returned to take power briefly once more in northern India, before dying in an accidental fall in 1556. This left his son, the 14-year-old Jalal-al-Din Muhammad Akbar, born when his father was a wandering exile, to consolidate Mughal power in Hindustan. Akbar managed to achieve this in a quite remarkable fashion in the first 15 years of his rule. Initially under the tutelage of the powerful Bairam Khan, then increasingly independent, he first defeated the autochthonous challenge of Himu Baqqal and the Afghans, and then set about systematically taming the power of the Rajputs in western India. A combined policy of carrot and stick, of marriage alliance and main force, meant that in the course of the 1560s, he was able to bring many of the main Rajput princely houses within the alliance-structure of the Mughal dispensation. By the early 1570s, the two old targets that Humayun had been unable to conquer properly – the maritime provinces of Gujarat and Bengal – had emerged once again as the next objects of Mughal expansion. The Mughal kingdom, at this point still a landlocked state in the plains of northern India, was about to enter the political scene of the Indian Ocean, and also transform itself from a fairly compact kingdom into a sprawling imperial state. Three major expansionary campaigns were to define this new profile, first the conquests of Gujarat and Bengal and then, in the early 1590s, the reduction of the autonomous kingdom of Sind astride the lower valley of the river Indus.

The Deccan context

The prospect of Mughal expansion was viewed with increasing alarm in Portuguese official circles from at least the 1570s. The 'natural' limits of the expanding empire were not at all obvious to such official observers as the minor chronicler António Pinto Pereira, writing his *História da Índia* in the 1570s; rather, it was feared that the power vacuum created by the collapse of Vijayanagara power in the south-western Deccan would occasion ever further Mughal inroads into the region of Goa.[9] Much has been written on Mughal-Portuguese relations during the reign of Akbar, particularly after the Mughal conquest of Gujarat in 1573. Three clear strands are visible in the historiography, even though they often appear intertwined. First, it is pointed out that the Mughal ports of Gujarat and Portuguese-controlled ports like Goa and Hormuz enjoyed important trade links in the last quarter of the sixteenth century, and that an accommodation of interests was necessary if the coastal *cáfilas* along the west coast or the annual fleets to the Persian Gulf were to ply. Both parties had an interest in the matter, the Mughals because Surat was thus supplied with silver *reales* and other goods, the Portuguese *Estado* because it received customs revenue, and Gujarati textiles brought to Goa could be carried back to Europe. Portuguese private traders settled at Surat, Rander, Cambay and other centres also formed a sort of pressure group which acted on the Goa administration.[10]

A second aspect of relations stemmed from the *hajj* traffic in which the Mughal state interested itself. Here, the Portuguese, as *cartaz*-issuing authorities, and the Mughals, whose ships received the safe-conducts, had to enter into dealings (paralleling those between the Portuguese and the Deccan rulers for the same purpose). Such dealings were, of course, a source of conflict, as the Mughals evidently did not accept *cartazes* with good grace and Portuguese officials for their part did not miss opportunities to squeeze benefits out of the arrangement. At the same time, an alignment with the realities of the balance of maritime power was necessary, if the *hajj* from Surat and other ports was to be maintained.

A further aspect, perhaps the best treated in the literature, can be traced to the late 1570s, with the beginnings of the Jesuit presence in Akbar's court, which lent a religious dimension to the dealings. The missionary Fathers hoped, in vain, to convert the ruler, or at least some of his prominent nobles. But they also served as a conduit between the authorities at Goa and the Mughal court, and were thus a convenient presence since the *Estado da Índia* and the Mughals did not maintain permanent diplomatic missions in each other's domains.

It is evident, even from the bald summary presented above, that relations between the Mughals and the Portuguese were potentially as much of conflict as of collaboration, since their basic interests were by no means congruent. We have to look no further than the *Mongoliecae Legationis Commentarius* of the Catalan Jesuit António Monserrate for a confirmation of this, for his account contains a detailed mention of the difficulties between Mughals and Portuguese in Gujarat and off the Konkan coast in the years 1581-2.[11] Abu'l Fazl's official Mughal chronicle, *Akbar Nama*, is no less explicit on the question.[12]

The Mughal-Portuguese equation, then, was an ambiguous one, even if we only consider Gujarat. Mughal expansion in other directions was not all that well received by the Portuguese either, as we see from Diogo do Couto's account of Raja Man Singh's expedition to the east in the 1590s, in *Década XII* of his huge chronicle, *Da Ásia*. It is all the more disappointing therefore that the surviving section of his chronicle says so little about the major Mughal expansion of the years 1597 to 1600, namely the incorporation of large parts of the Deccan, and in particular the Ahmadnagar Sultanate.[13] This is evidently in contrast to the detailed attention Couto pays to Nizam Shahi affairs in earlier parts of *Da Ásia*; the struggle for succession at the death of Burhan

Nizam Shah (r. 1508–54), the siege of Chaul in 1570–1, earlier Mughal threats to Ahmadnagar in the 1580s, and Portuguese-Nizam Shahi relations in the viceroyalty of Matias de Albuquerque (1591–7) all receiving their fair share of attention.[14] We should bear constantly in mind that the Portuguese, who had arrived in India a quarter-century before Babur turned his attention to Hindustan, were uneasy observers of Mughal expansion from their coastal enclaves, and invented in this process the collective myth of the omnivorous triumvirate of giants of south and south-west Asia, the Great Turk, the Great Sufi and the Great Mughal.[15]

Now, Mughal expansion into the Deccan, while it may have been contemplated as early as 1577, in fact only began in the 1590s. Conventional accounts link Akbar's decision to expand into Ahmadnagar with the quarrels between the ruler Murtaza Nizam Shah (r. 1565–88) and his brother Burhan, which led the latter, after a brief sojourn in Bijapur, to take shelter with the Mughals, who incorporated him in 1584 into their own hierarchy of notability by making him a *mansabdar-jagirdar*. It seems likely, however, that the Mughals would have turned their attention to the Deccan sooner or later, once they had secured the conquests of Bengal and Gujarat, and consolidated their northern and north-western frontier. Besides, it is useful to bear in mind that the succession struggle that ensued at Ahmadnagar on Murtaza's assassination in 1588 only set the seal on a process of fragmentation that had deeper roots; the effort by the *habashi* (or Ethiopian) element in the state to assert its autonomy, the recourse by others – especially Deccani notables – to a form of Mahdawi millenarianism, in view of the approach of the Hijri year 1000, all of these point to a political situation fraught with tension.[16] A reader of the two great chronicles of the epoch, the *Burhan-e Ma'asir* of Sayyid 'Ali bin 'Azizullah Tabatabai, and the *Gulshan-e Ibrahimi* of Muhammad Qasim Hindushah Astarabadi (better known by his *nom de plume* of Firishta), is left in no doubt as to this.[17] Both writers were witness to the situation in the late 1580s, and Firishta left Ahmadnagar for Bijapur soon after Murtaza Nizam Shah's death, apparently fearing the rise of the Mahdawis and its implications for Shi'as like himself.

Burhan returned to Ahmadnagar from his Mughal exile as Burhan Nizam Shah II in 1591. He did so with Akbar's blessings, but took the aid of Raji 'Ali Khan Faruqi, ruler of Khandesh, rather than that of the Mughals themselves, in order to improve his own legitimacy once in Ahmadnagar. On his return, he displaced and imprisoned his own son Isma'il, who had ruled for two years with the support of the Mahdawi leader Jamal Khan.[18] However, Mughal expectations that he would be little more than a quisling once in power were soon denied. Abu'l Fazl, in his *Akbar Nama*, expresses great disapproval of Burhan throughout his four-year reign, as the following passage demonstrates:

> When Burhan-al-Mulk prevailed over Ahmadnagar, he should have increased his devotion and gratitude, and been an example of obedience to other rulers in that quarter. The wine of success robbed him of his senses, and he forgot the varied favours he had received from the Shahinshah. In his evil fortune he set

himself to oppress the weak, and considered that his profit consisted in the injury of others.[19]

To force him back to a more submissive posture, Abu'l Fazl's brother Abu'l-Faiz 'Fayzi' was sent on a mission to the Deccan in the years 1591–3, leaving a valuable account to which we shall turn presently.[20] For reasons that await detailed analysis, the Mughals still held back militarily though, but did not conceal their amusement at Burhan's military failures – in respect of not only Bijapur but also with the Portuguese. One possible reason for Mughal reticence may have been the difficulties they faced in the early 1590s in Gujarat, where Muzaffar Shah once more led a resurgence of local chiefs, including those of Jamnagar, Junagadh, Sorath and Kacch. Akbar's foster brother Mirza 'Aziz Koka, newly appointed *subadar* of Gujarat, set about crushing this move, in a military action that endured from 1591 until well into 1592.

In the next year, 1593, Mirza Koka began to threaten the Portuguese settlements in Gujarat, in particular Diu. Thereafter, apparently disgruntled with the lack of favour shown him by the Mughal court despite his military success, he began to display rebellious tendencies, and eventually embarked in a Mughal pilgrim ship for the *hajj*, only returning in 1594.[21] This was the very year when Burhan Nizam Shah II entered into headlong conflict with the Portuguese over a fortress he had built on a tongue of land, overlooking their settlement of Chaul in the Deccan. The Persian chronicler Muhammad Qasim Firishta, in his near-contemporary chronicle, describes matters as follows:

> In the year AH. 1001 [AD 1592–3], Burhan Nizam Shah marched his army against the Portuguese of Rewadanda; and despatching a large force to the sea-port of Chaul, ordered that a fort should be built to prevent the entrance of the Portuguese into the harbour of Rewadanda, and this fort he called Korla. The Portuguese sailing during the night effected their escape, but they returned with reinforcements from many other ports which had also fallen into their hands (...). Burhan Nizam Shah now sent a body of about four thousand men, under Farhad Khan, to reinforce Korla; and as other troops were expected from Daman and Bassein, he appointed one Bahadur Khan Gilani, at the head of all the foreign troops, governor of the fortress of Korla, to blockade Rewadanda.[22]

The chronicler goes on to describe how the Ahmadnagar forces nearly got the Portuguese to capitulate; however, the 'tyranny' of Burhan caused many of his commanders to desist from taking the enterprise to its conclusion. The Portuguese meanwhile arrived in a fleet, carried out a landing and, after a prolonged fight in which 12,000 of the Ahmadnagar forces were killed, 'reduced the fort to ashes'. This event, according to Portuguese sources, took place in early September 1594; Burhan himself died on 18 April 1595. Thus far Firishta, who – in keeping with his disapproval of this particular monarch – does not tell us what prompted Burhan to act in such a manner, and so contravene the agreement that his brother Murtaza and the Portuguese had arrived at after the earlier siege of Chaul in the 1570s. Now Diogo do Couto, whose chronicle contains quite a detailed description of these events, is not much more helpful than Firishta in explaining what prompted the 'Melique' (i.e., Malik, the title by which he refers to Burhan and the Nizam Shahs in general), to build the fortress of the 'Morro' (the hill-top – referring here to Korla).[23] But whatever be the reasons for the act, there is little doubt that the episode of the 'Morro' precipitated a major crisis, leading eventually to serious Mughal inroads into the Ahmadnagar sultanate by about 1600. Although it would take them another three decades to complete the task of conquest, the years between 1593 and the death of Akbar in 1605 mark a decisive stage in the changing relations between the Mughals and the Deccan.

This takes us to the situation with regard to the other major Deccan sultanate, namely Bijapur, in these years under the rule of Ibrahim 'Adel Shah II (r. 1580–1627). Ibrahim had come to power after the controversial reign of 'Ali 'Adel Shah, who had entertained complex relations with the Portuguese. Initially, in the 1560s, he seemed rather favourably inclined to Goa, and had even encouraged a mission to his own court from the Archbishop, Dom Gaspar Pereira.[24] But later in the same decade, relations began to sour. Eventually, 'Ali had even undertaken an ambitious – if unsuccessful – campaign against the Portuguese, mounting an attack on Goa that posed a serious threat to the Portuguese for a time. However, by the time of his assassination, and Ibrahim's accession, it would have seemed clear to the most powerful elements in the Bijapur polity that the real threats came from the north rather than from the west. Residual Portuguese ambitions had more or less abated by then, and with the death of 'Ali bin Yusuf 'Adel Khan, the exiled son of Bijapur's founder who had sought refuge in Goa, even this element of friction no longer persisted. On the other hand, relations with the Mughals were quite another matter. For while the Mughal claim by the 1580s was that the whole of the Deccan fell under their suzerainty, the rulers of neither Bijapur nor Golkonda could countenance such a claim. In their titulature, their coinage, and other claims, they obviously saw themselves as rulers independent (if threatened) from the Mughals until at least the 1630s. Besides, from the early sixteenth century, there was the Safavid connection, and the fact that both Bijapur and Golkonda had periodically recognized in the Safavids a form of 'ritual suzerainty', often inserting the names of the rulers of Iran, for example, into the Friday prayers in their capital cities. The flow of Iranian migrants into the Deccan in the last quarter of the sixteenth century, and the fact that these migrants constituted a significant part of the elite in both Bijapur and Golkonda, only served to strengthen these ties. In correspondence with the ruler of Iran, the Bijapur ruler could write as late as 1613:

> This letter is from the humblest slave Ibrahim to the exalted emperor Shah 'Abbas. My forefathers had always great hopes in His Majesty's ancestors' love

and friendship and had banked on them. I, on my part, would do no better than to revive and strengthen those ties. The Deccan territories form as much a part of the Safavid empire as the provinces of Iraq, Fars, Khurasan, and Azarbaijan. Accordingly, the names of the Safavid monarchs have been recited in the [Friday] sermons and will continue to be recited in future. Our forefathers were appointed to rule over these territories and protect them, by His Majesty's ancestors. So our function is to rule the countries on His Majesty's behalf and defend them against foreign aggression.[25]

The manifest purpose of these letters was to complain about the 'ruler of Agra and Delhi', as the Mughal monarch is referred to. The project that is proposed, namely that the Safavids should attack the Mughals from the west (in the region of Qandahar), to divert them from attacks on the south, need not be taken too seriously. But it is clear that the Bijapur sultan, like his counterpart in Golkonda, hoped in some way to counterbalance the Mughal superpower by appeals to a countervailing threat. Here then is a clue as to how the Safavids were perceived from the viewpoint of the Deccan. It was clear of course that no military alliance was really possible that might straddle the distance between Chaul and Dabhol, and the ports of Fars, but other forms of real and symbolic affinity tied the predominantly Shi'i sultans of the Deccan to Iran rather than to the Sunni Mughals who were gradually encroaching upon them from the north.

Fayzi's mission to the Deccan, 1591–3

The reports of the Mughal poet-laureate, Abu'l-Faiz ibn Mubarak (better known as Fayzi Fayyazi), are a particularly valuable contemporary account for understanding the nature of Mughal-Safavid relations. The brother of the great chronicler and ideologue, Abu'l Fazl, Fayzi was personally close to Akbar himself, and thus failry faithfully represents the viewpoint of the Mughal court, while also bringing back crucial empirical information on matters in the Deccan for the benefit of his royal master. His despatch to the Deccan in 1591 was, however, neither as a Sunni Muslim (which he may not really have been), nor as a poet (which he most certainly was), but as an intimate of Akbar, who was thus charged to size up the situation in respect of the area of Khandesh (more or less a Mughal protectorate by then) and more particularly Ahmadnagar, Bijapur and Golkonda, regions that had a rather more ambiguous political position. It is in this rather delicate situation of contested sovereignties, that Fayzi found himself embroiled. Added to this was the fact that the ruler of Ahmadnagar, Burhan Nizam Shah, had spent some years in the Mughal court as an exile, and had returned to take charge as sultan having been a mere Mughal subordinate. This, then, is how Abu'l Fazl puts it in his *Akbar Nama*: [the pressing need was to bring around the] 'somnolent one [Burhan] and the other rulers of that quarter.

If they listened and apologised, he [Akbar] would withhold his hand from retribution. Otherwise a victorious army would be appointed, and chastisement would be inflicted'.[26]

Fayzi thus left Lahore on his travels to the Deccan on 24 August 1591 (the Hijri month of Shawwal 999), and returned to the court in May 1593, after an absence of a year and three-quarters.[27] In this time, he set down a number of reports for Akbar that touch on a diversity of subjects, ranging from the situation in crucial fortresses on the route, to gossip concerning the Safavid political situation gathered from fresh migrants to the Deccan, to an appraisal of the Deccan political scene itself. He also looked into the matter of persons in the Deccan, whether poets, writers or others, who might be recruited into Mughal service, thus acting as a sort of talent scout. Yet Fayzi's embassy to the Deccan was not considered a success from a diplomatic perspective, a fact which even his devoted brother Abu'l Fazl implicitly admits. Writing in the *Akbar Nama*, he notes:

> On the 28th [Ardibihisht] the standard of the seekers after knowledge, the *malik ush-shu'ra'* Shaykh Fayzi, returned from the Deccan, and after an absence of 1 year, 8 months, 14 days, did homage. He was exalted by various favours. He had gone on an embassy. Burhan in his arrogance and self-will had not listened to his counsels. He had not sent fitting presents and had prepared the materials for his own injury. Raji 'Ali Khan had to some extent listened to his commands, and had sent his daughter with choice bridal gifts for the wooing of the Prince Royal.[28]

The unofficial Mughal chronicler, Badayuni, who is much less sympathetic to Fayzi, notes that in Muharram 1002, four months after Fayzi's return, 'the other ambassadors arrived from the rulers of the Dakhin having succeeded in their negotiations; and paid their respects. And since Burhan-al-mulk had not sent any acceptable present, on 21 Muharram the emperor appointed the Prince Daniyal to this service, as *wakil* to the Khan-e Khanan (...) and other *amirs* with 70,000 specially assigned troops'.[29] There is a snide tone to this comment; the other ambassadors had 'succeeded', hence only Fayzi had failed. The failure consisted above all in that Fayzi was unable to persuade Burhan Nizam Shah to declare unambiguously that he was a vassal or subordinate of the Mughals, and that he was willing to pay regular tribute (or *peshkash*) to his powerful northern neighbours. In other words, in comparison to the Faruqi ruler of Khandesh, who received Fayzi with total self-abnegation, the Nizam Shah still showed signs that he saw himself as capable of being autonomous, partly through the privileged relations that he had with the Safavids. The final message to be derived from Fayzi's reports was that the Mughals had no real recourse left but military conquest.

Yet, this is to reduce a rich series of materials to a rather simple one-point programme. For Fayzi was able in four of his six reports to present a series of striking vignettes of various aspects of the Deccan, and also of the political situation in Iran.

They are all quite valuable and range from simple descriptions of the towns through which he passed, to evaluations of the court politics of the Deccan sultanates. We may take, by way of example, his brief but evocative description of Burhanpur, in his view no more than a small town (*baghayat tang*), but full of gardens and greenery (*bustan*).[30] No doubt Akbar and his sons found such information of interest when planning their military campaigns in the area, since they eventually used Burhanpur as a place of residence.

The first of Fayzi's reports, written largely while in Mughal territory, has its share of blunt condemnations, and recommendations of officials that he encountered; we do not know to what extent these ideas were implemented at court, and imperial servants transferred, promoted or chastized as a consequence. But the second report moves away from that tone and content. Instead, we get the following appreciation of the affairs of Ahmadnagar, from a time when Fayzi had taken up temporary residence in that city.

> Burhan Nizam-al-mulk is one of those who has been raised from the dust by Your Excellency, and who has been reared on your munificence. It is four months since he entered the *jagir* of 'Adel Khan in a part that is 25 *kos* from Ahmadnagar on the bank of the river Nahalwada or Bhima, a big river that separates them. And he has built two mud fortresses in the middle of the latter's territory. 'Adel Khan is still sitting in the fort of Bijapur, and has sent his army of 14,000 horsemen. There are skirmishes every day, and a large number of people are being slain on both sides.

Neither ruler of the Deccan is given the dignity of the title of 'shah', as we note, and their territories are treated throughout as mere *jagirs*, revenue-assignments deriving from the Mughals. Further, Fayzi notes that the uncle of Burhan Nizam-al-mulk (not 'Nizam Shah', we may stress again), a certain Baqir, who had been living in poverty in Bijapur, had been now promoted by the 'Adel Khan (not 'shah'), and sent against him with an army. He had been tempted by the idea of taking over Ahmadnagar. Meanwhile, Raji 'Ali Khan Faruqi had sent men to both the uncle and nephew, urging them to make peace. It was expected that a truce would be declared, but for the moment the war continued. Fayzi expresses great annoyance with the situation. For when Burhan had left Ahmadnagar on his Bijapur campaign, he had with great humility expressed his own sense of vulnerability, and declared that he was preparing the *peshkash* for the Mughals. However, Fayzi had since tried to persuade him to expedite matters, but he kept putting things off. Four months had passed in this manner, even though Fayzi had even met him twice in that connection. The Mughal envoy notes how distressed he was to find himself in the city of Ahmadnagar, full of mischief and commotion (*shor va sharr*), inhabited by seditionmongers and ruffians (*fitnasazan wa aubashan*). He had the impression of wasting his time, even though the wretched Burhan continued to write regularly to Fayzi, beseeching him to intervene to ensure that Akbar did not become angry. Each time, in his letters, he insisted he would return in a few days. Fayzi adds: 'Since Burhan is your disciple (*tarbiyat karda*), and has grown under your kind eye, I hope he will always remain on the correct path, and that his conduct will be acceptable to Your Excellency, and that it will all end well for him.'³¹

A description of the city of Ahmadnagar follows. Fayzi notes that the city was built by the father of Nizam-ul-mulk Bahri, grandfather of Burhan (himself son of Husain, son of Burhan, son of Ahmad). This last Ahmad had built a stone fort at a distance of four or five bowshots from the city, and the fort was the main seat of the ruler (*hakim*). Around the fort was a *maidan*, and open fields. The city was rectangular, and there were no city walls. At a distance of two *kos* was a lake, and a canal had been excavated to bring water from there to the city and then distributed to households. Some houses had tanks, others used well-water that was not particularly good. The Mughal envoy notes that when the late ruler Murtaza Nizam Shah had gone mad, a certain Salabat Khan had built a garden for him with tall cypress trees outside the town. In the middle of it was a covered pond or *hauz*, but Fayzi had not yet seen it.

Fayzi praises the good goldsmiths of the area, and weavers who were unparalleled, and mentions that in general very high-quality cloth was made in the Deccan. Patan is one centre and Dawlatabad another that he singles out. Clearly, the conquest of the area could bring major economic benefits to the Mughals. But, in contrast to the positive state of the climate and economy is the quite disastrous political ambiance. Of this matter, Fayzi writes:

> In the last few years, there were massacres (*qatl-e 'amm*) twice in this city [Ahmadnagar], in the course of which not a single person from abroad (*mardum-e wilayat*) was left alive. The killing spree lasted for three days. Good people like the learned men and traders, who had assembled here in this period, were all slain, and their houses were destroyed. And at another time, after the coming of Burhan Nizam-ul-mulk, a great plunder and loot was carried out with respect to the foreigners (*ghariban*). Whosoever had any goods was killed or wounded; the kith and kin of Shaykh Munawwar were ruined in this process, and were wounded. They are so ashamed that they do not dare come out of their houses. He expects favours from you. Lahori Afghan merchants too were plundered in large measure, and some of the servants of Salima Sultan Begam too were looted. How can the things plundered by these ruffians in this commotion be recovered?

These thugs, or *aubashan*, were still roaming the streets freely, a sign of how matters needed to be taken in hand in Ahmadnagar.

Having made it clear that Ahmadnagar under Nizam Shahi rule is a den of iniquity, Fayzi turns his attention to Ibrahim 'Adel Khan, the *hakim* (governor) of Bijapur, and now some 22 years old. He notes that in the early part of his reign, power had been exercised by a certain Dilawar Khan Habashi, a Sunni, but that he had then fled to the camp of Burhan. In a later section of the report, we learn more details, to the effect that Dilawar Khan Habashi had controlled Bijapur for ten to twelve years, to the point that 'Adel Khan did not even drink water without his approval and rarely stirred out. However, his misbehaviour had made the people of Bijapur miserable. Hence, the previous year, a large number of people had assembled there to kill him, with the connivance of 'Adel Khan himself. It was then that Dilawar Khan had fled to join Nizam-ul-mulk. In the meanwhile, 'Adel Khan invited him back and he returned, believing he would be well treated. Instead, when he reached there, his eyes were gouged out and his effects confiscated. His son, Muhammad Khan, was also wooed by 'Adel Khan, but when this failed, he too was blinded. Clearly, things in Bijapur were also on the decline. As for Golkonda, its ruler Muhammad Quli Qutb-al-Mulk was a Shi'a, who had made a new city called Bhagnagar, named after a certain Bhagmati, a hardened whore and his old mistress (*fahisha-e kuhna wa ma'shuqa-e qadim*), from which one can draw one's own conclusions.[32] The territories of the Deccan were thus broadly divided, in Fayzi's view, into the *jagirs* of these three men and some other *rajas*, who coexisted in a politic fashion (*mubassirana*). Fayzi claims that he has observed them carefully, and promises a fuller report at a later date. Yet his claims for Mughal suzerainty continue to colour every part of the account. 'This territory is part of the well-protected territories (*mamalik-e mahrusa*)', he writes, calling on Akbar to visit it once, since the mere sound of the arrival of Akbar will have a positive effect on these recalcitrant elements.

Yet Fayzi was also keen to use his time in Ahmadnagar to look beyond the politics of the sultanates of the Deccan and one of his primary tasks was to gather information on the situation in Iran. It turned out that in that particular year, six ships had arrived from Hormuz on the Konkan coast; a certain Khwaja Mu'ina'i, who was a merchant-prince (*'umdat ut-tujjar*), had made the 24-day voyage with his friends, bringing with him 200 Iraqi horses in three ships. However, it turned out that the Portuguese – here simply termed the *firangis* – had a rule that ships with horses were taken first to Goa, where they picked out the ones they wanted. Only then could the ships go on to the port of Chaul, which was in the *jagir* of Nizam-ul-mulk.[33]

Fayzi notes that some traders and some of the *qezelbash* (Turkoman military specialists) in Safavid service, on account of the turbulence in Iraq and Fars, had left for the Mughal domains, with the intention of 'kissing the threshold' of Akbar. The chief of them was a certain Husain Quli Afshar, a brave young man, who in the time of Shah Tahmasp held the governorship of some districts around Isfahan. Another important man was Husain Bayg, *lashkar-navis* (army registrar), who held a high position in the province of Fars when his particular friend Ya'qub Khan had been powerful in Iran. But after Ya'qub's death (more details below), he had been forced to leave. These two men had come with their followers, and were temporarily staying in the port of Chaul, pondering their future. They had written to Fayzi and he had replied to both of them in a single letter, a copy of which he sent to Akbar.

The image of Shah 'Abbas

Amongst the people on the ship was a certain Hamza Hasan Bayg, a relative of the great Mughal general 'Abdolrahim Khan-e Khanan, who planned to go to Thatta, where 'Abdolrahim was. Another migrant was Haji Ibrahim, a former *rikabdar* (cup-bearer) of Shah Tahmasp. There was also Haji Khusrau, a former personal slave of Shah Tahmasp and well known in the Mughal court. Some of these passengers eventually arrived in Ahmadnagar, and gave Fayzi information concerning the current situation in Iraq, Fars and Rum. This was hot gossip indeed, and he hastened to relay it to his master, the emperor. Fayzi writes:

> Shah 'Abbas has attained twenty years of age, and is aflame with the fire of youth. His horoscope and those of his two brothers, Abu Talib Mirza and Tahmasp Mirza, are hereby enclosed for your consideration. The court-astrologers will tell you the beginning and the end of the fate of these three. Shah 'Abbas is fond of hunting, polo (*chawgan*), shooting, and javelin-throwing (*neza-bazi*). He is keen on falconry. Last year, he fell down twice from his horse while javelin-throwing, once in Shiraz and the second time in Isfahan. Both times, his knee was severely injured. He is a brave man, and proud of himself (*ghayratmand*), and even if he is prey to the whims and passions of royal youth, he is still sober, and intelligent. He has still not taken over the reins of governance, and the fiscal and administrative affairs are so far left to the officials. Farhad Khan is his chief secretary (*vakil-e motlaq*), and his constant companion, and Hatim Bayg Urdubadi, who is very shrewd and economical, is the *vazir*.

'The time had come', writes Fayzi, 'when the shah would awake from his stupor and also emerge from the intoxication of youth'. This was therefore a dangerous moment for his rivals and neighbours. The shah was now very concerned that most of the lands of Khorasan had been lost on account of his carelessness, and was making efforts for its recovery.[34] The previous year, he had wanted to attack Khorasan; but when he reached Rayy, plague broke out, and some of his troops had bubos on their side, others on their thighs, the size of a gram. Shah 'Abbas himself had fallen ill with fever at the time, and rushed back to Qazvin.[35] Thereupon, Farhad Khan, with some notables, had come to Khorasan, recaptured some of the towns, and arrived in the vicinity of Mashhad, killing several thousand Uzbeks. The son of the Shaybani ruler, 'Abdullah Khan, then made a flanking attack from Herat and Farhad Khan retreated to Qazvin. Fayzi notes that the traders from Iran had clearly mentioned that 'Abdullah Khan's son only had 5,000–6,000 men and that if Farhad Khan had stood his ground he would have carried the day; the implication is that Safavid military capability left much to be desired. The role of astrologers in determining Safavid policy is also noted: in the previous year they prevented the shah from launching any expedition in Khorasan, but in the current year, they suggested that he could lead the army, and even predicted that he would emerge victorious. Fayzi also makes a point of providing a detailed estimate of the armies that the shah, is planning to use to make the attack on Khorasan. He estimates the total force at well over a 100,000 men, and gives details of the various commanders (who are often provincial governors), the central forces (*lashkar-e khassa*) of about 30,000, as well as the slave-forces directly under the command of the shah and numbering about 10,000.[36] Their breakdown appears as follows.

Safavid forces according to Fayzi

    Zu'lfiqar Khan with his brother Farhad Khan, *hakim* of Ardabil and Damghan, 10,000 men
    Farhad Khan, with one of his brothers, and Alvand Sultan, 10,000 men
    Husain Khan, the *hakim* of Ganja, and 'Ali Sultan, 50,000 men
    Husain Khan Qajar, with a Qajar force, 12,000 men
    Shah Quli and Sultan Shamlu, *hakim* of Hamadan, 4,000 men
    Chiragh Sultan, *hakim* of Rayy, 4,000 men
    Farrukh Khan, brother of Murtaza Khan Turkoman, 5,000 men
    Muhammad Quli Sultan, son of Murtaza Khan, 2,000 men
    Buniyad Khan, *hakim* of Shiraz and dependencies (*tavabi'*), 10,000 men
    The *hakim* of Yazd and dependencies, 5,000 men
    Amir Hamza Khan and Siyaush Khan, with infantry and cavalry, 4,000 men
    Malik Sultan Muhammad, 8,000 men
    Mahdi Quli Sultan Shamlu, 1,000 men
    Ahmad Quli Sultan Zu'l-qadr, 12,000 men
    Farrukh Husain Khan Shamlu, 5,000 men
    The son of 'Ali Khan, 1,000 men
    Yadgar 'Ali Sultan, *hakim* of Khwarazm and Simnan, with cavalry and infantry, 2,000 men
    Cavalry and infantry (*piyada wa savar*) from Isfahan, 2,000 men
    Infantry (*jama'at-e piyada*) from different cities, 15,000 men
    The *lashkar-e khassa*
        That is *qurchi khassa* etc., 8,000 men
        Yuzbashi, etc., horsemen, 15,000 men
        Piyada, 8,000 men
    The army of the slaves of the shah
        Dalw-e Jamshid of the *hakim* of Qazvin, 2,000 men
        Dalw-e Husain, 3,000 men
        Dalw-e Farrukh Khan, 3,000 men
        Dalw-e Abdal, 2,000 men

Yet it seemed that even with this powerful army, the Safavid realm was riven with internal dissension. For example, Dawlat Yar Kurd, sent to the area between Tabriz and Qazvin with 20,000 people, had rebelled. The shah then sent Husain Khan, the governor of Qom, with 15,000 men to quell him; Husain Khan had, however, been defeated, and it was thought that when the shah left for his campaign in Khorasan, Dawlat Yar would be able to advance as far as Qazvin. In the face of this threat, the shah himself attacked him, and persuaded some of Dawlat Yar's brothers to defect. Because of this reverse, Dawlat Yar surrendered and appeared before the shah, expecting clemency. But none was forthcoming. Instead, the shah kept him in a cage (*sanduq*), took him to Qazvin, and burnt him there. The ferocity of Shah 'Abbas I is thus a recurring theme in these letters. It is claimed that he even threatened to harm some Uzbek traders in Yazd, and only relented when the Uzbeks said that if they were harmed, Iranian traders would then face similar consequences in Shaybani territories.

Besides, it was said that the previous year, Shah 'Abbas had blinded his brothers, Tahmasp Mirza and Mirza Abu Talib, Isma'il Mirza and the son of Hamza Mirza with a hot iron. The last of these was so young that he died from the maltreatment. Shah 'Abbas himself had two sons, Mirza Safi and the infant Mirza Haydar, who had been born the previous year. The shah's father, Sultan Muhammad, was totally blind and lived in his son's camp in a separate tent. Arrangements had been made for his food and drink; he occupied himself with various forms of entertainment.

But most significant of all was the case of a certain Ya'qub Khan, briefly mentioned above. Fayzi reports that the year before last, Yaktash Khan, the governor of Kirman and Yazd, who had a considerable force at his command, had revolted against the shah. Ya'qub Khan Zu'l-qadr, the governor of Shiraz, had been sent by the shah to chastise him; he had killed Yaktash in the fight that followed, and a huge amount of property and goods fell into the hands of Zu'l-qadr, which had rather turned his head. He used to claim to be a 'product of Shah Tahmasp' (*man az Shah Tahmasp hasil shuda am*), and even stated that he would one day be ruler of Iran. In pursuit of this idea, in Shiraz near the tomb of Shaykh Sa'di, he had illegally built a fort. The shah sent for him repeatedly from Isfahan, and asked him to deposit the goods he had gathered, but he refused to send anything. So the shah gathered 12,000 men and attacked Shiraz; but Zu'l-qadr now went to Istakhr, where he took refuge inside the fort with 400 men. Shah 'Abbas besieged him there for four months, and he used to say to his companions in regret that he had had no better servant than Ya'qub Khan, but that enemies had frightened and misled him. This news reached Ya'qub Khan, so that at last he left the fort under the influence of the seduction and soft words (*afsun va afsane*) of the shah, and was for a time forgiven by 'Abbas. Yet rumours persisted that he was planning to kill the shah, and 'Abbas one day (while hunting) passed his hand over Ya'qub Khan's shoulder under an affectionate pretext and saw that he was wearing a coat of mail. Taking this as a sign of sedition, he at once claimed to have a headache and returned to the city, abandoning the hunt. The next day, he summoned Ya'qub Khan to the audience-hall (*divan-khane*) with all his important servants. It so happened that on that very day, a group of rope-makers had asked to show their skill at rope-play to the shah. The shah seated Ya'qub Khan by his side, jokingly took a stick in his hand, and said: 'Kingship is coming to

Ya'qub Khan. He shall be the king, and we his servant' (*Shahi ba Ya'qub Khan mirasad. Ishan shah bashand va ma nawkar-e an*). He then said aloud that 'Shah Ya'qub Khan issued the order that such-and-such a servant should be killed with a rope'. The man was strangled. In this way, the supporters of Ya'qub Khan were killed before his very eyes one after another, until at last, it was his turn. He was hung by a rope, his body was put to the rack (*dar shekanje kardand*) and after torture his flesh was fed in morsels to the dogs (*loqma-ye sagan sakhtand*).[37] Fayzi leaves us in little doubt that he considers this an act of quite gratuitous cruelty, explaining why men such as Husain Bayg (mentioned above) had decided to leave Iran for India.

In view of all this, it is clear that Fayzi believed that the Mughal court could quite easily recruit the best talent from Iran. Thus, amongst the scholars (*daneshmand*) of Iraq and Fars was a certain Mir Taqi'-al-Din Muhammad, famous under the name of Taqiya Nasaba. In Iran he was unmatched, and he was a disciple of the great Mir Fathollah Shirazi, who had highly praised him to Fayzi. It was believed that Mir Taqi'-al-Din was keen to come to the Mughal court, but lacked the means for the voyage; Fayzi therefore suggests that Akbar should issue a *farman* with some money and that this would persuade him to make the trip. Other names are also mentioned, such as that of the son of the *qazi* of Hamadan (a certain Ibrahim) who was a great scholar, or of Shaykh Baha'-al-Din Esfahani, resident in the Safavid capital, or the celebrated Chalpay Bayg, who had been educated in Shiraz and Qazvin.[38] Besides, there were the Iranian savants in Ahmadnagar itself, who included two poets, Malek Qomi and Mulla Zohuri, both of whom Fayzi believed should be invited to the Mughal court.[39]

Throughout his stay in the Deccan, Fayzi continued to gather intelligence on the Safavids. In a later report, he notes that letters from Hormuz traders to those in Ahmadnagar had recently arrived and that he had managed to read some of them. These letters claimed that Shah 'Abbas I had first gone to Gilan and, after quelling some rebels there, had set out for Khorasan, accompanied by 150,000 horsemen and foot-soldiers. There was a great battle (*jang-e 'azim*), and the shah had recaptured Mashhad and Herat from the Uzbeks. The letters stated that the Uzbeks had fled the battlefield; rivers of their blood were spilt by the Qezelbash army of Iran. Besides, the great merchant (*sawdagar-e bozorg*) Khwaja Baha'-al-Din had written from Chaul, stating that the captain (*nakhoda*) of a ship on its way from Hormuz to Goa had stopped at Chaul on some pretext and given him the latest news from Iran, to the effect that the shah had taken Khorasan and had decided to send an envoy with 60 Iraqi horses, expensive textiles and a large quantity of goods to Akbar. The envoy (*ilchi*) was still in Hormuz and was about to leave for the Mughal court via Sind. Another letter (*khatt-e digar*) claims that 100 severed heads of Uzbeks and 100 live Uzbek slaves were being sent to the Mughals. Rather extravagantly, Fayzi confidently asserts that in his letters Shah 'Abbas humbly states that he is a mere 'devotee' (*mokhles*) of the Mughal emperor who hopes for Akbar's kind attention. He even claims that the Safavids admit freely that their fortune and state (*Dawlat dar khandan-e safavi*) is due to the Mughals (*in dudman-e 'ali*), as is evident from the pages of history.⁴⁰ Here, Fayzi's imperial rhetoric exceeds itself, but this need not detract from the significance of certain other parts of his account.

Iran and the Iranian world feature quite prominently in Fayzi's account. The Portuguese are a more discreet presence. One anecdote does feature a Portuguese character. It emerges that Fayzi had heard a story of a *farangi* physician called Bajarz (perhaps Borges), who had been invited to Ahmadnagar in the early sixteenth century by Nizam-ul-mulk Bahri, and was employed by him as a confidant. One day, this *hakim* asked Khvajagi Shaykh Shirazi in the court of Nizam-ul-mulk the following question: 'If there were a fire at the end of the world, and there was nothing in between you and that place, and you were standing on mountain, you can see the fire. Yet you people say that before the sky (*falak*), where the moon is, there is a layer of fire. Why is that not visible?' The Shaykh replied this was on account of distance. The Portuguese then crudely mocked his reply. At that time, the celebrated Shah Taher Hosayni arrived and asked what was happening. When he was told, he replied that the Shaykh was wrong. When there is a mixture of elements, only then are things visible, as with the usual worldly fires, which had particles of earth in them. But the heavenly canopy of fire was made up of a pure element and hence invisible. This silenced the Portuguese completely.⁴¹ From these and other minor elements in the account, we can see that Fayzi set no great store by the Portuguese. At best, they were minor irritants, at worst arrogant troublemakers.

Ten years after

In the ten years that followed Fayzi's mission, the Mughals managed to make substantial inroads into the Deccan. Despite resistance mounted by the Ahmadnagar queen, Chand Sultana, and a certain Abhang Khan, Mughal forces had come close to taking Ahmadnagar by 1599, and they were only temporarily halted in this enterprise by the mysterious death of Akbar's son, Shah Murad, who headed the Mughal army. Letters from the Portuguese viceroy, Dom Francisco da Gama, written in 1599 suggest that the *Estado da Índia* may in fact have been implicated in the Mughal prince's death, since the viceroy believed that this death would increase internal dissension in the Mughal camp and draw their attention away from projects of conquest.⁴² In reality, this strategy did not bear any fruit, as the Mughal armies crushed the forces of Ahmadnagar, took the city and advanced their southern frontier as far as Bijapur. Akbar, having personally supervised this campaign, then left his son Daniyal in charge of the Deccan, together with the veteran general 'Abdolrahim Khan-e Khanan, and returned north. The main remaining resistance in Ahmadnagar was provided by a group of Ethiopians, including a person we shall encounter below – Malek 'Ambar.⁴³ Faced with this situation, the plight of Bijapur's Ibrahim 'Adel Shah can only be imagined. Certain observers, like the Flemish jeweller Jacques de Coutre who was in the Bijapur court in these years (and who also knew both the Safavid and Mughal courts at first hand), decried the sultan's cowardice, but it is clear that his only possible strategy was now a form of passive resistance through diplomacy. Coutre, who claims to have known the monarch closely (*con mucha familiaridad*) between 1604 and 1616, is nevertheless bitingly sarcastic, referring to him by turns as a coward, tyrant, arbitrary and obsessed with his harem of over 900 concubines 'who served him carnally when he wished'.[44] Indeed, Ibrahim's major virtue in Coutre's eyes is that he paid his debts promptly (*era ... puntual en lo que comprava*), was harsh in punishing bandits, and regular in paying his soldiers and household. Coutre noted that Ibrahim's way of dealing with the Mughals was simply to offer them 'gross gifts and tributes', and he further reported that the 'Adel Shah had justified this to his own vassals by claiming that instead of spending money and lives in making war, which always carried the risk of a loss, he would 'rather send him [the Mughal] the money in offering, and make him content, and be his friend, and remain in my house with my peace and quiet (*quedarme en mi caza con mi quietud y sossiego*)'.[45]

In fact, Ibrahim's strategy was rather more creative, but in order to understand this we need to turn to the account of a Mughal envoy to the court in 1603, a certain Asad Bayg Qazvini. Asad Bayg had been a loyal servant of Shaykh Abu'l Fazl, until the latter's assassination in 1602. Thereafter, his career was briefly under a cloud, but he had managed to regain royal favour and was sent out to deal with Bijapur in 1603. As he himself explains in his detailed account, the *Vaqa'e'-e Asad Beg*, the situation in that year was as follows.[46] When Akbar had been in Burhanpur in pursuit of his campaign against Ahmadnagar, he had decided to send a certain Iranian savant called Mir Jamal-al-Din Husain Inju Shirazi to Bijapur as an envoy. Mir Jamal-al-Din's principal task was to arrange a marriage between Ibrahim's daughter and Prince Daniyal, but instead of doing so expeditiously, the Sayyid from Shiraz remained at the Bijapur court for an inordinately long while, so that the emperor began to grow restive. Further, letters came from both the Khan-e Khanan and Mir Jamal-al-Din, in which the latter gave improbable reasons for his failure to return. The emperor at last grew angry, reports Asad Bayg, and decided to set him straight. It was decided to send an appropriate person and the royal eye fell on Asad Bayg. The instructions to Asad Bayg were simple: he was to bring Mir Jamal-al-Din back without even 'giving him a chance to take a sip of water'. Further, the envoy was told to bring back goods and wealth (*zar-o mal*) from the Deccan by way of tribute. A *farman* was also drafted for Mir Jamal-al-Din, which stated that if he did not return with Asad to the court he would face dire consequences for himself and for his children. Asad Bayg further asked for, and was given, a royal order addressed to Malek 'Ambar. Finally, Akbar instructed Asad Bayg to bring back an elephant called Atesh Para belonging to Ibrahim, which he had long promised but so far not given to Mir Jamal-al-Din Hosayn.[47]

The envoy set out for the Deccan by way of Ujjain, where the governor was the Timurid prince, Mirza Shahrokh. From there, he went on to Mandu, then to

Burhanpur, where he was received by Prince Daniyal himself and the Khan-e Khanan. The Mughal army seems to have been well settled in the Deccan by then, and the tone was rather relaxed. Evenings were spent with poetry, wine and music, rather than in any extended martial reflection. The Khan-e Khanan did, however, ask Asad Bayg to try and bring around Malek 'Ambar and a certain Hasan 'Ali Bayg, who, it appears, had a disagreement. The resistance in Ahmadnagar itself seems to have been at a low ebb. On reaching Bir, Asad Bayg then met with Hasan 'Ali Bayg and eventually it was decided that a reconciliation meeting between him and Malek 'Ambar would be organized. The Mughal envoy then first met the Ethiopian warlord (whom he already knew), presented him with the Mughal *farman*, and the two started reminiscing. As far as Asad Bayg was concerned, 'Ambar is the paragon of all good qualities, a wonderful host and a devout Muslim. Indeed, were he to recount the qualities of this bravest of the men of the time, a chapter – nay, a book – would be needed; Asad Bayg paints a very different picture from the malevolent image that the same Malek 'Ambar would acquire in Mughal texts of the 1610s and 1620s![48]

The Mughal envoy now departed for the south, accompanied by 'Ambar's own young nephew as far as the frontier with Bijapur (*ta sarhad-e Bijapur*). The place at which Asad Bayg entered 'Adel Shahi country was a short distance from the town of Mangalbedha, where Mir Jamal-al-Din and Mustafa Khan, the head of the Bijapur armies, were resident. Here, he was given a letter from Mir Jamal-al-Din in response to an earlier missive that Asad Bayg had sent him. This letter contained rather hypocritical declarations of joy at Asad Bayg's coming and stated that the next day Mustafa Khan's son would meet him with a force. The day after that, he would be welcomed by a certain Haybat Khan, and thereafter by Mustafa Khan himself with the nobles of Bijapur and men on elephants. Orders also arrived from Sultan Ibrahim on the reception to be given to Asad Bayg. The Mughal envoy was thus treated with due pomp and ceremony, as befitted the representative of a superior power.

Yet it soon became clear that things were not as they appeared on the surface. True, Mir Jamal-al-Din and the people with him displayed extraordinary hospitality. Over the days that followed Asad Bayg was invited out by the Bijapur nobles one after another and each took care of him after his fashion. From each he received Arab horses and high-quality Deccani gifts, but the Mughal envoy began to chafe at the bit, and declared that he needed to see Ibrahim urgently. But Ibrahim protested that such haste was unseemly and contrary to their custom. In keeping with Coutre's characterization, his agents even tried to tempt Asad Bayg with an offer of 200,000 *huns* if he would just stay on in Bijapur for some time. Asad Bayg refused, but it soon became clear that it was by such means that Ibrahim had managed to manipulate Mir Jamal-al-Din. This was the reason why the Sayyid from Shiraz was so reluctant to leave the Deccan. The fact, according to Asad Bayg, was that each year Mir Jamal-al-Din was making some 300,000 or 400,000 *huns* from Bijapur and Golkonda, as if he had a *jagir* of 5,000. But the corruption went further still. Asad

Bayg claimed that the Khan-e Khanan too was receiving like sums of money, and there was an agreement between him and Ibrahim to delay the departure of the palankeen of the Khanan's daughter from Mangalbedha. When asked about the delay, the Khan-e Khanan would claim that the threat of Malek 'Ambar made the roads unsafe. What Ibrahim was unable to achieve by force, he was thus able to do by the judicious use of money.

Asad Bayg's arrival on the scene was therefore a nuisance to all parties. When they saw that he was impervious to bribes, at last Ibrahim invited him to the city of Bijapur. The Mughal envoy now set out with quite elaborate presents, including some horses, camels, Kashmiri shawls, as well as European cloth (*parchaha-ye nafis-e velayat*) worth some 20,000 to 25,000 rupees in all. But Ibrahim continued to procrastinate. When Asad Bayg was a day short of Bijapur, he asked him to delay his arrival by two weeks, as there was an important festival to attend to. During this further wait, the lavish hospitality continued, with all sorts of food, drinks and fresh fruits, and good fodder for the animals. Besides, the custom was that the food would be brought in copper dishes (*degh*) and chinaware (*chini*), which were never taken back. Asad Bayg thus accumulated a number of vessels and utensils, which began to cause a nuisance, as it was not clear where to keep them. Besides, Ibrahim had ordered that everyday two men from amongst his principal courtiers (*az majlesiyan-e khasse*) would come and converse with Asad Bayg to keep him entertained. They included Malek Qomi and Mawlana Zohuri (whom we have encountered above in Fayzi's account), as well as Bichetr Khan, Mirak Mo'in-al-Din and many others.

Still, all of this was quite tiresome, and it was a relief when the festival of Shab-e Bar'at finally arrived and Asad Bayg was given permission to meet Ibrahim, and brought to a house that had been kept ready at the edge of the tank (*tal*) of Bijapur. Here, the Bijapur ruler was supposed to have a first formal meeting with him in order to ceremonially receive the *farman* from Akbar. But having agreed that he would enter alone, when the moment came, other courtiers also barged in, which Asad Bayg took to be an offensive breach of etiquette. Still, he carried on with the ceremony, which required Ibrahim to acknowledge Mughal superiority and also to perform the *sijda* and bow down in the direction of the absent Akbar. The *farman* was now opened and read, but at a certain moment Ibrahim began to find its contents offensive and started to comment in Marathi (*ba zaban-e Marhata*) to his chief Brahmin adviser, Antu Pandit. Asad Bayg was hence obliged to negotiate directly with Ibrahim, while sending the courtiers away. This posed a minor problem, for while Ibrahim 'understood Persian well, (...) he could not answer in that language, and spoke in a broken (*shikaste*) way'. Still, the conversation was conducted and when it ended Ibrahim insisted once more that Asad Bayg could not leave the same day as this was against their tradition (*rasm*). For his part, Asad Bayg insisted that he had to leave quickly and accompanied by both Mir Jamal-al-Din and Ibrahim's daughter. Finally, there was the question of the royal elephant Atesh Para. Ibrahim now replied that this particular elephant had been rendered useless (*bar taraf shode*) two years before, and that in its place, another elephant called Chanchal would be sent. This arrangement was accepted, and further gifts were ceremonially exchanged.

The following day, after Asad Bayg had spent several hours in festivities, a further message was brought to him, to the effect that Ibrahim was not happy to give him just one elephant as a gift. He had therefore decided to give him a rare black Arab horse, called Chini, which he had bought in Bijapur for 3,000 *huns* (equivalent to 9,000 Mughal rupees). He also invited Asad Bayg to the palace, to bid him a formal farewell. Here was an occasion for Asad Bayg to inspect the fort and he noted that it consisted of triple concentric fortifications. Beyond each moat, that was wide and full of water, was a double wall. Between each level of fortification were two lines of trees and quite some greenery. When they had passed the third door, there were two lines of gunners, archers and swordsmen to be seen. When the Mughal party reached the interior palace (*Dawlat-khane*), they passed through another gate. A great display had clearly been put on to impress the Mughal envoy, for there were expensive carpets spread out and vases. They then went into a courtyard, where they found themselves in a large open area, clean and sparkling, with decorated galleries and covered vestibules in parallel. The main gallery was two yards high and some 60 hands in width, but with no visible columns. In this gallery, there was a golden throne studded with jewels, near which was a seat, with a number of reclining cushions, and single and double lamps of gold and silver, some 20 in all. Small pieces of velvet and brocade were spread around and between every two lamps and incense-burners were trellises of gold or silver. Asad Bayg went and sat by the throne. After some time, a door opened at the other side of the palace and Ibrahim in all his splendour, accompanied by three or four persons, entered the place. Asad Bayg stood up to greet him and the Bijapur ruler advanced towards him. The sound of continuous music came from the door where he had emerged and Ibrahim's attention seemed engaged by that music. But since Asad Bayg was his guest, he began to make conversation with him. Parallel to this gallery, there were three niches, one very high and two somewhat smaller. In the largest was the elephant Chanchal. In the other two were two female elephants. All three were offered by Ibrahim to Asad Bayg to take back with him. Their conversation went on until two watches of the night and then Asad Bayg took his leave. The Mughal envoy tried to drive the hardest bargain possible, extracting as much by way of tribute in jewels and precious objects as he could. By the time he reached home, it was almost dawn. However, a bone of contention remained for Ibrahim had insisted on taking Asad Bayg's badge of discipleship (*shast-e moridi*), which he had received directly from Akbar, and refused to return it. It was only after elaborate negotiations that the Mughal envoy had this precious symbolic object returned several days later.

Affairs were thus concluded from the Mughal envoy's point of view. He had the elephant and horse, besides other significant tribute-goods, as he had been instructed. The only remaining question was how to deal with the recalcitrant Mir Jamal-al-Din. Asad Bayg put matters to him bluntly and told him the game was up.

He and the Khan-e-Khanan would now have to expedite matters with regard to the Bijapur bride. A letter was sent out to the Khan-e-Khanan, who reluctantly agreed that he would make his way to receive the princess. Still, Mir Jamal-al-Din tried a few more desperate delaying tactics, but to no avail. The Bijapur force that was to accompany them also persisted in dragging their feet. Rumours were periodically heard that Malek 'Ambar was on his way with a force to attack them. But, Asad Bayg managed to keep his head in the midst of all this and presently a Mughal party came along to accompany them as far as Ahmadnagar. Here, in the Ahmadnagar fort, the Sona Mahal was kept aside for Prince Daniyal and everything was decorated and prepared. Asad Bayg's good services were brought to the prince's attention and he was duly rewarded, with Daniyal's generosity being contrasted to the miserliness of the Khan-e-Khanan. The fact that Asad Bayg had managed to persuade Mir Jamal-al-Din to return, and brought back the daughter of the 'Adel Khan, besides the elephants and other *peshkash*, allowed him to return to the Mughal court in very good odour.[49]

In Asad Bayg's account, the Portuguese in Goa have an insignificant role to play. They appear on three or four different occasions: first, some European cloth appears among the gifts; then, a box of Portuguese manufacture (*sanduqche-ye farangi*) is mentioned in regard to the transport of some jewels; third, wine of Portuguese origin is listed among the return presents sent by Ibrahim for Akbar; and last, in the context of a discussion of tobacco and its qualities in the Mughal court. Where the third of these is concerned, Asad Bayg informs us that Chanchal, the female elephant, was used to drinking two Akbari *man* of wine a day, and that eventually two of the casks of high-quality Portuguese wine (*sharab-e nafis-e purtagali*) had to be broached to calm her down on the way to Agra. But if the Portuguese have a minor place, what is even more remarkable for our purposes is the almost total absence of the Safavids – who had played such a prominent role in Fayzi's account – in Asad Bayg's narrative, even though Asad Bayg himself was a migrant to the Mughal domains from Qazvin. Rather, one has the impression that the affairs of the Deccan have been reduced to a rather straightforward game between the Deccan sultanates and the Mughals, with the Portuguese as minor spectators at the fringes. The links of the old 'infernal triangle' had been loosened, if not entirely dissolved.

Conclusion

The remaining quarter-century of Shah 'Abbas's reign did not see a major alteration in this relationship, although the Safavid relationship with the Golkonda was probably strengthened somewhat in these years, with the inauguration of direct maritime links between Masulipatnam and the Persian Gulf.[50] It was only in the late 1620s that matters began to change, with the accession of Shahjahan corresponding broadly with the death of 'Abbas. To this extent, the reign of the emperor Jahangir (1605–27) can be seen as a hiatus where the Deccan policy of the Mughals is concerned and, in general, this is a reign where few major expansionary moves are contemplated or executed. This was also a matter of some relief for the Portuguese *Estado da Índia*, who had their hands full already with the Dutch in South East Asia and on the Coromandel coast, and with the English Company in Surat, to say nothing of major problems with a host of Asian polities, from the Safavids to the Tokugawas. The years from 1580 to 1630 thus mark something of a watershed in Portuguese relations with the Deccan. In the first three-quarters of the sixteenth century, the Bijapur sultanate was a major thorn in Portuguese flesh and one of the periodic threats to Goa, as well as to other Portuguese interests on the Konkan coast.[51] For the first time, from the 1580s, this equation definitely changed, and the change was principally because Bijapur and Goa finally had a common enemy in the Mughals, whose expansion into the Deccan both feared. This common fear helped define a vastly improved relationship between 1580 and 1630, when Portuguese private traders could enter Bijapur with impunity and take part in the lucrative diamond and textile trade of the Deccan, as Coutre's account amply helps us document.

But this idyll could not last. The pressure exerted by Shahjahan on his accession to the throne, culminating in the Treaty of Submission for Bijapur and Golkonda of 1636, the declining economic strength of Goa itself, and a series of other minor factors, meant that by the late 1630s the rulers of Bijapur were looking for other trading partners, a fact that eventually led to the opening of the Dutch East India Company factory in Vengurla. In the case of Mughal-Safavid relations, these came increasingly to centre on problems associated with the fortress of Qandahar, which emerged as a major bone of contention between the two powers. At the same time, after the fall of Hormuz to a Safavid-English alliance in 1622, trading relations between Bandar 'Abbas and Surat gained a new prominence and the supply of silver into the great Mughal port via the Safavid domains is one of the striking features of the middle decades of the seventeenth century.

In the first decade or so of Shah 'Abbas's reign, the Deccan played a far more prominent role in Mughal-Safavid relations than was to be the case later. This also brought the Portuguese *Estado da Índia* into the picture in a particular vein, for at this time the Portuguese imagined that the Mughals were their greatest threat and that the Safavids were a relatively benign power so far as they were concerned. The broad tone of their portrayal in these years hence tends to favour the Safavids over the Mughals, whom they see as a hidden threat (*inimigo encuberto*). Once into the seventeenth century, the balance shifted. The new expansionary policy of Shah 'Abbas meant a far more determined drive by the Safavids to take control of the Persian Gulf, as manifested in the contest with the Portuguese over centres such as Qishm and Kamaran (or Bandar 'Abbas), which they took in September 1614.[52] Interestingly, the captain of the Portuguese fort of Kamaran at the time of its fall was none other than the brother of the count of Vidigueira, namely Dom Luís da Gama. His letters at the time not only bemoan his own fate, and his public disgrace, but also represent a recognition that the Portuguese had greatly underestimated the threat that the 'Great Sufi' could represent. Lulled into a sense of security by the century of relatively amicable relations that they had had since the time of Shah Isma'il and Afonso de Albuquerque, the high authorities in the Portuguese *Estado da Índia* continued to believe that the real threats to their security came from the Ottomans and the Mughals. Yet, as Fayzi had so astutely pointed out, the 1590s were still a time when Shah 'Abbas was testing the waters and consolidating his own position. The years from 1600 to 1625 would then see the transformation of the external profile of the Safavid state in more senses than one, and the Portuguese would number among the victims of this transformation.

Notes

1. Letter of the count of Vidigueira to Philip III, British Library, London (henceforth BL), Addn. 28,432, fo. 14v.
2. Letter of the count of Vidigueira to Philip III, Biblioteca Nacional de Lisboa (henceforth BNL), Fundo Geral, Códice 1976, fo. 94v.
3. Abu'l Fazl, *Akbar Nama*, vol. III, trans. H. Beveridge, reprint (Delhi, 1989), pp. 972–3.
4. Letter of the count of Vidigueira to Philip III, dated 23 December 1599, BNL, Fundo Geral, Códice 1976, fo. 141v–142r.
5. BL, Addn. 28,432, fos. 16r–16v. Compare other letters on Hormuz affairs from Vidigueira to the king, dated April 1598 and December 1599, in BNL, Códice 1976, fos. 92v, 107v and 141v. For Persian materials on Portuguese-Safavid relations and the Portuguese presence in the Persian Gulf in the period, also see Jahangir Qa'im Maqami, *Asnad-i farsi 'arabi wa turki dar arshiv-i milli-yi purtughal, darbar-i hurmuz wa khalij-i fars*, vol. I, Teheran, 1354 AHs.
6. See Riazul Islam, *A Calendar of Documents on Indo-Persian Relations (1500-1750)*, 2 vols (Karachi/Teheran, 1978–82), vol. I, pp. 123–33. There is some variation in the precise names of ambassadors between these documents and the *Akbar Nama*, and I have generally preferred the former versions.
7. For an earlier essay on similar themes, see Muzaffar Alam and Sanjay Subrahmanyam, 'Uma sociedade de Fronteira do século XVI: Perspectivas Indo-Persas no Decão Ocidental', *Oceanos*, no. 34 (1998), pp. 88–101.
8. For an overview of political circumstances in about 1500, see Sanjay Subrahmanyam, *The Portuguese Empire in Asia, 1500-1700: A Political and Economic History* (London, 1993), chapter 1.
9. António Pinto Pereira, *História da Índia no tempo em que a governou o visorey D. Luís de Ataíde*, introd. Manuel Marques Duarte (Lisbon, 1987).
10. For an earlier analysis, see Sanjay Subrahmanyam, 'A matter of alignment: Mughal Gujarat and the Iberian world in the transition of 1580–81', *Mare Liberum*, no. 9 (1995), pp. 461–79.
11. H. Hosten, ed., 'Mongoliecae Legationis Commentarius', *Memoirs of the Asiatic Society of Bengal*, vol. III (1914), pp. 513–704; S. N. Banerjee and John S. Hoyland, trans. *The Commentary of Father Monserrate S.J. on His Journey to the Court of Akbar* (London, 1922).
12. Abu'l Fazl, *Akbar Nama*, pp. 409–10 (personal names have been modernized). Akbar's anti-Portuguese posture at this time is also echoed in his letter to 'Abdullah Khan Uzbek, for details of which see Mansura Haider, 'Relations of Abdullah Khan Uzbeg with Akbar', *Cahiers du Monde Russe et Soviétique*, XXII/3-4 (Paris, 1982), pp. 313–31. A later letter to 'Abdullah Khan, from 1586, again stressing the desire to expel the Portuguese, may be found in *Akbar Nama*, vol. III, pp. 754–60. For another view, see M. N. Pearson, 'The Estado da Índia and the Hajj', *Indica*, vol. XXVI (1/2) (1989), pp. 103–18, esp. pp. 117–18.

13. Diogo do Couto, *Da Ásia, Décadas IV-XII*, reprint (Lisbon, 1974). Couto's *Década Duodécima* is divided into five books, and a total of 63 chapters, all dealing with the viceroyalty of the count of Vidigueira (1597-1600). Of these, Malabar affairs dominate by far, but four chapters are Mughal-related. Two of these (pp. 24-39) are devoted to the affairs of Man Singh ('Manacinga'), and another two to the conversion of a prince of Badakhshan ('Abadaxam'), son of Mirza Shahrukh, to Christianity by the Augustinians at Hormuz (pp. 483-505).
14. But also see such contemporary letters as those in BL, Addn. 28,432, fos. 13r-16v; BNL, Códice 1976, fos. 117r-121v. The latter volume contains several other letters of interest for Mughal-Portuguese relations.
15. Elements of this portrayal, in respect of the Ottomans and the Safavids, may already be found in João de Barros, *Da Asia, Décadas I-IV*, reprint (Lisbon, 1973-4), and the legend of the 'Grand Turk' itself, of course, goes back at least to the fifteenth century; cf. Lucette Valensi, *Venise et la Sublime Porte: La naissance du despote* (Paris, 1987). For one of Couto's earliest uses of the term 'Grão Mogor', see Maria Augusta Lima Cruz, *Diogo do Couto e a Década Oitava da Ásia*, vol. I (Lisbon, 1993), p. 39, the context being a Mughal attack on Daman.
16. Mahdawi movements in the region are conventionally traced to Sayyid Muhammad Jaunpuri (1443-1505), who was born in the Sharqi sultanate of Jaunpur, and after performing the *hajj* in 1495-6, settled down in western India, where he attracted numerous followers and sympathizers in Gujarat and Ahmadnagar, including – it is claimed – Sultan Mahmud Begarha of Gujarat and Ahmad Nizam Shah. He was, however, expelled from the area by Sultan Mahmud, and died (or was killed) in Afghanistan. For details, see S. A. A. Rizvi, 'The Mahdavi movement in India', *Medieval India Quarterly*, vol. I (1) (1950), pp. 10-25; M. M. Saeed, *The Sharqi Sultanate of Jaunpur: A Political and Cultural History* (Karachi, 1972), pp. 284-92.
17. See T. Wolseley Haig, trans. *The History of the Nizam Shahi Kings of Ahmadnagar* (Bombay, 1923), pp. 201-3, an abridged translation of the third *tabaqa* of Sayyid 'Ali bin 'Azizullah Tabatabai of Samnan's chronicle, *Burhan-i Ma'asir* (the Persian edition is from Hyderabad, 1936-7). For the *Gulshan-i Ibrahimi* or *Tarikh-i Firishta*, by Muhammad Qasim Hindu Shah, see John Briggs, trans. *History of the Rise of Mahomedan Power in India*, 4 vols, reprint (New Delhi, 1989); earlier editions London, 1829, and Calcutta, 1908-10, in which volume III deals with the five post-Bahmani Deccan sultanates. A third, as yet unpublished, chronicle is the *Tazkirat-al-muluk* of Rafi'-al-Din Ibrahim Shirazi (1540/41-ca. 1620), written between 1608 and 1612; for a discussion of which see Iqtidar Alam Khan, 'The Tazkirat ul-Muluk by Rafi'uddin Ibrahim Shirazi: As a source on the history of Akbar's reign', *Studies in History* (N.S.), vol. II (1) (1980), pp. 41-55.
18. Firishta, in Briggs, *History of Mahomedan Power*, vol. III, pp. 168-71.
19. Abu'l Fazl, *Akbar Nama*, p. 909.
20. H. K. Sherwani, *History of the Qutb Shahi Dynasty* (New Delhi, 1974), pp. 352-53. Also see A. D. Arshad, ed., *Ensha'-e Fayzi* (Lahore, 1973), pp. 95, 101-3, and *passim*. An extensive discussion of this text may be found in Muzaffar Alam and Sanjay Subrahmanyam, 'A place in the sun: Travels with Faizi in the Deccan, 1591-93', in François Grimal (ed.), *Les sources et le temps/Sources and Time: A Colloquium* (Pondicherry, 2001), pp. 265-307.
21. Abu'l Fazl, *Akbar Nama*, pp. 979-82, 1006; 'Abd-al-Qadir Badayuni, *Muntakhab-al-Tawarikh*, trans. George S. A. Ranking, W. H. Lowe and T. W. Haig, 3 vols (Calcutta, 1884-1925); reprint (New Delhi, 1990), vol. II, pp. 400-1, 412.
22. Firishta, in Briggs, *History of Mahomedan Power*, vol. III, pp. 172-3 (proper names have been modernized). For Mughal responses to Burhan's defeat, see Abu'l Fazl, *Akbar Nama*, pp. 1023-5.
23. Couto, *Década XI*, pp. 164-73; also see Sanjay Subrahmanyam, '"The life and actions of Mathias de Albuquerque" (1547-1609): A Portuguese source for Deccan history', *Portuguese Studies*, vol. XI (1995), pp. 62-77.
24. On this mission, see Sanjay Subrahmanyam, 'Palavras do Idalcão: Um encontro curioso em Bijapur no ano de 1561', *Cadernos do Noroeste*, vol. 15, 1-2 (2001), pp. 513-24.

25. Translated in Nazir Ahmad, 'Adil Shahi diplomatic missions to the court of Shah Abbas', *Islamic Culture*, vol. 43/2 (1969), pp. 143-61; text in Nazir Ahmad, 'Letters of the rulers of the Deccan to Shah 'Abbas of Iran', *Medieval India: A Miscellany*, vol. I (Aligarh, 1969), pp. 280-300. For a general discussion, also see M. A. Nayeem, *External Relations of the Bijapur Kingdom (1489-1686 AD.): A Study in Diplomatic History* (Hyderabad, 1974).
26. Abu'l Fazl, *Akbar Nama*, p. 909.
27. Badayuni, *Muntakhab*, vol. II, pp. 389-90, mentions that four envoys were sent out: Faizi to Asir and Burhanpur, Amin-al-din to Ahmadnagar, Mir Muhammad Amin to Bijapur and Mir Munir to Golkonda.
28. Abu'l Fazl, *Akbar Nama*, p. 982.
29. Badayuni, *Muntakhab*, vol. II, pp. 402-3.
30. Arshad, *Ensha'-e Fayzi*, p. 97.
31. Ibid., p. 103.
32. For comments on this legend, and Faizi's recounting of it, see Sherwani, *History of the Qutb Shahi Dynasty*, pp. 339-48.
33. Goa is misread in the edited text as 'Kuda', and 'Chaul' as 'Jival'.
34. On the siege and capture of Herat by Shaybani or Uzbek forces in 1587-8, see R. D. McChesney, 'The conquest of Herat 995-6/1587-8: Sources for the study of Safavid/Qizilbash-Shibanid/Uzbak relations', in Jean Calmard (ed.), *Études Safavides* (Paris-Teheran, 1993), pp. 69-107.
35. On the peripatetic life of Shah 'Abbas I in this epoch and later, see Charles Melville, 'From Qars to Qandahar: The itineraries of Shah 'Abbas I (995-1038/1587-1629)', in J. Calmard (ed.), *Études Safavides*, (Paris-Teheran, 1993), pp. 195-224.
36. On this subject, also see Masashi Haneda, *Le Chah et les Qizilbaš: Le système militaire safavide* (Berlin, 1987).
37. Compare this description with the slightly later suppression of the Nuqtawis by Shah 'Abbas, described in Kathryn Babayan, 'The waning of the Qizilbash: The spiritual and the temporal in seventeenth century Iran' (Ph.D. dissertation, Princeton University, 1993), pp. 57-62.
38. On the issue of the migration of Iranian savants to Mughal India, see the details in Ahmad Golchin-i Ma'ani, *Karwan-i Hind (The Caravan of India: On Life and Works of the Poets of Safavid Era Emigrated to India)*, 2 vols (Mashhad, 1990).
39. Both poets are later to be found in Bijapur, as we see from Asad Bayg's account. For their work, see M. A. Ghani, *A History of Persian Language and Literature at the Mughal Court*, reprint (Westmead, 1972), vol. II, pp. 181-219.
40. This was, of course, the exact opposite of the real relationship between Babur and Humayun and the Safavid dynasty.
41. On Shah Taher, see the brief comment in Richard M. Eaton, *Sufis of Bijapur, 1300-1700: Social Roles of Sufis in Medieval India* (Princeton, 1978), pp. 68-9.
42. See Sanjay Subrahmanyam, 'The Viceroy as assassin: The Mughals, the Portuguese and Deccan politics, c. 1600', *Santa Barbara Portuguese Studies*, Special Number (1995), pp. 162-203.
43. On this personage, see B. G. Tamaskar, *Life and Work of Malik Ambar* (Delhi, 1978); also Radhe Shyam, *Life and Times of Malik Ambar* (Delhi, 1968).
44. Jacques de Coutre, *Andanzas asiáticas*, edited by Eddy Stols, B. Teensma and J. Verberckmoes (Madrid, 1991), pp. 174-98, 287-98; the quotation is from p. 297.
45. Coutre, *Andanzas*, pp. 296-97; for Ibrahim's relations with the Mughals in the early 1610s, see Khursheed Nurul Hasan and Mansura Haydar, 'Letters of Aziz Koka to Ibrahim Adil Shah II', *Proceedings of the Indian History Congress*, 27th Session (1965), pp. 161-7, containing a calendar of some diplomatic documents in 'Abdul Wahhab bin Muhammad Ma'muri-al-Husaini, *Gulshan-i Balaghat*, for a manuscript of which see Asiatic Society of Bengal, Calcutta, Curzon Collection, II, 312 (IvC 131).
46. For an earlier discussion (with manuscript references) of this important text, see Muzaffar Alam and Sanjay Subrahmanyam, 'Witnessing transition: Views on the end of the Akbari dispensation', in

K. N. Panikkar, Terence J. Byres and Utsa Patnaik (eds), *The Making of History: Essays Presented to Irfan Habib* (New Delhi, 2000), pp. 104–40.

47. Also see the earlier account by P. M. Joshi, 'Asad Beg's mission to Bijapur, 1603–1604', in S. N. Sen (ed.), *Mahamahopadhyaya Prof. D.V. Potdar Sixty-First Birthday Commemoration Volume* (Poona, 1950), pp. 184–96.
48. See, in this context, B. P. Saksena, 'A few unnoticed facts about the early life of Malik Amber', *Proceedings (Transactions) of the Indian History Congress*, 5th Session (1941), pp. 601–3.
49. Cf. P. M. Joshi, 'Asad Beg's return from Bijapur and his second mission to the Deccan, 1604–1606', in V. D. Rao (ed.), *Studies in Indian History: Dr. A.G. Pawar Felicitation Volume* (Bombay, 1968), pp. 136–55.
50. Cf. Sanjay Subrahmanyam, 'Persians, pilgrims and Portuguese: The travails of Masulipatnam shipping in the western Indian Ocean, 1590–1665', *Modern Asian Studies*, XXII/3 (1988), pp. 503–30.
51. See the discussion in Sanjay Subrahmanyam, 'Notas sobre um rei congelado: O caso de Ali bin Yusuf Adil Khan, chamado Mealecão', in Rui Manuel Loureiro and Serge Gruzinski (eds), *Passar as fronteiras: II Colóquio Internacional sobre Mediadores Culturais, séculos XV a XVIII* (Lagos, 1999), pp. 265–90.
52. On the loss of Kamaran, see the letters from Dom Luís da Gama in Instituto dos Arquivos Nacionais/ Torre do Tombo, Lisbon, Manuscritos do Convento da Graça, Tomo II-E [Cx. 6], pp. 161–73.

8

The Shaybanid Uzbeks, Moghuls and Safavids in Eastern Iran

Barat Dahmardeh

Introduction

The Mehrabanid Maleks, after assuming power in Sistan in the year 633 AH/1235–36 AD, maintained very close relations with the governing dynasties in Iran. However, in the late Timurid period they decided to seek independence. This led to direct Timurid intervention in Sistan and the flight of the Maleks to the Sarhadd area.[1] When the Uzbeks had ousted the Timurids, they attacked Sistan and its Timurid ruler fled. The Maleks then tried to return from Sarhadd to Sistan, but Uzbek power made that impossible (913 AH/1507–8 AD). The Safavid Shah Esma'il's advance into Khorasan and his victory over the Uzbeks at Merv resulted in the return of the Mehrabanid Maleks and the restoration of their power (916 AH/1510–11AD). Malek Mahmud ebn-e Nezam al-Din Yahya (916–44 AH/1510–38 AD), who had been living in exile in the Sarhadd for about 26 years, on learning about the Safavid penetration of Khorasan entered Sistan. He defeated and killed Shah Mansur-e Bakhshi, the Uzbek governor, and restored Mehrabanid Malek authority.[2]

Following official recognition of Malek Mahmud by Shah Esma'il I, a very close relationship was created between both sides. Shah Esma'il sent a deputy (*vakil*) to Sistan to show that he wanted close supervision of that province. Malek Mahmud did not initially oppose this supervision after the victory of the Safavids over the Uzbeks had occupied Sistan. But, after the stabilization of his position in Sistan he wanted more freedom of action and he expelled the Safavid deputy from Sistan (926/1519–20). Moreover, he supported the rebellion of Sam Mirza, the brother of Shah Tahmasb I in 941/1534–5. In reaction, Shah Tahmasb sent Ahmad Soltan Shamlu as his *vakil* to Sistan to impose an even tighter supervision. He also allotted the governorship of four regions in Sistan to Ahmad Soltan and the other regions to Malek Mahmud. Shah Tahmasb was quite aware that deposing Malek Mahmud might cause him to revolt or to seek asylum with the Moghuls and therefore he did not do so. But Malek Mahmud on learning this news left Sistan and went to India through Sarhadd.³

With Malek Mahmud's flight, direct Safavid rule began in Sistan and lasted for about 42 years (944–86 AH/1537–78 AD). The Mehrabanid Maleks wanted to restore their power during this period, but Safavid military power thwarted their plans. After Shah Tahmasb's death Safavid power diminished, and Malek Mahmud ebn-e Malek Haydar (986–98/1578–90) succeeded in expelling the Safavids from Sistan (986/1578). Internal conflicts among the Qandahar and Zamindavar mirzas provided a suitable opportunity.⁴ In addition, the presence of the Uzbeks in Khorasan increased the disturbance in the country.⁵

The crisis in south-eastern Iran

'Abdollah Khan II's attack of Khorasan in 996/1587–8 and his conquest of Herat in 997/1588–9 heralded a new phase of the extension of Uzbek power into Safavid territory. Shah 'Abbas I's problems with the rebellious Qezelbash tribes offered a suitable opportunity for the advance of the Uzbeks into other parts of Iran. For this purpose 'Abdollah Khan sent Shahom Qorchi Sepahsalar with 12,000 cavalry to occupy Qohestan and Sistan. Shahum Qorchi immediately marched south from Herat, and easily occupied Qohestan. He forced its governor, Amir 'Alam Khozayme, to provide guidance for his attack on Sistan. He had decided on a surprise attack on Malek Mahmud ebn-e Malek Haydar (986–98/1578–90), the ruler of Sistan, by advancing through western Sistan and the Dasht-e Lut which was a less travelled route. The Uzbeks first attacked Tabasayn,⁶ which was governed by Sayyedi Eqbal on behalf of Malek Mahmud. Due to severe resistance the Uzbeks could not do anything and proceeded to Sistan. Fortunately, Amir 'Alam Khozayme, the governor of Qohestan, who noticed that the Uzbeks were not familiar with the western route of Sistan, took them about 60 kilometres into desert towards Kerman. Although the Uzbeks killed Amir 'Alam Khozayme as soon as they found out his treachery, his courageous action saved Sistan from the Uzbek attack. Shahum Qorchi returned to Tabasayn being convinced that Malek Mahmud had been informed of his attack and because he had lost about 1,000 men and 2–3,000 horses, he immediately returned to Herat via Qayen (997/1588–9).⁷

The domination of the Uzbeks over most of Khorasan as well as the political instability in central Iran gradually created important political movements in south-eastern Iran. Yakan Khan Afshar, the governor of Farah, invited Rostam Mirza, the governor of Zamindavar, to Farah to jointly confront the danger of the Uzbeks. Rostam Mirza was in permanent conflict with his brother, Mozaffar Hosayn Mirza, governor of Qandahar. In accepting this invitation he decided to take his chances in southern Khorasan. However, he killed Yakan Khan Afshar three days after entering Farah and confiscated the properties of the Afshar chiefs showing that he could not be relied upon. Although the Afshars were very much incensed by this action, they did not react due to the danger of the Uzbeks. After having established himself over Farah, Rostam Mirza decided to extend his realm. His first step was to try and encourage Malek Mahmud to accept his authority by despatching a number of envoys. Through his envoy Abdollah Farahi, Rostam Mirza tried to gain some allies among Malek Mahmud's relatives. While negotiations were under way between the governors of Farah and Sistan, Baktash Khan, the governor of Kerman, also sent some envoys to Sistan. The mission of these envoys was to encourage Malek Mahmud to create a union of the governors of Fars, Kerman and Sistan to support the sultanate of one of the Mirzas. But Malek Mahmud, who had gone from Rashkak[8] to Mahkameh,[9] which was known as Chap va Rast, fearing a sudden attack by Rostam Mirza, rejected the requests of Baktash Khan, but he did not accept cooperation with Rostam Mirza either. Malek Mahmud's reaction was natural because expressing loyalty to Shah 'Abbas I who was far away in Qazvin and did not have much power was much more rational than accepting Rostam Mirza who was in nearby Farah and who was expected to attack Sistan.[10]

Rostam Mirza, in spite of the rejection of his overtures, continued to maintain friendly relations with Malek Mahmud. This was probably due to the presence of the Uzbeks in Khorasan. At the same time, a group of Uzbeks from Samarqand, who intended to occupy Farah, appeared in that area. Rostam Mirza, due to the brave resistance of the Qezelbash tribes, easily defeated the Uzbeks and killed about a thousand of them. This victory relieved Rostam Mirza's concerns about the Uzbeks, and provided a suitable opportunity for his advance towards Sistan. 'Abdollah Farahi had been successful in persuading Malek Zarif, who had power in Qal'e-ye Jarunak,[11] and was a cousin (son of paternal uncle) of Malek Mahmud, to rebel against his cousin. Malek Zarif also spread *cholera morbus* in Malek Mahmud's camp, which resulted in the dispersion of his troops, and this made Rostam Mirza determined to attack Sistan. The escape of Zo'l-Faqar Bayg Torkoman, the favourite of Rostam Mirza, to Sistan and Malek Mahmud's refusal to return him to Farah provided the necessary pretext for the forces of Rostam Mirza to enter Sistan in Jomadi-al-avval of the year 998 (March 1590).[12]

While the cholera infection was a great setback to the military power of Sistan, Malek Mahmud's uncertainty about how to confront the attackers increased the gravity of the situation. Finally, Malek Mahmud, disagreeing with the more rational view of Malek Jalal al-Din, his son, who believed that Qal'e-ye Fath[13] should be considered as the centre of confrontation with Rostam Mirza, went to Jarunak. Moreover, after entering that fort, being sure of its defences, Malek Mahmud began to live in pleasure and neglected the probable attack of Rostam Mirza. Under these circumstances Rostam Mirza easily entered Sistan on 25 Jomadi-al-avval 998 (22 March 1590) and besieged Jarunak.[14]

Although Malek Zarif, who had played an important role in Rostam Mirza's attack of Sistan, repented the siege of Jaranuk and resisted, he was forced to surrender after 17 days (12 Jomadi-al-thani 998/8 April 1590). Rostam Mirza killed Malek Zarif, his father Malek Nasr-al-Din and his brother Malek Gharib a day after seizing Jarunak and imprisoned Malek Mahmud, the ruler of Sistan, and Malek Shah Hosayn, the author of *Ehya al-Moluk*, and some of the other maleks. Undoubtedly, the presence of Malek Jalal al-Din, the son of Malek Mahmud, in Qal'e-ye Fath was instrumental in the survival of Malek Mahmud. Malek Jalal-al-Din was besieged in Qal'e-ye Fath, but he resisted strongly. Although Malek Jalal al-Din's forces were few in number in the first week, many joined him from the different regions of Sistan. The escape of Malek Shah Hosayn and some of the Maleks from Rostam Mirza's camp and their arrival at Qal'e-ye Taraqun[15] was another ray of hope. The people of the Zere district,[16] who had earlier refused to help Malek Jalal al-Din, were now ready to help of their own accord. Malek Jalal al-Din being informed of the readiness of the Zereids went to them and formed a corps of 10,000 men. He first attacked the Qezelbash forces which had besieged Qal'e-ye Fath and repulsed them and he then decided to confront Rostam Mirza.[17]

Given Malek Jalal al-Din's resistance in Qal'e-ye Fath and Malek Shah Hosayn's escape to Qal'e-ye Taraqun, Rostam Mirza's advisers suggested that he must kill Malek Mahmud to suppress the resistance of Sistan's people. Hence, Malek Mahmud was killed during the last night of Sha'ban 998 (23 June 1590); he was 63 years old. On hearing the news that his father had been killed by the invaders, Malek Jalal al-Din quickly turned to Rashkak, which had recently been occupied by Rostam Mirza. Feeling the general hatred of Sistan's people, Rostam Mirza quickly evacuated Rashkak and turned to Hirmand by way of Posht-e Zave.[18] After a short battle with Malek Jalal al-Din when he passed Hirmand, he proceeded to the Saraban district[19] and retreated from there to Zamindavar. After Rostam Mirza's escape, the Maleks and the emirs of Sistan performed the mourning ceremonies for Malek Mahmud and then gathered in Mahkame district to select the new ruler of Sistan and settled on Malek Jalal al-Din (17 Shavval 998/9 August 1590).[20]

The Uzbeks in Sistan

Malek Jalal al-Din tried to obtain the support of the maleks and emirs by donating many gifts and forgiving those who had cooperated with Rostam Mirza. This led to peace and stability in Sistan. But this period lasted for only eight months because the Uzbeks had gradually extended their control over south Khorasan down to Qal'e-ye Kah district[21] to the north of Sistan; they began their attack on Sistan in the middle of 999 (1590–1). The commander of the Uzbeks for these attacks was Najuli who with 5,000 cavalry selected Qal'e-ye Kah as the base of his attack on Sistan. Najuli first entered Sistan in a surprise attack; the Posht-e Zere[22] to Qal'e-ye Posht-e Zave districts were completely ravaged. During this attack, 500 herdsmen were killed and after the fall of Qal'e-ye Posht-e Zave, 500 inhabitants were massacred.[23]

Najuli's second attack took place later the same year; he entered Sistan with a force of about 2,000 troops. After a brief confrontation with the guards of Qal'e-ye

Taghrun,[24] the Uzbeks passed Hirmand and turned to Shayle.[25] They killed about a thousand people and enslaved another thousand. After these operations, Najuli plundered Posht-e Zave once more and then, passing Hirmand, moved towards Qal'e-ye Kah. But Amir Hajji Mohammad blocked his way to the Taghrun district. In the battle that followed, one of the Uzbek commanders, Dorman Bahador, was killed and the Uzbeks were defeated and had to retreat. Amir Hajji Mohammad, apart from freeing all the captives and retaking all plunder, killed 200 Uzbek soldiers and took 1,500 horses as booty.[26]

After this success, Amir Hajji Mohammad decided to rescue Uq's people, who were his relatives, and he requested help from Malek Jalal al-Din. The latter immediately sent a force of 10,000 under the command of Malek 'Ali to help him. Amir Hajji Mohammad therefore easily expelled the Uzbeks from Uq and this put a stop to Uzbek attacks for a while. Najuli, observing the recent successes of Malek Jalal al-Din, abandoned the policy of military occupation of Sistan and sent an envoy, Tursun Bahadur, to the ruler of Sistan. He tried to encourage him to accept Uzbek suzerainty through peaceful means. Although Malek Jalal al-Din did not want to accept Uzbek overlordship, he sent gifts and an envoy, Maqsud Dowlat, to Najuli to keep the door open for peace negotiations and at the same time to remain informed about Uzbek intentions. Finally, after many negotiations, a kind of peace agreement was concluded between the two sides that lasted for six months. During this period, the Sistanis, who were living fully prepared in their forts, created many obstacles in the various areas to confront the probable invasion of the Uzbek cavalry.[27]

Although Malek Jalal al-Din had sufficient capacity to confront the Uzbeks through the cooperation that had been established between the Maleks and emirs, this situation did not last long. Amir Hajji Mohammad opposed Malek Jalal al-Din under a pretext[28] late in 999 (1591) and went to Herat. Before leaving, he stated that he would go to Herat for peace negotiations, but there was much anxiety about his possible actions. For this reason, Malek Jalal al-Din decided to take the initiative by sending a mission to Herat. The mission was led by one of the Maleks named Malek Mahmudî. The purpose of the mission was to inform the Uzbeks that Malek Jalal al-Din was ready to accept Uzbek suzerainty and to pay yearly tribute in the form of gifts, provided that their attacks on Sistan ended. Thus, Malek Jalal al-Din gradually gave in to the Uzbeks due to their military pressure, internal conflicts and the weakness of the Safavids.[29]

Malek Jalal al-Din's mission went to Herat late in 999 (1591). After meeting with Amir Hajji Mohammad in Asfazar,[30] who joined the mission, it soon arrived at Herat. Although Mir Quli Baba Kukultash,[31] the governor of Herat, arrested and imprisoned the members of the mission, he soon freed them at the order of 'Abdollah Khan II and was instructed to respond to Malek Jalal al-Din's rapprochement to the Uzbeks with suitable behaviour. Although Malek Mahmudî and his retinue were freed, they were not allowed to leave Herat. This was because there were Uzbeks who were determined to occupy Sistan militarily and allot it to one of the Uzbek emirs and they were not interested in negotiations. Malek Mahmudî was well aware of that situation and therefore opposed appeasement with Malek Jalal al-Din; he apparently succeeded in obtaining Mir Quli Baba Kukultash's support. Mir Quli Baba Kukultash therefore consulted with him how best to occupy Sistan. Malek Mahmudî believed that the only way was to conclude a temporary peace agreement. He promised Mir Quli Baba Kukultash that after entering Sistan, he would arrest Malek Jalal al-Din at an opportune moment and deliver him to the Uzbeks. The governor of Herat was taken in by the words of Malek Mahmudî. He freed him and his retinue and sent him with an envoy to Sistan. However, after their departure from Herat he had second thoughts and ordered them arrested. He did not succeed because Malek Mahmudî, after leaving Herat, had travelled quickly to Sistan and arrived in Qal'e-ye Taghrun in two days and informed Malek Jalal al-Din of the Uzbek intentions (999–1000/1591–2).[32]

During 1000–2 (1591–4) Sistan was free from Uzbek attacks because they were preoccupied with the occupation of Zamindavar. It was under these conditions that the Moghuls, taking advantage of the internal problems of the Safavids, decided to take control over Qandahar and Zamindavar before the Uzbeks could do so. Akbar (963–1014/1555–1606) who had been considering the conquest of Sistan for a while, sent an army under Khan-e Khanan 'Abd-al-Rahim to occupy Qandahar in 999 (1590–1). But this, and the subsequent military expedition that took place under the command of Mirza Daniyal in 1000, did not succeed. What finally led to Moghul dominion over those areas was the voluntary submission of the mirzas of Qandahar and Zamindavar due to increasing Uzbek pressure. Rostam Mirza, who, after escaping from Sistan, had lost both his reputation and his troops, had been attacked in Zamindavar by the Uzbeks. He went to India and was well received by Akbar (1002/1593–4). Rostam Mirza's approach to the Moghuls and his respectful reception by Akbar made Mozaffar Hosayn Mirza interested in doing the same. What triggered his decision were the attacks of the Uzbeks. At that time Din Mohammad Soltan and Baqi Soltan, two Uzbek commanders, had been instructed by 'Abdollah Khan II to occupy Qandahar and Sistan. Therefore they carried out many attacks on Qandahar. Mozaffar Hosayn Mirza, who had become very weak because of the great loss of men he had sustained as a result of the Uzbek attacks, decided to rebuild his position by joining with Akbar. 'Abdollah Khan II, receiving information of Mozaffar Hosayn Mirza's decision, wanted him to give up that idea and promised to prevent Uzbek attacks on Qandahar. But as 'Abdollah Khan II did not undertake any effective action to prevent Uzbek attacks, Mozaffar Hosayn Mirza surrendered Qandahar to Shah Bayg Khan, one of Akbar's emirs, and went to India (1003/1594–5).[33]

With the Moghuls in charge of Zamindavar and Qandahar, it was natural that Uzbek pressure on Sistan would increase. In fact, a new round of Uzbek attacks on Sistan had begun after Rostam Mirza joined the Moghuls. Tengri Berdi Ughlan, the Uzbek commander, entered Sistan in 1002 with the intention of plundering Makran.[34] At the beginning he went to Zere and Ramrud[35] and plundered Makran by gathering a fighting force from those regions and then returned to Sistan. After that, Uzbek invasions began in Sistan and became very serious with the plundering on Saraban. On receiving information of the Uzbek attack on Saraban, Malek Jalal al-Din quickly marched from Mahkame and attacked the Uzbeks who were encamped in the Tirak desert.[36] He easily defeated them and returned to Mahkame after freeing many Saraban people they had enslaved.[37]

With the Uzbek control over Farah and then Uq at that time, Uzbek attacks on Sistan became severe as two groups of Uzbeks now attacked Sistan. The first group under Soltan Muhammad Ughlan was stationed in Farah and the second group under Tengri Berdi Ughlan had selected Uq as its base for attacks on Sistan. Because of increasing Uzbek attacks, Malek Jalal al-Din had to leave Mahkame and go to Se-Kuhe.[38] After having resided there for six months he went to Qal'e-ye Sabz[39] where he constructed many fortifications. The establishment of the Sistan ruler in Qal'e-ye Sabz made Tengri Berdi Ughlan decide to carry out attacks to capture that castle. Because he sustained many casualties and did not succeed in capturing it, he resorted to a war of attrition. He plundered several regions and then returned to Uq. He sent a small group to plunder the outskirts of Kuh-e Khaje Ghaltan,[40] but they were repulsed by Jalal al-Din before they could.[41]

Despite the return of the Uzbeks to Uq, Malek Jalal al-Din, who knew that Qal'e-ye Sabz was not strong enough to be defended, moved to the castle of Fath. After the gradual departure of the other Maleks and emirs of Sistan from Qal'e-ye Sabz, only Malek Shah Hosayn and his brother Malek Mahmudî remained in the castle with their relatives. The unrelenting pressure of the Uzbeks in during 1002–3 (1593–5) gradually made many Maleks, such as Malek Mohammad, consider abandoning Sistan and emigrating to India. Malek Mohammad even consulted with Malek Shah Hosayn about this, but before any decision was made, the Uzbek attacks resumed. This time the Uzbeks easily advanced to the region of Shaykhlang-e 'Olya,[42] which they selected as their encampment. Although they Uzbeks went first to Qal'e-ye Sabz, they returned to their encampment without any fight.[43]

The establishment of the Uzbek camp in Shaykhlang-e 'Olya was a sign of their significant penetration into Sistan. Although the Uzbek aim was the capture of Qal'e-ye Sabz, the failure of their previous attacks caused them to withhold from a direct attack on that castle, although it did not have good defences after the departure of Malek Jalal al-Din and the others. To deceive the guards of Qal'e-ye Sabz and to lure them out of the castle, the Uzbeks spread the rumour that they had left to take Qal'e-ye Fath and that therefore their encampment in Shaykhlang-e 'Olya was unguarded. Falling into the trap, about 150 defenders from Qal'e-ye Sabz set out to plunder the Uzbek camp in Shayklang-e 'Olya. Malek Shah Hosayn's efforts to dissuade them by warning that they would be trapped by the Uzbeks were fruitless and he was even forced to assume command of the raid. When he arrived at Band-e Modud,[44] the appearance of a force of 14,000 Uzbeks made Malek Shah Hosayn realize that he had been trapped. However, his efficient handling of the Sistani force allowed them to take refuge in the nearby jungle and save their lives. After various clashes between the two sides, night fell, and when help arrived Malek Shah Hosayn succeeded in retreating to Qal'e-ye Sabz.[45]

The presence of an Uzbek force of 14,000 in that attack shows that the Uzbeks were determined to conquer Sistan by force. However, the courage of the Sistanis in the Band-e Modud battle and the defensive tactics of Malek Jalal al-Din forced the temporary retreat of the Uzbeks to Uq. Mir Quli Baba Kukultash, the governor of Herat, after having been informed of Sistan's situation by Delir Ughlan, one of the Uzbek commanders stationed in Uq, sent a deputy, Molla Qara to Qal'e-ye Sabz to negotiate with Malek Mahmud. Meanwhile, 'Abdollah Khan II, who believed in the military occupation of Sistan, at the same time ordered troops from Khorasan's different regions to gather in Uq. But, after another Uzbek attack under Tangri Berdi Ughlan on Qal'e-ye Sabz was repulsed, Molla Qara took the initiative and opened peace negotiations. Based on the agreement concluded between the two sides at the foot of Qal'e-ye Sabz, the Sistanis accepted the establishment of an Uzbek commander, Qara Ughlan, in Posht-e Zere and agreed to pay him a stipend from the revenues of Posht-e Zere and Abkhuran.[46] Without any consultation with Malek Jalal al-Din, Malek Mahmudî eventually agreed to this arrangement because of the strong pressure exerted by the Uzbeks and in order to reduce their attacks.[47]

Despite the recent agreement, Tangri Berdi Ughlan continued to conquer other regions of Sistan. This forced Malek Jalal al-Din to prevent these attacks by appealing to 'Abdollah Khan II. He therefore sent envoys with many gifts to Bokhara. Although Malek Shah Hosayn considered this mission as a complaint against Tangri Berdi Uqlan's attacks, it may be argued that Malek Jalal al-Din's aim was to end Uzbek attacks by accepting the suzerainty of 'Abdollah Khan II. Unfortunately, the arrival of these envoys at Bokhara coincided with a new decision by the Khan of the Uzbeks about Sistan. As the victory over Sistan had not materialized, 'Abdollah Khan II had given the governorship of Qohestan and Sistan to Din Mohammad Khan, with the order to conquer Sistan as soon as possible and then hand it over to his little brother Baqi Mohammad Khan. Also, to resolve the Sistan problem rapidly, he had ordered Din Muhammad Khan to give the governorship of one of Sistan's forts and several regions to Malek Jalal al-Din and to avoid alienating the population of Sistan by harsh treatment. Most likely, 'Abdollah Khan II had issued this new order to prevent Sistan's rulers from taking refuge with the Moghuls as the mirzas of Qandahar and Zamindavar had done. Indeed, the delay in the return of Malek Jalal al-Din's envoys had made him decide to get military help from the Moghuls. For this purpose he sent one of Sistan's maleks, Malek Mohammad, to India. The fact that Malek Jalal al-Din was ready to accept the overlordship of the Uzbeks and Moghuls, on condition that he maintained his relative independence shows that he did not expect any help from the Safavids.[48]

With the arrival of Baqi Mohammad Khan in 1004 (1595–6), a new round of Uzbek attacks started. Because he paid attention to the defensive tactics of Sistan's people, there were not many who wanted to oppose the Uzbeks at that time, so that even Qal'e-ye Sabz, which did not have appropriate defences, was evacuated. The peaceful policy of Baqi Mohammad Khan who had taken up quarters in Nih[49] was one of the other reasons that people did not oppose him. This Uzbek commander summoned Amir Mahmud ebn-e Hajji Mohammad, who had assumed the leadership over Sistan's emirs after his father's death, and concluded a peace agreement with him. According to this agreement, Baqi Muhammad Khan undertook not to attack Sistan in that year, in return for which the emirs were obliged to pay him a portion of Sistan's tax and the remainder to Malek Jalal al-Din. As soon as Malek Jalal al-Din was informed of this agreement, he opposed it and even said that he would abdicate rather than accept. Therefore the emirs made other proposals to win him round. According to the first proposal, if Malek Jalal al-Din sent one of his first-rank relatives to Qal'e-ye Taghrun, the gathering centre of the emirs, they would defend Sistan against the Uzbeks. But this proposal was rejected because of Malek Jalal al-Din's fear of probable treachery by the emirs. The emirs' second proposal included the cession of Qal'e-ye Fath to them in recompense for their help in the defence of Sistan against the Uzbeks, but this proposal too was rejected by Malek Jalal al-Din. Baqi Mohammad Khan when informed of the conflicts between the emirs and Malek Jalal al-Din, sent an envoy, Ishum Bey Samarqandi, to Qal'e-ye Taghrun and called Amir Mahmud to Nih for negotiations. They reached an agreement that Ishum Bey Samarqandi be selected as Sistan's *kalantar*, while Baqi Mohammad Khan committed himself to not attacking Sistan in 1004 (1595–6). This agreement was also confirmed to some degree by Malek Jalal al-Din, since he remained in Fath and Tarqun forts and ceded the administration of Sistan's affairs to Amir Mahmud. During the one-year period that this agreement lasted the relations between Uzbeks and Sistanis was good and Ishum Bey Samarqandi did not create any problems for the commercial caravans traversing between Fath and Tarqun forts.[50]

Safavids or Moghuls?

At the beginning of the year 1005 (1596–7) Din Mohammad Khan, with his brother Baqi Mohammad Khan, entered Sistan. Because the leading men of Zere and Ramrud joined him, the Uzbeks had full control of Sistan, except for the Fath and Tarqun forts. Because Malek Jalal al-Din knew that in the end Uzbeks would attack these two forts he decided to request military help from the Moghuls once again. For this purpose, he sent Malek Shah Hosayn to Qandahar to discus the matter with its governor, Shah Bayg Khan. After Malek Shah Hosayn's arrival at Qandahar, Shah Bayg Khan immediately reported Sistan's situation to Delhi, but Akbar, who did not want to get involved with the Uzbeks in Sistan, ordered Qandahar's governor not to give military assistance to Malek Jalal al-Din. However, Malek Mohammad, who had gone to India for military aid in the year 1004 (1595–6), was able to interest Akbar in Sistan's affairs. However, he made it a condition of any decision in this matter that he receive more information about Sistan's situation. Malek Mohammad immediately invited Malek Shah Hosayn to Delhi to supply information to Akbar. While Malek Shah Hosayn was preparing to move to Delhi he was recalled to Sistan by Malek Jalal al-Din.[51]

The reason for his recall was that Malek Jalal al-Din had decided to ask for military help from the Safavids instead of the Moghuls. During Malek Shah Hosayn's stay in Qandahar, Malek Jalal al-Din had decided to attack Farah and expel the Uzbeks by mobilizing 5,000 men in Zere and Ramrud. But, after a short time, he abandoned the idea of attacking Farah, probably because he did not have enough troops and also because the people of Zereh and Ramrud were not interested in taking part in this military expedition. In the end Malek Jalal al-Din, in the early autumn of 1005 (1596–7), with the encouragement of the leading men of Zere and Ramrud, went to Isfahan via Bam and Kerman with a force of about 900 horsemen to ask for assistance from Shah 'Abbas I. Although Shah 'Abbas I paid Malek Jalal al-Din much respect, he did not give him any military help due to the opposition of Farhad Khan Qaramanlu. He argued that at the time of the planned military expedition to Khorasan during the following year, a force might be sent to Sistan. Malek Jalal al-Din requested to be allowed to return. Shah 'Abbas I gave him permission and ordered Ganj 'Ali Khan, the governor of Kerman, to help Malek Jalal al-Din transfer his relatives from Sistan to Kerman. But, despite Shah 'Abbas I's explicit order, Ganj 'Ali Khan did not comply due to Farhad Khan Qaramanlu's opposition. Therefore Malek Jalal al-Din returned to Tarqun without any result. According to the chronicle of Malek Shah Hosayn, the news of his return created such a clamour in Sistan that if a small number of Qezelbash troops had been in his retinue, the Uzbeks would have immediately departed.[52] Malek Jalal al-Din, having been disappointed by the Safavids, was determined to expel the Uzbeks from Sistan by relying on local forces. For this reason, he charged Malek Mohammad, who had just returned from India to Sistan, to attack Taghrun, the Uzbeks' gathering centre with 4,000 men. However, Malek Mohammad was defeated, which was a great shock to the morale of the people of Sistan and to Malek Jalal al-Din's military power. After this success the Uzbeks made preparations to attack the Fath and Tarqun forts. Malek Jalal al-Din, therefore, had no choice but to open peace talks and he succeeded in concluding an agreement with them. According to this agreement, Malek Jalal al-Din would cede Qal'e-ye Fath to the Uzbeks and in return they would cede Huzdar, Kondor and Ramrud to him. Thus, the domination of the Uzbeks over the eastern side of Hirmand was completed. Malek Mahmudî, the governor of Qal'e-ye Fath, evacuated the castle and retreated to Tarqun, the last base of resistance of the Maleks against the Uzbeks (late 1005/1597).[53]

Migration to India

Although the fall of the fort at Fath was a great blow to the morale of the Maleks, they lived in Taraqun for one more year, despite the food shortage. On New Year's day 1006 (1597–8) Malek Jalal al-Din despaired of ever receiving help from

Shah 'Abbas I and therefore decided to move to India. Because he could not count on Safavid assistance, he was ready to join the Moghuls. From Malek Shah Hosayn's explanations it is clear that Malek Jalal al-Din, after returning from Isfahan, at first intended to send Malek Shah Hosayn to Kerman and then to go to Qandahar. The probability of too much pressure from the Uzbeks on Tarqun, his last base, made him consider the possibility of taking military help from the Moghuls. After the fall of Qal'e-ye Fath and the expected fall of Tarqun, he completely lost hope in the Safavids and ordered Malek Shah Hosayn to go to Qandahar. Conflicts among the maleks during those critical times also made Malek Jalal al-Din and the other Maleks more resolute in abandoning Taraqun. But, due to unsafe roads, only Malek Jalal al-Din succeeded in leaving Taraqun with a small number of men and moving to Qandahar. For this reason Tarqun remained under the control of the Maleks until the ousting of the Uzbeks from Sistan.[54]

With the departure of Malek Jalal al-Din from Tarqun, its fall seemed certain. However, the death of 'Abdollah Khan II (1006/1597–8) and internal conflicts among the Uzbeks prevented it. Under these conditions, Malek Mohammad, who had remained in Taraqun, was determined to use the opportunity and expel the Uzbeks from Qal'e-ye Fath. He first went to Qal'e-ye Sabz and put a force together from the people gathered there. Then he went to Qal'e-ye Fath but he was defeated and killed in Saraban by the Uzbeks. The Uzbek victory in the battle of Saraban not only strengthened their position, which had become shaky after the death of 'Abdollah Khan II, but also resulted in the dispersion of those who had gathered in Qal'e-ye Sabz.[55]

Malek Jalal al-Din's arrival at Qandahar coincided with the new Moghul policy of intervention in Sistan, adopted after the death of 'Abdollah Khan II. For this reason, Shah Bayg Khan welcomed Malek Jalal al-Din. Moreover, Shah Bayg Khan made 2,000 soldiers available to him after 40 days to transfer his relatives from Tarqun to Qandahar. Malek Jalal al-Din left his son, Hamzez Mirza, and Malek Shah Husayn in Qandahar as hostages. He returned with that force to Sistan and on arrival, he was informed that Mohammad Khan Uzbek wanted to prevent this transfer of people. At first, the Uzbek Khan decided to oppose Malek Jalal al-Din but finally, at the advice of his counsellors, allowed him to transfer his relatives to Qandahar. Although Malek Jalal al-Din succeeded in reaching Qal'e-ye Sabz, he did not succeed in evacuating the emirs residing in that fort, due to the fear amongst the Moghul soldiers of confronting the Uzbeks. However, he succeeded in transferring all but 50 of the residents of Qal'e-ye Taraqun.[56]

The above-mentioned actions and Malek Jalal al-Din's willingness to go to Delhi and meet with Akbar showed his determination to join the Moghuls. Shah Bayg Khan, however, did not want the Sistan ruler to depart soon, for he was probably waiting for the result of the clash between the Uzbeks and Safavids. Shah 'Abbas I's victory at the battle of Robat-e Pariyan changed his mind about joining the Moghuls.[57]

Cooperation with the Safavids

Shah 'Abbas I, from the moment he had acceded to the throne in 1587, aimed to retake Khorasan. He had grown up there and it was one of the richest provinces of Iran. Moreover, Khorasan was a strategic geographical area and whoever controlled it controlled its neighbouring provinces. Although Shah 'Abbas I undertook five campaigns to Khorasan during 996–1006 (1587–8) he was not able to retake the province due to the internal problems. The death of 'Abdollah Khan II, the killing of his son 'Abdol-Mo'min Khan and internal dissension among the Uzbeks provided an excellent opportunity to retake Khorasan (1006/1597–8). With the advance of Shah 'Abbas I towards Khorasan, its Uzbek leaders retreated and gathered in Herat. In the battle that took place near Herat, at first Din Mohammad Khan succeeded in defeating the Safavid vanguard under Farhad Khan. But in the main battle, which took place in Robat-e Pariyan, the Uzbeks were totally defeated and Din Mohammad Khan was killed. After this heavy defeat, the Uzbeks evacuated Herat and all of Khorasan, except for Balkh.[58]

After this victory Shah 'Abbas I allotted the governorship of Sistan to Ganj 'Ali Khan, governor of Kerman. The possible reason for that decision was Malek Jalal al-Din's collaboration with the Moghuls. Malek Jalal al-Din, who had been preparing to go to Delhi immediately, went to Khorasan after receiving news of the Safavid victory. Although Shah 'Abbas I welcomed him and his retinue, he did not give him the governorship of Sistan. Probably Shah 'Abbas I was awaiting the outcome of Ganj 'Ali Khan's military operations in Sistan at that time. Shah 'Abbas I allowed only Malek Shah Hosayn to return to Qandahar to encourage the Sistanis there to return. When he left Khorasan, Shah 'Abbas I took Malek Jalal al-Din with him and kept him in his camp for more than a year.[59]

Ganj 'Ali Khan, the new governor of Sistan, occupied Qal'e-ye Fath which was still in Uzbek hands. After that he turned to Qal'e-ye Taraqun, but was opposed by its guards. Through the intercession of some Maleks he finally took Taraqun and sent the keys of all the forts of Sistan to Shah 'Abbas I as a symbol of Safavid control. Ganj 'Ali Khan informed Shah 'Abbas I that the people of Sistan were loyal to the Safavids and that the entire area had been destroyed. According to Malek Shah Hosayn, Shah 'Abbas I gave the governorship of Sistan to Malek Jalal al-Din on receiving that report. Malek Shah Hosayn's statement, however, is a superficial interpretation of Sistan's situation at that time. Undoubtedly in the beginning Shah 'Abbas I did not intend to give Malek Jalal al-Din the governorship of Sistan, but his allegiance to Shah 'Abbas I was an important factor in changing the shah's mind. The most important factor though was the presence of Malek Hamze, the oldest son of Malek Jalal al-Din, with a large number of Sistanis in Qandahar who, in spite of Shah 'Abbas I's order, had not yet returned to Sistan. If the governorship of Sistan was not given to Malek Jalal al-Din, they might create problems on the eastern border of Iran with the help of the Moghuls. The loyalty of the few guards of Taraqun, and their resistance against Ganj 'Ali Khan, showed that the people of that province were loyal to the Mehrabanid Maleks in spite of the difficulties they had experienced. The destruction of Sistan, due to the Uzbek attacks and the loyalty of Sistan people to the Safavids that Ganj 'Ali Khan had mentioned in his report, made it clear that the restoration of power to the Mehrabanid Maleks was the best possible action.[60]

Shah 'Abbas I, observing Sistan's situation in late 1007 (1598–9), officially made Malek Jalal al-Din governor of that province, but did not immediately send him to Sistan. Probably Shah 'Abbas I wanted to be informed of the reaction of the people of Sistan. The news caused happiness among the Sistani emigrants at Qandahar and Malek Shah Hosayn immediately returned to Sistan with them. They numbered about 5–6,000 families; he entered that province at the beginning of Moharram 1008 (beginning of August 1599). It was some time after their return that Shah Abbas allowed Malek Jalal al-Din to return and he entered Sistan on 1 Jamada I 1008 (19 November 1599).[61]

Thereafter Malek Jalal al-Din established very good relations with Shah 'Abbas I and took part in many of the shah's campaigns, such as the conquest of Marv, the attack of Balkh, the conquest of Tabriz and Qal'e-ye Erevan. He also took part in the campaign of Herat's governor to occupy Qandahar in the year of 1014 (1605–6), which took place after the death of Akbar and the outbreak of the succession troubles. But this campaign did not succeed despite the 11-month siege of Qandahar and the Iranian forces were forced to return on the arrival of Moghul reinforcements (1015/1606–7).[62]

During the stable governorship of Malek Jalal al-Din, Sistan's situation gradually improved. He enjoyed such power that in 1018 (1609–10) he decided to conquer Makran and besieged Mir Mohammad, its governor, in Qal'e-ye Dezak.[63] Finally, a peace agreement was concluded between the two sides through the efforts of Malek Shah Hosayn, which obliged Mir Mohammad, the governor of Makran, to pay a thousand tomans as tribute. Also, Malek Jalal al-Din forced Amir Afzal *sepahsalar-e Sarhadd* to obey him. Moreover, he took part in the campaign of Shah 'Abbas I against Qandahar and the conquest of that city in 1031 (1622) and increased his bonds with the Safavids.[64]

The precise date of Malek Jalal al-Din's death is not clear.[65] He went on the Hajj pilgrimage before his death.[66] Malek Shah Hosayn, who recorded events in Sistan up to the year of 1031 (1621–2), informs us that he was still alive at that time. His successor was his son Malek Hamze (1031–55/1621–46), who was very generous and kind and for this reason has been mentioned with respect in the local traditions of Sistan.[67] During his father's governorship, Malek Hamze had established close relations with Shah 'Abbas I and remained completely loyal to him. These good relations continued under Shah Safi I (1038–52/1628–43) and Malek Hamze regularly sent gifts to Isfahan.[68] However, after 'Ali Mardan Khan, the governor of Qandahar, defected to the Moghuls in 1047/1637–8, Malek Hamze's relations with the Safavids became strained for a while due to his relationship with Qulich Khan, the Moghul governor of Qandahar. Probably Shah Safi I's cruelty led to 'Ali Mardan Khan's defection and caused the establishment of this relationship.

Something of Malek Jalal al-Din's ideas may be discerned from a quatrain of his that has survived:

bigane nayam ta chu ghammam yari hast   gar raft ze dast-e sobhe zonnari hast
del-ju'i-ye Hamze gar be Iran nakonand   dar pahlu-ye u Hend jegar-khvari hast

> I am not a stranger until I have a friend like sorrow
> If the (Islamic) prayer-bead were lost, there would be the (Christian) waist string
> If they do not court Hamze in Iran
> There is an Indian sympathizer (ready) at his side.[69]

This discontent did not continue for long because, once Malek Hamzeh had been informed of the shah's anger by one of his friends at court, he discontinued his connection with the Moghuls and to show his loyalty he even made an unsuccessful attack on their realm. Finally, Malek Hamzeh died at the age of 70, at a time when he had very close relations with the Safavids. Also, his successors continued this good relationship with the Safavids. Safavid policy of granting the governorship of Sistan to the Mehrabanid Maleks ensured that the province remained an integral part of Iran.[70]

Conclusion

The above examination of the political, social and economic situation of Sistan has yielded the following results.

The military power of the Safavids, and their official recognition of the governorship of the Mehrabanid Maleks in Sistan, were the most important factors for the Maleks' loyalty to them. With the establishment of the direct governance of the Safavids in Sistan that took place after the support of Malek Mahmud ebn-e Nezam al-Din Yahya for Sam Mirza's rebellion, their relations deteriorated to such an extent that the Maleks, after expelling the Safavids from Sistan, were prepared to join with any other power and renounce their relationship with the Safavids. With the domination of the Uzbeks over Khorasan and their advance towards Sistan, Malek Jalal al-Din was ready to accept their suzerainty by sending envoys. But the Uzbek effort to occupy Sistan militarily and appoint an Uzbek governor made any kind of agreement impossible. The ten-year period of Uzbek attacks of Sistan had a major impact on the political, social and economic life of that province and as a result many people of Sistan migrated to other places, such as Qandahar. Although the governors of Zamindavar and Qandahar joined the Moghuls due to Uzbek attacks on eastern Iran, Malek Jalal al-Din who was interested in protecting his realm, seriously opposed them.

What finally drove him to join the Moghuls was the unrelenting military pressure of the Uzbeks, the weakness of the Safavids and the deterioration of the defensive strength of Sistan people. Although Akbar undertook some actions to conquer

Sistan, Shah Abbas I's victory over the Uzbeks in the battle of Robat-e Pariyan put a stop to this. Shah 'Abbas I was not pleased that Malek Jalal al-Din had taken refuge with the Moghuls. At first, therefore, he was not willing to give Sistan to him. However, the destruction of Sistan, the loyalty of the people of Sistan to the Mehrabanid Maleks, as well as the presence in Qandahar of Malek Hamze, who might create problems on the eastern borders in cooperation with the Moghuls, forced Shah 'Abbas I to grant the governorship of Sistan to Malek Jalal-Din. This decision and the military power of the Safavids ensured that Sistan remained a part of the Iranian state.

Notes

1. The Sarhadd consists of a mountainous district in Baluchistan and southern Seistan. This district is situated between Quetta and Kerman. Sykes, Sir Percy, *Ten Thousand Miles in Persia or Eight years in Iran* (London, 1902), pp. 92-3, translated to Persian by Hosayn, Sadat Nuri as *Safarname-ye Zheneral Ser Persi Sayks, ya, Dah hazar mil dar Iran* (Tehran, 1363/1984), pp. 126, 163.
2. C. E. Bosworth, *The History of the Saffarids of Sistan and the Maleks of Nimruz (247/861 to 949/1542-3)* (Costa Mesa, 1994), pp. 429-69; Barat, Dahmardeh, *Maleks of Seistan: A Study of the Political, Social and Economic Situation of Seistan (393-1148 AH)* Unpublished PhD thesis, University of Tehran (1379/2000), pp. 76-183.
3. Bosworth, *The History of the Saffarids of Sistan*, pp. 469-75; Dahmardeh, *Maleks of Seistan*, pp. 183-90.
4. These conflicts involved Mozaffar Hosayn Mirza and Rostam Mirza, the sons of Soltan Hosayn Mirza. Soltan Hosayn Mirza was the son of Bahram Mirza the brother of Tahmasb. Shah Tahmasb had appointed Soltan Hosayn Mirza to the government of Qandahar and Zamindavar in 965/1557 and he remained governor there until he died in 984/1576. He was succeeded by one of his sons. Eskandar Bayg Monshi, *Tarikh-e 'Alamara-ye 'Abbasi*, ed. Iraj Afshar, 2 vols (Tehran, 1350/1971), vol. 1, p. 57.
5. Dahmardeh, *Maleks of Seistan*, pp. 190-218.
6. Tabasayn was a small town in Sistan to the north of Lake Hamun, near the Bandan. Malek Shah Hosayn, *Ehya al-moluk*, ed. Manuchehr Setudeh (Tehran, 1344/1965), pp. 152, 172, 267-8.
7. Malek Shah Hosayn, *Ehya al-moluk*, pp. 267-8.
8. Rashkak was located near Qal'e-ye Nasrabad (Nosratabad, modern Zabol). Seistani, Mohammad A'zam, *Sistan: Sarzamin-e Maseha va Hamaseha*, 2 vols (Kabol, 1366/1987), vol. 2, p. 225.
9. Mahkama or Chap va Rast was located south of Lake Hamun. Malek Shah Hosayn, *Ehya' al-Moluk*, pp. 319-38, 378.
10. Eskandar Bayg Monshi, *'Alamarya-e 'Abbasi*, vol. 1, pp. 482-8; Malek Shah Hosayn, *Ehya al-moluk*, p. 269; Saburi, Naseh and Nuzhat, *Shajarat al-moluk*, Microfilm, Central library of Tehran University. No. 7411, fos. 90-2; G. P. Tate, *Seistan: A Memoir on the History, Topography, Ruins and People of the Country* (Calcutta, 1910-12) Persian translation by Sayyed Ahmad Musavi as *Sistan*, 4 vols. (Zahedan, 1364/1985: Edare-ye Koll-e Ershad-e Esami-ye Sistan va Baluchestan, 1362-64 H.Sh./ 1983-6, vol. 1, p. 141.
11. Jarunak village was located between Hozdar and Qal'e-ye Fath. Seistani, *Seistan*, vol. 2, p. 273.
12. Eskandar Bayg Monshi, *'Alamaray-e 'Abbasi*, vol. 1, p. 483; Malek Shah Hosayn, *Ehya al-moluk*, pp. 273-83; Saburi, *Shajarat al-moluk*, fo. 91; Tate, *Seistan*, vol. 1, p. 141.
13. Qal'e-ye Fath is located about 50 kilometres south of Zaran, Seistani, *Seistan*, vol. 2, p. 229.
14. Eskandar Bayg Monshi, *'Alamara-ye 'Abbasi*, vol. 1, p. 483; Malek Shah Hosayn, *Ehya al-moluk*, pp. 274-83; *Tazkere-ye khayr al-bayan*, Facsimile. No. 2113 V, fo. 426; Saburi, *Shajarat al-moluk*, fos. 91-2; Tate, *Seistan*, vol. 1, pp. 141-2.

15. Taraqun was located between the districts of Saraban, Ramrud, Zere and Bar-e Zere. Malek Shah Hosayn, *Ehya al-moluk*, p. 144.
16. Zere district was located south of Lake Hamun near modern Zabul. For further information see Sykes, Sir Percy, *A Fourth Journey in Persia*, in *Joghrafiya-ye tarikhi-ye Sistan. Safar ba safarname-ha*, trans. Hasan Ahmadi (Tehran, 1378/1999), pp. 467, 474.
17. Eskandar Bayg Monshi, *'Alamara-ye 'Abbasi*, vol. 1, pp. 483–4; Malek Shah Hosayn, *Ehya al-moluk*, pp. 282–307; *Tazkere-ye khayr al-bayan*, V, fo. 426; Saburi, *Shajarat al-moluk*, fos. 92–5; Tate, *Seistan*, vol. 1, p. 142.
18. Pushte Zave village was located between Huzdar and Qal'e-ye Fath. Sistani, *Sistan*, vol. 2, p. 273.
19. Saraban was one of southern districts of Zarang and Qal'a-ye Fath was its centre during the Safavid period. Sistani, *Sistan*, vol. 2, pp. 229–31.
20. Eskandar Bayg Monshi, *'Alamaray-e 'Abbasi*, vol. 1, p. 484; Malek Shah Hosayn, *Ehya al-moluk*, pp. 300–1, 307–311; *Tazkere-ye khayr al-bayan*, No. 2109, I, fos. 6–7, V, fos. 426; Saburi, *Shajarat al-moluk*, fos. 95–6; Tate, *Seistan*, vol. 1, pp. 142–3.
21. Qal'e-ye Kah (or Uq) was one of Seistan's districts; it was located north of Lake Hamun. Seistani, *Seistan*, vol. 2, p. 301.
22. Pusht-e Zere was located north of Lake Hamun and sometimes Uq was considered a part of that, Malek Shah Hosayn, *Ehya al-moluk*, pp. 81, 91, 97–102, 109.
23. Malek Shah Hosayn, *Ehya al-moluk*, pp. 321–2; Saburi, *Shajarat al-moluk*, fos. 96–8. According to this source, the Uzbek commander was called Janu and because of his attacks Jalal al-Din was forced to leave Seistan and go to Kerman and Isfahan. This source did not mention Jalal al-Din's migration to India that happened several years later.
24. Taghrun was located in the Pusht-e Zere district. Malek Shah Hosayn, *Ehya al-moluk*, pp. 322, 336, 345.
25. Shayle (Shayle Mahmud Abad) was located near Rashkak. Malek Shah Hosayn, *Ehya al-moluk*, pp. 180, 222, 293–5, 311, 456.
26. Malek Shah Hosayn, *Ehya al-moluk*, pp. 317–23.
27. Ibid., pp. 323–5.
28. The cause of Haji Mohammad's dissatisfaction was a famine in Seistan. Malek Jalal al-Din had much grain, but allocated only 100 *manns* (600 kilos) for Amir Hajji Mohammad. Malek Shah Hosayn, *Ehya al-moluk*, pp. 325–6.
29. Ibid., pp. 325–7.
30. Asfazar or Isfazar (Sabzavar) nowadays is located in Afghanistan and it is different from Iranian Sabzavar. G. Le Strange, *The Lands of the Eastern Caliphate*, Persian translation by Mahmud 'Erfan as *Jografiya-ye tarikhi-ye sarzaminha-ye khelafat-e sharqi* (Tehran: Bongah-e Tarjomeh, 1337/1959), p. 438.
31. Mir Quli Baba (Qul Baba) Kukultash was the foster brother of 'Abdollah Khan II and therefore the Uzbeks called him Kukultash. 'Abdallah Khan, after the conquest of Herat, appointed him as governor there. When 'Abdollah Khan died, his son 'Abdol Mu'men Khan killed Kukultash. Eskandar Bayg Monshi, *'Alamara-ye 'Abbasi*, vol. 1, p. 553; Malek Shah Hosayn, *Ehya al-moluk*, p. 353–6; *Tazkere-ye khayr al-bayan*, V, fo. 432.
32. Malek Shah Hosayn, *Ehya al-moluk*, pp. 326–9.
33. Eskandar Bayg Monshi, *'Alamaray-e 'Abbasi*, vol. 1, pp. 485–6; Saburi, *Shajarat al-moluk*, fo. 96; Riazul-Islam, *Indo-Persian Relations, A Study of the Political and Diplomatic Relations between the Mughul Empire and Iran* (Tehran, 1970), Persian translation by Mohammad Baqer Aram and Abbas Qoli Ghaffari-Fard as *Tarikh-e Ravabit-e Iran va Hind* (Tehran: Amir Kabir, 1373/1994), pp. 98–102.
34. Makran = (Makoran) is the southern part of Baluchistan, the littoral of the Sea of Oman. Le Strange, *The Lands*, p. 352; Sykes, *Ten Thousand Miles*, pp. 124–5; W. Barthold, *An Historical Geography of Iran*. Persian translation by Hamzeh Sardavar as *Tazkere-ye joghrafiya-ye tarikh-e Iran* (Tehran: Tus, 1372/1993), p. 168.

35. Ramrud was located in south-west Seistan and east of the Sarshayle River. Sykes, *Ten Thousand Miles*, p. 378; Rawlinson, Sir Henry C., 'Notes on Seistan', *Jogharafiyay-e Tarikhi-ye Seistan*, pp. 309, 313–14; C. E. Yate, *Khurasan and Seistan*, Persian translation by Qodratallah Rowshani and Mehrdad Rahbari as *Khorasan va Sistan* (Tehran, 1365/1986), p. 89.
36. Tirak was probably located in Saraban district. Malek Shah Hosayn, *Ehya al-moluk*, p. 334.
37. Ibid., pp. 333–5.
38. Se Kuhe is one of Shib-e Ab villages in Seistan. Zo'l-Faqar Kermani visited it in 1288/1871 and estimated its population at about 3,442 people. *Joghrafiya-ye Nimruz*, ed. 'Azizollah 'Atarudi (Tehran 1374/1995), p. 139.
39. Qal'e-ye Sabz (modern Jalalabad) was located near the Sahur-e Sheykh and Khvajeh Kan near the Bar-e Zere. Malek Shah Hosayn, *Ehya al-moluk*, p. 339; Sistani, *Sistan*, vol. 2, pp. 239–40.
40. Kuh-e Khvajeh Ghaltan is located in the middle of Lake Hamun.
41. Malek Shah Hosayn, *Ehya al-moluk*, pp. 337–41.
42. Sheykhlang-e 'Olya village was located west of the Hirmand and south of Lake Hamun. Malek Shah Hosayn, *Ehya al-moluk*, pp. 343, 345.
43. Ibid., pp. 341–3.
44. Band-e Mudud's location is not clear. It was probably located south of Lake Hamun and west of the Hirmand river. Malek Shah Hosayn, *Ehya al-moluk*, pp. 344–6.
45. Ibid., pp. 343–53.
46. Abkhuran was located at the south of Lake Hamun. Malek Shah Hosayn, *Ehya al-moluk*, p. 341.
47. Ibid., pp. 348, 353–7.
48. Ibid., pp. 357–8; Tate, *Seistan*, vol. 1, p. 144.
49. Nih (Neh) was one of the small towns of Seistan located at the Qohestan boundary. *Tarikh-e Sistan*, ed., *Malek al-Sho'ara Bahar* (Tehran, 1314/1935), p. 261, note 2.
50. Malek Shah Hosayn, *Ehya al-moluk*, pp. 359–62.
51. Eskandar Bayg Monshi, *'Alamara-ye 'Abbasi*, vol. 1, p. 487; Malek Shah Hosayn, *Ehya al-moluk*, pp. 363–9.
52. Eskandar Bayg Monshi, *'Alamara-ye 'Abbasi*, vol. 1, pp. 487, 529; Malek Shah Hosayn, *Ehya al-moluk*, pp. 369–78; Saburi, *Shajarat al-moluk*, fo. 98; Tate, *Seistan*, vol. 1, pp. 143–4.
53. Malek Shah Hosayn, *Ehya al-moluk*, pp. 378–86.
54. Ibid., pp. 379–82, 386–92; *Tadhkere-ye khayr al-bayan*, I, fo. 7; Tate, *Seistan*, vol. 1, p. 144.
55. Malek Shah Hosayn, *Ehya al-moluk*, pp. 394–5.
56. Ibid., pp. 392–5.
57. Ibid., pp. 396–9; *Tadhkere-ye khayr al-bayan*, I, fo. 7.
58. Eskandar Bg, *'Alamara-ye 'Abbasi*, vol. 1, pp. 381, 399–414, 443–5, 507–12, 553–74.
59. Eskandar Bayg Monshi, *'Alamara-ye 'Abbasi*, vol. 1, p. 576; Malek Shah Hosayn, *Ehya al-moluk*, pp. 399–400, 403–6; Tate, *Seistan*, vol. 1, p. 144; Röhrborn, Klaus-Michael, *Provinzen und Zentralgewalt Persiens im 16. und 17. Jahrhundert* (Berlin 1966); Saburi, *Shajarat al-moluk*, fos. 98–9. According to this source, Malek Jalal al-Din was in Isfahan at this time and when Shah 'Abbas I went to Khorasan he left for Seistan. After Shah 'Abbas I's victory at Robat-e Parian the Uzbeks left Seistan; Malek Shah Hosayn, *Ehya al-moluk*, p. 411; *Tazkere-ye khayr al-bayan*, I, fo. 7.
60. Malek Shah Hosayn, *Ehya al-moluk*, pp. 405–6.
61. Ibid., p. 406. Malek Shah Hosayn wrongly registered his entrance as the first day of Moharram 1007/4 August 1598.
62. Ibid., pp. 407–11; Riazul-Islam, *Indo-Persian Relations*, pp. 114–15.
63. Dezak (modern Saravan) is one of the villages of northern Baluchistan which has warm and unfavourable weather. E'temad al-Saltaneh, Mohammad Hasan Khan (Sani' al-Dowleh), *Mer'at al-Boldan*, ed. 'Abdol-Hosayn Nava'i and Mir Hashem Mohaddeth (Tehran, 1367/1988), p. 442.
64. Malek Shah Hosayn, *Ehya al-moluk*, pp. 412–13, 441–8, 485–6.
65. The date of his death in the *Shajarat al-moluk* is recorded as 1018/1609–10, fo. 104; Tate stated that it was in 1028/1618–19. Tate, *Seistan*, vol. 1, p. 147.

66. Saburi, *Shajarat al-moluk*, fo. 103.
67. Tate, *Seistan*, vol. 1, p. 146.
68. Vali Qoli Khan Shamlu, *Qesas al-khaqani*, ed. Sayyed Hasan Sadat Naseri, 2 vols (Tehran, 1371/1992), vol. 1, pp. 241–52; Tate, *Seistan*, vol. 1, pp. 146–7; Malek Shah Hosayn, *Ehya al-moluk*, pp. 420–1; Saburi, *Shajarat al-moluk*, fo. 103–104; Mohammad Ma'sum Esfahani, *Kholasat al-siya*, ed. Iraj Afshar (Tehran, 1368/1989), pp. 179–80.
69. For this poem see *Tazkere-ye Nasrabadi*, ed. Vahid Dastgerdi (Tehran, 1317/1938), p. 37; Ahmad Golchin Ma'ani, *Karavan-e Hend* (Mashhad, 1369/1990), vol. 2, p. 1549, note l; Shamlu, *Qesas al-khaqani*, vol. 2, p. 126 gives a slightly different version of this poem.
70. Tate, *Seistan*, vol. 1, pp. 150–2; Seistani, *Seistan*, vol. 2, p. 299; Riazul-Islam, *Indo-Persian Relations*, pp. 161–3.

9

Safavid Persia and Its Diplomatic Relations with Venice

Giorgio Rota

Diplomatic relations between the Republic of Venice and Safavid Persia began very early; one might say with the inception of the Safavid dynasty itself. As in the times of Uzun Hasan Aq Qoyunlu, both states were looking for an ally against the powerful common enemy – the Ottoman Empire. A sea-power like Venice needed the support of strong ground forces and the Safavids hoped to be supplied with artillery, while the Venetian navy could create diversions on the coasts of Anatolia. Attempts to build an anti-Ottoman military alliance remained a recurrent theme in the relations between Persia and Venice until the closing years of the seventeenth century, but there were also other concerns. Over time, Safavid-Venetian trade grew in importance (Persian silk and Venetian glass and luxury goods being the main items), and extant documents show both rulers repeatedly seeking protection for their own traders as well as offering the same to foreign merchants. In addition, starting at the latest from the middle of the seventeenth century, the Venetian Senate wrote several letters of recommendation on behalf of Catholic Armenians of Persia and foreign missionaries.[1] One may suppose that, in the course of that century, the Venetian government became more and more conscious of the necessity to preserve its own traditional role of protector and patron of the Catholics of the Middle East from the increasingly active and aggressive policy of the Holy See and France, and that this attitude concerned not only the territories of the Ottoman Empire but Safavid Persia as well.[2] In this chapter I have chosen to focus mainly on the question of the political relations between the two states, since I believe that at the present time there is not enough information available to allow even a brief discussion of the other two issues in their entirety. However, I am aware that trade, politics and religion were sometimes closely intertwined and were usually of mutual importance. Merchants, missionaries and men of religion in general often played a great part in the foreign relations of both Venice and Safavid Persia, as well as in those of the other polities of the period. My article will be concerned mainly with Safavid-Venetian relations in the seventeenth century, since those in the sixteenth century have drawn scholars' attention to a greater extent and are therefore relatively better known.

Marin Sanudo mentioned Shah Esma'il (1501-24) in his journal as early as 1501.[3] In 1502, the Republic entrusted a Greek from Constantinople, Costantino Lascari, with the task of collecting information on the new ruler of Persia. Lascari could not meet Shah Esma'il but he saw the latter's ally, the Karamanid pretender, whom he reassured about Venice's will to support him in his fight against the common enemy, the Ottomans.[4] In 1505 another Karamanid envoy, who carried a letter from the shah to the doge, visited the Venetian consul in Damascus, who subsequently sent a copy of the letter to Venice. The message was received in the city in the course of the following year.[5] In 1508, the Venetian governor of the Greek city of Nafplio (or Napoli di Romania, as it was known to Italians at that time) was visited by a Safavid envoy disguised in dervish garb.[6] Finally, the first Safavid ambassadors (the second of them together with a Karamanid envoy) reached Venice in March and May 1509, respectively.[7] Unfortunately, he arrived just a few months before the Venetians' disastrous defeat at Agnadello (14 May 1509), during the War of the League of Cambrai. Consequently, he received the Republic's expressions of affection and good will for the shah, but no military support. The following year (1510) Mamluk authorities in Syria arrested Nicolò Surier, who was coming back from Persia with letters from the shah addressed to the Venetian government and to some of its representatives in the Levant.[8] All these contacts, as well as others which took place during Shah Esma'il's reign, had one feature in common: the wish or the hope to set up a military alliance against the Ottomans. As previously stated, such hopes may have never died out completely, reappearing intermittently during the two centuries of Safavid-Venetian diplomatic relations. However, the Battle of Chalderan (1514), the death of the shah and the Venetian policy of appeasement towards the Porte brought about a lull in the relations between the two states.[9]

Diplomatic activity resumed as soon as new Ottoman-Venetian wars broke out in 1537 and 1570. In 1539 the Serenissima sent Michele Membré to Persia; in 1570 it was the turn of Vincenzo degli Alessandri and of the Persian trader, Khvaje 'Ali Tabrizi, who travelled to Qazvin separately. None of them succeeded in enlisting Safavid military help, but at least the two Italian envoys left important accounts of their missions.[10] In their turn, the Safavids looked again to Venice after they were attacked by the Ottomans in 1578. Two years later, the trader Khvaje Mohammad arrived in Venice as the envoy of Shah Soltan Mohammad Khodabande (1578-87). He informed the doge and the Senate that Persia was once again at war with the Ottomans and sought the Republic's 'moral support'. Khvaje Mohammad was cordially received and dismissed with kind words, but he achieved no practical result. The Serenissima had signed a peace treaty with the Porte just seven years before (1573), and the time was not right for a new war.[11] The last Safavid envoy to reach Venice in the seventeenth century was another trader, Asad Bayg, who arrived in the city in the year 1600. However, he was the first of a series of merchants-cum-envoys sent by Shah 'Abbas I (1587-1629) in the following decades.

He was followed by the Venetian Angelo Gradenigo (a Jew converted to Christianity) in 1602; by Fathi Bayg and Mohammad Amin Bayg (who had the title of *gerekyaraq-e khasse-ye sharife*) in 1603; by the Armenians Khvaje Kirakos and Khvaje Safar in 1609 and 1610 respectively; and by 'Ala'al-Din Mohammad and Khvaje Shahsavar in 1613. This last returned to Venice in 1622 together with other traders – all of them styled *gerekyaraqan-e khasse-ye sharife*.[12] It is interesting to observe that the only two 'pure' Safavid ambassadors sent to Venice in this period, Anthony Sherley and Hosayn-'Ali Bayg Bayat were not authorized to enter the city and present their credentials and letters to the doge (1601).[13]

In 1634, Venice was visited by 'Ali Bali, who announced the accession of Shah Safi (1629–42). He seems to have been the last Muslim to be sent as an envoy from the Safavid court to the Serenissima.[14]

The beginning of the War of Candia (1645), however, triggered a Venetian diplomatic offensive towards Persia. It was in that same year that the Republic sent Giovanni Tiepolo as its ambassador to the king of Poland. The following year Tiepolo handed a letter addressed to the shah from the Senate to the Dominican Father Antonio da Fiandra, who was to accompany a Polish envoy, Jerzy Ilicz to the Safavid court. The year 1646 also saw the Venetian government send another emissary to the shah, the merchant Domenico de Santis, who followed the Aleppo route. In November 1647 it was the turn of Father Ferdinando Gioerida (a Catholic priest and a relative of Pietro della Valle's first wife) to set off from Venice. Father Antonio presented himself to the Collegio at Palazzo Ducale on 28 March 1649; de Santis returned to Venice probably in 1651 (after a circuitous journey which took him from Isfahan to Tarku, where he was denied permission to cross Russian territory, Isfahan again, Hormuz, Goa, Lisbon and finally Venice); and Gioerida appeared before the Collegio on 28 March 1650, exactly one year after Father Antonio.[15] The three envoys carried back letters that confirmed the shah's friendship but contained no definite commitment to a military alliance.[16]

Afterwards, letters between the Safavid court and the Venetian Senate were exchanged mainly through missionaries or other representatives of the Catholic clergy. For instance, letters to the shah were entrusted to an anonymous messenger in 1661, to the Armenian *vardapet* Arakel in 1662 and to the Dominican Father Antonio Tani in 1663. The letter sent in 1661 contained a request to join Venice in the conflict against the Ottomans (the War of Candia ended only in 1669), while in 1663 the senators did not judge it appropriate to put such an exhortation into writing. Arakel had instructions to expose to the shah orally what he had learnt 'from the hearts' of the senators.[17] In 1669 the Archbishop of Nakhjavan, Mateos Avanik, went to Persia, and in 1673 two Armenian Dominican fathers arrived in Venice with letters from the shah and Archbishop Mateos. The latter reported to the Senate that he had pleaded with the shah for a Persian attack against the Ottomans 'according to the orders of Your Excellencies', but that the news of the fall of Candia (1669) and the end of the war had then come, to the disappointment of Shah Solayman I (1666–94) (thus implying that he was not averse to war). The two Dominicans were given a letter of response to the shah.[18] According to Berchet, this was the last Safavid diplomatic mission to visit Venice.[19]

In the following years (in particular, during the War of the Holy League, 1684–99), other letters were sent to Persia, carried by an unknown messenger in 1695, and by two papal envoys, Pietro Paolo Pignatelli in 1697 and Felice Maria da Sellano in 1699. Only the first of these letters urged the shah to enter the war, while the other two simply confirmed the Republic's good affection towards him.[20] It seems that no proposals of alliance were made to Persia during the last Ottoman-Venetian conflict, the War of Morea (1714–18). However, at the end of 1718 the Senate sent a letter to Shah Soltan Hosayn (1694–1722), requesting him to protect the Capuchin missionaries and the Catholic Armenians of Tbilisi from the attacks of the Gregorian Armenians.[21] This is, to the present state of my knowledge, the overall picture of Safavid-Venetian diplomatic relations. It is, however, far from complete and still needs a good deal of research.

Safavid-Venetian diplomatic relations can therefore be roughly divided into two different phases. During the first, corresponding to the years 1501–87, each of the two states still saw in the other a possible military ally against the Ottomans. Several missions were thus exchanged to this effect, but conditions favourable to war never occurred in both countries at the same time, thus preventing the formation of a league.

The accession to the throne of Shah 'Abbas I marked the beginning of a second phase, lasting throughout the seventeenth century. The Armenian priest Hakob Margarian, who had travelled to Persia around 1595 with the aim of concluding an anti-Ottoman alliance between the shah and the emperor, passed through Venice on his journey back to Europe in 1597 carrying Shah 'Abbas I's letters for the emperor himself and the Pope. However vague the shah's responses may have been (as it seems, they did not touch on the question of an alliance), it may be interesting to remark that Hakob had no letters at all for the doge.[22] Nearly all the Safavid envoys who visited Venice in the following years (starting with Asad Bayg in 1600) were merchants commissioned to sell limited amounts of silk and other goods on behalf of the shah and buy luxury goods for the court (for example, Carnival masks),[23] as well as carrying with them complimentary letters and gifts for the doge. Some of them also had more particular missions. For instance, Asad Bayg had to provide Anthony Sherley and Hosayn-'Ali Bayg Bayat with money, in case they needed it, while Gradenigo was to obtain news of the two ambassadors. Khvaje Kirakos and Khvaje Safar were to recover the goods Fathi Bayg had sent back to Venice when he passed through Syria on his way back to Persia after the outbreak of a new Ottoman-Safavid war in 1603, in order not to have them confiscated by local Ottoman authorities. None of them was charged with negotiating an anti-Ottoman alliance.

From the very beginning of his reign, therefore, Shah 'Abbas I must have considered Venice a commercial rather than a military partner. The last Safavid envoy to visit Venice with the aim of forging an alliance against the Ottomans had been

Khvaje Mohammad in 1580. Since he had been sent by Shah 'Abbas I's father, Shah Soltan Mohammad Khodabande, it would be interesting to know whether the former's attitude was influenced to any extent by the recollection of that failure. At any rate, Shah 'Abbas's views of Safavid-Venetian relations are, in my opinion, also demonstrated by what can be rightly called a forgotten historical episode; that is, the commercial venture of Alvise Sagredo to Persia.

Given the economic importance of silk exports and the state of the political relations between the Ottoman Empire and Safavid Persia, it is (as Willem Floor wrote) 'not surprising to observe that Shah 'Abbas I started looking for other routes for the export of Persian silk'.[24] It is perhaps a little more surprising (at least, from our point of view and with hindsight) to see that, among the possible partners, the shah singled out the Republic of Venice. The fact is, as it has already been noted, that diverting the entire silk trade from the Ottoman land route to Hormuz was not in the interests of Shah 'Abbas I or that of his successors: 'having two export routes gave the Shahs the opportunity to sell their silk to whatever route offered the highest profit'.[25] Pietro della Valle's assertion, according to which the shah intended to export raw silk to Europe 'without passing through Turkey at all',[26] did not correspond to the reality of facts, but rather mirrored what Shah 'Abbas wanted his neighbours and new commercial partners to think. The contacts between the shah and the Sagredo family must have begun well before 1608, the year in which Shah 'Abbas I appointed the Venetian consul at Aleppo, Giovan Francesco Sagredo (Alvise's uncle) as 'Persian consul' in the Syrian city.[27] Three years later, in 1611, he designated Giovan Francesco as his own 'general procurator' in the city of Venice and in the whole Venetian state.[28] Probably in 1626, Alvise Sagredo (who had served as vice-consul during his own uncle's period of tenure) wrote to Shah 'Abbas I about the possibility of sending his own agent, Alvise Parente to Persia to trade. The shah replied in 1627 inviting Alvise to go in person to Persia and trade freely.[29] The Senate authorized Sagredo's journey in 1629 and he left Venice in the same year, unaware that Shah 'Abbas I had died in the meantime.[30] In Aleppo he had to wait for new credential letters addressed to Shah Safi, and for a Persian passport.[31] Eventually he left Syria for Venice, at the latest in July 1631, it would seem because the Ottoman military campaign against Baghdad and then the retreat of the besieging army had blocked the way to Persia.[32] That there was a real interest on the Safavid side in having a Venetian commercial presence in Persia is confirmed, I believe, by the fact that Shah Safi mentioned Alvise Sagredo in the letter he sent to the doge through 'Ali Bali. In this letter the shah renewed his grandfather's invitation to Sagredo to go to Persia and start a trade 'like that of the English and the Dutch'.[33] Given the fact that five years before Shah Safi was still secluded in the Royal haram, someone else at court must have retained a memory of the invitation made by Shah 'Abbas as well as, it seems, a certain measure of interest in Sagredo's mission. As yet, I am not completely sure about what the aim of this mission was. However, from Shah Safi's letter, and from a few vague hints gathered from Venetian sources, I think it very probable that he considered establishing some sort of permanent trade mission in Persia in order to revive the overland trade in Persian silk via Aleppo to the benefit of Venetian traders. As for the attitude of the Venetian government, it was not particularly supportive. The Senate officially authorized Sagredo's journey and provided him with letters addressed to the shah, but did not get further involved in his mission. The same Senate, as well as Venetian diplomatic representatives in the Levant, praised Sagredo's 'desire' to help Venetian trade in Aleppo, thus implying that he was not an official representative of the Republic.[34] It is interesting to note that, in order to not arouse too much suspicion on the Ottoman side, Venetian authorities even claimed in their letters that another aim of the mission was the benefit of the Ottoman revenues and treasury; that is, precisely what the redirection of Persian silk trade via Hormuz was supposed to prevent.[35] Analogously, the fact that Sagredo was given the title of *khvaje* in Shah Safi's letter and not of *bayg* (like other Venetian envoys before and after him) suggests that the Safavid court saw him as a merchant rather than a diplomat.[36]

It is quite clear that Safavid interest in Venice dramatically decreased after 1629. In 1632, in order to inform the doge and the Senate of his own ascent to the throne, Shah Safi sent the trader 'Ali Bali, who reached Venice in 1634 after a journey which lasted about fifteen months. The very fact that it took three years for the shah to send an envoy to the Serenissima implies that such a mission did not rank very highly among State priorities. This is perfectly understandable, given the numerous problems Shah Safi had to face in the first years of his reign, at home and abroad. Despite the mention of Sagredo's name in the shah's letter, the main aim of 'Ali Bali's mission was clearly the recovery of the proceeds of the sale of 69 bales of silk and a certain quantity of woollen cloth belonging to the *sarkar-e khasse-ye sharife*, which had been deposited in the Venetian mint ten years earlier, following a squabble among the people engaged in selling them.[37] Even though Persia was at that time at war with the Ottoman Empire, there is no trace of a proposal for a military alliance in the shah's letter, neither in the speech 'Ali Bali delivered in the presence of the doge, nor in the record of his conversations with Venetian officials. We only read the customary offers of friendship and good relations.[38]

As for the attitude of the Venetian government, it replied only occasionally to Shah 'Abbas I's letters, and almost certainly sent no special envoy of its own to Isfahan. Persia had a very small role in Venetian anti-Ottoman political and military strategy. A scrutiny of the letters sent by the Venetian ambassador at the Porte between the closing months of 1638 and the beginning of 1639, at a time when the two states were on the verge of war and the ambassador himself was under house arrest, shows that the option Venetian diplomats and politicians considered more likely and helpful in case of conflict (of course, after an alliance with the major European states) was a diversion on the part of Poland, the ruler of Wallachia or the Cossacks.[39] Although the outbreak of a new war was seen as depending on the outcome of Murad IV's campaign against Baghdad (1638), the possibility of organizing a joint military action with Persia is never hinted at.[40] It is interesting to note that, unlike Father Antonio, de Santis and Gioerida, the Venetian envoy to Poland,

Tiepolo, was a fully-fledged ambassador. This was a direct consequence of the different standing of Persia and Poland in Venetian anti-Ottoman strategy; in the eyes of the Serenissima, the latter was more important as a potential military ally than the former. The other three were rather messengers, and they had been chosen as envoys to Persia first by other Christian rulers and then by the Republic of Venice: Antonio da Fiandra by the king of Poland and Gioerida by the Pope. As for de Santis, he left an account of his mission which, even though not as important as those written by Membré and degli Alessandri, aptly illustrates the importance of the human factor in seventeenth-century Persian-European diplomacy.[41] He became an envoy of the Republic in quite a fortuitous way, being ordered to carry a letter to the shah while he was in the city, waiting for a ship on his way to Persia as a messenger of the Pope, the emperor, the king of Poland and the Grand Duke of Tuscany.[42] Tavernier, who travelled with de Santis from Aleppo to Isfahan, accused him of being uncouth, inexperienced, avaricious and totally unfit for the task he had been chosen for.[43] The French traveller may have been personally biased against de Santis[44] and given that his account of the facts is incorrect on several points, it may also be unreliable as far as the description of the Venetian envoy is concerned.[45] However, de Santis's lack of experience emerges from his own version of the facts. For instance, he travelled for three months, between Isfahan and the Russian border, in the company of an ambassador of the Czar without even talking to him, and without ascertaining whether the passport and the credential letter issued by the shah would actually allow him to cross Russian territory. The modern reader has the impression that de Santis was very flattered by his encounters with kings (besides the shah, the king of Portugal and the exiled emperor of Ceylon), ambassadors and ministers, perhaps to the point of forgetting what the aim of his journey was. Tavernier states that de Santis narrowly escaped a severe punishment on the part of the Senate.[46] Certainly, the Venetian government must not have been pleased with the fact that he consistently styled himself 'ambassador' of the Republic, or with the detailed list of expenses he attached to his account of the mission and his request to be refunded. Venice was then at war with the Ottomans, and in general Venetian representatives ('real' ambassadors included) were supposed to dig into their own pockets if the resources allotted to them were not enough 'to preserve the prestige of the State'.[47]

In spite of their poor organization, the missions of Father Antonio, de Santis and Gioerida represented the last determined and coordinated attempt on the part of the Republic of Venice to forge an anti-Ottoman alliance with Persia. Indeed, as for the round of contacts which took place in the 1660s, Venetian attempts to draw Persia into the war seem somewhat more half-hearted than in the 1640s. Once again, the first input to Venetian overtures came from outside. Arakel, who offered himself to the Senate to negotiate a league with Persia, was a private individual and a foreign subject; Mateos was the Pope's envoy and Antonio Tani's journey was explicitly considered by Venetian authorities to be a mission organized by Tuscan diplomacy, to which the Republic contributed with a letter to the shah in order to satisfy a request of the Grand Duke. War was approaching its end, and it seems more than likely that the Venetian Senate did not consider it sensible to invest time and money (even a limited amount thereof) in trying to build a league which had proved impossible to create in the previous two centuries.

In conclusion, continued diplomatic relations between Safavid Persia and the Republic of Venice never brought about anything comparable to the joint military action which took place in the 1470s during Uzun Hasan's reign. During most of the sixteenth century, such an outcome was hindered by the political conditions that prevailed in Venice or Isfahan. Generally speaking, whenever one of the two states seriously addressed the other to obtain military help, the latter had just negotiated a peace treaty with the Ottomans or was engaged in a war against another external enemy. However, as far as the period after 1587 is concerned, we also perceive a lack of political will on the part of both states, as well as other and more contradictory features. For Venice, Persia was a diplomatic card which could be played without much hope of success, but also without great effort or expense. At the same time, Venetian official sources confirm the important role played by Safavid Persia in European politics owing to its relations with the Ottoman Empire. They also confirm that the diplomatic relations between Safavid Persia and any given European state should be looked at against the background of the European political context of the time in order to be fully understood. Furthermore, the presence of Safavid traders (be they Muslim or Armenian) in the city became increasingly appreciated as the Venetians had to face ever stronger English, French and Dutch competition in the Eastern Mediterranean and the Levant.

For Persia as well, Venice was a useful commercial outlet. Furthermore, their relations with the Republic allowed the Safavid shahs to put a moderate amount of diplomatic pressure on the Ottoman Empire, once again with very little effort. Yet the Serenissima does not seem to have been considered a viable military partner in the seventeenth century, and at best was seen as a part of the 'cordon sanitaire' of Christian powers surrounding the Ottomans.[48] The respective political 'function' of each of the two states was so well established during the course of the seventeenth century that not even two major conflicts such as the War of Candia (1645–69) and the War of the Holy League (1684–99), nor the Ottoman offensives against Persia during the reign of Shah Safi could cause a change. To keep their relations with Venice alive, the Safavid rulers regularly expressed their willingness to comply with any request on the part of the Venetian government. With hindsight, we know that they did not necessarily mean to wage war against the Ottomans, especially after the Peace of Zohab in 1639. The fact that Venetian envoys, conversely, almost invariably reported on the Safavid rulers' willingness to fight the Ottomans seems to me to be the result either of their desire to impress favourably the Venetian Senate, or of a misinterpretation on their own part, rather than of a deliberate deception by Safavid authorities. This leads us to one last point. In spite of a long tradition, Safavid-Venetian diplomacy suffered from the same faults which marred the relations between Persia and the other European states. Geographical distance was a matter of fact, as was the volatile international situation (especially in Europe), and as such they represented factors which could not be modified or easily overcome. The choice of envoys, however, remained arbitrary both in Venice and in Persia, as elsewhere, thus adding a further measure of uncertainty to diplomatic missions, which had to face so many odds in order to achieve their goals. This is particularly significant in the case of Venice, which certainly did not lack trustworthy and skilled state officials with a first-hand experience of both diplomacy and the Middle East. It is therefore not surprising if the last (and perhaps the only) such figure to be sent to Safavid Persia was Vincenzo degli Alessandri in 1570.[49]

Notes

1   Berchet, Guglielmo, *La Repubblica di Venezia e la Persia* (Turin, 1865), pp. 239–40, 243–5, 247–8. Recently I found a letter (dated 26 July 1692) written by the Senate upon the request of the Archbishop of Nakhjavan, 'Paolo Battista Avanisense' and on behalf of the local Armenian Catholics: cf. Archivio di Stato, Venezia (hereafter ASV), *Senato, Corti*, registro 69, fo. 163a (the text of the letter); ASV, *Senato, Corti*, filza 129, 19 July 1692 (the archbishop's petition), and 26 July 1692 (the first draft of the letter). This document was not known to Berchet, and others certainly await discovery in Venetian archives. On Paul Baptist Yovhanisean ('Paolo Battista Avanisense'), cf. van den Oudenrijn, M. A., 'Bishops and Archbishops of Naxivan' *Archivum Fratrum Praedicatorum* VI (1936), p. 182. However, as early as 1572 Vincenzo degli Alessandri mentioned the two patents (*patenti*) granted to the 'Archbishop of Erevan' by two different doges in 1561 and 1569: cf. Berchet, *Venezia e la Persia*, p. 174.
2. Venetian official documents clearly show how Venetian diplomats in the Ottoman Empire (the ambassador at the Porte, or Bailo, and the consul in Aleppo in particular) were engaged in political-religious squabbles, almost on a daily basis. Besides the usually tense relations between the Greek Orthodox and the Roman Catholic clergy, they had to deal with rivalries between competing Catholic religious orders as well as with a host of problems caused by the personal behaviour or the political stance of individual clerics.
3. Scarcia Amoretti, Biancamaria, ed., *Shah Isma'il nei 'Diarii' di Marin* Sanudo, vol. I (Rome, 1979), pp. 3–4. Since most of the bibliography relevant to the present chapter has been mentioned in my 'Diplomatic relations between Safavid Persia and the Republic of Venice: An overview', in Hasan Celâl Güzel, C. Cem Oğuz and Osman Karatay (eds), *The Turks*, vol. 2 (Ankara, 2002), pp. 580–7, the works which have been cited there will be mentioned here only occasionally, with the exception of Guglielmo Berchet's works, which are to remain standard reference works on the subject of Safavid-Venetian relations until new substantial contributions appear. Kausi 'Araqi, Mohammad Hasan, ed., *Asnad-e ravabet-e dawlat-e Safavi ba hokumatha-ye Italya* (Tehran, 1379), pp. 1–66 does not add much to our knowledge of Safavid-Venetian relations, even though it presents some interesting documents. Finally, cf. also Rota, Giorgio, *Under Two Lions: On the Knowledge of Persia in the Republic of Venice (ca. 1450-1797)* (Vienna, 2009) and idem., 'Safavid Envoys in Venice', in Ralph Kauz, Giorgio Rota and Jan Paul Niederkorn (eds), *Diplomatisches Zeremoniell in Europa und im Mittleren Osten in der Frühen Neuzeit* (Vienna, 2009), pp. 213–45.
4. Berchet, *Venezia e la Persia*, pp. 22, 153–7; *'Diarii'*, vol. 1, pp. 32–9.
5. Berchet, *Venezia e la Persia*, pp. 24, 158; *'Diarii'*, vol. 1, pp. 84, 91–2.
6. *'Diarii'*, vol. 1, p. 155.
7. Berchet, *Venezia e la Persia*, pp. 25–6; *'Diarii'*, vol. 1, pp. 134–5, 161–4.
8. On the serious diplomatic incident between the Republic of Venice and the Mamluk sultan caused by the arrest of Surier, cf. Berchet, *Venezia e la Persia*, pp. 26–7; Lucchetta, Francesca, ' "L'affare Zen"

in Levante nel primo Cinquecento' *Studi veneziani* X (1968), pp. 109–219; *'Diarii'*, vol. 1, pp. 167–75, 181–2, 190, 208, 210; Setton, Kenneth M., *The Papacy and the Levant (1204-1571)* (Philadelphia, 1984), vol. 3, pp. 25–33; Aubin, Jean, 'La crise égyptienne de 1510-1512: Venise, Louis XII et le Sultan', *Moyen Orient et Océan Indien*, vol. 6 (1989), pp. 123–50; Pedani Fabris, Maria Pia, 'Gli ultimi accordi tra i sultani mamelucchi d'Egitto e la Repubblica di Venezia' *Quaderni di Studi Arabi*, vol. 12 (1994), pp. 60–4.

9. For a relatively more detailed exposé of Safavid-Venetian relations in the years 1501-24, cf. Rota, 'Diplomatic relations', pp. 580–1.
10. Membré, Michele, *Relazione di Persia (1542)*, ed. Giorgio R. Cardona (Naples, 1969); Membré, Michele, *Mission to the Lord Sophy of Persia (1539-1542)*, English translation by Alexander H. Morton (London, 1993). Degli Alessandri's account was published first in Eugenio Albèri, ed., *Relazioni degli ambasciatori veneti al Senato* (Florence, 1844), serie III, vol. II, pp. 105–27, and then in Berchet, *Venezia e la Persia*, pp. 167–82. For further bibliographical references on the missions of Membrè, degli Alessandri and Khvaje 'Ali Tabrizi, cf. Rota, 'Diplomatic relations', pp. 581–2.
11. Berchet, *Venezia e la Persia*, pp. 38–9, 182–3, 183–91 (Khvaje Mohammad's account of his mission). According to the Armenian scholar Alishan, degli Alessandri met two Julfans in Qazvin who were to leave for Venice as Shah Tahmasp I's envoys: cf. Alishan, Ghevond, *Sisakan* (Venice, 1893), p. 386, quoted in Herzig, Edmund M., 'The rise of the Julfa merchants in the late sixteenth century', in C. Melville (ed.), *Safavid Persia* (London-New York, 1996), p. 315. However, in a letter written from Cracow during his journey back, degli Alessandri reported that he was questioned by some Armenian traders from Julfa who had sent their agents to Venice and had no news of them: cf. Berchet, *Venezia e la Persia*, pp. 31, 33, 36. Nothing in the printed text of the letter suggests that they were about to leave as the shah's envoys. For another Armenian merchant met by degli Alessandri in Qazvin, cf. Berchet, *Venezia e la Persia*, pp. 163–4. Julfans, however, were already well known in Venice by the time of degli Alessandri's mission to Persia. The first notarial record of a Julfa Armenian in the city dates back to 1570: cf. Herzig, 'The rise of the Julfa merchants', p. 308. A certain 'Mercevelin chiefalino' (i.e., from Julfa) received gifts from the consul in Aleppo, Pietro Michiel on 6 October 1583 and 13 April 1584: cf. ASV, *Capi del Consiglio dei Dieci, Lettere di rettori e di altre cariche*, busta 255, no. 6.
12. Berchet, *Venezia e la Persia*, pp. 43–50, 65–6, 192–215; Berchet, Guglielmo, 'La Repubblica di Venezia e la Persia. Nuovi documenti e regesti', *Raccolta veneta* I/2 (1866), pp. 7–18, 22, 28–31; Kausi 'Araqi: *Asnad-e ravabet*, pp. 35–7; Rota, 'Diplomatic relations', pp. 581–2. Unfortunately, the last article is marred by many misprints, some of which have altered the names of Safavid envoys. Thus we have Bayram Bayg 'Kavuqlu' instead of Chavushlu (the ambassador chosen to accompany Membré on his journey back to Venice), Khvaje 'Jafar' for Safar and Haji 'Eva' instead of 'Evaz (one of Khvaje Shahsavar's companions during his second journey): cf. Rota, 'Diplomatic relations', *passim*.
13. Among the huge amount of scholarly literature existing on the Sherley brothers, cf. Alonso O. S. A., Carlos, 'Embajadores de Persia en las cortes de Praga, Roma y Valladolid (1600-1601)' *Anthologica Annua* XXXVII (1989), pp. 66–7; Babinger, Franz, *Sherleiana* (Berlin, 1932), p. 24. It is usually assumed that the decision of the Senate was dictated by the presence in the city of an Ottoman diplomatic delegation, which had arrived shortly before Sherley and Hosayn-'Ali Bayg for important negotiations. Babinger, however, remarked that he could not find more precise information on this Ottoman mission. In fact, a list of Ottoman envoys sent to Venice for this period mentions only a Daud *chavush* (who arrived in May 1600 to protest against the damage caused by the Uskoks to Ottoman shipping and trade) and a doctor, Bartolomeo Coressi (who arrived on 12 April 1601 with the *fethname* of a campaign in Hungary and the 'announcement of a succession to the throne'): cf. Babinger, *Sherleiana*, n. 3 p. 24; Pedani, Maria Pia, *In nome del Gran Signore* (Venice, 1994), p. 208. The episode of the denied reception is investigated in Rota, 'Safavid Envoys', pp. 222–7.
14. Berchet, 'Nuovi documenti', pp. 31–4; Rota, 'Diplomatic relations', p. 582.
15. ASV, *Collegio, Esposizioni principi*, filza 61, 28 March 1650.
16. On their missions, cf. Berchet, *Venezia e la Persia*, pp. 50–2, 216, 218–28; Rota, 'Diplomatic relations', pp. 582–3. Father Ferdinando died before 18 August 1654, drowning in the Araxes river between Erzurum

and Erevan: cf. *A Chronicle of the Carmelites in Persia*, 2 vols (London, 1939), vol. 1, p. 388. On his family ties with Sitti Maani Gioerida, cf. *Carmelites*, vol. 1, pp. 344, 614 and n. 8 p. 442; Richard, Francis, *Raphaël du Mans missionnaire en Perse au XVIIe s.*, 2 vols (Paris, 1995), vol. 1, pp. 138-9 (in particular, n. 12).
17. Berchet, *Venezia e la Persia*, pp. 52, 55, 229-31, 243-4; Rota, 'Diplomatic relations', p. 583.
18. Berchet, *Venezia e la Persia*, pp. 52-4, 231-40; Rota, 'Diplomatic relations', p. 583. The two Dominicans, Antonis Nazar and Azaria 'Djahgetsi' were sent to Europe by Shah Solayman, together with a third Dominican brother who died along the way, with letters for the doge, the Grand Duke of Tuscany, the king of France and the Pope: cf. 'Itinéraire du très-révérend frère Augustin Badjétsi, évêque arménien de Nakhidchévan, de l'ordre des Frères-Prêcheurs, à travers l'Europe, etc.', trans. M. Brosset, *Journal Asiatique*, III série, III (1837), pp. 401-21 (in particular, pp. 415-16, 419-21). On Antonis and Azaria, cf. also Richard, *Raphaël du Mans*, vol. 1, n. 213 pp. 91-2 and n. 245 p. 234.
19. Berchet, *Venezia e la Persia*, p. 53.
20. Berchet, *Venezia e la Persia*, pp. 56, 241, 247; Rota, 'Diplomatic relations', p. 583. Interesting details on the Pignatelli and da Sellano missions are in Dallolio, Alberto, 'Un viaggio in Oriente alla fine del secolo XVII' *L'Archiginnasio. Bullettino della Biblioteca Comunale di Bologna* II/3-4 (1907), pp. 73-106; Donazzolo, Pietro, 'Viaggio in Oriente ed in Occidente (Sec. XVII-XVIII) del Fratello Francesco Maria di S. Siro' *Rivista Geografica Italiana*, vol. XIX (1912), pp. 337-54, 423-36, 530-7, 584-605. Cf. also Jacoli, Ferdinando, 'L'autore del "Viaggio in Oriente"' *L'Archiginnasio. Bullettino della Biblioteca Comunale di Bologna*, II/6 (1907), pp. 209-13.
21. Ibid., pp. 56-7, 247-8.
22. Margarian is mentioned by a number of scholars who have dealt with European, Persian and Georgian politics and international relations in the closing years of the sixteenth century. The most important works mentioning him are probably Alishan, Ghevond, *Hay-Venet* (Venice, 1896), *passim*; Gabashvili, Valerian, 'Kartuli dip'lomat'iis ist'oriidan (Sakartvelo da ant'iosmaluri k'oaliciebi XVI-XVII ss.)', *Masalebi Sakartvelosa da K'avk'asiis ist'oriisatvis*, vol. 31 (Tbilisi, 1954), pp. 59-128; Tardy, Lajos, 'Le roi Simon Ier à la lumière des sources d'Europe centrale contemporaines de son époque (IIe partie)' *Bedi Kartlisa*, XXXII (1974), pp. 147-74.
23. A list of such goods (including masks) dated 1613 is in Berchet, *Venezia e la Persia*, pp. 65-6 (a first draft of this list is in ASV, *Secreta, Documenti persiani*, busta 1, no. 21). Other lists are in Berchet, *Venezia e la Persia*, pp. 208-9 (dated 17 February 1610) and in ASV, *Collegio, Esposizioni principi*, filza 19, 28 May 1610.
24. Floor, Willem, 'The Dutch and the Persian silk trade', in C. Melville (ed.), *Safavid Persia*, p. 324.
25. Ibid., p. 358.
26. *Viaggi di Pietro della Valle*, 2 vols (Brighton, 1843), vol. 1, p. 696.
27. Berchet, *Venezia e la Persia*, pp. 73, 252-3.
28. Ibid., pp. 73, 254-5.
29. Ibid., pp. 73, 257-8.
30. Ibid., pp. 73, 259.
31. ASV, *Senato, Dispacci consoli, Aleppo*, filza 4, no. 1, fo. 152a (4 March 1630).
32. ASV, *Bailo a Costantinopoli, Lettere*, filza 109 (Aleppo, 13 July 1631).
33. Berchet, 'Nuovi documenti', p. 32; Fekete, Lajos, *Einführung in die persische Paläographie* (Budapest, 1977), pp. 502-3. Clearly, the text published by Berchet is either an abridged translation of the letter published by Fekete, or the translation of another document.
34. For instance, cf. ASV, *Senato, Deliberazioni Costantinopoli*, filza 22 (24 March 1629); *Senato, Dispacci consoli, Aleppo*, filza 3, no. 21, fo. 75b (12 October 1629); *Senato, Dispacci ambasciatori, Costantinopoli*, filza 110, no. 24, fo. 212a (8 April 1630).
35. ASV, *Senato, Dispacci ambasciatori, Costantinopoli*, filza 107, no. 214, fos. 545a-546a (4 August 1629); *Senato, Dispacci consoli, Aleppo*, filza 3, no. 21, fo. 75a (12 October 1629).

36. For 'Mika'il Bayg' (i.e., Michele Membré), cf. Scarcia, Gianroberto, 'Un documento persiano del 946/1539 nell'Archivio di Stato di Venezia' *Annali dell'Istituto Universitario Orientale di Napoli*, Nuova Serie, XVIII (1968), pp. 338–42; Membré, *Relazione di Persia*, pp. 185, 187–9; Fekete, *Einführung*, pp. 384–7, 390–3. For the mysterious 'Suburor Bayg Dasnan' (almost certainly, Domenico de Santis), cf. Fekete, *Einführung*, pp. 518–19, 522–3.
37. The story of the sale of the 69 bales of silk is summarized in ASV, *Senato, Deliberazioni Costantinopoli*, filza 26, 27 July 1634 and is the subject of Rota, Giorgio, 'A "bilingual" Persian-Italian Safavid document (1627) and its historical background' (forthcoming).
38. ASV, *Senato, Deliberazioni Costantinopoli*, filza 26, 1 June and 10 July 1634; Berchet, 'Nuovi documenti', pp. 31–3; Fekete, *Einführung*, pp. 500–3.
39. On the Cossacks, cf. for instance ASV, *Senato, Dispacci ambasciatori, Costantinopoli*, filza 119, no. 90, fo. 548a (24 September 1638), no. 93, fos. 590a–590b (6 October 1638), no. 95, fo. 635b (28 October 1638), no. 99, fo. 688a (13 November 1638); filza 120, no. 128, fos. 76a–76b (26 March 1639), no. 140, fos. 238a–238b (4 June 1639). On Wallachia, cf. ASV, *Senato, Dispacci ambasciatori, Costantinopoli*, filza 119, no. 105, fos. 767a–767b (18 December 1638); filza 120, no. 136, fo. 173b (15 May 1639). On Poland and Wallachia, cf. ASV, *Senato, Dispacci ambasciatori, Costantinopoli*, filza 119, no. 90, fos. 542a–542b (24 September 1638).
40. For example, in one case, the Bailo suggested that he and the ambassadors of the emperor and of the king of Poland ought to secretly contact the Safavid ambassador, who was soon to arrive in Constantinople, and convince him not to conclude a peace agreement with the Porte 'so easily', giving him the hope of a league among the Christian powers against the Ottomans: cf. ASV, *Senato, Dispacci ambasciatori, Costantinopoli*, filza 120, no. 142, fos. 284b–285a (25 June 1639). Cf. also ASV, *Senato, Dispacci ambasciatori, Costantinopoli*, filza 119, no. 93, fo. 593b (6 October 1638). On the Ottoman-Venetian crisis of 1638–9, cf. Rota, Giorgio, 'Una nota su Moldavia, Valacchia e la strategia anti-ottomana della Repubblica di Venezia nel 1638-1639', in Cristian Luca and Gianluca Masi (eds), *L'Europa Centro-Orientale e la Penisola italiana: quattro secoli di rapporti e influssi intercorsi tra Stati e civiltà (1300-1700)* (Brăila-Venice, 2007), pp. 207–25.
41. ASV, *Collegio, Relazioni*, busta 25, fascicolo Q, no. 1, fos. 1a–13a.
42. Berchet, *Venezia e la Persia*, p. 215.
43. Tavernier, Jean-Baptiste, *Les six voyages de Turquie et de Perse*, S. Yérasimos (ed), 2 vols (Paris, 1981), vol. 1, pp. 240, 263–75.
44. The two had become acquainted with each other for the first time in India, before meeting again in Aleppo on their way to Persia: cf. Tavernier, *Les six voyages*, vol. 1, pp. 264, 274.
45. For instance, the Venetian government was the last to entrust de Santis with a letter for the shah, unlike what is stated by Tavernier. Furthermore, the latter does not mention the Grand Duke of Tuscany among the rulers addressing the shah: cf. Berchet, *Venezia e la Persia*, p. 215; Tavernier, *Les six voyages*, vol. 1, pp. 263–4, 273–4. The same Tavernier gives a wrong date for his departure from Aleppo together with de Santis and the famous French missionary, Father Raphaël du Mans (1644 instead of 1647): cf. Richard, *Raphaël du Mans*, vol. 1, pp. 18–21. Francis Richard does not agree with Tavernier's claim that de Santis was associated with the French Jesuit Father Rigordi: cf. Tavernier, *Les six voyages*, vol. 1, p. 274; Richard, *Raphaël du Mans*, vol. 2, n. 18 p. 207 and n. 36 p. 214.
46. Tavernier, *Les six voyages*, vol. 1, p. 275. So far, I have not been able to find any document endorsing or contradicting Tavernier's claim.
47. I abstain from giving references to single passages of the original text of de Santis' travel account, which I am presently preparing for publication, in the hope that it will soon be available to readers in its entirety.
48. On the notion of 'cordon sanitaire' in Safavid diplomatic relations with Europe, cf. Matthee, Rudi, 'Iran's Ottoman diplomacy during the reign of Shah Sulayman I (1077-1105/1666-94)', in Kambiz Eslami (ed), *Iran and Iranian Studies. Essays in Honor of Iraj Afshar* (Princeton, 1998), p. 165.
49. Finally, I would like to thank Lidia Fersuoch and Justine Zara Rapaccioli for their most kind and decisive help.

10

The Embassy of Don García de Silva y Figueroa to Shah 'Abbas I[1]

Luis Gil

In a previous paper, I addressed the background, purposes and long preparations of the embassy sent in 1614 by Philip III, king of Spain and Portugal, to Shah 'Abbas I of Persia, and I published the reports sent to the Spanish Court by the ambassador, don García de Silva y Figueroa,[2] kept in the General Archives of Simancas (=AGS), section Estado (=E). I had studied only up to the ambassador embarking on a journey from Lisbon to Goa. In this chapter my intention is to provide a narrative of that embassy, for which we have abundant sources of information. The basic source, although scarcely known, is the account of the mission in a diary left by don García in imitation of Caesar (=*Com.*),[3] supplemented by his diplomatic correspondence. The other important sources are the Portuguese documents: those collected in the 'Livros das Moncões' (=LM) and the ten manuscripts 'Relaciones' by an anonymous soldier (=*Rel.*), perhaps Gutierre de Monroy, member of the ambassador's retinue, that are kept in the Torre do Tombo and the National Library of Lisbon (=BNL).[4] Equally important are the accounts provided by Pietro della Valle (=*La Persia* I, II),[5] fray Hernando Moraga (=*RBE*)[6] and the letters and manuscript reports of the Augustinian and Carmelite missionaries in Isfahan that are kept in the National Library of Madrid (=BNM) and in the General Archives of the Carmelites in Rome (=AGC).

The stay in Goa

Don García sailed from Lisbon on 8 April 1614 with Cocha Sefer[7] in the flagship of a fleet of five galleons. It was Cocha Sefer who made him aware of how Robert Sherley (the English adventurer whom Shah 'Abbas I had sent as his ambassador to several European courts in 1609), had falsified the letter of the king of Persia to collect the money that his agents in Europe owed him and also managed to convince him that Sherley was a complete liar. Arriving in Goa on 6 November 1614, don García could not leave for Hormuz until 21 March 1617, withheld either by adverse circumstances, or by the obstacles put in place to his departure by the viceroy, don Jerónimo de Azevedo, the archbishop and the captain of Hormuz, don Luis de Gama.

On his arrival, the ambassador found the city preparing for a war[8] against the Mogor (Mughal) and the Melique (Malek) of Chaúl. The Mogor, offended by the viceroy's seizure of his ship carrying pilgrims to Mecca, had decreed a commercial boycott of the Portuguese ports of Diu, Goa and Hormuz. This step was imitated by the Melique of Chaúl, irritated because the Portuguese had cut short the payment of certain commercial duties that he used to collect. Don Jerónimo de Azevedo was assembling a fleet (although he hid his intentions from don García) against the English in Surrate (Surat). Two English ships had come to trade in this port during the previous year, whereas four ships had appeared in September 1614, confirming don García's suspicion that Sherley had reached an agreement in England 'with some privateers and merchants'.[9] But don García had serious doubts about the operational capacity of the force marshalled by Azevedo.

Concerning his mission, don García mentioned that a few days after his arrival a letter from the captain of Hormuz had reached Goa, reporting the siege of the Portuguese fortress in Comorán[10] and demanding help from the Viceroy of India. For their part, the messengers from Hormuz gave an account of the invasion of Quéixome (Qeshm), and brought the news that the ambassador of the Hidalcán had announced that 'Abbas had requested all the kings of India to wage war against the Portuguese in order to prevent them from aiding their compatriots in Hormuz. In view of this unforeseen situation, the ambassador decided to await further developments, and even considered giving up if the situation became more serious.[11] Don García listed the reasons that had moved the shah to take the path of war, and added to the long report a *post scriptum* in his own hand. Trustworthy informants had reported to him that, on 13 December 1614, the viceroy had received reliable reports concerning the loss of the Comorán fortress and the island of Quéixome. The Persians were preparing a large number of *terradas*[12] to invade Hormuz. Don García discussed the matter with the viceroy without delay. At first the latter denied having received such a message, in the end he admitted it, but insisted that the fortress of Hormuz would not be lost because the enemy was lacking artillery.[13]

During the absence of the viceroy, don García was at the mercy of the city's Archbishop, who refused either to provide him with transportation for Hormuz, where don García expected new instructions, or to advance him any funds on account of the monies that he was supposed to collect in Hormuz. Time went by with exasperating slowness, and don García became increasingly convinced that His Majesty's ministers in India did not relish the ambassador's mission to Persia. This was quite understandable, given the situation. But he could see with his own eyes that there were other powerful reasons to explain why his presence would arouse such bad feeling among the authorities in India. Notably, the fear that a direct representative of the monarch, sent to uphold the interests of Portugal, would look into their deeds and give first-hand reports on their ineptitude, lack of foresight and rapacity. The repeated missives explaining the reasons for his delay that don García sent back to court, both by land and sea, never reached their destination.

After the viceroy's return from his disastrous expedition to Surate (Surat) in 1615, don García continued to pester him with his demands to move on to Hormuz. Once again, he failed. The same year, on 29 October 1615,[14] his nephew and lieutenant, don Fernando de Silva, and his servant, Bernardo de Heredia, were both involved in the murder of his butler, Baltasar Vázquez de Neira, an incident the ambassador shamefully skips in his *Comentarios*. The ambassador had to go through the humiliation of seeing them both escape punishment with the complicity of the Portuguese authorities, who facilitated their flight. At the end of February 1616, a new blow was to increase his restlessness. Robert Sherley and fray Redento de la Cruz, whom Shah 'Abbas I was sending to Spain as his ambassadors, were greeted in Goa with 'great pomp and honours', despite the ambassador's warnings that they were not to be welcomed, whether in Hormuz or in India. To win over the shah, the Carmelites of Isfahan, rivals of the Augustinians, had supported Sherley against the Augustinian fray Melchor de los Angeles, whom Shah 'Abbas I intended to send as his envoy to Spain[15] together with Asem Bec.[16]

Fray Melchor, however, was an obstinate man. He presented the Persian sovereign with a memorandum challenging the appointment. The memorandum was rejected, and he was not authorized to dispatch a friar of his order to either Spain or Goa, for the shah feared that they would convey a distorted portrayal of the situation. But, in the end, fray Melchor's stubbornness won, and both fray Juan Tadeo, vicar of the Carmelites, and Robert Sherley, in person, persuaded the shah to accept the request on condition that Melchor and the prior of his convent remain in Isfahan 'as hostages and prisoners'.[17] Don García learnt of all those intrigues and the offers that Sherley intended to make the king of Spain in his new mission through an Augustinian friar. Don García realized the danger threatening Hormuz, now that Shah 'Abbas I had taken hold of Bahrein (Bahrain), the kingdom of Lara (Lar) and the mainland of Comorán. He also noted that a fortress was being built in the inlet of Guadel (Gwadar), half way between Sinde (Sind) and Hormuz, attesting to Shah 'Abbas I's ambitions concerning Hormuz trade.

On 22 October 1616, the ambassador received a letter from the king ordering him to make his journey, since the war with Persia gave cause for it. He was also informed that the viceroy had been given instructions to provide him with all the necessary support in Goa.[18] With that letter in hand, he once more asked don Jerónimo of Azevedo for a ship, encountering the same deceits and hypocrisies he might have encountered in an enemy of his king.[19] As time went by and the risk of losing the monsoon of 1617 (which began on 15 February and finished in March) increased, he embarked on his own in a small ship belonging to a Basain (Bassein) merchant[20] and set course for Hormuz on 21 February.

The journey to Persia

After a hazardous trip and stopping en route in Mascate (Muscat), the ambassador arrived in Hormuz on 29 May 1617. The captain of the stronghold, don Luis de Gama, did not welcome him with excessive cordiality. Don García was increasingly convinced that he was heading for failure with his peace message for a king who 'despite friendly appearances, was essentially an enemy',[21] and only the royal order received in Goa, which urged him to comply with his mission, and another missive in the same terms that reached him in Hormuz[22] encouraged him to go ahead. Thus, he wrote to the governors of Bandel,[23] Lara (Lar) and Xiras (Shiraz) asking them to arrange the necessary camels and beasts of transport on the mainland. When he got news that they were ready and that the gifts from Spain and India had been embarked, he moved on to Bandel on 12 October 1617.[24]

There he was welcome by the governor Casem Bec (Qasem Bayg), and was offered accommodation in tents by the ruins of the Comorán fortress, which he stared at with a melancholy one can imagine. In Bandel he was forced to linger for a few days in order to purchase horses for himself and his retinue and assemble the long train of camels – about 400 – needed to transport the huge amount of equipment he carried about. The caravan left for Lara on the evening of 19 October.[25] To avoid the torrid heat, the distances between the different caravanserais in which they sought refuge were covered by night. With the precision of a geographer and naturalist, of an ethnologist, historian and antiquarian, don García describes everything that caught his eye each day. The impression of objectivity is such that the reader of the account is moved to think that nothing has been left out. However, he does not always proceed with the impartiality of a chronicler. Don García almost never refers to his collaborators by their names, and they are neither criticized nor praised. He omits the personal frictions during the journey or only mentions them in passing, minimizing their importance – for example, the disputes with his servants and the secretary of the embassy, Juan de Ozaeta. We know of these incidents from the ill-intentioned revelations of fray Melchor de los Angeles,[26] whose testimony portrays don García as an authoritarian, arrogant and distant with his subordinates. The slightest fault committed by his servants – remarks the friar[27] – would prompt the ambassador to call in the justice of the 'Moors' and deliver them to the authorities, so that they were thrown in jail. His penchant for scholarship and intellectual curiosity also induced don García to skip over some of his dealings, as if he had been sent on a scientific or archaeological expedition and not on a diplomatic mission. For example, he does not mention his letter from Hormuz to fray Melchor de Los Angeles, urging him to spread the news of his imminent arrival as direct ambassador of the king of Spain to prevent the shah from accepting the trade agreement that the English had come to negotiate with the Persian Court.[28]

However, these small defects do not diminish the quality of the *Comentarios,* which occupy a distinct place among travel books. Let us follow, then, *per summa capita* the itinerary of don García's caravan. Already on its way, on 27 October 1617, while resting in the caravanserai of Charchap close to Lara, fray Melchor de los Angeles arrived carrying 'detailed instructions' from Shah 'Abbas I, 'which in Persian language are called *parauana* (*parvane* ed.) so that the ambassador and all of his household, camels and horses receive sustenance and anything they should need for their journey'.[29] The following day the caravan made its entry to Lara, where governor Chamberbec (Qanbar Bayg) warmly greeted don García. From Lara to Xiras (Shiraz) the journey continued with some noteworthy incidents. In the city of 'Çafhra', don García took a short break, indulging in recollections of his native Zafra in Extremadura.[30] On 24 November, the caravan reached Xiras. As winter was approaching, don García decided to spend winter there and did not resume the journey until 4 April 1618. During the stay, he took the opportunity to visit the city and its surroundings. He could observe the treatment reserved by the shah for his prisoners in the person of the son of the king of the Chacatais (*Chaghatay*) and in that of the mother and two sons, aged eight and nine years, of Timuras I of Kakheti (called Tamarascan by don García). One could reproach don García for acting too cautiously, avoiding any contacts with the unfortunate lady and declining her attempts to approach him through her confessor, a friar of Saint Basil's order called Moysén.[31]

Don García forgets to mention that fray Melchor de los Angeles and at least one of the friars, fray Luis de Ribera, who joined him in Hormuz did not stay in Xiras, but continued their journey to Ispahán (Isfahan), undaunted by the rigours of the Persian winter. This detail does not lack importance. On 18 January 1618, fray Melchor provided fray Luis, heading for Spain by the land route, with a letter[32] for don Juan Ciriza, senior secretary of the Council of State, in which he harshly criticized the slowness of the ambassador. Don García's six-month delay in Hormuz had made the king of Persia mistrustful of his arrival and the king had bestowed the port of Jasques (Jask) on the English, agreeing with them a contract on very favourable terms for their commodities.

Don García resumed the journey from Xiras on 5 April 1618. Upon arriving in Margascán, he let the rest of the caravan proceed on its way, while he and a handful of his following took a detour to visit, under the guide of a '*deruís* or hermit', the ruins the natives called Chilminara (*chehel menar*), 'that in the Arabic language is tantamount to forty minarets or columns'.[33] The site contained nothing less than the ruins of Persepolis. Immediately aware of their importance,[34] he made a rough calculation of the location with the help of a sextant. Then, he took some iconographic documentation, ordering his painter to make sketches of the bas-reliefs and take samples of the cuneiform writing. This unforgettable archaeological excursion that lasted until dawn bore its fruit in chapter VI of the first volume of his *Comentarios*, expressively entitled by the publisher Manuel Serrano y Sanz 'Edifiçios Soberuios y antiquíssimos de Chilminara' (Superb and most ancient buildings of Chilminara), is the first scientific description made by a European of the ruins of Persepolis.[35]

Having satisfied his curiosity, don García continued the journey without any noteworthy incidents other than the very unpleasant one of finding Jusepe Salvador, the faithful Armenian interpreter who had served as a courier with Spain on several occasions, beheaded in Amanzada (*imamzade*: shrine) on 10 April 1618.[36] After this terrible loss, which could hardly be made up for,[37] he paused in the village of Jarustán, at a league's distance from Isfahan, where he arrived on the 19th. During the two days he remained there, while waiting to be formally admitted into the capital, don García was visited by the Augustinians and Carmelites established in it, as well as by the members of the European colony – a dozen English, three or four Italians, and two Germans.[38] Being told that the shah was at the time in Farabat (Farahabad, in Mazandaran on the Caspian coast), he dispatched letters to the monarch and his prime minister Agamir (Aqa Mir Taher), announcing his arrival and stating his feelings concerning the murder of Jusepe Salvador.[39] When the king got the missive, he had already received a report of his arrival by a courier of the city's *deroga* (*darughe*). Shah 'Abbas I received the letter while dining with Pietro della Valle, whom he asked if the ambassador was Spanish ('cioè del Regno di Castiglia') or Portuguese. The Italian answered that he had relatives on both sides, 'ma che d'inclinazione e professione era Spagnuolo' ('he was a Spaniard at heart and by profession').[40] On 1 May, the party entered Isfahan, the ambassador refusing (and forbidding his retinue) to prostrate before the royal palace, as Persian protocol required of foreign legations. He remained in the city, honoured by the authorities, until 28 May, the date on which, at the suggestion of Shah 'Abbas I, he headed for Casbín.[41]

As usual, don García records the incidents, sometimes irrelevant, of the journey and all the noteworthy things he saw on his way. On 13 June 1618, the caravan camped in Pole Sofián, two leagues from Casbín, and two days later the ambassador made a formal entry into the city, accompanied by Daur Cham (Da'ud Khan), the son of Alaverdecam (Allahverdi Khan) and brother of Emancolicám (Emamqoli Khan), the governor, and Usembec (Hosayn Bayg Zu'l-Qadar), the royal chamberlain. The ambassador, having sent part of his servants with the luggage and the present for the shah ahead of him, was surrounded by the rest of the retinue in full array, graciously dressed and wearing colourful panaches, as befitted the dignity of the embassy. Don García himself wore, in his own words, 'inappropriate garments for his age and taste'.[42] He was lodged in the house of the Cocha Sefer, the best residence in Casbín. The ambassador omits in the account of his entry that Pietro della Valle had come to greet him a mile from the city. Della Valle, who rode alongside don García and Daur Cham, accompanied the ambassador 'in camera', and talked with him for more than an hour.[43] This allowed him to sketch an excellent portrait of don García as a strong old man 'molto ben vestito' ('elegantly dressed'), an aspect that another eyewitness of the event, fray Hernando Moraga,[44] also emphasizes.

The meeting with Shah 'Abbas I in Casbín

The Spanish ambassador led an intense social life during the month and a half that he stayed in Casbín in the summer of 1618. He had the opportunity to meet four times with the shah and to interact with the principal personages of the court.

His house was open to every Portuguese returning by land to the Peninsula and to every foreigner in search of hospitality. Among the visitors were fray Hernando Moraga, custodian of the Franciscans of Philippines, and captain Mondragón, who carried letters for His Majesty from the governor of the islands, don Jerónimo de Silva, with the news of the victory obtained in Manila against the Dutch in 1617 and 'the painting depicting battle'.[45] Both had missed the departure of the ships from Goa and were now taking the Babylon (Baghdad) route for Spain.

However, it cannot be said that the stay in Casbín pleased don García. The shah behaved in an elusive way, and the instructions received in Spain had been rendered obsolete by the circumstances. Essentially, these instructions came down to convincing the shah to pursue the war against the Turks and asking him to return the occupied territories to the kingdom of Hormuz. But now it was necessary to demand satisfaction for the conquest of Quéixome and the destruction of the Comorán fortress, as well as to protest against the concession of the port of Jasques (Jask) to the English merchants of Surat, so harmful for the Portuguese trade in Hormuz and India. Don García was perfectly aware of the difficulty of his mission, warned as he had been by the friars of Isfahan and Pietro della Valle[46] that the shah was firmly determined not to give back any of the conquests, and so did not entertain false hopes concerning the success of the negotiations. This explains his eagerness to obtain permission to return, if possible in one of the ships that weighed anchor from Goa in December 1618, to the native land that he painfully longed for after four years of absence. All this was carefully noted by don García in his *Comentarios*. But still he left out some points which are elucidated in the account of the embassy rendered by fray Hernando Moraga on 30 January 1619, by order of His Majesty.

First, a slight chronological discrepancy between both testimonies stands out. Don García says that the Castilian friars and soldiers arrived in Casbín 'some days before the King's departure', giving him the chance to show the aforementioned painting to the royal chamberlain Usembec and to the secretary of state Agamir.[47] The idea was to use the news of this victory to restore the military prestige of the Portuguese in India, badly shaken by the disaster of Surat, due to the cowardice and incompetence of don Jerónimo de Azevedo, the Viceroy of India and general of that fleet.[48] According to this, the Castilian envoys would have entered Casbín in July 1618. Fray Hernando Moraga, on the other hand, claims to have resided almost two months in don García's household, officiating as his chaplain and confidant. If we are to believe Moraga, he was already in Casbín when the Spanish ambassador arrived in the city. Accepting the credibility of the friar's testimony is vital for a better knowledge of certain aspects of the embassy, like the description of the present offered to the shah.

After entering Casbín on 14 July, don García ordered the present to be unpacked on that very same day, but he was warned by the royal chamberlain that the delivery could only take place two days later. The protocol required that one man carry each piece, no matter how big or small it actually was. So more than 600 were necessary, according to don García (about 500, according to Pietro della Valle; 400, according to Moraga), to transport it in parade along the principal streets of Casbín, from the ambassador's residence to 'the garden and house' in which the Iranian monarch was to welcome him.[49]

The present was made up of (a) the objects and weapons pawned in Milan by Robert Sherley and whose redemption had been ordered by the king of Spain; (b) the gift proper from the Spanish monarch, to which 300 loads of pepper and a few more of cochineal had been added; (c) the gifts added by the ambassador at his own expense. Don García mentions in passing the first, not considering it perhaps as a true present for the Spanish monarch. Pietro della Valle did not pay particular attention to it either. On the other hand, nothing could draw Moraga's attention more than its spectacular nature. Unlike Pietro della Valle, Moraga has nothing to say of the personal gift of the ambassador, and the former, logically, is more explicit than the friar concerning the description of the weapons and cloths. Thanks to Moraga's account, we know the order in which the different elements paraded the streets of Casbín. The present from the king of Spain went first, preceded by the sword of Philip III. Next came the objects and weapons of the shah redeemed in Milan, followed by the gifts from the ambassador, and closing the parade the great mastiff the ambassador had brought from Spain.

A dinner in the king's garden that finished at midnight followed the delivery of the present. Shah 'Abbas I received the ambassador and the Chaus, or envoy of the Turks, simultaneously, with the deliberate intention that the latter should see the magnificence of the present sent to him by the king of Spain. During the meeting, after a small incident brought about by the long waiting time, don García had the chance to watch the monarch at ease, since the latter spent most of the time talking with the Chaus. He was struck by the Spartan austerity of the dinner, the simplicity of the garments and weapons, as well as the rather unrefined aspect of the host.[50] However, in the lively glance of Shah 'Abbas I and his way of laughing at puns, the ambassador was able to recognize the traits of a hypocritical and shrewd man.

Days went by, but the shah, with the excuse of having to deal first with the legation of the Turkish general, would not grant don García an audience, despite the latter's requests to the royal chamberlain. For don García, the situation was hardly bearable. The Europeans present at the court, notably the English merchants, might regard this as an attempt to flatter the Chaus and show contempt for the king of Spain. Rumour had it that the shah would leave for Soltania (Soltaniye) to join his army shortly. By 4 July, don García took the decision[51] to arrange a meeting with the shah at any price.

Don García had sent letters to the king of Spain through a courier, who, at three or four days' distance from Baghdad, interrupted the journey and returned to Hormuz. Claiming to be in need of a *paravana* to reach him and get the letters back, he kept looking for ways of getting in touch with the shah in order to obtain it, and he ran into him coming out of a bazaar in the square (*máydan*). Shah 'Abbas I seemed to be happy to meet him, and not only did he accept the request, but also invited don

García to join him in a garden that he owned nearby. They both took a seat in a small loggia, and the Persian sovereign began to complain that the princes of Europe did not duly make war on the Turks, that the Pope, as the head of their religion, did not call everybody to this enterprise, that the king of Spain, so powerful, only ordered his galleys to go privateering, instead of taking Cyprus, Rhodes or Negroponte. Don García was prepared to acknowledge in this the wicked hand of some Europeans, and he tried as hard as he could to give his host satisfaction for his complaints. The union of the European princes, each pursuing their particular goals, was not easy. The authority of the Pontiff was only spiritual and not worldly. Still his forces were always united with the forces of the king of Spain and of the princes of Italy, waiting for a suitable moment to attack the common enemy.[52] The Spaniards sailed the seas of the Levant without rest, causing great devastation on the coasts of Greece and Barbary, and forcing the Turks to divert their best armies to their defence.

But as Shah 'Abbas I did not stop extolling his triumphs and diminishing the action of the Europeans, don García, fed up, crudely suggested to him to consider without passion which of the two kings, the Persian or the Spanish, was more in debt to the other. The Persian struggled to recover his possessions; the Spaniard did not fight for reasons of necessity, but out of antagonism against the Turks and to honour his engagements.[53] At that moment, to avoid the conversation following such a dangerous path, Shah 'Abbas I had fray Juan Tadeo de San Eliseo, vicar of the convent of the Carmelites in Isfahan, come in with the Psalms of David and the New Testament which he had translated into Persian. And so, with his usual shrewdness, he diverted the conversation to spiritual matters,[54] and managed to play down the mounting tension. The food was served and the conversation took a different, worldlier turn. At the end of the meal, the king fell back in a contemplative mood and, as he drank, turned his eyes to the sky, prayed and shed abundant tears.[55] Suddenly, when no one could have expected it, he asked about the damage caused to the Turks by the galleys of the king of Spain. The ambassador answered by listing all the operations of Spanish fleets in the Levant and Barbary over the last 20 years. The shah asked for this account to be translated and written down in Persian. And when it seemed that the conversation was going to tackle the problems pending, the shah resumed his spiritual and devout concerns.[56] He mentioned the respect he had always felt for the temples and images of the Christians, and uttered such praise of the Virgin and the humanity of Christ that the ambassador felt obliged to assert that not without reason was the shah considered the head of his religion and that he set an example for the European Christians present there. In this way the banquet came to an end.

Reading the detailed account written by don García of this surprising interview with Shah 'Abbas I one is convinced that he omitted no detail. However, it is probable that in the course of the conversation other matters were touched upon that were later deliberately or involuntarily left out. For example, it is likely that don García asked Shah 'Abbas I for authorization to return to Spain by a different route, as can be surmised from the testimony of fray Hernando Moraga, who was informed of the audience by the ambassador himself and fray Juan Tadeo. The ambassador was so sore about the treatment received from the Portuguese, who had acted as if they were not vassals of the same king, that he requested the Iranian monarch to allow him to return to Spain by the Moscow route in order to avoid both Hormuz and Portugal. Shah 'Abbas I not only granted permission, but also promised to have him accompanied by a personal ambassador to the Moscow court in order to facilitate his way through Russia.[57]

In the days following this first contact, don García received daily visits from the *maimandar* (*mehmandar*: royal guest-keeper) carrying gifts of bread and game from the shah,[58] who also invited him twice to the maydán (square, market place), the first time towards 11 July to admire a present sent by the governor of Sirván;[59] the second towards 14 July, so that he could watch him 'play *chueca* [Spanish for a kind a hockey] on a horse (polo)'.[60] When taking their farewells, don García begged for an audience and the king promised to entertain him 'some other day'. On 19 July he got an invitation from the king to accompany him on his stroll through the maydán. Don García decided to take advantage of the situation to speak up openly, and warned his interpreter 'that he would have him killed, if he did not clearly translate everything he said'.[61] With this firm decision in mind, he began the conversation with Shah 'Abbas I while riding at his side. The king continued with his repeated complaints, and seeing that the evening went on without having solved anything, don García asked for permission to speak about the kingdom of Hormuz.[62] After receiving a reluctant permission, the ambassador censured the violation of the friendship ties with the king of Spain that entailed the occupation first of Bahrain, then of the lands of the Mogostán, and more recently of the Comorán fortress and the island of Quéixome.[63] Visibly irritated, the shah replied that he had only recovered his belongings. Don García retorted that those territories had been a possession of the kings of Portugal for more than 110 years, and that Shah 'Abbas I's predecessors had never extended their dominions to the coast. Through the embarrassment of the interpreter, don García realized that his words were being faithfully translated. This was confirmed by the angry reaction of Shah 'Abbas I who, without uttering a single word by way of answer, spurred his horse furiously and rode away.[64]

Back in his residence, accompanied by the *maimandar*, don García received, nevertheless, the usual gifts from the king. Some days later, towards 20 July, he was visited by Usembec with the news that Shah 'Abbas I was departing for Soltania, to welcome the embassy of the king of Laor (Lahore), and that, for this reason, he would be happy to entertain him there for three or four days and then grant him leave to go back to Hormuz.[65] The news filled the ambassador's whole household with joy. The following day, everything was ready for the journey and Shah 'Abbas I thanked him through his chamberlain for accepting the invitation.[66] The project, though, was ruined by misfortune. The very same day news arrived from the governor of Tabris (Tabriz) that the Turkish general had moved from Caramit (Qara Hamid) to Van with a huge army. The shah changed his plans and set out for Ardevil (Ardabil), transmitting to the ambassador the message that he could not pause in Soltania nor join the legation of the Mogor there. Don García, continued the message, should travel to Isfahan and wait for him in that city.[67] The annoyance of don García and his retinue was immense, since this would delay their return home for at least a year. Thus, there is no basis for Pietro della Valle's conjecture[68] that the long delay in the embassy's departure was due to one of these three reasons: either the king was taking revenge on the Spanish ambassador for having refused to accompany him,[69] or it was customary to entertain foreign legations for long periods of time, or finally don García wanted to ascertain the outcome of the war before taking leave from Shah 'Abbas I.

The ambassador departed from Casbín on the afternoon of 27 July 1618, when the arrival of the Mogor legation was imminent. The legation, which came to condole with Shah 'Abbas I on the death of his first-born son, whose killing had been commanded by Shah 'Abbas I himself, was so magnificent and large that, according to fray Hernando of Moraga, it resembled more the journey of the Hebrews through the desert than the embassy of a king to another.[70] Already on his way, don García received a letter from Philip III while resting in the caravanserai of Dawlatabad.[71] The monarch left at his discretion the decision to proceed or not to Persia. The letter, complains the ambassador, arrived too late. If he had received it in Hormuz, he would not have moved on to the mainland.[72] With resignation, then, he continued the journey, arriving in Isfahan on 13 August, where he patiently waited the shah's permission to return to Hormuz for the whole summer and autumn of that year, as well as the winter, the spring and a large part of the summer of 1619. Don García suspected that he was being held back until news was received of how Robert Sherley had been welcomed in Spain and a fortuitous fact confirmed his suspicions. An Armenian delivered an envelope to him with letters that had been entrusted to him by an Arab he had left seriously ill on the route to Baghdad with a request to carry to them to Isfahan. As 'the envelope' was written 'in letters of Francs' and he did not know who he was supposed to hand it to, he gave it to the ambassador. One of the letters was intended for fray Juan Tadeo and another for the king of Persia, both written from Lisbon by Robert Sherley a few days after his arrival and signed with the Persian name of Bezabda that the Iranian monarch had bestowed on him. In the letter addressed to the king, which was translated for him by a Persian *alfaquí* (*faqih*) or mullah that frequented his abode, Sherley reported having been greeted in an unfavourable manner and suggested delaying the ambassador in Persia until his return.[73]

During his long stay, the ambassador could feel the isolation to which he was subjected by the captain of Hormuz, don Luis de Gama, and the Portuguese Augustinians in Isfahan, who intercepted the letters he both sent to and received from Spain and did as much as they could to discredit him in the eyes of the Persians.[74] Nevertheless, his sense of duty forced him to take decisions that he considered pointless or hurt his pride as a Castilian nobleman. So, fully aware of the futility of the mission, he sent fray Melchor de los Angeles to Farabat, where Shah 'Abbas I was dwelling at the time, at the beginning of December 1618. Fray Melchor carried a letter from Philip III dispatched by the Council of Portugal in which both the silk deal proposed by Robert Sherley and the conveyance of a fleet to close off navigation in the Red Sea were accepted.[75] As he had foreseen, the shah refused to meet the friar, letting him know through his secretary of state Agamir that he did not need a fleet in the Red Sea, nor the silk deal, because he had already negotiated a peace with the Turks and intended to have all the silk transit via Aleppo. Furthermore, he was not willing to return a single handspan of the land he had gained.[76] Fray Melchor returned in a gloomy mood with the cold answer of the monarch and prepared to travel to Spain with it, where don García had already sent a message stating how little could be expected of the king of Persia.[77]

Shah 'Abbas I returned to Isfahan in the spring of 1619 and, without warning, dropped by the dwelling-place of the ambassador to greet him politely, for that was, in his own words, how friends deserved to be treated.[78] The unexpected visit is described by Pietro della Valle with much greater liveliness and sense of humour.[79] The day of the solemn entry of the ambassadors to the city, don García became impatient at not having met the king and returned to his residence. Once there, a servant arrived in haste to tell to him that the monarch was waiting for him with the ambassadors to eat in the palace.[80] During this banquet, attended also by the Carmelites fray Juan Tadeo and fray Juan Leandro, the Augustinians fray Diego de la Resurrection and fray Bernardo Azevedo, and the gentlemen in the ambassador's retinue, the Iranian monarch insisted that fray Juan Tadeo translate a credential letter that fray Bernardo had brought from the court for the Spanish ambassador. To the greatest displeasure of the Spanish ambassador the friar did so in front of all the other ambassadors. Shah 'Abbas I promised to grant him a long audience.

Finally, on Friday, 2 August 1619, Shah 'Abbas I convened all the ambassadors in the maydán, and approached the Spaniard to ask him what he sought on behalf of his king and what he wanted to ask personally.[81] Don García, believing that his intention was to hear him 'summarily', replied that he sought what he had told him in Casbín and through fray Melchor de los Angeles in Farabat. For his part, he simply wanted to be granted leave to set out for Hormuz. But the king insisted on talking with him more calmly and took him to a distant part of the maydán. There, in the presence of Persian dignitaries, as well as of fray Juan Tadeo and Domingo Rodríguez, an interpreter native of Hormuz, don García, in view of his good will, tried first to convince him to take advantage of the succession crisis of the Turks to make war on them.[82] But Shah 'Abbas I interrupted the reasoning, declaring that if the Christians did it in Europe, he would fight against them in Asia until he took Jerusalem, 'which he would later deliver to the Christians'.[83] The ambassador went on to recall his obligation to return Bahrein, Quéixome and Comorán to the king of Hormuz and not admit English or foreigners to the silk deal. Shah 'Abbas I, 'with a quiet and peaceful countenance', replied 'that the King of Spain, his brother, could not care less if those islands and fortresses were in his hands or in those of the King of Hormuz, for while both were Mahommedans, the latter was a Sunnite and, therefore, of a religious obedience more contrary to the Francs than his own one'.[84]

The ambassador, of course, found the reply 'a complete mockery', and insisted on the mutual obligation of the allies to return each other's possessions. But the king, as he used to do when he disliked the matter discussed, indulged in 'large praises of the humanity of Christ and the purity of Our Lady', and then asked don García if he wanted to ask for something personally. Don García only requested the necessary means for his journey to Hormuz and his permission so that both the Augustinians and the Carmelites could build their convents in Isfahan. Shah 'Abbas I promised to do this, and helping don García to stand up, 'he embraced him, calling him father and saying that he would always be a very dear friend'. Moved by the gesture, the latter 'kissed his hand, which he had never done until then'.[85] The king embraced him again and took leave of him.

An illness that kept the ambassador in bed for 20 days delayed his departure from Isfahan until 25 August 1619. On that occasion he was accompanied by all the Franks living in the city, except for Pietro della Valle, 'per la poca corrispondeza' (the little friendship)[86] he had had with him. Fray Dimas de la Cruz, an Italian Carmelite, and fray Manuel de la Madre de Dios, a Portuguese Augustinian, joined the party the following day. On 3 September, don García was reached by a soldier sent by the captain of Hormuz, don Luis de Sosa, in the belief that he was still in Isfahan. The soldier carried an envelope from the king of Spain that a courier had brought via Bassorah (Basra). It contained instructions for the ambassador,[87] a letter from Philip III and another from Robert Sherley to the Iranian monarch on the silk trade[88] through Hormuz and India and the blockade of the Red Sea by a fleet of the king of Spain.[89] The ministers of the monarch, disregarding the warnings of don García regarding the scant basis of Sherley's and fray Redento de la Cruz's proposals, believed that 'granted such conditions, the King of Persia would return Bahrein, Quéyxome and the Comorán fortress'. The galleons had already set sail with the said friar, leaving Sherley in Spain. Once more, although deeply disappointed, the ambassador complied with his duty, and dispatched the same messenger, with the missives of the Spanish monarch, a letter for Shah 'Abbas I in accordance with the received instructions and another for fray Juan Tadeo, which were to be delivered and read out to the shah.[90]

The correspondence was handed to the monarch on 16 September by fray Juan Tadeo, who was entrusted with its translation and was ordered to come back and read it out the following day. When the friar opened the correspondence at home, Pietro della Valle was next to him.[91] Della Valle, in possession as usual of first-hand information, discusses the reasons that led don García to deliver the correspondence to the Carmelite, and reliably describes the content of the letters from the king of Spain, Robert Sherley and the ambassador. The content of the first is already known, that of Sherley referred to the letter sent through fray Redento, and that of the ambassador contained a warning and a less veiled threat than the letter from the Spanish monarch. If the king of Persia did not restore the lands claimed by the Portuguese, the latter would help themselves by making use of their galleons.[92]

Having delegated the negotiation to fray Juan Tadeo, the Spanish ambassador made him familiar with the instructions he had received. The king of Spain did not insist so much on the return of the occupied territories, including Quéixome,[93] as on the condition that no other nations should be granted port facilities, and that no haven should be granted to privateers like the English.[94] Before reading the letters, Shah 'Abbas I asked fray Juan Tadeo to acquaint him with their 'substance', and once aware of it, he said that the silk business would be solved immediately.[95] On 17 September, after convening the Armenians of Julfa (Djolfa), the English and the father prior of the Carmelites, Shah 'Abbas I organized a public auction of the Persian silk, announcing that it would be awarded to the highest bid. First spoke fray Juan Tadeo, saying that he had no orders from Spain to make any offers. Neither had the English, and so the silk was awarded to the Armenians for a high amount.[96]

On 3 October, fray Juan Tadeo was called by Shah 'Abbas I to read out the letter from the king of Spain, without being granted an audience. The following day, the monarch had the *maimandar* bring the translation of the letters. The *maimandar* reported to the friar the monarch's reaction when he read them. Regarding the return of the territories, he remarked angrily that he had not stolen anything from the Portuguese; regarding the silk, that all the numerous conditions proposed just made him laugh; regarding the friendship of the king of Spain, that he cared little for it, and that he could have taken Hormuz with a single blow, if he had only wanted to. He seemed especially irritated with don García's letter, which he tore into pieces in the presence of his senior dignitaries, while showing evident signs of displeasure.[97] However, he ordered don García to be answered that the king of Spain should await the arrival of fray Redento with precise instructions to deal with these matters. Furthermore, he ordered an ambassador to make preparations to set out for Spain.[98]

Don García arrived in Xiras on 7 September 1619. He remained there for seven days and learnt of the execution of Moysén, the confessor of Timuras' mother,[99] falsely accused of adultery with the wife of Assenbec (Hosayn Bayg), the chancellor of the city's Chan. On 17 October, he was already in the Bandel, where he was visited by the governor Soltan Alaverdi (Allahverdi Bayg), who created difficulties and claimed 'some presents', as the governor of Lara had done previously. But when the ambassador was about to write to the Iranian monarch to report the incident, messengers arrived 'in haste'[100] to inform him that everything was ready for the transfer to Hormuz. On 19 October 1619 he was back on the island.

Don García remained in Hormuz during the winter waiting for the monsoon ships from Goa. The stay gave him the opportunity to become acquainted with the evils plaguing the island. Two long years of drought had served as a pretext for the governor of Comorán to increase the taxes on water and supplies, the inhabitants lived in fear of a Persian invasion, and the fortress was not big enough to lodge all the people to whom it was supposed to offer refuge and did not have provisions for more than 15 days. The captain did not take the right measures for an effective defence either and, to make matters worse, he incompetently spread the false rumour that don Hernando de Albuquerque,[101] governor in office of the state of India after the demise of the viceroy count of Redondo in November 1619, had set out for Hormuz at the head of a large fleet. The reaction of the shah was to order the Chan of Xiras to have 300 terradas and 15,000 men prepared on the western end of the island of Quéixome. In greatest fear the king, the sheriff, the judge and the finance inspector sought shelter in the fortress, and the affluent citizens deposited their monies and jewels in it. But the Persians, instead of attacking Hormuz, crossed over to Julpha in Arabia[102] and returned after destroying a petty little place where Alicamalun, Arab of the Niquilu in the coast of the kingdom of Lara, had settled due to disagreements with the shah and the chan of Xiras.[103]

Once the fear of attack was over, the ambassador began to prepare for his return to Goa, but only after dispatching his secretary Saulisante for Spain with letters to the king in which he reported on the events in Persia and the state of affairs in Hormuz. But, as a large part of March went by and the monsoon ships from Goa had not arrived, he decided to embark with part of his retinue on 5 April, in a small merchant ship coming from Cochín, and after a hazardous and eventful voyage punctuated by storms, dead calms and the menace of Malabar piratry, the ship arrived in Goa on 25 April 1620.

The second stay in Goa

The ambassador had already found accommodation when the servants he had left behind in Hormuz arrived in the monsoon ships on 10 May. Among them was Diego Lobo, who all thought to be dead, as he had been treacherously attacked the day on which the ambassador had embarked for Goa, suffering severe wounds from a sword and harquebus. 'Two notable things' combined in this case, remarks a sarcastic don García, the healing of the wounded against all odds and the absence of any investigation by the island authorities in order to clear up the incident.[104] In one of those ships also arrived Caya (Khvaje) Soltán, the ambassador that the king of Persia was sending to Spain, whose visit coincided with that of don García in Hormuz.[105]

As the stay in Goa, during which a plague epidemic broke out claiming numerous lives[106] and delaying the departure of the ships, continued longer than expected, the ambassador decided to embark in an old caravel that had just arrived from Portugal, against the opposition of the governor, who claimed to be in need of her sailors.[107] Thanks to the good offices of his friends, he was allowed to use her on the condition that he fitted her out at his expense and paid the crew. The ship was named 'Our Lady of Nazareth' and set sail on 19 December 1620 with the ambassador and his retinue. Crowded and overloaded, there was hardly any room to place the eight small cannons that she carried to deter attacks by Malabar pirates. The pirates indeed showed up in 11 *paroes* shortly after leaving the Goa sandbank. But the caravel managed to escape thanks to the timely intervention of Gutierre de Monroy, a servant of the ambassador, who observed that in high seas it would be easier to catch wind and leave the Malabar ships behind. The ambassador realized that he was right, and gave orders to continue the course, outrunning the Malabar *paroes*.[108]

The caravel arrived in Mozambique on 17 February 1621, but unable to continue the journey for Europe due to the violence of the headwinds, she set sail again for Goa on 14 March, arriving on 28 May. There, the pilot's lack of skill[109] almost brought about a disaster. The ship foundered on a sandbank, the rudder broke into pieces and the sails fell down, while the port pilot's boat was waiting alongside. At that moment, don García says, one of his servants took him by the arm and told him to save his life before the ship sank. The ambassador slid down to the boat that was waiting there and was picked up by another servant.[110]

One cannot forgive don García de Silva y Figueroa, always so particular about details, for not having mentioned the name of the 'servant' or 'servants' that took care of him. In this way, he would have revealed to us the identity of the author of the anonymous *Relaciones* of the National Library in Lisbon, whose version of the facts differs considerably, insofar as it is reported that he almost lost his own life in trying to rescue the ambassador in those critical instants, having first to go search for him in his cabin, then dragging him out by his shoulder, and finally being forced to jump onto a launch at the risk of drowning for he could not swim.[111] Notwithstanding the the lack of information provided by don García, we would venture to suggest, with all due caution, that the anonymous author is perhaps Gutierre de Monroy, on the basis of the following facts. Having direct access to a person so jealous of his authority as don García reveals a degree of familiarity improper of a simple servant. His speedy reaction on that occasion recalls that of Gutierre de Monroy before the Malabar pirates. The author of the *Relaciones* was present in the audience granted by the shah in Isfahan to the ambassadors, which was also attended by the gentlemen in the Spanish ambassador's retinue.

But let us return to our account. Once again installed in Goa, don García did not obtain from the Portuguese authorities the necessary support or the treatment he deserved. In addition, he had the misfortune to witness the accumulation of disasters that fell upon the state of India. On 22 August, the explosion of the powder-magazine, which caused serious damage to the city, shocked him. In 1622 he learnt about the failure of Ruy Freire in Quéixome and the loss of Hormuz. That same year the ship *Sancto Thomé* docked in Goa. Don García wanted her for his return to Spain.[112] But destiny had new delays in store for him. Most unfortunately, the Count da Vidigueira arrived as the new Viceroy of India. Da Vidigueira was one of the persons that had strongly opposed his appointment as ambassador, and in spite of his insistence on being given passage in the *Sancto Thomé*, the viceroy turned a deaf ear, occupied as he was 'in stealing their money from the wretched people of Goa by imposing on them incredible levies that had never been used before'.[113] His behaviour made don García suspect that he tried every possible way to prevent 'anybody from providing information about him in Spain, except for the people of his own choice'.[114]

Don García, having gone to see the master and the pilot of the *Sancto Thomé* in order to purchase a passage at any price,[115] was able in the event to embark on 28 January 1624.[116] During the voyage, faithful to his custom, he continued his daily notes, which are interrupted on 28 April. A final footnote in an incomplete copy of the *Comentarios* kept in the National Library of Madrid, published by Manuel Serrano y Sanz,[117] informs us that he died on 22 July 1624 at 8pm, of the 'disease of Loanda', at 35 degrees North and 110 leagues from the Flores and Cuervo islands. By an irony of destiny, don García was victim to the same 'disease of Loanda', or scurvy, that he saw and described in detail during his first journey to Goa.[118] Ailing in Goa and therefore unable to go on board with the ambassador, the author of the *Relaciones* regrets the loss of 'such a distinguished, pleasant, prudent and courageous gentleman', and deplores that 'his noble and elderly bones would find a tomb in the broad and salty sea'. With him, 'he took the true, sensible and dispassionate account' of the evils afflicting India and the possibility that, with its knowledge, His Majesty would have sought the necessary remedies.[119] It is hard to imagine a greater praise of the personality and the loyal but unsuccessful services rendered by don García de Silva y Figueroa.

Notes

1. Anthroponyms and place-names are written as they appear in the Spanish and Portuguese sources. The first time they appear I have added, when possible, the transliteration from Persian.
2. García de Silva y Figueroa, *Epistolario diplomático*. Edición y estudios preliminares de Luis Gil (Cáceres Institución Cultural 'El Brocense', 1989).
3. *Comentarios de D. García de Silva y Figueroa de la embajada que de parte del rey de España don Felipe III hizo al rey Xa Abas de Persia*. Los publica la Sociedad de Bibliófilos Españoles (Madrid, 1903), 2 vols.
4. Ms BNL, fondo geral 580, fos. 31r–83v.
5. *Viaggi di Pietro della Valle il Pellegrino. Descritti da lui medesimo in Lettere familiari all'erudito suo amico Mario Schipano, La Persia*, In Roma, A spese di Biagio Deuersin, MDCLVIII. All' Insegna della Regina. Con licenza de' Svperiori, et privilegio. 2 vols (parte prima, seconda).
6. Relacion breve de la embaxada y presente que la Magestad del Rey don Felipe Tercero Rey de las Españas, y Emperador del Nueuo mu(n)do, hizo a Xaabay Rey de Persia clarissimo: la qual Embaxada dio Don García de Silva y Figueroa su Embaxador, el año passado de 1618. Años, hecha por fray Herna(n)do Moraga, Custodio de la Prouincia de San Gregorio de Filipinas, que se halló presente en la Corte del Persiano y vio la dicha embaxada y presente: auiendo venido de Manila, a Malaca Azilan, Oromuz, Persia, Babilonia, y passado por el desierto de Arabia, Assyria, Tripoli, y de allí a Chipre, Candia, Malta, Francia y llegó a esta Corte este presente año de 1619. A 30. de enero y fue bien recebido de su magestad por cuyo mandado hizo esta relación: y otra de su viage, cosa marauillosa y digna de saberse.
7. Khvaje or Khoja Safar, *La Persia* II, 49.
8. *ED* doc. 16, p. 189
9. ibid., p. 189
10. Combru [Gombroon/Gamron in English sources of the period], *La Persia* II, 466, Hormozgan.
11. ibid., p. 191
12. From the Farsi *tarrak*, a type of boat without deck.
13. Combru [Gombroon/Gamron in English sources of the period], *La Persia* II, P.S., p. 194.

14. The file with the facts sent from Goa, can be seen in AGS E 437; cf. *ED*, docs 26, 28, pp. 22, 224.
15. *ED* doc. 30, pp. 228–9
16. Hosayn Bayg Zu'l-Qadr
17. ibid., p. 229
18. *Com*. I, p. 223
19. ibid.
20. ibid.
21. *Com*. I, p. 269
22. *ED* docs 28, 32, pp. 224 and 233, LM 11, fos. 111 and 12, fo. 484
23. Bandar, *Persia* II, p. 64
24. *Com*. I, p. 270, 8 May *Rel*. 31v
25. ibid., p. 274
26. 'Relación de la Jornada de Dom García de Sylua Embaxador, dada por Fr. Melchor de los Ángeles' (Madrid a 30-XII-1619) in ms.BNM 2348, fos. 519r–520v.
27. *Com*. I, fo. 520r–v
28. AGS E 265, unfoliated
29. *Com*. I, p. 287
30. ibid., pp. 321–3
31. ibid., p. 362
32. 'Aspan 1618. El Padre Melchor de los Ángeles a 18 de Enero a Jhoan de Ziriça, Secret(ari)o mayor del Consejo de Estado', AGS E 265, unfoliated.
33. *Com*. I, p. 369
34. ibid., p. 373
35. ibid., p. 389
36. *Com*. II, p. 10
37. Don García does not mention that the interpreter he had brought from Spain died in Hormuz and that he engaged Jusepe Salvador there. After his assassination, he did not want to take another very competent one in his service for the high price he asked for, and engaged another Armenian with a good command of Persian, but 'little knowledge of Spanish' (ms BNM 2348, fo. 519v). With his saintly intention, fray Melchor completes the missing information.
38. *Com*. II, p. 20
39. ibid., p. 24
40. *La Persia* I, pp. 250–1
41. Qazvin, *Com*. II, p. 51
42. *Com*. II, 79
43. *La Persia* I, pp. 324–5
44. RBE, fo. 1v
45. *Com*. II, p. 124
46. ibid., p. 121
47. *La Persia*, II, p. 105
48. *Com*. II, p. 124
49. ibid., pp. 82–3
50. ibid., p. 89
51. ibid., p. 97
52. ibid., p. 99
53. ibid., p. 101
54. ibid., p. 102
55. ibid., p. 105
56. ibid., p. 106
57. RBE, fo. 5r
58. *Com*. II, p. 107

59. Shirvan, *Com.* II, p. 110
60. *Com.* II, p. 113
61. *Com.* II, p. 118
62. ibid., p. 120
63. ibid., p. 120
64. ibid., p. 120
65. ibid., pp. 121–2
66. ibid., p. 122
67. ibid., p. 122
68. *La Persia* I, p. 347
69. According to fray Melchor de los Angeles, the king invited him to join him in his trip to Soltania, on the promise that he would grant him audience there. The ambassador, appealing to his old age and claiming to have ailing servants, presented his apologies, which irritated the shah. Aware of it, don García agreed to go along, but the king had changed his mind and ordered him to set out for Isfahan (ms. BNM 2348, fo. 519v).
70. *RBE*, fo. 7r
71. Doulet-abàd, *La Persia* II, p. 18
72. *Com.* II, p. 326
73. ibid., pp. 340–1
74. ibid., p. 359
75. ibid., p. 360
76. ibid., p. 360
77. In Madrid, on 30 December 1619, he tabled the already mentioned report on the embassy of don García (ms. BNM 2348, fos. 519r–520v).
78. *Com.* II, p. 363
79. *La Persia* II, p. 11
80. *Com.* II, p. 368
81. ibid., p. 407
82. ibid., pp. 408–9
83. ibid., p. 409
84. ibid., p. 410
85. ibid., p. 411
86. *La Persia* II, p. 61
87. It is certainly the long letter of LM 12, fo. 150 ('Descifrado de carta de S(ua) M(a)g(esta)de para o Embaixador de Persia dom Garçia de Silva e Figueroa, 14 de Março de 1619').
88. 'O que se ten assentado acerca da amizade que El Rey de Persia polo seu embaixador mandou offerecer a S(ua) M(a)g(esta)de e do comercio e tratto de seda, que tudo se ha de capitular, e assinar na Persia polo mesmo Rey e polo Embaixador de S(ua) M(a)g(esta)de em virtude dos poderes que se lhe manda' (LM 12, fo. 148). The different points of the agreement can be seen also in fray Redento's report to Rome (AGC, 234-e, fo. 5) and in the ms. BNM 2352, fos. 486r–488v and 11077, fos. 186v–187v. and their general guidelines in *La Persia* II, p. 64.
89. *Com.* II., pp. 418–19
90. ibid., pp. 420–2
91. *La Persia II*, p. 62
92. ibid., p. 65
93. ibid., p. 64
94. ibid., p. 62
95. ibid., p. 62
96. ibid., p. 67
97. ibid., p. 68
98. ibid.

99. *Com.* II, p. 425
100. ibid., p. 450
101. On 8 February 1620, Fernão of Albuquerque informed the king of the arrival of don García in Hormuz and that the 'veedor de fazenda' (tax inspector) complained that he was pestered by don García, who demanded the payment of what was owed to him. And he added that he did the same in Goa without being possible to satisfy him for lack of funds. With respect to the silk deal, he considered that Shah 'Abbas I would not comply with the agreement, because he had already signed a contract with the English who had arrived in Jasques with five ships that year (LM 12, fo. 140).
102. *Com.* II, p. 464
103. ibid., p. 467
104. ibid., p. 490
105. ibid.
106. *Com.* II, pp. 487–8
107. On the other hand, the governor don Fernão de Albuquerque in a letter to the king dated 16 December 1620 refers that don García did not want to go on board in the same ship as the shah's ambassador, for he considered that 'he would not be comfortably installed' and that he granted him the caravel in which he could sail back to the kingdom in May (LM 15, fo. 41).
108. *Com.* II, p. 501
109. ibid., p. 546
110. ibid., p. 557
111. *Rel.*, fos. 81r–82r
112. On 15 February 1622, Fernão de Albuquerque writes to the king telling him that, having assigned don García the 'gasalhados' (stateroom), the latter 'decided not to leave this year', as was attested by the copy of the document that he sent to the secretary who went on board. The document (not a copy, but an original autograph of don García, as I have been able to verify personally) reads as follows: 'Beso las manos a V(uesa) M(erced) por el cuydado y merçed del S(eñ)or gouernador, pero siendo ya tan tarde, que se aurá de hazer el viage fuera de monçion, y yo no me hallo con salud para lleuar los trabaxos q(ue) en los tales viages q(ue) fuera de tiempo se padecen, estoy resuelto de no embarcarme este año, aunq(ue) sea tan mala la vida que yo tengo en Goa. Dios guarde a V(uesa) M(erced). De mi posada, 15 de enero de 1622. Don García de Silva y Figueroa' (LM 15, fo. 233).
113. *Com.* II, p. 604
114. ibid., p. 607
115. ibid., p. 605
116. ibid., pp. 607–8. In a letter to the king dated in January 1624, Count Vidigueira informs: 'Dom Garcia da Silua [...] se embarca na nao S. Thome q(ue) ora vay para o Reino. E eu o procurey acomodar nella e lhe dei o anno passado mil pardaos de ajuda de custo.' In this way, history is written.
117. *Com.* I, p. XVII, note 1
118. ibid., pp. 85–6
119. *Rel.*, fos. 82v–83r

11

The Holy See, the Spanish Monarchy and Safavid Persia in the Sixteenth Century: Some Aspects of the Involvement of the Society of Jesus

Enrique García Hernán

Introduction

This chapter intends to analyse the diplomatic efforts of the Holy See and Spain to achieve a Persian alliance in their common fight against the Turks, particularly during the pontificates of Pius V, Gregory XIII and Clement VIII. The confrontation between Persia and the Ottoman Empire was perceived by the Catholic monarchy and the papacy as the best opportunity for the Persian Safavid dynasty to become a faithful ally despite their different religions. We shall concentrate mainly on the diplomatic activity of three Jesuits, Francis Borgia, Matías Bicudo and Francisco de Acosta. This new religious order was capable of serving both the Hispanic monarchy and the Holy See at the same time. The three of them were supporters of a determined military involvement. The Holy See would face numerous difficulties in its attempt to establish an efficient apostolic activity and fluid diplomatic relations. However, polarized positions and divisions among the religious orders would prove an insurmountable problem. We shall use mostly unpublished documentation from the General Archives of Simancas.

Shah Esmaʻil I (1500-24), who since 1510 had extended his dominion to all of Iran, Mesopotamia and Armenia so that it bordered the Ottoman Empire, realized the need to create an alliance with the European Christian powers to oppose the Ottomans. Charles V also analysed this possible alliance and was the first to take the initiative and, in his capacity as emperor of Germany, he contacted Esmaʻil in the decade of 1520 to find channels of cooperation. As a response to this approach, Shah Tahmasp sent him a letter in 1523 in which he expressed his hope that both armies would join to overcome the Ottomans. Thus, in the context of the international strategy of the Hispanic monarchs and of the Pontiffs, Persia was turning into a possible ally that, from a strategic point of view, presented the possibility of attacking the common Ottoman enemy on two fronts.

Later on, in 1566, emperors Maximilian II and Philip II decided to send an embassy to Shah Tahmasp offering friendship and alliance. Both needed the cooperation of the king of Portugal, don Sebastian, who was in contact with the king of Persia through the viceroy of India and the captain of Hormuz. In the cosmopolitan Portuguese city of Hormuz (1507–1622) Persians, Turks, Arabs, Armenians, Abyssinians, Indians, Chinese, Portuguese, Muslims, Jews, Christians and Hindus and other nationalities and religious communities met and mingled.[1] The Holy See was aware of what was going on there thanks to the Jesuits. The Dutch Gaspar Berze (1515–53) resided there for several years from 1549 to 1551. Francisco sent him to Hormuz with the duty of staying there, a true crossroads of the Orient, for at least three years. He observed that in Hormuz illicit arms traffic with Moors and Turks was taking place. This was prohibited by the Bull *In Coena Domini*, which sanctioned with excommunication the sale of arms, steel and sulphur to the 'enemies of faith'. The sulphur originated in Persia across the straights from the city of Hormuz. The orders of the Bull could be dispensed with under special circumstances. However, the Jews, true traders of weapons and other military goods, could act as intermediaries since as non-Christians they were not affected by excommunication. In Hormuz there were many Hispanic Jews, for the most part new Christians from Spain and Portugal who, coming through Venice, had arrived in the Persian Gulf and had regained the faith of their ancestors.

Father Berze saw that Hormuz had little apostolic success and therefore wished to go to Persia. As a matter of fact, he had thought of writing to Shah Tahmasp a detailed report about the mistakes of the Islamic religion and to beg him to send some of his doctors of divinity (i.e. *faqihs*) to Hormuz to have a conversation with him about their faiths. If Francisco Javier authorized him, he was prepared to go to Persia. Berze shared the general opinion with the Persians that the Christian princes demonstrated unjustifiable weakness in their reluctance to fight the Turks.

Around 1550 Berze had a public dispute with a Muslim philosopher of Persia, ambassador Ceide Maduny, who, coming from Chaul in an embassy from India, had arrived in Hormuz. Berze achieved the conversion of his wife and daughter. He also succeeded in sending a Portuguese embassy to Persia to renew the mutual alliance, despite the incident with Ceide Maduny, because the shah needed Portuguese artillery and arms in his fight against the Turks. One of the manners and customs that most amazed Berze was that the Persians considered the shah a god. He remarked with surprise that: 'the water with which he washes his feet they all use as relics to cure all sicknesses'.[2] Despite all efforts, there was no significant success and the provincial of India ruled that there should be a different priest in Hormuz every year given the unhealthiness of the place and the few apostolic results obtained. In spite of this ruling, the Society of Jesus would obtain privileged information about the situation in Hormuz.[3]

From the political perspective, the Persian alliance continued to be important for the Christian princes. In 1567 Philip II asked his ambassador in Lisbon to send him a detailed report about the best way to reach Persia, the personal qualities a potential ambassador might require, the emoluments of the ambassadors of the king of Portugal to that court, how to behave towards the shah, the language in which to write and the presents most valued by the Persians. The king wished to send an embassy together with the ambassador. This mission reached Lisbon too late, after the vessels departing for India that year had already set sail.[4] Another significant moment was in 1572, when on the occasion of the victory at Lepanto, the Holy See, Venice, Spain and Portugal sent emissaries to the king of Abyssinia and to the sovereigns of Arabia Felix and the Arabian border with Syria to encourage attacks on the Turks.[5]

In the same way as the Spanish monarchs tried to create a network of alliances with the enemies of the Sublime Port to mitigate their desire for conquest in the West, the Persians pursued the support of the Christian monarchs to hold back Ottoman advances in the East. Therefore, during the sixteenth century the Hispanic monarchy tried to create a stable alliance with those rulers who could serve this purpose, providing funds or sending emissaries to the Balkan peninsula, the north of Africa and oriental Europe and, of course, to Persia.[6] The viceroy of Portugal would recognize in 1601 that Philip II had always wished to stay in diplomatic contact with Persia with the sole purpose of establishing an alliance against the Turkish Empire.[7] In this sense, Spain and the Holy See could support each other to achieve the same objectives.

The pontificate of Pius V (1566–72)

The apostolic see started to favour requesting the cooperation of the Persians during the pontificate of Pius V, who had started a great offensive against the Turks by means of the Holy League (1571–3), a Hispanic-Venetian pontifical confederation, formed with the aim of regaining Jerusalem by any means.[8] After lengthy and complex diplomatic, legal and military negotiations, the three states became confederated to oppose the Ottomans under Selim II (1566–74). On the same day on which the most celebrated Holy League was signed, the Pope decided on his own initiative, without the counsel of his cardinals, to send apostolic legates to Spain and Germany. The Pope's nephew, Cardinal Alexandrine, was to visit Philip II, while Maximilian II would receive a visit from Cardinal Commendome.

The Alexandrine legate was also to visit Portugal and, depending on circumstances, France as well, as turned out to be the case. One of the aspects of the instructions – very zealously protected – linked Alexandrine with a person who was internationally admired, particularly in Spain. The Pope instructed his nephew that, as far as Portugal was concerned, he should follow the lead of the Jesuits' General, Father Francis Borgia; furthermore, he was plainly telling him that he was to converse with him about everything, to follow his advice and that he should only meet those whom Borgia specified.⁹ Borgia was brought into the Pope's ambitious plan to unite Christendom, to put an end to heresy, to restrain the Turkish advance and to expand Christendom throughout the world. Borgia was a key element in the pontifical governance system. His capacity as general of the Jesuits, his privileged position as former Duke of Gandía and, most particularly, his personal talents made him appear as particularly useful to serve the pontificate in particularly difficult missions.

Although initially some churchmen proposed that legates be sent to the Protestant princes to persuade them to cooperate in the fight against the Turks, the Pope very energetically opposed this: 'nullam concordiam vel pacem debere nec posse esse inter nos et hereticos' the council solemnly declared on 23 June 1571. The Pope was not inclined to ask the Lutherans and Calvinists for help, rather he was counting on help from the shah of Persia. As soon as the victory of Lepanto was known, he did not hesitate to request the shah's assistance.¹⁰ It was possibly the Portuguese Jesuit priest Matías Bicudo (Matías Furtado Bigudo) who inspired Pius V with the idea of requesting the cooperation of Persia since for several years Bicudo had resided in the Orient serving the Portuguese kings, and he knew the atmosphere and was now close to the Pope. Nevertheless, there are numerous unanswered questions about this individual, who appears to have belonged to a number of religious orders. It is difficult to be certain about his true activities for he was a shadowy figure to his contemporaries and has remained so for historians.¹¹

There are also doubts as to the real intentions of Pius V for, when the Spanish ambassador to Rome mentioned the Persian cooperation, he responded that he did not wish to write to Persia since it was not customary for the popes to relate to infidels. Philip took this to be a great contradiction and thought the Pope had forgotten that the negotiations had already been opened; this explains the king's reaction: '[His Holiness] must not have remembered', he wrote to his ambassador in Rome. The King already had in his possession the original pontifical document remitted to the shah.¹²

In those documents Pius V narrated to the shah the victory of Lepanto and encouraged him to take advantage of the favourable military circumstance and to raise an army to invade the enemy territory to make up for the losses his nation had suffered with the territories stolen from his ancestors by Suleiman in the regions of Mesopotamia and Syria. The pontifical chancellery was ignorant of the real situation in Persia, as the losses referred to in the document had occurred during the reign of Tahmasp I, in 1534, and not in that of his predecessors.¹³

One of the objectives of Francis Borgia in Portugal had been to persuade King Sebastian to second the strategic plans of Pius V.

From Lisbon he directly informed his friend the *condottiere* Marco Antonio Colonna, admiral of the pontifical fleet, who had succeeded in securing the entry of the Portuguese king into the Holy League by offering his military assistance. Furthermore, the Portuguese would attack the Turks not only from the Red Sea, but also from Persia and Ethiopia.¹⁴ Marco Antonio Colonna was thankful for the

Portuguese help for a future military campaign in Persia but asked Philip II – thus following the pontifical plans – to do anything possible to regain Constantinople, which was the main objective.[15] One must bear in mind that in December 1571 the king informed his ambassador in Rome to contrive the diplomacy to obtain Persia's cooperation. Thus, from Madrid, Lisbon, Rome, Venice and Messina, where the allied fleet was, all set to work to obtain the shah's cooperation.[16]

No sooner had he left Madrid, than the Alexandrine legate entrusted to the nuncio at the Spanish court, Castagna, some matters pertaining to Persia, five apostolic briefs and a letter for King don Sebastian of Portugal. They were sent to the pontifical collector in Lisbon, monsignor Aspra. The aim was to pursue the initiative of the allies, to persuade Persia, 'Ethiopia' and 'Arabia' to declare war on the Turks. For this purpose they could count on the help promised by King Sebastian, taking into account the many contacts he had with the allies due to the frequency of Portuguese voyages and travels. Aspra had to translate the apostolic briefs into the languages of their consignees.[17] King Sebastian accepted the proposals and sent a special ambassador to Persia with the letters from the Pope, the doge from Venice and the Catholic king.[18] Translating the apostolic briefs and documents into Persian was no easy task. Certainly there were Portuguese who spoke Persian, but they were usually not in Lisbon and for that reason it was decided eventually that an Armenian would translate them when they reached Hormuz.[19]

The man chosen to take the documents to Persia was don Miguel de Abreu, a Portuguese noble who had lived in India for many years. He would embark in one of the vessels that were to leave Lisbon in the month of March. In the instructions for Abreu, the king of Portugal ordered that, for the sake of all, he was to convince the shah to attack the Turks immediately since, further to the victory of Lepanto, the Christian allies would continue their fight in new fronts. The emperor and Poland would attack from Hungary, and the king of Portugal from India. Now a new front needed to be opened from the Red Sea and from Hormuz to cause the greatest damage possible and, as the instruction mentioned, 'que le faça toda la guerra que poder sea' (to wage war with all means available). Portuguese India had no doubts that it would so be done. The aim was to achieve on all possible fronts the total destruction of the Turks: 'sua total destruição'. The Christian princes were certain that they would find an ally in the shah with whom they would have friendship and trade.[20] Abreu would first travel to Goa, the Portuguese capital in India, from where the viceroy would grant him everything needed to continue his journey to Hormuz and from there to Persia.

It is true that King Sebastian was prepared to participate in the league against the Turks and to enter the war for Asia and the Red Sea by sending an army supported by Abyssinians, Arabs and Egyptians. He had ordered the readying of a great army of 4,000 men to support the Holy League in those territories. But before they embarked on this military adventure the king wanted the Dutch Calvinists who threatened his dominions to be neutralized. He knew that nearly 70 vessels were being prepared to attack the Portuguese in Brazil. Aside from the question of how to respond to the

Calvinist mobilization, doubts remained about whether it was strategically advisable to send 4,000 men to Asia. Some argued that it would be better to maximize the resources available to the Holy League and to direct all available forces to an attack on the very heart of the Ottoman Empire. The Venetian ambassador Tiepolo reasoned that these men would be better employed in the Mediterranean, rather than in such far away places, and therefore he requested the Portuguese authorities to indicate exactly the number of soldiers they would send 'non nelle parte delle Indie, ma delle parte d'Europa' (not from India but from Europe).[22] Don Sebastian decided that, for Christendom, the best he could send was 6,000 men to Asia, that it would be of little benefit for the league to send a reduced army to the Mediterranean. Don Juan of Austria, captain general of the allied forces of the Holy League, was also in favour of King Sebastian sending his army to Asia because the 2,000 soldiers, at the most, for the Mediterranean front would be nothing compared with the 6,000 who would come from Asia. Thereafter the Arabs and Persians would revolt little by little at the sight of Portuguese troops.[23]

The pontifical documents arrived in the hands of the Spanish ambassador in Lisbon – don Juan Borgia (son of Francis Borgia) – 12 hours after the vessels heading to India set sail from the port of Lisbon, early in the morning of 18 March 1572. All the diplomatic efforts seemed to have been in vain. However, several moves were made to ensure that those documents reached the hands of their cosignatories via the ambassadors. There is no evidence of how this was achieved, although there is a certain amount of information suggesting that the mission was successful.

On his side, Jesuit Matías Bicudo endeavoured on all possible fronts to ensure that Christian forces allied themselves with the Persians to attack the Ottomans. It is known that in 1571 he had already proposed to the viceroy of Sicily the establishment of negotiations with a distinguished gentleman of Cairo.[24] The proposal was successful because don Juan of Austria communicated to the king that he had sent to Egypt two spies that Bicudo had recommended.[25] At that time the Society of Jesus had already had several important apostolic missions in those territories. The first Jesuits in Egypt, Miguel de Nóbrega (1552–3) and Fulgencio Freire (1560–3), lived like slaves. Between 1561 and 1564 fathers Cristóbal Rodríguez and Giovanni Battista Eliano remained in Egypt as apostolic legates to the Coptic patriarch Gabriel VII with the intention of achieving unification between the Coptic and Roman churches. Bicudo was aware of these moves and envisaged a possible Coptic alliance in their fight against the Turks. We have no more news about the spies sent by Juan de Austria but there are records showing that one decade later the new patriarch, John XIV, was more inclined towards the union, hence Gregory XIII sent a new mission between 1582 and 1584 with expert Jesuits, fathers Francesco Sasso and Giovanni Battista Eliano. Although the Council of Menfis took place, it ended in controversy and failure, with the imprisonment of the Jesuits on 21 September 1584. They were released the following year.

While the Holy League lasted (1571–3) the Spanish politicians realized the need for the shah and other princes to join the confederation. It is possible that similar letters were sent to the duke of Moscow, to the king of Poland and to the Christian provinces of the Black Sea. Don Juan of Austria, at least, wrote to this effect to the Christians of Rhodes seeking the alliance of the Greeks of Maina.[26]

It is also known that in Rome Cardinal Amulio, Venetian ambassador to the Holy See, had an understanding with Matías Bicudo that was starting to raise suspicions amongst the Spaniards. He had planned an almost perfect scheme to seize Alexandria. The idea was also presented to the Spanish Cardinal Gaspar de Quiroga who, in turn, presented it to Philip II. No sooner had the sovereign heard the plan than he openly endorsed it. The king had personally seen the Portuguese Father Bicudo and believed he was trustworthy and, although he could not make a final decision about the proposal, Bicudo was right in what concerned the purposes of the enemy army and therefore he had to be taken into account for missions in the Orient. Philip II was in favour of the project but did not wish to leave any trace of his decision. The answer he gave to Quiroga was not registered in the chancery nor was the secretary, Antonio Pérez, aware of it. To the contrary, his answer was stamped in his own hand in Quiroga's very letter; the sovereign even wrote on the back: 'To the care of the Bishop', which was unusual for him. Indeed, the 'Prudent King' accepted the plan unconditionally, but he also wanted to know the opinion of his counsellors who were better informed about the events on the ground; this meant that the opinions and economic resources coming from Rome, Naples and Sicily needed to be set aside. Hence, Philip II was not acting on his own for 'with the wisdom and the caution of these three [Cardinal Quiroga, Cardinal Granvela and the marquis of Pescara] eventually some monies could be raised from there'. However, the plan was stopped precisely because the three of them did not consider it viable and Matías Bicudo was losing his reputation.[27]

The pontificate of Gregory XIII (1572-85)

Thus far we have seen how don Sebastian of Portugal sent an embassy to Shah Tahmasp of Persia through Miguel de Abreu de Lima, who also represented Pope Pius V, King Philip II and the doge of Venice.[28] Little is known about Abreu's mission. Robert Gulbenkian doubted he ever reached the Safavid capital. However, Augustinian Melchor de los Angeles reports that the mission was accomplished, although with limited success.[29]

Several years after the initiatives of the Holy League of 1571, at the insistence of Matías Bicudo, don Juan de Austria, decided on his own to send an embassy to Persia making use of the Greek Marcos Trastopulo, Luis de Portillo and the bishop of Stonj, who resided in Ragusa with Matías Bicudo.[30] Diplomatic preparations began and the proposal was sent to the ambassadors in Rome and Lisbon. In July 1573 the ambassador in Rome awaited the early arrival of Matías Bicudo with the aim of proposing to the new pope, Gregory XIII, that Luis de Portillo and the bishop of Stonj travel to Persia and Moscow. After the arrangements were completed an important last minute change in plans occurred which was not communicated to the Pope but only to the Greek, Marcos Trastopulo. The reason for this is still not clear, although it is thought that Juan de Austria did not consider the other two reliable enough. Bicudo arrived at Ragusa in the summer of 1575 and was able to establish an agent in Constantinople to inform him of the activities of the sultan and, as soon as he arrived, the agent started to prepare for his mission as secret agent in Persia.[31]

As for Abreu's mission in 1572, there are reliable sources that in November of 1576 the pontifical collector from Portugal communicated to the cardinal of Como that the preceding month a certain Horacio de Milan had returned from India. He had been imprisoned by the Turks during the siege at Famagusta in 1570 but had managed to escape to Persia where, in Casbin, he found a jeweller by the name of Mario Greco who accompanied the Portuguese ambassador sent to Persia by the Pope and King Philip II. Thereafter, Horacio de Milan returned to Europe by way of Hormuz and Goa. It appears that Mario Greco had an audience with the shah and then returned to Rome. Possibly, the ambassador referred to in this document was Abreu and Mario Greco was an envoy of Gregory XIII and Philip II charged with learning the results of the negotiations that started during the pontificate of Pius V.

We have a long passage dated December 1575 concerning what happened to a Hispanic-Portuguese-Pontifical embassy to Persia that confirms our suspicions. It is the mission of Francisco de Barros, sent in 1572; he was possibly a replacement for Abreu, but he had no success as the shah did not wish to establish an alliance. This prompted a report that a well-informed secretary in the Spanish chancery included in a marginal note on matters relating to the Orient, which we think is worthwhile transcribing for it provides specific details of Abreu's mission:

> Este embajador [Abreu] fue enviado por parte de Su Santidad, el rey nuestro señor y el rey de Portugal, al cual el Sr. Don Juan envió un hombre y cédula de 12.000 ducados para si hubiera menester dineros, y se partió de Portugal y se detuvo como dos años en llegar, y llegó el 26 de febrero de 1575, y el embajador llegó cuando éste partió de Hormuz. Que le tenían al embajador del rey en Casbin muy apretado y maltratado en una casilla que no se puede habitar y que el sobrino del rey, que es el que gobierna por ser el rey viejo, que se maravillaba cómo un rey tan grande como el de Portugal no había enviado al rey Xatamas [Tahmasp] que es tan poderoso que llega a los cielos presente de dos cuentos de oro. Y parece ser que llegó presente hasta de 16.000 ducados en dinero y joyas y piezas de ellas, se las devolvieron con una cama que valdría 500 o 600 ducados, la cual tiene consigo el embajador ... le mataron un criado armenio que era su comprador ... y estaba para matar al embajador y todos sus hombres que serían 20, y de miedo uno de ellos se tornó moro ... y que la causa dicen porque querían al embajador era porque había entrado en la mezquita de Hormuz y quemado los libros que allí había, y que el embajador respondió que porque ellos habían quebrado la cruz de la iglesia que los portugueses querían hacer, y que ellos respondieron que por causa de aquel palo habían de hacer aquel daño en la mezquita, y que el

embajador había dicho que por aquel palo habían sido redimidos los cristianos y que le habían dejado y se había tratado otra cosa y le tenían detenido allí. Que este rey es el rey de Persia. Que el rey de Persia le recibió muy bien y que después que le vio y entendió su embajada, que era para que rompiese guerra, se agravió y comenzó a hacer maltratamiento sin responder ni decirle nada a su embajada, y no se vio más con el rey ni le habló, sino a un sobrino.[32]

In 1576 king Philip II also sent to Persia an Armenian emissary, a Juan Bautista, who would also meet the shah. Meanwhile, in Persia, Tahmasp died in 1576 and, after a succession dispute during which several claimants briefly occupied the throne, Mohammad Khodabande finally succeeded (1577-87). He was considered a weak man. The Turkish sultan Murad III decided to attack Persia directly in 1578, prompting a series of defeats for the Persians. An emissary of the shah went to Portugal in 1579 to seek help. But the reality was that until 1580 Philip II had enjoyed a certain degree of peace with the Turks, mainly due to truces.[33] These truces were, to a certain extent, forced since the Turks had to challenge the Persians and Philip II had to confront the different pressures from England and France. The Turkish military companies transferred to the land.[34] Overall, there were sufficient notices alerting the Catholic king that in the summer the Turks would attack Spain with 300 galleys, which would entail more expense. These were confusing notices for it was known that in reality the Ottomans did not want to start a direct attack but rather, at most, to pursue skirmishes and to get Philip II to continue spending his wealth in defending himself from possible attacks. In any case, a well-informed confidant said that it was essential to be careful for one could not trust the promises of such foolish people as the Ottomans, let alone their good faith.[35] There were attempts at Hispanic-Persian cooperation that we must mention, albeit briefly. In 1582 Frei Simao de Moiras, prior of the Augustinian convent of Hormuz, handed the shah letters from Philip II, again proposing an alliance with the Turks.[36] This time the shah was inclined towards the exchange of ambassadors. The French resident in Madrid, Monsieur de Longlée, informed Paris in 1583 of the announcement of the arrival of a Persian embassy to Lisbon. A new diplomatic way seemed to be opening which could be useful. A few years later, in 1586, news of battles between the Turks and the Persians reached Europe. The Spanish poet Andrés Flores wrote verses about the Spanish feelings favouring the Persians, friends of the Christians. It was fantastic propaganda propitiating the view of everyone and referring to Persia with renewed interest. The poem asserts that, once the Ottomans were defeated, the Persians would distribute the booty:

> Tanta de la artillería
> tanto oro y plata labrada
> tanta joya y pedrería
> todo lo cual repartía
> con gente esforzada.

> Especial a los cristianos
> repartió gran cantidad
> que los quieren los persianos
> como si fueren hermanos
> y los muestra su amistad.

So much artillery/ so much carved gold/ so many jewels and precious stones/ all of them distributed by bravehearts/ especially to the Christians/ to whom he gave in such abundance/ that the Persians love them like brothers/ and so prove their friendship.

These verses were printed in Valencia and Burgos in 1586 and contributed to increasing the myth of all that related to Persia. Not more than four years later historian Antonio Herrera from Tordesillas chose a current event to gain the confidence of the king. He translated the works of Juan Tomas Minadoi (1540–1615) with the title *History of the War between Turks and Persians*, from Italian. The work had appeared for the first time in Rome in 1587 and it described the battles that took place between 1576 and 1585 with maps, names, and so on and printed at the works of Francisco Sánchez in Madrid in 1588. It was exaggerated propaganda in favour of the Persians, which originated in the court itself, for it was dedicated to the royal secretary Juan de Idiáquez, one of Philip II's most reliable men. It led to new and particularly memorable Spanish missions to the far-off court of Abbas I, which were to take place in the following reign.[37]

As for Matías Bicudo there is confirmation that, as of 1584, he was in contact with the French ambassador in Venice. He had abandoned the Society of Jesus and joined the Franciscan order and furthermore he had become a great defender of Portuguese independence from the Hispanic monarchy.[38] During that year he served the prior of Crato, don Antonio of Portugal, claimant to the Portuguese crown and therefore enemy of Philip II. He was sent by don Antonio of Portugal to Constantinople and travelled through France where he contacted a Jewish spy in the service of France by the name of Saul Cohen.[39] He secretly stopped in Venice but as soon as he was discovered, Philip II, through his ambassador in Venice, immediately ordered that all necessary steps be taken to make him a prisoner.[40] There were then a series of unfruitful attempts to extract him from Venice and to imprison him.[41]

Despite all these disappointments, the Holy See sought to send an ambassador to Persia. In 1584 Gregory XIII, inspired by Cardinal Ferdinand of Medici, requested the Florentine knight Giovanni Battista Vecchietti to go on an important mission to Persia. He was to convince the shah to persevere in the war against the Turks, promising military help from the Pope and Philip II. The king of Spain had already entrusted a similar mission to the Augustinian Father Simón de Moiras. The Pope finally sent a short accreditation to the shah dated 28 February 1584. One of its main missions was to obtain manuscripts in Arabic, Persian and Turkish.[42] Vecchietti arrived in Hormuz on 29 June 1587, fulfilled his mission carefully and returned to Italy passing through Madrid in 1589 to inform the king. It is known that the shah gave him a precious letter – written in golden letters, except for the shah's signature, as a gesture of humbleness – in which he wrote that he required two expert artillerymen, two architects to build fortresses and two sergeant majors who were expert cavalry tacticians. These demands were all-important since the shah was well aware of the military inferiority of his army. Shortly thereafter the Shirley brothers arrived, one of whom, Antonio, seems to have collaborated in the organization of the Persian army.[43]

Vecchietti carried with him a good number of Arabic books, amongst which was a Bible in Arabic that he left in Egypt the following year whilst on a pontifical mission. Gregory XIII took an interest in those books and instructed the Jesuit father of Jewish ancestry Giovanni Battista Eliano, an apostolic legate, to purchase them. The books cost 300 escudos.[44] Vecchietti returned to Persia in 1601; thereafter he stayed in Hormuz and became political counsel to the viceroy of Portugal Diego Núñez until 1603; subsequently he went to India. In Jaipur he became sick but was lodged and protected by the Jesuit Father Francesco, a Florentine like him, who had mastered the Persian language. This Jesuit was born in 1568, had joined the Order in 1587, was sent to Goa in 1599, and then was dispatched on a diplomatic mission to the Great Mogul of India.[45] He died in 1633 after 36 years of apostolic services in India. He was preceptor to the nephews of Emperor Jahangir in Uttar Pradesh and chaplain to the Armenian Prince Mirza Zu'lqarnayn, a soldier in the service of the Great Mogul. Having survived a number of risky adventures, Giovan Battista Vecchietti was able to return to Rome in October where he worked at the Oriental Library. He died on 8 December 1619.

It is worth pointing out that one of the instructions he had received from the Cardinal of Florence was to acquire in Persia books in Arabic, Arabic grammars in Persian and Turkish and vice-versa, and to obtain a book in Persian and Arabic with beautiful characters. He was passionate in his search for the Bible in Persian in 1606 he wrote to the Pope from Isfahan that he hoped to all the books of the New Testament in some city of Persia where Christians had resided, although he had already gotten hold of the Gospels in Persian. The future Pope Paul V, Camillo Borghese, met Vecchietti in Madrid when he was extraordinary nuncio in that court in 1593 and for several months they discussed the importance of Persia in the international context. Vecchietti's dreams had come true; he had learnt correct Persian and was translating the book of Esther, a Persian queen.[46]

The pontificate of Sixtus V (1585-90)

The Turks were at war against the Persians from 1578 to 1590, the Ottoman Empire gained dominion over Georgia, Yerevan and most of Armenia. The apogee of Murat III (1574-95) coincided with the decline of Muhammad Khodabande (1578-88).[47] This crisis would also have consequences for the Hispanic monarchy. In 1582 Philip II had asked the viceroy of India to reiterate the previous offerings to Shah Tahmasp, but he died in 1576 and was succeeded by Haidar Mirza who was assassinated that same year. Thereafter Khudabanda reigned. This demonstrates the great ignorance there was in Spain about the events taking place in Persia; the only important matter for them was to prevent the Turks going to war against Spain. The viceroy in Naples accepted the proposal by Philip II and again sent Juan Bautista with a personal letter and an emissary of his own. They arrived in India where the new viceroy, don Francisco de Mascareñas had been instructed to initiate negotiations with the shah. For this reason the viceroy requested the Augustinian Fra Simón de la Concepción de Moraes, who spoke Persian, to go to the shah's court to finally agree on an alliance. Fra Simón asked Gregory XIII to unite the Christian princes in the fight against the Turks at the same time as he narrated his mission in Persia. Shah Tahmasp appointed him his son's preceptor since he was an expert mathematician. The shah decided to send him off to the court of Philip II together with a Persian ambassador but the vessel taking them to Europe sank in 1585, although it is also possible, according to another version, that Fra Simón was poisoned by the Armenian accompanying them.[48]

In the heart of the Turkish Empire there was great fear of the Persians. More precisely, they were worried about the heavy expenses incurred. It could well be said that Persia represented for the Ottoman Empire what Flanders represented for Philip II, or Candia for the doge of Venice, or Ireland for Elisabeth I, precisely because the expenses incurred in defending and occupying those territories were enormous and the revenue tiny. Furthermore, the Turks no longer wanted the help of the Tatars, who had lost all hope that the Turks were about to start a war against the Muscovites in exchange for their help in fighting the Persians, as narrated in a letter addressed to Pope Sixtus V from a pontifical spy who had infiltrated the Turkish army fighting in Persia. The Turks, left with no cavalry because of the 'lunga e faticosa guerra di Persia' (the long and exhausting war with Persia), feared the military strength of the Georgians and the Muscovites who, if they united, could take Syria and Egypt. Furthermore, they had lost the alliance with the Tatars, as they were unable to attack Moscow. For this reason they sought peace with the Persians. But Murat II mostly feared Philip II rather than the shah for his potential to bribe the Ottoman military commanders.[49] Shortly thereafter, in 1601, the Persian ambassador Antonio Sherley would propose to Clement VIII an attack on Syria or Palestine, on account of their supposed vulnerability and in order to open up a war front where the troops of the shah could also be deployed.[50]

The Persian-Hispanic climate of understanding favoured the settlement of Augustinians in Persia, particularly since the accession to the throne of Abbas I in 1587, who established the capital in Isfahan. The aim was to take advantage in Europe of the bitter rivalry between the Persians and Turks, as had already been tried in the past. The new Shah Abbas, soon after ascending the throne, had to sign a peace treaty with the Ottomans in 1590, thereby losing a great portion of his north-western territories. Then the Armenians decided to ask the Holy See and the king of Spain for help. They wished to receive military reinforcements and in return were prepared to accept vassalage to the Pope and the king of Spain as well as receiving missionaries who would bring the Catholic faith. They promised to cooperate to regain the holy places in Palestine and Constantinople. This was not at all new; a similar situation can be found in Greece, Tunisia and even in Ireland. All were ready to become good Catholic vassals to the king of Spain. However, words were one thing and deeds another.

The pontificate of Clement VIII (1592–1605)

Despite the failure of previous missions, Philip II persevered in his aim of achieving a Persian alliance. In 1594 he instructed Matías de Albuquerque, viceroy of India to send an embassy to Shah Abbas I, thus agreeing to his wish to maintain diplomatic correspondence. Two years later he did the same with the new viceroy, don Francisco de Gama, although this time insisting on the fact that the envoy should be a noble, someone with the same qualities as Abreu, who had been sent by don Sebastian in 1571. The new Pope was attentive to these moves and well aware of the importance of counting on the support of the religious who had gone to those places: Augustinians, Jesuits and Franciscans. Clement VIII wanted finally to establish the Catholic mission in Persia.

The establishment of the Catholic missions in Persia was determined by the arrival of two Portuguese clerics in Isfahan, the Franciscan Alonso Cordero and the Augustinian Nicolás de Melo, and the presence of the Jesuit Father Francisco de Acosta. In 1599 Nicolás de Melo sent the interpreter Angelo to Europe. He was an Armenian who had worked for the duke of Mantua. Angelo was sent to alert the Pope, Philip III and the viceroy of India that the shah would send an embassy to the Christian princes to sign a defensive alliance. In 1598 he had defeated the Uzbeks in the province of Khorasan, and Qazvin was no longer the capital, which had been moved to Isfahan.

The clerics met there with the Sherley brothers who were involved in the diplomatic and military affairs of the shah. In 1599, Abbas I decided to send to the Pope and the Catholic princes an embassy lead by Hosayn 'Ali Beg and Antonio Sherley with the aim of consummating the coalition. With them was the Augustinian Father Nicolás de Melo. The journey lasted more than two years; they crossed Russia to Europe and on their way they began to suspect the hidden motives of Antonio Sherley. The negotiations concerning the anti-Turk league took place in Prague, Rome and Valladolid. In Rome the Pope decided to separate the ambassadors: Sherley was to return to Persia – in fact, he ended up remaining in Venice – whilst Hosayn was to travel to Spain and return to Persia from Lisbon.[51] In Valladolid, Hosayn was treated very well; he attended the baptism of the Spanish infanta; received a gift of 2,000 escudos, a chain worth 600 and four more worth 200 escudos to distribute to his favourite travelling companions, together with another 8,000 escudos for his return voyage. According to our witness, he left 'very pleased'.⁵²

At almost the same time the shah sent his emissaries, Francisco de Acosta and captain don Diego de Miranda who had been in Persia, to Rome to inform the Pope of the shah's good intentions towards Christianity. The truth is that in 1600 the Pope elected Francisco de Acosta and captain Diego de Miranda to go to Persia as ambassadors, which prompted a disagreement with Vecchietti, who accused Francisco de Acosta of having abandoned the Society of Jesus 'prete vagante' (priest without canonical permission) in Lisbon and Miranda of being an Indian, born in Hormuz, who had married a public prostitute in Rome. Despite the criticisms, the cardinal of Como decided to send three emissaries to Persia: the Spaniard Luis Félix, the Portuguese Francisco Acosta and Diego de Miranda.⁵³

With respect to the Persian legation, and to make a point about the contribution of the Society of Jesus, we need to draw attention to the fact that upon his arrival in Prague, Antonio Sherley, an Anglican, asked the nuncio to provide him with a confessor for he wished to return to Catholicism. The nuncio put him in contact with a Spanish Jesuit, Pedro de Buiza, a man of 'molto valore' (a man of great courage) – in the nuncio's opinion – and 'well known in the court' – as the ambassador to Prague told the king. He was a theologian with great diplomatic virtues. Sherley did not want the confessor to be a French or English Jesuit, but a Spaniard. It appears the two understood each other well and became friends.⁵⁴ In Rome he also befriended some English Jesuits, counsellors to Philip III, Robert Persons (1546–1610) and Joseph Creswell (1556–1623). The ambassador to Rome – the duke of Sessa – informed the king by way of a coded letter that Sherley and Persons were good friends. Sherley would not stop mentioning everywhere that the shah was prepared to cooperate with 60,000 infantrymen and as many cavalrymen in the fight against the Turks. In exchange, he requested specific cooperation, exchange of ambassadors, freedom of trade, military support and in particular that the bars of iron arriving at Hormuz be longer to allow the manufacture of swords according to the measures customary to the Persians.

According to what Francisco de Acosta told the Pope, Abbas I, who was the son and husband of Christians, seemed inclined to Christianity. His wife was the daughter of Simon Causeno – whose lineage could be traced back to the Kings of Georgia – and Allahverdi Khan was a friend to the Christians. The Jesuit wrote a long report about Persia that he handed to the ambassador in Rome, the duke of Sessa, who in turn sent it to Philip III.⁵⁵ On the other hand, Acosta held lengthy conversations with some Spanish Jesuits in Rome, with Bartolomé Pérez and Juan Álvarez, Spanish and Portuguese assistants to Father Acquaviva, and with Father Sebastian Rodríguez. The decision-making authorities of the Society of Jesus had doubts about Acosta's true intentions for he seemed too inclined towards the shah's military plan. Francisco de Acosta left the Society in 1598, although he was readmitted when he was sent as ambassador to Persia, for he had a duty to send to Persia, via Hormuz, a good number of Jesuits coming from India.[56]

In 1601 Pope Clement VIII was enthusiastic about the embassy and sent a diplomatic mission to Acosta in his capacity as legate *a latere* before Abbas. Acquaviva, on his side, was to obtain support from Philip III to facilitate Jesuit access to Persia. It must be taken into account that in 1600 Phillip III had already sent three Augustinians to Persia to ask the shah to pursue the war against the Turks, which is why royal favour to Jesuits caused some distrust amongst the Augustinians. The antipathy of the Augustinians towards the Jesuit mission was such that the archbishop of Braga, the Augustinian Agustín de Castro, threatened the king to stop favouring the Jesuit mission in Persia. The Augustinians thought they had exclusive rights because they had started their mission in Hormuz in 1571 when the Jesuits had abandoned the place because of its unsanitary conditions. In 1572 there were no fewer than 12 Augustinians in Hormuz and Goa, as a matter of fact they had established houses in Bandar Abbas, in Muscat and other places. The ambassadors sent by Philip II had been Augustinians, like Father Simón de Moraes. The progress of the order had been enormous, such that in 1600 they had more than 200 members. Sending Jesuits rather than Augustinians could be taken as an insult.[57] In short, due to the pressure he was under the king did not authorize the sending of Jesuits. Nevertheless, Acosta went to Persia accompanied by the soldier Diego de Miranda, although they parted in disagreement. Only Acosta reached Isfahan. He was presented by the Augustinians residing there as the apostolic legate. He became military counsellor to the shah and participated in the military campaigns against the Turks. This fact, which the shah himself disclosed in a letter to the Pope, reveals the military merits of Acosta. He was probably related to the Persian general Allahverdi Khan, who was considered a friend of the Christians.[58]

The preliminary arrangements for Acosta's legation were swiftly made but they did not, however, forget to point out that it was of the utmost importance to establish a permanent Jesuit mission in Hormuz, despite Philip III's opposition. Yet the Jesuits and Augustinians were not the only ones to report on the situation in Persia to the Pope, other reports came from different quarters. Since 1582 an Armenian by the name of Thomas, who mastered the Persian language, was working at the Vatican Library. When the embassy of Hosayn 'Ali Beg arrived he was appointed their interpreter. Besides, the Pope wanted Thomas to accompany the ambassador on his mission to Spain and Portugal as interpreter despite the fact that the ambassador himself spoke Turkish and that there was an official Turkish interpreter in Spain. It is known that during his stay in Spain the Persian's translator was not Thomas but Diego de Urrea. One of Hosayn's objectives in Lisbon was to ship back to Persia a significant amount of arms, which was permitted by the king. Four members of the ambassadorial party converted to Catholicism and subsequently remained in Spain and their Muslim 'chaplain' was killed in Merida.

Philip III's counsel of state determined in March of 1602 that, in response to Hosayn 'Ali Beg's embassy, once he had spoken to the provincial of the order of Castille, a Jesuit chosen by the cardinal of Seville was to be sent, together with a Portuguese noble, don Luis Pereyra de la Cerda. Nothing is known about the Jesuit, most likely he was not able to depart due to Augustinian opposition. However, we do know that in 1603 Luis Pereyra departed for Persia where he arrived the following year.[59] Given the great tensions between Augustinians and Jesuits the Pope was inclined to send some Capuchins to Persia as well to allow the Catholic mission a greater chance of success.[60] It was all getting complicated with the many different, individual interests of Jesuits, Augustinians, Capuchins and Carmelites; together with the tensions between the ambassadors and the Spaniards and the Portuguese. They did not realize that they were placing the prospective Persian alliance at risk.

On the other hand, it must also be taken into account that in 1600 Philip III had already sent three Augustinians to Persia to request the shah to pursue the war against the Turks. But the political and religious situation in Persia changed when a Carmelite mission, sent by Clement VIII, arrived in 1601. The Pope cancelled Acosta's mission when he learnt that he had acted with little fidelity to his instructions. The confusion was such that it could be said that no mission was safe. But on the Persian side something similar was happening. Their different embassies ended in failure due to the division of their members, such as the separation between Hosayn 'Ali Beg and Antonio Sherley who were growing further apart.[61]

Nevertheless, the shah, who gradually began to notice the religious divisions between the Spanish and Portuguese, decided to send Acosta as ambassador to Rome in 1605, where he arrived in 1607 via Moscow.[62] But it was all too late. In 1606 the emperor had signed a truce with the Turks and Philip III would not support the Persians in open warfare, either in the Mediterranean or in the Persian Gulf. The following year relations further deteriorated to the extent that the shah announced that he was prepared to expel the religious, persecute his Christian vassals and take Hormuz.

In 1614 the news arriving in Spain confirmed that Christians, Armenians and Syrians were being persecuted and that the Carmelites and Augustinians had left Persia. When the religious orders returned to Isfahan the tensions between Carmelites and Augustinians continued. There were several prominent incidents that reverberated in Spain through publications in 1611 and in 1624.[63] The main event was when the shah fulfilled his threat and, with English help, took Hormuz in 1622. In August of that same year a public auction took place in London to sell the goods seized during the conquest of Hormuz, which contributed to the increasing distrust that was building up in Madrid in relation to the possible wedding of the Prince of Wales to a Spanish infanta (princess).[64]

The clues to a political interpretation of these changes stem from two aspects. On one side the tensions between Augustinians and Carmelites and the distorting element of Francisco de Acosta; on the other, the constant disputes between the Spaniards and the Portuguese. In sum, the Augustinians confronted the Jesuits and the Spanish Carmelites confronted the Portuguese Augustinians. It should be noted that it was the shah who, in 1608, requested the help of the Christian powers, an appeal which once again led to the exchange of a number of embassies. The Carmelites arrived in 1607 and their apostolate with the Armenian Christians, Antonio de Gouvea, was the one who did the most to achieve the union of the Armenians.[65]

Conclusion

From the early-1570s Safavid sovereigns, the Habsburgs and successive popes explored the possibility of a common policy with regard to a common enemy. Contact between Persians and Spaniards was advanced by a number of Catholics such as Gaspar de Berze, Francisco de Acosta, Alonso Cordero, Nicolás de Melo and others. The dialogue that they began embraced a number of themes of great importance: Persian policies towards the Christian minorities within their domains and their common fight against the Ottoman Turks were addressed, as were the limits of the territorial and commercial expansion of the European powers in Asia. True, there are elements of this history which remain difficult to measure and others where the personal interests or prejudices of the diplomats predominated, such as in the tendency of some religious to advance (improbable) military schemes.

It has been the objective of this chapter to underline the importance of the role of a number of Jesuits in the approach to the Safavid shahs. Taking his lead from Pius V, Francisco de Borgia was in favour of the military alliance with 'the Persian'; however, he was sceptical about the more ambitious proposals advanced by some of his colleagues. Matías Bicudo and Francisco de Acosta, in contrast, were drawn to more extreme measures. These men were true crusaders. They did not limit themselves to mere apostolic activities or initiatives and readily involved themselves in military matters, espionage and plans for the conquest and division of Ottoman domains. The same outlook could be found in Persons and Creswell, the two Jesuits who contacted Antonio Sherley.

These Jesuits were, of course, exceptional figures, but the very fact that their letters, proposals, reports and pleas are to be found in the General Archive of Simancas gives an indication that their initiatives commanded attention in the highest echelons of political and military government in Spain. Their legacy was far from negligible, although it took a form that would have surprised and, perhaps, disappointed them. In the following century the Society of Jesus would take a different path, for the missionaries who succeeded in establishing themselves in Iran in 1648 were neither Portuguese nor Spanish. Instead, it was Frenchmen such as François Rigordi, Aimé Chezaud and Alexandre de Rhodes who marched forward as Christian soldiers into the heart of the Persian world.

Notes

1. Since the original preparation of this chapter, a number of important works have been published which cast further light on the area. Enrique García Hernán, 'The Persian Gentlemen at the Spanish Court in the Early Senventeenth Century', Jorge Flores – Ruddi Matthee (eds), *Portugal, the Persian Gulf and Safavid Persia* (Leuven, Peeters, 2011), pp. 283–300; Rafael Valladares, *Castilla y Portugal en Asia (1580-1680). Declive imperial y adaptación* (Leuven University Press, 2001); Luis Gil Fernández, *El Imperio Luso-Español y la Persia Safávida, Tomo I (1582–1605), Tomo II (1606–1622)*, (Madrid, FUE, 2006–2009). I have also published a shortened Castilian version of it, 'Persia en la acción conjunta del papado y la Monarquía Hispánica. Aproximación a la actuación de la Compañía de Jesús (1549–1649)', *Hispania Sacra* 73 (2010), pp. 213–241. On the Ottoman-Safavid conflict see A. Allouche, *The Origins and Development of the Ottoman-Safavid Conflict (906-962/1500-1555)* (Berlín, 1983); J. L. Bacqué-Grammont, *Les Ottomans, les Safavides et leur voisins*, (Estambul, 1987), y *The Persian Presence in the Islamic World*, edited by Richard G. Hovannisian and Georges Sabagh (Cambridge, Cambridge University Press, 1998). On the Catholic Church in Iran and its missionary activities, see Carlos Alonso, 'Clemente VIII y la fundación de las misiones católicas en Persia. Un capítulo previo a la penetración de los misioneros agustinos', *La Ciudad de Dios* 171 (1958) 196–239; Angelo Bugnini, *La Chiesa in Iran* (Roma, 1981); V. Preiss, *De restauratione missionum in Persia saec. XVII Poloniaeque partibus* (Diss. PUUrbanian, Roma, 1936). J. Escalera, 'Irán', in Ch. E. O'Neill – J. M. Domínguez, *Diccionario Histórico de la Compañía de Jesús* (Roma-Madrid, IHSI, 2001, 4 vols), IV, pp. 2066–2067. Concerning the following century, I am researching on other religious orders, such as Augustinians and Carmelites.
2. Georg Schurhammer, *Francisco Javier, su vida y su tiempo*, IV vol. IV, (Pamplona, 1992), pp. 484–519.
3. J. Aubin, 'Le royaume d'Hormuz au début du XVIe siècle', *Mare Luso-Indicum* 2 (Ginebra, 1973), pp. 77–179. Niels Steensgaard, *The Asian Trade Revolution of the Seventeenth Century* (Chicago, 1974); *Diccionario Histórico de la Compañía de Jesús* (Madrid-Roma, 2002), I, p. 427. See also N. Trigault, *Vita Gasparis Barzaei Belgae* (Antuerpiae, 1610 y Douai 1615).
4. AGS. E. 385, 54, 58, 59. Maximilian II to shah; instruction to Jacobo Draperis, 'lo que el emperador escribe sobre la embajada de Persia' y 'Apuntamientos del emperador sobre la embajada del persiano'. The ambassador en Lisbon was don Alonso de Tovar, see his 'Relación del viaje de Portugal a Persia, 7 enero 1567', en AGS. E. 385, 55. The king of Portugal was in contact with the shah through the viceroy of India and the captain of Hormuz. The fleet sailed from Lisbon to Goa once each year in March or April, and the convoy went from Goa to Hormuz in November–December and again towards the end of March. The journey in winter passed through India to Hormuz, and in spring through Rosalgate. Both involved a month of travel.
5. Carlos Alonso, 'Embajadores de Persia en las cortes de Praga, Roma y Valladolid (1600–1601)', *Anthologica Annua* 36 (1989), pp. 11–271; Carlos Alonso, *La embajada a Persia de D. García de Silva y Figueroa (1612-1624)* (Badajoz, 1993). On Spain and Persia see B. Alonso Acero, *Sultanes de Berbería en tierras de la cristiandad. Exilio musulmán, conversión y asimilación en la Monarquía hispánica (siglos XVI-XVII)* (Barcelona, Bellaterra, 2006); Mas, A., *Les Turcs dans la littérature espagnole du Siècle d'Or* (París, 1967), y Bunes Ibarra, Miguel Ángel de, *La imagen de los musulmanes en la España de los siglos XVI-XVII. Los caracteres de una hostilidad* (Madrid, 1989).
6. José María Floristán Imízcoz, *Fuentes para la política oriental de los Austrias: la documentación griega del Archivo de Simancas, 1571-1621* (León, 1986); A. G. Hess, *The Forgotten Frontier* (Chicago, 1978); C. Rodríguez Joulian de Saint-Cyr, *Felipe III y el rey del Cuco* (Madrid, 1954).
7. AGS. E. 493. Cristóbal de Moura to Philip III, Lisbon, 27-X-1601. 'Y así las veces que el rey, que haya gloria, le escribió, nunca trató de otra cosa que de animarle contra el turco y ofrecerle que por acá sería gallardamente ayudado, para que todos en un mismo tiempo hiciesen daño al enemigo común'. Vid. Alonso, 'Embajadores de Persia'.
8. Carlos Alonso, 'Nueva documentación inédita sobre las misiones agustinianas en la India y en Persia (1571–1609)', *Archivo Agustiniano* 33 (1970), pp. 253–7; P. Z. Novoa, 'El M.R.P. Fr. Melchor de los Ángeles,

agustino, primer misionero en Persia', en *Archivo Agustiniano* 45 (1951), pp. 263–75; Enrique García Hernán, 'Pío V y el mesianismo profético', *Hispania Sacra* 45 (1993), pp. 83–102.

9. ASV. Miscell. Arm. II, 82, 392. 'Conferirete il tutto co' il sudetto P. Generale, governandovi secondo il suo consiglio, parlando con chi a sua paternità reverenda parerà a proposito et expediente'. See Enrique García Hernán, *La acción diplomática de Francisco de Borgia al servicio del Pontificado* (Valencia, 2000).
10. ASV. Senado, dispaci, Roma, 7, 113, Soriano-Soranzo to Dux, Roma, 3 junio 1571. Sobre la elección de Alejandrino, véase ASV. Act. Miscell. 36. During the consistorial meeting of 23 May the Pope decided to send legates to the Christian princes, and on 18 June Alexandrine was elected officially. For some documents detailing his legacy see ASV. Reg. Vat. 2014, 9 (to Philip II) and 15 (to Sebastian), dated 18 June; another copy in BAV. Barb. Lat. 2412. AGS. E. 390, 83. Pius V to the Shah, 12-XII-1571.
11. About Bicudo, see Marqués de Azebedo, *Apontamientos históricos ... de la provincia de San Paulo*, 2 vols (Rio de Janeiro, 1879). A very famous member of this family was Hidalgo, who died in 1650. See G. Pereira Esteves e Rodrigues, *Portugal. Diccionario histórico*, 7 vols (Lisbon, 1904–15).
12. AGS. E. 918, 150, Juan de Zúñiga to Philip II, Roma, 14-III-1572.
13. On Lepanto, see David y Enrique García Hernán, *On Lepanto, el día después* (Madrid, Actas, 1999).
14. *Monumenta Borgia* (Madrid, 1911), V, p. 647, Francis Borgia to Marco Antonio Colonna, Lisbon, 10-XII-1571. 'Quanto a la liga, che questo principe ci entra molto volontieri, et non solamente per il Mar Rosso et Persico, et per la Ethiopia, vole far guerra al turco, ma anche per questa parte vol dar aiuto alla armata christiana'.
15. AGS. E. 918, 271. Marco Antonio Colonna to Philip II, Rome, 20-I-1572.
16. AGS. E. 917, 121. Philip II to Zúñiga, 22-XII-1571. 'en lo que toca al Sofi, no hay duda sino que importaría mucho que por todas estas partes se apretase al turco para mayor daño y destrucción suya, y para procurar persona a propósito para esto se hará diligencia por vía de Portugal; y para ello he mandado que se escriba a mi embajador y también para que por parte del rey de Portugal se haga esta diligencia y se advierta al legado para que él ayude por su parte, si ya no fuere partido'.
17. ASV. SS. Spagna 5, 50. Castagna to Flaminio Donato d'Aspra, Madrid, 12-I-1572. Another copy of this documents in AGS. E. 390, 82-83-83; 157-158-159, y en ASV. Arm. XLIV, 19, 441. Letter of Philip II to kings of Persia, Ethiopia an Arabia en AGS. E. 390, 148–150, (15 March 1572). *Rudimenta linguae Persicae authore Ludovico de Dieu; accedunt duo priora capita Geneseos ex persica translatione Iac. Tawusi* (Lugduni Batavorum, ex Officina Elseviriana, 1639), [8], 95 p. 4, Madrid, Palacio Real, Pas. Arm. 1/99 (1).
18. AGS. E. 390, 80. Sebastian to the shah, Lisbon, 26-II-1572. Archivo General de Simancas. E. 390, 81. Copy of the instruction to Miguel de Breu. AGS. E. 3990, 161. Philip II to Juan Borgia, 28-II-1572. See Carlos Alonso, *A los orígenes de las relaciones entre la Santa Sede y Persia (1571-72)*, en *Dalla Chiesa antica alla Chiesa moderna. Miscellanea per il Cinquentesimo della Facoltà di Storia Ecclesiastica della Pontificia Università Gregoriana*; M. S. I. Fois, Monachino, V. S. I. and Litva, F. S. I. (eds), (Roma, 1983), pp. 215–29. See also, Luis Gil, 'Embajadas de Felipe II a Persia: inútil búsqueda de un aliado contra los turcos', *Historia 16* 178 (1991), pp. 39–46.
19. Fr Juan Tadeo de San Eliseo O.C.D. knew Persian language. Lodewijk de Dieu (1590–1642) published in Leyden in 1639 the *Rudimenta Linguae Persicae*. In 1649 the *Elementa Linguae Persicae* edited in London by John Greaves (1602–52). See also the *Alphabetum persium, cum oratione dominicali et salutatione angelica* (Romae, typis Sac. Congreg. de Propag. Fide, 1784). In Spain one of the few people who knew the Persian language was the Basque Francisco de Gurmendi, who in 1612 was the translator at the royal court for Arabic, Turkish and Persian.
20. AGS. E. 390, 80. Sebastian to the shah, Lisbon 27-II-1572. AGS. E. 390, 81. Instructions to Miguel de Abreu.
21. ASVen. Archivio Proprio Spagna 6, 152, Copia tradotta dalla risposta all'Ambasciatore.
22. ASVen. Archivio Proprio Spagna 6, 147, Tiepolo to Mocenigo, Almeirin, 19-I-1572.
23. ASVen. Annali, 1571, (old signature Cod. di Brera, 339) 302, 303. Sebastian to the dux. 24-I-1572 (collaborating with the holy league). Another in 31-I-1572 (sent one ambassador to the king of Persia). ASVen. Archivio Proprio Spagna, 6, 153, Tiepolo to Mocenigo, 13-I-1572.

24. AGS. E. 1135, 66 y 67.
25. AGS. E. 1138. Juan de Austria to Philip II, Mesina, 2-II-1572. 'A Alexandría de Egipto he enviado yo dos hombres que Mathías Bicudo, aquel portugués que el año pasado andaba en esa corte me ha dado a entender lo que por allí se podría hacer, daré aviso a V. M. de la relación que de ellos tuviere. A Rodas, a Corón y a África y a Trípoli y a Constantinopla he enviado estos días hombres a entender el estado en que se hallan allí las cosas, y con algunas pláticas, y tratado. Hasta ver si tienen fundamento de sustancia no quiero cansar a V. M. con escribir las particularidades de ellas'.
26. *Colección de Documentos Inéditos para la Historia de España*, (Madrid), III, 351. Don Juan de Austria a los cristianos de la isla de Rodas, Mesina 15 de enero 1572.
27. AGS. E. 153, 155. Bishop of Cuenca to Philip II with the answer inside: 'entendido lo de la liga y lo que hace el Turco, que no podrá dejar de saberse pronto, podremos ir con quienes será bien tratar de esto, y creo que entonces lo será escribir al cardenal Granvela, que tiene mucha noticia de estas cosas, que las tratase con el cardenal Amulio, y que entre ambos desde allí [Roma] se comunicasen con el marqués de Pescara [virrey de Sicilia] a quien también se podrá escribirle sobre ello'. AGS. E. 1134, 164. Juan de Austria to Philip II, Mesina, 25-XI-1571. 'V. M. se debe acordar de un portugués que andaba en esa corte cuando yo partí de ella que se llama Matías Bicudo, el cual fue encaminado por el cardenal Amulio al obispo de Cuenca y trataba de ser parte para rendir en los confines del Cayro y Alexandria un gran señor vasallo del Turco. Este se halla al presente en Roma y escrito a don Juan de Zúñiga que me lo envíe con intención de que haga el viaje que ha ofrecido, particularmente así que el negocio tiene algún fundamento de agora tiempo de intentarlo. Llegado aquí pienso despacharle y avisar a V. M. de lo que con él se tratare ...' See Enrique García Hernán, *La armada española en la Monarquía de Felipe II y la defensa de Mediterráneo* (Madrid, Tempo, 1995).
28. AGS. E. 390, 80. 'Copia de la carta que el serenísimo rey de Portugal escribió a Xathamas, rey de Persia', 26-II-1572. AGS. E. 390, 81. 'Copia de la instrucción que el serenísimo rey de Portugal dio al embajador que envió al rey de Persia, Miguel Dabreu'.
29. *L'Ambassade en Perse de Luis Pereira de Lacerda et des Pères Portugais de l'Orde de Saint Agustin Melchor dos Anjos et Guilherme de Santo Agostinho, 1604-1605* (Lisbon, 1972), p. 28. Véase AGS. E. 495. 'Lo que dicen los dos padres agustinos que han venido de Persia acerca del estado en que está aquella, Melchor de los Ángeles y Juan de San José, 6 enero 1614'.
30. Is Bonifacio de Esteba O. Min. Obs., born in Ragusa, bishop of Stonj, (17-XI-1561 till 1582, year of his death). Conradus Eubel, *Hierarchia Catholica* (Monasterii, 1923), III, 304.
31. There are six letters of Bicudo (Ragusa, 29-VIII; 13-IX; 1-X; 26-X; 9-XI; y 1-XII.). AGS. E. 1517., 1, 9, 23, 24, 27 y 30.
32. AGS. E. 1517. 12-XII-1575. This ambassador [Abreu] was sent by His Holiness, the king our lord and the king of Portugal, to whom Don Juan sent a man and a bill of exchange for 12,000 ducats should he need the money. They departed from Portugal and travelled for two years, arriving on 26 February 1575, the ambassador arriving when he left Hormuz. The king's ambassador in Casbin was rather ill-treated, (lodged) in a hut which could not be inhabited, and it was the king [of Persia's] nephew who was governing, for the king/[shah?] was old; he wondered how a king such as that of Portugal had not sent king Xatamas [Tahmasp] who is so powerful he could reach the skies, presents of two million ducats in gold. And it seems he arrived with presents worth up to 16,000 ducats in monies, jewels and other pieces; and in return he received a bed that could be worth 500 or 600 ducats which the ambassador has in his possession ... they killed an Armenian servant of his who was his shopper ... and decided to kill the ambassador and all his men who were about 20 and, out of fear, one of them turned Muslim ... and they say the reason they wanted (to kill) the ambassador was because he had entered the mosque in Hormuz and burned the books that were there, and the ambassador replied it was because they had broken the Cross of the church that the Portuguese wanted to build there. And they responded that on account of that pole were they to inflict such damage in the mosque, and the [Portuguese] ambassador said that by 'that pole' the Christians had been redeemed, and [at this] they moved onto another matter but

kept him detained there. And this king to whom I refer is the king of Persia, who had received him excellently although having welcomed him and understood that his embassy was for a war, [the king] was offended and started the maltreatment without responding or saying anything to this ambassador, and he never again saw or spoke to the king, but only to his nephew.

33. The first truce started in 1577 and was subsequently renewed until 1593. Juan de Marigliano (born in Milan) was the representative of the Spanish monarchy in Constantinople. Henry II of France did everything in order to destroy these negotiations, with the collaboration of the Holy See. The Turks sought to mislead the French, denying the existence of this truce, Henry III to Abbé de Lile. Poistiers 7-IX-1577. García Hernán, *La armada española*, pp. 55–60.
34. BAV. Urb. Lat. 831, 487. 'Le provincie presse dal gran Turco, cominciando dall'anno 1577'.
35. 'Cartas y avisos diferentes a don Juan de Zúñiga en 1581'. *Colección de libros españoles raros o curiosos* (Madrid, 1887), p. 18.
36. See, Carlos Alonso, El P. Simón de Moraes, 'pionero de las misiones agustinianas en Persia', en *Analecta Agustiniana* 24 (1979) 343–72
37. Andrés de Flores, *Relación muy verdadera: que trata de las brauas y cruelisimas batallas, y balerosos rencuentros, y las crueles muertes de tantos y tan soberuios Turcos tan balerosos y Capitanes y famosos Basanes que en las batallas a dado el baleroso Rey de Persia al soberuio y poderoso campo nunca visto, que el gran turco embio a la Persia...*, (Burgos, por Santillana, 1586), 4 hoj., 4º, en la BNM, VE/193–8. Minadoi, Giovaani Tommaso, trad. Herrera y Tordesillas, Antonio, *Historia de la guerra entre turcos y persianos..., comenzando del año de 1576 que fueron los primeros motivos della, hasta el año de 1585* (Madrid, Francisco Sánchez, 1588) 1932 h, 4º. BNM, R/23810.
38. AGS. E. 1517, 1, 9, 23, 24, 30.
39. AGS. E. 1260, 94. Mathias Bicudo to the French ambassador in Venice, Ferrara, 4-V-1585. AGS. E. 1260, 98 y 100 two letter of Bicudo to Saúl Cohen.
40. AGS. E. 1340, 26, 33, 37, 73. 1583–4.
41. AGS. E. 1341, 83. 'Juan Bautista de Tassis me escribió a los 20 y 21 de febrero como don Antonio enviaba a Constantinopla a un fraile que se llama Matías Bicudo, que antes que tomase el hábito de San Francisco sirvió a V. M. por orden de don Juan de Austria, que está en el cielo, en Ragusa, y otras partes el año 73 y 74...y le detuviese como fraile apóstata'. Cristóbal de Salazar a Felipe II, Venecia, 2 mayo 1583. AGS. E. 1341, 4. En lo de tomar a Matías Bicudo no se pudo efectuar por haber mudado de parecer el embajador de Francia y también porque le socorrieron agora para pasar en Constantinopla con 700 ducados, como Saúl Cohen me ha dicho, dejándose ir a Ferrara por esto, y aunque con el nuncio he hecho toda diligencia posible para que se prendiera, por ser nuevo y haber sido dos fiestas juntas ayer y anteier no se ha podido hacer diligencia en el oficio de la inquisición para prenderle, y ha sido necesario a los 24 de éste dar información de cómo andó sin hábito y que está fuera de la religión, porque a otra manera no se diera licencia para prenderle, porque es menester el brazo seglar y siempre se hace así, y ha sido gran impedimento, porque la inquisición no tiene ministros para prender, no obstante que se ha visto por una carta que el papa ha mandado se prenda. Y hanme avisado que partió anteier el Matías sin saberse por qué parte salió de aquí, ni aun de los mismo de la casa del embajador, porque salió sin ser visto, sino de uno que le abrió la puerta antes del amanecer, Cristóbal de Salazar to Philip II, Venice, 27-VII-1585.
42. The details of the journey were published by Ugo Tucci, 'Una relazione di G. B. Vecchietti sulla Persia e sul regno di Hormuz 1587', *Oriente Moderno* (1955), pp. 149–60.
43. For more details on the letter to the shah, see E. Rossi, 'Elenco dei manoscritti persiani della Biblioteca Vaticana', *Studi e Testi* 136, (Città del Vaticano, 1948). Two letters of Abbas to Clement VIII (ASV. Vat. Pers. 164 y 165).
44. Roberto Amalgià, 'Giovan Battista e Gerolamo Vecchietti, viaggiatori in Oriente', *Atti della Accademia Nazionale dei Lincei* 9 (1956), pp. 313–50, 319; A. Vaccari, 'Una bibbia araba per il primo Gesuita venuto al Líbano', *Mélanges Université Saint Joseph* 10 (1925), pp. 79–104.

45. E. Hambye, 'Francesco Corsi', *Diccionario Histórico de la Compañía de Jesús* (Madrid-Roma, 2002), I, p. 969.
46. BAV, Cod. Barb. Lat. 4602, 190. G. B. Vecchietti a Paulo V, Ispahán, 15 julio 1606, en Roberto Amalgià, 'Giovan Battista e Gerolamo Vecchietti', pp. 313–50, 348–50.
47. Rhoads Murphey, *Ottoman Warfare, 1500-1700* (London, 1999), p. 4. Abbas I recuperará Tabriz en 1603 y Erivan en 1604.
48. Carlos Alonso, 'Nueva documentación', pp. 309–93. Arnulf Hartmann, OSA, 'The Agustians in golden Goa. A manuscript by Felix of Jesus OSA', *Analecta Agustiniana* 30 (1967), p. 13.
49. ASV. Varia Politicorum, 159, 61–82. Relatione di personaggio qualificato sopra lo stato del turco. 'Havendo S. M. tanto oro dall'Indie non gli corrompa i ministri per intendere i suoi secreti et anco per divertire le guerre da suoi paesi caricandoli altri, et di più per causargli alcuna sollevatione ne suoi stati et fino nei propri figlioli ...', 68v.
50. ASV. Borghese IV, Vol, 52, 334–7, in Carlos Alonso, 'Embajadores de Persia en las Cortes de Praga, Roma y Valladolid (1600–1601)', *Anthologica Annua* 36 (1989), p. 212.
51. On Nicolás de Melo (1578–1615), see Gregorio de Santiago Vela, *Ensayo de una biblioteca ibero-americana de la Orden de San Agustín,* (Madrid, 1920), V, pp. 373–7; and Carlos Alonso, 'El P. Nicolás de Melo, OSA. Embajador y Mártir', *Misionalia Hispanica* 15 (1958), pp. 219–44. On Antonio de Gouvea (1575–), see Joseph Metzler, 'Nicht erfüllen Hoffnungen in Persien', in *Sacrae Congregationis de Propaganda Fide Memoria Rerum* (Freiburg 1971), I/1, pp. 680–705, Gregorio de Santiago Vela, *Ensayo de una biblioteca ibero-americana,* pp. 253–79; Gil, Luis and Floristán, J. M., 'Las misiones luso-españolas en Persia y la Cristiandad armenia (1600–1614)', *Sefarad* 46 (1986), pp. 207–19; J. M. Floristán, 'Carta del Patriarca armenio David IV a Felipe III', *Safarad* 46 (1986), pp. 197–205.
52. Luis Cabrera de Córdoba, *Relaciones de las cosas sucedidas en la corte de España desde 1599 hasta 1614* (Junta de Castilla y León, 1997), p. 122.
53. Roberto Amalgià, 'Giovan Battista e Gerolamo Vecchietti', pp. 313–50, 324.
54. ASV. Borghese III, 87, 133. Nuncio de Praga, Spinelli, al cardenal de San Jorge, Praga, 13 noviembre 1600. AGS. E. 707, 23–4. Guillén de San Clemente a Felipe III, Praga, 10 marzo 1601. Vid. Carlos Alonso, 'Embajadores de Persia'. Pedro de Buiza (Medina de Rioseco 1561–†Toledo 1626), theologian, practised his profession in Rome in 1600 and was later confessor of the count of Fuentes, governor of Milan. He died as superior of the religious house in Toledo.
55. We have not found in AGS the report sent by Acosta to Philip III. There is a detailed report to the Pope. ASV. Borghese, II, 20, 158–9, 'Informatione di Francesco da Costa, sacerdote portuguese, venuto dall'India, alla Santità di Nostro Signore intorno all'ambasciata del Persiano', publicado por Carlos Alonso, 'Una embajada de Clemente VIII a Persia (1600–1609)', *Archivum Historiae Pontificiae* 34 (1996), pp. 7–125, 77–9.
56. AGS. K. 1630. Relación de la embajada que el rey de Persia envió con don Antonio Sherley y Cusán Alibey, persiano. Roma, 8 junio 1601, publicada por Alonso, 'Embajadores de Persia', pp. 223–6.
57. Carlos Alonso, 'El P. Simón de Moraes', pp. 343–72.
58. See *Encyclopaedia Iranica.* The Jesuits were well acquainted with the arts of war. See also *Diccionario Histórico de la Compañía de Jesús* (Madrid-Roma, 2002).
59. AGS. E. 191. Philip III to Cristóbal de Moura, viceroy of Portugal, Valladolid, 6-III-1602.
60. AGS. K. 1631, 217. Duke of Sessa to Philip III, Rome, 25-XI-1602.
61. See *A Chronicle of the Carmelites in Persia and the Papal Missions of the XVIIth and XVIIIth Centuries* (Londres, 1939); Carlos Alonso, *Ángel María Cittadino, OP, arzobispo de Naxiwan (+1629). Una iniciativa de Propaganda Fide a favor de armenia* (Roma, 1970); Pietro Della Valle, *I viaggi di ...* , (Roma, 1668); A. de Gouvea, *Relaçam em que se tratam as guerras e grandes victorias que alcançou o grande rey de Persia Xa Abbas do grao turco Mahometto & seu filho Amethe ...* , (Lisbon, 1611); R. Gulbenkian, *L'ambassade en Perse de Luis Pereira de Lacerda et des Perès Portugais de l'Ordre de Saint-Augustin, Melchior dos Anjos et Guilherme de Santo Agostinho, 1604-1605* (Lisbon, 1972); San J. de Miguel, *Crónica de la provincia franciscana de San*

Miguel (Madrid, 1989); A. Da Silva Rego, *Documentação para a história das missoes da padroado português do Oriente* (Lisbon, 1955–8).

62. Carlos Alonso, 'Una embajada de Clemente VIII', pp. 7–125.
63. Obispo de Cirene Antonio de Gouveia (O.S.A.), *Relaçam em que se tratan as guerras e grandes victorias que alcaçon o grande rey da Persia... por mandado... del Rey D. Felippe segundo de Portugal fizerao alguns religiosos da Ordem dos Eremitas de S. Augustinho a Persia / composto pello padre F. Antonio de Gouuea religioso da mesma ordem...*, (Impresso em Lisboa, por Pedro Crasbeeck: vendese na rua romana en casa de Simao de Carualho...*, 1611). [13], 226 [i.e. 213], [4] h.; 4º, in Madrid, Real Academia de la Historia, 5/1708. Prospero del Espiritu Santo, (O. C. D.), *Breve suma de la Historia de los sucessos de la mission de Persia de los Carmelitas Descalços, desde el año de 1621 hasta el de 1624 / escrita por el Padre Fray Prospero del Espiritu Santo... de la misma orden [Carmelitas Descalzos]*, (Madrid, por la viuda de Alonso Martin, 1626). 10 [i.e. 6] h.; Fol. Madrid, Palacio Real III-6474(9). *Relación cierta y verdadera de la feliz victoria y prósperos sucesos que en la India Oriental han conseguido los Portugueses, contra armadas muy poderosas de Olanda, y Persia este año de 1624, la fecha en la ciudad de Goa, cabeça de aquel Reyno a 27 de Março, del dicho año*, (Impresso en Madrid, en casa de Bernardino de Guzman, 1625). BNM, Mss./2355.
64. Martín Fernández de Figueroa, *Conquista de las Indias de Persia e Arabia que fizo la armada del rey don Manuel de Portugal e de las muchas tierras, diversas gentes, extrañas riquezas y grandes batallas que allá hubo: en sumario del bachiller Juan Agüero de Trasmiera*; introducción, edición crítica y notas de Luis Gil Fernández (Valladolid, Secretariado de Publicaciones e Intercambio Editorial, Universidad, 1999). García de Silva Figueroa, *Epistolario diplomático*; edición y estudios preliminares de Luis Gil, (Cáceres, Institución Cultural 'El Brocense', 1989). Véase: Niels Steensgaard, *The Asian Trade Revolution*. Biblioteca Real de Madrid, Ms. II/2590, 16, 32–33. Marqués de Hinojosa a Juan de Ziriza, Londres, 30-X-1623. 'Sobre que no se le ha respondido al particular de la hacienda que llegó allí robada a portugueses y de los despojos de Hormuz'.
65. B. Zimmel, 'Vorgeschichte und Gründung der Jesuitenmission in Isfahan, 1642–1657', in *Zeitschrift für Missionswissenschaft und Religionswissenschaft* 53 (1969), pp. 1–26.

Part III

Commercial Connections

12

Arduous Travelling: The Qandahar-Isfahan Highway in the Seventeenth Century

Willem Floor

Introduction

This chapter takes you on a trip from Qandahar to Isfahan. Its purpose is to acquaint you with the reality of travelling in the Safavid period. For, when discussing trade, cultural and other contacts, scholars inform their readers that goods were transported, traders and artists travelled, but these studies do not provide you with a sense of how easy or difficult travel was. To that end, I therefore intend to discuss in some detail one of the important highways connecting India with Iran, to wit: the road between Qandahar and Isfahan. This description will not only give a feel for what traders and other travellers had to go through, but also that profits made the world go round in the Safavid era just as today. There was no obstacle, no mountain too high, no terrain too difficult or too dangerous, that people in the seventeenth century were not willing to overcome to move goods from one point to another. In addition, the chapter will, where possible, identify the stages along this commercial route, as well as some alternative stretches that were taken by travellers during the Safavid period.

Importance of trade with India

Trade between India and Iran was conducted both by land and sea before the Europeans arrived in the Indian Ocean. By 1500, India's foreign trade was already predominantly transported by the maritime route. Merchants trading with Iran continued, however, to have a choice of either route to maximize their profits. This pattern did not change after the Portuguese arrived in the Persian Gulf nor when they were ousted from Hormuz in 1622. For the Dutch and English, after emasculating the Portuguese in the Persian Gulf by 1630, found that they also had to compete with the already long-established, inter Persia-India land trade.[1]

The land route between India and Iran started at Lahore, but I will only discuss the part between Qandahar and Isfahan. The reason being that the road from Lahore to Qandahar is quite well known and has been described in detail by several travellers.[2] From Qandahar to Farah travellers to Persia followed the same route. However, at Farah travellers had two options. They could take the route we are going to travel together, or they could travel onwards to Herat and Mashhad. From Mashhad the route would take the traveller via Semnan to Tehran, and then south via Qom and Kashan to Isfahan, or continuing from Tehran via Qazvin to the Ottoman Empire, either via Hamadan to Baghdad or via Tabriz to Erzerum. We have, as yet, not enough data to determine which of these two routes was more important than the other, although the road via Mashhad was a much easier one to travel. This northern route was indeed much frequented, for Paul Simon, the Carmelite papal ambassador, observed in 1607 that Kashan 'is much frequented by traders from being on the road to Khorasan, to the Mughal's territories and to India, whence many valuable goods are brought'.[3] Tavernier, some 60 years later, wrote that this route was little used, because you had to traverse deserts and often march for three days without finding water.[4] However, this does not sound very convincing. Tavernier, as far as we know, never travelled this route, and it was a well-provided countryside in terms of caravanserais, water cisterns and villages. Also, this route continued to be used and was considered an important trade route throughout Safavid times and later periods. In fact, it was a much more comfortable route than Tavernier wants us to believe. His compatriot Le Gouz wrote that the caravan from Qazvin via Qandahar to Lahore (i.e. the route via Mashhad) left every two months and that the voyage lasted six months. He did not mention the route via Tabas at all.[5]

Qandahar was an important location where several trading routes met. According to Babur (d. 1530), former ruler of Samarqand and founder of the Moghul Empire in India,

> there are two trade-marts on the land-route between Hindustan and Khurasan; one is Kabul, the other Kandahar. To Kabul caravans come from Kashgar, Farghana, Turkistan, Samarkand, Bokhara, Balkh, Hisar, and Badakhshan. To Kandahar they come from Khurasan. Kabul is an excellent trading center; if merchants went to Khita [China] or to Rum [Ottoman Empire], they might make no higher profit. Down to Kabul every year come 7, 8, or 10,000 horses and up to it, from Hindustan, come every year caravans of 10, 15, or 20,000 heads-of-houses, bringing slaves (*barda*), white cloth, sugar-candy, refined and common sugar, and aromatic roots. Many a trader is not content with profit of 30 to 40 on 10 [300 to 400 per cent]. In Kabul can be had the products of Khurasan, Rum, Iraq, and Chin (China); while it is Hindustan's market.[6]

From Babur's description it is clear that Kabul and Qandahar, as well as Herat, which he refers to as Khorasan, were important links in the trade between India and Iran (and Central Asia) and that despite the high mountain ranges and desert roads, the caravans were successful in overcoming these barriers. English merchants who visited the city around 1609 also attest to the continued commercial importance of Qandahar. 'Candhar is a Citie of importance, which is frequented with Merchants out of Turkie, Persia and other parts of India.'[7] To Iran, Qandahar was a very important source of revenue, and its importance may also explain why there were intermittent military conflicts between the Moghuls and Safavids about who controlled the city.[8]

For India, exports and imports to and from Iran mostly started and ended in Lahore (situated in the rich agricultural centres of the Himalayan foothills and the Gangetic plains of northern India). Richard Steel and John Crowther, two merchants in the service of the East India Company, wrote in 1614: 'At this present the Merchants of India assemble at Lahore, and invest a great part of their monies in Commodities, and joyne themselves in Caravans to passe the Mountaines of Candahar into Persia, by which way is generally reported to passe twelve of fourteen thousand Camels lading, whereas heretofore scarsly passed three thousand, the rest going by way of Ormus.'[9] In 1621, the German traveller von Poser observed that there was a daily coming and going of thousands of camels, which, of course, although a gross exaggeration, indicates a very high and lively level of commercial activity. He also noted the buying and selling of textiles in the bazaars, the heavy 'drinking' of tobacco and booze, and, finally, the wantonness of the prostitutes. Steel and Crowther confirm the latter, for they wrote that Qandahar 'is much inhabited with lewd people'.[10]

Road protection

To stimulate land-based trade the Moghul emperors had improved the roads to Kabul and Qandahar. The main overland trade routes from India to the north-west were (a) via the Sanghar and later the Khaybar pass and Kabul (b) via the Bolan pass and Qandahar and (c) via the Gumal pass, though this last was not used for trade with Iran. Large caravans moved along those routes, escorted by guards, because of attacks by the wild, mostly non-Moslem, Pathans and other tribes. To promote trade, the governor of Qandahar had orders to protect travellers and traders and keep highway robbery and banditry in check. This was no empty command, because the mountains around Qandahar were inhabited by 'Agwans or Potans, great Robbers, accustomed to cut off whole Caravans. But at present partly for feare of the Mogoll, and partly through sweet found by commerce (in venting their graine, sheepe and Goats, of which they have great store, and buying of coarse Linnen and other necessaries) they are become more civill.'[11] There was even coordination of effort between the Moghuls and the Safavids to keep the roads secure, certainly in terms of exchange of information. The fact that Qandahar was a bone of contention between the Moghuls and Safavids at times meant that tribal chiefs in the frontier areas preying on caravans could find shelter with the other side.[12]

There were other reasons why the governor of Qandahar wanted to make sure that merchants arrived unmolested at his town. In addition to customs duties and the money that caravans spent in the city, the governors had developed other ways to add to their income. They tried to delay caravans from leaving too soon and to get in exchange for some entertainment a valuable present.[13] The presence of the caravans was also good for the local economy. Manrique reported when in Farah, 'on the second day of our stay we were visited by the officials and ministers of that inland harbour, who at once began to deal in such goods and merchandise as they had. Meanwhile we were also visited by the villagers, who brought us from the neighbouring villages an abundance of foodstuffs and other necessaries for sale, so that the Caravan was well stocked with all that was required.'[14] Steel and Crowther further observed that Qandahar, 'by reason of frequent passage of Caravans is much enlarged lately, that the suburbs are bigger than the Citie. For within this two years, that the way of Ormus is stopped up by the wars betwixt the Persians and the Portugals, must of necessitie goe by this place. And here they do hire Camels to go into India, and at their returne for Persia.'[15]

Land versus maritime route

In 1611, Coverte reported: 'There is a great and continuall traffique by land, from Persia, Indestand, Mesopotamia, and from all partes betweene that and China, with all sorts of merchandize and commodities which those Countries yeelde; For there are continually 7. or 8. thousand Camels about the Citie [of Qandahar] which trade to and fro with merchandize.'[16] This number of camels given by Coverte is not as outrageous as it may sound. Steensgaard has estimated that around 1600, caravans of mules and camels transported some 6 million lbs or 2,700 tons of Asian goods.[17] This amount of goods required more than 10,000 camels, which tallies with what is known about the size of the Indian caravans coming to Iran and beyond in years when a large part of the normal maritime trade was channelled via the land route. Seistani reported that when Amir Mohammad Amin Mashhadi, who, as *qafele-bashi*, returned after a stay of many years in India, he passed through Sistan with a caravan of close to 10,000 camels. However, in normal years, the size of these caravans was barely 3,000 camels, according to Steel and Crowther.[18] Klein reports even the arrival of oxen caravans from India, which, though a rare occurrence in Iran, was not entirely unknown.[19] I have dealt with the topic of the relative importance of the land versus the maritime route elsewhere. Suffice it to say that the land route continued to offer a viable, and even a flourishing, alternative, albeit a less important one.[20]

The overland route had become safer because of the military might of the European companies. This is clear from the shift in trade that occurred as a result of the Persian-Portuguese hostilities, which led to the conquest of Gamron in 1614 and of Hormuz in 1622. Steel and Crowther, passing through Qandahar on their way from India to Iran, reported that prior to the start of these hostilities, around 1614, not more than 3,000 camels used to ply the India-Qandahar-Iran trade route annually, while after that year their number increased to 12,000 and even 14,000. According to Steel and Crowther the value of the goods per camel was 120–130 rupees, so the total value of trade that year was about 1.4–1.8 million rupees (16–20 metric tons of silver). On the other hand, an outbreak of hostilities between the Moghuls and Safavids over Qandahar had a negative impact on the volume of trade on the overland route and increased maritime trade.[21]

Merchants could choose between transport by land or by sea. Under normal conditions the choice, depending on one's location, between the routes was about the same from a cost point of view. Most merchants chose the maritime route. Those who continued to use the land route also traded en route, and thus tried to increase the profitability of their enterprise. Many of these merchants only travelled part of the road and then sold their goods to other merchants, returning to their place of origin with goods purchased from the same or other merchants. According to Steel and Crowther: 'Trade it yeelds not of it selfe, but accidentally by the meeting of Indian, Persian, and Turkie merchants, who are not willing to travell further at twentie per Cento profit.' '[The caravans into Persia broke into] smaller Companies: for in many places greater they would not find provision. For all Persia, especially betwixt this and Spahan, is barren, where sometime in two or three dayes travel, there is no greene thing to be seene; only some water, and that also often brackish, stinking and naught.'[22] This en route trading not only occurred in in Farah, as we have already discussed, but even in such out of the way places as the Biyabanak district in the salt desert. Manrique mentioned that his caravan stayed there four days during which period 'the merchants purchased various kinds of silk, and especially velvet, which is made throughout this Kingdom of Corazane. They brought for sale to the Caravan, throughout this region, the very richest carpets of wool and silk, interwoven with designs in gold and silver and all at most moderate prices.'[23]

What influenced all merchants in their choice of route was security (risk of pirates or bandits), war, and a change in transportation cost, including tolls. When, for example, the overland route via Qandahar was blocked in 1639, due to the war between the Safavids and Moghuls over the city, merchants immediately shifted to the maritime route. The English in Surat remarked: 'never to any man's remembrance were soe many merchants and goods present at any one time in Surat.'[24] Although customs duties at Qandahar ranged from only two to three per cent, in Bandar 'Abbas some 10 per cent was levied; the difference in rates alone was not sufficient for merchants to prefer one route over the other. For customs fees also had to be paid when passing through major towns in addition to various fees to be paid for road-guards.²⁵

Road equipment

To facilitate travel along the commercial routes, which only permitted quadrupeds (camels, mules, horses and oxen) and no wheeled transportation, both shahs and private individuals built caravanseries, water tanks and bridges. At the caravanseries, often near villages, the traveller found water, food, fodder and shelter. In the 1640s, Manrique remarked that part of the route had been equipped with water cisterns.

> At the places where the Caravans were accustomed to halt, some of the wells were so deep that the water (also bitter and saline) was very difficult to get up. We also met with some reservoirs along this dry route, but all were empty, due, they said, to the scanty rainfall of the two years past. These reservoirs were pious works which certain followers and devotees of the Alcoran had had constructed to relieve their consciences and for the good of their souls.²⁶

He also mentioned that Shah 'Abbas, to facilitate the passage of his armies, had road markers erected; the distance between them was such that they could be seen, to make sure that the road user did not get lost.²⁷ This may have been the case in the 1640s, but not in 1598, when Allahverdi Khan travelled from Shiraz, via Robat-e Khoranaq, Posht-e Badam, Robat-e Shotoran and Tabas to Mashhad to join Shah 'Abbas's expeditionary force against the Uzbeks.²⁸ In fact, Molla Jalal Monajjem wrote about this march: 'Never has an army traversed this [route], because of the lack of water.'²⁹ In 1614–15, Steel and Crowther still had to worry whether they would get lost between Tabas and Ardakan. They also had to dig for water on one leg of their voyage because the water cisterns were not always found or were dry.³⁰ There is also, as yet, no archaeological evidence that shows that road markers, called *mil*, were actually built on this road. The only detailed and comprehensive study of the Dasht-e Lut mentions the existence of the remains of only four *mil*s. Of these four, two are of Sasanian origin (*mil-e Baluchan* and *mil-e Mohammad 'Ali Khan*, also called *mil-e Rahim Dad*). The other two date from Seljuq times (*mil-e Farhad*, also called *mil-e Kharaban* and *mil-e Naderi*). These road markers are found elsewhere in Iran, such as the *mil-e Ayaz* (near Daragez- Khorasan) mentioned by MacGregor, which is built of good burnt brick and is 80 feet high, but probably is a minaret to a nearby shrine rather than a road marker. There is also a *mil* in the Zangi-Ahmad desert (southern Lut).³¹

During high season a traveller would meet other caravans on the road consisting of scores of pack animals. Steel and Crowther, for example, when leaving Tabas, joined a small caravan of 100 camels.³² The Persian camels lived long, were patient in travel, gentle in handling and of great strength, they carried about 1,000 lbs, and were content with little food of the meanest sort.[33] The difference in the weight carried by camels, as mentioned by contemporary sources, is due to the fact that there were two kinds of camels, the larger ones carried up to 1,300 lbs, and the smaller ones about 700 lbs. Camels usually did not do more than four leagues (one league = about 10 km) per day, while horses and mules travelled five to six leagues.[34]

The daily distance travelled, usually between four to six leagues was also impacted by halts wherever there was water, while every fourth day, at least according to Steel and Crowther and implied by Manrique, was a rest day to allow the animals to regain their strength.[35] During moments of forced immobility, such as at border posts, the animals were usually sent to nearby pastures to recuperate and gain strength for the next arduous days of travel. In addition to forage found en route, the camels were fed 'ardua, the flour of barley pounded fine and made into balls, which is given to camels morning and evening.'[36] Of course, the speed also depended on the age and the kind of animal, the type of goods, the terrain and weather. The length of the Persian *farsakh* usually equals 6 km, but actually it was the distance an animal could travel during one hour.

Travel through the mountains in Afghanistan during winter was very difficult, if not impossible. The route was often difficult for other reasons such as lack of provisions, because the area was sparsely inhabited and caravans often moved over difficult and inhospitable tracts for days at a time. The *karavan-bashi*s would try to cross the Helmand River and its tributaries when the river was fordable and to avoid sandstorms. In particular, they wanted to avoid the *bad-e sad-o-bist ruz*, the 120 days' wind, which was a violent sandstorm (with velocities of 110 km/h or more) in the Farah area blowing from the end of May or mid-June to about the end of September.[37] The road therefore probably had peak and slack seasons. It would seem that caravans coming from India mainly arrived between May and July, while those leaving for India moved between July and September. Steel and Crowther and Manrique travelled in May and Coverte in June, and von Poser between July and September. Tavernier did not provide dates for his journey.

Because of the heat during the day, caravans usually travelled by night, leaving sometime before sunset and stopping at sunrise. It was difficult to sleep because of the unpacking to be done, the pitching of tents and all the other necessary activities that made a great deal of noise.[38] Finally, the horror of the road brought people from different backgrounds and religions together in a more than usual cooperative spirit, and, thus it would seem, that Mother Nature is an equal opportunity provider and equalizer. The English merchants, Richard Steel and John Crowther, left Qandahar in May 1614 with a group of 12 Persian Moslem merchants and 3 Armenians.[39] During one of the more difficult parts of his route (between Cres and Pena) von Poser did not have enough water with him and there was hardly any in the desert. He was saved from this lack by Indian co-travellers. Von Poser fell ill in Farah, but a fellow traveller, Estichbeg (Eshaq Bayg?) from Ardabil, helped him and offered to share his food. His fellow travellers ascribed von Poser's illness to eating meat and drinking wine and brandy and told him to eat fresh fruit and milk products like them. When he had another bout of fever at the very moment that his caravan left Qandahar, a merchant from Yazd helped him find a donkey and made sure that he was not left behind.[40] The Portuguese Augustinian monk Sebastian Manrique travelled in the company of people he considered pagans. But, when he fell into the Helmand River and thoroughly soaked all his clothes, 'the Pagan merchant carried me off, as soon as I got ashore, to where he was encamped, to his tent, in order to get me to change my wet clothes.'[41]

The Qandahar-Isfahan route

Only two scholars have so far dealt with the Qandahar-Isfahan route, and then only with its commercial aspect.[42] However, none have dealt in any detail with the geography, logists and travel aspects of this route. According to Siroux, who, in the 1940s, made a study of the historical caravanserais in Iran, the Qandahar-Isfahan route, although traversed by various travellers, had not as yet been researched from an archaeological and historical point of view. Fifty years later, his 'successors', Kleiss and Kayani, indicate in their book on Iranian caravanserais that most of the buildings along the Qandahar-Isfahan highway had been studied. They did not indicate which route (the one via Mashhad or via Tabas) they referred to. From the map in their book, however, it is clear that they meant the route via Mashhad, for they indicate only one caravanserai on the Farah-Berjand route; that is, outside the urban areas. In fact, the Berjand-Biyabanak-Saghand route is not even shown on their map. This is not surprising, because this part of the country was invariably shown as a white spot on maps up until recent times.[43]

We do not have many description from the Safavid era of the Qandahar-Isfahan route. As far as I know, we have only one contemporary Persian, and very cursory, description of part of the route by Siyaqi-Nezam in his *Fotuhat-e Homayun*. He briefly described the arduous march of Allahverdi Khan's troops in 1598, from Shiraz, via Robat-e Khoranaq, Posht-e Badam, Robat-e Shotoran and Tabas to Mashhad.[44] The first European who described this route was the Spanish ambassador Gouvea, who, in 1602, took the road from Yazd to Torbat-e Haydari via Tabas, but without providing any particulars about it. We also have two very short descriptions of the route in 1609 between Qandahar to Isfahan by Salbancke and Coverte, both working for the East India Company (EIC), and, although they published two separate accounts, they travelled this part of their journey together. In addition, there is a more detailed, although still succinct, description of the route travelled by Steel and Crowther, two EIC staffers travelling in 1614 from Qandahar to Isfahan, and a similar description by von Poser, who made the trip from Isfahan to Qandahar in 1621. The monk Manrique traversed the route from Qandahar to Isfahan in 1642; he too provided very little information on the stations that he passed. Finally, Tavernier provided us with a list of all stations along the same route from a journey he made around 1650.[45] Although some of the travellers went from Isfahan to Qandahar, others travelled in the opposite direction. I nevertheless have decided to take Qandahar as the point of departure. This also means that some of the reporters seem to travel backwards compared to the text of their account.

The Qandahar-Isfahan route seems to have been the least likely axis for a major caravan route. In fact, Siyaqi-Nezam stated: 'Never, have more than 1,000 persons travelled this road, because of lack of water.'[46] Nevertheless, despite its inadequacies it appears to have been an important caravan route and since this road is hardly known, even to scholars of Safavid Iran, it is of interest to discuss it in some detail. The Qandahar-Tabas-Isfahan road was so inhospitable and gruelling that even Europeans rarely travelled it. In fact, after Tavernier and Manrique traversed the route from the 1640s to the 1650s, there do not seem to have been other Europeans who travelled this road in Safavid times; at least, they have not left us any account of their travels. It is only in the Qajar period that descriptions of this route appear again. In Kinneir's book there is an enumeration of the stations on the route from Shiraz via Mashhad to Kabul. Mohammad Sadeq, a Persian employed by Sir John Malcolm travelled the route and listed the stations. Captain Christie also travelled part of it around the same time.[47] Khanikof travelled a small part of the route in 1859; Macgregor in 1875, who also gave the most detailed description. Stewart, who travelled part of Steel and Crowther's route in 1880, has provided both a description and map, while Sykes took the same road in 1902. Finally, there were Vaughn and Stahl who covered part of the road in 1889 and 1895 respectively, as did Sven Hedin in 1906.[48]

On leaving Qandahar our sources do not agree on the designation of all the halting stations, or the distances. According to Coverte, one farsang equals one league; and one league equals two courses, while Steel and Crowther stated that every farsang equals 2.5 Indian course. Part of the road they travelled after Tabas also diverged, because each traveller took a different route through the desert. This had to do with the fact that caravans usually broke up in to smaller groups when entering Persia, because of their different destinations (Isfahan or Yazd), as well as the limited capacity of the countryside along the routes, which meant that large caravans could not easily be provisioned and accommodated. As you will see, the road was difficult. It went over mountainous terrain, flat gravel, sand plains and howling deserts, but the main problem was water.

Description of the highway's halting stations

Because it is sometimes difficult to identify the names of the locations mentioned by our sources I have decided to split the route in to distinct parts to facilitate comparisons. There are seven stages: (1) Qandahar to Gereshk; (2) Gereshk to Delaram; (3) Deleram to Farah; (4) Farah to Tabas; (5) Tabas to Berjand; (6) Berjand to Hawz-e

Shah; (7) Hawz-e Shah via Biyabanak to Isfahan; (8) Hawz-e Shah via Posht-e Badam to Yazd.

The country between Qandahar and Gereshk was not easy to traverse. There was only a narrow strip of land available, cut off on the south by a desert of sandhills, and on the north by hilly country that was a sea of rocks, which was even difficult for pedestrians to travel through. Water was difficult to obtain.[49] Coverte stated that, 'Leaving Qandahar, after eight courses the traveler came to a river [Argand Ab], with towns on each side of the river. One of these towns was called Langor.'[50] Langor, which does not appear on any map, must have been a village, not a town. Steel and Crowther noted that after ten courses they arrived at a village called Seriabe. Coverte's Langor therefore may be a copyist's error for Sangor, while Steel's Seriabe may also be a corrupt rendering of the correct form of the halting place referred to, mostly likely Sungzirie, according to a nineteenth-century map, or Sinjiri, as it is called nowadays.[51] From here to Gereshk took three days or at least 26 courses, according to Coverte. During the first two days his party camped in the field. 'The third day, traveling 12 courses, there was a river which was the border between Iran and the land of the Puttans.' Here customs had to be paid for the camels. After taking a ferry over the river Sabbaa,[52] the road led one course to a castle near a town called Grees [Gereshk], the first Persian town, 'where the Persian hath a Garrison of a thousand souldiers.'[53] Steel and Crowther noted that after Seriabe, a village, their party travelled 20 courses to Debage (Deh-Bagh or garden village?), which they called a small village or *dea* (*deh*). Then, after eight courses they arrived at Cushecunna, which was a small castle with a Moghul garrison, for it was the border town. Tavernier also mentioned this town, and referred to it as Kouskienogout.[54] Manrique only mentions one location between Qandahar and Gereshk, which he calls Cushecunam.[55]

From there it took Steel and Crowther another 17 courses to the border river, which, according to the map, must be the Helmand, and then another four courses to Greece [Gereshk], a castle. Here a fee of five '*abbasi*s per camel was levied, unless you had a letter from the Moghul governor of Lahore, as Crowther had. Salbancke did not specify the amount to be paid, but Von Poser had to pay five and a half *shahi*s without even having his goods searched or inspected.[56] After leaving Qandahar, von Poser travelled via Jekata and Cushkina, hamlets where supplies were cheap. The third day he crossed into Persian territory and the day after his caravan crossed the Helmand River. One day later he was in Grista (Gereshk). Von Poser observed the impressive fortress, which was claimed by the Moghuls because of its strategic importance in protecting that area against marauding Baluchis, Chagathays and Uzbegs. The commercial traffic passing through Gereshk yielded enough revenue to maintain a garrison of 2,000 men, von Poser reported.[57] Manrique, who confuses Gereshk with Cushecunam or Khashk-nakhod, wrote that it was the last outpost of the Moghuls with a fortress on a stony plain surrounded by rugged mountains. 'This fort has as its normal garrison one company of a hundred horsemen, under a Captain, and some small guns in poor order. The object of this cavalry force is, I fancy, rather to collect the dues paid by Caravans entering and leaving Persia and Indostan, than for guard duty, as thirty good musketeers could have taken the post without being put to any unusual exertions. We were two days here while the officials in the custom-house examined all our property.'[58]

The crossing of the Helmand River at Saaba (i.e. Abbazaw) could be a time-consuming undertaking. The caravan in which Manrique travelled (100 camels and 40 horses) took four days to cross, although the *karavan-bashi* had hired all the available boats. During spring the water of the river was swollen and swift due to the melted snow that came running down the mountains. The animals sometimes slipped on the smooth stones in the river and, as Manrique experienced, fell with rider and goods into the water.[59]

The slight disagreement between our sources as to the distance travelled may be due to their using a different speed and halting station rather than a different caravan track. For there is general agreement about the number of days travelled between the major halting places. Salbancke, Coverte, Steel and Crowther, and von Poser, all travelled from Qandahar to Gereshk in five days. Tavernier's list suggests that he travelled this stretch of the route in three days, but this seems unlikely, because he also gives a shorter distance. See Table 12.1 for details of halting stations and distances between Qandahar and Gereshk provided by various sources.

After having departed from Gereshk, Coverte slept the next day in the field again (six farsangs). The day thereafter, after six farsangs, he arrived at a castle, where they rested. This was probably Dalkhak, as mentioned by Tavernier. The following day he travelled five farsangs through a plain and slept in the field. Finally, after four farsangs, Coverte arrived at the town of Doctoreham – that is, Delaram – which is located at 90 miles NNW of Gereshk. Between Gereshk and Delaram, Tavernier passed the villages of Dexkah[60] and Chaquilan,[61] while Steel and Crowther mentioned a village called Malgee,[62] after two *farsakh*, then, after ten *farsakh*, they slept in an open field, the next day, after five *farsakh* they reached Gazichan,[63] which was a small castle. Another day, after five *farsakh*, Steel and Crowther reached an old ruined fort, where there was only stinking water to be had. Finally, the next day after five *farsakh*, they reached Delaram, an old fort, where 1.5 *'abbasi* per camel had to be paid. Here they stayed to rest the animals, 'which is called making Mochoane'.[64] As to Gereshk, von Poser made the interesting observation that people drank so much 'tobacco and coffee [kaffe], which make you half raving'.[65] Having left Gereshk, von Poser, after one day, slept at a place called Schuttap, which does not occur on any map and the term probably refers to a waterhole.[66] There were only a few shepherds with their flocks; nevertheless, figs and coagulated milk could be had. The next day von Poser arrived at Delaram, which was situated on the banks of the Hoschrot River, now called the Kash Rud. He stayed in an inn called Dalchech, which I have not been able to identify.[67] The distance was 21 *farsakh* according to Coverte, 27 *farsakh* according to Salbancke and at least 20 *farsakh* according to Tavernier. The

Table 12.1 Halting stations and distances (in *farsakh*) between Qandahar and Gereshk

Steel and Crowther	Distance	Tavernier	Distance	Coverte	Distance	Manrique	Von Poser	Modern name
Candahar	5	–	12	Candahar	4	Candahar	Candahar	Qandahar
Seriabe	10	–	–	Langor	3.5	–	?	Sinjiri
–	–	–	–	Field	3.5	–	?	Hawz Medad
Debage	4	–	–	–	–	–	Jekata	?
Cuschecunna	13.5	Kouskienogout	10	–	–	Cushecunam	Cushkina	Khoshk-Nakhud
Border River	2	–	–	Saba River	1	Sabaa	Hilma River	Abbazaw Helmand
Greece	–	Girichk	–	Grees	–	–	Grista	Gereshk
Total distance	34.5		22 +		12 +			

Table 12.2 Halting stations and distances (in *farsakh*) between Gereshk and Delaram

Steel and Crowther	Distance	Tavernier	Distance	Coverte	Distance	Von Poser	Modern name
Greece	2	Ghirichk	12	Grees	6	Gres	Gereshk
Malgee	10	–		Fields	6	?	Malgir
Fields	5	Dexkhak	4	Castle	5	?	Dalkhak
Gazichan	5	Chaquilan	4	Fields	4	Schuttap	Sangilan
Old fort	5	–	–	–	–	–	
Delaram		Dilaram		Doctoroham		Delarum	Delaram
Total distance	27		20 +		21		

halting stations and distances for this route, as provided by different sources, are listed in Table 12.2.

From Delaram, Coverte and Salbancke continued their voyage, and reached the 'next day after 5–6 farsang to the town of Sehawe [Siyah Ab]'.[68] Thence they continued to a town called Vea 'where are great store of Feltmakers which also make felt Carpets & weauvers of Turkie Carpet, there are also great stores of Dates, and all sorts of fruits'.[69] The next day they travelled six *farsakh* to 'a fair city called Parra [Farah] where they waited for a caravan'. Steel and Crowther travelled seven *farsakh* via Bacon (Bukwa), an old castle, and then camped two days in the open fields where nothing but water was to be had, covering eight *farsakh*, to arrive the fourth day, after four *farsakh*, in Farra, a total distance of 19 *farsakh*, seemingly a greater distance than Coverte. However, the latter forgot to note the distance between Bukwa and Siyah Ab. Tavernier travelled four days and 22 *farsakh* from Delaram to Farah via Bakou,[70] Siaba,[71] and then via KhurMalek (Khurmaliq), which must be Vea (given that the distance to Farah is the same), which neither von Poser nor Tavernier mention at all.[72] Manrique does not provide any locations. Von Poser travelled via Schat and Gre, which were locations in the desert where only some nomads were to be seen. Schat may be the same term as Schuttab, used by von Poser earlier to refer to a waterhole. Water was available at both locations and dates at Gre but these were not ripe yet. He noted that the people called the river there, Ferrahruh (Farah Rud), which yielded good whetstones. That same day von Poser arrived at Farah, after having passed Schadalbnis, Bischabarandak and Baschen, none of which have I been able to identify.[73] The halting stations and distances for this route, as provided by different sources, are listed in Table 12.3.

Coverte and Salbancke agreed about the importance of Farah, where, according to Coverte, there was 'a great trade of merchandize, and great store of raw silke'.[74] Steel and Crowther observed: 'Fara is a little Towne walled with a high wall of brickes about, having a pretty Bazar vaulted over-head to keepe from raine, wherein all necessaries are sold. It stands in good soile, and has plenty of water, without which in this Countrey nothing is to be had: At this Towne all Merchants which go to Persia,

Table 12.3 Halting stations and distance (in *farsakh*) between Delaram and Farah

Steel and Crowther	Distance	Tavernier	Distance	Coverte	Distance	Von Poser	Modern name
Delaram	7	Delaram	6	Doctoroham	6	Delarum	Delaram
Bacon	4	Bakou	4	–		Schat	Bukwa
Open field	4	Siabeh	6	Sehawe	?	Gre	Siyah Ab
Open field	4	Khourmalik	6	Vea	6	Baschen	Khurmaliq
Fara		Fara		Parra		Ferra	Farah
Total distance	19		22		12 +		

are forced to stay seven, or eight, or ten daies together, where the King's Treasurer seeth the weight of all their packets, and esteemes them at so much the Maune (*mann*), as he thinks fit, and takes three per cento custome.'[75] Steel and Crowther stayed for two days in Farah where their Armenian fellow travellers left their company. Von Poser observed that Farah, which was situated near a hill called Kurdgi, had a deep moat and no attractive buildings, except for that of the governor. The town was surrounded with vineyards and fruit gardens that had very large fruits, which were irrigated from the nearby river. Von Poser was also quite happy to drink some good wine at Farah during the few days that he stayed there.[76] Manrique mentioned that, 'although a small place with not more than four thousand inhabitants, it is still much frequented by foreign merchants and strangers, as well as by the troops which are usually posted there owing to the presence of the Kanes or Viceroys of the Province'. He further mentioned that the customs officials examined the goods and processed the payment of fees.[77]

Although there is, once again, a difference in the recorded distance of travel amongst these travellers, there is agreement on the eight days travelled between Gereshk and Farah.

Coverte and Salbancke are not very specific about the route they took after Farah. Salbancke only reported: 'From Parra we spent eigtheene dayes to Jesd, a Citie of Persia, passing through a very desolate countrey.'[78] Coverte provided some more information, but only of a very general nature. Having departed from Farah, he noted that, 'The next day two farsangs over the mountains; another day 4–5 farsangs over the mountains next days 7 farsangs; next day 5 farsangs; next day 10 farsangs over mountainous terrain; next day after 3 farsangs he arrived at a town called Banda [possibly is Birjand], being but a harbor or lodging place.'[79] Steel and Crowther, von Poser, Manrique and Tavernier all took the same route, and they all (except for Manrique who hardly mentions any stops) agree that the next major stop was Birjand. Von Poser went via the river (at Farah) and camped for two stops in the field and the third stop was Duruh. Tavernier went via Zela, Chechmeband to Duruh. No such place as Zela is found on any maps. There are two possible sites for its location, one is Qal'e-Kah and the other Imam Zeid. Steel and Crowther, as well as von Poser, went one *farsakh* to the Helmand River, then continued one day in the fields (travelling seven *farsakh*) and then the next day after four *farsakh* reached a small village, where they found supplies. Then the next day they were less fortunate, they travelled four *farsakh* and had to dig for water. Continuing another day for eight *farsakh*, they arrived the day thereafter, after five *farsakh*, at Draw (Duruh), a village. Here 'we stayed a day, which is the custome once in foure dayes, for such as travel with laden Camels, to rest.'[80] From Duruh they continued one day for three *farsakh*, and another day four *farsakh*. Finally, after another day of five *farsakh* of travel they made a stop at Zaidabasha (Sarbishe), where many carpets could be had. Carpets were also produced and offered for sale at the next stop, Mude, or Mud as it is now known. They finally arrived, after five *farsakh*, at Birchen (Berjand).[81] Tavernier stopped at Mont, which probably is not a name, at least it does not occur on any map, but just the French word for mountain. This is not surprising, as it is clear from the remarks made by Coverte and Salbancke about travelling over mountains, as well as by the physical reality of the terrain, that this was a very mountainous area. The next stop was Sarbicha (Sarbishe), and after that Moud (Mud).[82]

After Farah, von Poser moved for two days through desert-like terrain. There were some gardens scattered here and there but, apart from other travellers, he did not see anybody. Although very uninviting, the area offered good grazing for the animals as well as water. The first day he mentioned being at a location called Galaka (Gala Chah), which is an important well, located 15 miles north of Dagh Namadi, also referred to as the Naomid desert. This area is a swampy depression, through which small streams run during spring, but which is dry and covered with alkali and salt during summer.[83] The next day in the same desert the caravan passed a location, which, according to the Indians in the caravan, was called Tschesmenbudi. This is possibly what is now called Chashme-ye Garm, a small spring of good water on the Naspanda-Duruh road, 35 miles from Duruh.[84] The following day, von Poser arrived at the village of Duro, where there was a fortress on top of the hills and, more importantly, wonderful grapes and almonds available. Having spent the night here, the caravan moved on to Prunck (Purang) where only some nomads and their flocks were seen. The next day von Poser arrived at Serbescha, where the inhabitants produced carpets and felts, and trees such as *Anabat* (probably the *'anab* or jujube tree) and *Singit* (probably the *senjed* or oleaster tree) were found. The next stop was in the village of Müt (Mud), which traded with Berjand. Because of its gardens von Poser liked the village very much. The caravan arrived a day later at Birgian (Berjand). Here von Poser noted the rather large castle for protection against Uzbeg raids, the good water hauled by windmills, as well as the production of carpets and other floor covers made with goat hair.[85] At Berjand, fine felts and carpets of camel hair could be bought for two to five *'abbasis* per *mann* (about 3 kg). Steel and Crowther stayed there one day.[86]

All travellers covered the distance between Farah to Berjand in seven days, except for Steel and Crowther who took ten days, due to a slower pace, and the fact that they had to search and sometimes dig for water. According to Coverte the distance was 44+ *farsakh*, while Steel and Crowther estimated it at 54 *farsakh*, and Tavernier at 56 *farsakh* (see Table 12.4).

From Berjand to Tabas the road continued through a gravel waste. The route went via Deazaid, probably Deh-e Sayyed or a village of sayyeds – that is, descendants of the prophet Mohammad – 'where they pretend to be all religious, and have store of Carpets to sell at cheape rates'.[87] The halting stations were Tesaitan, which is not on any map and may be Dastajerd. Steel and Crowther made a stop in the fields after three *farsakh*. After Berjand, Tavernier continued to Cors, and Steel and Crowther, after five *farsakh*, to Choore, an old ruined town. Given the limited choice this must be Khur, where Tavernier stayed. From Khur, Tavernier's road went via Talkeave or Tulkah as it now known on the maps, or, in the case of Steel and Crowther, via two stops in the open field and ten *farsakh*, where only brackish and stinking water was to be had. From this village the next stop was Douhouk (Duhuk) and the caravan was getting close to Tabas. Steel and Crowther did not mention the distance, but they arrived at Dehuge (Duhuk), 'where is a prettie streame of hot water, which being put into any vessel, becomes coole and health-some'. To Duhuk, Tavernier travelled for two days and 16 *farsakh*, and Steel and Crowther three days and 10+ *farsakh*. From Duhuk, Steel and Crowther's road went seven *farsakh* via Dea Curma (Deh-e Khorma or the date village), or via Espak, Espaque (Esfake, Aspak) in the case of Tavernier, and then after five *farsakh* to Tobaz (Tabas). In both cases it was a trip of two days and 12 or 13 *farsakh*, and then finally Daralit (which had a serai and some supplies in the nineteenth century) at the Ashego pass. Having gone through this pass, the caravan arrived at Tabas. Here travellers would stay for some time, because now the most difficult part of the route began, part of which skirted and part passed through

Table 12.4 Halting stations and distance (in *farsakh*) between Farah and Berjand

Steel and Crowther	Distance	Tavernier	Distance	Coverte	Distance	Von Poser	Modern name
Fara	1	Fara	10	Parra	2	Ferra	Farah
River	7	–		Mountains	5		Helmand
Open field	4	Zela	10	Mountains	7		
Small village	4	–		Mountains	5	Galaka	Galachah
Field	8	–		–		–	
Field	8	Chechmeband	6	Mountains	12	Tschesmebudi	
Draw	3	Dourouh	12			Duro	Duruh
Field	4	–		–			
Field	5	Mont	7	Mountains	10	Prunck	Purang
Zaidebashe	5	Sarbicha	5			Serbescha	Sarbishe
Mude	5	Moud	7	Mountains	3	Müt	Mud
Birchen		Birdjand		Banda		Birgian	Berjand
Total distance	54		57		44 +		

the *kevir* or salt desert as well as a Saharan-type sand desert. Steel and Crowther state that all caravans stayed for four or five days for the animals to rest and prepare for the four day journey through the salt desert, 'wherein many miscarry'.[88] At Tobaz (Tabas) and in Dea Curma (Deh Khorma or date village) 'are store of Dates, and three thousand Maune yearely of the finest Silke in Persia, which is carried to Yades, a faire Citie, where they have the like, and is made into Taffatas, Sattens and Damaskes. The King will not suffer it to be transported, especially into Turkie, but the Portugalls carried it into Portugall.'[89]

Having left Berjand, von Poser arrived in the village of Tagaer (?), where the chief's name was Mir Neʻmatollah (Mirnamathola). The next day he lodged at the village of Jeka (?), and the day thereafter at Chur (Khur), where there was good water and other necessary supplies. The following day led through the Telchau desert, where, although water was found, nobody wanted to drink. Continuing, von Poser came the next day to Gala Degu (Qalʻe-ye Duhuk), where he celebrated his 24th birthday by drinking the best water he had ever had from a spring in the rocks. It was a cultivated village. The caravan then moved to Ispas, which was situated on a hill and where travellers could get all kinds of fruit. Finally, von Poser's caravan arrived at Tabes (Tabas) where he had to pay six *bisti*s or 30 *kreuzer* per camel. The money changed here, and one *shahi* equalled 12 *caspeger* (*sic*; *qazbegi*).[90] The details of halting stations and distances between Berjand and Tabas, as provided by the travellers, is listed in Table 12.5.

Two days after Tabas, the travellers took different routes, which indicates that there was not one commercial route. The choice of route was probably determined by the availability of pack animals, water, guides, and whether you wanted to go to Isfahan rather than Yazd. The route after Tabas is not very well described by our sources. In fact, Tavernier is the only one who continues to provide us with the names of the halting stations he stopped at. The others rarely provide names, and, if they do, they are mostly unintelligible. Nevertheless, based on the data provided

Table 12.5 Halting stations and distance (in *farsakh*) between Berjand and Tabas

From/to	Distance	Tavernier	Distance	Von Poser	Modern name
Birchen		Birdjand	7	Birgian	Berjand
Deazaid	3	Tesaitan	9	Tagaer	Taghab
Field	5	–	–	Jeka	
Choore	3	Cors	10	Cuhr	Khur
Fields	7	Talkeave	6	Telchau	Tulkah
Fields	?	–	–	–	–
Dehuge	7	Douhouk	6	Gala Degu	Duhuk
Dea Curma	5	Espaque	7	Ispas	Aspak
Tobaz	–	Tebbes	–	Tebes	Tabas
Total distance	30+		45		

by the travellers it is clear that they did not follow the same route. Everybody had to travel to Cheshme-ye Shah and Ja'fari. Then travellers could go to Isfahan via Biyabanak, or to Yazd via Robat-e Khan and Posht-e Badam. Manrique and Tavernier travelled via Biyabanak and onwards to Isfahan. The rest all took the Yazd road, but after Saghand, Steel and Crowther went via Ardekan to Isfahan, the others continued to Yazd. I will first discuss the Biyabanak-Isfahan route and then the Robat-e Khan-Yazd to road.

Because Tavernier's description is the most complete one, we will follow his lead for that part of the road they all travelled to Ja'fari. Where possible, there will be details of halting stations as given by the other travellers. Tavernier's first stop after Tabas was Karte, which is probably Kerdabad,[91] one of the villages near Chaharde, a small settlement consisting of several villages and hidden by palms.[92] The next stop was Shorab, also known as Robat-e Gur.[93] There was a direct route via the salt desert, but caravans skirted this desert and arrived at Shorab, which had a small *serai* and some salt water from a riverbed that was generally dry. This location is not mentioned by Tavernier. From here the next stage was 14 miles to Chechme-Cha or Cheshme-ye Shah, which had a very fine spring and, given the horribly bitter taste of most of the water along this route, had the best water.[94] In 1598, Allah Verdi Khan's army, after having traversed the most difficult part of their march, finally arrived at Cheshme-ye Hasan. I have not been able to identify this spring on any map, but given that their next stop was Chaharde, I think it may be identified with Cheshme-ye Shah. At this stop, Allahverdi Khan's soldiers only found a small source of brackish water, which was just enough for their animals. The men therefore did not drink anything themselves. By chance a fusilier saw a goat and followed it and then over the hill he saw a paradisical field with an abundant source of clear water. The army was saved and it is likely that from then onwards this source of water was known as Cheshme-ye Shah, although neither Siyaqi-Nezam nor any other source has reported this.[95] From there the caravan passed Safurria (i.e. Ja'fari), a small hamlet, after two miles and, continuing via the Miyan pass, arrived at the start of the pass at Doree, a hamlet, which was called Sadarou by Tavernier.[96] Allahverdi Khan took a different route. Rather than going to Biyabanak in a more or less straight line to the west, he took a turn towards the left, in a south-western direction to Posht-e Badam via Robat-e Khan. MacGregor had travelled this route in 1875, Stewart in 1880 and Sykes in 1902.[97] I return to this route later, but let us first complete the route via Biyabanak.

After Sadarou, Tavernier's route continued over a road that was very trying for the camels[98] to the next well, known as Tchah Mehdji according to Tavernier, or Chah Mehjee.[99] It had a tower, which in the nineteenth century was in ruins. More importantly, it had a 150-feet deep well and, if you were lucky, a rope. However, the water was bitter salt water. The well itself was situated on a waste of sand hills and was a most desolate place. Although the gravel and stony terrain had been a challenge so far, now the terrain turned into soft sand, which made for very hard going. After some miles the caravan had to cross part of the *Kevir*. The salt desert does not have 'one blade of grass, not one leaf of any kind, not a living thing of any sort. It is composed of dark soil, which looks as if it had been turned up by the plough a year before, but which is covered with a thick salt efflorescence, which glitters painfully to the eyes.' There were also many potholes making it difficult for the animals.[100] Finally, the salt desert ended and the road became gravel and sand, difficult for the animals to tread.

> On the third day God ordained that the wind should fall, on which we began to enter those sandy Sirtes, [i.e. sand desert] which by the mere movement of the feet of the men and animals forming the Caravan rose in great clouds of that finely divided sand, so that it was necessary to keep the eyes, mouth, and the nostrils covered, in order not to clog them and be stifled. To this hardship another was added, as when we were about to halt at the end of the first day's march, we found ourselves without any of the small stock of good water we carried with us solely for drinking, the leather water-bags being stuck together and as wrinkled as if they had never held water.[101]

After ten miles there was an old cistern, called Hawz-e Mirza, but, as was the case in 1875, it did not always have water. Tavernier did not mention this cistern, but Caseni (?) as his next stop, which I have not been able to identify. It may have been another well nearby.[102] Tavernier's next stretch only had water after 20 *farsakh* or 60 to 70 miles. The caravan then had to move onwards to Mehrjan, a miserable place in a wasteland, with indifferent water and where supplies were difficult to get.[103] The next stop for the travellers was Biyabanak, or Biyabanact as Tavernier called it.[104] Manrique, who did not mention any stations en route, only describes his arrival at Biyabanak, as follows: 'We thus reached some deserts called by the people Biabonas or the desert of Biabanac, which they say are a part of the sandy Lybian wastes. Though not so very extensive, it took us four days to march across them, which seemed to me four thousand!'[105] It is, therefore, not surprising that people were elated to find some temporary relief from their hardship that had seemed to be never-ending.

> So welcome was its [the City of Biabanac] sight to all of us that we congratulated each other on our excellent journey, forgetful in our present joy of the hardships passed. Then, about a musket-shot's distance, before the City was reached, we came upon a swift, lovely, and pleasant stream of good clean water, which flowing down from the neighbouring mountains, spread away through a wide level plain dotted with green gardens full of fruit-trees and covered with leafy palms laden with bunches of sweet luscious dates, which, however, could not be eaten, as they were not yet in season.[106]

However, there was an abundance of melons and watermelons, which the villagers brought for sale.[107]

Although Manrique and Tavernier mention that they arrived at Biyabanak, it would appear that such an oasis did not exist. Despite the fact that, for example, Hedin has a village called Bijabanek on his maps right at the location where one expects it to be, MacGregor maintains that it is more likely that they arrived at Khoor, a small oasis 'situated amidst of a waste of stony plains and rocky hills'.[108] For in the nineteenth century, Biyabanak was an administrative district not a village. MacGregor visited the district and reported:

> Beeabunnuck is a sub-division of Semnan, Khoor being its principal place. It has eight villages-viz. Khoor; Junduck, fifteen farsangs north of Beyaza, with fifty houses; Ferukhi, forty houses, three farsangs north; Gurmab, five farsangs; Oordeeb, forty houses, six farsangs west; Iraj, seven farsangs west, fifty houses; Mehrjan, 100 houses, six farsangs east; and Beyaza, sixty houses, ten farsangs from Khoor...
>
> These are all situated separately, generally at the foot of hills in the midst of a howling wilderness. There is no village of the name of Beeabunnuck, or hills or valleys; but it is only a collection of small oases, having no topographical connection with each other. From this it is sixty farsangs to Semnan, while Naeen is forty-five farsangs; Yuzd, fifty farsangs; and Tubbus, forty farsangs.[109]

Despite the fact that the seventeenth- and the nineteenth-century travellers mention an oasis called Biyabanak, which is clearly situated south of Khur, MacGregor's evidence is very convincing. Biyabanak is not found on modern maps, in the *Historical Gazetteer*, in Razmara's *Farhang-e Joghrafiya-ye Iran* nor in Mostawfi's *Shahdad*, which is the most detailed modern geographical description of the area in question. Also, Hedin and others who put Biyabanak on the map never physically checked out its existence, which MacGregor did. I therefore have to conclude that MacGregor is right and that the travellers confused one of the eight villages, Beyaze, with Biyabanak, the name of the administrative district. Table 12.6 provides details of the stages between Tabas and Biyabanak district, as provided by Tavernier.

After Biyabanak, Tavernier lists the following stages: Abiger, Basabad and Anarek, which probably was the more traditional route to proceed to Isfahan. From the Biyabanak district the road went through gravel and stony land, alternating with sand hollows. Tavernier continued to a station called Abiger, which is found on the maps as Ab-e Garm or Warm Water, and is situated at five *farsakh* from Khur. From here the route took Tavernier to Basabad, a location found on a map printed by Hedin (Abbassabad) and Gabriel. After this the road continued via Muschudseri (Mashhad-e Sar?) to Anaraka large village.[110] From here, in easy stages, Tavernier travelled via Na'in, Mouchena de R(ahdar) (Mushkinan?), and Sakunegi (Sagzi?) to Isfahan.[111] There was also an alternative, direct road from the Biyabanak district to Saghand, a total distance of 60 miles.[112]

Table 12.6 Halting stations and distance (in *farsakh*) between Tabas and Biyabanak district

Tavernier	Distance	Modern name
Tebbes	4	Tabas
Karte	14	Korit – Kardabad
–		Shorab
Chechme-Cha	8	Chasme-ye Shah
Sadarou	15	Darre-ye Daru
–	–	Hawz-e Mirza
Tchah-Mehdji	10	Chah Mehji
Casena	5	Mehrjan?
Biabanact	5	Biyabanak District or Beyaze village
Abiger	5	Garmab
Total distance	66	

From Cheshme-ye Shah, whence Manrique and Tavernier had continued in a western direction to Biyabanak, others, such as Allahverdi Khan's army, Salbancke, Coverte, Steel and Crowther, as well as von Poser, took the southern route towards Yazd. Their road had to go to Robat-i-Khan via Ja'fari. From here the route went to Pusht-e Badam, through tracts 'of true desert not surpassed by any in the world'.[113] This stretch of the route measured 48 miles and was, according to Stewart, 'the worst part of the journey' and a 'howling desert'.[114] After 11 miles there was a tower and a tiny spring, and from here the road ascended. After eight miles the road descended and another nine miles took the traveller to Hawz-e Shah 'Abbas, which may have been the location that von Poser called Gala (i.e. *qal'e* or fortress).[115] Continuing for another 14 miles there was a hamlet with brackish water, and finally Posht-e Badam, or Postobatan as von Poser called it. According to MacGregor, it was 'a hideous village, at the bottom of an equally hideous stony valley'. After about 12 miles, the only water available during the entire stretch of 42 miles was at Hawz-e Charfarsakh.[116] It was during this part of the journey that von Poser was in dire need of water, and was helped by his Indian fellow travellers.[117] After 15 miles, the traveller reached Allahabad, which had no water and was in ruins in 1875, but in 1810 Christie recorded it as a stage, while in 1880 it had a good well with brackish water.[118] The next station was at Saghand, after 17 miles, which had a caravanserai and good water. Between Yazd and Saghand, a distance of 50 miles, there were only three springs, and here and there a water cistern (*hawz*). Saghand was situated around a spring.[119] Table 12.7 provides details of the stages between Tabas and Saghand, as provided by the travellers.

The above description is mostly based on nineteenth-century travel accounts. They do not differ in their basic experience from von Poser who mentioned that he had to go for six days through a terrible desert.[120] Siyaqi-Nezam wrote that

Table 12.7 Halting stations and distance (in *farsakh*) between Tabas and Saghand

Steel and Crowther	Distance	Coverte	Distance	Von Poser	Modern name
Tobaz	12	Plains	3	Tebes	Tabas
Desert		Plains	5	Pena	Pahalonj
Desert	5	Plains	7.5	desert	Chasme-ye Shah
Small castle	9	Sunday		–	Robat-e Khan
Field	5	Plains	7.5	Postbatan	Posht-e Badam
Field	10	Plains	9	desert	
Seagan	4	Seafta	5	desert	Saghand
Fields	10	Gusta	4	Cres	Khuranaq
Total distance	55		41		

Allahverdi Khan's army passed this part of the route on 21 June 1598, the hottest time of the year. The troops suffered because of the heat and lack of water. Only the best troops, the royal slaves (*gholam*), were able to endure the heat. 'Fifty *farsakh* of desert, so hot and short of water as the seventh hell (*sajin*), separates Posht-e Badam from Tabas.'[121]

From Saghand, Steel and Crowther travelled via the fields, as they called the wilderness, to Irabad, which may be identified as Ebrahimabad.[122] They then continued to travel via the fields and then arrived at Ardakan, a well-known halting station. From here their route went via Sellef (Sarv?), Agea Gaurum (Agda?), the fields, Beavas (Kuhpa?), and Goolabad (Golnabad). Continuing their journey, they probably travelled the same route as Tavernier, if Tavernier's Moucena de Radar (Mushkinan?) is Steel and Crowther's Morea Shavade, which I have not been able to identify. The road continued via Cupa (Kuhpa), Dea Sabs (Deh-e Sabz or Green village, but more likely as Deh Sagzi), and a last stop in the fields, before arriving at Isfahan.[123]

After Saghand, Salbancke, Coverte and von Poser, continued to Yazd. They arrived at Rezab after 13 miles, which offered shelter and brackish water, but there was still a stretch of 40 miles. The road was gravel and started to ascend after six miles.[124] The caravan arrived at Hawz-e Miyan-Taq, which in the nineteenth century no longer had any water. According to Stewart, after 28 miles at the start of a great ravine, there was some water at Doh Kulli. After eight miles the road started to ascend and went through an eight-mile-long defile until it arrived at Robat-e Khoranoq. This location may be the same as Coverte's Gusta and von Poser's Cres, which the latter described as having a lot of fruit and good water.[125] From here one could either continue to Yazd, or take the road to the right and continue to Ardakan. Stewart traversed this part of the route between Khoranoq and Ardakan, a distance of 32.5 miles. The road led for 11.5 miles through a pass between hills and arrived at a domed well called Cheshme. After 11 miles it arrived at Hawz-e Safid, which allowed men and beasts to take in water for the last time before reaching Ardakan after 20 miles.[126]

Khoranoq was a small village with a caravanserai and 80 families, around 1880. From here it was still 22 miles to Yazd according to Christie, but MacGregor had calculated it as 44 miles.[127] The country was entirely barren of any vegetation, there were no streams, and only the presence of cisterns, or *hawz* as they were called in this part of the country, made it possible for people to live there. After seven miles of gravelly terrain there was Chah-e Naw, which had water. The route continued through rocky hills and stony valleys without any vegetation. MacGregor passed two cisterns neither of which had water. 'The country passed on this day was just like that which one sees from the deck of a P. and O. steamer going up the red Sea.' as he graphically described the landscape. Finally, the weary caravan arrived at Anjirak, which had a simple caravanserai with a good spring of water.[128] Yazd was close by and held out hope for rest and comfort. The road slowly ascended through hills known as Kuh-e Tarunah. At first the terrain was hard sand and gravel ridges, alternating with soft sand hollows, but on nearing Yazd it changed into heavy sand, like the Sahara desert, up to Naranj Qal'a, two miles from the Yazd oasis. The last stop on this route before Yazd was at Hawz-e Jaq'far (ten miles from Yazd), after leaving the Kuh-e Tarunah.[129]

Von Poser went from Yazd, where much silk was cultivated, via Jesdeschat (Huddschetabad? = Hojjatabad) to Ardakan, which was very populous and fertile, but its water tasted peculiar; then onwards to Agda (Aghda), where his caravan got dates, figs, very large melons and grapes. The next stop was Arekan (Arakan), which he described as a collection of huts and some ploughing farmers. The grapes were good, although the people were unpleasant. After Arakan came Misra Kasi (Mazra'e Kasi?). This village was situated in the rocks, surrounded by vineyards; the next stop was at Merdeschebat (Mordeshabad?), which had all the necessities and water, where the traveller paid one *'abbasi* per camel. On this stretch of the route, where there were villages there was cultivation otherwise the country was an utter wilderness. The caravan then arrived at Cupa (Kuhpa) where there was good water and many gardens, and from there it was onwards to Serna (Sagzi?), where von Poser had to pay a road fee (*rahdari*). Finally, von Poser arrived at Isfahan via Bummen (unidentified), Gulnabat (Golnabad), and Merdebat (Murzabad?) on the Zayande Rud.[130]

Conclusion

Travelling from Qandahar to Isfahan was an adventure. Although the road was well travelled, it was very hot, very uncomfortable, very unpleasant for man and animal, and dangerous because the route was unmarked so that one could easily lose one's way. Steele and Crowther concluded: 'For all Persia, especially betwixt this and Spahan, is barren, where sometime in two or three dayes travel, there is no greene thing to be seene; only some water, and that also often brackish, stinking and naught.'[131] But travellers had little choice. You either took the roundabout way via Mashhad, or the more direct route to Isfahan. I have further shown that during the last stretch of the route there was more than one way out of the gravel and sand desert that skirted the great salt desert *kevir* to reach the road linking Yazd and Isfahan. Despite the fact that the road was much travelled by pilgrims, not just by traders, it is amazing that it was not a well-serviced one. There were hardly any caravanserais such as those that dotted the other major commercial routes in Iran. Although there were water cisterns along the route both their condition and their water was bad, in general. The road was not properly marked either, and no trace remains of the pillars allegedly erected by Shah 'Abbas on part of this road. You had to be really determined to make a living, or maybe because you had no choice, if you decided to take this highway to Isfahan. Finally, I have identified the stages mentioned by Steel and Crowther, von Poser, Manrique, and Tavernier, but not all of those mentioned by Coverte and Salbancke on the last part of their route. As such, this chapter has also tried to make a contribution to the historical geography of Iran.

Notes

1. Willem Floor, *The Economy of Safavid Persia* (Wiesbaden: Reichert, 2000).
2. See, for example, Temple, Richard, 'The highway from the Indus to Candahar', *Proceedings of the Royal Geographical Society* IX (1880), pp. 529–48; Michael A. Biddulph, 'Pishin and the routes between India and Candahar', *Proceedings of the Royal Geographical Society* IX (1880), pp. 212–46; James Sutherland Broadfoot, 'Reports on parts of the Ghilzi country and on the route from Ghazni to Dera Ismail Khan by the Ghalwari Pass', *Royal Geographical Society, Supplementary Papers* I (1885), pp. 341–400. In general, see S. Dale, *Indian Merchants and Eurasian Trade, 1600-1750* (Cambridge: Cambridge University Press, 1994), pp. 49–55.
3. Anonymous, *A Chronicle of the Carmelites in Persia and the Papal Mission of the Seventeenth and Eighteenth Centuries*, 2 vols (London: Eyre and Spottiswood, 1939), vol. 1, p. 120.
4. Jean-Baptiste Tavernier, *Voyages en Perse et description de ce royaume* (Paris, 1930), p. 340.
5. See, for example, the map showing the high density of caravanserais on this route in Wolfram Kleiss and Mehdi Yusof Kayani, *Fehrest-e Karavansarayha-ye Irani*, 2 vols (Tehran, 1368/1989); Francois Le Gouz, *Les Voyages et Observations du Sieur de la Boullaye-Le Gouz* (Paris: Francois Clousier, 1653), p. 62.
6. A. S. Beveridge, trans. *Babur-Nama*, 2 vols in one (London, 1928 [New Delhi, 1989]), p. 202.
7. 'The voyage of M. Joseph Salbancke through India, Persia, part of Turkie, the Persian Gulfe, and Rabia. 1609', in Purchas, Samuel (ed.), *Hakluytus Posthumus or Purchas His Pilgrims*, 20 vols (Glasgow, 1905), vol. 3, p. 85 (henceforth cited as Purchas, vol. 3).
8. Floor, *The Economy*, pp. 200–1, 207–10.
9. A journall of the journey of Richard Steel and John Crowther from Azemere in India, the place of the Great Mughals residence, to Spahan the Royall Seat of the King of Persia, in the affaires of the East-Indian Society. Anonymous 1615, 1616, in Purchas, Samuel (ed.), *Hakluytus Posthumus or Purchas His Pilgrims*, 20 vols (Glasgow, 1905), vol. 4, pp. 268–9 (henceforth cited as Purchas, vol. 4).
10. Heinrich Von Poser, *Lebens- und Todes Geschichte* (Jehna, 1675), unpaginated (entry 21 September); Purchas, vol. 4, p. 273.
11. Purchas, vol. 4, p. 272.

12. Riazul Islam, *Indo-Persian Relations* (Tehran, 1970), p. 172, notes 3-4; Ibid., *A Calendar of Documents on Indo-Persian Relations*. 2 vols (Tehran/Karachi, 1979), vol. 1, pp. 264-70; Dale, *Indian Merchants*, pp. 49-55.
13. Raphael Du Mans, *Estat de la Perse*, ed. Ch. Schefer (Paris: Leroux, 1890), p. 193.
14. Sebastian Manrique, *Travels of Fray Sebastien Manrique*, trans. C. Eckford Luad and H. Hosten, 2 vols (London: Hakluyt, 1927), vol. 2, pp. 343-4.
15. Purchas, vol. 4, p. 272. Herbert also mentions that many caravans imported all kinds of goods coming from Hindustan, Tartary and Arabia. Thomas Herbert, *Travels in Persia, 1627-1629*, ed. W. Foster (New York, 1929), p. 255.
16. Robert Coverte, *The Travels of Captain Robert Coverte*, ed. Boies Penrose (Philadelphia, 1931), p. 74. This represented about 2,000 tons if one assumes the carrying capacity of a camel at 100 kg. According to W. Hinz, *Moslem Weights and Measures*, pp. 14-15, a camel pack was on average 250 kg.
17. Steensgaard, Niels, *Carrack, Caravans and Companies* (Copenhagen, 1973), p. 168.
18. Seistani, Malek Shah Hosein b. Malek Ghayath al-Din Mohammad b. Shah Mahmud., *Ehya al-Moluk*, ed. Manuchehr Setudeh (Tehran, 1344/1966), p. 220; Purchas, vol. 4, p. 269.
19. Klein, Rüediger, 'Caravan trade in Safavid Iran (first half of the 17th century)', in Calmard, Jean (ed.), *Etudes Safavides* (Paris/Tehran, 1994), p. 311, n. 22. See Floor, *The Economy*, p. 206, for examples of the use of cows as pack animal in Safavid Iran.
20. Floor, *The Economy*, pp. 200-9.
21. Purchas, vol. 4, p. 268; Danvers, Frederick Charles, *The Portuguese in India: Being an History of the Rise and Decline of their Eastern Empire*, 2 vols. (London, 1894); William Foster, ed., *The English Factories in India 1618-1669*, 13 vols (London, 1906-27), p. 242 (1637-41); pp. 203, 207-8, 246, 261, 266, 307-8, and so on (1646-50). See also W. Moreland, *India at the Death of Akbar* (London, 1920), p. 56. For more examples, see Floor, *The Economy*, pp. 203-8 as well as Niels Steensgaard, 'The route through Quandahar: The significance of the overland trade from India to the West in the seventeenth century', in Sunil Chaudhury and Michel Morineau (eds) *Merchants, Companies and Trade* (Cambridge: Cambridge University Press, 1999),
22. Purchas, vol. 4, p. 273.
23. Manrique, *Travels*, vol. 2, pp. 351-2.
24. R. W. Ferrier, *British-Persian Relations in the 17th Century*, unpublished dissertation (Cambridge University, 1970), p. 363.
25. H. Dunlop, *Bronnen tot de geschiedenis der Oostindische Compagnie in Perzië* (-s'Gravenhage 1930), p. 480 (1634); Floor, Willem, *A Fiscal History of Iran in the Safavid and Qajar Periods, 1500-1925* (New York: Bibliotheca Persica Press, 1998), pp. 159-65; John Emerson and Willem Floor, *A Fiscal History of Iran in the Safavid and Qajar Period*. New York: Bibliotheca Persica, 1999.
26. Manrique, *Travels*, vol. 2, p. 352.
27. Ibid., p. 349.
28. Chahryar Adle, editor and translator, 'Siyaqi-Nezam – Fotuhate Homayun – "Les Victoires augustes"', 1007/1598 2 vols (Sorbonne – Paris: unpublished thesis, 1976), vol. 2, pp. 442-4.
29. Molla Jalal al-Din Monajjem, *Ruzname-ye 'Abbasi ya Ruzname-ye Molla Jalal*, ed. Sayfollah Vahidniya (Tehran, 1366/1967), p. 165.
30. Purchas, vol. 4, p. 275.
31. Ahmad Mostawfi, *Shahdad va Joghrafiya-ye Tarikhi va Dasht-e Lut* (Tehran: Daneshgah-e Tehran, 1351/1972), pp. 70-1, 74, 139, 145, 326-36; MacGregor, *Narrative*, vol. 1, p. 276 (plus drawing); Alfons Gabriel, *Weites Wildes Iran* (Stuttgart: Strecker und Schröder, 1940), p. 65 (photo); Idem., 'The Southern Lut and Iranian Baluchistan', *Geographic Journal* 92 (1938), p. 203 (photo); Government of Great Britain (Naval Intelligence Division), *Persia*, Geographical Handbook Series B.R. 525 (n.p.; 1939-45), p. 162, photo 137 ('eroded "Mil" marking the southern entrance to the ancient route across the Southern Lut.').
32. Purchas, vol. 4, p. 275.
33. Herbert, *Travels*, p. 50.
34. Jean Chardin, *Voyages*, ed. L. Langlès, 10 vols (Paris, 1811), vol. 3, p. 376; vol. 2, p. 320. According to Hinz, Walther, *Islamische Masse und Gewichte* (Leiden: Brill, 1970), one camel-load was on average 250kg.

Jenkinson's camels carried 180 kg. Camels carried normally 40–50 *mann-e Tabriz*, though they could carry more, but this was seldom done, according to Charles Lockyer, *An Account of the Trade in India* (London, 1711), p. 236. 'Ordinary camels take 100 waight, Persian camels load usually 800–900 waight.' Robert Coverte, *A True & Almost Incredible Report of an Englishman That Travelled by Land through Many Kingdoms* (Philadelphia, 1930), p. 80. In the nineteenth century, Persian camels carried between 400 and 480 lbs = 180 and 216 kg, while mules and ponies carried 200–250 lbs = 90–112 kg, while donkeys could carry about 130 lbs = 58 kg. Issawi, Ch. *The Economic History of Iran 1800-1914* (Chicago, 1971), p. 195. Barker, the EIC agent recommended that goods destined for Persia be packed in bales of 130 lbs two of which constituted a donkey load, three a mule-load and four a camel-load. The normal silk load was 200 kg or 441 lbs, Steensgaard, *Caravans*, pp. 31–2.

35. Cornelius Le Bruyn, *Travels into Moscovy, Persia and Part of the East-Indies*, 2 vols (London, 1737), vol. 1, p. 147; Purchas, vol. 4, p. 275; Manrique, *Travels*, vol. 2, p. 341.
36. Manrique, *Travels*, vol. 2, p. 341.
37. Dale, *Indian Merchants*, p. 37; Purchas, vol. 4, p. 269; Manrique, *Travels*, vol. 2, p. 344; E. Ehlers, *Iran. Grundzüge einer geographischen Landeskunde* (Darmstadt, 1980), pp. 68, 362, 442; Moreland, *India at the Death of Akbar*, pp. 205–7.
38. Manrique, *Travels*, vol. 2, p. 341; Von Poser, *Lebens- und Todes Geschichte* (entry on 12 September).
39. Purchas, vol. 4, p. 273.
40. Von Poser, *Lebens- und Todes Geschichte* (entries on 12, 17, 21 September).
41. Manrique, *Travels*, vol. 2, p. 341.
42. Steensgaard, 'The route', pp. 55–73; Floor, *The Economy*, pp. 200–10.
43. Maxime Siroux, *Anciennes voies et monuments routiers de la region d'Isfahan* (Cairo, 1971), p. 19; Wolfram Kleiss and Mehdi Yusof Kayani, *Fehrest-e Karavansarayha-ye Irani* 2 vols (Tehran, 1368/1989).
44. Adle, *Fotuhate Homayun*, vol. 2, pp. 442–4. Eskander Bayg Monshi, *Tarikh-e 'Alamara-ye 'Abbasi*, ed. Iraj Afshar, 2 vols (Tehran 1350/1971), vol. 1, p. 564 only mentions that Allahverdi Khan was ordered to march from Fars and Kerman via Yazd and Biyabanak to Khorasan. For an English translation see R. M. Savory, *History of Shah 'Abbas the Great* (translation of Monshi) 3 vols (Boulder, 1978), vol. 2, p. 748. The same information is provided by Monajjem, *Ruzname*, p. 165 (Yazd-Khoranoq, Robat-e Posht-e Badam, Robat-e Shotoran-Tabas).
45. It would seem that George Strachan also travelled the land route to India and back, but there is no account available of this trip, if there ever was one. G. L. Dellavida, *George Strachan, Memorials of a Wandering Scottish Scholar of the Seventeenth Century* (Aberdeen: Third Spalding Club, 1956), pp. 69–70.
46. Adle, *Fotuhate* Homayun, vol. 2, p. 442.
47. John Macdonald Kinneir, *A Geographical Memoir of the Persian Empire* (London, 1813 [Arno, 1973]), pp. 403–4.
48. Nicolas de Khanikoff, *Mémoire sur la partie meridionale de l'Asie Centrale* (Paris, 1861); C. M. Macgregor, *Narrative of a Journey through the Province of Khorassan and on the N.W. Frontier of Afghanistan in 1875*, 2 vols (London: Wm. Allen & Co, 1879); C. E. Stewart, *Through Persia in Disguise* (London, 1911); Percy M. Sykes, 'A fifth journey in Persia', *Geographical Journal* 28 (1906), pp. 452–3, 560–1; Sven Hedin, *Zu Land nach Indien durch Persien, Seistan, Beluchistan*, 2 vols (Leipzig: Brockhaus, 1910); H. B. Vaughn, 'Journeys in Persia, 1890–91', *Geographical Journal* 7 (1896), pp. 24–41 and 163–75; Idem., 'A journey through Persia, 1887–8', *RGS Supplemental Papers* III (1893); A. F. Stahl, 'Reisen in Nord- und Zentral-Persien', *Petermanns Mitteilungen, Ergänzungsheft* nr. 118 (Gotha, 1896).
49. R. Beaven, 'Notes on the country between Candahar and Girishk', *PRGS* IX (1880), pp. 548–52.
50. Coverte, *A True*, p. 74.
51. 'Sinjiri on the road to Girishk 11.2 miles.' The next stop was Khoshk-e Nakhod. Adamec, *Historical Gazetteer of Afghanistan*, vol. 5, p. 457. On Biddulph's map the village is called Sungzirie located on the banks of the Argand Ab; on the other side of the river the village of Kokoran was located. Biddulph, 'Pishin and the routes.'

52. Probably Abbazaw, a small village on the left bank of the Helmand, south of Girishk, 78 miles from Qandahar. Adamec, *Historical Gazetteer of Afghanistan*, vol. 2, p. 15.
53. Gereshk, 75 miles west of Qandahar. Adamec, *Historical Gazetteer of Afghanistan*, vol. 2, p. 92; Coverte, *A True*, p. 75; Purchas, vol. 3, p. 85.
54. Tavernier, *Voyages*, p. 341. Khush-e Nakhud, 45 miles from Kandahar and 6 miles from Mis Karez. Adamec, *Historical Gazetteer of Afghanistan*, vol. 5, pp. 302–3. There is also a village called Khoshkhane, which, around 1880, was half a mile south-west of Qandahar, but given its position cannot be the location referred to here. Ibid., vol. 5, p. 289.
55. Manrique, *Travels*, vol. 2, p. 342.
56. Purchas, vol. 4, p. 273; Ibid., vol. 3, p. 85 ('Here we paid a custome for our Cammels.'); Von Poser, *Lebens- und Todes Geschichte* (entry on 16 September); Tavernier, *Voyages*, p. 341.
57. Von Poser, *Lebens- und Todes Geschichte* (entry on 14 September).
58. Manrique, *Travels*, vol. 2, p. 342.
59. Ibid., p. 341.
60. Dalkhak see Adamec, *Historical Gazetteer of Afghanistan*, vol. 2, p. 61 at 48 miles from Delaram.
61. Hasan Gilan or Sangilan, an old fort on the desert road from Gereshk to Delaram, about 63 miles from Gereshk, and about 12 miles from Delaram. Adamec, *Historical Gazetteer of Afghanistan*, vol. 2, p. 106.
62. Malgir see Adamec, *Historical Gazetteer of Afghanistan*, vol. 2, p. 195, a village below Gereshk on the left bank of the Helmand River.
63. I have not been able to find a village or location called Ghazi Khan on any map or in any publication. There is a location called Saghi, a chauki in Bakwa on the Girishk-Farrah road (Adamec, *Historical Gazetteer of Afghanistan*, vol. 2, p. 253), but it is more likely that the name refers to the village of Sangilan (see above). Manrique, *Travels*, vol. 2, p. 342 also mentions Gazichan, but from the context it is clear that he meant Gereshk. Manrique, also at other parts of this stretch of his travels, often omits and confuses places and names, which the translators of his travels understandably ascribed to a loss of notes and details. Ibid., vol. 2, p. 353, n. 14 (5).
64. Purchas, vol. 4, p. 274. For Delaram see Adamec, *Historical Gazetteer of Afghanistan*, vol. 2, p. 66.
65. Von Poser, *Lebens- und Todes Geschichte* (entry on 17 September).
66. The term *shatt* refers to the rivers of ooze beneath the salt (*shatt-ab*), which are very dangerous to cross, and even impassable, other than in summer. Government of Great Britain, *Persia*, p. 88, photos 63–64.
67. Von Poser, *Lebens- und Todes Geschichte* (entry on September 11); Adamec, *Historical Gazetteer of Afghanistan*, vol. 2, p. 34.
68. 'Siah Ab or Siah Ao.' Adamec, *Historical Gazetteer of Afghanistan*, vol. 2, p. 280 at 39 miles east of Farah.
69. Coverte, *A True*, p. 76; Purchas, vol. 3, p. 85.
70. Clearly the same as Coverte's Bacon, or Soltan Bukwa, a halting place see Adamec, *Historical Gazetteer of Afghanistan*, vol. 2, p. 285 at 116 miles from Gereshk and 51 miles from Farah.
71. Most likely the same as Coverte's Sehawe or Siyah Ab.
72. For Farah see Adamec, *Historical Gazetteer of Afghanistan*, vol. 2, p. 76, and for Khurmaliq see Ibid., p. 167 which was situated at 23 miles from Farah.
73. Von Poser, *Lebens- und Todes Geschichte* (entries on 2–6 September).
74. Coverte, *A True*, p. 76; Purchas, vol. 3, p. 85.
75. Purchas, vol. 4, p. 274.
76. Von Poser, *Lebens- und Todes Geschichte* (entry on 3 September).
77. Manrique, *Travels*, vol. 2, pp. 343–4.
78. Purchas, vol. 3, p. 85.
79. Coverte, *A True*, p. 77.
80. Purchas, vol. 4, p. 275.

81. Purchas, vol. 4, p. 275.
82. Tavernier, *Voyages*, p. 341; Purchas, vol. 4, p. 275.
83. Von Poser, *Lebens- und Todes Geschichte* (entry on 31 August); Adamec, *Historical Gazetteer of Afghanistan*, vol. 2, pp. 58–60 (map 7B).
84. Adamec, *Historical Gazetteer of Iran*, vol. 4, p. 96.
85. Von Poser, *Lebens- und Todes Geschichte* (entries on 25–30 August); Adamec, *Historical Gazetteer of Iran*, vol. 4, p. 349 (Purang, a hamlet) map 3C.
86. Purchas, vol. 4, p. 276.
87. Ibid., p. 276.
88. Ibid., p. 275; Tavernier, *Voyages*, p. 341.
89. Purchas, vol. 4, pp. 275–6.
90. Von Poser, *Lebens- und Todes Geschichte* (entries on 16–25 August). On the coinage see, Floor, Willem, *The Economy of Safavid Persia* (Weisbaden, 2000), chapter four.
91. See map III in Sven Hedin, *Eine Routenaufnahme durch OstPersien* 2 vols (Stockholm: Generalstabens, 1918); Hedin, *Zu Land*, vol. 2 (map inserted at end); also Adamec, *Historical Gazetteer of Iran*, vol. 2, map II-36-B; Adle, *Fotuhat-e Shah*, vol. 2, p. 443.
92. Stewart, *Through Persia*, p. 279; Mostawfi, *Shahdad*, p. 283; Adle, *Fotuhat-e Shah*, vol. 2, p. 444; Hedin, *Zu Land*, vol. 2, pp. 43–6 (map inserted at end).
93. Mostawfi, *Shahdad*, pp. 283–4; Hedin, *Zu Land*, vol. 2, p. 34 (photo), 37–41 (map inserted at end); also Adamec, *Historical Gazetteer of Iran*, vol. 2, map II-36-B.
94. Tavernier, *Voyages*, p. 340.
95. Adle, *Fotuhat-e Shah*, vol. 2, p. 443.
96. Tavernier, *Voyages*, p. 340; Durra Dhri according to Stewart, *Through Persia*, p. 278; Hedin, *Zu Land*, vol. 2, p. 33 (Dschaffaru and Duri – map inserted at end); Duri or Dehri, see Adamec, *Historical Gazetteer of Iran*, vol. 2, p. 162.
97. According to Stewart, *Through Persia*, pp. 275, 278, 15 miles after Robat-e Khan was a village called Jefferabad through a stony path, named Durra Dhri, which was very trying for the camels. For a map see Hedin, *Eine Routenaufnahme*, maps III and V; Stewart, *Through Persia*, pp. 274–5.
98. Stewart, *Through Persia*, p. 278.
99. Tavernier, *Voyages*, p. 340; Hedin, *Zu Land*, vol. 2, p. 29 (Tscha-Medschi; map inserted at end); C. M. Macgregor, *Narrative of a Journey through the Province of Khorassan and on the N.W. Frontier of Afghanistan in 1875*, 2 vols (London: Wm. Allen & Co, 1879), vol. 1, p. 103; also Adamec, *Historical Gazetteer of Iran*, vol. 2, p. 102 (map II-36-B).
100. MacGregor, *Narrative*, vol. 1, p. 101.
101. Manrique, *Travels*, vol. 2, pp. 348–9.
102. MacGregor, *Narrative*, vol. 1, p. 100; Hedin, *Zu Land*, vol. 2 (map inserted at end); Hedin, *Eine Routenaufnahme*, map III. The latter map shows a cistern a little beyond Hawz-e Mirza, and just marks it as Haus (=hawz or cistern), which may be Tavernier's Caseni.
103. MacGregor, *Narrative*, vol. 1, pp. 97, 99; Hedin, *Zu Land*, vol. 2 (Mehredschan- map inserted at end); Hedin, *Eine Routenaufnahme*, map III.
104. Tavernier, *Voyages*, p. 340; Adle, *Fotuhate Shahi*, vol. 2, p. 442.
105. Manrique, *Travels*, vol. 2, p. 348.
106. Ibid., pp. 350–1.
107. Ibid., p. 351.
108. MacGregor, *Narrative*, vol. 1, pp. 93–4; Hedin, *Zu Land*, vol. 2 (map inserted at end) shows a location called Biyabanak; Hedin, *Eine Routenaufnahme*, map III shows Bijabanek; Eskander Bayg Monshi, *Tarikh-e 'Alamara-ye 'Abbasi*, ed. Iraj Afshar 2 vols (Tehran 1350/1971), vol. 1, p. 564, also mentions an oasis called Biyabanak at this location. For English translation see Savory, *History of Shah 'Abbas*, vol. 2, p. 748. For a description and photos of Khur see Ibid., vol. 2, pp. 1–14 and figs. 110–23.
109. MacGregor, *Narrative*, vol. 1, pp. 91–2.

110. Tavernier, *Voyages*, p. 340; Hedin, *Zu Land*, inserted at the end of vol. 1; Hedin, *Eine Routenaufnahme*, vol. 1, pp. 33–45 and map III.
111. Tavernier, *Voyages*, p. 430.
112. MacGregor, *Narrative*, vol. 1, p. 87.
113. Stewart, *Through Persia*, p. 271; MacGregor, *Narrative*, vol. 1, pp. 90, 92; Adamec, *Historical Gazetteer of Iran*, vol. 2, p. 571.
114. Stewart, *Through Persia*, pp. 274, 271.
115. Ibid., pp. 274–5; Von Poser, *Lebens- und Todes Geschichte* (entry on 11 August).
116. MacGregor, *Narrative*, vol. 1, p. 89; Stewart, *Through Persia*, p. 273 (46 miles); Mostawfi, *Shahdad*, pp. 287–9; Von Poser, *Lebens- und Todes Geschichte*.
117. Von Poser, *Lebens- und Todes Geschichte* (entry on 11 August).
118. MacGregor, *Narrative*, vol. 1, p. 88; Stewart, *Through Persia*, p. 272; Mostawfi, *Shahdad*, pp. 289–90.
119. MacGregor, *Narrative*, vol. 1, p. 87; Stewart, *Through Persia*, p. 272; Mostawfi, *Shahdad*, pp. 290–1.
120. Von Poser, *Lebens- und Todes Geschichte* (entries on 10–15 August).
121. Adle, *Fotuhate Shah*, vol. 2, p. 442.
122. Stewart, *Through Persia*, p. 272 mentions a village called Illahabad, which is 17 miles from Saghand. It had a good well, but very brackish water.
123. Purchas, vol. 4, p. 275; Tavernier, *Voyages*, p. 340.
124. Stewart, *Through Persia*, p. 271; MacGregor, *Narrative*, vol. 1, p. 86.
125. Stewart, *Through Persia*, p. 270; MacGregor, *Narrative*, vol. 1, p. 85; Adle, *Fotuhate Shah*, vol. 2, p. 442; Monajjem, *Ruzname*, p. 165; Von Poser, *Lebens- und Todes Geschichte* (entries on 8–9 August).
126. Stewart, *Through Persia*, p. 268; Kinneir, *A Geographical Memoir*, p. 404.
127. MacGregor, *Narrative*, vol. 1, p. 85; Mostawfi, *Shahdad*, pp. 291–2.
128. MacGregor, *Narrative*, vol. 1, pp. 83–4; Mostawfi, *Shahdad*, p. 292.
129. MacGregor, *Narrative*, vol. 1, p. 81; Kinneir, *A Geographical Memoir*, p. 404.
130. Von Poser, *Lebens- und Todes Geschichte* (entries of 18 July–1 August).
131. Purchas, vol. 4, p. 273.

13

Trade between the Ottomans and Safavids: The Acem *Tüccarı* and Others

Suraiya Faroqhi

In Turkish, grammatical constructions resembling the term Acem *tüccarı* can mean traders doing business *in* a given country or geographical area, regardless of origins. Thus the Avrupa *tüccarı* of the late eighteenth and early nineteenth centuries were not Europeans subject to foreign rulers, but non-Muslim subjects of the sultans doing business in Europe and who had been accorded privileges in order to dissuade them from seeking foreign protection.[1] However, a term formed according to the same grammatical rules can also denote foreign traders with whom the Ottomans had come in contact: the expressions Hind *tüccarı*, İngiliz *tüccarı* or Venedik *tüccarı* refer to merchants from India, England or Venice. However, as far as I can tell, the expression Acem *tüccarı* always means traders *from* Iran; there does not seem to be a specific term signifying those Ottoman traders who must have visited Tabriz, Tiflis or Ganja. In these cases, it was necessary to use a more complicated turn of phrase, such as 'Acem diyarından gelen tüccar taifesi' (a group of traders coming from the land of Acem).

The silk trade around 1500: In the shadow of interstate conflict

The earliest Ottoman records referring to the presence of Iranian traders come from the kadi registers of Bursa, of which a few volumes date from the closing years of the fifteenth century. At this time, the Bursa silk manufacturers were already fully active, but as yet no silkworms were being raised locally, and the necessary raw material was all imported from Iran.[2] However, after 1514, due to the war between Shah Esma'il I (İsmail in Ottoman sources) and Sultan Selim I, this branch of commerce came to a total standstill, for Selim I attempted to diminish the revenues his rival obtained from customs duties by forbidding all importation of silk from the territories ruled by Shah İsmail. For a short while, importation continued by way of Aleppo, which was on Mamluk, and thereby neutral, territory.[3] But by his campaign of 1516/17, Sultan Selim had conquered the Mamluk sultanate, and for the next 400 years, Aleppo became an Ottoman city; thus no Iranian silk could be brought into the empire since it was supposedly of Syrian origin. Not only was the silk trade interrupted, but merchants who had been incautious enough not to immediately leave Ottoman territory when war was declared had their goods taken away and were imprisoned.

However, Selim I died in 1520 and his successor Süleyman the Magnificent quickly reversed the dead ruler's policy on the silk trade. Apparently, the new sultan had been informed that taking away the goods belonging to private persons, even if subject to an enemy ruler, was an act of flagrant injustice. This consideration must have carried some weight with a sultan who, to later generations, was to be known as Kanuni, or the Lawgiver. But more prosaically, the embargo on Iranian silk must have severely disrupted Bursa's trade and, with many merchants about to go bankrupt or already having ceased operations, numerous poor people must also have lost their jobs. Moreover, the court depended on the Bursa silk manufacturers for its supply of valuable textiles and Sultan Süleyman, during the first years of his reign, was by no means the austere personage he appeared to later.[4] Last but not least, in the 1520s the young ruler led a series of successful campaigns not against Muslim, but against western rulers such as the Knights of St John, the kings of Hungary and the Austrian Habsburgs. For the time being at least, these priorities must have made it seem less urgent to diminish the customs revenues of the shahs of Iran and presumably all the considerations mentioned here played no small role in the reopening of the silk trade.

However, throughout the sixteenth century, the Ottoman authorities were very much concerned with the possibility that emissaries of the shahs, in their capacity as leaders of the Safaviyye dervish order (Turkish *halife*/Persian *khalife*), might appear in Anatolia and gain the loyalty of local nomadic and semi-nomadic tribesmen. After all, some of the latter had, during previous decades, shown their disaffection by several rebellions and even mass emigration to Safavid territory.[5] This accounts for the campaigns of state-sponsored repression against Anatolian and Rumelian heterodox dervishes, to say nothing about ordinary subjects of the empire. These men and women were banished to Cyprus, imprisoned in fortresses, or even executed. Paranoia about possible 'subversive' activities by Iranian visitors, be they pilgrims or ambassadors, is apparent from numerous sultanic commands in the Mühimme Defterleri, or central chancery registers, which survive from the mid-sixteenth century onwards.[6] We even know of cases in which the central administration ordered the assassination of suspected spies, more or less convincingly disguised as attacks by highway robbers.[7]

From war to trade and back again: The contacts of Anatolian Muslim traders with the Safavid territories

When the sultan's council (*divan-ı humayun*) formulated policy recommendations, usually accepted by the ruler, commercial considerations were normally a major part of the equation. Like many other sovereigns the world over, the Ottoman sultans had established a list of 'forbidden goods', for the most part potentially of military significance, which could not be legally exported. There have been quite a few studies of these export prohibitions. But they all concern European countries, highlighting the manner in which traders, both foreign and Ottoman, quite often circumvented these regulations.[8] For it happened quite often that the remuneration offered by exporting merchants was more attractive than the administratively imposed prices paid by the naval arsenal, the janissary corps or even ordinary artisans working for the Istanbul market. In such instances, even repeated inspections and threats of dire punishment were unable to halt the smuggling.

All this had been familiar territory for quite some time, but it is less well known that similar policies were also applied against Iran. Here the key goods were not so much cotton or leather, so often mentioned when it came to illegal trade with Europeans, but rather horses, arms and Ottoman coins (both *akçe* and *guruş*). More generally, purchasers in the Safavid state were interested in metals above all, namely iron, silver and especially copper.[9] To mention just one particularly vivid example of the illegal iron trade, we hear that before 1570, a supposed *halife* of the Safavids had shown up in the eastern Anatolian town of Divriği, located close to an iron mine. With the intention of securing a regular supply of horseshoes for Iran, he had appointed three local men as *halifes*, and they apparently fulfilled his expectations.[10] For even though the claim that every year, the Divriği *halifes* had expedited over a 100,000 horseshoes to Iran should probably be taken with a grain of salt, the deliveries must have been substantial.[11]

Even more often do we hear of copper being sold 'up over the border' (*yukaru canibe*), although, as always when dealing with prohibited goods, it is impossible to specify the quantities involved; we will never know whether the illegal copper trade was greater or lesser than that in smuggled iron. However, Iranian demand must have been high, for not only was the product of Anatolian mines such as Küre-i mamure (today: Küre) being smuggled out, but also copper mined in Hungary, in the very north-west of the empire's European provinces. Küre is located close to the Black Sea in fairly inaccessible territory and thus must have been convenient for smugglers. But it is hard to imagine how Hungarian copper could have traversed the entire length of south-eastern Europe without attracting the attention of Ottoman officials. Of course, we must ask ourselves whether the claims made in the relevant sultanic commands were realistic and were not merely a figment of the imaginations of over-zealous bureaucrats and also of certain ordinary taxpayers, often with axes of their own to grind. In any event, the sultan's council warned the dependent princes (*voyvodas*) of Transylvania, Wallachia and Moldavia that, according to information received, certain dealers in

Hungarian copper were not carrying this metal to Istanbul, but smuggling it to Iran. The three princes were enjoined to lay hands on this copper on behalf of the Ottoman fisc, and report the merchants to the authorities.[12] In addition, the coppersmiths of Istanbul had complained to the sultan that certain merchants were buying up copper to sell to Iran in such quantities that they themselves were having trouble finding sufficient raw material.[13] In response, traders on their way to Iran were strictly forbidden to buy copper and those who did not comply were threatened with arrest, quite apart from the confiscation of their wares.[14]

In addition, Ottoman coins were in demand 'beyond the frontier', presumably on account of their silver content; Ottoman attempts to prevent this outflow by overvaluing their own currency seem to have met with qualified success.[15] Complaints reached Istanbul that the Erzurum mint, which transformed raw silver from the nearby mine of Canca, was located in an isolated spot; as a result, it was easy for merchants to carry off its product to Iran.[16] Other Ottoman coins travelled to Iran by way of the commercial centre of Aleppo.[17] As there were no mines in this region, local mints must have produced the coins from silver that European traders had brought into the area, primarily to fund their purchases of Iranian raw silk. According to the sultan's command, merchants smuggling silver to Iran acquired silver at low prices and made substantial profits. If caught, they were first to pay a fee to the local mint (*darbhane hakkı*), and then half the remaining silver was to be confiscated. While this was a serious penalty, it was still more lenient than that threatening the copper dealers, who were repeatedly warned that in case of contravention, they would lose their entire consignments.[18]

Large-scale smuggling is never possible without the connivance of customs collectors, and the Iranian case was no exception. When rumours circulated that metals were being smuggled into Iran, the so-called *gümüş arayıcıları* (searchers of silver) should have patrolled the border and prevented it from happening.[19] But apparently that was far from the case, although the smugglers of metals avoided the more frequented highways and, by this very act, should have aroused suspicion, they were allowed to proceed; in fact the sultanic rescript emphasized that the paths used by smugglers were well known to the provincial authorities in Erzurum. Moreover, the governor himself was involved at times; for in 982 (1574/75), this high official was told that he should not allow illegal trade to continue with the excuse that he had not been given any orders in this matter.[20] A few years earlier, the governor of Rum, in north-central Anatolia, had been accused of a similar collusion: no less than 182 wagonloads of copper and iron had supposedly passed through his province without eliciting any official response whatsoever.[21]

Iranian luxury goods and insubordinate border lords

When Ottoman state officials attempted to repress the sale of metals to Iran, an important role fell to the Kurdish lords (ümera-yı Ekrad) whose territories lay close to the Ottoman-Iranian frontier. When the central government attempted to prevent smuggling, these magnates, who ruled broad sweeps of territory, often with minimal interference on the part of the central power, were specifically called upon to intervene against the offending traders. But in this matter, the material interests of the Kurdish lords might well have proven stronger than injunctions from the sultan's council. Thus, it was not rare for the lords to offer merchants cheaper customs rates than those charged in the official stations of Erzurum and Diyarbekir, in order to profit at least marginally from the traffic across their borders.[22]

But the converse was equally probable. Thus, we find traders who needed to travel back and forth from central Anatolia to Iran complaining that, after they had paid the legal dues to the Ottoman central government (*bac, gümrük*), a second sales tax (*bac*) was demanded from them. The culprits were the sub-governor of an unidentified locality in the province of Diyarbekir and his counterpart officiating in Mahmudî (province of Van), who probably belonged to local dynasties in addition to being servitors of the sultans. As a pretext, the governors claimed that the merchants in question had passed through their particular territories.[23] A rather similar case occurred in the early seventeenth century, as apparent from the official answer to a complaint from the Iranian merchant Hodadad, head of a traders' caravan.[24] Here the issue was a due named *pişkeş* (tribute) demanded from merchants over and above the regular dues on the route between Diyarbekir and Van, but it is not quite clear by whom. All we learn is that the authorities in Istanbul also considered this tribute illegitimate, in contradistinction to the legally assessed market dues (*bac*) and customs duties (*gümrük*). Whether frontier lords and governors obeyed Istanbul's injunction to stop molesting the merchants remains unknown.

More detailed information on how the border lords might have obtained Iranian luxury goods is found in a sultanic rescript detailing the activities of Elvend-zade Mustafa, governor of a sub-province subordinate to Mosul.[25] A report by the governor and kadi of Baghdad forms the basis for a command from the sultan's council, the only evidence of this affair still in existence. Elvend-zade Mustafa had sent silver with a Mosuli trader to the value of 8,000 gold pieces (*filori*) that were tracked down by the local *gümüş arayıcıları*.[26] But the Mosuli trader, probably under Elvend-zade's orders, refused to give up the silver, even going so far as to give the officials who had the temerity to demand it a good beating. In due course, the merchant returned from Iran with 20 loads of valuable cloth, which had presumably been purchased with the smuggled silver. But, before he could reach Mosul, Sultan Hüseyin, at that time governor of Imadiyye, reported the caravan to the authorities. So the goods were impounded in Baghdad and placed under seal, until such time as Elvend-zade consented to pay a double customs duty. However, by the date of the surviving record, that had not yet happened; on the contrary, an infuriated Elvend-zade had appeared in Baghdad, declaring that he was not willing to pay a single duty, let alone two. The final result remains unknown, but the sultan's council commanded that henceforth, attempts at smuggling should generally be punished by a double payment.

But who was to control the borderlands? Our rescript tells us that to compound his insubordination, Elvend-zade had opened the *semt yolları*, paths known only to the locals, by which they could cross the border without attracting attention. Certainly, the authorities in Istanbul ordered that these should be closed again. But, in the absence of rivalries similar to that between Elvend-zade and Sultan Hüseyin, it is doubtful that the traffic on such roads was even reported to the Ottoman capital.

After all, the local resources at the disposal of these various lords were strictly limited, while luxury goods from both Iran and Istanbul passed temptingly close to their residences. Many magnates did not let these opportunities pass them by. As an example, we may refer to the wealth of Abdal Khan of Bitlis who, in 1655/56, negotiated with Melek Ahmed Paşa, the relative and patron of the well-known travel writer Evliya Çelebi (1611–some time after 1683). When this Ottoman vizier left Bitlis, he was presented with jewelled muskets from Mazenderan, three Isfahan carpets with gold thread worked into them, three felt carpets from Nakhshevan and 'ten droves of Gilani mules'.[27] Now, it is probable that the distinguished visitor from Istanbul was given items he was not likely to find at home; and the treasury of the khan, seized by Melek Ahmed Paşa after the ruler of Bitlis had lost a small-scale war against the Ottomans, did in fact contain luxury goods of Istanbul and European provenance. But pride of place went to Iranian textiles: there were 200 silk carpets and, in addition, 70 felt coverings from Isfahan, all embellished with embroidery.[28] To amass these treasures, Abdal Khan must have maintained quite close relations with Iran, especially the Safavid court.[29] Probably some of the items confiscated by Melek Ahmed Paşa must have come to Bitlis as diplomatic gifts, but merchants had doubtless brought in the remainder.

On the other hand, received wisdom must have prompted the sultans' councillors not to insist too drastically on the cooperation of the Kurdish lords against smugglers; in the early seventeenth century an Ottoman official, experienced in the affairs of the Iranian frontier, suggested that it was always wise to avoid alienating these people as they were staunch Sunnis and therefore reliable allies against the Safavids.[30] If the border lords were prepared to allow the Ottoman armies to pass through their territories unmolested, make available food and other necessities and even send contingents of armed men if required, presumably they could be allowed a few profits from smuggled trade.

Iranian luxuries and raw silk at the Ottoman centre

There is some evidence that the magnates of eastern Anatolia were interested in Iranian luxury goods and, to a more limited degree, this is also true of the wealthy inhabitants of Istanbul, Bursa and Edirne. But even in more provincial environments, there was a demand for textiles 'from across the border'. Certain central

Anatolian nomads were accused of highway robbery because of the Iranian fabrics found in their possession, which they had tried to sell in the markets of Ankara and Çorum; apparently the authorities assumed that such costly goods could not have been acquired through legitimate trade.[31] In addition, the inventory of the former sub-provincial governor (*mirliva*) Sinan Bey, who died in Edirne in or just before 1553, contained a woollen cloak in the Iranian style, 'with leopard' – that is, either decorated with leopard fur or with a design reminiscent of leopard spots.[32] Another *mirliva*, resident in the same city, owned a belt of Iranian workmanship (*miyanbend-i acem*).[33] Among the precious goods left by an Edirne goldsmith and moneylender, we encounter a bracelet probably from Iran, or in the Iranian style (*bir Acem bileziği*).[34] A felt tapestry of Iranian workmanship, probably used to keep off the sun and not very costly, was part of the estate inventory of the wealthy *poursuivant* Hasan Çavuş.[35] But overall, Ottoman estate inventories of the sixteenth and early seventeenth centuries do not contain major quantities of Iranian luxury goods, possibly because the numerous years of war impeded importation.

As to the Ottoman palace, apparently Iranian rugs arrived mainly as diplomatic gifts, while the sultans do not seem to have made any effort to acquire these precious items by way of trade. While merchants in palace service visited both England and Russia, evidence of direct court purchases in Iran has not as yet come to light.[36] Once again, it has been suggested that the vicissitudes of war were responsible; the transfer of the Iranian capital to Qazvin and then to Isfahan made it more difficult for Ottomans to become familiar with the spectacular sixteenth-century novelties in Iranian rug design.[37] Moreover, wealthy Ottomans living in the central provinces but not part of the palace circle may have found textiles and carpets of Safavid make rather expensive, given the cost of transportation by caravan and the relative weightiness of woollen rugs.

Thus, the most important item among Iranian goods marketed in the Ottoman Empire was doubtless raw silk. Until the end of the sixteenth century, this was the major input needed by the famous manufacturers of silk cloth in Bursa, and probably also by the workshops operating in Istanbul proper. However, during the last quarter of the sixteenth century, the prices of Iranian raw silk steadily increased. To some degree, warfare must have been responsible; not only did war-induced dislocations discourage, and sometimes even prevent, the laborious process of raising the silkworms and unwinding the cocoons, but the plundering of large portions of certain silk harvests must also have discouraged the producers.[38] More importantly, competition from European traders, in a period when silk industries were developing in England, France and elsewhere, was the principal factor driving up prices.[39]

Even worse, the Bursa producers were unable to pass on their increased expenses for raw material; this was partly due to the political clout of their customers, with the palace and high dignitaries purchasing an appreciable share of the industry's output. In addition, silk was after all a luxury for which cheaper substitutes were readily available; in the years around 1600, as political and financial crises ate into the purchasing power of even the well-to-do, raising prices could only serve to limit the market yet further. All this resulted in a profit squeeze, which some silk weavers tried to cope with by producing lighter and cheaper silks.[40] But once again, the Ottoman palace's demand for the heavy and more costly varieties limited the possibilities of adapting to market conditions. On the contrary, masters who tried this solution were constantly reviled and penalized for not adhering to the established standards of the guild.[41]

Yet, in the course of the seventeenth century, the Bursa silk industry did adjust to the new situation. Turning to a different kind of workforce was part of the solution. In the fifteenth and sixteenth centuries the Bursa industry had employed numerous slaves, a high-cost solution in an industry demanding a skilled labour force, in the seventeenth century entrepreneurs increasingly turned to the local inhabitants, whose number had much increased in the course of the sixteenth century.[42] Alternatives to high-cost Iranian raw silk were also found, as the countryside around Bursa turned into an important producer of raw silk, a role it was to continue up to World War I. As a result, after the crisis of the years around 1600 had been overcome, at least partially, Bursa was able to regain some of its previous importance as a silk manufacturing centre, even if the palace now figured less prominently among its customers. The fact that, during the later seventeenth and early eighteenth centuries, English traders turned away from the Mediterranean and concentrated on Indian and Chinese raw silks also served to lessen the upward trend of the prices of Iranian raw silk in the Ottoman Empire. As a result, the Bursa manufacturers enjoyed something of a breathing space.[43] In the seventeenth century, Iranian raw silk and the local product were apparently used side by side in the Bursa industry.

Trade conditions, or trials and tribulations along Ottoman roads

Merchants from Iran could enter Ottoman territory by land, passing through the customs stations of Erzurum and Diyarbekir. Those who arrived by sea, must have entered through the port of Basra quite often. In the sixteenth century, this was a well-frequented commercial centre, visited by merchants from India, Yemen and Acem.[44] Once again, our documents only provide indirect evidence of this trade, namely in their responses to complaints from merchant visitors. For, when a trader died, the local officials in charge of heirless property (*beytülmalcı*) typically tried by every means at their disposal to confiscate the dead man's goods. Even when appropriate witnesses were present and the estate should have been turned over to the heirs, the *beytülmalcıs* would claim that the value of the inheritance was superior to 10,000 *akçe* and therefore all disputes concerning it had to be heard in Istanbul.[45] Given the cost of travelling from Basra to the capital, this must often have amounted to confiscation pure and simple.

It is thus worth noting that a rule which European states often inserted into their capitulations, because it protected their merchants against arbitrary actions by local powers, operated in exactly the contrary fashion where merchants arriving from territories to the east of the Ottoman borders were concerned.[46] Because the rulers involved maintained no permanent representatives at the Ottoman court, they could not protect their merchants in the same fashion as did the French, Venetian, Dutch or English governments, while the distance between Istanbul and Basra formed a significant deterrent to all those who needed to seek justice at the gates of the *padişah* in person.[47] Thus, it was not the shahs of Iran or the Mughal emperors who intervened in order to protect Indian or Iranian traders going to Basra, but the higher-level Ottoman authorities themselves. For, similar to the central government's reaction towards complaints about the overcharging of Indian merchants by the Şerifs of Mecca, these officials also took the wider view with respect to the port of Basra. After all, as seen from Istanbul, continued harassment would simply cause the foreign traders to become disgusted (*nefret etmek*) and therefore avoid the ports where they had been mistreated.[48] Such developments could, in the end, only result in an overall loss of customs revenues. Therefore, the sultan accepted a suggestion from the governor-general of Basra that the local judges should be authorized to hear disputes involving inheritances not just up to 10,000 but all the way to 50,000 *akçe*.

Nor did the troubles of the merchants from the *vilayet-i Acem* end once they had passed border checkpoints and the lands of semi-independent frontier lords, and were securely on Ottoman territory. Some information is available on the misadventures of merchants from Iran who travelled through the Ottoman lands. In 1040 (1630/31), caravans went from Iran to Istanbul and Edirne, and from there continued all the way through the Balkans as far as Venice. There the traders exchanged the goods they had brought for fabrics and woollen cloth; we do not know whether the latter was of Venetian manufacture or of northern, possibly English origin.[49] On their way back, the merchants stopped in Edirne for a few days' rest, but, as they claimed in their letters of complaint, without opening their bags or doing any business. In the past, traders in this position had not been required to pay customs duties in Edirne, but recently, this practice had changed. This, the merchants claimed, was detrimental to their interests and they asked for a return to previous practice.

Presumably textile sales in Edirne were limited, while in Istanbul, which was the major centre of consumption, turnover must have been much higher. Certainly, merchants who already had paid dues in a provincial town could often get a rebate when dealing with the Istanbul customs officials or tax farmers, though presumably there was no guarantee that this really would happen. Moreover merchants probably had little cash available after their purchases in Venice, and would have had to take up loans in order to tide them over until their Istanbul customers paid their bills. From the central authorities' viewpoint, it probably did not make much difference whether the duties were paid in Edirne or in Istanbul, provided they were paid in full. At least this is how I would interpret the surviving order from the sultan's council to the kadi of Edirne. This judge was told that if traders from Iran had, on their way out, paid their dues in Istanbul and had continued their travels with the permission of the relevant official, on their way back, those who did not do any buying or selling in Edirne should not be interfered with. Once again, the dominant consideration must have been the continuance of the caravan trade; after all, if molested once too often, the traders from Iran might decide to go to Aleppo instead of Istanbul and load their goods upon a Venetian boat, or even use the services of English shippers visiting Bandar 'Abbas or other ports on the Gulf.[50]

Such alternatives were not available to the Acem *tüccarı* who travelled on the Anatolian caravan routes to sell their goods, and especially their raw silk, in Bursa and Istanbul.[51] Some of them attempted to ward off the attentions of the Bursa tax collectors by opening their bales in small towns to the east of the city, like Borlu (today: Safranbolu) or Geyve; presumably they had made arrangements with some of their business partners in advance, who would come to these places and make their purchases.[52] While this was quite obviously a subterfuge, the situation was somewhat different in the case of traders wishing to market their wares in Bursa itself. For in the mid-seventeenth century, there existed a local silk industry of some importance in this city, and thus there should have been a – albeit limited – market for the silks brought in by the Acem *tüccarı*. However, perhaps due to the confusion caused by the unbalanced Sultan Ibrahim's demand for expensive luxuries, the needs of the Bursa artisans were not taken into consideration at all. Under threats of dire punishment, the Acem *tüccarı* were enjoined to carry all their wares to the capital and pay their customs duties in this city.[53]

Trade without politics: The Acem tüccarı

Without inordinate exaggeration, we can thus say that the Ottoman-Iranian trade of the period between 1550 and 1650 survived due to the continuing importation of raw silk and, in the Ottoman territories, it was mainly the Acem *tüccarı* who kept the trade going. Research on these merchants has typically focused on their roles as commercial employees of the Safavid rulers and also as highly competitive business partners of the European traders active in the Middle East.[54] That they also had dealings with Ottoman merchants and consumers has, in contrast, remained in the shadow. For admittedly, Ottoman economic history is a latecomer compared to its French or English counterparts and, in addition, primary sources on the Ottoman trade of Iranian merchants are few and far between. In this part of our study, we will present an analysis of some sultanic rescripts that cast at least a small ray of light on the activities of the Acem *tüccarı* as suppliers to Ottoman silk cloth manufacturers.

Given the overall political situation, it is perhaps not surprising that, while there had been quite a few Muslim Iranians trading in Bursa before the Safavid takeover, after the 1520s their place was largely taken by Christian, usually Armenian, subjects of the shah.[55] After all, these men could not be suspected of being Safaviyye *halifes* in disguise and, in the overheated atmosphere of the sixteenth century, this made all the difference. However, contrary to Ottoman bureaucratic custom in many other contexts, our documents do not differentiate between Muslims and non-Muslims. In itself, this would seem to indicate that there were few Muslims involved in the silk trade for, had it been otherwise, their names would have preceded those of their Christian fellow traders. Certainly some Muslim merchants from Iran must have ventured into Ottoman territory, but we know very little about them.[56]

Only in the – not so very frequent – cases that the traders under discussion are mentioned by name, can we deduce anything at all about their religious or ethnic backgrounds? In the surviving texts, we find men named Bedros, Balı, Kirkor, M-nlas or M-las, Şeker and D-rar.[57] Apparently Christian subjects of the shahs did not have the quality of *müstemin* (temporary visitor not subject to payment to the poll tax or *cizye*) normally assigned to the merchants from western Christian states. Instead, they were counted as *zimmi*s, similar to the Christian subjects of the Ottoman sultan.[58] It is not so surprising to find these men active in Üsküdar and Galata, that is within Greater Istanbul, or else in Manisa. After all, this last was an important centre of textile production located very close to Izmir, where many of the Acem *tüccarı* did business with European exporters of raw silk. But it is rather unexpected to find Acem *tüccarı* on the seventeenth-century island of Midilli (Lesbos), where there is a record of a merchant having trouble collecting the inheritance of a deceased cousin. Moreover, these traders also spread out into the countryside of north-western Anatolia, selling fine cotton cloth (*tülbend*) in small towns such as Kandıra, Şeyhlü or Taşköprü. Unsurprisingly, the local merchants were not especially delighted with the competition, and claimed to possess an order from the sultan excluding 'outsiders'. However, the authorities in Istanbul confirmed the right of the Acem *tüccarı* to do business in these places. Occasionally, a few Indian traders also hawked their wares in the depths of the Ottoman provinces.[59]

Conclusion

As so often happens, our documents reflect the activities of traders between the Ottoman Empire and Iran purely from the government's point of view. This means that political and fiscal aspects are highlighted while issues like commercial profit or business organization remain in the shadow. For the Ottoman authorities in the sixteenth century the paramount objective was to prevent the outflow of silver, copper and iron to a potential military opponent. Yet, from the mid-seventeenth century onwards, this ceased to be a concern. Presumably after the Kızılbaş (Qezelbash) tribes had lost their former power, due to Shah Abbas' reorganization of his state and the treaty of Kasr-ı şirin (Zuhab) in 1639 establishing what turned out to be a long-lasting peace, the Safavids were no longer regarded as a probable enemy. In addition, with the elimination of the Kızılbaş, the heresy' issue also receded into the background. Now the main motivation for official Ottoman interest in the trade with Iran was fiscal; the Acem *tüccarı* were viewed as a source of customs duties and, for that reason, their presence was considered desirable.

Moreover, the duties paid by the Acem *tüccarı* were, more often than not, a cause of dispute between the central authorities and provincial governors. As the latter were increasingly expected to find the financial means needed for their administrations themselves, the inclination to invent new taxes must have increased. In the territories controlled by Kurdish chieftains, a glance at the map shows that they were encouraged to tax Iranian merchants because so many desirable luxuries could be obtained from Iran more easily than from Istanbul. In addition, taxable resources in these relatively infertile lands were few and the traders, if they could be persuaded to pass through the chieftains' territories, obviously formed an external source of revenue, which the latter desperately needed in order to keep their followers happy and control of their lands intact. On the other hand, the officials of the central government, with their access to the empire's budgets and an understanding of its overall financial situation, must have been more concerned about not killing the goose that laid the golden eggs.[60] These different perspectives explain the tension between burgeoning taxation on the local level and a paternalistic extension of protection to the Acem *tüccarı* by the Ottoman central power.

More remarkable is the Istanbul government's intervention in favour of the Acem *tüccarı* when it came to the complaints submitted by provincial Ottoman shopkeepers. For as a rule, the demands of artisans who claimed to have been hurt by the activities of foreign merchants found a ready response among Ottoman officials. Probably in this case, the crucial difference was that, while the European traders who fell foul of Ottoman regulations were known to be exporters of goods produced within the Ottoman Empire, this did not apply to the Acem *tüccarı*. On the contrary, the latter *imported* essential goods, raw silk and cotton fabrics among others. Thus, they were regarded as supplying the domestic Ottoman market with desirable wares and this basic fact made them seem worthy of protection, even against competitors who were themselves Ottoman subjects.[61]

Notes

1. Bruce Masters, 'The sultan's entrepreneurs: The Avrupa *tüccarı* and the Hayriye *tüccarı*s in Syria', *International Journal of Middle East Studies* 24 (1992), pp. 579–97.
2. Fahri Dalsar, *Türk Sanayi ve Ticaret Tarihinde Bursa'da İpekçilik* (Istanbul, 1960), p. 127 analyses documents that demonstrate the importance of the silk trade even in the fifteenth century.
3. Dalsar, *Bursa'da İpekçilik*, pp. 130–6.

4. On the courtly celebrations of Süleyman's early years, compare Mehmet Arslan, *Türk Edebiyatında Manzum Surnameler (Osmanlı Saray Düğünleri ve Şenlikleri)* (Ankara, 1999), p. 12. On the same ruler's tendency, in his later years, to withdraw from public view, see Gülru Necipoğlu, *Architecture, Ceremonial and Power, The Topkapı Palace in the Fifteenth and Sixteenth Centuries* (Cambridge, MA, 1991), pp. 25-6.
5. Hanna Sohrweide, 'Der Sieg der Safawiden in Persien und seine Rückwirkungen auf die Schiiten Anatoliens im 16. Jahrhundert', *Der Islam* 41 (1965), pp. 95-223; Colin Imber, 'The persecution of the Ottoman Shiites according to the Mühimme Defterleri 1565-1585', *Der Islam* 56 (1979), pp. 245-73.
6. Mühimme Defterleri (from now on: MD) 6, p. 355, no. 761, 972 (1564/65). This register has been published: compare Ismet Binark *et al.*, eds, *6 Numaralı Mühimme Defteri 972/1564-65*, 3 vols (Ankara, 1995).
7. For an example compare Bekir Kütükoğlu, *Osmanlı-İran Siyasi Münasebetleri*, vol. I (Istanbul, 1962), p. 11.
8. Ömer Lütfi Barkan, 'The price revolution of the sixteenth century: A turning point in the economic history of the near East', *International Journal of Middle East Studies* VI (1975), pp. 3-28; Suraiya Faroqhi, 'Die osmanische Handelspolitik des frühen 17. Jahrhunderts zwischen Dubrovnik und Venedig', *Wiener Beiträge für die Geschichte der Neuzeit* 10 (1983), pp. 207-22 (which contains references to further secondary literature). See also Suraiya Faroqhi, *Towns and Townsmen of Ottoman Anatolia, Trade, Crafts, and Food Production in an Urban Setting 1520-1650* (Cambridge, 1984), pp. 135-7.
9. MD 21, p. 216, no. 517 980 (1572/73) contains a list of the goods not to be exported to Iran.
10. MD 7, p. 725, no. 1988 975/76 (1567/69). This register also has been published: compare Şener Murat *et al.*, eds, *7 Numaralı Mühimme Defteri 975-976/1567-69*, 3 vols (Ankara, 1997).
11. Faroqhi, *Towns and Townsmen*, p. 188.
12. MD 58, p. 204, no. 772, 993 (1585).
13. MD 7, p. 763, no. 2086, 976 (1568/69).
14. MD 21, p. 216, no. 517, 980 (1572/73).
15. Şevket Pamuk, *A Monetary History of the Ottoman Empire* (Cambridge, 2000), pp. 93-104.
16. MD 26, p. 199, no. 549, 982 (1574/75).
17. MD 28, p. 11, no. 22, 984 (1576).
18. See, for example, MD 58, p. 204, no. 772, 993 (1585). However, in another instance, and for reasons unknown, the penalties were less severe: some people who had been caught with 700 *batman* of copper by the governor of Van were merely ordered to sell their copper in the town itself. Moreover when the dealers complained to the sultan's council that their packhorses had been unjustly impounded, the authorities in Istanbul ordered the animals turned over to their proper owners: MD 48, p. 330, no. 970, 991 (1583).
19. MD 21, p. 216, no. 517, 980 (1572/73). In the context of this sultanic order, the *gümüş arayıcıları* seem to have been officials in charge of finding stores of illegally transported silver. The text tells us that these men were charged with the duty to secretly observe possible smugglers of silver to Iran. However, they themselves were not considered really trustworthy, so that other servitors of the sultan were to supervise them; these measures indicate spies of some kind. However, in the late fifteenth century, the *gümüş arayıcıları* were *essayeurs*; that is, specialists entrusted with checking the purity of silver. Compare Nicoară Beldiceanu, *Les actes des premiers sultans conservés dans les manuscripts turcs de la Bibliothèque Nationale à Paris*, vol. II (Paris, Den Haag, 1964), documents no. 12, 13, 14 and 19.
20. MD 26, p. 113, no. 291.
21. MD 7, p. 705, no. 705, 976 (1568/69).
22. MD 21, p. 33, no. 92, 980 (1572/73); MD 36, p. 107, no. 311, 987 (1579/80).
23. MD 14, p. 233, no. 333, 978 (1570/71). Evliya Çelebi, *Evliya Çelebi in Bitlis, the Relevant Sections of the Seyahatname, Edited Translation, Commentary and Introduction* by Robert Dankoff (Leiden, 1990), pp. 168-9 refers to the Mahmudi Ekradı.
24. MD 79, p. 475, no. 1219, 1020 (1611/12).

25. MD 21, p. 155, no. 379, 980 (1572/73). In the late 1500s, a member of this family became the governor of Aleppo: compare the manuscript Revan 1943 in the Topkapı Sarayı Library (Istanbul), catalogued in Fehmi Edhem Karatay, *Topkapı Sarayı Kütüphanesi Türkçe Yazmalar Kataloğu*, 2 vols (Istanbul, 1961), vol. 1, p. 232, no. 702. When I consulted this manuscript, I found that the documents in it were unnumbered, but provisionally, I have given the relevant text the number 46.

    The name of the sub-province to the uninitiated looks rather like 'Zekiyye', only there is no *liva* of that name in the province of Mosul; nor does the map showing the state of the province in 1530 contain any locality whose name might be read in this manner. Compare *998 Numaralı Muhâsebe-i vilâyet-i Diyâr-i bekr*... ed. Murat Şener et al. (Ankara, 1998), p. 123.

26. On trade in Iraq during this period, compare Dina Khoury, 'Merchants and trade in early modern Iraq', *New Perspectives on Turkey* 5–6 (1991), pp. 53–86.
27. Çelebi, *Evliya Çelebi in Bitlis*, pp. 154–5.
28. Ibid., pp. 304–5.
29. Ottomans tended to view the custom of filling the treasury with valuable textiles, rather than with arms, as a rather dubious custom. Compare the comments of the Ottoman naval captain Seydi Ali Reis when shown the treasury of Shah Tahmasp, in which silks, rugs and carpets figured prominently: Seyyidî 'Ali Re'is, *Le miroir des pays*, ed. Jean-Louis Bacqué Grammont (Paris, 1999), pp. 124–5. Abdal Khan, as Evliya Çelebi's description shows, possessed both varieties of treasure.
30. ['Azîz Efendi], *Kanûn-nâme-i sultânî li 'Azîz Efendi, Aziz Efendi's Book of Sultanic Laws and Regulations*... , ed. Rhoads Murphey (Cambridge MA, 1985).
31. MD 21, p. 981, no. 735, 980 (1572–3). However, at times the shoe might be on the other foot: in 1090 (1679/80), villagers from the district of Bayramlı in the province of Erzurum complained that some 'Acem eşkiyası', who supposedly had come to the region for trade, had in fact attacked them: MD 96, p. 176.
32. Ömer Lütfi Barkan, 'Edirne Askeri Kassam'ına ait Tereke Defterleri (1545–1659)', *Belgeler* III/5–6 (1966), pp. 1–479, see p. 117. As some Bursa velvets showed designs reminiscent of leopard's fur, presumably the scribe meant the Iranian variant of this particular design. See Hülya Tezcan and John Michael Rogers, *Topkapı Sarayı Museum, Textilien* (Herrsching am Ammersee, 1986), p. 40.
33. Barkan, 'Edirne Askeri Kassam'ı', p. 149.
34. Ibid., p. 202.
35. Ibid., p. 371.
36. On official Ottoman fur traders in Russia see Alexandre Benningsen and Chantal Lemercier-Quelquejay, 'Les marchands de la cour ottomane et le commerce des fourrures moscovites dans la seconde moitié du XVIe siècle', *Cahiers du monde russe et soviétique* 11/3 (1970), pp. 363–90.
37. Tezcan and Rogers, *Topkapı Sarayı Museum*, pp. 151–9 and the exhibition catalogue *Onbin Yıllık İran Medeniyeti ve İkibin Yıllık Ortak Miras* (Istanbul, 2009).
38. On the transportation of silk collected in Şirvan for the benefit of the Ottoman sultan see MD 69, p. 3, no. 4 1000 (1591/92).
39. Murat Çizakça, 'Price history and the Bursa silk industry: A study in Ottoman industrial decline, 1550–1650', reprinted in *The Ottoman Empire and the World Economy*, ed. Huri Islamoğlu-Inan (Cambridge, Paris, 1987), pp. 247–61.
40. Ibid.
41. Dalsar, *Bursa'da İpekçilik*, pp. 293–343. Dalsar's pioneering work is based on documents the author has found in the Bursa kadi registers.
42. Haim Gerber, *Economy and Society in an Ottoman City: Bursa, 1600–1700* (Jerusalem, 1988), pp. 66–70; Suraiya Faroqhi, 'Bursa at the crossroads: Iranian silk, European competition and the local economy 1470–1700' in idem., *Making a Living in the Ottoman Lands 1480–1820* (Istanbul, 1995), pp. 113–48.
43. Murat Çizakça, 'Incorporation of the Middle East into the European world economy', *Review* VIII/3 (1985), pp. 353–78.

44. Murat Çizakça, 'An introduction to the economic history of the city of Basra during the Ottoman era, 1550-1690, some hypotheses', in Hans Georg Majer and Raoul Motika (eds), *Türkische Wirtschafts- und Sozialgeschichte von 1071-1920* (Wiesbaden, 1995), pp. 35-50. See also Khoury, 'Merchants and trade', p. 58.
45. On similar behaviour of the *beytülmalcıs* accompanying the pilgrimage caravan to Mecca, compare Suraiya Faroqhi, *Pilgrims and Sultans* (London, 1994), p. 45. The Armenian merchant Simeon, who travelled in Anatolia at the beginning of the seventeenth century, reports a similar experience. He had to recover some of his belongings that he had entrusted to a companion who died shortly afterwards, and the *beytülmalcı* was not very willing to hand over the valuables he had seized: *Polonyalı Simeon'un Seyahatnâmesi*, trans. Hrand Andreasyan (Istanbul, 1964), pp. 84-5.
46. For an example, compare Alexander De Groot, *The Ottoman Empire and the Dutch Republic, A History of the Earliest Diplomatic Relations 1610-1630* (Leiden, Istanbul, 1978), p. 251. This was the first capitulation the Ottoman sultan granted to the Dutch; it specified that all disputes involving Dutch subjects, regardless of the amounts of money involved, must be decided in Istanbul. However, there was no such clause in the Polish capitulations, compare Dariusz Kołodziejczyk, *Ottoman-Polish Diplomatic Relations (15th-18th Century), An Annotated Edition of 'Ahdnames and Other Documents* (Leiden, 2000).
47. While this title mainly denoted the sultans themselves, it could be accorded to other rulers if the Ottoman administration wished to honour them; thus official documents occasionally refer to the França *padişahı*.
48. On the problems of traders in Jiddah compare Faroqhi, *Pilgrims and Sultans*, pp. 162-3. On the overcharging of merchants on the Ottoman-Iranian land frontier, see above.
49. Domenico Sella, 'The rise and fall of the Venetian woollen industry' in Brian Pullan (ed.), *Crisis and Change in the Venetian Economy in the Sixteenth and Seventeenth Centuries* (London, 1968), pp. 106-26.
50. Niels Steensgaard, *The Asian Trade Revolution of the Seventeenth Century, The East India Companies and the Decline of the Caravan Trade* (Chicago, London, 1973), p. 60 discusses this competition among the providers of protection.
51. On seventeenth-century Acem *tüccarı* carrying raw silk to Izmir for sale to English and other exporters, see Daniel Goffman, *Izmir and the Levantine World, 1550-1650* (Seattle, London, 1990), p. 53.
52. MD 89, p. 89, 1053 (1643/44).
53. MD 89, p. 23, 1052 (1642/43).
54. Kéram Kévonian, 'Marchands arméniens au XVIIe siècle, à propos d'un livre arménien publié à Amsterdam en 1699', *Cahiers du monde russe et soviétique* 16/2 (1975), pp. 199-244; Ina Baghdiantz McCabe, *The Shah's Silk for Europe's Silver, the Eurasian Trade of the Julfa Armenians in Safavid Iran and India (1530-1750)* (Atlanta/Georgia, 1999); Rudolph P. Matthee, *The Politics of Trade in Safavid Iran, Silk for Silver 1600-1730* (Cambridge, 1999).
55. Halil İnalcık, 'Bursa, XV Asır Sanayi ve Ticaret Tarihine Dair Vesikalar', *Belleten* XXIV (1960), pp. 45-102; Dalsar, *Bursa'da İpekçilik*, p. 139.
56. MD 7, p. 144, no. 369, 975 (1567/68).
57. MD 95, p. 30, no. 1075 (1664/65); ibid., p. 32, p. 42, p.56 (same year); MD 98, p. 148, 1089 (1678/79).
58. MD 95, p. 32, no. 1075 (1664/65).
59. On the activities of Acem *tüccarı* as documented by the customs registers of late seventeenth and early eighteenth-century Erzurum, see Neşe Erim, 'Trade, traders and the state in eighteenth-century Erzurum', *New Perspectives on Turkey* 5-6 (1991), pp. 123-50.
60. On the growing financial resources of Ottoman provincial governors during this period, compare Metin I. Kunt, *The Sultan's Servants, The Transformation of Ottoman Provincial Government, 1550-1650* (New York, 1983), pp. 88-93.
61. Halil Inalcık, 'Capital formation in the Ottoman Empire', *The Journal of Economic History* XIX (1969), pp. 97-140 and Inalcik, 'The Ottoman economic mind and aspects of the Ottoman economy', in Michael Cook (ed.), *Studies of the Economic History of the Middle East* (London, Oxford, 1970), pp. 207-18.

14

Sweden, Russia and the Safavid Empire: A Mercantile Perspective

Stefan Troebst

Introduction

The Secret Prussian State Archives in Berlin contain a file on trade relations between Brandenburg-Prussia and Iran via Muscovy, dated 1697/98 and labelled *Acta, betreffend Handel aus Persien nach seiner kurfürstlichen Durchlaucht Landen* (Documents on Trade from Persia to His Electoral Highness's Territories).[1] What is unusual about this file is that it contains a short addition summing up the commercial result of this project: *woraus nichts geworden* (which did not materialize). Until recently international historiography had written off most attempts by greater and smaller European powers to direct Iranian trade along the Russian route through their own territories as failures. The various forays of Denmark, Poland-Lithuania, Brandenburg-Prussia, Holstein-Gottorf and Courland in the seventeenth and early eighteenth centuries were more often than not collectively dismissed as unsuccessful and John Foran has explicitly characterized Stockholm's trade policy towards Iran as a 'non-starter'.[2] Even the Swedish orientalist, Gunnar Jarring, was of the opinion that in the seventeenth century no Iranian transit trade of any size took place via Sweden.[3]

However, recent research based on Western, Muscovite, Iranian and Armenian sources has demonstrated that the long-distance trade route via Russia was indeed an alternative for transporting raw silk and other commodities from Iran to northwestern Europe.[4] One of the two routes from Moscow to Amsterdam ran through Narva; that is, across Swedish territory.[5] The other one, however, from Archangel on the White Sea around the North Cape into the Northern Sea, remained beyond Sweden's reach.

From the late sixteenth century to 1703, the Muscovite State had no access to the Baltic Sea because the entire Gulf of Finland, as well as Livonia, were in Swedish possession. Also Sweden temporarily blocked Poland-Lithuania and the northern parts of the German Empire from such access. So the driving forces behind Sweden's expansion, and her ultimate rise to Great Power status in the early modern period, were economic and financial ones. The peripheral, poor, backward and sparsely populated country tried to compensate for its paucity of resources by controlling the main arteries of East–West trade in order to increase its revenues by levying high customs fees on goods passing along these routes.[6]

Thus, Sweden during its Great Power period can be compared to Safavid Iran, as the two shared many similarities. For both, their rise and fall took place from the sixteenth to the eighteenth centuries; trade was a core factor in their achieving Great Power status; and their mercantile expertise was mainly imported from abroad. Both made serious attempts to centralize the state government and create an efficient bureaucracy; in both countries, long periods of interregnum did not erode monarchic rule; and under weak rulers, royal power slowed down reform and put their international standing at risk.

The main target of Sweden's policy of trade control was Russia's trade with the West; that is, with England, the Netherlands and Germany. From the mid-sixteenth century to the early eighteenth century, the re-routing of Russian foreign trade from Archangel to Swedish ports on the Eastern Baltic Sea was a core element of Sweden's foreign policy. In the second half of the sixteenth century, the Swedish experts who were focused on Russia's export to north-western Europe realized that commodities from Iran were a major component of the Tsar's trade with the West. Accordingly, Swedish policy makers developed a sustained interest in Safavid Iran in general, and in Persian trade with Europe in particular. This interest is amply reflected in the rich holdings of the *Riksarkivet* – the Swedish National Archives in Stockholm. Yet, while the *Diplomatica Persica*, a series of diplomatic documents on Swedish-Persian relations, that is housed there consists of only two slim volumes,[7] the files of the *Kommerskollegium* (College of Commerce) – that is the Swedish Ministry of Trade established in 1651 – contain large numbers of documents on bilateral Swedish-Iranian relations.[8]

Swedish trade policy towards Iran: 1616–74[9]

In 1616 Gustav II Adolf, king of Sweden from 1611 to 1632, tried for the first time to talk Tsar Mikhail Fedorovich and his father Filaret into giving the green light to transit trade from Iran to Amsterdam via Narva – instead of Archangel. Although the king was not successful, during the 1620s, Muscovite merchants from north-western Russia did occasionally transport Iranian raw silk to Sweden's Baltic provinces. In addition to a number of direct initiatives in Moscow, Swedish diplomats teamed up with Holstein-Gottorff on the Holstein Project of 1632 to 1635/41, which resulted in the Brüggemann-Crusius-Olearius mission, a plan to establish a trade route from Isfahan in Iran, via Russia and Sweden, to Friedrichstadt in Holstein. The project as such was not successful. But it had at least one important medium-term effect on Sweden: one of the envoys, Philip Crusius, stayed on in Swedish Livonia, which became, as was said at the time, his *Blievland* (the land where he would stay for good). Crusius, who was soon ennobled and given the name von Krusenstiern, became the Swedish crown's most important expert on Iran. Until his death in 1676, he wrote numerous memoranda on transit trade to Isfahan, held high-ranking administrative positions in Sweden's Baltic provinces, and took up diplomatic missions to Moscow. Above all, he constantly urged the crown to send a mission to the Iranian shah (Shahs Abbas II and Safi II) to firmly establish bilateral diplomatic and commercial relations.[10]

In the 1640s, von Krusenstiern was instrumental in reforming the Swedish customs system in the trans-Baltic ports, which resulted in an increased flow of trade from Russia to Nyen, Narva, Reval and Riga. Merchants in Reval who traded with Russia now began including Persian raw silk in their mercantile transactions. The silk was bought in Moscow and Novgorod and then exported via Sweden to Amsterdam. At the same time, merchants in north-western Russia started to export raw silk to Sweden, which would go on to Lübeck and the Netherlands. Between 1600 and 1650, this trade amounted to 50 to 100 bales of Iranian raw silk annually. However, the Russian-Swedish War of 1656 to 1661, and later Sten'ka Razin's Cossack rebellion in the Lower Volga Region, as well as the Tsar's determination to cling to the port of Archangel, prevented Iranian commodities from being transported through Swedish territory.

Sweden's interest in trade with Iran, however, did not diminish. In 1658, when Sweden was temporarily in possession of parts of Norway, and thus also in a position to control Russian trade through Archangel, Harald Appelboom, Swedish envoy to the Netherlands, wrote to King Charles X Gustav:

> Your Royal Majesty has the chance of getting not only all of the Muscovite trade but also a large part of the Persian trade in Your hands. This would bring Your Royal Majesty many millions and an incredible richness, so in the future Your Royal Majesty would need no more French or English subsidies and payments.[11]

When in late 1673 a Swedish mission to the Tsar learnt of his recent trade agreement with the Armenian merchants of Isfahan, it immediately excited the new Swedish king Charles XI's interest in the Persian connection. Alas, the plan to dispatch veteran expert von Krusenstiern to Isfahan could not be realized: the former Holsteinian envoy to Isfahan, now at the biblical age of 77, declined the offer of another mission to Iran because of health problems. It was not until 1677 that Charles XI again embarked on the Iranian project. By that time, a replacement for von Krusenstiern had been found in the person of the Dutch expert on Iran and Muscovy, Major Ludvig Fabritius.

The missions of Ludvig Fabritius[12]

Between 1679 and 1687, Fabritius undertook his first two missions to Isfahan on behalf of the Swedish crown. In negotiations with the grand vizier and Armenian merchants, Fabritius succeeded in whetting his counterparts' appetites for the Baltic route. In addition, in 1687, he managed to obtain the agreement of the Tsar's chancellor that subjects of the shah could use transit trade routes via Novgorod and Narva to Amsterdam. In return, on 23 September 1687, Charles XI of Sweden issued an *Octroi* (charter) to the Armenian merchants of Isfahan, which granted them low customs tariffs and the privilege of using Sweden's Baltic port of Narva, including the right to operate a *Persianisches Haus* (Persian house), a warehouse cum hostel in the centre of town. By doing so, the Swedish crown not only hoped to increase its custom revenues but also to increase Swedish exports. When asked by Swedish officials whether the Armenian merchants would consider buying European commodities for the Iranian market in Narva instead of Amsterdam, the head of the Armenian delegation, Safar Nersisjan, reacted positively:

> The old Armenian emphasized to strive for no lesser aim than to turn Narva into the same staple town as Amsterdam; and if they get their retour commodities in Narva then they would be very satisfied with that.[13]

From 1690 on, the *Octroi* triggered a fairly regular transit trade in raw silk from Iran, via Russia and Narva, to Amsterdam carried out by Armenian merchants. Occasionally, up to 50 merchants and their staff stayed in Narva. According to Swedish statistics, between 1690 and 1697 an annual average of 250 bales of raw silk, approximately four per cent of all of Iran's raw silk exports, were shipped via Sweden.

From the mid-1690s on, internal economic competition among the Armenian merchants of Isfahan resulted in the emergence of Courland and Poland–Lithuania as competitors for the Narva route. Thus in 1697, the Swedish crown sent Fabritius once more to Isfahan. According to Fabritius' report, Shah Sultan Husayn I agreed to direct Persian transit trade through the Swedish ports on the Baltic, and even responded positively to the Swedish request for permission for Swedish merchants to trade in Iran and to open their own permanent trading house in Isfahan. However, the outbreak of the Great Northern War in the summer of 1700, the founding of St Petersburg in 1703 and the Russian occupation of Reval and Riga in 1710, brought an end to the Narva route. As the Swedish historian of architecture, Sten Karling, describes it:

> The idea to open a trade route via Russia to Persia was dominating Sweden's trade policy throughout all of her existence as a Great Power. This daring project was almost completely realized when Russia under Peter the Great usurped it. Narva is the monument for this grandiose mercantile intermezzo.[14]

With the exception of mercantile information, Swedish archival sources contain very little on other aspects of Swedish-Iranian relations or, more accurately, Swedish-Armenian relations. In particular, almost nothing is known about how Armenian merchants, Swedish authorities and the inhabitants of Narva got along with each other. What is known is that religion was a problem to the Swedes. After many years of trying, English merchants in 1684 finally received permission to operate their own church in Narva. The Armenians, however, who had repeatedly made the same request, never did receive permission.[15] It is also known that in addition to the numerous Russian translators in Narva, Armenian and Farsi translators were now in demand. In 1696 one of them, Jochum Ekebohm, complained to the king in Stockholm that he was completely overloaded with work and, as compensation, asked for and received permission to do petty trading with the Armenian merchants.[16] Finally, the outbreak of hostilities between Russia and Sweden in 1700 prevented a number of Armenian merchants from returning home via Moscow. They were put up in Stockholm, and the Swedish crown bore their expenses throughout the 21 years the war lasted, and some of them remained in Sweden permanently.

The Great Northern War ended Sweden's status as a Great Power. But another emerging power in the region adopted the Swedish plan to draw Iran's trade with western Europe to the Baltic Sea; in 1708, Brandenburg-Prussia used the Swedish *Octroi* of 1687 as the blueprint to attract a group of Armenian merchants to Königsberg. Despite increased Prussian diplomatic activity in Isfahan and Moscow, no substantial trade developed and in 1720 the project was cancelled.[17]

Notes

1. Acta, betr. Handel aus Persien nach S. Kurfürstl. Durchl. Landen, woraus nichts geworden. 1697/98. In: Geheimes Staatsarchiv Preußischer Kulturbesitz, Berlin: Hauptabteilung 1, Repertorium XI, 203: Persien, Faszikel 4. See also Michael Hundt, *'Woraus nichts geworden'. Brandenburg-Preußens Handel mit Persien (1668–1720)* (Hamburg, 1997).
2. John Foran, 'The making of an external area: Iran's place in the world system, 1500–1722', *Review. A Journal of the Fernand Braudel Center for the Study of Economies, Historical Systems, and Civilizations* 12/1 (1998), pp. 71–199, here p. 106.
3. Gunnar Jarring, 'Vidgat horisont', in Gudrun Ekstrand (ed.), *Tre Karlar. Karl X Gustav, Karl XI, Karl XII* (Stockholm, 1984), pp. 138–51, here p. 145.
4. See, first of all, Rudolph P. Matthee, *The Politics of Trade in Safavid Iran. Silk for Silver, 1600–1730* (Cambridge, 1999), and Ina Baghdiantz McCabe, *The Shah's Silk for Europe's Silver. The Eurasian Trade of the Julfa Armenians in Safavid Iran and India (1530–1750)* (Atlanta, GA, 1999), as well as Willem Floor, *A Fiscal History of Iran in the Safavid and Qajar Periods 1500–1925* (New York, 1998); idem, *The Economy of Safavid Persia* (Wiesbaden 2000); Nina G. Kukanova, *Ocherki po istorii russko-iranskich torgovych otnoshenii v XVII – pervoi polovine XIX veka* (Saransk, 1977); Stefan Troebst, 'Isfahan – Moskau – Amsterdam. Zur Entstehungsgeschichte des moskauischen Transitprivilegs für die Armenische Handelskompagnie in Persien (1666–1676)', *Jahrbücher für Geschichte Osteuropas* 41/2 (1993), pp. 179–209, and Michel Aghassian and Kéram Kévonian, 'The Armenian merchant network: Overall autonomy and local integration', in Sushil Chaudhury and Michel Morineau (eds), *Merchants, Companies and Trade. Europe and Asia in the Early Modern Era* (Cambridge, 1999), pp. 74–94.
5. Stefan Troebst, 'Narva und der Aussenhandel Persiens im 17. Jahrhundert. Zum merkantilen Hintergrund schwedischer Grossmachtpolitik', in Aleksander Loit and Helmut Piirimäe (eds), *Die schwedischen Ostseeprovinzen Estland und Livland im 16.-18. Jahrhundert* (Uppsala, 1993), pp. 161–78.

6. Artur Attman, *Swedish Aspirations and the Russian Market during the 17th Century* (Göteborg, 1985). For an alternative view stressing security reasons see Michael Roberts, *The Swedish Imperial Experience, 1560-1717* (Cambridge, 1979). This historiographic controversy is covered by Klaus Zernack, 'Schweden als europäische Großmacht der frühen Neuzeit', *Historische Zeitschrift* 232 (1980), pp. 327–57, and Stefan Troebst, 'Debating the mercantile background to early modern Swedish empire-building: Michael Roberts versus Artur Attman', *European History Quarterly* 24/4 (1994), pp. 485–509.
7. Cf. Sören Tommos, *The Diplomatica Collection in the Swedish National Archives* (Stockholm, 1980), p. 138.
8. For examples see Artur Attman et al. (eds), *Ekonomiska förbindelser mellan Sverige och Ryssland under 1600-talet. Dokument ur svenska arkiv* (Stockholm, 1978).
9. The following account is based on Troebst, *Handelskontrolle - 'Derivation' - Eindämmung. Schwedische Moskaupolitik 1617-1661* (Wiesbaden, 1997), pp. 167–203, 369–91, 459–60 and 486–90, and Troebst, 'Russland als 'Magazin der Handlung zwischen Asien und Europa'? Die Frage des Orienthandels bei der schwedischen Moskaugesandtschaft 1673/74', *Forschungen zur osteuropäischen Geschichte* 58 (2001), pp. 287–300.
10. Benigna von Krusenstiern, *Philip Crusius von Krusenstiern (1597-1676). Sein Wirken in Livland als Rußlandkenner, Diplomat und Landespolitiker* (Marburg/L., 1976).
11. Harald Appelboom to Charles X Gustav, The Hague, 28 May/7 June 1658 in Riksarkivet Stockholm, Diplomatica Hollandica, vol. 50: Harald Appelbooms brev till K. M:t 1658 (Maj-juli till K. M:t och maj-november till rådet), fo. 4r-v.
12. The following account is based on Stefan Troebst, 'Die Kaspi-Volga-Ostsee-Route in der Handelspolitik Karls XI. Die schwedischen Persien-Mission von Ludvig Fabritius 1679–1700', *Forschungen zur osteuropäischen Geschichte* 54 (1998), pp. 127–204. See also Johan Kempe, *Kongl. Swenska Envoijen Ludwich Fabritii Lefwerne* (Stockholm, 1762).
13. Protocol of the session of the College of Commerce in the afternoon of 13 September 1687 in Riksarkivet Stockholm. Kommerskollegium, Huvudarkivet, Protokoll (A I a 1), vol. 33: 1687.
14. Sten Karling, *Narva. Eine baugeschichtliche Untersuchung* (Stockholm, 1936), p. 34.
15. Jaroslav R. Dashkevitch, 'Armiano-shvedskie kontakty v XVII v.', in Aleksandr O. Chubarian et al. (eds), *Vsesoiuznaia konferentsiia po izucheniiu istorii, ekonomiki, literatury i iazyka skandinavskich stran i Finliandii. Tezisy dokladov*, pt. I (Moskva, 1989), pp. 49–50.
16. Letter by the combined Colleges of Chamber and Commerce to Charles XI. Stockholm, 10 March 1696, in Riksarkivet Stockholm, Kommerskollegium till K. M:t, vol. 13: 1696.
17. The 'woraus nichts geworden' file in the Prussian State Archives contains more on the results of this undertaking.

15

The Armenian Colony in Amsterdam in the Seventeenth and Eighteenth Centuries: Armenian Merchants from Julfa before and after the Fall of the Safavid Empire

René Arthur Bekius

Since publications by Macler[1] and van Rooy,[2] it is well known that Amsterdam housed a small Armenian merchant community in the seventeenth and eighteenth centuries. After passing the Nieuwmarkt, dominated by a characteristic medieval building – originally one of the entrance gates to the city – the pedestrian enters the Koningsstraat. An attentive observer could discover, at number 27, a renovated house with an interesting small gable stone depicting a chalice. Beneath the chalice, there is a text in a peculiar script. The script is Armenian and reads: 'In the year of Jesus Christ 1765'. To the left and right sides of the text, you can see the Latin letters A and P, abbreviations of the Armenian words Holy Chalice.[3] Who could have been the owner of this house? It turns out that it was inhabited by several Armenian priests in the eighteenth century, the most famous being Johannes di Minas.

The interested tourist might wonder what else is left of the Armenian merchant community from olden days. At the end of the Koningsstraat, you can discover one of the most picturesque small canals in Amsterdam, the Krom Boomssloot.[4] Just a couple of metres from the corner of the Koningsstraat and this canal, you will see a large, white building at number 22. If you take a close look at the entrance door, you will discover a nameplate indicating the function of this building: Apostolic Armenian Church. If you pass by on Sunday mornings, you will hear clearly the hymns of the present-day devout Armenian community attending a service. The same songs that a passer-by would have heard in the early eighteenth century.

The original Armenian Church dates back to 1714. However, the building has undergone several architectural changes in the course of its history. The most recent was in the late nineteenth century, when an extra storey was added to the existing building. From 1890 until 1989 the building was used as a Catholic primary school. In 1989 the school moved to a new building nearby. Due to the initiative of the late Mr V. Kinebanian and a grant from the Armenian General Benevolent Union, the original historical building was bought back by the Armenian Apostolic Church Foundation. The classroom, which once housed the original eighteenth-century Armenian Church, was again transformed into a church. The Armenian painter Krikor Momdjian – originating from Lebanon – was commissioned to decorate the walls with frescos and on 26 November 1989 the church was consecrated by the Armenian archbishop of Paris, K. Nakachian.

Between its foundation and its second consecration as an Armenian church, the building experienced a series of vicissitudes. On 9 March 1874 it was publicly auctioned and sold for 10,000 guilders and until 1890 the building was not used. In the course of the nineteenth century Dutch curators rented the Armenian Church to several denominations, such as the Old Lutheran Church, served by minister Pogge, and the Free Church of Scotland, served by the converted Jew, Dr C. Schwartz.[5]

Several decades earlier, in 1835, the last member of the Armenian Church in Amsterdam, Stephan di Gabriel, married to Christina Birmer, died childless. In his will Stephan declared that, according to article 1 of the rules written down by the church ward Alexander di Massé dated 1 June 1788, the last church member was entitled to administer the church building and objects. In addition, the rules stated that the Patriarch of Armenia was recognized as religious leader, but not as the ultimate possessor of the church and its goods. On 30 September 1840 a new inventory was made by notary K. Schlosjer, who asked Mr J. Lublink to act as curator. Finally, in 1874, the patriarch of Etchmiadzin, Kevork IV received an overview of the financial transactions of the several curators.

By the early nineteenth century, there was no use for an Armenian church in Amsterdam. The situation in the previous century had been different. In 1749, during the last flourishing days of the Armenian colony in Amsterdam, Johannes di Minas, an Armenian priest from Amasia, took the initiative to embellish the church facade by placing an elegant gable stone with an Armenian inscription above the exterior head entrance.[6] In addition, he replaced the old staircase with a new doorstep decorated with ironwork in rococo style. This restoration was carried out at Minas' own expense.

On 30 January 1714, during the second flourishing period of the Armenian community in Amsterdam, the Amsterdam Burgomasters gave the Armenians official permission to build an Armenian church visible from the street.[7] In the margin of the letter of permission, there is the following: 'Armenian merchants granted a church'. Then follows the content of the permission: 'On the request of the Armenian merchants at this place, has been approved after deliberations to grant them within this town to buy a house, in order to make a church to perform their religion'.

This decision was in line with the liberal policy of the protestant Amsterdam Burgomasters. Other religious minorities – like the Portuguese Jews, the German Jews and the Lutherans – had already built their official churches. Only Catholics were not allowed to hold services in churches recognizable as such from the street and had to perform services in private homes until the late eighteenth century.

Immediately after official permission was granted by the city council, the Armenian churchwardens, Babasan di Sultan and Nicolaes di Theodoor, acted quickly. On 28 February 1714 they bought a warehouse and properties from the inheritors of Joosten Baan and Dieuertje Haringkarspel. The warehouse was situated at number 3, the Dwarsboomsloot (currently called the Krom Boomssloot), between the Keizersstraat and a house situated on the north-western side of the Dwarsboomsloot.

A year later, on 7 May 1715, 40 Armenian merchants testified before the notary Gerrit van der Groe.[8] They officially ratified the purchase of the warehouse and the costs incurred by the two responsible churchwardens to transform the building into an official church. Simultaneously, the merchants donated a gift to compensate for the costs. However, the size of each donation is not specified. A considerable number of these merchants came from Safavid Iran. One of the beneficiaries was a certain Sarhad di Stefan. I believe this is the same person who wrote a detailed accountbook[9] on his silk transactions with foreign and Armenian merchants on his route from Isfahan, Tabriz, Samachi, Astrakhan, Moscow, Archangelsk[10] and Amsterdam between 1711 and 1718.

In addition, a notarial act of 7 May 1715 contained two explicit stipulations. The first stated that the Armenian Church had to serve current and future Armenian merchants. The second stated that the church could only be sold under two conditions: if the City of Amsterdam were to forbid the free practice of the Armenian religion; or if the entire Armenian community were to move elsewhere to trade. The money received from the sale should then be sent back to the Patriarch of Echmiadzin, who had the right to decide where to erect a new church. The Armenian Church is sometimes referred to as the Persiaansche Kerk (Persian Church).[11]

The story of the Armenian merchant colony in Amsterdam does not stop at 1714. From the early 1620s until 1714 there was a first wave of Armenian merchants. Armenian migration to Amsterdam could be split into two phases. In the first phase merchants only stayed in the city temporarily. In the second phase, around the mid-1660s, they gradually settled permanently.

Like other denominations of minorities they had to perform religious services in private homes. The first hard evidence that Armenians held services in private houses dates from a notarial act of 1703. This church was situated in the Koningsdwarsstraat, most probably the dwelling of the Armenian priest Johannes de Oe Goer Loe. In the presence of the notary, the priest appointed three administrators, Thessali de

Agasar, Pieter Avedt and Nazar van Leuwen, to take care of the Armenian Church artefacts after his death. The inventory distinguishes between objects belonging to the Armenian Church and the private property of the priest. The church space in this private house must have been rather big, given all the objects described and several church pews. The main objects fall into three categories: metal and copperware; printed Armenian books, including a folio Armenian bible with silver decorations; and finally 15 paintings, large and small. Some of these objects can be identified in an etching depicting the Armenian Church in the mid-eighteenth century, the work of the official city historian Wagenaar.[12]

Armenian merchants did not only leave architectural traces. Early in the seventeenth century they were depicted on allegorical etchings illustrating Amsterdam as a trade metropolis. One example is a panoramic view of Amsterdam etched by Claes Jansz Visscher in 1611 in which Armenians, or Persians, are depicted. Throughout the seventeenth century certain Dutch painters specialized in Amsterdam city views, depicting official buildings like the town hall and the Stock Exchange and painted orientals, mostly two or three people engaged in conversation, centrally placed at the foreground. It seems most likely that they were Armenian merchants from Persia and the Levant. They symbolized the cosmopolitan element of both locations. In addition, the paintings illustrate that Armenians were a fundamental part of street life in Amsterdam.

However, the most impressive traces that Armenians left in Amsterdam were printed Armenian books, which have been described and investigated by several authors.[13] Armenian printers settled in Amsterdam for various reasons: to evade the severe censorship of Rome; to learn technical printing skills from local Amsterdam printers, who made Amsterdam the leading printing centre of Europe; and to make use of the excellent transport facilities needed to export their books to the Middle East.

Between 1664 and 1718 Armenian priests printed a total of 48 Armenian books. In the literature, Armenian printing is quite often seen as covering a single, united period. In reality, it was active at intervals. Between 1658 and 1661, Matt'eos Tsarets'i was the first person to print books in Armenian; he was followed from 1661-4 by his successors, Awetis Ghllitsents Erevants'i and Karapet Andrianats'i. The most productive period was between 1664 and 1669, when Oskan Erevants'i was the most prominent printer. In 1666, he produced the famous printed Armenian Bible,[14] illustrated with etchings by the Dutch engraver family van Sichem.

From 1685-92 a new era in Armenian printing started under the guidance of Matte'os Yohannes Vanandets'i. Subsequently, from 1695 to 1718, T'omas Vanandets'i and his nephew, Ghukas Vanandets'i, were the leading figures in Armenian printing. In 1695, the first Armenian world map was printed by T'omas Vanandets'i, who commissioned the brothers Adriaan and Petrus Damianus Schoonebeeck to engrave the map on copperplates.

Right from the start, the various Armenian printers active in Amsterdam used the names Surb Echmiadcin and Surb Sargis Zoravar. Several remarks can be made on the connection between these printers and Safavid Iran. Most of the priest-printers, often assisted by family members, came from Iran. Most printed Armenian books were intended for export. The first destination was the Ottoman Empire (Smirna). From there books were transported, through colporteurs, overland to eastern Anatolia and Iran. The main goal of the Armenian printers in Amsterdam was to educate Armenian readers in Iran. The main client was the Armenian Patriarchate, while the leading financiers were rich Armenian merchants from Safavid Iran. I have traced nine names in the publication information of Amsterdam Armenian prints. Other financiers were the Amsterdam priest-printers.

First Armenian-Dutch contacts in the Middle East

The first contacts between Dutch merchants and Armenian silk traders from Iran were made in the early seventeenth century in Aleppo. It was here that the Dutch became acquainted with Iranian silk. Soon the Governor-General Jan Pieterszoon Coen and Jacob van Dedel, admiral of the Dutch-English defensive fleet, who drove the Portugese from Hormuz in 1621, saw the importance of setting up a factory in Persia. On Dedel's recommendation, the first manager of the new Dutch factory in Isfahan was appointed. The choice fell on Hybert Visnich, the son of a textile-dyeing family from Dordrecht, who had built up considerable expertise on the overland silk trade from Persia to Aleppo whilst active as a merchant in Aleppo, where he also mastered Arabic and Turkish. Right from the start the Verenigde Oostindische Compagnie or Dutch East India Company (VOC) in Iran employed Armenians as interpreters[15] and in other functions.[16]

Visnich played an important role in concluding the first Dutch-Persian capitulation with Shah 'Abbas I during 1623. The agreement was quite favourable to the Dutch. It was agreed that the silk from the Caspian area had to be delivered by the shah's silk factor directly to the Dutch Lodge in Isfahan. If they failed to deliver on time the shah had to finance the transport costs himself. A series of disputes arose between the shah's silk factor, Molaym Bek (Molayem Bayg), and Visnich on the irregular silk deliveries and price agreements. That is why Visnich started travelling regularly to the silk producing areas to arrange his affairs on the spot. Visnich competed directly with Armenian silk merchants. Perhaps he was in an advantageous position since he was married to an Armenian wife from Julfa. From this marriage he had two sons. Visnich, being a skilful merchant, successfully did business for the VOC from 1603 until 1628. In 1629 his position became intolerable through intrigues of his successor Delcourt and the Dutch court painter van Hasselt. Both accused Visnich of damaging the VOC cause by doing private business. In addition, in 1629, his main protégés, Shah Abbas I and Jan Pieterszoon Coen passed away. Delcourt soon discovered that he lacked the knowledge to deal efficiently with the royal factor, Molaym Bek. Therefore, he needed Visnich's expertise to conclude a new capitulation with Shah Safi. However, Visnich was not willing to cooperate. Delcourt took revenge by laying an embargo on Visnich's personal possessions, and by persuading Shah Safi not to provide Visnich with a safe conduct. Visnich then decided to return to the Dutch Republic to report back to the Dutch East India Company on his administrative activities while working for the Company in Iran. With the help of Armenian relatives and other European friends he tried to escape through Turkey. While crossing the border he was arrested as a spy and murdered.[17] This case study illustrates the start of a complex triangular relationship, between the Dutch East India Company, state officials of the Safavid Empire and Iranian Armenian silk dealers, which continued over a period of two centuries. In addition, it shows that in rare cases Dutch VOC officials got direct access to the silk producing areas, thereby circumventing Iranian Armenian brokers and state officials.

According to McCabe's hypothesis the English and Dutch companies were no real match for Armenian silk dealers in Iran, since the Armenians completely dominated the silk market. From 1618, European companies did not control the flow of silk to Europe, but the New Julfan Armenians totally controlled the supply of Iranian silk to the Levant. This viewpoint is also shared by Matthee. With regards to the advantage enjoyed by the Europeans because they were able to internalize their protection costs on the European maritime route, I would even go a step further than Matthee.[18] Here too, the Europeans lost out to their Armenian competitors. Once Armenian merchants had settled down in Amsterdam, they made use of the same protection costs as the Dutch by arranging insurance for their transports.[19]

However, McCabe's hypothesis on the competition between the Armenian silk traders and the European trade companies in the seventeenth and eighteenth centuries is not underpinned with hard quantitative data – based on Armenian or Iranian sources – indicating roughly how many silk bales were exported by Armenians on a yearly basis overland from Iran to the Levant. Nor roughly how many silk bales Armenians exported from Iran to Europe, either directly or via the Russian route, circumventing the West European companies. McCabe refers to the existence of European records but does not make use of them or compare the statistical silk data from the VOC sources, to assess the extent of the competition between the Armenian silk traders and their main competitor, the VOC.

This exercise is partly done by Floor,[20] who has compared the silk exports of the VOC and the East India Company (EIC) from Persia to the Dutch Republic between 1624 and 1714. These data show that the exports were more profitable in certain years than others. Peaks occurred in 1624-8, 1638-41, 1652-4, 1669-77, 1681-2 and 1695. From 1696 to 1714 there were hardly any exports.

The story about the competition between the Armenian silk traders and the Dutch VOC becomes even more complicated when looking in time series to the export of Iranian silk bales by the VOC to other factories within Asia. In her study of the eighteenth-century inter-Asiatic trade of the VOC, Jacobs has drawn up several time series of products in which the VOC dealt, of which silk was only one.[21]

Three Dutch archival sources on Armenian silk merchants

The competition of the Armenian silk dealers with European trade companies in Iran and the Levant can only be studied in a fruitful way by combining Western archival sources and non-Western Ottoman, Armenian and Iranian sources. From the Dutch perspective there are several useful sources that shed a better light on the interaction of Armenian traders with the Dutch. For Iran, this can be done by using the archives of the VOC and for the Levant by consulting the Dutch Levant Archives. Dutch travelogues[22] describing both empires provide additional information.

However, a third source could be added. The local Amsterdam notarial acts provide additional information on trade interactions between the Armenian merchants residing in Amsterdam and their fellow traders in Iran and the Levant. In addition, these notarial acts shed light on a series of related topics not easily found in the archives of the trade companies, such as: different Armenian migration flows to the Dutch Republic; residential settlement patterns in Amsterdam; patterns of mixed marriage; the range of Armenian import and export products; the practical problems of silk storage; changing patterns in different silk imports; temporary trade associations that were formed among Armenians themselves and between Armenian and Dutch merchants in Amsterdam; the pattern of Armenians active in inter-European trade; ways in which transaction costs were guaranteed (minimizing trade risks), and so on.

In the Amsterdam notarial acts Armenian merchants are indicated by several terms. The most common designation is armeender, armener, or armeniër (Armenian) or Persian merchant. However, in the archives of the Dutch East India Company, Armenians from Iran are quite often called Giofalynen, Solfalynen of Jolfalijnen.[23] These names are different spellings of New Julfa, a suburb of Isfahan, the place of origin of most Armenian merchants.

From the Amsterdam notarial acts I have tried to chart the whole Armenian community – in total some 800 persons,[24] including the names of Dutch wives and children from mixed marriages – over two centuries. For each person I have made a record with relevant data on the place of origin, date of birth and death in Amsterdam, sex, marital status, home address and knowledge of languages and specialization in trade products. I have tried to quantify the country of origin where it was explicitly stated in the acts. To measure the average period of stay in Amsterdam of Armenian merchants, I have taken the first and the last year per person referred to in the acts.

Why did Armenian merchants come to Amsterdam?

Why did Armenian merchants come to Amsterdam and not to other main European trading cities in the course of the seventeenth century? Were they led by economic considerations because of the rise of Amsterdam as a trade metropolis in the world economy? Did they want to escape the religious or political oppression of the Safavid and Ottoman empires? Or were they attracted to the liberal political and religious climate in the Dutch Republic?

It is not plausible that the first Armenians coming from Iran to the Dutch Republic in the early seventeenth century fled their country due to political or religious oppression. On the contrary, the Armenian merchant elite received from Shah Abbas I all kinds of trade privileges. They were crucial, as international silk traders, to the Iranian economy. So the profit motive was the driving force for Armenians to come to the Dutch Republic. In addition, the arrival of Armenians in Amsterdam was also stimulated by several protectionist economic measures taken by the Dutch. Around the 1630s a rule was introduced by which it was forbidden to transport goods from Iran and Turkey in foreign ships. In order to protect their interests Armenians started to load their goods on Dutch ships.

Armenians were also attracted to Amsterdam because they were then less prone to protectionist economic measures taken by France or England. Patents of the Turkey Company in London from 1581 and 1661 excluded foreigners in the trade between England and the Levant. In the course of the eighteenth century France also introduced economic measures that made transactions with France by foreigners more complicated. French captains were not allowed to accept goods belonging to foreigners or that were addressed to foreigners in France. In addition, the French government levied an import tax of 20 per cent on goods arriving on foreign ships. Counting up all these protectionist measures it was more profitable for Armenians to do business in Amsterdam.

The first Armenian merchants only came on a temporary basis and left Amsterdam after having done business. From 1650, however, we notice an influx of Armenian merchants mentioned in the notarial acts. In the 1660s and 1670s the Armenian colony in Amsterdam reached its first peak. In 1668 there were 66 Armenians. After 1687 a decline set in. In the first two decades of the eighteenth century there were just over 50. In 1715 there were 71 Armenians in the city, the all-time maximum. In 1731 the number declined to 26 and between 1740 and 1750 there were about 45 persons. After the mid-eighteenth century a gradual decline set in and in 1810 there were only five Armenians left.

Based on the indications given in the notarial acts about the country they originated from it is possible to discern three main migration flows of Armenian merchants coming to Amsterdam. The first came from Iran, the second from the Ottoman Empire and the third from Russia.

The residential pattern of Armenian merchants in Amsterdam

Relatively little is known about how Armenian merchants settled in the main European towns in the course of the seventeenth and eighteenth centuries. Is it possible to discern a general pattern as to why they chose certain quarters in European cities to settle down in? In which quarters of Amsterdam did the Armenians settle and what can be told about the history of the changes in their residential patterns in the city? Who acted as interpreters and brokers for the merchants?

Armenian merchants arriving in Amsterdam were faced – like most temporary foreign businessmen – with a number of practical problems: where to stay and how to do business without knowing the language. Most Armenian merchants solved these problems in a very practical way. They rented rooms in the houses of Armenian interpreters who made a living from receiving these temporary guests. The interpreters acted not only as brokers but also as moneylenders, providing starting capital up to 1,000 guilders. Since it was common practice among Armenian merchants to trust each other by word of mouth these transactions between the Amsterdam Armenian brokers and Armenian merchants coming from abroad were not laid down in written form before a notary. After the client had done his business successfully the broker received back his money, with interest. This specific Armenian trade custom[25] was testified to and explained by 11 Armenian merchants before an Amsterdam notary in 1717.

The urban history of Armenian merchants in Amsterdam can be partly mapped from notarial acts providing data on 110 street names where Armenians were living. Obtaining specific data on the selling and buying of houses by Armenians is possible through cadastral research, combined with data on municipal taxes on houses. It turns out that, spread over two centuries, the core of the Armenian merchant community in Amsterdam, in total 71 persons, remained concentrated in city quarters 10, 11 and 12. These quarters were situated east of the Nieuwmarkt, around the Kromme Waal, Koningsstraat, Rechtboomssloot and Krom Boomssloot, the so-called Lastage. The Jewish district was adjacent to this quarter. Only after 1750 did a percentage of Armenians, with a known address, gradually move out from their old area to other parts of town.

Why did Armenian merchants settle in these three specific quarters in town? Several explanations could be given for their choice of settlement. From 1591 the Amsterdam municipality designated this part of town to factories specializing in dying silk fibres and silk fabrics. Since most Armenian merchants, in particular in the first part of the seventeenth century, were exclusively dealing in silk it seems logical that they preferred to live near the silk factories.[26] Armenian merchants could rent sufficient warehouses in this area to store their silk bales.

Armenian silk traders, not knowing the Dutch language at first, hired Portuguese Jews, who knew both Persian and Dutch, to act as brokers and interpreters. These brokers went with the merchants to notaries to testify on trade transactions. A recorded example is one Cogie Saharat, who hired the interpreter Isaac (or Isack) Chamis in 1627. Through Chamis, Saharat conveyed to the notary that he was happy with a trade transaction he had concluded with the Dutch merchant Gerrit Alewijn.[27]

In the initial period, Armenian merchants settled in the same quarters, helped by colleagues renting out rooms. At a later stage, they spread out in these quarters, renting rooms from Dutch families. During the final stage, Armenians bought houses in the area. This can be substantiated by analysing data from the notarial acts and from the Amsterdam city tax department in 1742.[28] It is not surprising therefore that the Armenian Church was later erected in this part of the city. Armenians remained faithful to this urban area since it was very close to the economic and administrative heart of Amsterdam. The extent to which they clung together in one quarter of town testifies to a limited integration.

Two rich Armenian merchants possessed, like the Amsterdam merchant elite, country houses in a wealthy rural area called the Watergraafsmeer, just outside Amsterdam. Alexander di Massé owned a country house called Weltevreden, with a double pleasure garden, and the Iranian Armenian merchant Johannes di Jacob Galdar possessed a similar country house in the Schagerlaan. Country houses were bought as investments and to escape the stinking Amsterdam canals in summertime.[29]

Social life

Reconstructing Armenian social life in Amsterdam in the seventeenth and eighteenth centuries can only be done in a fragmented way, by using those notarial acts which shed light on these aspects. I have not yet looked at legal records, which might shed more light on social conflicts.

Most Armenian merchants arrived in Amsterdam at a young age to do business. Once they settled down they started to look for local marriage partners. Further investigation might reveal from which social strata Armenian merchants recruited their brides. It is difficult to assess how the local Amsterdam population perceived Armenian-Dutch mixed marriages. However, there are indications that some locals, in particular those living in the Armenian quarter, looked down on mixed marriages. This can be illustrated by one case in which the head officer of the city wanted to obtain official testimonies from several Dutch witnesses. They had seen how Agneta Sluyters, housewife of Albert Jansen, but formerly with an Armenian merchant, was first harassed by a close neighbour, the tailor Harmen Bavinck. He shouted at her and branded her as 'a whore and a Persian thief'. Subsequently, Harmen Bavinck wounded Agneta severely by throwing a foot-stove with hot burning coals on her body. This act of aggression took place in the Krom Boomssloot where Agneta Sluyters and Harmen Bavinck were living.[30]

The Armenian Church and its control over Armenian social life in Amsterdam

Unlike the parnassim of the Jews, who had both religious and partial judiciary control over the Jewish community, Armenian priests dealt only with spiritual matters and incidentally acted as arbiters in trading conflicts among Armenians. All other matters were dealt with by local Amsterdam municipal institutions.

The Armenian Church in Amsterdam played an important role in holding together the social fabric (identity) of the Armenian merchants passing through or living permanently in Amsterdam. However, sometimes conflicts erupted. The first type of conflict arose between Armenians priests and their flock. Excommunication, the Church's ultimate threat to exclude a churchgoer, was generally not widely applied by the several denominations in the Dutch Republic. However, I have found two cases of Armenian merchants being excommunicated by Armenian priests in Amsterdam. This is surprising, taking into account the small number of Armenian merchants in the city in the seventeenth century.

I have found no evidence that members of the Armenian Church were excommunicated in the eighteenth century. Most probably due to mixed marriages, it was harder for the Armenian Church to maintain a grip on their flock. The first excommunication letter was drafted by the famous printer and bishop, Oskan Erevants'i, in 1668 directed towards the merchant Martiros.[31] The second excommunication case dates from 1684 and is directed towards a certain Adgj Jesuf, residing in Smirna.[32]

These two cases of excommunicated Armenian merchants in the Dutch Republic of the seventeenth century are difficult to interpret. Only by comparing similar excommunication cases in other Armenian communities in Europe and in Safavid Iran in the same period might one discover on what grounds Armenian merchants were excommunicated, or try to quantify these cases for several European countries. My hypothesis – based on Kaplan's research on excommunication practices among Dutch Jews[33] – is that Armenian priests applied the excommunication weapon more often when they thought they were losing control over a modernizing Armenian community and when priests were afraid to lose their grip on Armenian men due to increasing mixed marriages in the diaspora societies.

Another type of conflict which could easily arise was within the management of the Armenian Church, when new churchmasters were elected to take over the financial management from their predecessors. Such a conflict erupted in 1748 between the new churchmasters'm Matheus di Ouan and Petrus di Babgian, and the former senior churchmaster, Johannes di Jacob Galdar. The new appointees filed a complaint with the notary that the recently received financial account of Johannes di Jacob Galdar was not congruent with the same oral and written account presented at the church council meeting when the two new officials were elected. Johannes di Jacob Galdar was requested to deliver an accurate account of his financial management on the income and goods of the Armenian Church as soon as possible. Simultaneously, Galdar was warned that if he failed to come up with a proper account he would have to pay the costs of the damage as well as interest.[34]

Armenian merchants making use of the international information infrastructure in Amsterdam

According to Lesger,[35] Amsterdam developed into a world trade centre thanks to its concentration of trade information, the speed of information exchange and a geographical concentration in the centre of the town of a series of specialized services, which merchants could use at any time: the Stock Exchange, the notaries, the specialized Stock Exchange newspapers, news tidings, publishers, specialized schools and brokers. In this respect Armenian merchants residing in Amsterdam were better and more quickly informed than their colleagues in Iran and the Ottoman Empire.

According to Floor,[36] Persian and Asian merchants kept up correspondence with agents in other countries but generally they had less access to trade information than the European trade companies, who received relevant trade information from all over Asia. Armenian merchants compensated for this lack by using middlemen and agents. It seems plausible that Armenian traders in Iran used two information flows on the latest marketing developments. One information flow was based on the local knowledge of the vicissitudes of the internal Iranian trade market. This local information flow was supplemented with an external marketing information flow, provided by Armenians who put together directly relevant information, obtained from specialized services in the European towns, with their network of agents in Iran and the Levant.

What were the locations in Amsterdam where Armenian merchants regularly did their business? The main financial and trade institutions were situated in the centre of Amsterdam at Dam square, in walking distance from the Armenian quarter. Armenians could be spotted regularly in the cellar of the town hall doing business with the Amsterdam Exchange Bank (Wisselbank). Or they might pay a visit to the Commissarissen van Zeezaken en Verzekeringen (Maritime Affairs and Insurance Commissioners),[37] also located in the town hall, receiving back their money when ships were wrecked or lost at sea. And when Armenian merchants married Amsterdam locals, they had to register their marriages in the usual way.

However, most frequently they could be spotted daily at fixed hours at the Stock Exchange, situated not very far from the town hall. Like all local and foreign traders the daily rhythm of Armenian merchants was dictated by the short opening hours of the Stock Exchange from 12.00 to 13.00. 'During this hour one could do more than one could do during a whole day' according to the well-known Amsterdam broker and merchant, Isaac le Long, in his well-known description of the functioning of the international trade institutions in Amsterdam.[38]

The major transactions in the Stock Exchange took place in an open inner courtyard surrounded by arcades supported by 46 pillars constructed of blue ardyn stone. The Stock Exchange organized the transactions of merchants along a system of pillars in the inner courtyard. Each pillar corresponded with a specific type of product or nation. Newcomers could find their way in this building by consulting posters of sworn specialized brokers and the map indicating the spots where specific products were sold.[39] At the main entrance of the building one could meet wine sellers, French merchants, actionists and Portuguese Jews. At pillars two and three one could find German Jews, while Armenian and Persian merchants, dealing in silk, had their fixed spot between pillars 13 and 14. At pillars 39 and 40 one could meet Eastern dealers specializing in trade to Russia. Undoubtedly, Armenian merchants must have been active at this spot as well. Von Zesen refers to Armenian merchants dealing at the Stock Exchange in the mid-seventeenth century in his chapter on this institution in his work on the history of Amsterdam.[40]

The Stock Exchange was an important meeting point for all merchants to exchange the latest news on trade. In addition, they could read relevant written information on the pillars concerning public auctions of goods and, news about shipping transports. Trade information could also be obtained through the specialized Stock Exchange newspapers. The Stock Exchange did not levy Stock Exchange Tax nor register the number of merchants paying regular visits to this institution, so I cannot provide statistical data about how many Armenian merchants visited the Stock Exchange.[41] Armenians at the Stock Exchange did not deal exclusively in silk but also traded in stocks, bills of exchange and bonds.

Transactions of Armenian merchants did not take place exclusively at the Stock Exchange. I have also found evidence in notarial acts that merchants sold goods at several inns, like the St. Crispina[42] and the Brakke Grond, selling Turkish yarn. In these inns public auctions took place of all kind of merchandise regulated through official ordinances from the city council. In particular the Ouden Heeren Logement on the Fluwelenburgwal must have been a place where Armenian merchants were seen quite frequently. At this place several products such as cloth, silk, woollens, diamonds and jewels were auctioned.

How did the silk bales of the Armenians finally arrive in their warehouses? After clearing customs the silk bales were weighed at the Weighing House in front of the town hall on Dam square. Armenian merchants, like their Dutch counterparts, hired specialized porters to transport the silk bales from the Weighing House to the warehouse cellars or attics, either on sledges or by boats. The porters themselves worked for specific companies.

Wearing special clothes they could be split up into distinct categories: Amsterdam, Moscovian and even Arabic porters. If a porter was not in, one could leave a message by writing it up on a slate.[43]

In the early eighteenth century Armenian merchants were well acquainted with the ins and outs of business in Amsterdam. To accumulate wealth they also took an active part in Dutch lotteries. Like their Dutch fellowmen Armenian merchants were eager to win a prize. When leaving the country on a business trip they designated solicitors who could receive their money if they won.[44]

Bookkeeping practices

Although we have found only one case from 1718 it seems most probable that a certain category of Armenian merchants in Amsterdam delegated their business administration to professional Armenian bookkeepers who they hired for a certain number of years. Such labour contracts were registered in the presence of a notary. The case I found refers to the Armenian bookkeeper, Johannes de Michael, who contracted himself to work on a part-time basis for six years at the office of the Armenian merchant, Satur di Petrus, in Amsterdam.[45] The terms of payment as well as the working hours were laid down in a contract that closely resembles a contemporary labour contract. The bookkeeper was to appear five days per week at the office of Satur di Petrus. From Monday to Thursday he worked three hours in the afternoon. At the end of the week Armenian merchants presumably had to register their weekly transactions. In the contract it was stipulated that the bookkeeper had to work on Fridays from 7 a.m. until noon and then for another three hours in the afternoon.

Sarhad's diary

In Amsterdam, Armenian merchants maintained their bookkeeping system in the Armenian language until well into the eighteenth century. In addition to this regular bookkeeping system, Armenians kept additional account-books when travelling. In these account-books they wrote down their business transactions and only a few have been preserved. One example is the account-book of Sarhad, running from 1711 to 1718, who traded with Amsterdam. This account-book has been published by Khach'ikyan.[46] Sarhad had trade contacts with 23 Dutch merchants, whose names I could trace through Khach'ikyan's name index.

Sarhad's knowledge of Dutch must have been minimal. Most Dutch names, rendered phonetically in Armenian, are difficult to decipher. I have checked if these 23 names are mentioned in the alphabetical index of the account-books of the Amsterdam Exchange Bank. I could trace nine persons[47] who Sarhad refers to in his diary.

Other Armenian merchant habits

The Amsterdam notarial acts provide much more information on Armenian merchant habits than we can deal with in this chapter. However, I should like to elucidate one point.

Focusing on commercial property belonging to young boys, McCabe[48] raises two questions. The first is whether Armenian women were trading in the names of their sons to protect their own family's capital from their husbands. The second is whether Armenian merchants can establish a capital base for young sons? If my interpretation of the following notarial act is correct than the second question can be answer positively.

The schooling of young boys abroad was laid down in fixed customary rules deeply embedded in family values. Before the Amsterdam notary Hendrick Rosa three Armenian merchants, at the request of the Armenian merchant Badbagan Petro Balthasar, testified as follows. It is customary in their countries (I interpret this as both the Ottoman and Safavid empires) that if a son is sent abroad to study at a school or to learn something, that he takes with him some goods or some business, which will be given to either a factor or a correspondent or a friend, until the young person in question is capable of dealing with these goods (no mention is made about the age). In addition, it is stipulated that a son can receive these goods from either his mother or his father. Explicitly, it is stated that neither the brothers nor the sisters of the boy are entitled to claim the rights on these goods. The goods given by the parents remain exclusively in the hands of the young person who is sent abroad.[49]

Trading networks of Armenian Iranian merchants in Amsterdam

The Amsterdam notarial acts give a relatively good, though not complete, insight into the trade transactions of Amsterdam Armenian merchants. Armenian merchants in Amsterdam, coming from the Safavid and Ottoman empires or through Russia, were involved both in long-distance trade with several countries in Asia and in the inter-European trade network. Armenian merchants in Amsterdam regularly exported specific Dutch products like cloth, tiles, chandeliers, and so on to other European countries and imported specific products from Russia, Italy, France, Spain and Portugal by bartering products with an extensive network of Armenian merchant colonies in these countries.

Over two centuries Armenian Iranian merchants settled down temporarily or permanently in the Dutch Republic in Amsterdam to deal in a wide range of products while keeping on contact with their network of families and business partners in Iran. I will illustrate this with two case studies of Armenian Iranian merchants involved in both long-distance trade and in inter-European trade. The first case deals with Godge Sarhad (Khvaje Sarhad), one of the first Armenian Iranian merchants to come to the Dutch Republic to sell silk in Amsterdam around the mid-1620s. The second case deals with the Armenian Iranian merchant, Johannes di Jacob Galdar, who was active between the 1740s and 1760s in Amsterdam.

Godge Sarhad

One of the first Armenian silk merchants, originating from Iran, operating both in Amsterdam and the Levant was a certain Godge Sarhad (coagie Saarhat), who cooperated closely with the Dutch merchant Johan Schaep in the early 1620s in Amsterdam. From the Levant, Sarhad sent nine bales of silk to Amsterdam, in a Dutch ship owned by Captain Claes Pietersz Spangiaert. The Amsterdam merchants Johan Schaep and Matthijs Aertsen were involved in selling these bales for Sarhad. The total worth of these nine silk bales amounted to 16,843 and a half reals. Johan Schaep, acting on behalf of Sarhad, sent back to Sarhad 5,000 reals of eight, from Genua to the Levant, in a Dutch ship called Sampson, under command of Captain Adriaen Pietersz Losken from Enkhuizen. The sum was a part of the total sum of this silk transaction. Before the notary Sarhad testified that the silk transaction with Schaep went smoothly and that Schaep had met his financial duties. The two witnesses, Johan Lucas van Hasselt and Isack Chamis, the Jewish broker, both testified to having rendered the content written down by the notary, to Sarhad in Armenian and Turkish, having a knowledge of both languages.[50]

Another transaction between Sarhad and the Dutch merchant Schaep can be obtained from a notarial act in which Schaep testified, at the request of Sarhad, that approximately five years ago, in the presence of Seloe Saarhat and a certain Armenian merchant Aganier, he had sold 40 bales of silk on behalf of Sarhad. Schaep declared that Sarhad had met his financial obligations towards him.[51]

Right from the beginning of the seventeenth century until well into the second half of the eighteenth century, Armenian Iranian merchants were firmly embedded in Dutch economic life by concluding temporary trade partnerships with Dutch merchants, as well as with Armenian merchants residing in Amsterdam. Sarhad serves as the first case to illustrate the first Dutch-Armenian silk trade contacts. The Armenian Iranian merchant Galdar is taken as a second case to illustrate Armenian-Dutch silk transactions in the mid-1750s. This case illustrates that Armenian Iranian silk transactions to the Dutch Republic did not come to a halt after the collapse of the Safavid Empire.

Johannes di Jacob Galdar

Most probably Johannes di Jacob Galdar arrived in Amsterdam from Iran in the early 1740s and was active to about 1764. This merchant specialized in exporting Dutch imperial cloth (imperialen lakenen and saijen/zayen) and woollen cloth[52] both to Russia and to several Asian countries. Galdar's name can be traced for the first time in the Amsterdam tax assessment register[53] of 1742. During his stay in Amsterdam, Galdar lived in at least at two different locations. The first can be traced in a tax assessment register of 1742 in which he is assessed as a 'half capitalist'. His dwelling is situated on the Buitenkant, in city quarter number 11, not far from the Armenian Church. He possessed one servant and he paid 500 guilders rent, as his capital is assessed at 2,000 guilders. His second dwelling was not situated in the Armenian quarter but in a wealthy street on a canal, called Fluwelenburgwal, currently called Oudezijds Voorburgwal.

Subsequently, Galdar is mentioned several times between 1744 and 1764 in several Amsterdam notarial acts. In addition, his name appears quite regularly as a member of the Amsterdam Exchange Bank[54] between 1742 and 1764. After 1764 Galdar's name can no longer be traced in the alphabetical books of the Exchange Bank. On 7 September 1762 Galdar's wife was buried in grave 1049/129 in the Oude Kerk in Amsterdam. It could well be that Galdar left the Republic after his wife's death to return to Iran.

In a later stage of my research I hope to have more information on the complex trading networks between the Amsterdam Armenian merchants and their Dutch counterparts. Judging from the data I have seen, it seems that the Armenians of Amsterdam had an intricate trading network with important local Amsterdam merchant houses. In order to spread his trading risks Galdar imported a range of profitable luxurious products like silk, diamonds and cornelian stones.

It is difficult to quantify the silk imports brought to Amsterdam by Armenian merchants from the Levant and the Safavid Empire or Russia on the basis of the limited availability of information relating to Armenians in the Amsterdam notarial acts. Selling prices differed in every period, depending on the scarcity of the silk imports. Nevertheless, it is possible to indicate roughly the trends in the imports of silks by Armenians by scoring the silk imports according to the country of origin. In the case of Galdar's silk transactions in cerbassi and ardasette silks, it seems that in the 1740s and 1750s most of Iranian silk he imported came to Amsterdam via the Russian route through Moscow or St Petersburg.

On 25 November 1744 Galdar agreed to sell only 16 bales of cerbassi silk to the Amsterdam merchant Balthazar Rijke. The original deal was that Rijke would buy 48 bales. Since the major part of these silk bales still had to be transported from St Petersburg to Amsterdam, Balthazar Rijke was able to cancel the sale. It was common in these types of trade conflict for two or more persons to act as arbiters, either Dutchmen or a mixed committee composed of Armenian and Dutch merchants.[55]

Merchants continuously had to cope with unexpected trading risks. For some risks, like shipwreck, they could insure themselves in advance. However, sometimes merchants were confronted with unexpected surprises. This was the case in a diamond transaction in which Johannes di Jacob Galdar was involved. On behalf of Galdar, two Armenian colleagues, Aratun de Sarat Sceriman and Johannes di Aritun (or Joannes di Arituin), went on 14 June 1744 in Amsterdam to the Hamburg post office (postcomptoir) where all the mail coming from Hamburg and eastern Europe arrived. Galdar was expecting a set of diamonds sent by the Armenian merchant Aratun di Nazaret from Moscow. To their surprise, the two delegates from Galdar had to establish that, notwithstanding the announcement in the accompanying letter, there were no diamonds when they opened the four sealed envelopes. Both witnesses concluded in front of the notary that the sender had forgotten to put the diamonds in the four parcels and that any theft had to be excluded.[56]

Galdar's trading network also stretched to the east coast of India, to the city of Tranquebar. On 20 August 1760 Galdar and the Dutch merchant Bendix Cantor appeared before a notary to draw up a contract on the delivery of a shipment of cornelian stones.[57] Both agreed to import from Tranquebar a batch of approximately 79,000 cornelian stones, split up in four distinct assortments, to arrive in Amsterdam through Copenhagen. The notary described in detail, based on four specimens attached to the notarial act, that one bunch of black stones were to the account of Galdar. Subsequently, the notary specified the colours and amount of the second, third and fourth consignments that Galdar had to sell to Bendix Cantor, apparently a Jewish merchant. The risk management arrangements for this transaction were also agreed in advance. If the first or second ship was wrecked the deal would be automatically dissolved. In addition, the payment schedule between the two parties was established in advance. Payment would take place in three instalments, at intervals of four months after the arrival of each of the four consignments. Even in the early 1720s Amsterdam Armenian merchants, like Milchom di Bibi, traded with Tranquebar in India.[58]

Why did Armenians transport cornelian stones from India through Copenhagen and not directly to Amsterdam? Since 1620 the Danish Asiatic Company[59] had conquered Tranquebar. Gradually the Danish set up a whole network of trading posts along the Coromandel Coast and in Bengal using Tranquebar as the central operating base. So it was logical that Armenian merchants importing products from Tranquebar and its surroundings made frequent use of Danish vessels to transport their goods to Amsterdam.

In order to minimize trading conflicts, Armenian merchants in Amsterdam quite often went to notaries in Amsterdam to lay down their transactions in detail. In rare cases disputes arose among Armenian merchants about the illegibility of Armenian characters on Armenian bills.[60] In 1755 Satur di Jacob Galdar, the brother of Johannes di Jacob Galdar, also residing in Amsterdam, got into a dispute with two other Armenian merchants, Joannes di Aritun and Makar di Manidgar. Satur refused to pay a bill in the name of both Armenian merchants because he did not understand some incomprehensible characters on the back of the bill, originally written in Armenian and translated into Italian. To solve this problem both merchants showed the original bill written in Armenian, with the notary as witness. They admitted that they themselves could not decipher the characters but that most probably these characters attested to the validity of the signature of the bill. Johannes di Jacob Galdar advised his brother Satur, before he paid the bill, to claim a valid translation of the incomprehensible Armenian characters on the bill in an understandable language.

The clue to this conflict is complicated. It turns out that Satur di Jacob Galdar, like his brother, had regular contacts with Armenian merchants in India. During Satur's stay in Calcutta he had a business transaction with Wattandi Parzigu on 7 January 1748 in which he signed a contract. However, Satur did not keep his promise to pay Wattandi. Wattandi took action by writing a letter of complaint to his brother, Nazar Artemjeff residing in Moscow, and asking his brother to take action against Satur di Galdar in Amsterdam. Nazar Artemjeff contacted the Dutch notary, Andreas Linde, in Moscow with the request to delegate this case to two Armenian merchants residing in Amsterdam, Joannes di Aritun and Makardi Manidgar. They in their turn contacted the Amsterdam notary Phaff who requested Satur to pay his back bill running from 7 January 1748 to 21 March 1750, amounting to 490 rubles and 18 kopek. With his brother Jacob di Galdar acting as interpreter, Satur answered the notary that he was only willing to pay if he received a copy of the bill.[61] This case shows quite clearly that in conflicts over long-distance trade Armenian merchants had to wait for years to receive their legitimate share.

Galdar's will

The ties of Armenian Iranian merchants residing in Amsterdam to their homeland, even after the fall of the Safavids, remained strong. One way to deduce these ties are in the wills of Armenian Iranian merchants. It turns out that Johannes di Jacob Galdar not only had strong ties with his family members in Iran but also with clerical Armenian institutions.

On 22 September 1753 Johannes di Galdar invited the notary Daniel van den Brink[62] to his home on the corner of the Fluwelenburgwal and St Agnietenstraat. Being ill but compos mentis, he made up a new will with two persons as witnesses. From this will several remarks can be made on the Armenian bookkeeping system, the distribution of money and property to direct family members and friends in the Republic and Iran and to religious institutions in both countries, and about the educational system of Armenian youth abroad and in Iran.

Galdar declared in front of the notary that his ledger and journals were meticulously up to date to December 1752, written in his own handwriting. In this ledger all his transactions were justified, in addition to his properties. The business transactions that took place between December 1752 and 14 September 1753 are described by Galdar in his journal (Kleinboek).

In Galdar's will we can discern four distinct parties to inherit money. The first category is the family in the Dutch Republic and in Iran. The first person mentioned in his will is his wife Azat, who was in Isfahan when the will was made. She was to receive 200 Toman directly when Galdar died and another 210 Toman until all the children reached the age of 25. The will also stated that the children should obey their mother unconditionally. Furthermore, Galdar stated that his wife Azat was entitled to administer the total fortune, if his daughter Hanai, currently in Isfahan, married Gregori di Gotschamel Galdar in Moscow. In addition, Galdar stated that his daughter Hanai was to receive the legitimate portion of 700 Toman, to be distributed yearly by the executors of the will for her support. The surplus had to be remitted to her once she reached the age of 25 if she remained in Isfahan. In addition, Galdar stipulated that if the amount of money was not enough for her that his sons were obliged to assist her financially, as Christians ought to. The two most important heirs were his sons Johannes and Jacob Jean de Johannnes Galdar. However, Galdar explicitly stated that his son Johannes de Stephan Galdar owed him 1,000 guilders and that this sum should be deducted from his legacy if the amount was not reimbursed.

The widow and children of his brother Gregori received 30 Toman each. His sister Wartini got 30 Toman and his five brothers, being alive, all received the amount of 20 Toman. In particular, his brother Avet was to get his borrowed money back, as well as 20 Toman. Galdar also bequeathed 20 Toman to Aswazatur, the son of his nephew Martins Aga de Murat in Astracan and 5 Toman to Jacob de David Galdar, also living in the same place. Galdar possessed two gardens in Julfa in Isfahan. One garden called Jalalens and the other Ottarens. In his will Galdar stipulated that the revenues and usufruct of the latter went to Gatum Tatuk, widow of his late brother Gregory, and her children as long as they live.

The second category consisted of immediate friends and his personnel in the Republic. Galdar was quite generous towards his faithful Dutch servants. His maid Clara would get 250 guilders if she still lived at Galdar's house when he died. If she left Galdar's house before, the amount would be 50 guilders. His gardener Dirk and his spouse got 100 guilders between them, while Anna the cleaning lady would receive 30 guilders and Pieternel the servant, who was out of service, would receive 30 guilders. Another ex-servant, Christina, who had lived in his house would also receive 30 guilders. Finally, Galdar stated in his will that the children of a close friend living nearby on the Rusland would receive 50 guilders.

The third category to which Galdar's money went were religious institutions in the Republic.

The most important institution in Amsterdam to which Galdar left an unspecified amount of money was the Armenian Church. The gift was to finance the priest's living. In addition, 100 guilders went to the Foundation for the Armenian Poor of the Church.

On top of this, the priest Johannes di Minas of the Armenian Church in Amsterdam received 100 guilders. Galdar not only sent gifts to the Armenian religious institutions in Amsterdam but, interestingly, he also donated 500 guilders to the Diaconate of the Poor of the Reformed Dutch Church.

The fourth category to inherit Galdar's money were religious institutions in the Ottoman Empire and Iran. The first institution mentioned is Jerusalem, to receive ten Toman. Subsequently, the same amount is given to the Patriarch of Etchmiadzin. Seven religious Armenian institutions all situated in Isfahan are endowed. The biggest Armenian monastery in Isfahan got ten Toman, followed by a gift of five Toman to the monastery of Ofam Wartabit situated in Julfa and the same amount to the nunnery of Julfa, with interest. In particular, the priests of the Pertowin church, most probably the church where Galdar went regularly when he was in Julfa, received 15 Toman and on top two Toman as long as his children were living to perform a weekly mass to remember their father. The priest Gatthatur de Zatur of the Pertowin Church received in addition three Toman. Priests belonging to other Armenians churches in Julfa received two Toman each. In addition, Galdar paid attention in his will to the poor of Julfa and he gave money for poor relief consisting of 1000 guilders and a certain unspecified amount plus a half per cent per month interest per year.

The executors of the will consisted of two parties. Galdar's brother Avet di Jacob Galdar and Maxim Philip were responsible for distributing his legacy among his minor children and heirs in Astracan. While the main executor of Galdar's will in Amsterdam was Wattan di Bazilius. He was entitled to sell Galdar's country house, situated in the Schagerlaan just outside Amsterdam,[63] as well as all his houses, furniture and jewellery in public auctions. Finally, Galdar states in his will that his brother in Amsterdam take good care of his two sons by giving them the proper schooling and education needed in later life.

Decline of the Armenian colony in Amsterdam

Why did the Armenian colony in Amsterdam come to a halt at the end of the eighteenth century? This question cannot be answered with one explanation. Several factors played a role. From the notarial acts it becomes clear that the decline in the Armenian community set in after the 1750s. One cause is the gradual decline of the Amsterdam staple market. In 1763 and 1772-3 there were big financial crises in the Dutch Republic. In addition, trade with Persia declined in the mid-eighteenth century. Due to protectionist measures by the Dutch in the Levant, the relative transaction costs became higher for Armenian merchants. Gradually it became more attractive for Armenian merchants to deal with other European countries offering them more favourable trading conditions. The Ottoman sultans concluded several treaties with Poland and Sweden (1737), Sweden and Naples (1740), Hamburg, Denmark and Prussia (1761) and Spain (1782). The terms of these treaties opened trade facilities to Ottoman subjects, Armenians, Jews and Greeks. Due to this economic decline it was not attractive for new Armenian traders to visit or to settle down in Amsterdam. Those who came earlier integrated socially with the local population. This integration led ultimately to the extinction of the Armenian community in Amsterdam.

Conclusion

There was a continuity in the trade relations of Iranian Armenians with the Dutch Republic, in particular with Amsterdam, starting under Shah Abbas I and continuing into the late 1760s and 1770s, long after the fall of the Safavids.

It is no coincidence that just in the first quarter of the eighteenth century, when the Safavid Empire fell, a second wave of Armenian merchants came from Julfa and settled down in Amsterdam around 1715 to continue their international trade activities.

Armenian merchants were not exclusively engaged in long-distance silk trade. They were actively involved in the inter-European trading network as international businessmen like their European counterparts. It is striking that they spread their risks by dealing in a wide range of products.

I found no evidence supporting McCabe's hypothesis of the existence of a centrally-led Armenian trading company, based in Julfa in the Safavid period, directed by a board of directors comparable to western trading companies. If Armenian Iranian merchants residing in the Dutch Republic stayed in contact with such an organization, then obviously this type of trade network or cooperation would have been regularly reported in the Amsterdam notarial acts.

Armenian merchants in Europe did not exclusively focus on their Armenian international trading network but participated actively in Dutch international long-distance trade and inter-European trading networks as well, once having become integrated into the Dutch Republic.

Against Matthee's hypothesis, that the Dutch did not compete fiercely with Armenian merchants in Iran, it may be pointed out that in the early seventeenth century at least one representative of the VOC did so according to archives of the VOC in the Netherlands.

The complex trade activities of Armenian merchants, operating from the Safavid and Ottoman empires in the seventeenth and eighteenth centuries, in western Europe, Russia and the Indian Ocean, would benefit from setting up a standardized international Armenian merchant database, fed by researchers working on specific countries or regions.

Notes

1. Frédérique Macler, 'Note sur La Hollande et les Arméniens', in F. Macler, *Quatre conférences sur la Hollande et les Arméniens* (Paris, 1932), pp. 236–79.
2. Sylvio van Rooy, 'Armenian merchant habits as mirrored in the 17th and 18th century Amsterdam', *Revue des Etudes Arméniennes*, NS 3 (1966), pp. 347–57.
3. Onno W. Boers, *De gevelstenen van Amsterdam* (Amsterdam, 1992), p. 108.
4. The name Krom Boomssloot is derived from the sixteenth-century shipbuilder Cornelis Pieterz Boom. To connect his wharf with the surrounding waters he dug two waterways, the Rechtboomssloot and the Krom Boomssloot. See Martha Bakker, ed., *Stadsatlas Amsterdam. Stadskaarten en straatnamen verklaard* (Amsterdam, 2002), p. 21.
5. Hendrik Frederik Wijnman, *Historische gids van Amsterdam* (Amsterdam, 1974), p. 200.
6. Translated into Dutch by Prof. Jos Weitenberg. See René Arthur Bekius, 'De Armeense kolonie in Amsterdam in de 17e en 18e eeuw', *Ons Amsterdam* 37 (1985), p. 328.
7. Regeering en Oud-Burgemeesteren van Amsterdam, 1714, fo. 35.
8. NAA: Notarial Archives of Municipal Archive of Amsterdam. NAA, G. van der Groe inv. 6626 7.5.1715.
9. Khachikyan, Shushanik, ed., *Shavelu vordi Sarhadi hashvematyaně* (Yerevan, 1994). See Ina Baghdiantz McCabe, Book review Shushanik Khach'ikyan (ed.), *Shavelu vordi Sarhadi hashvematyaně Revue des Etudes Arméniennes* 25 (1994/1995), pp. 451–3.

10. McCabe states that the duration of the passage from Archangelsk to Amsterdam is difficult to estimate. See Ina Baghdiantz McCabe, *The Shah's Silk for Europe's Silver. The Eurasian Trade of the Julfa Armenians in Safavid Iran and India, 1530-1750* (Atlanta: 1999), p. 285. However, the duration data are known. To be on time at the annual market in Archangelsk, held from the beginning of June until the beginning of September, ships left Amsterdam either in June or in July. From Amsterdam ships sailed to Archangelsk within 16-20 days and a maximum of one month. See Jan Willem Veluwenkamp, *Archangel, Nederlandse ondernemers in Rusland 1550-1785* (Amsterdam, 2000), p. 113.
11. Samuel van Emdre, *Historisch berigt van alle gezindten, die buiten onze gereformeerde kerk, in ons vaderland vrijheid van openbare godsdienstoefening hebben waar in kerkelijk der zelven leerstukken en kerkelijke plechtigheden worden gegeven* (Utrecht, 1784), p. 66.
12. J. Wagenaar, *Amsterdam in zijne opkomst* (Amsterdam, 1756), pp. 124-6.
13. For example, Frédérique Macler, 'Les livres imprimés arméniens dans la bibliotheque de l'Université d'Amsterdam' *Revue des Etudes Arméniennes* 6 (1926); Frédérique Macler, *Rapport sur une mission scientifique en Belgique, Hollande, Danemark et Suede, juillet-septembre 1922* (Paris, 1924); Raymond H. Kévorkian, *Catalogue des incunables arméniens (1511 1695) ou chronique de l'imprimerie arménienne* (Geneve, 1986), pp. 39-66 and pp. 80-101.
14. Alice Taylor, *Book Arts of Isfahan. Diversity and Identity in Seventeenth-Century Persia* (Malibu, 1995), pp. 69-77; Vrej Nersessian, *The Bible in the Armenian Tradition* (London, 2001), pp. 32-4.
15. H. Dunlop, ed., *Bronnen tot de geschiedenis van den Oostindische Compagnie in Perzië. Deel 1: 1611-38.* ('s-Gravenhage, 1930), p. xi – I disagree with McCabe that it is a misconception that Armenians worked for Western trade companies. See McCabe, *The Shah's Silk*, p. 339.
16. This point leads to the topic of the dhimmis in Islam. According to Lewis, Bernard, *Jews of Islam* (London, 1984), p. 28 'minorities tended to congregate in certain places and to concentrate in certain professions, in particular those requiring skills that Muslims needed and did not possess themselves or did not care to acquire'. Lewis continues that 'dhimmis in certain periods were heavily engaged in trade and finance, vocations scorned by hero military societies. Later on dhimmis were represented in dirty trades'. Finally, Lewis states that 'these dhimmi professions included what was also, for a strict Muslim, something to be avoided – dealing with unbelievers'. For the Ottoman Empire Suraiya Faroqhi affirms that the Ottoman central administration looked down on doing commerce with foreign merchants. To avoid direct contacts matters were delegated to subordinate officials as much as possible, Suraiya Faroqhi, 'Crisis and change', in Halil Inalcik and Donald Quataert (eds), *An Economic and Social History of the Ottoman Empire, 1300-1914* (Cambridge, 1994), p. 481. Little attention has been paid so far in the literature to explain why Muslim Iranians (Azeris), dominating the silk trade from the fifteenth till the first half of the sixteenth century in the Ottoman Empire, were pushed away this trade sector by the rise of Iranian dhimmis (Armenians) in the mid-sixteenth century. The existing literature does not clearly explain why and how Armenians got involved in the trade and cultivation of the sericultures in Iran between 1550 and 1603.
17. M. A. P. Meilink-Roelofsz, 'The earliest relations between Persia and the Netherlands', *Persica, Jaarboek van het genootschap Nederland-Iran* 6 (1972/1974), pp. 1–50.
18. Rudolph P. Matthee, *The Politics of Trade in Safavid Iran, Silver for Silver, 1600-1730* (Cambridge, 1999), p. 238.
19. Amsterdam notarial acts on Armenian trade activities related to Iran could possibly shed some more light on the lack of data on the silk transactions by Armenian Iranian merchants to which Matthee is referring in his last chapter on the politics of trade in Safavid Iran.
20. Willem Floor, 'The Dutch and Persian silk trade', in C. Melville (ed.), *Safavid Persia* (London, 1996), pp. 323-68.
21. Els Jacobs, *Koopman in Azië, De handel van de Verenigde Oost-Indische Compagnie tijdens de 18e eeuw* (Zutphen, 2000), p. 240.

22. René Arthur Bekius, 'Armeense dhimmi's in Perzië aan het begin van de 18ᵉ eeuw. Waarnemingen van een Nederlands reiziger', in A. H. de Groot (ed.), *Het Midden-Oosten en Nederland in historisch perspectief* (Muiderberg, 1989), pp. 33–51.
23. Dunlop, *Bronnen tot*, pp. 800–2.
24. According to van Sylvio van Rooy, about 80 per cent of the Amsterdam notarial acts have been retrieved. In my research I hope to discover the other 20 per cent. I am now adding additional names from the notarial acts not seen by S. van Rooy into my database.
25. NAA, G. van der Groe inv. 6631 25/26–10–1717.
26. Further research has to elucidate to what degree Armenian merchants in Amsterdam sold their silk exclusively to specialized silk traders or to other merchants as well.
27. NAA, J. Meerhout inv. 233/194 26.11.1627.
28. W. F. H. Oldewelt, *Kohier van de Personele Quotisatie te Amsterdam over het jaar 1742* (Amsterdam, 1945).
29. Tirtsah Levie and Henk Zantkuyl, *Wonen in Amsterdam in de 17e en en 18 e eeuw* (Amsterdam, 1980), p. 38.
30. NAA, G. van de Groe inv. 6633 20.7.1718.
31. NAA, H. Outgers inv. 3196/14 1.10.1668.
32. NAA, P. de Witt inv. 4963/1120 5–10–1684.
33. Yosef Kaplan, 'The social function of the herem', in Y. Kaplan, *An Alternative Path to Modernity: The Sephardi diaspora in Western Europe* (Leiden, 2000), pp. 108–42.
34. NAA, B. Phaff inv. 10243/135 16.2.1748.
35. Clé Lesger, *Handel in Amsterdam ten tijde van de Opstand. Kooplieden, commerciële expansie en verandering in de ruimtelijke economie van de Nederlanden ca. 1550–ca. 1630* (Hilversum, 2001), pp. 236–41.
36. Willem Floor, *The Economy of Safavid Persia* (Wiesbaden, 2000), p. 120.
37. Isaäc le Long, *Den Koophandel van Amsterdam* eerst ontworpen door wylen Le Moine de l'Espine, nu... in andere ordre gebragt en... verm. door I. le Long (Amsterdam, 1714), p. 133.
38. Ibid., p. 13.
39. Ibid., p. 126.
40. Philipp von Zesen, *Beschreibung der Stadt Amsterdam: darinnen von derselben ersten Ursprunge bis auf gegenwärtigen Zustand, ihr unterschiedlicher Anwachs, herrliche Vorrechte, und in mehr als 70 Kupfer-Stücke entworfene fürnehmste Gebäude...* (Amsterdam, 1664), p. 233.
41. H. Brugmans, *Amsterdam in de Zeventiende Eeuw* (Amsterdam, 1897–1904), p. 172.
42. NAA, F. Tixerandet inv. 3864/378 15.6.1676.
43. Long, *Den Koophandel*, pp. 137–40.
44. NAA, A. Baars inv. 8572/837 08.05.1725.
45. NAA, G. van der Groe inv. 6632 3.3.1718.
46. Khach'ikyan, *Shavelu vordi*.
47. Cornelis Fellinger; Jan de Man; Jan van Horsten; Nicolaas Calkoen; Pieter Mentink; Coenraad Sprick; Jan Welsingh Isaac Soon; Willem Hendrik Kerkringh; Jacob Vorsterman.
48. McCabe, *The Shah's Silk*, pp. 248–50.
49. NAA, H. Rosa inv. 3109/122 15.8.1672.
50. NAA, S. Cornelisz inv. 633/43–45 1.5.1626.
51. NAA, W. Cluyt inv. 370/601 27.11.1626.
52. NAA, D. van den Brink inv. 10455/1405 22.09.1753.
53. Oldewelt, *Kohier*, p. 64.
54. Currently I am inventorising Amsterdam Armenian merchants, who were members of the Amsterdam Exchange Bank, dealing with Dutch merchant houses.
55. NAA, H. de Wolff inv. 8969/1083 25.11.1744.
56. NAA, D. van de Brink inv. 0359/957 16.6.1744.
57. NAA, S. Dorper inv. 10787/1022 20.08.1760.
58. NAA, A. Baars inv. 8606/1031 01.09.1724.

59. P. C. Emmer, ed., *Wirtschaft und Handel der Kolonialreiche* (München, 1988), p. 156.
60. NAA, B. Phaff inv. 10271/41 28.1.1755.
61. NAA, B. Phaff inv. 10271/11 11.1.1755.
62. NAA, D.van de Brink inv. 10455/1405 22.09.1753.
63. NAA, D. van den Brink inv. 10455/1405 22.9.1753.

16

Sarhad's Account-Book as a Source for Studying the Commercial Activities of New Julfa Merchants in the Eighteenth Century

Shushanik Khachikyan

From ancient times, the merchants of Armenia played an important role in East-West trade. This role grew after the mass deportation of the population of Eastern Armenia to Iran by Shah 'Abbas I in 1604–5. By his order the inhabitants of Erevan, Old Julfa, Agulis, Dasht and other commercial centres of Armenia were settled in the vicinity of Isfahan, where a new town called New Julfa (Nor Jugha in Armenian) emerged in the early seventeenth century.

The merchants of New Julfa, having inherited the commercial traditions of Old Julfa, outran their predecessors and became well known for the prominent role they played in the international trade of the seventeenth and eighteenth centuries. Having expanded their commercial activities as far as Holland, Britain and Portugal in the West and China, Tibet, India and Indonesia in the East, they controlled most of the silk export from Iran to Europe and were major players in the export of oriental goods to Europe and the import of European goods into eastern countries.

Among the various documents concerning the commercial activities of New Julfa merchants, their account-books are of special value and contain reliable information on the goods traded, their quantities and prices, the duties and taxes levied, the freight charges, the means of communication, the commercial routes and other relevant matters.

So far the only account-books to be published are those of Hovhannes Ter-Davt'ean Joughayets'i, who traded in South-eastern Asia in the years 1682–93;[1] Shahveli Bandorean's son Sarhad, who traded in Europe in 1711–18;[2] and the trading activities of the Lazareans' family firm in Russia and Holland in 1741–59.[3]

The subjects of this chapter are the transactions of Sarhad and his family in Russia and Holland as reflected in his account-book.

The document, preserved in the Matenadaran, the Institute of Ancient Manuscripts in Yerevan, under #6241, is made up of 79 sheets (*fards*), each 33 cm long and 22 cm wide. The *fards* are subdivided into paragraphs, called *numray* (numbers) 130 in all. Each paragraph begins with the summary of the dealing, followed by detailed accounts, which are put down in two columns, those of credit and debit (*amat* and *eraft* respectively). For example, *numray* 33 of *fard* 15 reads: 'By God's will I wrote in the year 98, on 30 Nadar (18 August 1713), that of our 13 bales of Gilan silk six (bales) weighed 25 litres (and) seven weighed 20 litres each, 13 bales in all. On 20 Nakha (9 June) of the same year they were loaded on six ships in Archangel (and) arrived safely in Amsterdam. What is written below is the account of the expenses of these 13 bales. May Lord Jesus grant good trade. Amen.'[4] Another example: '*numray* 47. By God's will in the year 98, on 24 Aram (10 December 1713) I wrote that Mat'os's sons Aghatsatur and Avet, the agents of Mr. Margar Khaldarents', authorized me to purchase 30 lengths of wide-brimmed cloth, to prepare and dispatch it in the same year and gave me 7,400 guldens ... The account is as follows ...'[5]

To denote numbers the author of the ledger used the system of letters of the Armenian alphabet, common in medieval Armenia. The Arabic figures, though very rarely, are also attested in the account-book. The dates in the ledger were marked according to the calendar of Azaria Jughaets'i, which was the calendar most commonly used by the merchants of New Julfa. The first year of this calendar, referred to as small number, or merely number, begins on 21 March (2 April in New style) 1615. The year consisted of 12 months of 30 days each and a supplementary (*aveleats'*) month of five (or six in a leap year) days.

The ledger is compiled in the New Julfa dialect of Armenian and abounds in Persian, Arabic, Turkish, Russian and European terms, often distorted; for example, *khrid* for Persian *kharid* (purchase), *tankhay* for Persian *tankhvah* (capital), *ch'up'ayi* for Persian *chaharpa* (four-legged, pack animal), *snjaf* for Persian *sanjab* (squirrel), *k'iuliay* for Arabic *kulliya* (all), *chet'ver* for Russian *chetvert* (quarter), *soruk* for Russian *surok* (marmot), *p'odich'e* for Russian *podacha* (present, bribe), *damojni*, for Russian *tamozhnia* (customs-house), *vesl* for Dutch *wissel* (bill, promissory note), *frghat'* for Italian *fregatta* (frigate), *p'otr* for Dutch *poeder* (powder), and so on. The polyglot character of this dialect considerably complicates the deciphering of the text.

The ledger has preserved the brief contents of the contract concluded between Shahveli's family and their investors. It reads: 'In Isfahan, from *khoja* Ohan's sons *agha* Mr. Murad [and] Mr. Hakobjan and *khoja* Margar's son Hovhannes, I, Bandor's son Shahveli and we [in the text: I], Shahveli's sons Sarhad and Khojamal, took a sum of 900 *abbasi tumans* for trading, by God's will. Whatever profit Lord God, the Creator of all, grants, the profit from 675 *tumans* out of the capital of 900 *tumans* will go to our *aghas* [i.e. investors, masters] Mr. Murad, Mr. Hakobjan and Mr. Hovhannes, the profit from 150 *tumans* will be mine, Bandor's son Shahveli's, the profit from 60 *tumans* will be mine, Sarhad's, [and] the profit of 15 tumans will be mine, Khojamal's. May Lord Jesus grant good luck: fortune and misfortune are in God's hand. We were given the sum, we got 900 *tumans*.'[6]

Thus, in accordance with the contract, Shahveli, together with his sons Sarhad and Khojamal, received on credit from wealthy merchants 900 *tumans*, equivalent to 328.5 kg of silver, on the terms of repaying the creditors 75 per cent of the profits, while the rest (25 per cent) was to be shared among his sons and him in the following ratio: 16.6 per cent would go to Shahveli, 6.8 per cent to the author of the ledger and 1.6 per cent to Khojamal.

As follows from the account-book, Sarhad, via Shamakhi, one of the important sericultural regions in the Caucasus, arrived at the wharf of Nizovaia (called Nizovoy in the ledger) on the Caspian Sea and got aboard a ship on 2 August 1712. It should be noted that one of the most important commercial routes from Iran to Europe lay through Russia. It began at Astrakhan, near the mouth of the Volga River, and ended at Arkhangel, on the White Sea. The Russian route was especially frequented after 1711, when Tsar Peter I reaffirmed the privileges granted by the Russian government to Armenian tradesmen in 1667 and 1673.

This policy of the Russian government, aimed at attracting Armenian (Iranian) merchants towards the Russian route and thus increasing the influx of finances into the state treasury, proved effective. According to the aforementioned agreements between the Russian administration and New Julfa merchants, the duty imposed on each *pood* (16.38 kg) of imported raw silk was as high as one ruble in Astrakhan, 1.5 rubles in Moscow and two rubles in Arkhangel. Thus, the rate of taxes levied for the transit of silk from Astrakhan to Moscow amounted to 2.5 rubles per pood and that from Astrakhan to Arkhangel to 4.5 rubles.[7] Hence, the author of the ledger, one of the numerous merchants who had chosen the Russian route, according to our estimates, must have paid the Russian treasury 4,280 rubles (equivalent to approximately 122 kg of silver). It should be noted for comparison that in those times the annual salary of workers in textile manufacture in Russia was about 30 rubles, that of skilled workers in the metal industry was 20–120 rubles, whereas that of unskilled labourers did not exceed 1 ruble 47 kopecks.[8]

As mentioned above, Sarhad set out from Nizovaia in August 1712. Via Saratov on the Volga River and Lomovka in the Penza province, he reached Moscow and in the same year he continued on his way to Holland via Arkhangel. Arriving in Amsterdam on 5 February 1713, he stayed there for 14 months, selling the commodities he had imported and purchasing a large amount of local articles. He left Amsterdam on 19 April 1714. Sarhad's further itinerary was as follows: Arkhangel-Vologda-Arkhangel-Moscow. In November 1716 we find him back in Amsterdam. In 1717 he returned to Astrakhan, in August of the same year he was in Shamakhi, in October he left for Tebriz, whence, in August 1718, he made his way back to Shamakhi.

The main item of Sarhad's trade, as of most of New Julfa merchants, was raw silk. Because the silk industry was not developed in Russia, it was mainly exported to western Europe and only a small amount was sold in Russia. It was not until the 1730s to 1740s, that, in view of the development of silk manufacture in Moscow, the Russian market absorbed the major part of the imported Iranian silk.

Thus, during the years 1711–17 Sarhad exported 132 bales of raw silk, weighing about 15,586 kg, out of which only nine bales, weighing 1,031 kg were sold in Russia.

The weight of the silk in the ledger is given in *litres* and *stils*. Besides the shah's *litre* and *stil*, which were equivalent to 5.8 kg and 120.9 g respectively,[9] Sarhad also mentions Shamakhi and Gilan *litres* in his records. Owing to the few cases in which the weight of the bales is given in Russian units, along with that in Shamakhi and Gilan *litres*, it was possible to calculate their weight: the Shamakhi *litre* was equivalent to 7.7 kg and that of Gilan weighed 4.5 kg.

Not willing to over burden the chapter with an analysis of the abundant information on quantities of goods, their prices, duties paid, freight charges, and so on, I will confine myself to presenting some results of this analysis:

- the sale price of raw silk in Amsterdam exceeded its purchase price by 44 per cent, while the profit from the deal did not amount to 18 per cent;

- the freight charges of raw silk from Shamakhi to Nizovaia were as high as 1.5 per cent of its purchase price;

- the rate of expenditure from Astrakhan to Arkhangel, as well as from Arkhangel to Amsterdam fluctuated by 22 to 26 per cent. For example, expenditure from Astrakhan to Archangel was about 16.7 g of silver per 1 kg of silk in 1712 and 12.37 g in 1713, from Arkhangel to Amsterdam it amounted to 4.75 g per kg of silk in 1712 and to 3.7 g in 1713. Thus, in 1712 Sarhad's expenditure from Astrakhan to Arkhangel and thence to Amsterdam exceeded those of 1713 by 26 per cent and 22 per cent respectively.

Another important item of Iranian export was gems (such as diamonds, rubies, sapphires, pearls, garnets, agates), the import of which was not taxed in Russia (a privilege the Russian government granted to New Julfa merchants and aimed at attracting them towards Russia as already mentioned above).

A special place in the trade of New Julfa merchants, besides raw silk, belonged to incense. Thus, Sarhad's profit from selling 28 *poods* 15 pounds (464 kg) of incense amounted to 53 per cent.

Other commodities imported into Russia were wool, various textiles, such as *zarbaf* (gold- and silver-woven fabric), taffeta, satin, brocade, atlas, velvet, kerchiefs (*aghlukh*), carpets, blue, fruit, rice, coffee, and others.

The New Julfa merchants exported from Russia furs, leather, honey, wax and grain. Sarhad's family was also engaged in the fur trade. The ledger contains many records of purchasing different amounts of sable, marmot, white hare and so on. Thus, according to a record, Sarhad sold two sable fur-coats to the khan of Shamakhi at the price of 30 *tumans*, whereas 12 pairs of sable were sold for 1 *tuman* 8000 *dians* each.[10]

From Europe to Russia and Iran various manufactured goods, such as woollen fabrics, calico, women's clothing, lace, clocks and many other articles were exported. The tradesmen of the Bandorean family exported from Holland a considerable amount of cloth, lace, needles, pen-sharpeners, candlesticks, cutlery, porcelain, jewellery, pictures, clocks, mirrors, leather gloves and belts, door-locks and so on.

Sarhad's records are rich in information on the prices of these goods. Thus, an ordinary clock could be purchased for 45 guldens, a good one cost 64 guldens, the Armenian map, printed in Amsterdam in 1695 was bought for 12 guldens, six diamond rings for 226 guldens, 16 pictures for 104 guldens and so on.

The ledger abounds in data on loans, money transfer (*yolborji*), bills of exchange, and so on, thus providing interesting information on financial operations used in the milieu of New Julfa merchants.

The remittance charge from Moscow to Shamakhi, as well as from Moscow to Amsterdam varied from 20 to 38 per cent, though there are cases when it was lower. Thus, in Moscow Sarhad's father took 10 *tumans* from a certain Grigor on condition he repay 9.5 *tumans* in Shamakhi. The *yolborji* charge in this case amounted to five per cent of the sum. The remittance charge from Moscow to Shamakhi, received from a certain Horum was as high as 16 per cent. In all probability, the rate of the charge was lowest when the partners in the operation were either members of the New Julfa community, or economic associates.

During the period covered by the account-book, Sarhad was in contact with over a hundred merchants, manufacturers, functionaries and political figures. For example, in the records of 1715–17 we read: '201 [*tumans*] 5000 *dians*: in *fard* 81 *numray* 4 on 17 Ovdan [2 February] is written, [that] I took from the governor of Moscow Naryshkin 201 *tumans* 5000 *dians*, drew up a bill, [according to which] in six weeks, in Amsterdam, Markos, from [the sum] I have sent, shall repay to prince Vasili Vladimirovich Dolgorukov 1000 gold [coins]. I got each coin for 2015 *dians*.'[11]

This record is significant not only for mentioning the governor of Moscow, prince Cyrill Naryshkin, a close relative of Peter I, and the Russian field marshal prince Vasily Dolgorukov. It is also interesting for the fact that the sum taken by Sarhad was equal to that to be paid in Amsterdam, 1000 gold coins being equivalent to 201 *tumans* 5000 *dians*. Perhaps, in this case the rate of interest on the sum of 1000 gold coins, borrowed in Moscow from Naryshkin, was as high as the remittance charge for that very sum Sarhad's agent Markos was to pay off in Amsterdam to Vasily Dolgorukov.

From another record we learn that Sarhad's father received in Moscow 40 *tumans* (equivalent to 2000 guldens) from Kalantar's son Hovhannes. In Amsterdam 1560 guldens – that is 72 per cent of this sum – were to be paid off to Petros Gilanents,[12] who was the founder and commander of the Armenian squadron formed in Astrakhan in 1722 that took part in the Persian campaign of Peter I.

The ledger also provides clear evidence that its author and his relatives, like other New Julfa merchants of the seventeenth and eighteenth centuries, were not only deeply involved in international trade, but also active participants in a wide variety of financial operations.

Notes

1. Levon Khachikyan and Papazyan, Hakob, *Hovhannes Ter-Davt'yan Jughayets'u hashvetumare* (Yerevan, 1984).
2. Shushanik Khachikyan, *Shahvelu vordi Sarhadi hashvematyane* (Yerevan, 1994).
3. Shushanik Khachikyan, *The Ledger of the Lazareans' Trade Company (1741-1759)* (Yerevan, 2006).
4. Khachikyan, *Shavelu*, p. 84.
5. Ibid., p. 93.
6. Ibid., p. 33.
7. Vardan Parsamyan, ed., *Armiano-russkie otnosheniia v XVII veke* (Yerevan, 1953), pp. 62-3.
8. E. I. Zaozerskaia, *Manufaktura pri Petre I* (Moscow-Leningrad, 1947), pp. 117-19.
9. Valter M. Khints (Walther M. Hinz), *Musulmanskie mery i vesa s perevodom v metricheskuiu sistemu* (Moscow, 1970), p. 30.
10. Khachikyan, *Shahvelu*, p. 152.
11. Ibid., pp. 111-12.
12. Ibid., p. 92.

Part IV

Cross-Cultural Perceptions and Exchange

17

Mapping the *Regnum Sophorum*: Adam Olearius's Representation of the Safavid Empire (1647)

Elio Brancaforte

One of the distinguishing characteristics of the early modern era in Europe is the development of cartography. Within a relatively short time span – approximately the two centuries from 1450 to 1650 – maps developed from the schematic T-O world maps of the Middle Ages to the early modern depictions of a globe that is divided into segments by coordinate grids as a result of numerous voyages of exploration.

This chapter will examine the cartographic contribution of the German Baroque humanist, Adam Olearius, who is best known for his monumental travel account, the *Vermehrte Newe Beschreibung der Muscowitischen und Persischen Reyse* (The Expanded, New Description of the Muscovite and Persian Journey) of 1656,[1] his depiction of an embassy that journeyed through Muscovy and Safavid Persia and sought to bring Persian silk to northern Europe. Less well known are the cartographic works that accompanied the travel account, in particular Olearius's new and improved map of Persia, the *Nova Delineatio Persiae et Confiniorum*. This map, which will be examined here in some detail, represents a significant achievement in the history of cartography, especially due to its portrayal of the Caspian Sea. Olearius's map – in contrast to the other European Baroque maps of the Caspian – begins to show the sea more correctly, namely as being longer from north to south than from east to west. This is due to the author's eyewitness observations, as well as his use of Islamic sources.

Olearius's *Nova Delineatio Persiae* is comprised of both visual and textual elements, and thus represents a type of text, or discourse, that needs to be analysed in detail in order to be read correctly.[2] It also needs to be examined in conjunction with the travel account for which it was produced. By investigating some of the different component elements of this particular map, I shall address some of the following questions:

1) How is the exotic other represented visually and is it typologically categorized?
2) What are the signs of royal patronage in Olearius's map of Persia and how does the author position himself with regard to his patron?

3) What is new about Olearius's depiction of the Caspian Sea?
4) And finally, how does the author inscribe his presence in the map and explain his methodology and manner of collecting information?

My analysis thus hopes to show how Olearius's map of Persia marks a transition from the classical/medieval era to the Enlightenment, and points the way to a geographically accurate representation of this hitherto relatively unexplored land for western Europe.

Adam Olearius (1599–1671) was the secretary of a trade mission sent by Duke Frederick III of the small northern German duchy of Holstein-Gottorf. The mission lasted from 1635 to 1639 and went through modern-day Estonia to Moscow, down the Volga, across a small portion of the Caspian Sea and on through Shamakha, Qazvin, Qom, Kashan to Isfahan. Olearius had planned to explore the entire Caspian coastline, but had to land near Baku because of a shipwreck. Upon his return to Gottorf, Olearius published an account of the journey, the *Offt begehrte Beschreibung Der Newen Orientalischen Rejse* (The Oft-Requested Description of the New Oriental Journey), in 1647, in which his map of Persia appeared for the first time. The much-enlarged second edition of 1656 includes information from the disciplines of ethnography, history and literature.[3] It consists of more than 800 folio pages and 120 engravings, with scenes from the journey and cityscapes, as well as a number of maps (e.g. one depicting the course of the Volga, which was used well into the eighteenth century), and the Persia map, which is almost identical to the one in the 1647 edition.

The Nova Delineatio Persiae

The *Nova Delineatio Persiae* (Figure 17.1) is a dense document, containing several layers and types of visual and verbal cues, the excess of which may overwhelm a viewer: the document represents a kind of Baroque *horror vacui* (or fear of the void) and there are very few empty areas on which the eye can rest. Now I will examine some of its specific elements while drawing parallels with the text of the travel account. The layout of the travel account proceeds as follows: first the frontispiece or title page, then the dedications, followed by the body of the text. My reading of Olearius's cartographic text will follow the same pattern, by analysing the corresponding features on the map.

The title

I thus begin my reading at the bottom left hand side of the map with the title (Figure 17.2). It is contained within an ornate strapwork cartouche and corresponds to the title page of the written travel account. Olearius's emphasis in the cartouche is on accuracy and novelty; the description of Persia will not simply repeat the

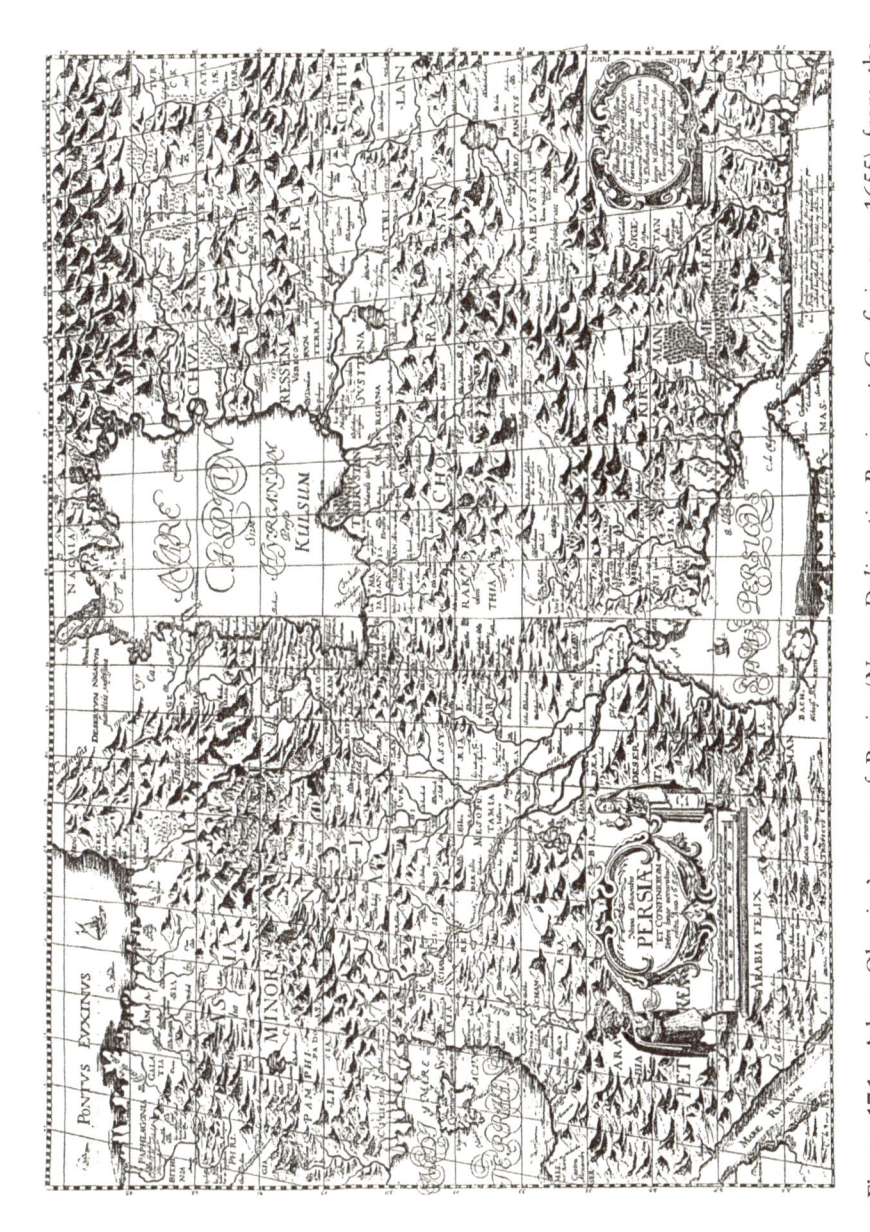

Figure 17.1 Adam Olearius's map of Persia (*Nova Delineatio Persiæ et Confiniorum*, 1655) from the *Vermehrte, Newe Reysebeschreibung*

Figure 17.2 Title Cartouche; detail from Adam Olearius's *Nova Delineatio Persiæ et Confiniorum* (1655)

representations of older, classical authorities such as Ptolemy. The cartouche rests on a kind of architectural base in which a scale bar is contained, and above which we read: 'Miliaria Germanica & Persica quae Farsang vocant.' (German and Persian miles, which they call farsang.) – this addresses the idea of translation for a West European audience.

Two inhabitants of the country on either side of the cartouche represent the native population. On the left, a moustachioed nobleman, wearing a cloak and *mandil* (turban) grasps the cartouche with his right hand, and with his left holds up a bowl. His legs are spread apart and his torso seems to turn towards the written inscription of the title, thus conveying a sense of movement. His counterpart, a Persian noblewoman, stands demurely on the right side of the cartouche, her visage uncovered for the benefit of the (European) viewer. Her left hand rests on the cartouche and in her right hand she holds a flask up to her head. This simple gesture – the anticipation of a drink – can be construed as a gesture of welcome or hospitality to the reader who is entering into this exotic world. As representatives of their land, the Persian couple stands not only for the entire population, but they also introduce the reader to the ethnographic information included within the travel account. For example,

Figure 17.3 Persian costumes from the *Vermehrte, Newe Reysebeschreibung* (1656)

Olearius devotes an entire chapter to Persian clothing in his work, and even infers moral character traits of the inhabitants from their clothing styles (Figure 17.3). In short, the Persian couple depicted on the cartouche lead the interested viewer to a series of related subjects in the travel account that concern both the exterior and interior traits of the inhabitants.

It was a common practice in early modern maps to depict iconic couples dressed in native costumes, meant to represent the inhabitants of a particular region (as in the topographic city views of Georg Braun and Franz Hogenberg, and the world maps of Willem and Joan Blaeu, which often include natives in costume on the borders of the map). In this context we should also note the importance of early modern costume books, which supplied much of the visual material for the cartographic literature. To give just one example, in the frontispiece to Hans Weigel and Jost Amman's *Trachtenbuch* of 1577 (Figure 17.4), we find male figures who are chosen to represent the continents: from the bottom left we notice a streaking European tailor carrying a bolt of cloth, who points his scissors rather menacingly at the Persian satrap's midsection, who stands for Asia. Next to him we find the representatives of America (a chieftain) and Africa (an Ottoman warrior). Inside the costume book, we find the Persian satrap again – portrayed quite accurately – in contrast to the depiction of a Tatar warrior (Figure 17.5), who does

Figure 17.4 Frontispiece to Hans Weigel and Jost Amman's *Trachtenbuch* (1577)

TARTARICVS MILES.

CLXXIIII.

Also gehen die Tattern in jrer Tracht vnd Rüstung.
Die Tattern zur Heeres macht / Vnd ist das jr Rüstung in gmein /
Gehen daher mit solchem Tracht. Wann sie wider den Feindt auff sein.

X r ij

Figure 17.5 Tatar warrior from Hans Weigel and Jost Amman's *Trachtenbuch* (1577)

not seem to be a native of the Eurasian steppe, but looks as though he has been plucked from the pages of *Asterix and Obelix*.

The Persian couple in the cartouche thus performs the same function as the figures on a frontispiece: in visual form, they provide the viewer with an iconic image of two 'typical' inhabitants and their form of dress. This cartographic convention has lasted to the modern day. In a recent National Geographic Society map from 1999, we can still find counterparts to the early modern iconic couples (Figure 17.6). The map has a very orientalist title – 'Caspian Region: Promise and Peril' – that

Figure 17.6 Detail from National Geographic map 'Caspian Region: Promise and Peril' (1999)

alludes to the riches to be found in the area, mainly in the form of natural resources, as well as to the dangers encountered there, from such factors as ethnic conflicts, nationalism and religious fundamentalism. If we look only at the couples associated with Olearius's travel account we find a Russian couple at work (a female doctor and a male fisherman in a rather small format). The couple associated with Iran has a larger format and corresponds to pre-established views that a typical US reader might hold. A forbidding-looking mullah, dressed entirely in black is seen praying, while flames from an oil well spout forth behind his shoulder. The spectre of religious fundamentalism is given visual form. An Iranian woman in native dress can be found below the mullah, in a smaller format. Neither of them is smiling, nor shown to be engaged in productive activity as a number of the other representatives in the image are.

The dedicatory cartouche

After this short excursus, let us turn now to the other strapwork cartouche located at the extreme right side of the Persia map (Figure 17.7). It contains a Latin inscription written in italics, that dedicates the work to Duke Frederick III, and

Figure 17.7 Dedicatory cartouche and 'Candide Lector'; detail from the *Nova Delineatio Persiæ et Confiniorum* (1655)

also names the author, Adam Olearius, and the engraver, Christian Lorens. The forms of address in the dedicatory cartouche echo – in condensed form – the dedication of the travel account, which is located directly after the frontispiece and title page. In the dedication to the travel account, the author gives the reasons for the journey and praises his patron for his wisdom in sponsoring the mission and having the foresight to publish the work for posterity. The map's dedicatory cartouche thus reiterates the duke's various attributes (outlined in the text), but in a shorthand form.

Let us first consider how the patron is addressed, since he occupies the position of primary importance. All the letters of the ruler's name, FRIEDERICO, are capitalized, and a special style of italics is used just for his name. Even the typography plays a role in emphasizing the importance of the dedicatee. The titles of the duke (*Domino … Hæredi Norwegiæ … Duci … Comiti*) are all mentioned, along with the different territories under his control (*Sleswicensi Holsatiæ Stormariæ & Delmenhorsti*). This establishes the duke's geographical purview and serves to link the duchy with the foreign territories depicted on the map – even though the link is a rather fictitious one, belonging to the realm of wish-fulfilment, since the duke was ultimately unable to obtain the exclusive rights to import silk from the Persian empire. The cartouche containing the ducal name represents a kind of seal of authority (indicating ownership of the map and approval for the enterprise) and stands as a symbol for the link between political power and modes of representation during the early modern era.

Below the seven lines dedicated to the duke we read '*dedicat Auctor M. Adam Oleari*', thus the author inscribes his own name and his own presence on his work. Just below Olearius's name, squeezed in almost as an afterthought, we find '*Christian Lorens fecit*', written in a smaller typeface. The engraver's position as a workman is clearly established by the placement of his name below the patron and the author. Olearius, as the inventor of the work, has a different status, what one could term a very pronounced sense of self.

Tom Conley, who, in his work *The Self-Made Map: Cartographic Writing in Early Modern France* analyses the intersections between literature and cartography in early modern France, makes a number of observations that can apply to Olearius's situation as well. Conley notes that one of the main features for the development of cartography during the early modern age

> might be located in the new importance afforded to the emerging self and to the self's relation to the idea of national space. In this domain, which appears to be situated between raw perception and the creative imagination, there seems to be a correlation between mapping and the growth of a new medium – literature – in early modern print culture. New modes of surveying and plotting the world influence representations of the private and public domains of the individual writer. What Erich Auerbach once called the 'drama' of European literature (1984) may indeed have been, in the changes between the 15th and

17th centuries, an unforeseen theatricalization of the self, which acquired a consciousness of its autonomy through modes of positioning that are developed into both textual and gridded representations of reality.[4]

While the role of autobiography in the travel account needs a separate treatment, suffice it to say that Olearius is an author who indeed marks his presence in the text, and who does not shy away from stating his own ideas, which are based on his own observations. The multiplicity of genres found in the travel account results in a multiplicity of roles that the author must play in order to present his information. To mention but a few of these roles, Olearius writes as historian, ethnographer, philosopher, naturalist, artist, geographer, traveller and tourist, merchant and diplomat. These many roles find expression in the multiple points of view found in the text. Olearius switches constantly from the first person singular (*Ich*) to an objective third-person observer, and moves to the first person plural, especially when recounting adventures that relate to the entire group.

Candide Lector

If we now return to the map, we see that the presence of the author is further emphasized in a direct address to the reader, located just below and to the left of the dedicatory cartouche, at the very bottom border of the map (Figure 17.7). The very position of this text – in the bottom right-hand corner of the map – marks it as a kind of signature, as the locus that corresponds to where an artist would sign his name. As mentioned above, Olearius considered himself to be fulfilling a number of roles and he blurs the boundaries between these different functions.

The Latin text, translated into English, reads as follows:

> Illustrious Reader,
>
> This map shows the location of these significant provinces, cities, mountains and rivers with roads and modern names – that is, as they derived partly from the Persians and partly from my own observation – to which are attached also the places where great events took place especially the [more] illustrious ones of Alexander the Great.

Olearius inserts himself into the text by talking directly to his *Lector* or reader, and emphasizes the fact that both old and new can be found on the map.

Let us now turn to Olearius's assertion that his new information (the location of the sites) is based on information received from the Persians as well as from his own observations. To this end, we shall examine Olearius's depiction of the Caspian Sea, and discuss some of the issues relating to the history of the depiction of this body of water.

The Caspian Sea

On Olearius's map of Persia, the Caspian Sea is referred to as 'MARE CASPIVM Sive HYRCANVM Persis KÜLSUM', and in the text of the travel account the author devotes a lengthy passage to other names that have been used for this sea in the past and in the present (e.g. Mare Chosar, Bohar Corsun, Mare de Baku).[5] After mentioning these different possibilities, Olearius proceeds to discuss the question of whether the Caspian is in fact a lake. Olearius lists all the writers before him who had assumed that the Caspian Sea was connected to other bodies of water, but he ultimately agrees with Aristotle and Herodotus, who say that it is an independent body of water.

Olearius goes on to describe the physical characteristics of the sea (e.g. whether it has a tide or not; the number of tributaries flowing into it; the salinity of the waters; and the fact that there are few good harbours). He also observes that no one had yet been to the centre of the Caspian Sea. Olearius also denies the reports that the water on top is as black as tar, as Petrus Petraeus contends in his *Muscovitische Chronica* of 1620. Regarding the fauna, he rejects ancient eyewitness accounts that there are enormous snakes in the sea.

However, the most significant feature of Olearius's map of the Caspian is its shape. As far as I know, he is the first northern European to, underline the fact that the sea is longer from north to south than from east to west. I say northern European, because some fifteenth-century Italian maps depict the Caspian more accurately, but Olearius does not seem to have been aware of them. The dimensions that Olearius gives for the sea are 120 German miles long and 90 miles wide. The shape of the sea provided by Olearius is radically different from those of previous representations, and he stuck to his calculations because of his observations and research, despite later criticism he received from colleagues and friends all over Europe.

Until Olearius returned from his voyage to Persia, the Ptolemaic depiction of the Caspian reigned throughout Europe. For example, in the collections of the immensely popular Sebastian Münster (Figure 17.8), whose encyclopaedic *Cosmographia universalis* went through 27 different editions from 1553 to 1628, as well as in the works of Abraham Ortelius and Gerard Mercator and in the other dominant cartographic literature of the seventeenth century (produced by the Hondius family, Jan Jansson, and the Blaeu family). It is only at the beginning of the eighteenth century that maps begin to show the Caspian in a way that is familiar to the modern viewer (e.g. in a map by Johann Baptist Homann, ca. 1725, Nuremberg, Figure 17.9).

Olearius and Islamic influence

Finally, I would like to discuss briefly the kinds of sources Olearius may have consulted in creating his map of Persia. The author insistently repeats the claim that his map is based on his own observations and the measurements that he took with his

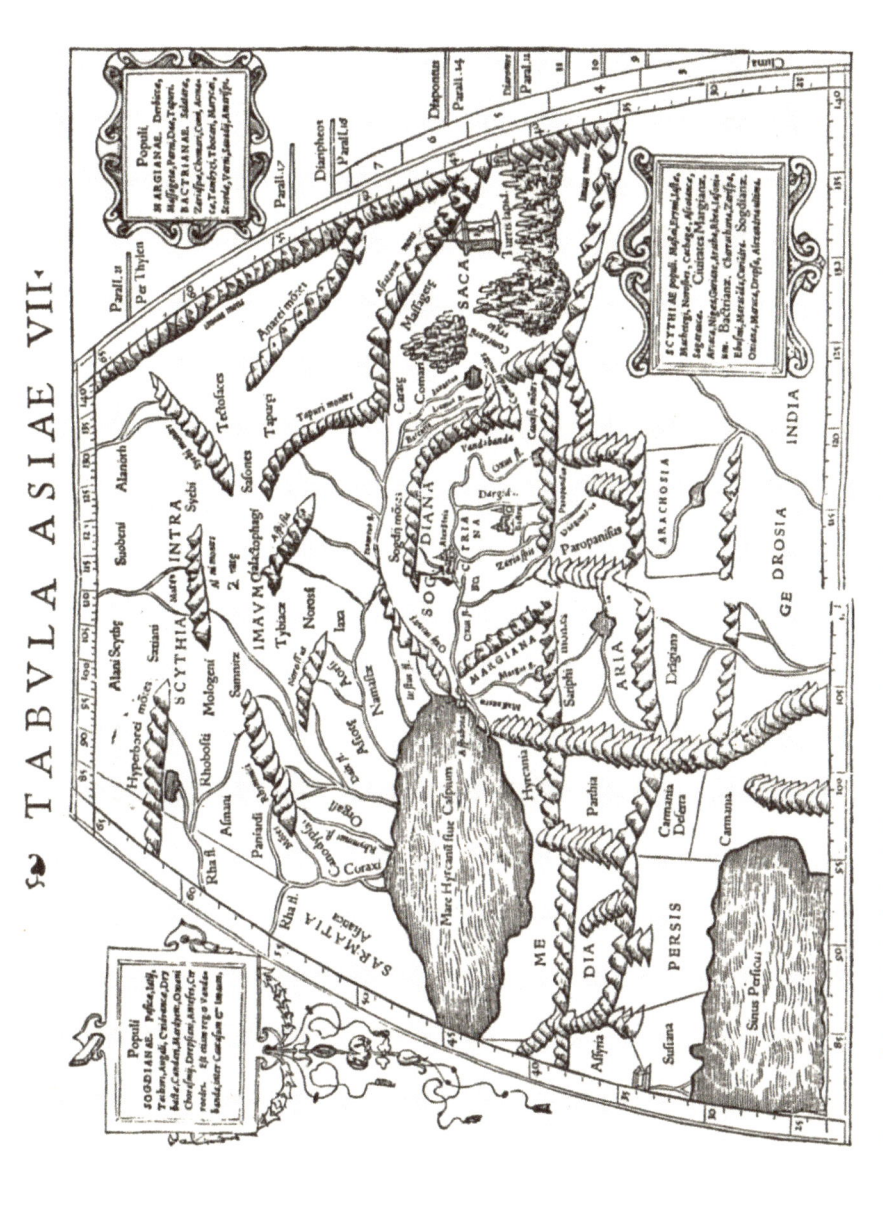

Figure 17.8 Tabula Asiae VII of Ptolemy's *Geographia*, Sebastian Münster (ed.), (1540)

Figure 17.9 Map of Persia by Johann Baptist Homann (ca. 1720)

astrolabe, but since he only travelled along half of the sea's west coast and in a very small portion of the Safavid Empire itself, Olearius realizes that he may have a problem with credibility. He therefore assures the reader that his information is based on information received from Europeans he befriended in Isfahan (mainly monks, who had a good knowledge of the country), as well as his houseguest Haqverdi, the secretary of a Persian embassy, who defected and remained in Gottorf in 1639. In addition, in an extensive bibliography at the beginning of the travel account, Olearius also lists the authorities, both classical and contemporary, that he consulted in writing his work.

With regard to the geographical coordinates (and shape of the Caspian Sea) on his new map of Persia, the author observes that he consulted Persian and Arabic sources. Where his own observations accorded with those sources, he used those same sources for the areas where he was not able to travel himself. Nowhere, however, does he mention exactly which Islamic sources he used. Olearius notes that while he was in Shamakhi, he befriended a certain Mullah Moheb 'Ali, who provided him with geographical coordinates, as well as maps, but again, Olearius does not provide any specifics.

A clue regarding this subject may be found in the works of the Oxford orientalist, John Greaves (1602–52), whom Olearius cites at different stages in the second edition of his travel account. Greaves had collected Islamic manuscripts during a journey to the Middle East from 1637 to 1640, approximately the same time as Olearius's journey to Persia. During his travels to Istanbul, Alexandria and Cairo, Greaves took measurements of the pyramids, and bought works written in Greek, Arabic and Persian, including copies of the astronomical tables of Nasir al-Din al-Tusi, as well as five Persian manuscripts of the Samarqand Tables by Ulugh Bayg. Greaves's translations into Latin of the tables of Ulugh Bayg and al-Tusi – the *Binae Tabulae* ... (1652) – interest us most in our discussion concerning the influence of Islamic science on Olearius's map of Persia.[6]

An analysis of the city coordinates on Olearius's map – derived both from the text and the locations of the cities on the map itself – suggests that the German author made use of an Ulugh Bayg table in plotting the cities on his map. Since – to my knowledge – there is no documentation from the author detailing which maps or geographical tables he referred to in placing the cities on his map, one can only guess which works he used. Olearius's admiration for John Greaves's works, and the fact that Greaves's opinion is frequently quoted throughout the travel account suggests that the German author made frequent use of the Oxford orientalist's tables, which he may have received from Greaves in manuscript form before they were published.

In conclusion, in my reading of some of the different elements of the *Nova Delineatio Persiae* I have tried to show some of the subtexts, as it were, that are to be found beneath the surface of the engraved image. The signs and symbols, the scratches and numbers on the surface are all part of a larger story, involving questions of patronage, authorship, naming and unattributed borrowing from different cultures and traditions. Olearius's cartographic work combines with his travel account to form a visual and discursive nexus, and a unique expression of early modern subjectivity.

Notes

1. For an introduction to Olearius and his account, see Dieter Lohmeier's Afterword to Adam Olearius, *Vermehrte Newe Beschreibung der Muscowitischen und Persischen Rejse* (1656), Dieter Lohmeier, ed., *Deutsche Neudrucke 21* (Tübingen, 1971). See also Samuel Baron, *The Travels of Olearius in Seventeenth-Century Russia* (Stanford, 1967), which provides a modern scholarly translation into English of the Russian section of the journey.
2. For a more detailed investigation of Olearius's map of the Caspian Sea, see Elio Brancaforte, *Visions of Persia: Mapping the Travels of Adam Olearius* (Cambridge, MA, 2003), which also discusses the relationship between word and image in the German author's works.
3. Besides a number of German editions, the travel account was also translated into Dutch (1651), French (1656), Italian (1658) and English (1662). Regarding the various editions of the travel account, see John Emerson, 'Adam Olearius and the literature of the Schleswig-Holstein missions to Russia and Iran, 1633–1639', in Jean Calmard (ed.), *Études safavides* (Paris, 1993).
4. Tom Conley, *The Self-Made Map: Cartographic Writing in Early Modern France* (Minneapolis, 1996), p. 2.
5. Regarding the multiple names for this sea, see Xavier de Planhol's useful entry, 'Caspian Sea', in Ehsan Yarshater (ed.), *Encyclopaedia Iranica* (Costa Mesa, CA, 1992), pp. 48–61, where he notes that there were more than 37 different designations for the Caspian in Islamic geographical texts.
6. See John Greaves, ed., *Binae tabulae geographicae: una Nassir Eddini Persae altera Ulug Beigi Tatari* (London, 1652). Greaves also befriended the celebrated orientalists of Persian and Arabic, James Golius in Leyden and Edward Pococke at Oxford. For a complete listing of Greaves's publications, see the *Dictionary of National Biography*, s.v. 'Greaves', pp. 481–2.

18

The French Presence in Safavid Persia: A Preliminary Study[1]

Jean Calmard

Outline of early Franco-Persian relations

French presence in Persia naturally inscribes itself within the history of Franco-Persian relations and more generally within the framework of contacts between Orient and Occident. Further to the launching of the Crusades, when France emerged as a powerful Christian entity in the thirteenth century, Persian lands had to face the Mongol invasions. Despite their disastrous effects, the Mongol conquests enabled the renewal of contacts between Europe and the Orient. Whereas the Mongols repeatedly required allegiance from Christian powers and the papacy, Christian Europe thought they could in turn be converted, as had been the case with other barbarians. Christian missionaries were dispatched to the Il-khans of Persia (1256–1335), mainly from France, and diplomatic relations were established. Together with the papacy and England, France sought an Ilkhanid alliance against the Mamluks and the Turks. Although these projects came to nothing, the idea of forming a European alliance with the rulers of Persia against growing Muslim power in the East Mediterranean was revived by the Venetians who tried to attract the Turkmen Aq Qoyunlu confederation into an alliance against the Ottomans. The Safavids were, in many ways, a successor state to the Aq Qoyunlu confederation. Not surprisingly, the founder of the dynasty, Shah Esma'il, sought an anti-Ottoman alliance with the Portuguese, Charles V and Ludwig of Hungary. Safavid assistance against the Turks was also reciprocally demanded of Shah 'Abbas I by the Sherley brothers and other envoys from Europe (see the chapters by Rota, Gil and Hernan in this volume).[2]

With the persistence of the Crusader spirit, strong links remained between religion and politics. After obtaining a firm foothold in Europe, the Ottomans came to symbolize Islam: to be a Turk was to be a Muslim or a Moor; that is, an enemy of Christianity. Shah Esma'il's imposition of Twelver Shi'ism in his realm kindled political opposition towards the Sunnites (Ottomans, Uzbeks, internal opponents).

From the outset, Europeans perceived the Safavids as having pro-Christian leanings. Shah 'Abbas I was also allegedly said to be willing to abjure Islam and become a Christian.[3]

While the Venetians retained some of their influence, the Portuguese established themselves at Hormuz (1507–1622). Friendly relations were also developed between Persia and Spain (suzerain of Portugal, 1580–1640). To counteract Charles V's hegemony over Europe, François I (1515–47) formed an alliance with the Ottomans. The French were granted extra-territorial rights (capitulations, operational from 1669) in the Echelles du Levant; that is, the ports of the Levant. They also obtained rights of protection over Christian minorities. While being profitable to French commerce and influence, the Franco-Ottoman alliance hampered the establishment of Franco-Persian relations. The renewal of capitulations (1604) prevented Henri IV from responding to overtures made to him by Shah 'Abbas I. However, Henri IV was interested in developing French-Oriental relations. His despatch of a gentleman of his court to China was probably part of that policy. While passing through Persia, Henry de Feynes was warmly received by Shah Abbas I at Isfahan (see the conclusion to this chapter for further information about de Feynes time in Persia).

The first attempt to direct Franco-Persian relations was made under Louis XIII, by a former courtier of Henri IV, Louis Deshayes de Courmenin (Cormenin, d. 1637). According to his instructions (February 1626) he was to obtain from Persia advantages similar to those obtained from Turkey about the protection of Christian minorities and commercial rights detrimental to those granted to Britain, Holland and Spain. Deshayes's mission was rendered impossible by the French ambassador to the Porte, de Césy, and the Ottoman grand vizier. An attempt to establish franco-commercial links via Russia, entrusted to Deshayes's son in 1629, was also a failure. Having sided with Gaston d'Orléans, Deshayes's son was eliminated by Cardinal de Richelieu.[4]

The Catholic missionaries who settled in Persia from 1603 were mostly Portuguese Augustinians and Spanish or Italian Carmelites. But the great missionary upsurge (le grand élan missionnaire) came from Paris, with the policy set up by Richelieu and his éminence grise, the influential Father Joseph, after the latter had found his ambitious project for a Crusade unrealizable. They despatched two Capuchin fathers, Pacifique de Provins and Gabriel de Paris, to the court of Isfahan, who reached there towards the end of 1628. Shah 'Abbas I sent Father Pacifique back to France to negotiate various projects and the purchase of a printing press. These projects were abandoned after the shah's death (1629). However, Pacifique's negotiations and Gabriel's activities at Isfahan enabled the Capuchins to establish themselves in Persia, at Isfahan and at Tabriz (1656, Gabriel de Chinon); the convent at Tabriz remained active for almost a hundred years.[5] The most important of these Capuchin fathers was Raphaël du Mans, notably for his role at the Safavid court and as a link between the Safavid court and European travellers (for further information about du Mans see the section on travellers, temporary settlers and residents, below).

Missionary activities in Persia, often in competition with one another, interested the Pope who tried to establish a bishopric for Latin Catholics at Isfahan. This resulted in further rivalries among missionaries originating from different nations. A further development of missionary activities came again from Paris, with the creation of the Société des Missions étrangères (approved by Pope Alexandre VII in 1664). This Société decided to found a diocese in Persia. This mission was entrusted to François Picquet, a former layman and French consul at Aleppo. Picquet was commissioned both by the Pope, as bishop of Babylon (Baghdad) and by Louis XIV who sent him in embassy to Shah Sulayman (1666–94). His credentials were obtained through the Jesuits. During his stay at Isfahan (July 1682–May 1684), Picquet was essentially occupied with sacerdotal matters. The answer to Louis XIV that he obtained from the shah concerned only the Jesuits and their privileges. Picquet was joined by two young priests of the Missions étrangères, Jean-Baptiste Roch and François Sanson. As Turko-Persian relations were then tense, Picquet and the two priests settled in Hamadan. A Theatine monk sent from Rome, Louis-Marie Pidou de Saint-Olon, joined them. After Picquet's death (Hamadan, 1685), Sanson negotiated his succession with the Safavid court, and the Société sent another priest from Paris, Martin Gaudereau. After protracted negotiations, hampered by the Capuchins and other missionaries, Gaudereau obtained from the shah the authorization to establish missions at New Jolfa and Hamadan (1692).[6]

With the evolution of French-Oriental policy, missionaries were increasingly entrusted with diplomatic missions. Pidou, who had succeeded Picquet as Louis XIV's representative in Persia, was consecrated bishop of Babylon (Isfahan, May 1694). He disagreed with Gaudereau, who continuously pressed for French intervention in the Persian Gulf after an attack from Muscat Arabs on Bandar-e Kong (1695). However, some religious orders kept apart from politics. Initially commissioned to foster the Persian anti-Ottoman alliance, the Carmelites remained essentially involved in their apostolic mission. Despite the opposition they met from the Armenian clergy of Jolfa, they maintained themselves until the middle of the eighteenth century and occupied the mission established by Picquet at Hamadan (1712–46).[7]

The French East India Company

In parallel with the missionary upsurge France launched a Compagnie des Indes Orientales set up by Louis XIV's minister, Colbert, in 1664. The next year, representatives of that company (entitled *députés*) were sent in embassy to Shah Abbas II. Three merchants, Nicolas Mariage, Jean de Bebber (also Béber) and Nicolas Dupont, were to carry out the mission and, as a matter of prestige, two noblemen, Nicolas Claude de Lalain and François de La Boullaye-Le Gouz (hereafter La Boullaye), were to conduct negotiations on behalf of Louis XIV. However, these men kept quarrelling with each other. The efficient help they received from Isaac Boutet de L'Estoille (or l'Estoile), a French jeweller, and Father Raphaël du Mans, who obtained the necessary farmans and their renewals, could not save this mismanaged enterprise from failure. There also remained a rivalry between Atlantic oriental sailors and merchants, and those preferring the traditional Mediterranean crossing to the Levant and overland route to Persia.[8]

Colbert's projects towards establishing Franco-Persian relations were renewed by Jérôme de Pontchartrain (1699–1715), Trade and Navy Secretary of State. A daring merchant from Marseilles, Jean Billon de Canserilles undertook on his own a voyage to Persia to revive overland trade with Persia through the Levant route. Although he was received by Shah Soltan Hosayn at Isfahan (December 1704) and further endeavoured to promote his project, his mission had no impact on Franco-Persian relations.[9] Another Marseillais, Jean-Baptiste Fabre, led an official mission. After much wandering in Turkey (1705–6), the mission of this 'most unsuited' ambassador (as Lockhart dubbed him) ended abruptly with his death at Erevan, on 16 August 1706. Continued by Fabre's adventurous mistress, Marie Petit, the mission was taken over by another Marseillais, Pierre-Victor Michel. While meeting strong opposition from the Dutch and English companies, Michel obtained from Shah Soltan Hosayn the first official treaty between France and Persia (16 September 1708).[10]

Despite renewed privileges granted to Saint-Malo merchants, no French ship appeared in the Persian Gulf. Upon Persia's initiative, Mohammad Reza Beg, Kalantar of Erivan, was sent in embassy to France. With much difficulty and the efficient help of the French ambassador to the Porte, Pierre des Alleurs and his astute dragoman, Etienne Padery, Mohammad Reza Beg was conveyed to Marseille and Versailles, where he was lavishly received at court (February 1715). The new treaty (13 August 1715) included more favourable provision for the French trade, which could have been promoted by the creation of the new Compagnie des Indes by the adventurous banker John Law (1716–69). This company fostered the Ocean route. Two consuls appointed as its representatives, Ange de Gardane (chief consul at Isfahan) and Padery (consul at Shiraz) totally differed on the Muscat affair. Despite his dismissal upon Gardane's demand, Padery obtained from Shah Sultan Husayn the ratification of the Treaty of 1715 shortly before the Afghan invasion (1722).[11] This sealed the fate of the Safavid dynasty and of Franco-Persian relations, which were only temporarily resumed in 1808, with the sending by Napoleon of a diplomatic and military mission to Fath 'Ali Shah, entrusted to Ange de Gardane's grandson, Claude-Mathieu de Gardane.[12]

French travellers, temporary settlers and residents in Safavid Persia

Long before the appearance of the French on the Safavid scene, there had been, through diplomatic and commercial contacts, a long tradition of European travel accounts about Persia. Italian, Venetian and Spanish precursors of the fifteenth and early sixteenth centuries were soon followed by Portuguese and English travellers, the latter being merchants, diplomats or adventurers, such as the Sherley brothers.[13] Although they benefited from the experience of their predecessors, from the seventeenth century, European travellers visiting Persia were more diverse in their background and motivation. Besides religious men, diplomats or merchants, some laymen undertook their voyage out of curiosity for themselves and their European contemporaries. Such is the case with Jean de Thévenot (1633-67) who, like the Roman patrician Pietro Della Valle, was a traveller of independent means. Before reaching Persia, he travelled extensively in Europe and in the Middle East. He had a good command of Turkish and acquired some knowledge of Persian.[14] This was also the case with the adventurous and restless traveller, La Boullaye (see below, *in fine*).

The best possible knowledge of foreign lands was part of an adequate cultural background of the European Renaissance humanist or the French 'honnête homme'. Such knowledge could be acquired or completed through serious observations provided by travel books. French travel accounts to the Levant and especially to Safavid Persia, often have very long titles giving a quasi-summary of their contents. They were thus conveying to French readers the idea they could form about Persia.[15] From the mid-seventeenth century, travel literature was eagerly sought after. In addition to their original accounts, some travellers (such as Tavernier) used the help of professional writers. Others were only compilers or editors or translators of travel accounts, letters, notes or memoirs of those who had gone to Persia. This was notably the case with Melchisedech Thévenot, Jean de Thévenot's uncle, who edited travel accounts, mainly in French translations, from various European and Oriental sources.[16]

Like all travel literature, French accounts about Persia should therefore be used cautiously. The main problem lies with the origin of the information gathered by observers or shaped in literary form by authors. In the absence of copyright rules before the French Revolution of 1789, there was also much plagiarism, or at the least unacknowledged authorship, grateful mention of informants, and so on. For over 40 years, Father Raphaël du Mans's memoirs (then unpublished) and his personal communications were among the major sources for a series of travellers passing through Isfahan, notably Tavernier, Chardin, Fryer, Kaempfer and, probably Thévenot.[17] Whereas his opinion differed from du Mans on many points, Chardin benefited in his research from the Capuchin father. Their mutual respect and admiration was further nurtured by their correspondence after 1667.[18] From his early years, Chardin had been fond of travel literature. In his writings, he repeatedly cites the classics and his contemporary predecessors, notably Pietro Della Valle and Olearius, both available in French translations.[19] He gratefully acknowledged his indebtedness to Father du Mans.[20] In an anonymous unpublished memoir, Chardin also recognized that for 40 years, du Mans provided travellers passing through Isfahan with 'the best part of their works'.[21] Translations of travel literature also had particular problems. Although they were much read in their original Italian text, Pietro Della Valle's letters soon became famous through their French, German and Dutch translations.[22]

Abraham de Wicquefort translated from Spanish the Persian embassy of Don Garcia de Silva Figueroa, from English Thomas Herbert's travels in Persia and India, from German Olearius's travels in Russia and Persia.[23] Many shortcomings and errors mar De Wicquefort's French translation of Olearius. Unfortunately, further translations of Olearius's voyage were made from that French translation (published in 1659), notably used by John Davies for his English translation of 1662.[24] Translations made from either the original or a translated text also varied in quality. This is particularly the case with the voyage of the adventurous Dutchman Jan Struys to the Caucasus and Persia in the 1670s. Translations from the Dutch original (1676) were soon made in German (1678), French (1681) and English (1683). This text soon became a kind of bestseller, mainly through its French translation, although that was the least reliable of the several published versions.[25]

From the beginning of the eighteenth century, and particularly after the Persian embassy to Louis XIV at Versailles in 1715, the French public developed such a curiosity about Persia that more and more travel accounts, letters, reports and even diplomatic material were published, including in series and periodicals (e.g. *Le Mercure Galant,* from 1672), sometimes without mention of authorship.

The shortest itinerary from France to Persia was through the Mediterranean and Turkey. This was the most dangerous yet the most frequented route. Alternative routes via Muscovy and the Caucasus or the Caspian were also used, as well as the route from Constantinople to Georgia, via the Black Sea (taken by Chardin in 1672). Some travellers also reached the Persian Gulf directly, via the Ocean route from Europe or from the Far East. Overland travel was made by caravan (horses, mules, camels). Some travellers employed private guides and even a private escort (such as Chardin). Routes, construction works (wooden and stone bridges) and caravanserais were frequently described.

The travellers also described the geography of the country, sometimes with maps. Some narrated the history. They were, however, more reliable on the contemporary events they personally witnessed, or heard about through local sources, rather than on ancient history. The French were mostly well-versed in the classical authors, both Greek and Latin. This sometimes influenced their views on local customs or monuments. But to lead their readers from the well-known to the unknown, they often compared Persian cities with those of France. Their observations on archaeological sites and modern buildings, sometimes with drawings, remain precious. But the most outstanding description of seventeenth-century Safavid Persia, in all its cultural and economical aspects, was provided by Jean Chardin. He notably gave us the best description and mapping of Isfahan, as well as an account of Safavid economy, political institutions, religion, customs and manners, and so on. Among the travelling merchants, Chardin had probably the longest Persian experience. Between his two main voyages, he spent altogether nearly ten years in Persia.[26] This is, however, rather a short time compared with the long stay of many monks and missionaries, above all Raphaël du Mans, who spent 50 years at Isfahan (1647–96) where he died. As shown by Francis Richard's studies, missionary activities in Persia, although they delivered poor results in the matter of conversions (mostly among Armenians changing their obedience), they had a long-standing cultural influence. Although the imprint of an Augustinian Portuguese presence remained from Shah 'Abbas I time, French missionaries and monks were increasingly present, notably among the Capuchins, the Carmelites and the Jesuits. While they were important observers of political and social events, they were also very active in studying languages (Arabic, Persian and Turkish) and produced a number of important scientific works on grammar, lexicography, religious controversies, traditional pharmacology and medicine and so on. They lodged travellers and helped them as informants and translators. Some of them played a part in diplomacy.[27]

Most of the monks or missionaries of different nationalities settled in Isfahan. But there were important convents in Tabriz (Capuchins), Shiraz and Hamadan (Carmelites). In the absence of local archival records, the number of French monks or missionaries remains debatable. Apart from some letters they sent to their congregation in France or Italy, very few of them wrote about their Persian experience. The Carmelite Ange de Saint-Joseph (Joseph Labrosse, Angelo Labrosse, 1636–97), born in Toulouse, who lived in Isfahan between 1664 and 1678 was a gifted and curious man. Besides his *Pharmacopoeia Persica* (translation of *Tebb-e shefa'i*), Paris 1681, he gave us the *Gazophylacium linguae Persarum* (Amsterdam 1684), a multilingual dictionary (Italian-Latin-French-Persian). More than a simple linguistic tool, it is a kind of Encyclopaedia, confronting European and Oriental visions of culture and religion.[28]

Besides these religious men of the robe, European laymen were attracted to Safavid Persia where there existed good prospects for skilled craftsmen and artisans such as clockmakers, jewellers or gunnery experts. Reading authors like Chardin implies that the French felt at home. However, unless some new documents are discovered, it appears that very few French laymen stayed there permanently. Some artisans, goldsmiths or jewellers established themselves at Isfahan. Some time between 1647 and 1649, La Boullaye met five or six Frenchmen there, among them the jeweller Isaac Boutet de L'Estoille.[29]

Mgr Pallu, bishop of Heliopolis, while passing through Isfahan in 1662, wrote a detailed report on Christians living in Isfahan. Apart from Isaac de L'Estoille, he found five other Frenchmen in the shah's service ('Abbas II); four of them were married, two were Huguenots. There were two clockmakers, two armourers and one engraver. Tavernier (around 1665) mentions five Frenchmen in the shah's service: Marais (engraver and arquebusier); Jean Bernard (armourer); Sain (goldsmith); Didier Lajis/Lajisse and (Philippe?) Varin (two clockmakers). In 1684, Kæmpfer mentions seven Frenchmen, who had come upon the demand of 'Abbas II. They were living at the shah's expense, with their families in Jolfa. There were also some rare passing merchants. Ten years later, in 1694, the number of French residents at Isfahan had not noticeably increased. Besides François de l'Estoile and his family (see below), five of them are mentioned: MM. Jourde, Varein (Varin), Grangier, Vincent Definot (a Calvinist from Lyon), Sein (or Sain, also a Calvinist).[30]

The influential family de l'Estoile[31]

The family de l'Estoile (also spelt l'Etoile, l'Estoille and Lestoille) entertained relations with all the European community through commercial interest and intermarriage. The first member of that family to come to Persia was Isaac Boutet de l'Estoille, who was a Calvinist Huguenot, apparently originating from the Charente (western France),[32] or from Lyon.[33] Circumstances and dates of his arrival in Persia remain unclear. He apparently served Abbas I as a goldsmith before retiring from royal service and resuming his private business. He returned several times to France, probably before and after 1652.[34] When staying in Paris in 1657, he obtained from Louis XIV a letter of recommendation for Shah 'Abbas II. In 1665, he accepted the mentorship of Louis XIV's *députés* to Persia, the agents of the newly created Compagnie Royale des Indes (see above). He provided very effective help to these envoys in matters of lodging, money, providing them with expensive embroidered clothing, and so on.[35] They apparently borrowed a considerable sum of money from him.[36] He married an Armenian woman with whom he already had children. The priest who consecrated the marriage, Father Valentin d'Angers, in 1643, required him to have his children educated in the Catholic faith. Isaac Boutet de l'Estoille died and was buried at Jolfa (28 July 1667).[37] Before dying, he converted to Catholicism and entrusted the care and education of his children to Raphaël du Mans. The Capuchin father taught catechism, Turkish and fencing to his sons Louis and François. In a letter to Colbert, Isaac declared that he wanted to attach his children to the service of France.[38]

Among his children, his eldest son was apparently Louis-Guilherme de L'Estoile (d. Jolfa, 16 June 1701), who was engaged, upon his father's demand, as interpreter (*kalamchi*) by the representatives of the French Company. Louis was well versed in commerce and languages. He could speak French, Persian, Turkish, Armenian and 'Indian'.[39] He maintained strong links with the Company, notably as interpreter, although its activities in Persia were negligible. When he became the Company's agent at Isfahan, he feared that its establishment in Persia would be cancelled. While conducting his own business at Surat, in 1673, he met one of the directors of the French factory, Claude Guêton (Gueston), who had been pressed upon by Father du Mans, in his letters, to send an embassy and presents to the Persian court. Louis convinced him to undertake this diplomatic mission to Persia. Guêton embarked on the *Saint Paul* with valuable gifts, partly bought on credit (March 1673). On his way, he became sick and died at Shiraz, in the Carmelite convent, leaving his party of about 20 in disarray. The Carmelites suggested that Guêton's party leave the gifts in their custody and return to Surat. Louis strongly opposed this project, as did Father du Mans who sent a letter to Shiraz urging the mission to proceed to Isfahan. Louis at first thought he would replace the Company's envoy, but the choice fell upon the young captain of the *Saint Paul*, Siméon de Jonchères, who took over as head of the mission (though he behaved with flippancy, according to Chardin's testimony). This embassy was received by the shah (September 1673) and obtained the renewal of its privileges for three years. After this time limit, the Company had to send a new envoy and further presents.⁴⁰ No concrete result came out of this costly embassy. No French ship appeared at Bandar 'Abbas where the Company's house was soon deserted. The missionaries were disappointed while witnessing the decline of French influence in Persia, since they placed great hope in Louis XIV's protection. With the renewal of the Company's privileges, Louis de l'Estoile was granted the right to make wine at Shiraz for his own use and to export five horses each year from Bandar 'Abbas.⁴¹ Louis and his brother Jacob were Shiraz wine merchants. They also took care of the mail of the French community and probably of other Europeans.⁴²

The Venetian traveller Ambrogio Bembo (1652–1705) met Louis at Jolfa in 1674. He said he had three other brothers. One of them, Jacques (Jacob), had spent seven years at Venice, on the Rialto, at the house of Pietro Calderari, a watchmaker and jeweller. Another one was in the shah's service at Qazvin. The third one had gone to France. Apart from the last one, all were married at Jolfa, where they lived in a comfortable house contiguous to the house of the Chief of the French Company. The women were secluded in several apartments. The garden, arranged in the European fashion, was the most carefully prepared that Bembo saw in the country.⁴³

According to a letter written from Isfahan by the three merchants of the French Company to their directors (November 1665), François de l'Estoile, then about 20 years old, was living in Paris and desired to enter the Company's service. In 1684, while he was probably acting as a Company agent, he is reported to have seven children. One of them may have been, as mentioned during the embassy of Michel in 1708, 'Isaac de l'Estoille, fils de François'. In 1689, François is mentioned as 'officier du Roi de Perse' (probably as a goldsmith).⁴⁴ Louis had a son, André, who likewise joined the Compagnie des Indes. He was buried at Jolfa in December 1745.⁴⁵ Louis maybe had another son, Alexandre, also in the Company service (see below).

Isaac Boutet de L'Estoille had several daughters. One of them married, before 1664, the shah's clockmaker Didier Lagisse (or Lagis), from Geneva. He apparently returned home towards the end of 1672.⁴⁶ Another one, Angela, married Eshaq Khan, son of Zenus, interpreter at the English company. Under the influence of the Carmelite Ange de Saint-Joseph, she converted to Catholicism before dying. Many other sons, daughters and further descendants or relatives of Isaac were buried at Jolfa and questions remain about that prolific family. In 1705, Mgr Pidou de Saint-Olon writes that the de l'Estoile family at Jolfa fills up the Church of the Jesuits, whereas the 'Sherimani' family's number diminishes.⁴⁷ Reine de L'Estoile, who was maybe Louis's daughter, married in 1737 Jacob (or Jacques) Rousseau, a clockmaker and jeweller from Geneva settled in Paris. He had accompanied the ill-fated Fabre mission to Persia (1705–6, see above). He settled at Isfahan in 1708 and became the shah's first clockmaker.⁴⁸ Jacob was the cousin of the great philosopher of French enlightenment Jean-Jacques Rousseau (1712–78) whose father, Isaac Rousseau (1672–1747) was a watchmaker. In the Calvinist Republic of Geneva, Isaac belonged to the plebeian class. In 1704, he married the well-born Anne Suzanne Bernard who gave him a son, François (15 March 1705). Being a passionate, restless man, unsuccessful in his profession, Isaac moved to Constantinople (June 1705) where he remained about six years, working as a watchmaker, apparently for the seraglio (in the St Gervais quarter where he lived later, he was referred to as 'the watchmaker to the harem'). He may also have worked for a watchmaker in town (at Pera). After his return to Geneva, in September 1711, Suzanne gave him his famous son Jean-Jacques (b. 28 June 1712), and she died (7 July).[49] We are ignorant of the main reason for Isaac's sudden move to Constantinople and whether he was in touch with his first cousin Jacob who preceded him in Turkey on his way to Persia. We also don't know whether Jean-Jacques Rousseau had any contact with his cousin Jacob living in Persia. Jean-Jacques certainly shared the fascination for the Orient then prevailing in Europe. From the 1760s, he adopted the Armenian mode of dress, as often observed by his contemporaries.

At Isfahan, Jacob and Reine had a son, Jean-François-Xavier Rousseau (1738–1808), who was to play an important diplomatic part as chief of the French factory at Basra. He was commissioned by the Minister of Navy, the Duc de Praslin (1712–85), to open commercial negotiations with Karim Khan Zand. He renounced commerce and remained in charge of French interests in Persia and in the Pashalik of Baghdad. He maintained correspondence with Turkish and Persian authorities, the Imam of Muscat, the agents of the French establishments in India and French ministers. He left us a memoir, dated 1804, on Franco-Persian relations, 1708–15, written from French diplomatic documents that have now disappeared.[50] At the beginning of the nineteenth century, as French Consul at Baghdad residing at Aleppo, he played a major part in the renewal of Franco-Persian relations leading to the Gardane mission of 1807–9.[51] When he returned to Basra in 1772, having lost in the previous ten years, his wife, mother and daughter, he married Anne-Marie Sahid, daughter of an interpreter at the Dutch East India Company (the VOC). Her father may have been François Sahid, mentioned by Mgr Pidou (in 1705 and 1712) as first interpreter at the VOC. He was a 'catholic zélé et exemplaire interprète'.[52] In 1722, François Sahid had, however, been succeeded by his son Joseph as dragoman of the VOC at Bandar 'Abbas.[53] François's father, Da'ud (b. Sa'id Esfahani, d. Isfahan, 1684) had served Louis XIV as interpreter (he was in Paris in 1640–4). He had also served the VOC as dragoman for 34 years.[54] Jean-François-Xavier Rousseau and Anne-Marie Sahid had a son, Jean-Baptiste-Louis-Jacques, called Joseph (1780–1831), who was French consul at Aleppo for a long time. He was, with his father, among those who prepared the Gardane mission in which he participated.[55]

The last representative of the East India French Royal Company was Isaac de L'Estoile's grandson Alexandre. He obtained from Shah Soltan Hosayn the confirmation of customs privileges and the right to export through Bandar 'Abbas as much wine as he wanted and five horses per year. This was of no avail. The director of the French factory at Surat, Etienne-Louis Pilavoine, preferred the advantages of private trade (although they were limited) and the post of the

French Company's representative in Persia was suppressed (1705). Alexandre died four days' walk away from Bandar 'Abbas, where he had gone to fetch the company packets (July 1707). A certain Bastard, a clockmaker from Geneva at the shah's service, accompanied him.[56]

The decline of the French presence

The persistent presence of the French Company, whose commercial transactions were non-existent, already puzzled the Dutch Company agent in 1677. At the same time, the British traveller John Fryer thought that only their qualities as interpreter and the profit they derived from the wine trade justified the presence of a French factory at Bandar 'Abbas.[57] Apart from the family de l'Estoile and Armenian merchants, other French wine dealers were apparently present at Isfahan. Father du Mans mentions a Marseillais, named Mouillon, who brought to Bebber a quantity of wine that was sold by the pint or the pot. Slanderers publicly said that the French Company only came to Persia to sell wine.[58]

The difficulties faced by the French Company were further aggravated by the fact that its representatives, except Nicolas Mariage, met an untimely death, shortly after their reception at Isfahan in 1665. Dupont died near Shiraz, in October or November 1665[59]; Lalain died near Bandar 'Abbas, in May 1667;[60] Bebber died at Goa, in 1669[61]; and La Boullaye also died in India (see the conclusion, below). Another major drawback came from the tentative settlement of the French Company at Madagascar that turned out to be a disaster. This added to financial problems arising from the expensive wars of Louis XIV in Europe, and particularly the War of Spanish succession (1701–14).

With the second French East India Company, privileges about wine remained. While Isfahan was living under the threat of an imminent Afghan invasion in August 1721, Padery was preparing the implements, storehouses and cellars to make good wine at Shiraz.[62] Ange de Gardane's brother, François, was also a wine dealer in Shiraz and was at Isfahan during the Afghan siege (March–October 1722).[63] During the siege and resultant famine in Isfahan, even Ange de Gardane lacked sufficient money to buy food and was obliged to send his own brother and French secretary away from his table and resort to selling wine to Georgians.[64]

Apart from the missionaries, among the few Frenchmen present in Persia in the early eighteenth century, there was a soldier of fortune, Philippe Colombe. A native of Paris, he had served in the Russian army and had left it to go to Persia. During the decisive battle against the Afghans, at Golnabad (March 1722), Colombe headed the artillery corps with 24 cannons, although he was nominally under Ahmad Khan, the *tupchi-bashi*.[65] Left unprotected, the artillery was fiercely attacked by the Afghans who killed Colombe and his men.[66] We have very scanty information about the French presence at Isfahan during the protracted Afghan siege. Through his secretary-interpreter, Joseph Apisalaimian, Gardane had recognized the Afghan Mahmud 'in advance as Shah of Persia'. Mahmud gave orders (not respected) to protect French subjects and interests.[67] However, Gardane was not invited to join the Dutch and English in welcoming Mahmud's triumphant entry to Isfahan (25 October 1722) because he had eaten his horse during the famine and could not appear at this solemn occasion on foot.[68]

Conclusion

As shown in this brief survey, apart from the missionary establishments, the French presence in Safavid Persia remained very limited. Whereas in Ottoman Turkey, there was, from the time of François I onwards, almost without interruption, a French ambassador with authority over politics, commerce, and religious activities (i.e. the protection of missionaries and Christian subjects), in Safavid Persia this kind of diplomatic protection only began in the 1660s and was intermittent and mostly ensured by missionaries. Father du Mans and other religious men surely would have preferred to see French commerce placed in the hands of good Catholics who could have favoured the evangelization of the country.[69] The importance of the French presence could, however, be seen more positively. After analysing the reason for the poor results of a French commercial connection with Persia, Lockhart points out the positive effect of the presence of French consular representatives at Isfahan until 1730, for the maintenance and security of the missions (for the last troubled years this was assured by Gardane and his brother François, from 1726). Regarding the cultural sphere, Lockhart pays homage to the success of France, then far ahead of other nations in the knowledge of Persian culture and its dissemination in Europe.[70] However, about the benefits that Persians could derive from Franco-Persian relations, one must say that the Persian elite was generally lacking the intellectual curiosity to learn from direct contact with Europe or from missionaries in Persia.[71] Apart from religious proselytism, some missionaries at least could provide tuition in languages and science (notably mathematics and astronomy). French presence and influence in Persia took an another aspect when, under the early Qajars (beginning of the nineteenth century), part of the Persian elite began to be attracted towards French culture, renewed by the Enlightenment and by the revolutionary process.[72]

Like the Safavids, who were at odds against the Sunnites, the French had their own sectarian problems. The effects of Counter-Reformation, at work in France from mid-sixteenth century, were felt in French communities in the Orient, among both travellers and settlers. As we have seen, many travellers, temporary settlers and residents had a Huguenot background. Many of them came from the Calvinist Republic of Geneva and were mostly clockmakers and jewellers. They were not organized in a community, like the Genoese residing at Constantinople, who were placed under the protection of the French ambassador to the Porte. They were also kept under the strict control of Calvinist ministers, mainly to protect them from any attempt at conversion to Papism made by Catholic missionaries. The numerical importance of the Constantinople community is explained by the increasing demand for clocks or watches, far beyond the needs of the Ottoman sultan and his officials. From the beginning of the eighteenth century, middle-price watches were sought after by the nascent bourgeoisie. Although they were in fashion at the Safavid court, clocks and watches became more common in Persia only in the nineteenth century.[73] The Calvinists residing in Persia were also theoretically under French diplomatic protection. Whenever it existed, it was, as we have seen, mainly in the hands of Catholic missionaries. These few Calvinists were apparently left without guidance from ministers and there was strong pressure from Catholic missionaries to convert those who wanted to settle in Persia. This was particularly the case with Isaac Boutet de l'Estoille and his descendants. By marrying Armenian Catholic women, the de l'Estoile belonged to the Armenian community of Jolfa. With their intimate knowledge of the country and the languages, and through their business relationships, they rendered a valuable service to French commercial interests. This was finally overlooked by Pilavoine, chief of the French factory at Surat, who dismissed Alexandre de Lestoille and suppressed his post (see above).

Our information about the French or Franco-Armenian community in Persia may be found essentially in diplomatic and missionary sources, the missionaries repeatedly interfering or directly dealing in diplomacy. For this survey, I made extensive use of the annotated biography and works of Father du Mans edited by Francis Richard. Since the missionaries kept the family archives of their parishioners, much more would be known about them and their background in France if we chanced to discover more archival documents.

About the various questions connected with the availability and reliability of observations on Safavid Persia, one may remark that, apart from some missionaries and mainly Father du Mans, permanent settlers seldom wrote about their personal experience. Among the laymen, we may note that Isaac Boutet de l'Estoille said to La Boullaye in Paris that he would write his memoirs as soon as he returned to Persia. Isaac may have discussed this project with Father du Mans who, perhaps, was thus incited to write his *Estat de la Perse*.[74]

Among the various problems linked with travel literature and authorship remains information about the background on some travellers, the real motivation pushing them to undertake long and hazardous journeys, and the difficulty they sometimes experienced to reinsert themselves in their communities or families upon their return. Some of them left their family and country at an early age. In this respect, a parallel could be drawn between de Feynes and La Boullaye.[75] Henry de Feynes (1573-1647) was the first French layman sent on an official mission to the Far East. His family originated from Beziers and Montpellier (south of France). Educated as a Protestant, he converted to Catholicism, like Henri IV whose army he served in and who sent him on his mission to China. He probably left France in 1606 and passed through Persia in 1606-7. Upon his return (November 1609), he was imprisoned at Lisbon and at the Jativa fortress near Valencia until 1613, charged with spying against Portuguese and Spanish interests. After such a long absence, on his return home to Montpellier he had to fight against his brothers and sisters who had deprived him of his inheritance. He then entered the service of the Duc de Nevers and later that of Louis XIII. His education was limited and he had to use the help of 'writers' to publish his travel account (first in English, London 1615, then in French, Paris, 1630).[76] Although easily available, de Feynes's observations about Persia have seldom been used, perhaps because of uncertainties regarding their dates. He was apparently very well received at Isfahan by Shah 'Abbas.[77] He was probably among the first Europeans to observe the shah's taste for spectacular, gladiatorial displays of might. He has left us a vivid description of the festivities organized at Isfahan, on the great maydan, after the shah's victorious campaigns against the Ottomans in Azerbaijan and the Caucasian provinces in the years 1602-7. These celebrations, lasting for several days, took place in November 1607.[78] According to de Feynes, the inhabitants of Isfahan wanted to demonstrate their grateful rejoicing to the shah for his glorious reconquest of the 'four provinces' from the Turk. On the square, in front of the palace, they built four great fortresses, full of fireworks and linked by ropes. By some mechanical device, artificially made animals (dragons, bears, leopards, crocodiles, lions) ran along the ropes and fought each other with so much vigour that they almost looked alive.[79]

François Le Gouz, Sieur de La Boullaye et du Gœuvre, was born in 1610 at Baugé (Anjou). After finishing his studies at the College de la Flèche, he served with the French troops in the service of Charles I of England. After travelling extensively in Europe (1643) he settled in Paris. Out of curiosity, he undertook a voyage to the Orient (1644-50, Italy, Greece, Constantinople, Persia, India) and returned through the Persian Gulf, the Levant and Egypt to Italy. He settled for a while in Rome, being lodged in his palace by Cardinal Capponi, keeper of the Vatican library. There he learnt about his father's death. Hastily returning to Anjou, he found that his brother-in-law had dispossessed him of his heritage. A lawsuit followed and, to further his cause, La Boullaye, then renowned as a great traveller, was presented to Louis XIV in his Oriental dress. As we have seen, he was among the *députés* of Colbert's Company sent by Louis XIV to Persia in 1665. After leaving Persia, he continued his mission for the Company at Surat. He was received at the Mughal Court by Aurangzeb, together with Bebber (December 1666). Bebber returned to Surat where he quarrelled with Thévenot and the Capuchin Father Ambroise de Preuilly. La Boullaye remained for a while at Agra, where he met Tavernier. He apparently intended to carry out his old project to go to China through Bengal. When taking his leave, he obtained 12 bottles of old wine from Tavernier. He went to Patna where he embarked for Dacca with a party of Persian soldiers. His baggage, which contained only books, attracted their attention. He was assassinated, probably during his sleep, just before reaching Dacca.[80]

Simplified genealogy of the family de l'Estoile - Rousseau

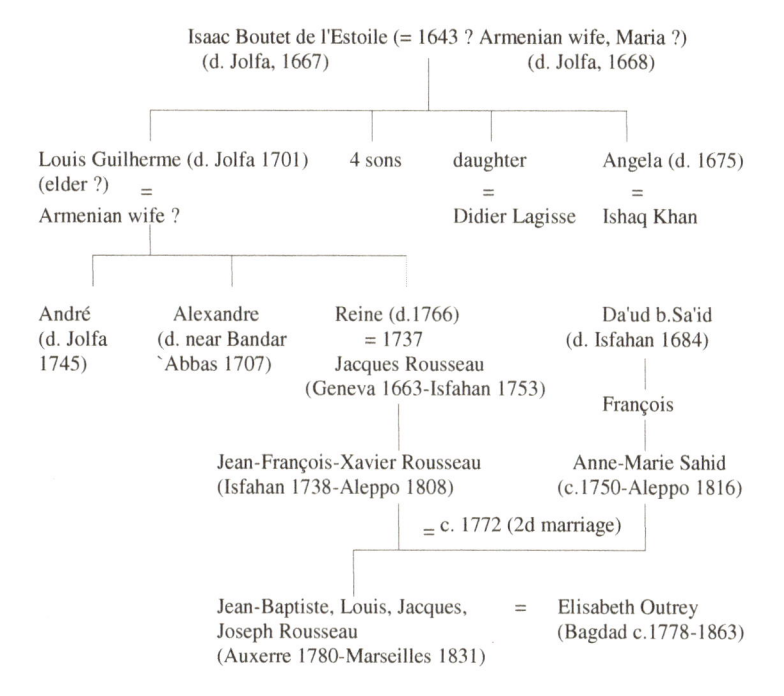

```
         Isaac Boutet de l'Estoile (= 1643 ? Armenian wife, Maria ?)
              (d. Jolfa, 1667)                (d. Jolfa, 1668)
    ┌────────────────────────┬──────────────┬──────────────┐
Louis Guilherme (d. Jolfa 1701)   4 sons    daughter    Angela (d. 1675)
(elder ?)                                      =              =
    =                                     Didier Lagisse   Ishaq Khan
Armenian wife ?
    ┌──────────┬──────────────┐
  André     Alexandre      Reine (d.1766)       Da'ud b.Sa'id
 (d. Jolfa  (d. near Bandar  = 1737            (d. Isfahan 1684)
  1745)    `Abbas 1707)    Jacques Rousseau
                         (Geneva 1663-Isfahan 1753)
                                                  François

              Jean-François-Xavier Rousseau    Anne-Marie Sahid
              (Isfahan 1738-Aleppo 1808)       (c.1750-Aleppo 1816)
                       = c. 1772 (2d marriage)

              Jean-Baptiste, Louis, Jacques,  =  Elisabeth Outrey
              Joseph Rousseau                    (Bagdad c.1778-1863)
              (Auxerre 1780-Marseilles 1831)
```

Notes

1. The general character of this chapter precludes any extensive documentation. Being only a part of a piece of original research, it intends to summarize the best available studies dealing with different aspects of the subject. References to primary sources, in manuscripts or printed works (archives, memoirs, travelogues, etc.), are therefore to be found in the references given in the notes and in the bibliography.
2. On early Franco-Persian relations, see J. Calmard, 'France: i Introduction, ii. Relations with Persia to 1789', *EIr*, X, pp. 127ff. For over 40 years, researchers depended mainly on Lockhart's pioneering work *The Fall of the Safavi Dynasty and the Afghan Occupation of Persia* (Cambridge, 1958), pp. 426ff., on Franco-Persian relations up to 1730. This was followed by his contribution to the *Cambridge History of Iran*: L. Lockhart, 'European contacts with Persia, 1350-1736', in *CHI*, VI.
3. On the alleged conversion of Shah 'Abbas to Catholicism, see Lockhart, 'European contacts', pp. 389ff.
4. On Deshayes de Courmenin, father and son, see Roman d'Amat, *Dictionnaire de Biographie française*, vol. X, (Paris: Letouzey et Ané, 1933), pp. 1380f.
5. On early French missionary activities in Safavid Persia see F. Richard, *Raphaël du Mans, missionnaire en Perse au XVIIe s.*, 2 vols, *MOOI*, IX (Paris, 1995), I, pp. 16ff. See also F. Richard 'Carmelites in Persia', *EIr*, IV, pp. 832-4; 'Capuchins in Persia', *EIr*, VIII, pp. 787f.
6. Richard, *du Mans*, I, pp.125-7. On Gauderean, see A. Kroell, *Nouvelles d'Ispahan*, ed. Société d'Histoire de l'Orient (Paris, 1979), pp. 52ff.; J. Calmard-Compas, 'Gaudereau', *EIr*, X, pp. 331-2.
7. Kroell, Anne, *Louis XIV, la Perse et Mascate* (Paris: Société d'histoire de l'Orient, 1977), pp. 8ff. Pidou died at Isfahan in 1717. See Richard, *du Mans*, I, p. 131.
8. Kroell, *Louis XIV*, pp. 5ff.; A. Kroell, 'East India Company (The French)', *EIr*, VII, pp. 647-9.

9. See Anne Kroell, 'Billon de Cancerille et les relations franco-persanes au début du XVIIIe siècle', in *Le Monde iranien et l'Islam*, II, Paris-Genève, 1974, pp. 127–56.
10. On the missions of Fabre and Michel, see Lockhart, *The Fall*, pp. 437ff.; Kroell, 'Louis XIV', pp. 24ff.
11. On Franco-Persian relations from 1708 to 1730, see Lockhart, *The Fall*, pp. 453ff. On Padery's missions as dragoman and consul, see Touzard, Anne-Marie, *Le Drogman Padery: émissaire de France en Perse, 1719-1725*, (Paris: Geuthner, 2005). On John Law's company, the fall of the Safavids, its aftermath and further Franco-Persian relations, see Calmard, 'Relations', pp. 12f.
12. See J. Calmard, 'Gardane mission 1807-1809', *EIr*, X.
13. See Lockhart, 'European contacts', pp. 373ff.
14. Ibid., pp. 399f. Thévenot died at Miyana, 28 November 1667.
15. For a detailed analysis of these titles and a thematic survey of the subjects they cover, see A.-M. Touzard, 'Image de la Perse. La thématique des titres des récits de voyages français en Perse, publiés entre 1600 et 1730', in *Studia Iranica*, 26/1 (1997), bibliographical list, pp. 94ff.
16. See ibid., p. 109.
17. See Richard, *du Mans*, I, pp. 74ff.; Richard, 'Du Mans', in *EIr*, VII, pp. 571f.
18. Richard, *du Mans*, I, pp. 98ff.
19. See D. Van der Cruysse, *Chardin le Persan* (Paris, 1998), p. 22f.
20. See Lockhart, *The Fall*, p. 428, n. 2.
21. Richard, *du Mans*, I, pp. 100f., identifying Chardin's authorship of the memoir in which he refers to both Tavernier and Thévenot having used du Mans in their travel accounts.
22. On the French translations by Fathers E. Carneau and F. Le Comte, see Touzard, 'Image de la Perse', p. 97; see also J. Gurney, 'Della Valle', in *EIr*, VII, pp. 251–4.
23. Touzard, 'Image de la Perse', pp. 109f.
24. See J. Emerson, 'Adam Olearius and the literature of the Schleswig-Holstein mission to Russia and Iran, 1633-1639', in Calmard, *Etudes Safavides*, pp. 31–56, pp. 49ff.
25. See W. Floor, 'Fact or fiction. The most perilous journeys of Jan Jansz. Struys', in Calmard (ed.), *Etudes Safavides*, pp. 57–68, 65ff.
26. Chardin's movements in Persia and India are difficult to retrace. He probably stayed in Persia in 1666-7 and between 1673 and 1677. See Emerson, John, 'Chardin, Sir John' in *Encyclopaedia Iranica* (online). Cruysse, *Chardin*, pp.46ff.
27. See F. Richard, 'L'apport des missionnaires européens à la connaissance de l'Iran en Europe et de l'Europe en Iran', in Calmard (ed.), *Etudes Safavides*, pp. 251–66.
28. On his *Gazophylacium*, partially edited by Michel Bastiaensen (Brussels, 1985), see review by J. Calmard, in *Abstracta Iranica* 9 (1986), p.97f.
29. See Kroell, 'Louis XIV', p. 4, n. 5.
30. See Richard, *du Mans*, I, p. 54, n. 127.
31. See the family tree entitled 'The family de l'Estoile – Rousseau' at the end of this chapter. It is based on research made by Francis Richard, and partly by Lockhart and Anne Kroell.
32. From Saint-Jean d'Angély? See ibid., p. 203, n. 170.
33. Lockhart, *The Fall*, p. 432, n. 1; Cruysse, *Chardin*, p. 39 (no reference provided).
34. Richard, *du Mans*, I, p. 150, II, p. 222, n. 62 (with reference to) Poullet, *Nouvelles Relations du Levant*, Chardin and La Boullaye Le Gouz.
35. See A. Kroell, 'Alexandre de l'Estoille dernier agent de la Compagnie royale des Indes en Perse', in *MOOI*, I (1984), p. 65.
36. See Richard, *du Mans*, I, pp. 150f., n. 47. Richard suggests that his wife may have been a certain Maria (d. Jolfa, 1668).
37. Ibid., p. 203, n. 170.
38. Ibid.; Kroell, 'L'Estoille' ,p. 65, n.6 and 7.
39. Ibid.; Richard, *du Mans*, I, p. 151.

40. Kroell, 'Louis XIV', pp. 6f.; Richard, du Mans, I, pp. 94ff.; Cruysse, Chardin, pp. 190ff (with further reference to strong criticism made by Chardin, who was then present at Isfahan, about Father du Mans who awkwardly 'forged' the Persian letters to be presented by de Jonchères to the shah, pp. 198ff).
41. Cruysse, Chardin, p. 200, n. 47, referring to the 'lettres patentes' integrally quoted by Chardin.
42. Kroell, 'Alexandre de Lestoille', p. 65, n. 6, 7, 8.
43. Richard, du Mans, I, p. 203, n. 170.
44. Ibid. and p. 207, n. 173.
45. Lockhart, The Fall, p. 433; Richard, du Mans, I, p. 203, n. 170.
46. Richard, du Mans, I, pp. 137, n. 5, 141, 148, n. 39, 150, n. 47, 203, n. 170; II, p. 251, n. 119.
47. Ibid., I, p. 203, n. 170.
48. Lockhart, The Fall, pp. 76, 78, 433, n. 3; Kroell, 'Louis XIV', p. 30, n. 101.
49. See Raymond Trousson, Jean-Jacques Rousseau. Heurs et malheurs d'une conscience (Paris, 1993), pp. 10ff.
50. See Touzard, 'Image de la Perse', p. 90; J. Perry, Karim Khan Zand. A History of Iran, 1747-1779 (Chicago, 1979), pp. 268f; 'Rousseau (Jean-François-Xavier)', in Larousse, Grand dictionnaire universel.
51. Calmard, 'Gardane mission', 293.
52. Richard, du Mans, I, p. 256, n. 298. See also 'Rousseau, Jean-François-Xavier', in Michaud, Dictionnaire de biographie universelle.
53. W. Floor, The Afghan Occupation of Safavid Persia 1721-1729, Cahier de Studia Iranica 19 (Paris, 1998), p. 98. Joseph Sahid had served for five and a half months as dragoman during Mohammad Reza Beg's embassy to France, in 1714-15 (see Richard, du Mans).
54. Da'ud b. Sa'id was a Catholic, probably belonging to a Jacobite family settled at Isfahan, and his family is further called Sahid in European sources (see Richard, du Mans).
55. See 'Rousseau (Jean-Baptiste-Louis-Jacques)', in Larousse, Grand dictionnaire universel; Calmard, 'Gardane mission', pp. 293f.
56. Kroell, 'Alexandre de Lestoille', p. 67, n. 23, 24, 25.
57. Ibid., p. 65, n. 8.
58. Richard, du Mans, I, p. 187.
59. Ibid., I, p. 174, n. 94.
60. Ibid., I, pp. 186f.
61. Ibid., I, p. 144, n. 25.
62. Touzard, Les missions de Padery, pp. 221f.
63. Floor, Afghan Occupation, p. 142.
64. Ibid., p. 152, 160
65. Lockhart, The Fall, p. 135.
66. Ibid., p.142. Colombe is called Coelang/Coulang in Dutch sources: see Floor, Afghan Occupation, pp. 86, n. 169, 92.
67. Lockhart, The Fall, p. 468.
68. Floor, Afghan Occupation, p. 174.
69. Richard, du Mans, I, p. 73.
70. Lockhart, The Fall, p. 469f.
71. See R. Matthee, 'Europe, Persian image of', in EIr, VIII, pp. 70-6.
72. See Calmard, 'Gardane mission', p. 296.
73. See W. Floor, 'Clocks', in EIr, V, pp. 713-18, p. 716.
74. Richard, du Mans, I, p. 203, n. 170.
75. As suggested by Béguin Billecoq, de Feynes, I, pp. 20f.
76. On his origins, biography, and bibliography, see ibid., pp. 10ff.
77. de Feynes, Henri, Voyage fait par terre depuis Paris iusques a la Chine... (Paris: Pierre Rocolet, 1630), p. 68.
78. See Eskandar Beg Monshi, Tarikh-e 'Alamara-ye 'Abbasi, trans. R. M. Savory, History of Shah 'Abbas the Great, 2 vols (Boulder, 1978), II, pp. 947f.

79. De Feynes, *Voyage*, pp. 50-2. De Feynes expresses his admiration for the man who artfully engineered these scenes. They are tentatively represented in an engraving in the upper part of the frontispiece of his travels (Paris, 1636): see Béguin Billecoq, *de Feynes*, vol. II, opposite p. 232.
80. See H. Castonnet des Fosses, *La Boullaye Le Gouz. Sa vie et ses voyages*, Angers, 1891 (pp. 47ff. about his mission in Persia and India). A different report about the circumstances of his death is given by Richard, *du Mans*, I, p. 188, n.128, referring to a letter of Father Ephrem de Nevers, who says that La Boullaye intended to return to France and was killed by thieves near Lahore.

References

Béguin Billecoq, X. *Henry de Feynes (1573-1647). Le premier Français en Extrême-Orient*, thesis (Université de Provence, 1999), 2 vols.
Calmard, J., 'France: i Introduction, ii. Relations with Persia to 1789', *EIr*, X, pp. 126-31.
—— 'Gardane mission 1807-1809', *EIr*, X, pp. 292-7.
—— (ed.), *Etudes Safavides* (Paris-Téhéran, 1993).
de Feynes, Henri, *Voyage fait par terre depuis Paris iusques a la Chine...*, (Paris: Pierre Rocolet, 1630)
EIr = *Encyclopædia Iranica*, ed. E. Yarshater, New York.
Floor, W., *The Afghan Occupation of Safavid Persia 1721-1729*, Cahier de Studia Iranica 19 (Paris, 1998).
Jackson, P. and Lockhart, L. (eds), *The Cambridge History of Iran*, vol. VI (Cambridge, 1986).
Kroell, A., *Nouvelles d'Ispahan*, ed. Société d'Histoire de l'Orient (Paris, 1979).
—— 'Alexandre de l'Estoille, dernier agent de la Compagnie royale des Indes en Perse', in *MOOI*, I (1984), pp. 62-72.
—— 'East India Company (The French)', *EIr*, VII, pp. 647-9.
Lockhart, L., 'European contacts with Persia, 1350-1736', in *CHI*, VI, pp. 373-411.
—— *The Fall of the Safavi Dynasty and the Afghan Occupation of Persia* (Cambridge, 1958).
'Louis XIV, la Perse et Mascate', *Le Monde iranien et l'Islam*, IV (1976-7), pp. 1-78. Reprinted with a map, an index, and same pagination, by Société d'Histoire de l'Orient, Paris 1977.
MOOI = *Moyen Orient et Océan Indien*, ed. Société d'Histoire de l'Orient (Paris, from 1984).
Richard, F., *Raphaël du Mans, missionnaire en Perse au XVIIe s.*, 2 vols, *MOOI*, IX (Paris, 1995).
Touzard, A.-M., *Diplomatie française en Perse au début du XVIIIe s. Les missions du drogman Padery*, *MOOI*, XIII (Paris, 2003) (in the print).
—— 'Image de la Perse. La thématique des titres des récits de voyages français en Perse, publiés entre 1600 et 1730', in *Studia Iranica*, 26/1 (1997), pp. 47-110.
Van der Cruysse, D., *Chardin le Persan* (Paris, 1998).

19

The Presence of Ancient Secular and Religious Texts in Pietro della Valle's (1586–1652) Unpublished and Printed Writings

Sonja Brentjes

In 1561, on his second journey to the Safavid Empire, Anthony Jenkinson carried a letter from Queen Elizabeth that greeted Shah Tahmasp in the following manner:

> Elizabeth, by the grace of God, queene of England, &c. To the right mightie, and right uictorius prince, the great Sophie, emperor of the Persians, Medes, Parthians, Hyrcanes, Carmaranians (*sic*), Margians, of the people on this side, and beyond the river of Tygris, and of all men and nations between the Caspian sea and the gulph of Persia, greeting, and most happie increase in all prosperitie.[1]

From the maps of the world, Asia and the Safavid Empire drawn by Giacomo Gastaldi between 1546 and 1562 in Venice, the early modern observer could learn that the realm of the Safavids consisted of very different provinces from those Elizabeth had imagined. For instance, the map called *Persia Nova Tabula,* drawn by Gastaldi for the Italian edition of Ptolemy's *Geography* in 1548, is covered in ancient Greek names such as Partia, Persia or Ircania, but a reader could also find new names such as Azimia, Corazani, Lar or Mar di Bachau.[2] The Iranian territories on the map in the first part of Asia (that is the region from the Black Sea and the eastern part of the Mediterranean Sea to Kabul) that Gastaldi produced 11 years later are purged of ancient Greek names and covered with local names such as Servan, Gilan, Taperistan, Mesandaran, Cusistan, Lurestan, Arach, Chirman, Corasan, Sigistan or Mare de Bachu. Some of the names are incorrectly spelt such as Tares, Tarsi, Mare Coruzum or Adilbegian, while others are misplaced, outdated, explanatory or misunderstood such as Rabia, Djargument, Ieselbas or Circan. All of these names go back to local toponyms used in the medieval or the early modern period in Iran.[3]

Gastaldi's maps were very successful. They influenced western European cartographical portrayals of Safavid Iran until its demise in the eighteenth century. Cartographers adopted both ways of naming Iran and her parts found in Gastaldi's maps – in some cases, mixing ancient Greek with medieval, plus early modern Persian names in transliterations of all kinds and, in other cases, applying exclusively transliterated medieval and early modern Persian names. Western European cartographers of the early modern period loved to indulge themselves and their clients with local names from as many foreign languages as possible. One example of this preference for native names in the case of Iran is the legend inscribed in the area of the Caspian Sea on the maps of Abraham Ortelius (1570 and following editions) and Gerhard Mercator as edited by Jodocus Hondius (1607 and following editions).

> For the Hyrcanian or Caspian sea, one has need of various names today. The Ruthenians call it Chualenska (*sic*) More; the Mores Bohar Corsun (*sic*) (a word shared with the Arabian gulf), which means closed sea. I see that it is called by others in other ways, as the sea of Bachu, Cunzar, Giorgian, Terbestan, Corusum, namely after the denomination of the neighbouring regions and places. The lake is the largest of the entire world and salty. It is rich in fish.[4]

Elizabeth's letter, as well as Gastaldi's, Ortelius's and Mercator's maps, set the stage for the discussion that follows. When we compare early modern printed travel accounts with early modern maps produced in Catholic or Protestant Europe, we discover that cartographers and map-printers more often preferred the use of local names, while authors of printed travel accounts clearly favoured ancient names. This does not mean that cartographers and map-printers after Gastaldi never used ancient names. But, when they used them they identified them mostly as names of the past by writing, for instance, 'Fars (or Farsistan) olim Persis'. Authors of printed travel accounts, in contrast, employed ancient names as guiding principles, because for them these were the names that truly mattered. The local names, which were used, were mostly presented as of secondary, derivative relevance and as needing placement in the context of the ancient names in order to be meaningful. The structural dominance of ancient names over medieval and contemporary local names was accompanied by explanatory and interpretive stories taken from ancient secular and religious sources. These stories strengthened the ascription of meaning to localities in Safavid Iran (as well as in the Ottoman Empire). They also identified the Safavid present as replicating the Achaemenid past, as seen through the eyes of ancient Greek and Latin writers.

Modern historians tend to take the dominance of ancient geography and history in early modern printed travel accounts about Safavid Iran at face value. They often declare that the geographical knowledge of early modern travellers about Iran was solidly anchored in ancient geography. They accept so-called eyewitness accounts of nature, culture and peoples as descriptions of observations made and told by the early modern traveller himself. They tend to repeat evaluations of Safavid society given by early modern travellers without questioning the validity, context and history of these evaluations. This readiness to trust the narrator is particularly strong when scientific subjects are described and judged.

The extant papers of one of the most eminent early modern west European travellers to Safavid Iran, Pietro della Valle (1586–1652), prove beyond doubt that the picture drawn in printed travel accounts is a construction of censorship and academic aspirations. This construction did not permeate the system of beliefs of the Italian traveller, as is shown by his unpublished private and semi-public writings. While travelling, Pietro della Valle was much more interested in learning local names, histories, customs and modes of life than remembering what ancient authors had written. A comparison of della Valle's unpublished letters to his friends and family, his original letters to Mario Schipano before they were printed, his travel diary with the printed letters and with his Latin geography of Iran prepared for print, reveals that the printed letters misrepresent della Valle's views and activities to such a degree that his beliefs, as expressed in the non-printed sources and in the brief biography attached to the printed letters, underwent radical alteration on three major points: the image of the Orient, the image of della Valle himself and the image of ancient secular and religious knowledge and values. Introducing quotes from, and references to, ancient authors and texts achieved this profound reconfiguration of della Valle's letters to Mario Schipano. Below, I present the results of my comparative analysis of the four types of text that della Valle produced in Iran and in Italy in order to prove these claims.

Della Valle's published letters to Mario Schipano

Della Valle quoted from, or referred to, 83 ancient, medieval and early modern texts or authors in his letters published in 1650, 1658 and 1663. Ignoring della Valle's references to his own letters, the remaining 82 texts comprise the Bible, the Qur'an, four other books on religious subjects, texts by 38 classical Greek and Latin authors, 31 books by medieval and early modern Catholic writers (more than half of them editions and collections of, or comments on, classical authors), seven works by medieval and early modern Muslim scholars and one book by a medieval Armenian Orthodox-turned-Catholic writer. Thus, the majority of the works quoted by della Valle in his printed letters deal with secular and religious topics of Greek and Roman antiquity, of Judaism and Christianity. The prevalence of this kind of literature is also shown when we look at which texts or authors are most often quoted by della Valle (see Table 19.1).

Table 19.1 Texts and authors quoted by della Valle

Title/author	Letters from the Ottoman Empire	Letters from the Safavid Empire	Letters from India
The Bible	112	33	–
Strabo	26	16	10
Virgil	26	21	–
Pierre Bélon	44	–	–
D. Siculus	15	19	4
Herodotus	17	9	3
Xenophon	6	18	–
Filippo Ferrari	10	12	–
Pierre Gilles	16	–	–

Since all the quotes from Ferrari are used in order to identify a certain town, region, river, mountain or king with an ancient name, and since most quotes from Bélon and Gilles either concern Egyptian antiquities, ancient identities of early modern Arabic towns, villages and rivers or refer to Byzantine monuments in Istanbul and environment, it is not an exaggeration to say that most of della Valle's references to books and manuscripts serve to structure, interpret and identify the places, objects and peoples he had encountered on his voyage as well as their histories, beliefs and customs in terms of ancient classical and biblical perspectives.

Della Valle used Ferrari, Strabo and Siculus to introduce his own ideas about which contemporary Arabic, Turkish or Persian geographical name corresponded to which ancient Greek or Latin name, to criticize what he considered wrong identifications by Ferrari and to remind his readers of shared geographical perspectives on the Safavid Empire, as well as the two other regions he visited. He wrote, for instance, about Mazandaran:

> But before we go ahead I will describe the location of Mazanderàn in general that it may be possible for you to recognize it on geographical maps and to see whether it is truly ancient Hyrcania or a part of Hyrcania or another province close to that as I think it more likely.[5]

Della Valle applied Herodotus, Xenophon, the Bible, Strabo and Diodorus Siculus to connect contemporary customs and habits in the Ottoman Empire, the Safavid Empire and western India with customs and habits described by the ancient authors. The second identification more than the first creates the impression that nothing had changed in those countries since classical times, an insight not left to the reader's astuteness, but formulated explicitly more than once.[6] The value of this judgement is not explicitly negative. The absence of historical change in any of the visited territories and cultures does not mean immobility and backwardness to della Valle. His rhetoric points more to continuity, reliability and accessibility for the outsider endowed with classical sources. When discussing the ethnic origin of the Mughals, della Valle wrote, for instance, about the heirs of Genghiz Khan:

> This Cinghiz, ..., having made himself finally the master of a huge state and quasi of all Tatary which encompassed the one and the other Scythia; divided it when dying among his sons. To Giagatà, who was his second-born son, he (gave) the country of Samarcand with the entire Sogdiana and diverse other areas (close by); & these were called after his proper name Giagataio and Giagataini all the people which remained under his rule. It is a most ancient custom of the Scythians to give to the countries subjected by them the name of their princes as one can see well in Diodorus Siculus.[7]

The qualitative picture sketched in the published letters about della Valle's scholarly attitude towards the areas he had visited and lived in for several years is one of personal experience safely secured within the boundaries of ancient secular and religious knowledge and wisdom. The personal experience is portrayed as one of cultural superiority of the traveller himself and of his native country. That country is most often identified with the hometown of his correspondent, that is Naples. Most towns and cities della Valle visited were less beautiful than Naples. Only Isfahan was comparable to at that Italian city. Most inhabitants of the Ottoman and the Safavid empires that della Valle met were less civilized than he was. Even Shah 'Abbas, to whom della Valle devoted a eulogy, was less witty and less well-mannered than the Roman patrician. Della Valle portrayed himself as superior because he adhered to the only true faith, was the only one who spoke a cultured, courteous language and adored women in a more appropriate style than the natives. Ancient knowledge lent authority to his information about contemporary Ottoman and Safavid geography, culture and history. Arabic and Persian texts and authors are portrayed as reliable when della Valle wished to point out the false beliefs of contemporary Italian writers on geography and history, but were of no great use when the ancient history of Iran was discussed. They remain a minority voice in della Valle's printed letters. The modern geography of the Ottoman and Safavid empires that della Valle wrote about to Mario Schipano was in no need of justification and legitimation by Arabic, Turkish and Persian scholarly works. It was della Valle's personal experience of these territories that provided the new knowledge, and it was his own intellectual capacity that could equate the new knowledge with the familiar knowledge found in ancient works and in recently printed books brought from Italy.

When looking at the relationship between ancient secular and religious works and early modern Oriental names in della Valle's printed letters from a quantitative angle, ancient geography and history drowns in a flood of early modern Oriental names and activities. Numerous letters do not contain a single reference to any work, while Oriental names appear frequently. Lacking any kind of reference to ancient sources, they are free of classical imprisonment. Thus della Valle's attempt to relate Ottoman or Safavid geography, history and customs to ancient textual authority did not produce a consistent result. Despite the immense work he carried out in Rome to enhance the status of his letters by quoting many ancient authors and texts, he could not and perhaps did not wish to suppress his genuine efforts to learn the local contemporary geography on its own terms while he was travelling.

Ancient authority in della Valle's Latin geography of Safavid Iran

The anchoring of contemporary Iranian geography in ancient knowledge and wisdom is much stronger in della Valle's Latin geography of Iran, titled in English *About the regions subjected by the recent empire of the Persians*. He wrote a first, apparently lost, version of this treatise for the Jesuit Vincislaus Pantaleone Kirwitzer (d. 1626), a missionary in China and the Philippines, whom he had met in Goa. As soon as he returned to Rome, della Valle decided to publish the text.[8] This intention was never implemented despite della Valle's continual efforts to improve the text. The text of the fine copy prepared in 1628 shows many parallels with the printed letters and was apparently revised accordingly. The frame of della Valle's description of each of the 17 territories he dealt with consists of identifying the contemporary local name of the region with an ancient designation and providing an etymology for the local name that, more often than not, is wrong. This frame is filled with different items such as the physical and natural endowments of the area, major cities, major monuments, borderlines and political events.

> The region of Babylon, together with some of the adjacent territories, which is called until today in the Holy Scriptures by the ancient name is called by the contemporary Persians Araq. The meaning of this name is sweat, first, because the heat in these areas is impetuous during summer time. Furthermore, too perhaps, because these areas are made fertile again by letting in brooks not only from the rivers, but with much sweat too after they are completely soaked after some few rainfalls. As a matter of fact, however, Araq is a double name, i.e. Araq of Arabia and Araq of Agiamia (they call namely Agiam or Agem all those regions which are subjugated to the power of the Persians). Araq of Arabia means Babylonia and the adjacent areas which are subjugated today to the empire of the Turks. When (you) turn toward the east, you travel from there straight through the high rising mountains of the region of Kurdistan. They go from north to south, with the Taurus Mountains so to say as a branch, and separate the Persian Empire from the Turkish (one). Immediately, Araq of Agiamia presents itself as the first region in Persian subordination and as a part of it (appears) the province of Hamadan. Its capital is the city of Hamadan. (This province) is, as I assume, part of ancient Persia or Susiana in the borders of the Medes.[9]

The framing of Iranian geography with ancient concepts and spatial arrangements reminds the reader – through continuous repetition – that the guiding principle of geographical writing had to be ancient knowledge.[10] Authors were not of prime importance, they are almost invisible in della Valle's text.

He only quotes three times from Virgil, once from Strabo and once, perhaps, from Pliny (without saying so) and refers to Diodorus Siculus. Throughout the text, however, he keeps the reader engaged in a debate about what ancient identity could and should be ascribed to each and any contemporary Iranian town, river or mountain. In this debate della Valle insists upon his personal experience and, occasionally, on the authority of Persian and Arabic texts for deciding cases in dispute; for instance, the troublesome question of whether the ancient Portae called Caucasia, Ferrea and Caspia were built at one and the same place and whether this place was modern Derbent at the western shores of the Caspian Sea.[11]

Della Valle's travel diary

Della Valle's notes from and about his travels, contained in Ms Città del Vaticano, Biblioteca Apostolica Vaticana, Ottobonianus latinus 3382 (from now abbreviated as Ms Ottobonianus lat. 3382), are almost void of any authority except his own and that of other travellers from Catholic and Protestant Europe whom he met in the Ottoman and Safavid empires. A few late medieval and early modern authors and once or twice the Bible are mentioned in the text of the diary, while the few references to ancient authors were almost all added as an afterthought and hence can be found in the margins or between the lines. The authors della Valle mentions in the entries are Torquato Tasso, Pierre Bélon and Filippo Ferrari. Once, he also mentions the Persian treatise *Ketab-e vajebat-e zaruriye*.[12]

In the margins, della Valle refers to two classical authors, Strabo and Justinus, to four early modern writers – one French and three Portuguese – Pierre Bélon, Pedro Teixeira, Father Negrone and a father whose name I cannot decipher correctly, and to four Persian books – the *Ketab-e masalek al-mamalek* of Abu'l-Hasan Sa'id (b. 'Ali al-Jurjani) (d. ca. 881h/1476), the *Si fasl* by Naser al-Din Tusi (d. 672h/1272), the *Taqvim* by 'Enayat, the brother of the astronomer Mulla Zayn al-Din from Lar, and Yahya's (b. 'Abd al-Latif al-Qazvini) (d. 962h/1552) *Lobb al-tavarikh*.[13]

There is only one exception; in the entry of 13 October 1621, which reports on della Valle's journey to Chehel Menar after the crossing of the river Kur via the so-called new bridge; that is, Pol-e no. In this entry, della Valle claimed that the people of the country did not possess any sound knowledge of ancient history. However, Don Garçia da Silva y Figueroa, ambassador of Spain and a man well-versed in history had told him that Quintus Curtius did mention the place, but not as one that was already very ancient in his day.[14] Della Valle added that he had no access to Curtius's book nor could he consult any other book.[15] Later, when the traveller discovered that the author the ambassador meant was not Quintus Curtius, but Diodorus Siculus, he wrote the latter's name in between the lines. A second reference to Diodorus Siculus in between the lines is found earlier in this very same entry where della Valle talked about the location of Chehel Menar with regard to some mountains. This interlinear addition is marked by a siglum to be integrated into the original text of the diary.[16] All of these references are verbal; that is, they seldom refer to the title of a precise work and they never contain any specific indication of the number of the book or chapter where the remembered remark could be found, except for the two references to Strabo and Justinus in the margins.

The style of della Valle's references to authors and texts differs in the various textual environments where they appear: the diary (the text, margins and space between the lines); the original letters (the text, margins, interlineal space and notes); and the printed letters. In the text of his diary, della Valle simply wrote remarks such as 'che descrivo il Tasso', 'come dice Belonio', 'della quale Belonio fa mentione' or 'come benissimo dice L'Epitome Geografica'.[17] In the margins, all references are marked as notes. As a rule, they say 'See the book of this or that author'. In the case of the two ancient authors, the references are more specific saying 'Vedi Strabone lib. 16. in principio' and 'Vedi Giustino hist. lib. 32 ...'.[18] The two interlinear references to Diodorus Siculus correspond to the references in the text of the diary.

Most of the notes in the diary can be recognized as later additions. Some have clearly been added a long time after the entry had been written. One such case is della Valle's note to the entry for 19 October 1616 in which he referred to his Latin translation of the Shi'i creed carried out three years later in Isfahan.[19] A second example is his reference to al-Jurjani's *Ketab-e masalek al-mamalek* at a moment when he had not yet left the Ottoman Empire, not yet learnt Persian and not yet bought the manuscript.[20] A third example is the reference to Negrone's book on India, which, according to della Valle's note, was at that time still in the process of being printed in Rome. It is attached to the entry for 8 December 1618 at the end of the folio, separated from the text by a siglum and dated by della Valle's remarks that Negrone passed through Persia in 1619 and that he saw him later in his place, that is in Goa. The form in which della Valle wrote about this later meeting suggests that he made the addition to his diary quite a long time after the meeting. I am inclined to assume that he did it in Rome. In this added reference, della Valle used the first form of his quoting style for the margins: 'Vedi de gli Indiani le relazioni del Pre' Fra Francesco Negrone francescano, scritte in portoghese ...'.[21] A fourth note in della Valle's diary confirms that this comment was added only after he had returned to Rome, since variants are also found in Ms Città del Vaticano, Biblioteca Apostolica Vaticana, Ottobonianus latinus 3384 (from now abbreviated as Ms Ottobonianus lat. 3384), a collection of remade letters and excerpts from studied books and manuscripts, and in Ms Città del Vaticano, Biblioteca Apostolica Vaticana, Ottobonianus latinus 3385 (from now on abbreviated as Ms Ottobonianus lat. 3385), a two volume-manuscript with long excerpts from books and manuscripts studied by della Valle.[22]

In his printed letters, too, a few general references similar to those in the text of the diary can be found, but all references discussed in section 1 have in the margin a note like 'Lib. 8', 'Lib. 1, cap. 2' or 'Gen. Lib. 2'. Hence, the diary's references to the ancient authors may have been added only when della Valle had made up his mind about the form of quotation to be used in the published version of his letters, that is in Rome.

The almost complete absence of references to ancient secular and religious authors and texts in the text of the diary – if we ignore the Bible and the reference to Quintus Curtius – and their very occasional presence in the diary margins is truly surprising. Given the small number of della Valle's references to any author in the text of his diary, a few remarks in the text pointing to a Greek or Latin poet, historian or geographer and some references to the Bible could be regarded as a mere difference of genres. Della Valle's almost complete silence about his classical and religious education and beliefs, however, implies that some force stronger than literary convention caused the differences between his manuscripts and the printed letters, in particular since it is not only the authors and books that are absent. The geographical and historical frame guiding della Valle's geographical treatise and its predominant use is also rarely visible in his printed letters. In his diary, when writing about the territories he passed through with the caravans, he used a style where local names, often misspelt and later corrected, prevail over classical learning. In territories better known to early modern travellers, such as Istanbul or the Arab provinces, he rarely bothered to give an ancient name. Only in cases such as Homs or Hama did he write, 'A tre hore di giorno arriuammo ad Hhams, ouero "hams" (in Arabic letters), che anticammente si chiamaua Emissa' and 'a tre hore di giorno o poco più arriuammo ad Hhamà anticamente detta Apamea'.[23] In the case of territories less familiar to della Valle, his major effort was directed towards learning the local names of towns, villages and camps and trying to memorize them by writing them down in Latin and Arabic according to what he had understood by listening.[24] He remembered smaller rivers, villages and small towns only by the local names. When he discovered that allegedly correct identifications between ancient and local names proved to be wrong, such as identifying Baghdad with Babylonia, he made a note saying so.[25] Provinces, major rivers and mountains of the Ottoman Empire he often described by their ancient names.[26] Early on in his journey in the Safavid Empire he combined ancient and native names, as in his identification of Arac with Parthia and Mazandaran with Hyrcania. In this state of mind, the diary continues until 1619/20. Then, ancient names occur only very rarely, as, for instance, when discussing the problem of the two rivers called Kur. Only very rarely did della Valle seem to feel the desire to check with Ferrari's lexicon for what the ancient name of a town, province, river or mountain may have been. Even his excursions into ancient Persian history, in particular his visit to Persepolis and Naqsh-e Rostam, did not induce him to mention a single author in the long notes describing his observations.

Authors and books, in particular ancient authors and printed books from his own culture, were not at the forefront of della Valle's mind while living in the Ottoman and Safavid empires.

Della Valle's original letters to Mario Schipano

A comparison of the diary with the single letter attached to it and with the material found in Mss Ottoboniani lat. 3383-3385 and Archivio Della Valle - del Bufalo 51 - shows that the character of the text of the diary corresponds more closely to that of the original letters of della Valle than to that of the printed version of the letters. These manuscripts reveal that the character of the printed letters was the result of della Valle's intensive study of ancient secular and religious texts, as well as of medieval and early modern texts in several languages. This study was almost entirely carried out after his return to Rome. The only exceptions were his studies of Persian, Arabic and Turkish manuscripts in Iran and India that he continued after he returned to Rome and which were partially integrated into his printed letters.

These manuscripts also show that references to ancient secular and religious authors are more visible in the original text of the letters than in the diary. In the letter from Farahabad, dated 25 July 1618 Qazvin, della Valle quoted implicitly from Virgil (2), Plato (1), the Bible (1), Ovid (1) and explicitly from Ferrari (5).[27] He did not add references to individual books or chapters, as we would expect of a person writing letters rather than the manuscript for a book proper. When he decided to have his letters printed rather than rewrite them as a coherent monograph, the situation changed. Now, explicit references to books were not only appropriate but necessary if the contemporary standards of scholarly bookwriting were to be met. These standards were apparently less formalized and less standardized than one often assumes. Della Valle at least, when starting to prepare his letters for print, had no clear rules in mind that he wished to follow. As the changes in, and the notes to, della Valle's letter from Farahabad illustrate, the revision of the letters was not done all at once, but evolved over time. Explicit and numerous quotes from ancient books were not among the changes della Valle started with. A number of newly produced versions of his original letters contained in Ms Archivio Della Valle - del Bufalo 51-do not yet show a single explicit quote. References to ancient and early modern authors can be found in the revising notes attached to the letter from Farahabad/Qazvin, but they are only a fraction of what can be found in the printed letter purporting to have been sent from Qazvin. The references also do not yet appear in the form used in the printed letters. The 42 numbered, and several other additions penned in six folios, including one long addition at the beginning of the letter covering the description of 'Ashura, contain seven references: ancient authors (5), the Bible (1) and Ferrari (1). Six of them are in the verbal style of the text of the diary. The seventh is in the later style of the printed letter. In the additions found in the margins of the letter, there is a second new verbal reference to Ferrari.[28] In the printed letter, only one verbal reference to an ancient author (Virgil) can be found, while there are 29 references to ancient authors, five references to the Bible and eight references to modern authors, seven of which concern Ferrari. Hence, della Valle decided, possibly within a first round of serious work on his letters, that ancient authors needed to be seen more often. He may have shown his first revision to some friends who may have suggested that he increase the visibility of ancient texts. Thus, della Valle rewrote his annotated and reworked letters fully, in his own hand, and then started a new round of annotations and corrections introducing more and more quotations from, and references to, ancient authors and texts. Another possible explanation of the multiple corrections that della Valle introduced into his letters may lie with the person who signed the imprimatur for the first volume of the letters, those from the Ottoman Empire, Leo Allaci. Allaci was a well-known scholar with a high reputation in the classics. Della Valle, with his close relationship to the papal court and the Propaganda fide, may well have learnt while working on the letters that Allaci was going to decide upon the fate of his letters and hence may have decided to make the letters correspond more closely to the tastes and interests of this one special reader.

Additions were not the only changes della Valle imposed on his original letters. He formatted their outward appearance by numbering them, giving them a title, omitting the letter-style heading and dividing them into numbered sections. He corrected Italian, Latin, Arabic, Turkish and Persian spelling, kept only the transliterated forms of the Oriental words, omitted several drawings found in the original letters as well as in his diary, worked on the elegance of his style and deleted numerous passages. The deleted passages often talked about geographical, historical and political subjects without being too intimate, provocative or revealing as della Valle had pretended in the preface to his letters.[29] Some of these passages were replaced by newly formulated statements, which repeated some of the previous information. In the case of the letter from Farahabad/Qazvin, della Valle deleted 23 passages rephrasing only three or four of them. One major result of the process of deleting original passages is the decreased visibility of the Orient and of della Valle's continuous and intense efforts to get to know the foreign lands in their own languages and concepts. One important example of this editorial suppression of Oriental landscapes and della Valle's newly acquired knowledge, is his cancelling of two folios of Persian toponyms describing his itinerary from Isfahan to Farahabad and his efforts to assemble a list of Safavid provinces and districts and equate them to classical names.[30] Finally, the printed letters occasionally contain additional material, which has not been indicated in the notes and comments to the original letters. The printed letter from Farahabad/Qazvin shows one such unannounced addition with two summarizing quotations from Justinus.[31] These unannounced additions indicate a third round of proofreading and correction of before the letters were given to the printer.

Mss Ottoboniani lat. 3384 and 3385 contain the by-products of della Valle's extensive reading. They show that he spent much time copying quotations from the Bible, Strabo, Herodotus, Xenophon, Diodorus Siculus and many other authors, including some, such as Schickard or Gassendi, whom he did not integrate into the printed version of the letters. Almost all the authors and books he quoted in the printed letters are present in these two manuscripts. Ms Ottobonianus lat. 3384 also contains several new versions of della Valle's letters under the label of 'Rimesse'.[32] It is here that he first adopted the form of reference to the books he used that we later find in the printed version. This form is also present in two folios of quotations from 30 ancient and modern books, including one about Persian history.[33] Immediately after this list, a new one follows entitled: 'Modo, come cito in margine gli Autori'.[34] The list starts with Virgil and offers two options: 'Eneid. 3./ouero Virg. Eneid. 3/Egl. 2.'[35] A look at della Valle's printed letters shows that he worked with both variants.[36] Folios 76a–80b in Ms Ottobonianus lat. 3384 contain a list entitled: 'Noue de mettersi nell' India'.[37]

After della Valle had finished the extensive revision of his letters to Schipano, he gave them to his sons to produce fine copies. Then the letters went to the Inquisition to receive the imprimatur, at which point numerous changes were demanded, as Gaetano and Lockhardt have indicated in their new edition of the first five letters written from Safavid Iran.[38] We may conclude that the enormous amount of time and labour invested by della Valle in revising his original letters was caused in part by expectations about possible demands from the Propaganda fide for the imprimatur. Della Valle wished to make sure that this time the Inquisition would allow his work to be printed and not, as had happened many times before, withhold its permission or worse, put the printed book on the index as happened to his book about Shah 'Abbas printed in 1629. A second factor that might help explain his extensive revision efforts may have been his assumption that a good history needed to be based on ancient authors, at least for the members of the Republic of Letters. A third factor, apparently, was his ambition, as della Valle wrote time and again, to become famous and immortal by publishing his letters. He surely considered the money, time and ink he spent on substantially revising many of his letters a wise investment.

Reflections on the conflicting usage of ancient authority in della Valle's writings

In the printed letters, della Valle complained occasionally about the lack of books that prevented him from identifying the ancient name of a certain river or mountain.[39] One of these complaints appears in the letter from Farahabad/Qazvin. There it is encapsulated within a passage referring to ancient authors and their books in the form he chose in Rome.[40] This location might indicate that we ought to consider the complaint as a later addition as well and regard it as almost topical. However, such regret is explicitly expressed in his original letters too; for instance, in one written from Baghdad on 23 December 1616. In this letter, he reports on his arrival in a town called by the Arabs 'el Her'. His Arab informants also told him that Jews founded the town in the time of Solomon. Della Valle doubts that one can trust the tradition and history as told by the 'ignorant Arabs'. God alone knows. 'But he himself', della Valle sighs, 'cannot recover the truth from the mist of change because beside the "Epitome geografica" I have no other book nor any help in these countries.'[41] Other than Filippo Ferrari's *Epitome geografica*, della Valle mentioned Pierre Bélon's travel report, Giovanni Battista Raimondi's Arabic alphabet, the French translation of Pietro Andrea Mattioli's commentary on Dioscorides' *Materia medica*, Franciscus Raphalengius' Latin-Arabic dictionary, Thomas Erpenius' Arabic grammar and a book by Marc Anton in French translation, which he either brought from Naples or encountered in Iran.[42] His cursory way of talking about encounters with European books while he was in Iran indicates that he did not search for them. It also indicates that most of the sources he quoted in his printed letters were not directly accessible to him while travelling, even if we allow for his using some books available in the libraries of the French and Venetian ambassadors in Istanbul and those of the missionaries in Isfahan or Goa. The lack of any quotation from ancient secular and religious sources in his printed letters from India, except the first one from Surat, suggests that we ought to reject the hypothesis that della Valle used such libraries when writing his original letters to Schipano. Although he browsed occasionally in his copy of Ferrari's geographical dictionary in order to identify modern Iranian rivers, towns or mountains while writing his letters in Iran, his only explicit statement that he spent time in the Carmelite convent of Isfahan explains that the purpose of his visit was to work on his translations of Persian treatises into Latin while sitting at a table, because there was no European-style table in his house.[43] Some of his rare references to Ferrari in his original letters imply that in the first years of his travels he identified this book as the authority guiding him on his difficult travels through the less familiar parts of the Ottoman Empire and Safavid Iran.[44] Later letters from Iran indicate that della Valle's attitude changed over time. He encountered too many contradictions between the early modern geographical and historical reality of the two Muslim countries and the knowledge found in Ferrari's book and in western European maps. He became increasingly sceptical about such information and began claiming that the knowledge he collected while visiting the region himself, and while reading and translating Persian and Arabic sources, could contribute substantially to correcting such faulty Western views.[45] Parallel to his rising distrust in early modern western European knowledge of Iran, della Valle's original letters not only express an increasing familiarity with the landscape of Iran and its nomenclature, but also a decreasing need for comparing this nomenclature with names found in ancient sources.

Della Valle also integrated ideas and judgements other than his references to ancient, medieval and early modern authors and texts into his letters when preparing them for print. A striking example is his report about a meeting with Father

Negrone, a Portuguese Franciscan, in Goa. This report is part of his letter from Surat written before della Valle ever set foot on Goan soil. Hence, this report cannot have been a part of his original letter. If he had carried this first letter to Goa and then added the report, it would have appeared as a postscript since this is how he proceeded in similar cases. The presence of this report in his letter from Surat can only mean that della Valle added it in Rome when preparing his letters for print. The function of this added report is to open the way for a comment. In this comment della Valle declared that good historical texts, particularly those concerning Indian matters, had to be based upon two elements: first, ancient history and geography and second, other humanistic studies and local sources accessed by the writer himself after having learnt the local languages. In both respects, della Valle exclaimed, Negrone was lacking and so were his books.

> But I had a somewhat longer talk with him in Goa, something I did not do in Persia. I found him of very little foundation in matters of ancient history and geography in accordance with all the religious (men) from Spain, and mostly the Portuguese, who give themselves little to other studies except to those that serve for preaching. I do not know, (however), how it can be possible to write good histories, and in particular about things of the Indians, about which he could gather information only through an interpreter, a method – as I have proved by experience – through which one often accumulates many errors.[46]

Della Valle's methodological claim, by virtue of having been added to the letters only when they were prepared for print, suggests that it was meant to apply only to printed histories, not to every kind of report about India and, by extension, Iran or the Ottoman Empire. Hence, the fact that della Valle's private and semi-public writings show a fundamentally different outlook indicates that the high visibility of ancient secular and religious references in his printed letters and his Latin geography of Iran does not signify an intellectual mentality, but a convention of printed learned literature propagated by the Republic of Letters and kept in place through various forms of censorship.

Because the printed letters differ in many aspects from the originals sent by della Valle to Schipano, the question arises whether they differ also in spirit. Della Valle denied this, assuring his readers that he only omitted private and politically sensitive statements, but given the enormous difference when it comes to references to authors and books in the two versions of the letters, this question can only be answered in the affirmative. The letters as originally composed by della Valle had a more individual and more Oriental outlook than the letters given to the printers. Many aspects of the original Oriental character of the letters were annihilated, including della Valle's researches into the administrative geography of Safavid Iran. As a consequence, the prominence of ancient geographical and historical names, quotations and judgements is much stronger than in the original letters. The description of Safavid Iran as a replica of the old Iranian empire of Cyrus or Darius is exclusively the result of della Valle's reading in Rome. Concepts of ancient geography, however, were present in the original letters and never disappeared completely. Della Valle was often preoccupied in his letters with determining whether a certain ancient name, territory, mountain, river or city corresponded to one he encountered in his own time. The original letters also indicate that the longer he lived in Iran the more reluctant he became to trust Filippo Ferrari's knowledge of Oriental geography. He repeatedly criticized Ferrari, explicitly or implicitly, for not being correct in spelling of Oriental names, the location of places and even their existence.

Della Valle's printed letters were used by French geographers in the second half of the seventeenth century as sources of new knowledge about the Ottoman and Safavid empires, which could allow them to modernize their maps. If they had worked with the original letters, rather than with the French translation of the printed ones, the impact of della Valle's knowledge acquired while travelling would have been much greater. However, the French mapmakers restored, to a degree, the spirit of della Valle's original letters since they ignored all references to ancient names and concepts and focused upon local contemporary knowledge.

The difference between ancient sources, contemporary Oriental geography and della Valle's own role as an agent of knowledge results from the fact that in the original letters, as written from the Middle East, ancient authority was almost completely absent. Della Valle had no use or need of ancient books while travelling through the Middle East. The books were not only too heavy to carry around, but they also made no sense when travelling with a caravan through the Arabian Desert, or riding with his new wife to inspect the ruins of ancient Babylonia in order to prove that Baghdad was a different city. Even remembering what he had learnt by heart from ancient religious and secular books was rarely worth the effort.

Notes

1. Jonas Hanway, *An historical account of the British trade over the Caspian sea: with a journal of travels from London through Russia into Persia; and back through Russia, Germany and Holland. To which are added, the revolutions of Persia during the present century, with the particular history of the great usurper Nadir Koala...* (London, 1753), vol. 1, p. 6.
2. *La geografia di Clavdio Ptolemeo Alessandrino,* Con alcuni comenti & aggiunte fatteui da Sebastiano Munstero Alamanno, Con le tauole non solamente antiche & moderne solite di stamparsi (Venice, 1548).
3. Iacopo Gastaldi 1559, Prima Parte della Asia; Re-edition Antonio Lafreri (Rome, 1570).
4. Abraham Ortelius, *Theatrum Orbis Terrarum* (Amsterdam, 1570), *Persici sive Sophorum Regni Typus*. Staatsbibliothek Berlin, Preussischer Kulturbesitz, Berlin, B 219.
5. 'Ma, prima che passiamo innanzi, descriuerò il sito del Mazanderàn, in generale; accioche V. S. possa riconoscerlo nelle carte Geografiche, e veder, se veramente è l'antica Hircania, ouero parte dell'Hircania, ò pur altra prouincia a quella vicina, come io più tosto penso.' *De'Viaggi di Pietro della Valle il Pellegrino Descritti da lui medesimo in Lettere familiari All'Erudito suo Amico Mario Schipano. Persia, Parte Prima* (Roma, 1658), p. 177.

6. When, for instance, telling Schipano that the Safavids take their dinner on the ground sitting on fine carpets, della Valle commented: 'Ma, che maraviglia? Anche in tempi anchissimi, non ci narra Senofonte (1) che quella bella ed onestissima Pantea, moglie del re de'Susiana, quando fu presa dall'esercito di Ciro, fu trovata ne suo padiglione, insieme con le sue ancelle, in terra a sedere? E che i tappeti servissero in Tiro a'suoi tempi appunto per sedervi sopra, non l'abbiamo da Ezechiel profeta (2)? ... (1) Cyropaed., lib. V. (2) Ezech. XXVII, 20.' Della Valle, *Viaggi*, vol. 1, p. 632. An analogous statement can be found only a few pages later when talking about ambassadorial gift-giving in Safavid Iran: 'Ed è costume fra di loro antico, poichè Filostrato ci accenna che i re medi, anche al tempo di Apollonio (1) non si andavano a vedere senza doni. ... (1) De Vita Apoll., lib. I, cap. 19' Della Valle, *Viaggi*, vol. 1, p. 650. There are several more remarks of this type in other letters of della Valle, all of them connected with quotations from, or references to, ancient authorities.

7. 'Questo Cinghiz, ... , fatto si al fin padrone di vn'immenso stato, e di quasi tutta la Tartaria, che comprende l'vna e l'altra Scithia; lo diuise poi morendo à suoi figliuoli. A Giagatà, che era suo figliuol secondogenito, toccò in sorte il paese di Samarcand, con tutta la Sogdiana, e diuerse altre terre di là intorno; & egli dal suo nome proprio lo chiamo Giagataio, e Giagataini tutti i popoli che restarono sótto al suo gouerno. Costume antichissimo de'Scithi, di dare à i paesi à loro soggetti il nome de'lor Principi, come ben si vede in Diodoro Siculo. Lib. 2', *De' Viaggi di Pietro della Valle il Pellegrino Descritti da lui medesimo in Lettere familiari All'Erudito suo Amico Mario Schipano. Parte Terza cioè L'India co'l Ritorno alla Patria* (Roma, 1663), p. 38.

8. 'Li II. Aprile per essere il giorno del mio Natale, feci di questo dì la data della lettera dedicatoria nel mio Trattato. *De Regionibus subiectis recentiori Persarum Imperio*, che haueuo animo di mandare in luce.' Penultimate letter to Schipano, Roma, 11 July 1626. Della Valle, *Viaggi* III, p. 498.

9. 'Babylonia regio, cum aliquot ex adiacentibus terries, a recentioribus Persis ad hanc usque diem antiquo nomine in sacris litteris memorato, Araq nuncupatur; cuius nominis interpretatio est sudor tum quia vehemens in illis terries calor est aestivis temporibus, tum etiam fortasse quia paucis admodum humefactae pluviis, non nisi deductis a fluviis magno quidem sudore rivis, terrae illae fertiles redduntur. Verum quia Araq nomen duplex est: Araq nimirum Arabia<e> et Araq Agiamia<e> (Agiam enim, sive Agem, universas Persarum dominio subiacentes dicunt regiones); pro Araq Arabia<e> Babyloniam et adiacentes terras Turcarum hodie imperio parentes intelligunt. Unde recto tramite si orientem versus proficiscaris superatis montibus regionis Kurdistan qui, Tauri quodammo rami, a septemtrione in meridiem excurrentes Persicum imperium a Turcico disterminant, statim Persicae dictionis prima occurrit regio Araq Agiamia et eius pars provincia Hamadan, cuius metropolis est Hamadan civitas eaque pars, ut opinor, antiquae vel Persidis vel Susianae in finibus Medorum.' P. Della Valle, 'De recentiori imperio Persarum subiectis regionibus', ed. Gamalero, E. *Studi Iranici* 17 (1977), pp. 287–303; 288; the acute parentheses indicate a correction of the edited text on the basis of the manuscript. The English translation is from Sonja Brentjes and Volkmar Schüller, 'Pietro della Valle's Latin Geography of Safavid Iran (1624–1628): Introduction.' *Journal of Early Modern History* 10 (3), 2006, pp. 169–219, see p. 189.

10. See, for another example, della Valle's description of Azerbaijan:
    'Adherbaigian, cuius interpretatio est ignis cultores, procul dubio Media est antiquorum seu potius, ut melius dicam, pars eius praecipua et magna; regio est montana, per quam institutum superius iter norduestem versus prosequenco, transgresso primum haud <spernendae magnitudinis> fluvio qui in Caspium excurrens persice nunc Sepid-rud, hoc est albus fluvius, turcico vero nomine vulgo Qizil-uzen, quasi rubeus natans vel aureus natans appellatur, sed quis nam esset apud antiquos non facile reperio, praeter alia permulta loca minus memoratu digna, insigniores reperiuntur civitates duae: Ardebil nempe magis ad orientem sita, peregrinationis meae ex ea parte terminus, Persarum hodie sanctuarium regumque hisce temporibus in Perside regnantium mausoleaum ob insignem quemdam ex eorem maioribus virum celebremque populis sanctimoniae fama quem, licet ipse rex non extiterit, nescio tamen an religionis an progeniei dignitatis gratia seu quia proprio sic nomine vocaretur, passim Sciah Sofì, hoc est regem selectum et sincere amicum sive religiosum, quod idem est apud illos, appellant et regum qui nunc

regnant progenitorem et Sciaitarum sectae in Agiamia nisi primum auctorem, praecipuum certe resuscitatorem ibi sepultum.

Magis vero ad occidentem in eodem quasi paralelo sita est Tebriz civitas, sedes et ipsa olim regum, frequentibus bellis inter Persas ac Turcas saepe vastata, saepius hinc inde capta, saepissime oppugnata, adhuc demum permanens iisdem de causis fama super aethera nota. Reliquas Adherbaigian civitates, cum eas ipse non viderim, sub silentio praetereo; tantum subiungam Adherbaigian regionem habere ab oriente maiore ex parte Araq Agiamia<e>, ab occidente septemtrionem versus Armeniam, cuius portio Persici imperii pars est hodie et Turcis confini, a septemtrione autem Ghilàn et alias antiquae Mediae supra mare Caspium magis septemtrionales partes, ubi olim Caddusii, Mardi et his similes memorabantur, a meridie vero Araq similiter partes, ni fallor.' Gamalero, 'Della Valle', pp. 288–9; the acute parentheses indicate a correction of the edited text according to the manuscript.

(Translation from Brentjes and Schüller: 'The Safavid court in the 17th century')

'Adherbaigian, the translation of which is 'the worshippers of the fire' is doubtless the ancients' Media, or rather, as I put it better, its excellent and great part. The region is mountainous. If one follows the upper way towards north-west, one transgresses first a river of remarkable size that flows into the Caspian Sea. (This river) is called now in Persian Sepid-rud, i.e. the white river, but in Turkish it is designated by the ordinary name Qizil-uzen, i.e. that which generates blackberry-red or golden-coloured. Which (river) this may be according to the ancients, I cannot discover easily. Beside many other places that are barely worth mentioning there are two more important cities: Ardebil, indeed, is farther east, the terminus of my peregrination in this area. (There is) today the sanctuary of the Persians and the mausoleum of the kings who reign today in Persia because of some man who stood out among their greatest and was famous among the population through the legend of (his) pious life, even if he himself was not a king. I do not know, however, whether he was called everywhere Sciah Sofì, i.e., 'the chosen and upright friendly or pious king' – which is the same for them – due to the faith and the dignity of descent or because of his proper name. They also call him the ancestor of the currently reigning kings and, if not the first founder of the sect of the Shi'ites in Agiamia, at least the outstanding restorer who is buried there.

Situated more towards the west, on almost the same parallel [as Ardebil] is Tebriz, once the royal seat, often devastated through the repeated wars between Persians and Turks, often captured by this or that party, more often besieged, and widely known due to these reasons. The remaining cities of Adherbaigiàn I pass over with silence since I have not seen them myself. There is so much the region of Adherbaigian borders on: in the east, the larger part of Araq of Agiamia, in the west, towards the north, Armenia which today is partly a member of the Persian Empire and is limited by the Turks, in the north too, Ghilàn and other more northern parts of ancient Media at the Caspian Sea – there where once the Caddusians, Mardians and the like were (placed) – but in the south in (again) parts of Araq, if I do not err.'

11. 'Alia est Derbend, quod nomen persice sonat quasi <P>ortae <L>igamen, ut ut Latinius <seu Caspiae> seu Caucasia<e> seu Ferrea<e> Porta<e> nuncupe<n>tur. Sed cum confusione scriptorum et quoad situm et quoad nomen huius urbis aliqua inducta sit obscuritas, non incongruum mihi videtur quod repperi apud orientales auctores hic aperire. Tria haec profecto valde confundunt Latini civitatum nomina ita ut non facile sit dignosci quae fuerint antiquorum Porta Ferrea, quae Porta Caspia et quae Porta Caucasia. Turcae hanc de qua loquebamur Derbend, portae nominis, ut puto, similitudine inducti, eorum lingua Demir-capì, Ferream nimirum Portam communiter appellant, unde forsitan recentioribus nostris orta est confusio. Arabes vero et Persae geographi, Turcis procul dubio eruditiores, alteram ab altera clarius distinguunt, nam quae a Persis Derbend nuncupatur ab Arabibus dicitur Bab el abvàb, id est porta portarum et diversa nimis recensetur a Porta Ferrea; quam, huiusmet significationis vocabulo, Arabes Bab el hadìd, Persae autem Der Ahanin appellant et longe admodum a Derbènd, Caspioque mari magis orientalem, in tractu quarti climatis reponunt, plusquam

viginti sex graduum longitudinis; et septem fere latitudinis differentia. Derbend enim quam commemorabamus in quinto climate ab iisdem constituitur, ad litus, ut dixi, Caspii maris occidentale; et cum illa sub imperio Chacqàn (magni scilicet cuiusdam orientalium Tartarorum Regis) describatur, haec Persis paret et ultima est hodie Persarum ditionis prope Caucasios <M>ontes', Gamalero, 'Della Valle', p. 291.

(Translation from Brentjes and Schüller: 'The Safavid court in the 17th century': 'The other (city) is Derbend. This name means in Persian something like the belt of the door even if it is called by the Latins either <Caspian>, Caucasian or Iron door<s>. But because of the confusion among the writers with regard to the position as well as the name of this city, a certain want of clearness has been created. (I)t does not appear inappropriate to me to present here what I have discovered in the (books of) oriental authors. The Latins confuse indeed very greatly these three names of (cities), so that it is not easy to differentiate which (cities) the ancients (have named) Porta<e> Ferrea<e>, Porta<e> Caspia<e>, and Porta<e> Caucasia<e>. The Turks usually call in their language that (city) which we spoke of as Derbend Demir-capì, induced by the similarity of the name "door" as I believe. (This) is undoubtedly Porta Ferrea which perhaps has caused the confusion among our contemporaries. The Arabs, however, and the Persian geographers, who are without doubt more learned than the Turks, differentiate the one clearly from the other. The one, which the Persians call Derbend, the Arabs call Bab elabvàb – that is, door of the doors. It is found to be completely different from Porta Ferrea. This one the Arabs call literally Bab elhadìd, but the Persians Der Ahanin. They situate it far away from Derbènd and farther east from the Caspian Sea, namely more than 26 degrees longitude and almost seven degrees latitude away, in the fourth climate. Derbend namely, which we have mentioned, is put into the fifth climate, at the western border of the Caspian Sea, as I said. While that (city) was described as being under the rule of the Chacqàn (i.e. of the great king of these eastern Tatars), this one is subject of the Persians. Today, it is the outermost border of the Persians' dominion, near to the Caucasian mountains.'

12. Ms Città del Vaticano, Biblioteca Apostolica Vaticana, Ottobonianus latinus 3382, fos. 3b, 7b, 12a–13a, 15a, 22a, 36a, 36b, 38a, 38b, 124b.
13. Ms Ottobonianus 3382, fos. 24a, 39a, 52a, 59b, 83a, 84a, 138a, 150b, 154b.
14. Ms Ottobonianus 3382, fo. 150b: 'Don Garzia da Silua y Figheroa, che fu in Persia Ambas.r di Spagna, et era huomo dotto d'historia, diceua che Quinto Curtió ne fa mentione come di cosa antichissima anco altro tempo;...'
15. Ms Ottobonianus 3382, fo. 150b '...; Io non ho qui Quinto Curtio per uederlo, ne altro libro da potei consultare,...'
16. Ms Ottobonianus 3382, fo. 150b: '...Cehil minar a pie (sic) del Monte che gli sta congiunto per leuante, ʌ e della cui pietra é facta la fabrica,... ʌ: come a conto dice Diodoro Siculo...'
17. Ms Ottobonianus 3382, fos. 22a, 36a, 38a, 38b.
18. Ms Ottobonianus 3382, fos. 52a, 165a.
19. Ms Ottobonianus 3382, fos. 47a, 124b.
20. Ms Ottobonianus 3382, fo. 55b.
21. Ms Ottobonianus 3382, fo. 83a.
22. 'Ho qualche... che possono esser la ruina di C... fonte Citta famosa... Vedi la Geographia Persiana intitolata (in Persian: Mesalik-e Memalik) alla Città (in Arabic: Mada'in).' Ms Città del Vaticano, Biblioteca Apostolica Vaticana, Ottobonianus latinus 3382, fo. 55b; 'Mesalik Memalik Geografia Persia: Medain, che in Arabico uel dir due città, uuol che sin. Tesofontes in Persiano, dunque bene, secondo Strabone, Seleucia e Tesifonte. erano... in un luogo: e però due città p<er> (?) Clima 3. Madain.' Ms Città del Vaticano, Biblioteca Apostolica Vaticana, Ottobonianus latinus 3384, fo. 79b; 'Medain <repeated in Arabic>/ Tesdid.../ Medain é Ctesiphon secondo la Geografia Persiana.' Ms Città del Vaticano, Biblioteca Apostolica Vaticana, Ottobonianus latinus 3385, vol. 1, fo. 64a.
23. Ms Ottobonianus 3382, fos. 38a–b.
24. Ms Ottobonianus 3382, see, for instance, fos. 64a, 67a, 68b.
25. Ms Ottobonianus 3382, fo. 48a.

26. Ms Ottobonianus 3382, fos. 40a, 45b, 77b.
27. Ms Ottobonianus 3382, fos. 263b, 265b, 266a, 285b, 286a, 290b.
28. Ms Ottobonianus 3382, fo. 277b.
29. Ms Ottobonianus 3382, see, for instance, fos. 265b, 278b, 281b.
30. Ms Ottobonianus 3384, fos. 130a–131a.
31. Ms Ottobonianus 3382, fo. 291a.
32. See, for instance, Ms Ottobonianus 3384, fos. 33a–37b (Rimesse nella 3 Lettera da Sphahan), 53a–56b (Rimesse nelle Lettere della Persia. Lra. i. Sphahan), and 57a–b.
33. Ms Ottobonianus 3384, fos. 70a–71b.
34. Ms Ottobonianus 3384, fos. 72a–72b.
35. Ms Ottobonianus 3384, fo. 72a.
36. See, for instance, *Viaggi di Pietro della Valle Il Pellegrino Descritti da lui medesimo in lettere familiari all'erudito suo amico Mario Schipano divisi in tre parti cioè La Turchia, La Persia e l'India colla Vita e Ritratto dell'Autore* (Brighton, 1843), vol. 1, pp. 12–13.
37. Ms Ottobonianus 3384, fos. 76a–80b.
38. 'Il testo ... non è passato integralmente nelle varie edizioni per gli interventi della censura ecclesiastica che modificò alcune espressioni che sembrarono troppo vivaci o sconvenienti e cancellò alcuni passi che attaccavano un certo tipo di politica missionaria ovvero apparivano equivoci o compromettenti; solo dopo queste modifiche – poco numerose per la *Turchia* e per l'*India*, molto più frequenti e importanti per le *Lettere dalla Persia* – l'opera fu data alle stampe.' *I Viaggi di Pietro della Valle. Lettere dalla Persia.* Tomo I. A cura di F. Gaeta e L. Lockhart (Roma, 1972), pp. XIX–XXI.
39. See, for instance, della Valle, *Viaggi*, vol. 1, pp. 448, 625, 646, 780.
40. Della Valle, *Viaggi*, vol. 1, p. 780.
41. Ms Città del Vaticano, Archivio Segreto, Archivio Della Valle – del Bufalo 51, letter from Baghdad, 18 December 1616, unpaginated. Della Valle kept this passage unaltered in his printed letters, see della Valle, *Viaggi*, vol. 1, p. 357.
42. See, della Valle, *Viaggi*, vol. 1, pp. 509, 605, 737; vol. 2, pp. 50–1.
43. Ibid., vol. 2, p. 226.
44. See Ms – del Bufalo 51, letter from Istanbul dated 27 June 1615, where della Valle calls Ferrari's book 'our Epitome geografica', although it did not provide him with what he was looking for – the name used in western Europe for Bitlis.
45. See della Valle, *Viaggi*, vol. 2, pp. 219, 264 and so on. In his letter from Shiraz written on 27 July 1622, for instance, della Valle distanced himself from the very same book, now calling it 'Ferrari's Epitome': 'Fra Filippo Ferrari nella sua Epitome geografica attribuisce il nome di Bendemir al fiume, il quale crede (1) che dai Latini fosse detto *Bagradas* o Brisoana, ma s'inganna, chè Bendemir è nome del ponte, e non del fiume, ed io nel suo libro che ho appresso di me ve l'ho notato in margine.' Della Valle, *Viaggi*, vol. 2, p. 264.
46. 'Ma hauendo io in Goa discorso con lui più à lungo, che non feci in Persia, l'hò trouato molto poco fondato nelle materia d'historie antiche, e della Geografia, conforme à tutti i Religiosi di Spagna, e massime di Portogallo, che poco si danno ad altri studij, fuorche à quel che serue à predicare: onde senza buon fondamento d'historia antica, e di Geografia, e d'altre lettere humane, non sò come possa scriuer bène historie, e particolarmente delle cose degli Indiane; de'quali anco solo per Interprete hà potuto informarsi; nel qual modo io per isperienza hò prouato, che si pigliano spesso molti errori.' Della Valle, *Viaggi* III, p. 85.

20

The Image of the Safavids in English and French Literature (1500–1800)

Parvin Loloi

The 2002 summer special exhibition at the Uffizi Gallery in Florence was devoted to the Myth of Europa. Towards the end of the exhibition there were a group of portraits by Cristofano dell'Altissimo (1530–1605) of the world's important personalities. The explanatory labels in English read:

> In the course of the 16th Century, the cornerstone in political history of Europe, the 'political Europe' was invested with images that were very different from those of the ancient myth... In an important painting, *The Allegory of the Abdication of Charles V* (by Frans Francken II, Circa 1636) the 'political' Europe is a beautiful lady endowed with Imperial emblems: together with the rest of the world, including Oceans, she is present at the historical event which gives shape to Modern Europe, to Europe that comprises distinct, autocratic states or those strengthened by the subdivision of the Empire. Together with a reproduction of the painting, there is a selection of portraits, all originating from the collections of Florentine galleries, depicting the rulers of the main European states and of Italy in 1555, the protagonists and important witnesses of the great event, including Suleiman the Magnificent, the aggressive challenger to European Christianity.

Among these portraits (though not exhibited) are those of Shah Ismail (1501–24) and Shah Tahmasp I (1524–76). This changing image and attitude was reflected in all aspects of European life and was naturally employed by writers in the West.

The founder of the Safavid dynasty was introduced to the West as early as 1508 by Giovanni Rota. His *La Vita del Sophi, Re de Persia et de Media* was translated into French by Jean Lemaire de Belges a year later as *L'histoire moderne du prince Schach Ysmail, dit Sophy Arduelin*. This was reprinted in many editions of Lemaire's various works during the first half of the sixteenth century.[1] Jennifer Britnell in her introduction to a 1997 edition of the works of Lemaire writes, 'Lemaire impose au phénomène qu'est le prince Isma'il une interprétation antipapale' [Lemaire attaches an antipapal interpretation to the phenomenon that is Prince Isma'il].[2] In contriving to give an anti-papal twist to his history of the Persian king, Lemaire set a precedent for later European writers by employing the Safavids to mirror and criticize the social and political life of the West. As the sixteenth century progressed, more published works, especially travellers' accounts (along with ideas and information transmitted orally), became important sources for both French and English writers. The adventures of the Sherley brothers from England and the later visit of Mohammad Reza Bayg, Shah 'Abbas's envoy, to the court of Louis XIV seem to have inspired the writers of the two countries, an inspiration that manifests itself in a variety of literary forms.

The dominant sixteenth-century British view of Persia was the same as that of the classical era. The traditional medieval and Renaissance image of Persia was, as Anthony Parr writes, of a 'land of wealth and luxury, with a glorious imperial past, [Persia] was for Western writers a genuinely exotic country, not a malign and unknowable neighbour but a fabulous resource'.[3] This is exactly how English writers sought to present the Persian court and the Sophy, both to amuse and to enrich their own works. Anthony Jenkinson's description of Shah Tahmasp's court is included in Michael Drayton's long poem *Poly-Olbion*. Drayton writes that Jenkinson:

> Adventured to view rich *Persias* wealth and pride
> Whose true report thereof, the *English* since have tride.[4]

Fabian, in Shakespeare's *Twelfth Night* says: 'I will not give my part of this sport for a pension/of thousands to be paid from the Sophy' (II, v, 180–1). Later on in the play, in a duel scene between the disguised Viola and Sir Andrew Aguecheek, Sir Toby Belch remarks: 'They say he has been fencer to the Sophy' (III, iv, 283–4). The first of these passages refers to Anthony Sherley and the second to his brother Robert. Shakespeare probably had first-hand knowledge of the Sherley brothers' adventures in Persia through Will Kemp, the famous actor and comedian of the time, who met Anthony Sherley in 1601 in Rome and was probably a relation of the Sherley family.[5] Another one of Shakespeare's references to the Sophy worth mentioning is when the prince of Morocco, in *The Merchant of Venice*, claims that he has taken part in the wars between the Turks and the Persians and, exhibiting a scimitar, says:

> by this scimitar
> That slew the Sophie, and a Persian Prince
> That won three fields of Sultan Solyman[.]
> (II, i, 24–6)

Dr Samuel Johnson, in annotating this passage, believed that Shakespeare's geography was at fault and wrote ironically that the Prince of Morocco must have travelled far to kill the Sophy of Persia.[6]

The lives of Anthony and Robert Sherley prompted several English writers to try their hand at either biographical sketches or plays. The most notable of these is *Travels of the Three English Brothers*, by John Day, William Rowley and George Wilkins. It is closely based on Anthony Nixon's pamphlet, *The Three English Brothers* (1607), which is believed to have been commissioned by Thomas Sherley who, after being freed from a Turkish prison, had returned to England in December 1606. Although the play was performed a few weeks before Nixon's pamphlet was published, it is thought that the dramatists must have had access either to Nixon's manuscript, or to a common source also employed by Nixon.[7] The play, apart from glorifying the chivalric deeds of the brothers, is heavily based on the notion that Persia could join forces with Europe to fight the Ottoman expansion, and that the Islamic religion of Persia was rather different from that of the Turks. In 1609 Thomas Middleton, in a pamphlet to promote Robert Sherley's embassy to Europe, 'carefully omits from the description of Persia any reference to Islam and almost all suggestion of hedonistic luxury. This is a spartan state in which Persians "seem more like Protestants than like Turks in their religion" and customs, and are thus a worthy ally against the Ottoman threat. The writers of *Travels* are altogether more eclectic in their portrayal of Europe's potential war partner. Like Middleton they make use of pre-Islamic descriptions of Persian society – many of which were reproduced in supposedly up-to-date geographies and ethnographies'.[8] The play also has its share of Renaissance stereotypes – with the brutal Turk and the caricatured Jew – but, as has been suggested by Anthony Parr,

> they co-exist with, and in a sense help to support, a fairly complex dramatization of cultural encounter. Cultural difference is in fact the play's principal theme. The English negotiations at the Persian court, which span politics, religion, the ethics of war and mixed marriage, provide a sort of frame for arguments between Persians and Turks over Islamic doctrine, Christian-Jewish antipathy in Venice, and an encounter between the two great acting traditions of English stage and the Italian *commedia dell'arte*.[9]

Two later plays, *The Sophy* (1642) by Sir John Denham, and *Mirza, A Tragedy* (1647 or 1655) by Robert Baron, are based on the life of Shah 'Abbas and the blinding of his son. The plays are inspired by Thomas Herbert's *A Relation of Some Years Travaile* (London, 1634). The supposed occurrences at the court of Shah 'Abbas are described on pages 97 to 99 of Herbert. In one passage (marked by a marginal note reading 'The Kings cruelties') Herbert typically presents Shah 'Abbas as rather 'a bloudie Tyrant, than so famous a King' (p. 99). Here, in the eyes of a relatively unsophisticated and badly informed traveller, the historical 'Abbas has been turned into the most enduring stereotype 'of medieval and renaissance thought – the cruel Oriental tyrant. Such figures peopled the pages of historians such as Richard Knolles, in his *Generalle Historie of the Turkes* (1603), and strode the stages of Elizabethan and Jacobean London in play after play. Most such figures are Turkish'.[10] The same is true of French thought and literature, of which I will write later. There are certainly some historical inaccuracies in the account Herbert gives. In the introduction to my editions of these plays I have written in some detail about these inaccuracies. Of the two plays Denham's *Sophy* is more successful. It became very popular and was performed both at court by the King's Men and at Blackfriars. It is a fine example of verse drama and it was called 'one of the best tragedies of its time'[11] by A. W. Ward. Denham was a staunch royalist and many passages in the play refer to contemporary political events and situations, such as when the following words are put into the king's (Abbas's) mouth:

> Talk not to me of Treasures, or Exchequers
> Send for five hundred of the wealthiest Burgers
> Their shops and ships are my Exchequer.
> (I, ii, 52–5)

The allusion here is to Charles I's attempt to raise funds through the imposition of ship money.

Baron's *Mirza* is a generally inferior play. There is no record that it was ever performed. At the time of writing *Mirza*, Baron was a young man of 25 and inexperienced; it is not surprising, then, that his verse lacks the maturity of Denham's, but it must be said that he follows the events described in Herbert more closely. The introduction of a ghost to torment the protagonist in the opening scene reminds one of *Hamlet*, and his 'villain has something of Iago's appreciation for the ironies of his clever plots'.[12] It is hard to see any substantial relation with contemporary events in *Mirza*, but Baron's readers and supporters clearly saw such links. In a dedicatory poem by John Quarles, a fellow of Peterhouse, Cambridge, we read:

> Our *Isle a Mirz'* and *Allybeg* can give.
> Thus Text and Time doe sute, and whilst you tell
> Your Tale, wee'l easily find a parallell.[13]

While Denham's *Sophy* has ancestors and predecessors in the tradition of serious ethical drama, Baron's '*Mirza* belongs almost wholly in the line of chamber or closet tragedies'.[14] They both, however, represent the vogue in palace intrigue, which became very popular in the literature of the seventeenth and eighteenth centuries.

William Cartwright's play *The Royal Slave* was perhaps the most performed and successful of the plays written about Shah 'Abbas's life. There is no written evidence of its source but more than likely the intriguing and sensational story of Shah 'Abbas' election of a temporary king in 1591 to replace him on the throne for a few days before executing him was transmitted orally by one of the Englishmen long resident in Persia (such as the Sherleys, Powell, Ward, Herbert). It was first performed in front of Charles I and his Queen, Henrietta Maria, on 30 August 1636 at Christ Church, Oxford. The elaborate scenery and the Persian costumes were designed by Inigo

Jones (unfortunately, these designs have not survived), and the music was composed by Henry Lawes. The writer and the other performers were students at Christ Church at the time. The performance was liked by the royal party: 'the Lord Chamberlain was so transported with it, that he swore mainly he never saw such a play before.'[15] In November it was played by the King's Players and, at the request of the Queen, at Hampton Court. Its success probably owed much to its exotic and elaborate scenery and costumes, as well as to its music. The story is transposed to ancient times and Platonic love is its underlying theme. The Ephesian prisoner behaves so nobly as a temporary king that he 'win[s] the admiration of the Persian court and a divine and royal reprieve'.[16] The three main characters 'conduct themselves with absolute rationality, justice, and virtue. Nonetheless, in adapting to ancient times the story of Shah Abbas and the "mock king", Cartwright preserves some emphasis on themes of rule and justice.'[17] Dryden must have had the 'mock king' in mind when he wrote in his play *Aurang-Zebe* (1675):

> ... I'm to die in state.
> They lodge me as I were the *Persian* King:
> And with luxurious Pomp my death they bring.
>
> (IV, i, 6–8)

After the Restoration a renewal of interest in all things Persian was evident in British life. Samuel Pepys, the famous diarist and courtier, wrote on 8 October 1666, that '[t]he king hath yesterday in council declared his resolution of setting a fashion for clothes, which he will never alter. It will be a vest, I know not well how. But it is to teach the nobility thrift, and will be good.'[18] John Evelyn wrote, ten days later, of 'it being the first time of his *Majesties* putting himselfe solemnley into the *Eastern fashion* of Vest, changing doublet, stiff Collar, [bands] & Cloake &c: into a comely Vest, after the *Persian* mode with girdle or sash, & Shoe strings & Garters, into bouckles, of which some were set with precious stones, resolving never to alter it.'[19] It must have been a spectacle to see the whole of the British court clad in Persian costume, as they rushed to follow the king's example. It did not last, however, and the king had 'to alter it' soon after. The choice of Persian costume was part of a campaign of reaction against excessive French influence on courtly fashions. There were both economic and anti-French messages in the action. In retaliation, Pepys writes on 22 November, 'the King of France [Louis XIV], hath, in defiance to the King of England, caused all his footmen to be put into Vests, and that the noblemen of France will do the like'.[20]

However, there was no similar competition between the two countries in literature. Rebecca Joubin in her excellent article observes that,

> [w]riting in the context of a French society that had been captivated by all things Oriental since the 17th-century Eastern travels of such French voyagers as Jean Baptiste Tavernier and Sir John Chardin, and Antoine Galland's translation into

French of *A Thousand and One Nights* (1704-17), the philosophes established a subgenre of Orientalist discourse in 18th-century French literature that used the topos of Oriental as Other as a lens through which to provide an indirect, albeit potent, means of cultural self-criticism. One example is Charles de Secondat de Montesquieu's *Lettres Persanes* (1721).[21]

After Lemaire's History, and before the appearance of Montesquieu's book, there were at least a dozen novels and plays featuring Persian characters, but the greater part of French Oriental literature was Turkish-based as Pierre Martino writes:

> le persan ne se distingua jamais bien du Turc: ils voisinaient tous deux géographiquement; leur religion était pareille d'aspect, et leurs moeurs semblables; il n'y avait point de voyageur qui visitât un de ces pays sans parcourir au moins les provinces frontières de l'autre. Le Persan fut donc une variété du Turc, si l'on peut dire; et jamais il n'obtint un premier rôle. Il eut bien quelques succès passagers, d'abord vers 1720 à la venue d'une ambassade persane et lors de la publication des *Letters persanes*.[22]

> [The Persian was not very distinct from the Turk: geographically they were neighbours; their religion appeared similar and their customs alike; there was no traveller who visited one of these countries without having at least traversed the frontier provinces of the other. One might say, then, that the Persian was a kind of Turk; and he never took a leading role. He had, for sure, certain passing successes, starting around 1720 with the coming of a Persian embassy and then with the publication of the *Persian Letters*.]

The first of these works worthy of mention is a short novel or român, entitled *Tachmas, Prince de Perse, nouvelle historique arrivée sous le Sophy Séliman aujourd'hui règnant* (Paris, 1676). The author signs himself H.F.M. It was translated into English in the same year by P. Porter as *Tachmas Prince of Persia: An Historical Novel, which happen'd under the Sophy Seliman who Reigns at this day*. Andrée Mansau provides a detailed study of the book in his article 'La Perse ou la Castration de L'Imaginaire au XVIIéme Siècle'. The novel is based on Chardin's description of un *Courennement du Roi de perse Soliman II* (1671). It is supposedly based on the life of Shah Safi II (Sulaiman).[23] *Tachmas* is in effect a romance about palace intrigues which could happen as readily at the court of Louis XIV as at the Persian court. Mansau writes:

> la peinture de la Perse présentée dans *Tachmas* montre le renouvellement des formes du roman baroque à la nouvelle classique, mais surtout l'effacement de l'imaginaire, du vraisemblable et des ornements étrangers au profit d'une peinture des sentiments ... La connaissance des civilasations et des moeurs persanes

ne l'empêche pas de peindre des amants qui possèdent le langage et la psychlogie en usage à la Cour de France.²⁴

[The picture of Persia presented in *Tachmas* shows the revival of the forms of the baroque romance in a new classicism, but above all the erasure of the imaginative, the authentic and of foreign embellishments in favour of the portrayal of sentiments... Knowledge of Persian culture and customs does not hinder the portrayal of lovers who possess the language and psychology current at the French court.]

Mezetin grand sophy de Perse was performed on 20 July 1689. In it the author Delosme de Monchnay dresses the French bourgeoisie in Persian costume, although the setting of the play is, in fact, Chinese – the first signs of the West's interest in Chinoiserie. Like most French comedies of the period, however, it is little more than a replica of Italian comedy, despite its exotic setting.²⁵ At the end of 1715 the visit to Paris of Mohammad Reza Bayg, the Persian ambassador, provoked the curiosity of the Parisians. His strange behaviour (in French eyes) is recorded by Saint Simon in his *Memoires*,²⁶ and also prompted the production of *Amazolide* (1716), a satirical novel in which the vulgar (and secret) adventures of the Persian ambassador are related.²⁷ Saint Simon's account of Mohammad Reza Bayg was also very influential on Montesquieu's *Persian Letters*. Much has been written on the *Lettres Persanes*,²⁸ where Montesquieu introduces a new genre to the mainstream of French literature. Despite his critical attacks on both Persian and French social orders, he speaks (through Usbek) rather affectionately of Shah Abbas:

Le monarque qui a si longtemps régné n'est plus. Il a bien fait parler des gens pendant sa vie; tout le monde s'est tu à sa mort. Ferme et courageux dans ce dernier moment, il a paru ne céder qu'au destin. Ainsi mourut le grand Chah Abas, après avoir rempli toute la Terre de son nom.²⁹

[The monarch who has reigned so long is no more. Certainly he made some people talk when he was alive; everyone fell silent at his death. Firm and courageous in this last moment, he appeared to give in to fate alone. Thus died the great Shah Abbas, after having filled the whole world with his name.]

Voltaire, on the other hand, seems to be somewhat ill-informed and confused in his discussion of Persia in his *Essai sur les Moeurs et l'Esprit des Nations*. At one point he thinks that the great cities in Persia, such as Isfahan were built by Arabs,³⁰ and later on he writes '[t]out ce qu'on nous dit de la Perse nous persuade qu'il n'y avait point de pays monarchique où l'on jouit plus des droits de l'humanité.' [Everything that we have been told about Persia convinces us that there is no monarchical country where one enjoys more human rights.] He adds further, '[i]l le fut, à ce qu'on prétend, sous le règne de Sha-Abbas, qu'on a appelé *le Grand*. Ce prétendu grand homme était très cruel; mais il y a des examples que des hommes féroces ont aimé l'ordre et le bien public. La cruauté ne s'exerce que sur des particuliers exposés sans cesse à la vue du tyran, et ce tyran est quelquefois par ses lois le bienfaiteurs de la patrie.'[31] [It has been claimed that during the reign of Shah Abbas he was called *the Great*. This supposed great man was very cruel; but there are some examples of violent men loving order and the public good. Their cruelty is only visited on those individuals constantly exposed to the tyrant's view, and this tyrant is sometimes through his laws the benefactor of the country.]

The works I have mentioned here – however briefly – provide examples of how the Safavids were presented in French and English literature. Traditionally, Western authors have looked to the East in order to enrich their own work. The works of both English and French writers, though often fanciful and remote from the historical accounts transmitted by historians and or travellers are, nevertheless, complex in character. They seek both to transmit cultural differences and similarities and, through the use of Persian themes, comment on contemporary events in Europe. In seventeenth-century England, stories from Safavid Iran provided a coded language in which, in the years around the Civil War, political issues and personalities (too dangerous to discuss openly) could be examined. In France, the Safavids were often employed as a means of self-criticism, of satirical observations of French habits of thought and behaviour. Satire is the most powerful and in some ways ruthless form of criticism and French writers in particular developed the form to its highest degree; it also did not escape the attention of some of the English writers. I will end this chapter by quoting a few lines from Samuel Butler (1612–80), the well-known English poet and satirist of the seventeenth century. In a satirical poem on women, he writes:

> The Sophy give's his Bauds Commission
> To Leavy, for his own Provision
> The Brightest Bewtys, and to choose
> Those that are fittest for his use
> With Power, by Privy-search, to try
> Their fitnes, and Ability
>
> If they Rest quietly t'explore
> Or in their sleep break winde, or snore.[32]

Notes

1. These include Lemaire's major work, *Les Illustrations de Gaule et singularitez de Troie* (first published 1509), and *Traicté de la différence des Schismes et des conciles de l'Église* (first published 1511).
2. Jean Lemaire de Belges, *Traicté de la différence des Schismes et des conciles de l'Église avec l'Histoire du Prince Sophy et autres oevres*, ed. Jennifer Britnell (Genève, 1997), p. 44.
3. Anthony Parr, ed., *Three Renaissance Travel Plays* (Manchester, 1995), p. 11.
4. Michael Drayton, *The Works*, ed. J. William Hebel, vol. IV, *Poly-Olbion* (Oxford, 1961), p. 403.

5. Samuel C. Chew, *The Crescent and the Rose: Islam and England during the Renaissance* (New York, 1965), pp. 275-6.
6. Quoted in Chew, *The Crescent and the Rose*, p. 253.
7. Parr, *Three Renaissance Travel Plays*, pp. 7-8.
8. Ibid., pp. 11-12.
9. Ibid., pp. 12-14.
10. Parvin Loloi, ed., *Two Seventeenth-Century Plays*: vol. I, *The Sophy* by Sir John Denham; vol. II, *Mirza, A Tragedy* by Robert Baron (Salzburg, 1998), the quotation is taken from the introduction to *The Sophy*, p. xvii.
11. Loloi, *The Sophy*, p. lv.
12. Linda McJannet, 'Bringing in a Persian', *Medieval and Renaissance Drama in England*, 12 (1999), p. 255.
13. Loloi, *Mirza*, p. 3.
14. Ibid., p. lix.
15. Quoted in Chew, *The Crescent and the Rose*, p. 515. Also see Stephen Orgel and Roy Strong, *Inigo Jones; the Theatre of the Stuart Court*, vol. 2 (California, 1973), pp. 828-9.
16. McJannet, 'Bringing in a Persian', p. 252.
17. Ibid., p. 523.
18. Robert Latham and Mathews, William, eds, *The Diary of Samuel Pepys*, vol. VII, 1666 (London, 2000), p. 315.
19. E. S. De Beer, ed., *The Diary of John Evelyn* (London, 1959), p. 501.
20. Latham and Mathews, *The Diary of Samuel Pepys*, vol. VII, p. 379.
21. Rebecca Joubin, 'Islam and the Arabs through the Eyes of the *Encyclopédie*: the "Other" as a Case of French Cultural Self-Criticism', *IJMES*, 32/2 (2000), pp. 197-8.
22. Pierre Martino, *L'Orient dans la Littérature Française au XVIIE et au XVIIIE Siècle* (Genève, 1970), p. 177.
23. There seems to be some confusion on whether Safi II was Sulaiman II or III. See H. R. Roemer, 'The Safavid period', in *The Cambridge History of Iran*, vol. 6 (1997), pp. 304-10.
24. Andrée Mansau, 'La Perse ou la Castration de l'Imaginaire au XVIIème Siècle', *Proceedings of the Xth Congress of the International Comparative Literature Association, New York 1982*, vol. I (New York and London, 1985), pp. 465-6.
25. Martino, *L'Orient dans la Littérature Française*, p. 231.
26. Saint-Simone, *Mémoires (1714-1716), Additions au Journal de Dangeau*, ed. Yves Coirault, vol. V (France, 1985), pp. 169-71 and 409-13; also see notes to these pages on pp. 1186-8 and 13314-17. Also see, Marie-France Hilgar, 'Mehemet Riza Beg, ambassadeur persan à la cour du roi soleil', in J. Charron and M. L. Flowers (eds) *Actes de Lexington: Actes du XXVe Colloque de la North American Society for Seventeenth-Century French Literature* (Paris, 1995), pp. 165-9.
27. Martino, *L'Orient dans la Littérature Française*, pp. 276-7.
28. See, for example, M. H. Karimi, 'Persia in the writings of Montesquieu', *The Durham University Journal*, 38/2 (June, 1977), pp. 231-7; and Gustave L. Van Roosbroeck, 'Persian letters before Montesquieu', *Modern Language Notes*, 20 (1925), pp. 433-42.
29. Montesquieu, *Lettres Persanes*, ed. Jacques Roger (Paris, 1964), p. 151, 'Lettre XCII'.
30. Voltaire, *Essai sur les moeurs et l'esprit des naions et sur les principaux faits de l'histoire depuis Charlemagne jusque'à Louis XIII*, Tome II (Paris, 1963), p. 771.
31. Ibid., p. 773. For further information on Voltaire's view of the Persians see Bonnerot, *La Perse dans la littérature et la pensée française au XVIIIe siècle* (Paris, 1988), pp. 201-15.
32. Samuel Butler, *Satires and Miscellaneous Poetry and Prose*, ed. René Lamar (Cambridge, 1928), p. 221.

21

Farang, Farangi and Farangestan: Safavid Historiography and the West (907–1148/1501–1736)

Mansur Sefatgol

Jean Chardin, who spent several years in Iran, claimed that Safavid government officials were poorly informed about conditions in Europe and that most courtiers took Europe to be a little island in the Northern Seas.[1] Considering Chardin's considerable knowledge of the cultural and political conditions of Iran during the Safavid period, especially the seventeenth century, this claim must be taken seriously. But it seems that the question of Iranian knowledge of the West during the Safavid period needs more research. The principal aim of this study is to explore the understanding of Iranians of the West during this period. This study will investigate both Safavid chronicles and other historical documents.

The establishment on the Safavid state in Iran coincided with the overseas expansion of the countries on Europe's Atlantic seaboard, and the beginning of direct relations between Iran and the West. Two main factors, war with the Ottomans and trade, led to the establishment of close relations between the Safavid kingdom and European states. Through the presence of Westerners in Iran as travellers, merchants, adventurers, diplomatic envoys and missionaries, the Iranian elite and courtiers changed their views and understanding of the West.

Despite the persistence of traditional opinions about the West, which Iranians inherited from the pre-Safavid period,[2] it appears that they changed their understanding gradually and names such as *Farang* (Europe), *Farangi* (European) and *Farangistan* were re-defined. This was because of, first, direct contact with Westerners in Iran; second, events relating to the military and political conditions of the Ottoman Empire; and finally, land and maritime contacts with the Indian subcontinent. For the subject of this study, the most important question is, how did Safavid chroniclers represent past and present information about the West in their work?

It seems that during the sixteenth century, because of the presence of the Portuguese and the Spanish in the East, the Safavid historians were familiar with those two names. Although there were no close diplomatic relations between the Safavid state and Portugal, and the Safavids did not send diplomatic envoys to Europe in this period, there were common interests which gave rise to relations between Iran and the West. However, this had little effect on the composition of Safavid chronicles. Up until the end of the sixteenth century, there were no details concerning Europe in Safavid historical writings.

The first, but not very extensive, Safavid work that contains some details on *Farang* and *Farangi* is that written by Hasan Rumlu. He presents his information in two ways: as a short account of the presence of the Portuguese in Hormuz,[3] in which he mentions the name of Dan Sebastin[4] as the king of *Farang*, the first time that the name of a European king appears in a Safavid chronicle; he also refers to *Farang* in his accounts of the Ottoman-European war, which he usually describes as a war with the unbelievers (*koffar*).[5] He also added some geographical information about European countries and cities.

Among the Safavid chroniclers, only 'Abdi Bayg of Shiraz presented a geographical description of the West. Although he follows Rumlu's narrative structure in his general history, which is still unpublished, he devotes a section to the Christian kings, who, according to him, were popes and *Qeyseriye* (emperors).[6] Then he presents a geographical description of *Farang* as: 'At the end of the land of Rum, there is a land with the name *Efranj*, which is known as *Farang*. The *Farang* are located on the West and North side of the *Rob'e-ye Maskun* one side of this land is the Roman Sea and its western-end is the ocean (*Awqyanos*).'[7]

During the reign of Shah 'Abbas I, direct contacts with Europe reached their zenith. The number of Europeans that resided in Iran increased and Iranian society, especially the elite, had opportunities for direct relations with them. Despite the increase in direct contact with Europe and Europeans, there is no sign that Safavid historians tried to include new information on the West in their works. It appears that the historians of the seventeenth century generally followed previous accounts of the West, though they differed from their predecessors in that they present some new details concerning the land of *Farangestan* and its political situation.

The best example of a seventeenth-century chronicle is that of Eskandar Bayg Monshi. who, while following the information presented by Rumlu, especially before the reign of his patron, refers to Europeans in the manner already mentioned. Eskandar Bayg Monshi does not present any geographical description of *Farang*. However, it seems he knew the differences between European dynasties and countries[8] in contrast to previous historians who usually used the term *Farang* in a general manner and did not show any detailed knowledge of Europe. In connection with events in Hormuz, for the first time in Safavid historiography, the name of England appears in the *'Alamara-ye 'Abbasi*.[9] He also refers to the religious differences between the English and the Portuguese.[10] Meanwhile, Eskandar Bayg Monshi describes his feelings about the Europeans. Relating the decision of the shah to accept the help offered by the English in his conflict with the Portuguese, he says, 'Although water from the Christian well is impure, it only washes a dead Jew, so what is there to fear?'[11]

It is interesting that while Eskandar Bayg Monshi describes the Portuguese as the enemies of the Safavid state, he praises their skill in building castles and weapons. For the first time in Safavid historiography, Eskandar Bayg Monshi presents some details concerning the position of the Pope amongst the Christians.[12] He also mentions the name of European countries such as *Namse* (Austria),[13] *Faranse*, *Volandis* (Holland), *Englis* (England) and others.[14] Perhaps this seems unremarkable, but no Safavid historian before or after Eskandar Bayg Monshi mentioned the names of Europeans countries in this manner.

An analysis of Eskandar Bayg Monshi's comments relating to *Farang* and *Farangestan* makes it clear that, in contrast to sixteenth-century Safavid historians, he, at least, had a new perspective on the West. However, he does not present many details. What is most important though is that he refers to the Iranian diplomatic envoys, whom Shah 'Abbas I sent to Europe. He does not, however, mention anything about the Sherleys, Anthony and Robert.[15] Neither he, nor any historian after him, mentions the two brothers. But we know through Safavid archival documents of their affairs in Iran.[16] It seems that these are the only Iranian sources which refer to the Sherleys. It is noticeable that after Eskandar Bayg Monshi, other Safavid historians did not make much effort to add to his account. In fact, they did not give much detail about the West at all.

In addition to the Safavid chronicles, another Safavid source material exists in the form of documents. These are also very important for the study of the Safavid understanding of the West. Chronologically, we can divide Safavid documents in the same way as the chronicles. They contain geographical details,[17] some references to the political situation in Europe and to religious conditions. From the political point of view, the documents show that the Safavid state knew that the European countries had their own separate states. The well-known method of government was monarchy with which the Safavids were familiar. Apart from some exceptions[18] it shows that for the Safavids, all European countries had royal families. They even referred to the Pope as the greatest king of *Farangestan*.[19]

Religious conditions in Europe were a major subject of interest to the Safavids. Through the investigation of Safavid documents, it becomes clear that they were interested in the religious situation, and that they usually asked European clerics, resident in Isfahan, about this topic. One of the most important pieces of evidence for such interest is a document from the reign of Shah 'Abbas I. According to this document, the Safavid king invited a group of European religious leaders, consisting of Catholic monks and a group of Englishmen, together with Safavid courtiers, to conduct a dialogue about the religious situation in Europe, especially the differences between the Roman and English churches. It is interesting that in the presence of the Safavid king, the Catholic monks included the English amongst those who were unbelievers in the Christian faith. The English, in contrast, tried to defend their doctrine.[20] This document is the most important piece of evidence demonstrating that the Safavids were aware of both Catholicism and Protestantism. However, there is no use of these two terms in the documents. They usually refer to the Christian sects by national identity. Above all, it is very interesting that, according to a recently discovered world map from the Safavid period, we can say for the first time that some Safavid learned people were aware of the discovery of the New World, which they called *Yengi Donya* (literally, new world).[21] Both the Safavid chronicles and documents can be considered as information about the West from the perspective of those inside the Safavid realm. We can also investigate the writings of those Iranians who travelled to Europe, or other parts of the world, during this period.

Rudi Matthee has pointed out that when the Iranian state began to send ambassadors to the West, this did not lead to the emergence of written works on the situation in European countries. He says: 'It is not surprising that Safavid envoys to Europe (such as) Husayn Ali Bayg, who represented Shah Abbas I on a mission to Portugal in 1601, Musa Bayg who went to Holland in 1626 and Muhammad Riza Bayg, who visited France in 1714–15 – showed a conspicuous lack of curiosity in the world they visited except for its women... Neither Muhammad Riza Bayg, nor any of his colleagues, seem to have recorded their impressions of their European journeys... Don Juan of Persia (Uruch Bayg) is an exception in having left a travelogue, but, having adopted Christianity, he never intended to return to Iran and his writings were therefore not aimed at an Iranian readership'.[22]

I think Matthee's conclusion is, in general, right. However, it was not just lack of curiosity about the places they visited. There were other reasons. Although Uruch Bayg did not write his travelogue in Persian, he says that his intention was to present his book to the shah when he returned to Iran.[23] Perhaps he was ordered to prepare a description about the situation in the countries he visited.

On the other hand, the Iranian government only began to send ambassadors to Europe from the time of Shah 'Abbas I and even then very few; most of them were sent during his rule, and one of them during the reign of Shah Soltan Hosayn. Most of them were executed or faced many problems on their return.[24] It may be that they wrote accounts of their journeys but that these were later destroyed or were not presented officially.

At the end of the seventeenth century, Iranian elites at least had an opportunity to consult an excellent work, which contained more details on Europeans, especially the English, than those written previously. Mohammad Rabi', a member of Shah Solayman's diplomatic embassy to Siam (Thailand), is the best example of Iranian curiosity in the world he visited. In his travelogue, *Safine-ye Solaymani*, he presented an excellent description about the *Farang* and *Farangiyan*, who were in Siam and India. Mohammad Rabi' did not visit England, or any other European country. However, because he met Europeans who were in India and in South and South East Asia, he was able to present a brilliant and detailed account of them.

Mohammad Rabi' describes the situation of the English[25] in Madras and in Siam. He also mentions other Europeans, but because he started his travels in an English ship, most of his information was about them and their conflict with the Portuguese. One of the most interesting parts of Mohammad Rabi's work is a description of a ceremony held in the garden of the English governor of Chinapatam or Madras, on the coronation day of the new king of England, James II. At this event, Mohammad Rabi' gives us a detailed account of the 'Franks' Feast' and a description of their manners and behaviour and also a description of the 'Frankish women'.[26] The information given by Mohammad Rabi' about the religions of the Franks is very extensive. Except for the Safavid documents mentioned above, it seems that for the first time in Safavid historiography, an author refers to the differences between Catholics and Protestants, though still without using those terms. This is clear from his statement about confession: 'It is the custom of the Portuguese, for instance, that every week, month and year, the men and women go before a priest in private and confess all their sins'. He says that some other Christians do not have such a ritual.[27]

There is another interesting travelogue, of which I hope to publish an edition in the near future. This travelogue belongs to an Iranian who went to Europe during the reign of Shah Solayman in a personal, not an official capacity, and returned during the reign of Shah Soltan Hosayn. Although the text is mainly his private memoirs, it contains a brief account of the author's journey to Venice. The author, 'Ali Akbar, an Armenian who converted to Islam during the reign of Shah Solayman,[28] says that when he became a Moslem his family tried to encourage him to return to Christianity. They thought if they asked Abkar, the previous name of 'Ali Akbar, to go to Venice, where their relatives lived, perhaps he would return to his previous faith. 'Ali Akbar went to Venice. He describes his journey and presents some details about the city, together with a short description of the trading office of his relatives. He did not, unfortunately, provide much more detail about the city.

Conclusion

The picture of *Farang* and *Farangi* in Safavid sources varies according to the nature of the source. To some poets, the *Farangi* was the supreme example of beauty of which they said,' *Farangi*: idol or moon?'[29] From the commercial point of view, there were those who came to Iran with gold and silver coins to purchase the Safavid silk and other commodities. As for the Safavid government, sometimes they were allies against the Ottomans.

Within the framework of traditional Safavid historical writing, the focus of which was significant dynastic events, there was no reason to include much information about the West. As, for the most part, European commercial, political and military developments remained marginal to Safavid affairs, it is not altogether surprising that Safavid histories only very rarely mention the names of European kings and rulers. Many of the existing written sources about the West concern religious polemic. These demonstrate the attempts of the religious leaders to refute Christianity.[30]

It seems that Safavid Iran had an ideology they considered to be superior and purer to that of foreigners, so they did not need to refer to the others generally. For them Iran was the centre of the universe and the Safavid kings were its pivot. They believed that they were the only true believers on earth. Safavid Iran was a rich and flourishing country and it seems that because of this pride and perhaps negligence, they did not concern themselves with problems like the growing European naval and commercial power.

On the other hand, although Iranian curiosity about new subjects was recorded by the European travellers, it seems that the motivation that caused the Europeans to begin a new understanding of the world was not present amongst the Iranians to any great extent. An analysis of Safavid sources makes it clear that in the period from the reign of Shah 'Abbas I to the final years of Safavid rule, a considerable and increasing number of people travelled abroad, but the main destination was India. There is not much detail about those who travelled to Europe. The cases of Uruch Bayg or 'Ali Akbar are exceptions. We do not have any information about the person who, as a secretary (*monshi*), accompanied Olearius. Furthermore, I have not studied the writings of those Armenian merchants who travelled to most of the major European cities.[31] It would be interesting to know whether they left any travelogues describing their feelings about the West.

It seems that during the last years of Safavid rule, the Iranians began to investigate other parts of the world, but only gradually. However, the fall of the Safavids led to a long interruption to this process.

Notes

I wish to thank Dr. John Gurney of the Oriental Institute of the University of Oxford who read part of the draft of this chapter and made valuable comments on it. Also, I would like to thank Dr Robert Gleave of the University of Bristol and Mr. Majid Tafreshi who both helped me to prepare this chapter. I also wish to thank Mr. Farhad Hakimzadeh and the Iran Heritage Foundation through whose support I had the opportunity to visit the British Library to continue my research.

1. Jean Chardin, *Voyages de M. Jean Chardin en Perse, aux Indes et autres Lieux d,orient*. Persian translation by Eqbal Yaghma'i as *Safarname-ye Shardan* (Tehran, 1374/1995), vol. 2. p. 776.
2. See, for example, 'Abdol-'Ali Berjandi, *Resale-ye Abad va Ajram*. Ms. 8426. Central Library of Tehran University, fos. 19b, 28b–29a, 29b, 31a, b; Mohammad Taher Ebn Abu al-Qasem Balkhi, `Ajayeb al-Tabaqat. Ms. 2018/3. Central Library of Tehran University, fos. 34b, 39a, b, 158b.
3. Hasan Bayg Rumlu, *Ahsan al-Tavarikh*, ed. 'Abdol-Hosayn Nava'i (Tehran, 1357/1979), p. 133.
4. Ibid., p. 592.
5. Ibid., pp. 55–7.
6. 'Abdi Bayg Shirazi, *Takmilat al-Akhbar*. Ms. 3890, Malek Library. Tehran. fo. 155; Abdi Bayg Shirazi, *'Takmil-e al-Akhbar*, ed. 'Abdol-Hosayn Nava'i (Tehran, 1369/1990).
7. Ibid., fo. 155.

8. Eskandar Bayg Monshi, *Tarikh-e 'Alamara-ye Abbasi*, ed. Iraj Afshar, 2 vols (Tehran 1350/1971), vol. 2, pp. 665, 667; vol. 1, pp. 513, 116–17, translated into English by Roger N. Savory as *History of Shah Abbas* (Boulder, CO: Westview Press, 1978).
9. Savory, *History of Shah Abbas*, vol. 2, pp. 1202–3.
10. Ibid., vol. 2, p. 1203.
11. Ibid., vol. 2, p. 1204.
12. Ibid., vol. 2, pp. 1304–5.
13. Savory identified *Namse* as Germany. Ibid., vol. 2, p. 1305.
14. Ibid., vol. 2, p. 1305.
15. Eskandar Bayg Monshi only mentions the name of Iranian envoys and the execution of Dangiz Bayg, Shah 'Abbas I's ambassador to the European courts. Eskandar Bayg Monshi, *Tarikh-e 'Alamara-ye Abbasi*, vol. 2, pp. 862–3; Savory, *History of Shah Abbas*, vol. 2, pp. 1074–6.
16. Mohammad Hasan Kavusi Araqi, ed., *Asnad-e ravabet-e dowlat-e Safavi ba hokumatha-ye Italiya* (Tehran: Markaz-e asnad va tarikh-e diplomasi, 1379/2000), pp. 38–9, 40–1, 95–6, 99–100, 223–4, 248–9, 254.
17. 'Abdol-Hosayn Nava'i, ed., *Asnad va mokatebat-e tarikhi-ye Iran az sal-e 1105-1135* (Tehran: Mo'assese-ye motale'at va tahqiqat-e farhangi, 1363/1984), pp. 9, 92–3.
18. Safavid historians and scribes usually referred to European rulers as the kings of *Farangestan*. They even included the Dutch amongst them. According to a document issued by Shah Safi I to the ruler of the Holland, he first called him as '*Estandal Jenderal*' (States-General) and '*Nazem-e omur-e dawlat-e Olandisi*' ('Governor of Dutch state affairs') but in the text he addressed him as 'Hazrat-e ... padeshah-e vallajah ... velayat-e Olandis' (the king of Holland). Jahangir Qa'em Maqami, ed., *Yeksad-o panjah sanad-e tarikhi* (Tehran: Setad-e bozorg arteshtaran, 1348/1969), p. 39.
19. Kavusi Araqi, *Asnad-e ravabet-e dowlat-e Safavi*, p. 182.
20. Ibid., pp. 258–70.
21. *Majmu'e-ye Mirza Taher Vazir of Adharbayjan*. Ms. Or. 12974. British library fo. 98b. There is a map in this folio which, though prepared according to the traditional style of mapmaking of Iranian geographical view, has a remarkable addition to it. The mapmaker included the name of '*Yengi Donya*' – (New World). I think this is the first time in the Safavid period that this name appears on an Iranian map, showing that Iranian scholars were aware of the discovery of the New World. There are some other details on this subject in another Safavid document. Kavusi Araqi, *Asnad-e ravabet-e dowlat-e Safavi*, p. 191.
22. Rudi Matthee 'Between aloofness and fascination: Safavid views of the West', *Iranian Studies* 31/2 (1998), p. 242.
23. *Don Juan of Persia, a Shi'ah Catholic 1560-1604*, trans. G. le Strange (London, 1926). Persian translation by Mas'ud Rajabniya as Uruch Bayg Bayat, *Don Zhuan-e Irani* (Tehran: Bongah-e tarjome va nashr-e ketab, 1338), p. 313.
24. Eskandar Bayg Monshi, *Tarikh-e 'Alamara-ye Abbasi*, vol. 2, pp. 862–3, where Eskandar Bayg Monshi describes the reasons for Dangiz Bayg's execution.
25. Muhammad Rabi, *The Ship of Solomon (Safine-ye Sulaymani)* trans. John O'Kane, Persian Heritage Series, No. 11 (London, 1972), pp. 33–5.
26. Ibid., pp. 36–9.
27. Ibid., pp. 40–1.
28. 'Ali Akbar, *E'teraf Name*, Ms. 6487, Central Library, University of Tehran, fos. 5a.b, 6a.b.
29. *Kholasat al-tavarikh*, vol. 1, p. 201; Z. Sabetiyan, *Asnad va name-ha-ye tarikhi-ye dawre-ye Safaviye* (Tehran: Ebn Sina, 1343 H.Sh.), pp. 166–7.
30. 'Abdol-Hadi Ha'eri, *Nakhostin ruyaru'iha-ye andishegaran-e Iran ba do-ruye-ye tamaddon-e borzhvazi-ye gharb* (Tehran: Amirkabir, 1367/1988).
31. We now know that some Armenians who travelled to Europe left diaries. One of them, Zakaria of Agulis described his feelings about the West, but did not provide much information about the European cities, such as Amsterdam and Venice, which he visited. See *The Journal of Zakaria of Agulis (Zakaria Aguletsu Oragrutyune)* Annotation, Translation and Commentary by George A. Bournoutian (Costa Mesa: Mazda, 2003). Thanks to Willem Floor who kindly sent me a copy of the text.

22

The Augustinians in Hormuz (1573–1622)

Carlos Alonso Vanes

During the sixteenth century and the first decades of the seventeenth century, the island of Hormuz formed the central and focal point of relations between Portugal and Iran. This is amply testified to by the bibliographical references found in the commemorative volume published in Lisbon in 1972, by the Calouste Gulbenkian foundation, on the 2,500th anniversary of the Iranian monarchy.

After the retreat of the Jesuits (of Father Barzeo and others) from the island in 1569, the Augustinians founded a monastery in compliance with the desire expressed by King Dom Sebastian. The monastery continued to exist until 1622, when the Portuguese lost the island. We shall briefly indicate the important moments in the Augustinian presence on the island over half a century. Many – Augustinians and others – passed through this place on their way from India to Europe or entered Persia from here. Among the non-Augustinians, three persons deserve special mention: the two Jesuit fathers, Monserrate and Páez, who spent some time here in 1588 on their way to Ethiopia on their way to Ethiopia; and Nicolao Orta Revelo who passed through Hormuz on his return journey to Europe in the beginning of the seventeenth century.

It was Father Simón de Moraes who founded the monastery of Hormuz in 1573; he came to the island from the coast of Africa at a period when the first Augustinians were leaving for India. In 1573, other Augustinians, like fathers Antonio de la Pasión and Anselmo del Paraíso, also travelled to Hormuz from Goa. Their first job was to build the church and then the monastery, dedicated to Our Lady of Grace. Besides the persons mentioned above, many other Augustinians also worked on the island during this initial stage. We do not know them all by name, but there were probably more than 30 present on the island at this period.

The most famous person during these early years was Father Simón de Moraes. As Vicar Provincial, he was already residing in Goa in 1584. Chosen as an emissary by Philip II, he was entrusted with a letter to be taken to Khoda Banda (Mohammad Khodabande), the blind king of Persia. A good amount of information is available both on his stay in the Persian court and on his return to Goa through Europe. It is believed that he converted a Persian philosopher to Christianity and baptized him. We are certain of some of his letters to Pope Gregory XIII and to the Spanish king. But the mission did not succeed due to a shipwreck in 1585, on his way to Europe.

We also do not know the complete list of the priors of the monastery, but some have left behind cherished memories of their sanctity and apostolates; the abovementioned Father Moraes is one of them. The others to be included in the list are Father Marcos da Graça and Father Leonardo da Graça, who later became a great missionary in Bengal.

An important part of this history is centred on Father Sebastian de S. Pedro, who much later became the bishop of Mylapur, Cochin, and the archbishop of Goa. He started his work on the island as a simple religious, and resided there for some seven years as administrator of the order and collector of incomes deriving from a rich inheritance left to the Augustinians of Lisbon by Alfonso Nuradim, a noble of Hormuz, and his sister Felipa Morada. We know of four letters written by Father Sebastian during this period, of great importance to the history of the monastery as well as of the island.

The rather large Augustinian community at Hormuz carried out all the possible kinds of apostolate: ministry to the Portuguese Catholics on the island, to the sick soldiers in the hospital, to the rest of the Christians living on the island or passing by, and to the crew of the ships sailing through those waters. One special activity recorded in historical sources was that of the missionaries boarding the Arab vessels that frequently arrived on the island taking children to Persia to be sold as slaves and rescuing them. The missionaries used to gather the children together and instruct them in a minor seminary, which they themselves had established for this purpose; there are frequent references to this activity for and among the orphan children in the surviving letters.

A group of islanders was converted to Christianity around 1600; they were all taken to Goa and baptized in a solemn ceremony with Archbishop Meneses officiating. Among those being baptized was a member of the Persian royal family, who became an Augustinian in Portugal, returned to India and continued to live for many years in the order. His baptismal name was Jerónimo Joete, but no record of his Muslim name prior to his conversion, or other information about him survives.

A Portuguese Augustinian working with the Spanish Augustinians in the Philippines passed through Hormuz in 1599 on his way to Europe. This was Nicolás de Melo, the procurator of that province. In order to facilitate his journey to Europe, he took the route through India and the Persian Gulf. Once in Hormuz, he heard about a delegation of the Persian king, Shah 'Abbas I, preparing to leave to meet the Pope and various European rulers. He proceeded to Isfahan and succeeded in getting admitted as a member of the delegation. However, he was detained in Russia, while the rest of the delegation continued its journey; Melo died some years later in Russia.

The delegation sent by 'Abbas and led by Sir Anthony Sherley and Hosayn 'Ali Bayg arrived in Rome and was received by Clement VIII; Hosayn 'Ali Bayg was also received by Philip III in his court at Valladolid in 1601. The Persian delegation returned home in 1603, after passing through Portugal and India. However, some members of the delegation were converted to Christianity and stayed in Italy and Spain. The best known member of the converts is Juan de Persia, the author of an account of this voyage.

In response to the Persian delegation, both Clement VIII and Philip III undertook to send their own envoys to the Persian ruler. Whereas the Pope's delegation took the Russian route, Philip III sent his letter of reply via India. Three Augustinians were designated to take the letter from Goa to Hormuz. The most renowned among them was Father Antonio de Gouvea, the author of *Relaçam en que se tratam as guerras e grandes victorias...* (of the Persian king), which gives a detailed account of this journey. The book was published in 1611 in Lisbon, during Gouvea's visit to Europe with another Persian delegation, to which we shall refer later.

Hosayn 'Ali Bayg returned to his country in 1605 and was chastized by Abbas. Three Augustinians accompanied him on his voyage from Goa to Isfahan. One of these was Father Diego de Santa Ana, who remained in Persia and became a great missionary. The other two returned to Goa, together with another Persian delegation, and with Luis Perira de Lacerda who was officially designated to accompany the delegation from Hormuz to Goa. In all these journeys, the envoys and delegations had to pass through Hormuz; the Augustinian monastery there served as a place of rest and a base of operations.

In 1607, Gouvea had already been in Goa for two years; he was also a councillor of the Vicar Provincial. He was, therefore, chosen to return to Persia where numerous apostolic activities would be opening up to the Augustinians thanks to the transmigration of the Armenians to Isfahan – ordered by Abbas as a defensive measure against the Turks. In 1608 Gouvea arrived in Persia and remained there for a few months. During this period, two great missionaries died in Hormuz in 1609: Father Jerónimo de Cruz, one of the pioneers to leave for Persia in 1602, and Father Matthias of the Holy Spirit, an Englishman, who attempted in vain to enter Iraq to work among the Mandaeans.

The Augustinian, Alejo de Meneses, was still the archbishop of Goa during this period. The king of Hormuz presented him with a precious crystal chest and valuable pearls, the only gift the great archbishop ever accepted during his 15 years of episcopate in Goa. Meneses sent this treasure to Lisbon, in order to be used as a tabernacle in the Augustinian church of Our Lady of the Grace. It is preserved today in the National Museum of Lisbon.

Gouvea had to leave Persia for a second time in 1611, in order to accompany the Persian delegation of Dangiz Bayg, who was to travel to Europe with a good many rolls of silk and a letter of reply to the Spanish crown. In 1611, the delegation passed through Hormuz where the customs took note of the accompanying merchandise and left a declaration that it was destined not for sale, but as a gift to the Spanish king.

The delegation reached Spain, but Philip III did not let it proceed to Rome; he himself sent 'Abbas's letter to the Pope through the Spanish ambassador in Rome. In the meantime the Holy See appointed Antonio de Gouvea as bishop of all Christians in Persia. The episcopal consecration took place in Lisbon, in 1612.

Finally, the Discalced Carmelites founded their monastery in Hormuz in 1612. Their letters mentioned the passage of Gouvea and Dangiz Bayg through Hormuz on their way back to Persia. Upon Dangiz Bayg's arrival at Isfahan, 'Abbas ordered him to be executed under the pretext that he had not paid back the price of the silk rolls advanced to him on the outset of the journey to Europe. Gouvea, for his part, remained in the Persian capital only for a few months. Finding himself insecure and threatened, Gouvea left Persia for Hormuz in the same year, 1613, without informing the king of his departure; this evidently angered the monarch.

In 1614 in Hormuz, Gouvea initiated the process of beatification for his companion in Persia, Father Guillermo de S. Agustin, who had been assassinated by the khan of Nakhichevan at the end of a heated debate on religious issues.

In 1615, the Carmelite Father Redento de la Cruz and Sir Robert Sherley passed through Hormuz on their way to Europe, as envoys of Abbas to the European monarchs. Sherley had previously conducted the delegation of 'Ali Qoli Bayg to Rome in 1609; on that occasion, they were received festively on their arrival in Rome and at the subsequent audience with the Pontiff. In Goa, Father Redento and Sir Robert chanced upon the envoy sent by Philip III to Persia in 1614 but detained in Goa for some years by the Portuguese authorities. This was García de Silva y Figueroa, who wrote an extensive description of the journey entitled *Commentarios* and published in two volumes in Madrid at the beginning of the twentieth century (see Chapter 10).

García de Silva stayed in Hormuz for several months and lodged mostly in the Augustinian monastery; he participated extensively in their life and activities, which he later described. During his visits to the interior regions of Persia, he was accompanied by the Augustinians. On his return to India in 1619, he again stopped over on the island for another six months, but the Augustinian monastery is not mentioned on this occasion in the *Commentarios*.

In 1621, Pietro della Valle (see Chapter 19), the Roman patrician, passed through Hormuz, or at least pretended that he had to and hence required the help of the Portuguese, in order to reach India. Father Sebastian de Jesús speaks of della Valla's departure from Isfahan, in a letter to Francisco de Souza, the captain of Hormuz. However, in his comments, Pietro della Valle does not mention this passage through the island. In his letter, Father Sebastian makes mention also of Father Nicolás Perete's journey from Isfahan to 'Abbas's camp to ease the difficulties with the Persians over the customs at Hormuz. He also comments on the preparations undertaken by both the Persians and the English to assault and conquer Hormuz.

In fact, by then the plan for the conquest of Hormuz by both parties was already much advanced. The Portuguese were aware of the plan and had been preparing to defend the island since 1620. Indeed, when General Ruy Freire de Andrade launched the defence of Qeshm, which also was attacked, he assigned the Augustinian Friar Rodrigo de Jesús to the front line to cheer up the soldiers. But Friar Rodrigo died on 5 May 1620 during one of the assaults before the conquest.

In December 1621, the English and the governor of the Persian province of Fars agreed upon their strategy to assault the island. According to the agreement, both parties were supposed to provide an equal number of soldiers and funds for the war, and would profit equally from the conquest. The assault lasted from January to May 1622. Hormuz was conquered; the Portuguese definitively lost the island, which they had possessed for more than a century. The Augustinian who acted as vicar of the Island of Qeshm was taken prisoner by the English.

According to an account of 1640, three Augustinians continued to reside for some time in Hormuz even after its fall, in order to attend to the wounded soldiers. But the monastery was lost and abandoned; the Carmelite monastery also suffered a similar fate. The Augustinian house had lasted for almost 50 years.

All attempts at reconquest by Portuguese vessels were in vain. Yet some Augustinians continued to reside in remote areas of the Arabian coast near Hormuz. A vicariate, for example, was founded in Suhar (Oman) in 1622; and another in Qurayyat (today in Saudi Arabia), and so on. The monastery founded in 1598 on the fortifications of Muscat along the coast of Oman, lasted until 1648.

23

European Catholic Missionary Propaganda among the Armenian Population of Safavid Iran

Kristine Kostikyan

Overview

European Catholic missionaries began their penetration into Iran from the second half of thirteenth century, eventually concentrating their activities on the local Armenian population. In the fourteenth century the Catholic community of Iran had its own episcopacy. Its first centre was in Sultanie and in the mid-fifteenth century it shifted to Nakhichevan.

Missionary activities in Iran intensified in the late sixteenth century. Shah 'Abbas I, interested in developing socio-economic and political relations with European countries, did not interfere with the arrival of the Catholic missionaries in Iran. They were allowed to settle in Iranian towns, build churches and freely spread Catholic religious propaganda.

The socio-economic and political situation of the Armenian people was such that by the mid-seventeenth century the Catholic missionaries had gained numerous converts among the Armenian subjects of Safavid Iran. The Armenian Catholics lived in separate communities from the Armenian Gregorians and did not enjoy the protection of the Apostolic Church, which was much needed under the rule of Moslem governors.

In the early eighteenth century, the Armenian Gregorian clergymen, having obtained royal decrees, began to fight the Catholic missionary propaganda among Armenians and achieved some success. This led to a decrease in the number of Armenian Catholics. The majority migrated to Ottoman Turkey and to Europe, or returned to Gregorian Christianity.

Missionary activity in Iran began in the Ilkhanid period in the fourteenth century, when the Mongol empire reached the shores of the Mediterranean Sea, and the Mongols established direct contact with Europe. As a result, people living in the Ilkhanid state became the target of Catholic expansionism. European Catholic missions in Iran and among the Armenian population date back to the second half of the thirteenth century.[1] Missionaries from the Franciscan and Dominican orders were the first to arrive, settling in Tabriz. In 1318, Soltanie became the centre of a newly formed Catholic bishopric.[2] Between 1320 and 1329, residences for Catholic bishops were established in Maraghe, Tabriz and Tiflis. In 1350, Nakhichevan also became the residence of a Catholic bishop and a century later, following the decline of Soltanie, the centre of the Catholic bishopric shifted to Nakhichevan around 1450.[3] In the late Middle Ages the Armenian people had been under the rule of Ottoman Turkey and Iran and were in danger of losing their national, cultural and religious independence. In the seventeenth century, another danger presented itself to the Armenians in both the east (under the rule of Iran) and west (under the rule of Ottoman Turkey) in the form of widespread Catholic missionary propaganda. During the early seventeenth century, this propaganda intensified during the reign of the Safavid Shah 'Abbas I, when the shah, seeking European allies in the war against Ottoman Turkey, established close economic and political relations between Iran and Europe, particularly Venice, Spain, France and the Russian Empire. Thus, for both political and economic reasons, the Safavid court did not interfere with the missionaries' activities. In addition to disseminating Catholic propaganda, the missionaries played an important diplomatic role, acting as intermediaries in the relations between the Safavid shahs, the European monarchs, and the Popes of the period, Clement VIII (1592–1605) and especially Paul V (1605–21). The missionaries supplied essential economic and political information about Iran to European political leaders and merchants, thus paving the way for colonial penetration into Iran, and also represented the interests of their countries at the Persian court.

Thus the Vatican and the Catholic clergy and their missions played a major role in the penetration by western European countries of Asia and Iran, in particular. The Catholic Church made efforts to win, and the court granted, special privileges for the missionaries that supported their activities in Safavid Iran, including:

1. the right to own private property;
2. immunity from paying taxes;
3. the freedom to practice free trade;
4. freedom to travel in the country;
5. political immunity;
6. to be treated with respect by state officials;
7. to be granted an audience with the shah at any time;
8. freedom to practice their Christian faith;
9. permission to open ecclesiastical, educational and other institutions;

10. the right to communicate freely with all Christians living in Iran; and
11. special juridical immunity for all clergymen subordinate to the Pope.[4]

Although the Safavid shahs and Muslim clergy did not tolerate Christian missionary activity among Muslims, they did not object to Catholic propaganda among the heterodox Christian minorities of Iran, particularly the Armenians.[5] Consequently, the Safavid government allowed Catholic churches to be constructed in the Iranian towns of Isfahan, Shiraz, Bander-'Abbas, Tabriz, and elsewhere.[6]

Indeed, Rome took special notice of the Armenians, who made up the majority of the Christian population of Safavid Iran, and the Catholic missionaries found ways to work effectively with them.[7] Taking advantage of the privileges granted to them by the Safavid court, the missionaries were successful in spreading Catholic propaganda and the Church gained numerous followers throughout Iran and Eastern Armenia, which was subject to the Safavid state. Several factors contributed to the dissemination of Catholicism:

1. The lack of an Armenian state and thus of state protection for its Apostolic Christian church.
2. The authority and power of the Pope to order and orchestrate the Church's efforts to convert the people of Iran and Asia, and the Church's wealth, which enabled the missionaries to offer the Armenian people charity, free education, free medical treatment and so on, thereby winning their sympathy.[8] With royal permission, European missionaries opened schools in Shiraz, Isfahan[9] and various Armenian settlements, including Jahuk and Aparaner,[10] whose purpose was to teach Catholicism to Armenian school-age children and adolescents.
3. As already noted, the Catholic missions enjoyed the political support of the Safavid state and their missionaries were granted the aforementioned privileges to aid them in carrying out their work.
4. The Armenian Catholic communities were also afforded special privileges by the Safavid shahs that had been negotiated for them by European sovereigns and the Pope. The Armenian Catholic settlements of Nakhichevan were *khasses*,[11] personal estates of the shah, and paid their taxes directly to him.[12] This in effect gave the settlements a protected status. No local nobleman (*beglarbeg*) or governor (*hakim*) had the right to interfere in the affairs of the Armenian Catholic settlements or collect taxes from them.
5. In the sixteenth century, Armenians and the leaders of the Armenian Apostolic Church had hoped to gain the support of European countries in their efforts to rid themselves of their Persian and Turkish yoke. The European rulers led them to believe that if the church submitted to the power of the Pope, they would organize another crusade and help Armenia gain independence from Safavid Iran and the Ottoman Empire.[13] This prospect was so tempting that in the seventeenth century some members of the Armenian Gregorian clergy were inclined towards Catholicism and submission to the Pope.

The dissemination of Catholicism among Armenians was a dangerous phenomenon for a stateless nation under Moslem rule. The Gregorian church united the Armenians and protected their rights. The intensified missionary activities in Safavid Iran in the sixteenth and seventeenth centuries resulted, among other things, in an increase in the number of Catholic Armenians, thereby dividing the Armenian population. Armenian Catholics were outsiders; they were called *Frangs* (Franks) and lived separately from Armenian Gregorians. They gradually became estranged from Armenian life and, consequently, many assimilated into foreign environments, especially in Europe.

By the beginning of the seventeenth century, there were 19,000 converted Catholic Armenians living in three towns and 12 villages in the Nakhichevan, Ernjak and Jahuk regions.[14] They were served by ten Catholic churches. Nevertheless, during the decline of the Safavid Empire that began in the second half of the seventeenth century, when the religious intolerance of senior Muslim clerics, as well as the illegal deeds and abuses by state officials, increased, the situation for the Catholic community of Nakhichevan deteriorated. The majority of Nakhichevan Armenian Catholics were forced to adopt Islam; others returned to the Apostolic Church or migrated to Izmir, Bursa, Constantinople and other towns in Ottoman Turkey.[15]

At the end of the seventeenth century, Yerevan province also became a centre of Catholic missionary activities. Catholicism had been disseminated among the Armenian population of Khachen and Karabagh, Ganja, Shamakhi, Shirvan, Baku, Derbend, Nukhi,[16] Tabriz,[17] Shiraz[18] and Isfahan.

Catholic missionaries tried various methods to convert senior Armenian clergymen and Catholicoses or to promote to high positions Gregorian clergymen who promised to take the Catholic side in conflicts with the Apostolic church, and they were sometimes successful. In the second half of the seventeenth century, Catholic propaganda had penetrated even the Holy See of Etchmiatsin.[19] The Catholic missionaries profited from the discord among Armenian clergymen, supporting one or other of them in promoting a union of the Armenian (Apostolic) and Catholic churches. Although they achieved a measure of success, the candidate they had supported, Nahapet Catholicos, nevertheless disappointed the Catholic missionaries: even after achieving high office he was unable to go against the desire of the majority of the Armenian population and the Apostolic Church clergymen to maintain independence from Rome.[20]

Catholic missions also made a great effort to convert the rich and influential merchants of New Julfa, the Armenian suburb of Isfahan, hoping to benefit from their wealth and power. There were seven Catholic churches in Isfahan, four of them in New Julfa.[21] Nevertheless, the majority of the Armenian Gregorian clergy of New Julfa fought tirelessly against Catholic propaganda, forbidding Armenians from contacting missionaries or attending their missionary schools.[22] Thus, as a result of efforts by Stepanos Jughayetsi, the bishop of the Apostolic Church in New Julfa, Shah Solayman ordered the expulsion of the Jesuit missionaries from Isfahan and the destruction of the Carmelite church.[23] The Armenian clergy of New Julfa also published books refuting the Catholic faith and promoting the principles of the Apostolic Church, and opened schools and libraries.[24]

The struggle between the Armenian Gregorian clergy and the Catholic missions of Iran intensified at the beginning of the eighteenth century, when Russia emerged as Armenia's liberator from Iranian and Ottoman Turkish rule. Soon afterwards the Armenian liberation movement changed its allegiance from Europe to Russia. The high clergymen of the Armenian Apostolic Church stepped up their fight against Catholic missionaries, trying to restrict Catholic propaganda among the Armenian Safavid subjects living in Iran and Eastern Armenia. Alexander Catholicos (1706–14), a leader of the Armenian Apostolic Church was one of the most active in the struggle against the activities of Catholic missionaries. In February 1709, he wrote a letter to Pope Paul V suggesting that the Church end its missionary propaganda among Armenian people.[25] However, that letter had no effect on the Pope and there was no change in Catholic missionary activities.

The activities of French Catholic missionaries in Iran intensified during the reign of Louis XIV (1643–1715). At the end of the seventeenth century, Shah Soltan Hosayn had reaffirmed the privileges of French missionaries, but their efforts to subordinate the Armenian Apostolic Church to the Pope failed.[26] In 1700, the French court and clergy opened the college of Louis le Grand in Paris to educate young Armenian and Greek men in Catholicism and spread the Catholic faith in the East.[27] At the beginning of the eighteenth century, Pierre-Victor Michel, the plenipotentiary French ambassador in Iran, renewed the privileges of French merchants and adjusted Iranian–French commercial relations. According to paragraph 27 of the 1708 treaty between Iran and France that was concluded through Michel's efforts, French missionaries were given the right to perform church services and to pray freely, on condition that they would not try to spread religious propaganda among the Moslems, try to convert them to the Catholic faith or commit any deed contrary to the Shi'a faith out of their houses and churches. They could, however, worship, spread religious propaganda and try to convert Christians or Jews in the towns of Iran and the Caucasus.[28] Michel intervened to protect the missionaries in their squabbles with the Armenian subjects of Safavid Iran and the Catholic missions. As a result of his efforts, the Shah Sultan Husayn sent a letter to the khan of Shamakhi demanding protection for the missionaries in Shamakhi.[29] In 1708 Michel obtained royal decrees addressed to Vakhtang, the king of Georgia, and to the *beglarbeg* of Tabriz declaring that anyone who interfered with missionary activities would be punished.[30] These decrees prohibited interference with missionary work and also meant that Armenians could no longer be prohibited from worshipping in Catholic churches.

But the Safavid shahs were two-faced in their dealings with the Catholic missionaries and the Armenian Apostolic Church. They preserved the rights and privileges of Catholic missionaries to retain their friendly relations with European countries. But, to maintain their supremacy over the Armenians, they took steps to curb the rising influence of Catholics. This dual policy can easily be traced in their decrees.

One group of these decrees, obtained by the missionaries, protected their rights to practice their religion in the territory of Safavid Iran.

Another group of decrees, issued at the request of the Armenian Apostolic Church and clergy, restricted the Catholic missionaries' rights with respect to the Armenian population of Safavid Iran. Three decrees in this group, issued by Shah Soltan Hosayn at the request of Alexander and Astvatsatur Etchmiatsin Catholicoses are kept in Yerevan Matenadaran. Of these, two were issued due to the efforts of Alexander Catholicos.

The first of the anti-Catholic decrees, issued in May 1710, referenced a report by Alexander Catholicos of Etchmiatsin saying that Catholic missionaries were settling in Armenian settlements, teaching Armenians the Catholic faith, marrying Armenian women and converting them to Catholicism. These actions had split the Armenians into two hostile groups, Apostolics and Catholics, contrary to the Muslim religious law (shar'ia), according to which Armenians were obedient subjects of Iran, pledged to permanently pay *jezye*[32] for the right to practice their faith. Therefore, the May 1710 decree made it illegal for Catholic missionaries to teach Armenian children in Catholic schools, force Armenian women into marriage, or facilitate the conversion of the Armenian people to Catholicism. These illegal deeds by missionaries were to be prevented everywhere in the territory of the Safavid state, particularly in Isfahan, Georgia, Tabriz, Hamadan, Ganja, Karabagh and Chokhur Sa'ad (Yerevan province), where Catholicism was the most widespread.

The shah also stipulated that the May 1710 treaty took precedence over the 1708 treaty between Iran and France. The missionaries had to follow it, and not violate it by misinterpreting the terms of the treaty. They had no right to interfere in the religious affairs and customs of the Armenians, or to build churches in Armenian settlements. According to the decree, Armenians could buy their houses and property at 'current prices'.

The second decree, issued in 1712, was even stricter. It not only confirmed the first decree, but this time Shah Soltan Hosayn also entrusted the local governors and officials with the responsibility of executing his order. He demanded that the governor of Tabriz return the fine of 50 tumans which had been collected from each of 25 Armenian Georgian clergymen who had violated an earlier, pro-Catholic decree by forbidding Armenians to visit the houses of Catholic missionaries and their church.

It is important to note that these anti-Catholic decrees were issued during the decline of the Safavid dynasty in Iran, when the shah was unable to keep order. Nevertheless, those decrees had probably given Alexander Catholicos of Etchmiatsin the power to cause damage to the activities of the Catholic missions at Tabriz, Tiflis, Ganja and so on.[33]

The third decree, issued in 1718[34] at the request of Astvatsatur Catholicos of Etchmiatsin, upheld the 1710 decree and ordered the local governors and officials to enforce it and to forbid any Armenian from adopting Catholicism.

Apart from the aforementioned decrees, we know about the existence of one from 1653 issued by Shah 'Abbas II prohibiting Catholic missionaries from building churches in New Julfa,³⁵ also Shah Soltan Hosayn's decrees of 1710, 1711 and 1712 concerning marriages between Armenians and Catholics or Protestants and missionary propaganda.³⁶

Thus the beginning of the eighteenth century was marked by an intensified struggle led by the Armenian Apostolic Church against Catholic missionary propaganda among Safavid and Ottoman Armenian people subject to Safavid Iran as well as to the Ottoman Empire. The decrees were used by the Armenian Georgian clergymen to wage an effective fight against the Catholic missionaries and quell their destructive activities among the Armenian subjects of Iran.

Notes

1. A. U. Martirosyan, *Armyanskie poseleniya na teritorii Irana v XI–XV vv* (Yerevan, 1990), p. 135 (in Russian).
2. A. V. Bayburdyan, 'Arevelyan Hayastanum misionerneri gortsuneutyan patmutyunits', *Patmabanasirakan handes* (Yerevan 1989), 2, p. 148 (in Armenian).
3. *Tarikh-e Iran: dawre-ye Safaviyan* (Tehran, 1380), p. 182 (in Persian).
4. M. G. Panakhiyan, *O rezhime kapitulyatsii v Irane (1568-1715)*, abstract of thesis (Moscow, 1962), p. 15 (in Russian).
5. Martirosyan, *Armyanskie*, pp. 135–6; V. A. Bayburdyan, *Armyanskaya koloniya Novoi Julfi v XVII veke* (Yerevan, 1969), p. 124 (in Russian).
6. M. Mir Ahmadi, *Din va dawlat dar asr-e Safavi* (Tehran, 1329), p. 104.
7. T. H. Hakobyan, 'Hayeri paykare katolikakan misionerneri asimilyatorakan dzgtumneri dem Iranum (XVII–XVIII darerum)', *Arevelagitakan zhoghovatsu* (Yerevan, 1960), p. 267 (in Armenian).
8. Bayburdyan, *Armyanskaya*, p. 125.
9. L.A. Semenova, 'Orden karmelitov kak orudie proniknoveniya evropeitsev v Iran', *Sbornik statei* (Moscow, 1962), p. 99 (in Russian).
10. B. Eghiayan, *Hay haranvanutyants bazhanume* (Antilias, 1971), p. 96.
11. The *khasse-e sharife* were the royal estates, workshops and other assets belonging to the shah and royal family (H. D. Papazyan, *Matenadarani parskeren hrovartaknere*, vol. 1 [Yerevan, 1956], p. 110 [in Armenian]).
12. Bayburdyan, 'Arevelyan', p. 150.
13. Ashot Hovhannisyan, *Drvagner hay azatagrakan mtki patmutyan*, vol. 2 (Yerevan, 1959), p. 175 (in Armenian).
14. Hakobyan, 'Hayeri paykare', p. 267.
15. Bayburdyan, 'Arevelyan', pp. 150–1.
16. Ibid., p. 155.
17. H. Ajemyan, 'Patmakan Tavrizi hin hayutyune', *Divan Atrpatakani hayots patmutyan*, vol. 1 (Beyrut, 1980), p. 73 (in Armenian).
18. Semenova, 'Orden karmelitov', p. 99.
19. *Hay zhoghovrdi patmutyun*, vol. 4 (Yerevan: HSSH GA Hratarakch'ut'yun, 1972), p. 122 (in Armenian).
20. Hovhannisyan, *Drvagner*, p. 304.
21. H. Hovhanyants, *Patmutyun Nor Jughayu vor Haspahan*, vol. 2 (Nor Jugha 1881), p. 265 (in Armenian).
22. Semenova, 'Orden karmelitov', p. 100.
23. Hovhanyants, *Patmutyun*, pp. 266–7.
24. Bayburdyan, *Armyanskaya*, p. 143.
25. Maghakia Ormanyan, *Azgapatum*, vol. 2 (St. Etchmiatsin, 2001), p. 3205.

26. *Tarikh-e Iran*, p. 212.
27. Eghiayan, *Hay*, p. 97.
28. Nava'i, 'Abdol Hosayn, *Ravabet-e Syasi-e Iran va Orupa dar 'asr-e Safavi* (Tehran, 1372), p. 273 (in Persian).
29. Hovhannisyan, *Drvagner*, p. 582.
30. Ibid.
31. Yerevan Matenadaran, Archive of Catholicosate, 1g, f. 268.
32. Jezye was the capitation tax collected from every non-Muslim adult male. Jezye was paid by every village, and the level was calculated and recorded in the tax registers. Apart from the general sum, once in several years some percentage, called 'tafavot-e jezye', was added to the fixed sum and collected separately (Papazyan, *Matenadarani*, vol. 1, p. 118).
33. Ormanyan, *Azgapatum*, p. 3207; Ajemyan, 'Patmakan', p. 78.
34. Yerevan Matenadaran, Archive of Catholicosate, 1g 272.
35. L. G. Minasyan, and *Divan Surb Amenaprkich vanki 1606-1960* (Nor Jugha, 1983), p. 111 (in Armenian).
36. Ibid., pp. 115-16.

24

The Safavid Presence in the Indian Ocean: A Reappraisal of the *Ship of Solayman*, a Seventeenth-Century Travel Account to Siam

Christoph Marcinkowski

Preliminary remarks

The present contribution by someone involved in Iranian *as well as* South East Asian Studies advocates a quasi holistic approach with regard to research on the spread of Iranian civilization in the eastern Indian Ocean region and South East Asia. Cross-cultural contacts between Iran and that region during the pre-Islamic and early Islamic periods have already been the subject of scholarly work.[1] Lesser known, however, are the political, diplomatic and cultural activities of Safavid Iran (1501–1722) in the eastern Indian Ocean region, in particular in Siam, present-day Thailand. Previous works have so far mostly focused on Safavid-Mughal contacts, such as Riazul Islam's magisterial study *Indo-Persian Relations* (which also contains momentous material related to southern India).[2] With regard to Thailand it should be mentioned that I have already referred to the lack of interdisciplinary approaches at several international conferences,[3] and I am looking forward to observing the progress in this field at forthcoming meetings. This present chapter is intended to summarize my observations hitherto.

The Ship of Solayman

The *Safine-ye Solaymani* (Ship of Solayman), the English translation of which has been out of print for some time, constitutes to date the only extant Persian source of which we have knowledge, for the extensive Safavid contacts with the region in question. The relevance of the Safavid-Siamese connection to the history of the

Indian subcontinent, southern India in particular, shall also be addressed after a summary of the *Ship of Solayman*.

The *Ship of Solayman* is a Persian travel account of an embassy sent by the Safavid ruler Shah Solayman (r. 1666–94) to the court of the kingdom of Siam in the year 1685. Iran's Safavid dynasty, which ruled that country from 1501 to 1722,[4] is mainly remembered today for the introduction of the Twelver Shi'i brand of Islam as the State religion and for reuniting Iran. The *Ship of Solayman* was written by the embassy's secretary Mohammad Rabi' (b. Mohammad Ebrahim), who in the pertinent literature is usually referred to simply as Ebn Mohammad Ebrahim. The work is considered an outstanding document to the historical and cultural presence of Iran in the eastern Indian Ocean region. With regard to the importance of the Persian language in the investigation of historical sources, Professor David K. Wyatt of Cornell University, a well-known scholar on Thai studies, has stated:

> [S]ome years ago, intrigued by comments I had made about the origins of the Bunnag family, one of my students suggested she might study the Persian language and investigate Thai relations with Persia in the seventeenth century. My response must have carried with it a hint of ridicule, for she never mentioned the subject again. I am now embarrassed to have to tell her that the study of Persian would have repaid her efforts [...][5]

The *Ship of Solayman* was translated for the first time into English about three decades ago by John O'Kane and published in the *Persian Heritage Series*,[6] based on a manuscript kept in the British Museum.[7] O'Kane's translation, especially his introduction and comments, and the almost entire lack of annotations and bibliography, received some criticism from scholars of Thai studies as well as Iranologists, including the present writer.[8] Apparently, O'Kane had no access to the Thai language and did not consult a scholar of Thai studies.[9] According to Jean Aubin, a second manuscript copy of the *Safine-ye Solaymani* is said to be extant in Iran.[10] In 1977, Dr 'Abbas Faruqi published his edition of the Persian text, which was reprinted in 1999, and to which I had access.[11]

The *Ship of Solayman*[12] consists of four main parts, which are referred to as *tohfe* (gifts) in the Persian text, but translated as jewels by O'Kane. The work is headed by an introduction containing a glorification of the Almighty and His bounties[13] and a eulogy to the Prophet and 'Ali (b. Abi Taleb), his cousin, son-in-law and the first Emam of the Shi'ites.[14] After this, the author refers to his own name and profession, 'Ebn Mohammad Ebrahim Mohammad Rabi''[15] [i.e. Mohammad Rabi' Ebn Mohammad Ebrahim] 'scribe to the contingent of the royal musketeers',[16] which refers apparently to the *tofangchi* or musketeer-corps.[17] This is followed by ornate praise of Shah Solayman, Iran's then reigning monarch.[18] Particularly touching, however, is the way in which he refers to the Siamese king:

> Good rulers, therefore, take a further step on the path toward world harmony. With ambassadors and delegations as their key they unlock the doors

of world-wide friendship. Such was the intent of the Siamese king, possessor of the white elephant and the throne of solid gold. For he loves all Muslims and was overawed seeing that our king [i.e. the Safavid Shah Solayman], the brilliant luminary of world rule had risen into the Heavens of eternal sovereignty, our king who is the noble planet of good fortune, adornment of the throne of omnipotence and bearer of Chosroes' crown and the cap of Kayan. Thereupon the Siamese monarch hastened to open the accounts of friendship and affection, 'May Allah bless him and guide him into the fold of Islam'.[19]

The name of Siam's King Narai (r. 1656–88), however, does not appear throughout the account. Moreover, the introduction refers to the purpose of the Iranian embassy,[20] which was in reply to a Siamese embassy to Iran in 1682 led by an Iranian, as we shall see later. Ebn Mohammad Ibrahim mentions furthermore that he had been appointed to the post of official scribe for the delegation.[21]

The First Gift (and in fact the whole account) is written in a highly embellished style and reports on the travel from the Persian Gulf port Bandar 'Abbas to India, which started on 25 Rajab 1096/27 June 1685.[22] Ebn Mohammad Ibrahim served as the embassy's secretary. He presents a dramatic account of the storms that occurred during the crossing of the Sea of Oman, as well as of other severe problems arising from a shortage of drinking water, great heat (caused by the end of the monsoon season), and too strong or low winds, respectively. He adds that the travel was carried out on an English ship.[23] Throughout the entire account we come across Qur'anic quotations and lines of Persian poetry, which had been inserted into the narrative by Ebn Mohammad Ebrahim. The ship arrived at Muscat after a journey of 14 days.[24] Along with a description of that city, the author refers to previous fights between the Portuguese and the local Khariji Arabs, which had resulted in the expulsion of the former from the region about the middle of the seventeenth century. As a devout Twelver Shi'ite, he cannot resist using this occasion to indulge in some kind of theological speculation on the Khariji sect.[25] Despite his obvious contempt for the Kharijis, however, he refers to the Omanis as tolerant people. After a three-day stay at Muscat, the ship sets sail for India.[26] The author informs us that the ship was new and that the first 20 days of that part of the journey passed smoothly, due to favourable winds. Thereafter, however, he complains of severe storms again. In this connection, he refers to the death of an Iranian merchant of Mazandarani origin, who went overboard during a typhoon. Interestingly, he refers to the unfortunate man as a Mecca pilgrim, who was on his way back to India, which was apparently his permanent residence.[27] After a turbulent journey of 47 days the ship arrives at the city of Chinapatam – that is, Madras – in south-east India, a port which was then controlled by the English. Ebn Mohammad Ibrahim gives a detailed description of the fort and elaborates on the respectful reception given to them by the English. He refers to the inhabitants of the city as 'of various racial backgrounds' but adds that 'most of them are Telegu Hindus', as well as 'Portuguese Franks'.[28] He reports, that the nearby city of Maylapur, too, had been previously under the 'Franks' (in this case the Portuguese), but that it was reconquered by the Qotbshahis, to whom he refers interestingly merely as '*valis*' (governors).[29] Moreover, Ebn Mohammad Ebrahim also mentions that news of the death of King Charles II (on 6 February 1685) reached Madras during his stay there.[30] Full of contempt, our author also gives his impressions of Frankish dinner customs, dancing and religious practice. Nevertheless, he finds some words of admiration for the Western women, but disapproves their open participation in public life, in comparison with his home country.[31]

The Second Gift elaborates on the travel from India to the then Siamese port of Tanasuri – that is, Tenasserim in present-day Burma – by crossing the Gulf of Bengal, and from Tenasserim, via land, first to Ayutthaya and then to Lopburi, which was at that time the residence of the Siamese King Narai. The ship with Ebn Mohammad Ebrahim and the Iranian embassy on board left Madras on 17 Shavval 1096/16 September 1685. They encountered similar difficulties as those during their journey from Bandar 'Abbas to India. This time they almost suffered shipwreck near the coast of the Burmese kingdom of Paig – that is, Pegu – which Ebn Mohammad Ebrahim refers to strangely as a part of Khita, Cathay – that is, China – however, with a 'separate king'.[32] Finally, they arrived at the Siamese port of Mergui,[33] where the Iranian Hajji Salim, a representative of the Siamese king and former ambassador to the court to Iran,[34] welcomes them. Hajji Salim introduces them to some aspects of Siamese custom and protocol. Their reception by Siamese officials present at that port is described as particularly respectful. Interestingly, our author mentions an Iranian, Mohammad Sadeq, as governor of Siamese Mergui and the entire adjoining province,[35] who functions as their host during their stay in that city. After some days rest, the embassy continues its journey by boat to Tenasserim. It is remarkable, that Ebn Mohammad Ebrahim sometimes refers to the entire country of Siam as Shahr-e Nav,[36] but on other occasions he applies that expression only to its capital, Ayutthaya. With regard to Tenasserim, our author states that it was inhabited by Siamese, Indian Sunni Muslims (he mentions explicitly their respective *hanafi* and *shafi'i* legal rites), Hindus and Franks.[37] Interestingly, the Persian word for Frank, referring to a Westerner, entered the Thai language as a loan word and is still used today.

At that time, the governor Mohammad Sadeq appears to have been with them still. Here, our author reports that the Iranian ambassador Hosayn Bayg had succumbed to a disease on 12 Moharram 1097/19 December 1685, following the various illnesses of other members of the delegation.[38] From Tenasserim the remaining members of the embassy continue their journey to the Siamese capital, Ayutthaya, taking one and a half months, the normal time supposedly being 25 to 26 days.[39] For 25 days of that journey they were in a boat floating on 'a great river',[40] perhaps the Tenasserim River. Finally, having crossed the peninsula, they arrive at Paj Puri – that is, Phetchapuri – where they are received by a Sayyed Mazandarani, another Iranian governor in Siamese service.[41] From there, they proceed to a city that Ebn Mohammad Ebrahim refers as Suhan, on the 'river to Shahr-e Nav', situated at one-day's boat travel from the capital.[42]

The present writer is not certain about its exact location, but the river mentioned by Ebn Mohammad Ebrahim seems to be the Chao Phraya. The governor, *raje*, in charge of that town was another Muslim, referred to by the author as 'Chelebi'. According to Ebn Mohammad Ebrahim, he was 'from Rum'; that is, an Anatolian Turk, who had recently 'converted' to Shi'ism.[43] Professor Anthony Reid of the Center for Southeast Asian Studies at the University of California, Los Angeles seems to identify the area administered by Chelebi with that of today's Bangkok.[44] There the travellers are also greeted by members of the local Iranian community.[45] Soon after, they proceed upstream on the Chao Phraya River, to the royal capital, Ayutthaya. There they are informed of the fact that the king had left for Lub – that is, Lopburi. Having arrived at that city, our author describes it as a strong fortress and mentions a certain Khvaje Hasan 'Ali Khorasani, supposedly a descendant of Khvaje 'Abd al-Latif, a former Safavid *vazir* of Khorasan, as the head of the Iranian community residing in Siam and the successor in that position to Aqa Mohammad, who had died earlier.[46]

Particularly disturbing throughout the entire account is the author's severe contempt for Siamese customs and manners,[47] especially when compared with the distinguished examples of respect and hospitality on the part of the Siamese towards the Iranian guests, to which even Ebn Mohammad Ebrahim refers on numerous occasions.[48] Interestingly, however, the lodgings for the Iranian guests in Lopburi are described by our author as Iranian in style, furnished with *hammams* and carpets and so on.[49] During their stay at Lopburi, Ebrahim Bayg, a *gholam*[50] of the imperial Safavid *khasse*, or Household,[51] is chosen as successor to the deceased Iranian ambassador, to the disappointment of Ebn Mohammad Ebrahim.[52] Also very important is his account of the background to the Iranian community's loss of influence and favour with the king, which our author considers the result of the machinations of a new favourite, the Greek Constantine Phaulkon, to whom he does not refer by this name, but rather by the contemptuous expression 'the evil Frank'.[53] Ebn Mohammad Ebrahim even claims that it was Phaulkon who influenced the king's not meeting the Iranian embassy *en route* and then postponing the audience.[54] Finally, a first audience does take place, whose formalities are described by our author, focusing particularly on the manner of how the letter of the Safavid shah was presented to the Siamese monarch.[55] About the actual contents, however, the reader is left in the dark. It follows a description of several hunting expeditions and dinner invitations at which the Iranians participated.[56] Subsequently, the king moves to his capital, Ayutthaya, and the Iranian embassy has to follow him.[57] Again, Ebn Mohammad Ebrahim reiterates, they are lodged in Iranian houses, with Siamese and Iranian attendants.[58] Soon thereafter, the members of the Iranian embassy decide to embark on their return journey and, in order to save time, they choose not to return by land to Tenasserim, but to go directly by sea.[59] Before that could happen, however, the king invites them on another hunting expedition, this time to the aforementioned Suhan, followed by similar activities to before.[60] At this point, Ebn Mohammad Ebrahim inserts important information about the custom of the Iranian community in Siam of performing *ta'ziye* or mourning ceremonies and performances in memory of the death of the Prophet's grandson Hosayn (b. Ali b. Abi Taleb at Karbala). These ceremoniees were paid for by the (Buddhist) Siamese monarch, who also provided a special building and other facilities for that purpose.[61] The French traveller Guy Tachard, who was at the Siamese capital about the same time, has left us an impressive account of such a performance of particularly Shi'i religiosity which is worth citing in full:

> [T]he Moors [the Shi'ite Muslims resident at the Siamese capital] made great Illuminations for eight days together, in Honour of their Prophet Mahomet [i.e. Mohammad] and his Son [sic!62], whose Funerals they celebrated. They began to solemnize the Festival the Evening before about four of the Clock at Night, by a kind of Procession, wherein they were above two thousand Souls. There they carried the Figure of the Tombs of those two Impostors, with many Symbols of a pretty neat Representation, amongst others, certain great Cages covered with painted Cloth, and carried by Men that marched and continually turned in cadence to the Sound of Drums and Timbrels. The quick and regular Motion of these huge Machines which we saw at a distance, without perceiving those that carried them, occasioned an agreeable Surprise.
>
> At the Head of this great Confluence of People, some Grooms led three or four Horses in rich Trappings, and a great many People carrying several Lanthorns at the end of long Poles, lighted all the Procession and sung in divers Quires after a very odd manner. With the same Zeal they continued this Festival for several Nights together till five of the Clock in the Morning. It is hardly to be conceived how these Porters of Machines, that uncessantly turned, could perform that Exercise for fifteen or sixteen Hours together, nor how the Singers that raised their Voices as high as was possible for them, could sing so long. The rest of the Procession looked modest enough, some marched before the Singers, who surrounded Coffins carried upon eight Mens Shoulders, and the rest were mingled in the Croud with them. There were a great many Siamese Men and Women, Young and Old there, who have embraced the Mahometan Religion [i.e. Islam]. For since the Moors have got footing in the Kingdom, they have drawn over a great many People to their Religion, which is an Argument that they are not so addicted to their Superstitions [a derogative remark referring to Theravada Buddhism?], but that they can forsake them, when our Missionaries have had Patience and Zeal enough to instruct them in our Mysteries. It is true, that Nation is a great Lover of Shows and splendid Ceremonies, and by that means it is that the Moors, who celebrate their Festivals with a great deal of Magnificence, have perverted many of them to the Sect of Mahomet.[63]

Other audiences with the king and the exchange of gifts followed, although our witness complains of the supposedly lower value of the Siamese presents, which was in his view again due to the machinations of the 'evil Frankish minister', that is, Phaulkon.⁶⁴ Finally, the Iranian embassy left Siam for Iran by ship on 22 Safar 1098/18 January 1687.⁶⁵

The Third Gift amounts to a 'report on the interior affairs of the kingdom of Siam'. Ebn Mohammad Ebrahim begins this part by referring to the terms *Chin* and *Machin* as they appear in Muslim geographical literature of earlier times,⁶⁶ but, more interestingly, he gives an explanation for the expression *Shahr-e Nav* for the country of Siam and, more specifically, for its then capital Ayutthaya.⁶⁷ We shall return to this subject later. Our source then refers in some length to the conflict of Siam with neighbouring Pegu.⁶⁸ Worthy of special note is Ebn Mohammad Ebrahim's statement that Iranians were highly respected in the kingdom and that they were even considered responsible for the enthronement of King Narai.⁶⁹ According to him, Iranians used also to exercise a strong cultural influence over the private habits of the king, such as his choice of dishes and drinks as well as his clothes.⁷⁰ Moreover, King Narai used also to surround himself with lifeguards from India, most probably Iranians, or at least Shi'i Indian Muslims from the southern part of the subcontinent.⁷¹ He refers at some length to the conflict between the rising fortunes of Constantine Phaulkon and his 'pro-French leanings' and the affairs of the Iranian community.⁷² The third part contains also 'information', or more accurately 'comments', from our author on Siamese religious practice,⁷³ the legal system,⁷⁴ as well as the holidays and festivals, the marriage and funeral rites,⁷⁵ official titles, criminal investigations and kinds of punishments,⁷⁶ but all this from a somewhat haughty perspective of supposed cultural superiority. After reporting on the suppression of a revolt started by the resident community of Macassar Sunni Muslims,⁷⁷ he closes the third part of his account with a lengthy reference to what he perceived to have been the daily routine,⁷⁸ income,⁷⁹ and expenses⁸⁰ of the Siamese monarch, and adds to this some remarks on the economy and the major trade goods,⁸¹ as well as the life and food of the common people.⁸²

The importance of the Third Gift lies in the fact that it highlights the role played by various members of the local Iranian community as supporters of the Siamese ruler, who is portrayed as an extreme Iranophile. This portion is extremely valuable with regard to the earliest history of today's still influential Bunnag family, which traces its roots back to Iranian ancestry, and which was influential at the Siamese court during the following centuries. We will refer again to this point below.

The Fourth Gift refers in a rather general fashion to some of Siam's neighbours, such as the Philippine islands, the Dutch possessions in what is now Indonesia, and even China and Japan, all of which is mostly based on hearsay. He starts this section with a geographical part, containing observations on Siam's flora and fauna, and what he perceived to be the effects of the tides, which is, however, generally more bizarre and fantastic than really informative.⁸³ His knowledge of the island of Ceylon, which he must have passed on his way to Siam, as well as on his return, is also based on hearsay, by quoting earlier Muslim geographers and historians.⁸⁴ He has also a part on the kingdom of Achi – that is, Acheh in northern Sumatra – and states explicitly that he had seen it,[85] most probably on his way back to Iran. He refers to the supposed Arab descent of its kings,[86] to fabulous amounts of gold to be found in that country,[87] and to the supposed 'treacherous nature' of its inhabitants.[88] He proceeds to the Andamans, whose inhabitants he believes were cannibals,[89] and thence to Nakbari – that is, the Nicobars.[90] This is followed by remarks on countries he certainly did not visit, such as the Philippine islands, which he refers to strangely as allah,[91] but whose capital city he rightly identifies as Manile – that is, Manila.[92] He identifies the Castilians, Spaniards, as its rulers and gives quite a detailed (and generally somewhat admiring) account regarding the instalment of its governors and the presence of Chinese settlers, but this is followed by the, one is tempted to say, usual references to gold treasures.[93] To this he adds what he had heard about Japan, aside from the usual fantastic stories, in particular on the activities of the Dutch and Portuguese in that country, and that only the Dutch were able to retain some favour there.[94] In a similar style he refers to Siam's then neighbours Pegu and China[95] (with regard to the latter he even has a section on supposed visits by Alexander the Great to that country[96]).

With regard to his return travel, he states that he passed Pattani, the rebellious Siamese vassal and one of the petty Malay principalities, whose inhabitants adhere to the *shafi'i* legal rite.[97] His quite accurate account of the custom of sending a golden flower (Malay: *bunga mas*) to the kings of Siam as a sign of loyalty is interesting.[98] Ebn Mohammad Ebrahim refers also to the then Dutch port of Malaqe – that is, Malacca – but states that he did not land there.[99] Moving on to India, he makes reference to Kuchi – that is, Cochin – then also under the Dutch, and the Malabar coast, called by him Malivar. His report on the customs of the local people is again rather bizarre, but he states that the Dutch had recently taken over the port from the Portuguese.[100] The returning Iranian delegation had to stay six full months at Cochin,[101] since they missed the season for sailing directly to the Persian Gulf. Instead, they embarked on a ship bound to Surat and were attacked on the way by pirates, resulting in the death of some passengers.[102] While trying to enter the port of Surat, they found it under a blockade by an English fleet, due to a conflict with the Mughals.[103] The English forced the ship to sail to Mumbai, which was under their control, and the Iranians stayed there for three and a half months, although they were apparently treated with respect by the English.[104] Ebn Mohammad Ebrahim refers in this connection to the circumstance that the city was given by Portugal as dowry to the English King,[105] Charles II (on the occasion of his marriage with Catherine of Braganza). Finally, the embassy left Mumbai on 5 Jumada II 1099/8 April 1688 on a ship bound for the Persian Gulf.[106] After surviving another attack by pirates *en route*, they arrive safely at Bandar 'Abbas on 24 Rajab 1099/14 May 1688.[107]

The Fourth Gift is followed by a quite detailed Appendix on the Mughal conquest of Haydarabad – that is, Hyderabad on the Deccan, the capital of the Golconda kingdom, ruled by the Shi'i Qotbshahs – which happened on 21 September 1687.[108] News of this momentous event had apparently also reached the returning Iranian mission, which was passing close by. The earlier fall of the kingdom of Bijapur on 12

September 1686 was also noticed by our author.[109] Remarkably, he refers to the rulers of both kingdoms merely as 'governors'.[110] The *Ship of Solayman* closes with the mention of the escape of the Mughal prince Akbar to the court of Iran,[111] which took place in 1682.

Ayutthaya, the 'city of boats and canals'

Throughout his account, Ebn Mohammad Ebrahim refers to the kingdom of Siam and to its then capital Ayutthaya with the Persian expression *Shahr-e Nav*. At least, O'Kane has offered this vowelling throughout his English translation. Modern (in particular Western) scholars, however, tend to refer to the variant form *Shahr-e Naw* (literally new city), which is said to have been applied since the fourteenth century throughout Muslim geographical literature (Persian and, remarkably, Arabic as well) when in fact referring to Ayutthaya, which was founded in 1351 as the country's new capital[112] and named after the sacred city of Ayodhya in India.[113] However, it appears that there existed a variety of different spellings of the Persian name, which it is important to note since different meanings are to be derived from them. Besides the form *Shahr-e Naw*, there exists also the variant *Shahr Nawi*, which we come across in the poetry of Hamze Fansuri,[114] the most enigmatic Malay mystical poet, who flourished in the sixteenth century, and furthermore in the sixteenth-century Malay chronicle *Sejarah Melayu*.[115] *Shahr Nawi* is said to be derived from the form *Shahr-e Naw*, new city.[116] In addition to that, Tibbetts records the form *Shahr Nawa*.[117]

To add to the confusion, we find throughout Ebn Mohammad Ebrahim's account the already referred to *Shahr-e Nav*. It is highly significant that this means literally, city of boats and canals.[118] We have elsewhere discussed the alternatives to Ebn Mohammad Ebrahim's *Shahr-e Nav*.[119] Here, we would like to reiterate our view that *Shahr-e Nav* should be the correct form. At this point, it should suffice to see what Steve Van Beek has to tell us about the etymology of the city's full Thai name:

> [...] from the beginning, Ayutthaya's destiny was written in water. Its Sanskrit name, Krung Thep Dvaravati Si Ayutthaya, is derived from the Mon word *krerng*, meaning 'canal' or 'river'. Although located in the heart of a fertile rice region, it sat on level ground, open to enemy attack. U-Thong [the founder of the city] compensated for this disadvantage by turning his city into a mini-Mont-Saint-Michel, a citadel ringed by a wall of earth and water, much like the mythical Phrasumen Mountain which, according to Hindu cosmology, occupied the centre of the universe. Ayutthaya's distance from the river-mouth protected it from sea-borne invasion. The rivers and canals which radiated from it were arteries for transport and were its principal avenues of contact with a further world.[120]

At any rate, Ebn Mohammad Ebrahim himself has emphasized the character of Ayutthaya as a city of boats and canals, when referring to the Persian name for the city:

> The name *Shahr-i Nav*:[121] The mainstay of travel and transportation in that whole region is the boat. In fact the name of the country and the capital means city of the boat. However, the local inhabitants call the city Ajaudia, which in their language means big city [sic!]. Finally, the Franks and men of learning who have gone more deeply into this subject refer to the city in their books as Siam.[122]

Ayutthaya was indeed a city dominated by boats and canals,[123] as was also the case with Thailand's present capital Bangkok far into the nineteenth century.[124] At any rate, Ebn Mohammad Ebrahim, when referring to Ayutthaya, conveyed in *The Ship of Solayman* the appropriate meaning of city of boats and canals by spelling it *Shahr-e Nav*.[125] In this context it is interesting to note that even according to Europeans who visited the region during the late seventeenth century, Persian was the *lingua franca* in the trading world of the Gulf of Bengal and the eastern Indian Ocean rim.[126] The rendering as 'new city', derived from a wrong reading (and vowelling), as done by most Western writers with no access to the Persian language, is therefore inappropriate and ought to be corrected in future studies.

Safavid-Siamese contacts and the Iranian community in the Siamese Ayutthaya kingdom

Ayutthaya's early history from the fourteenth century onwards has been studied in detail by Professor Charnvit Kasetsiri of Bangkok's Thammasat University,[127] Thailand's leading scholar on the history of the Ayutthaya Empire (1351–1767), and by Professor David K. Wyatt of Cornell University.[128] Ayutthaya is situated at a distance of only about 140km from the Gulf of Siam, at the lower course of the Chao Phraya river, which was then navigable even for larger vessels.[129] The city, which today is one hour's drive on a highway from Bangkok, is still an island[130] surrounded by rivers. Its location near the coast made it easily accessible to foreign merchant ships and destined it to become one of the major trading emporia of South East Asia. Ebn Mohammad Ebrahim stated that '[s]ince Siam is close to the ports of India and is situated on the sea route to China and Japan, merchants have always been attracted to settle there'.[131]

However, the foundation of Malacca (although at least nominally Siam's vassal) as well as the occupation of that port by the Portuguese in 1511[132] forced the rulers of Ayutthaya to search for other gateways for trade with the western Indian Ocean region. Therefore, during the 1460s Siam assumed control over Tenasserim, which was followed by Mergui in 1480,[133] thus gaining direct access to the Gulf of Bengal.

Further west, the first decades of the sixteenth century had seen the gradual stabilization of Mughal rule over northern India.[134] Only towards the beginning of the seventeenth century, however, did the Mughals gain full control over Bengal and Orissa[135] and become major players in the Bay of Bengal.

Highly significant in the context of the activities of Iranians in the eastern Indian Ocean rim is the emergence of Shi'ite kingdoms in the Deccan as successors to the Bahmanid Empire (1347–1525),[136] among them the Golconda kingdom of the Qutb Shahi dynasty (1512–1687).[137] This is not the place for a detailed discussion of the consequences of this development, but what should be kept in mind is that the Qutb Shahis, as well as their Muslim neighbours, adhered to Twelver Shi'ism and fostered strong political and religious ties with Safavid Iran. In line with this, the names of the Safavid rulers were even mentioned alongside the names of the Twelve Emams in the sermon during Friday prayers.[138] Those Shi'ite Deccan kingdoms, which were strongly influenced by Iranian culture,[139] were to attract Shi'ites from abroad, in most cases Iranians from Iran, but also from northern India. Sanjay Subrahmanyam of the École des Hautes Études en Sciences Sociales (EHESS), Paris, has provided numerous evidences for the massive economic, political and literary presence of Iranians in the Golconda kingdom of the Qutb Shahis.[140] By the second half of the sixteenth century there existed trade links between Golconda's main port Masulipatam (or Matchlibandar)[141] and Siamese Tenasserim.[142] The southern Indian Qutb Shahi kingdom also served as an important gateway to South East Asia, to the Thai empire of Ayutthaya in particular. In the light of the dominating role of Persianized Muslim states on the subcontinent, it is not surprising that the Siamese trading emporium of Ayutthaya should have been known under a Persian name to the mainly Muslim merchants.

I have dealt with the circumstances for the emergence of an Iranian community in Siam, in particular at the capital Ayutthaya, in some detail elsewhere,[143] where it has also been stated that Iranians might have been present in the kingdom at least since the early sixteenth century. The presence of Iranians at the Siamese capital Ayutthaya, however, seems to have been rather limited in number up to the beginning of the seventeenth century.[144] The political instability on the Deccan, the extension of international Safavid trade under Shah 'Abbas II (r. 1642–66),[145] as well as the expansion of Siamese trade with East Asia, in particular Japan,[146] which resulted in Ayutthaya becoming an important entrepôt for trade with that region, seem to have been the major factors for an increased Iranian immigration, whether directly from Iran or via India. It has been argued, moreover, that the increased economic and geopolitical significance of Ayutthaya necessitated the introduction of maritime laws along with clearly outlined responsibilities for officials dealing with foreigners,[147] which were now placed under the responsibility of a minister who was known in Thai as *Phra Khlang*, an office for which Breazeale has created the ingenious English translation, Ministry of External Relations and Maritime Trading Affairs.[148] This office became known to seventeenth-century European traders under various corrupted forms, such as Berklam[149] or Barcalon.[150]

The structuring of this important office has been studied by Breazeale and shall not concern us here.¹⁵¹ According to him, however, an Iranian, a certain Shaykh Ahmad 'of Qumm' had been in charge of the affairs and restructuring of the *Krom Tha Khwa* department since the year 1610, referring to that part of the ministry dealing with trade with 'the West' – that is, the Indian Ocean rim. More detailed information on the mysterious Shaykh Ahmad can be obtained from genealogical studies into the (ethnic) origins of Thai nobility carried out by Professor Wyatt.¹⁵² In the present context, it is only important to note that Shaykh Ahmad's descendants played momentous parts in Thai history during the eighteenth and nineteenth centuries. Wyatt also supplied in one of his contributions a genealogical table of Shaykh Ahmad's offspring.¹⁵³

More significant for a proper understanding of the historical background to the *Ship of Solayman* is the aforementioned transformation of Ayutthaya into a major hub of international trade in Asia. The presence of numerous foreign merchants there, as well as geopolitical considerations, might have driven Siam's kings to seek diplomatic contacts with other countries with an interest in Indian Ocean trade, perhaps also to counterbalance the growing power of Mughal India. In line with these considerations, the court of Golconda, for instance, received in the year 1664 a splendid Siamese embassy.¹⁵⁴ In 1669, only five years later, another Siamese embassy, sent by King Narai (r. 1656-88), arrived at the court of the Safavid Shah Solayman (r. 1666-94).¹⁵⁵ E. W. Hutchinson asserts also, that another Siamese trade mission was sent to Iran in 1680/81.¹⁵⁶ A letter by the Apostolic Vicar and titular Bishop François 'of Caesaropolis', a French missionary residing at Isfahan, to his sovereign Louis XIV, dated 20 January 1683, refers also to a Siamese embassy which was present that year at the Safavid court.¹⁵⁷ Kaempfer, too, who visited Iran, prior to his stays in Siam and subsequently Japan, reports in July 1684 that (another?) Siamese embassy was present at the shah's court, at the park of Sa'dabad.¹⁵⁸ According to Kaempfer,¹⁵⁹ the leader of the Siamese embassy was 'Persian born', apparently the Hajji Salim Mazandarani referred to in the *Ship of Solayman*.¹⁶⁰ Thus, it appears that the Iranian embassy of 1686 to Ayutthaya recorded in this account was in fact to reciprocate the visit of the Siamese mission to Isfahan in 1684 and not the earlier Siamese visit of 1669.¹⁶¹ The sixteenth- and seventeenth-century network of Iranian merchants, which was virtually controlling the eastern Indian Ocean maritime trade and was operating from southern India cannot be dealt with here in detail, but has recently been studied comprehensively by Subrahmanyam, referred to earlier, and by Jean Aubin.¹⁶² That the presence of Iranians in Siam, in particular at Ayutthaya, was rather limited until the mid-seventeenth century is attested to by both Western observers¹⁶³ and by Ebn Mohammad Ebrahim:

> From the time merchants first arrived until just before the present king came to power [i.e. King Narai, in 1656], about thirty Iranians had settled in Siam due to the great profits to be made in trade. Each of these Iranians was honored

with the utmost respect, presented with a house and given a specific position in the Siamese king's administration.[164]

In this context, it is worth noting that Ebn Mohammad Ebrahim did not, even once throughout his account, refer to Shaykh Ahmad by his name or as the alleged 'founder of the Iranian community' in Siam.

It is again Subrahmanyam, who has given the most comprehensive summary of the complex development that led to the increase in significance of Siam's Iranian community in the course of the seventeenth century.[165] Accordingly, King Narai is said to have been under Iranian cultural influences in terms of his daily food and dress and his preferred architectural styles.[166] The fortunes of Siam's Iranian community were checked by the rise of the Greek Constantine Phaulkon to royal favour, which happened about the time of Ebn Mohammad Ebrahim's visit to Siam, but which is beyond the present scope.

At any rate, perhaps the services rendered by the Iranian community to their host-country Siam should mainly be understood in the originally rather quietistic context of Shi'i Islam.[167] In the view of Professor Anthony Reid, it appears that the rulers of Ayutthaya were aware and appreciative of the loyal attitude of their Iranian subjects.[168] As we have seen earlier, the steady increase of the Shi'i community in Siam, in the capital in particular, might furthermore have been the result of an influx of Shi'is, especially Iranians, from the strongly Persianized Shi'i states of the southern Indian Deccan, which, as discussed above, was a direct result of the constant threats from the staunchly Sunni Mughal empire, which in the course of the 1680s was actually to annex them to its territory.[169] With regard to the conditions of the Muslim communities in the sixteenth-/seventeenth-century Ayutthaya kingdom, Guy Tachard, a French visitor to Siam in the 1680s, mentioned in great detail the public performance of the Shi'i *'Ashura'* mourning ceremonies (*ta'ziye*)[170] in the Siamese capital, as we have seen above.[171] In addition to this, the usually reliable Engelbert Kaempfer, who visited Ayutthaya in 1690, refers to the Persian language as the *lingua franca* in Siam.[172] Perhaps this refers to matters pertaining to the trade with the Muslim states in India, since the Malay language seems to have been applied in dealing with the Malay-Indonesian world.[173]

It cannot be established with certainty how many Iranian Muslims actually lived in Ayutthaya towards the second half of the seventeenth century, until the destruction of the city and kingdom by the Burmese invaders in 1767. Perhaps, from reports by Western travellers, such Frenchman Guy Tachard (who is thus perhaps not under suspicion of being all too sympathetic towards things Shi'i), and from Ebn Mohammad Ebrahim's statements in his *The Ship of Solayman*, it can be inferred that the majority of Muslims living in the then capital ascribed to Twelver Shi'ism, although there might also have been present a substantial number of Sunnis, especially from the Malay-Indonesian archipelago. It appears that the relations between Ayutthaya's Shi'i Muslim community and their Buddhist environment was marked by mutual respect and tolerance, a circumstance which is further substantiated by the fact that since the first half of the seventeenth century various dignitaries from among the resident Persian community served in the highest administrative positions of the kingdom, as discussed above.

In the year 1994, a conference had been conducted on the role of the mysterious Shaykh Ahmad and the Iranians residing in Siam during the seventeenth century. The one-day meeting in Ayutthaya was organized by the Cultural Center of the Iranian Embassy in Bangkok. Unfortunately, the proceedings of this meeting (published in Thai with selected English abstracts) record meagre results.[174] The compound of Ayutthaya's Rajabhat Institute Phranakhon Si Ayutthaya, the city's teacher training institution, situated near the modern Ayutthaya Historical Study Center where the conference took place, houses today a little park with a structure believed to mark the grave of Shaykh Ahmad. According to Professor Charnvit Kasetsiri,[175] it is rather doubtful whether that is the actual spot of Shaykh Ahmad's grave. Professor Charnvit Kasetsiri seems to prefer a location outside the city compound. At any rate, a memorial tablet, one of three, in Thai and situated at one of the entrances to the park indicates the place as the tomb of 'Chaophraya Boworn Rajnayok (Shaykh Ahmad of Qumm)'. Another tablet with a Thai inscription and an English translation is situated at the centre of the park. The English text runs as follows:[176]

> Chao Phya Boworn Rajnayok (Sheikh Ahmad), Shia-Ithna Ashari [i.e. Twelver Shi'ite] Muslim, was born in 1543 A.D. in the Paeene Shahar district of Qum, the Islamic centre of Iran. Towards the end of the reign of King Naresuan the Great [r. 1590–1605], Sheikh Ahmad and his retinue migrated to Ayudhya and set up their residential and trading quarters in the Ghayee landing district. His business prospered and he became very wealthy. He was married to a lady named 'Chuey', who bore him two sons and a daughter. As a result of his contribution to the development of the port administration in the reign of King Songdham [Song Tham, r. 1610/11–1628], Sheikh Ahmad was appointed by royal command to be Phya Sheikh Ahmad Rattana Rajsethee, Head of 'Krom Tha of the Right' in charge of foreign trade and responsible for the settling of disputes among foreigners other than Chinese, and as Chula Rajmontri [i.e. *Shaykh al-Islam*], the leader of the Muslim community, he was the first holder of the 'Chula Rajmontri' title and was recognized as the person who introduced the Shia-Ithna Ashari sect [i.e. Twelver Shi'ism] to Thailand. Subsequently, Sheikh Ahmad, together with his devoted friends, helped suppress an uprising in Ayudhya when a group of foreigners seized the Grand Palace. This dangerous deed let to his promotion by the king to the title 'Chao Phya'. He thus became Chao Phya Sheikh Ahmad Rattana Dhibodi, holding position of the 'Principle Minister for Civil Affairs (North)'. During the reign of King Prasartthong [r. 1629–56], when Sheikh Ahmad was 87 years old, the king appointed him 'Emeritus Councillor for the Civil Affairs' with the new

title of 'Chao Phya Boworn Rajnayok'. He passed away one year later in 1631 A.D. at the age of 88.

Both inscription tablet and tomb structure are relatively new. In fact, the tomb construction seems to have been carried out in connection with the said conference and is perhaps based on a kind of agreement between the Iranian and Thai authorities. However, the information provided on the tablet raises rather more questions on Shaykh Ahmad's actual identity than it answers. Shaykh Ahmad who is said to have arrived at Ayutthaya in 1602,[177] usually features as the ancestor of the Bunnag family in nineteenth- and twentieth-century Thai works on the genealogy of Siam's nobility.[178] The tablet refers to him as Shaykh Ahmad of Qumm – that is, of Qumm in central Iran. However, according to some research carried out by Associate Professor Pitya Bunnag, his actual place of origin is far from being established.[179] However, Shaykh Ahmad seems indeed to have been the first *Chularajmontri* or *Shaykh al-Islam* of Thailand. The emergence of that office in the Siamese context, a very exciting subject which gives further evidence for the influence of Iranians in the subsequent periods of Thai history, has been addressed elsewhere.[180]

Along with their countless other Buddhist compatriots, Muslims must have suffered during the total destruction of Ayutthaya by the Burmese in 1767.[181] However, apparently some of Shaykh Ahmad's descendants did survive this disaster, since political influence exercised by personalities originating from families of Iranian descent continued even in the subsequent Bangkok period.[182] The main branch of Shaykh Ahmad's family converted to Buddhism during the Bangkok period and featured in the court society of that period as the Bunnag family.[183] Today, members of the Bunnag family continue to serve their country in high positions, such as H. E. Professor Marut Bunnag, until recently President of Thailand's National Assembly and Speaker of the House of Representatives, who also attended the previously mentioned 1994 meeting in Ayutthaya.[184] The second branch of the family, however, remained Twelver Shi'ite Muslims, since until 1945 the office of *Chularajmontri* or *Shaykh al-Islam* used to be bestowed upon a descendant of Shaykh Ahmad.[185]

Conclusion

With regard to the overall significance of *The Ship of Solayman*, its uniqueness (as far as we know), and in particular its consequence for the study of Thai history, Professor Wyatt, stated in the 1970s:

> *The Ship of Sulaiman* deserves to be included among the most important primary sources for the history of Siam in the reign of King Narai. It is particularly

welcome because it should serve to open up new avenues of inquiry that have previously been neglected.[186]

From the point of view of the present writer, the *Ship of Solayman* provides also meaningful and significant information on the collapse of the southern Indian Shi'i kingdoms under the Mughal onslaught, since Ebn Mohammad Ebrahim happened to be in the region not much later. Ebn Mohammad Ebrahim's observations on the activities of Western powers in the Indian Ocean region are also substantial, in particular the Dutch, English and the waning fortunes of the Portuguese. From the perspective of Iranian as well as South East Asian and Thai studies, the account is particularly rich in information on Siam's Iranian community, making it a kind of *Who's Who* in this field. However, it provides no answer to the burning question of *who* really were the very first Iranian visitors to the country. Moreover, it does not contribute to our knowledge on Shaykh Ahmad of Qumm (whose name does not appear even once throughout the account), the ancestor of the powerful Bunnag family and Siam's first *Shaykh al-Islam*, but it does refer to his early successors.

References to flora and fauna, as well as to countries which Ebn Mohammad Ebrahim certainly did not see, such as China, Japan and the Philippines, but also to some regions which he did visit – Acheh, for instance – are usually unreliable, since they are based on hearsay. The *Ship of Solayman* is furthermore full of contempt for Siamese (Thai) customs and beliefs, giving evidence of its author's complete lack of understanding of, and sympathy for, the country and its hospitable people. He refers constantly to a supposed cultural superiority of Iran and its religion. There are, however, no traces of ethnic bias in the text. Finally, Thai expressions, if he bothers to refer to them at all, appear mostly in a corrupted and at times unintelligible form.

It is hoped that I will be in the position to present in the near future an analysis of the *Ship of Solayman* that is more detailed than has been possible in the framework of this contribution. Ultimately, it will be an interdisciplinary approach and exchange with scholars working in various interrelated fields, such as on Muslim southern India, maritime relations in the Indian Ocean rim, as well as Iranian and Thai studies, which will be able to add further to our knowledge on the activities of Iranians in that region during the Safavid period.

Notes

This chapter is dedicated to Professor Charnvit Kasetsiri as a token of respect.

1. See, for instance, Brian E. Colless, 'Persian merchants and missionaries in medieval Malaya', *Journal of the Malaysian Branch of the Royal Asiatic Society* (henceforth *JMBRAS*) 42/pt. 2 (1969), pp. 10–47, and especially Brian E. Colless, 'The traders of the Pearl. The mercantile and missionary activities of Persian and Armenian Christians in South East-Asia', *Abr Nahrain* (henceforth *AN*) 9 (1969–70), pp. 17–38; *AN* 10 (1970–1), pp. 102–21; *AN* 11 (1970), pp. 1–21; *AN* 13 (1972–3), pp. 113–35; *AN* 14 (1973–4), pp. 1–16; *AN* 15 (1974–5), pp. 6–17; *AN* 18 (1978–9), pp. 1–18, furthermore G. R. Tibbetts, 'Pre-Islamic

Arabia and South-East Asia', *Journal of the Malaysian Branch on the Royal Asiatic Society* (henceforth *JMBRAS*) 29/pt. 3 (1955), pp. 182–208; G. R. Tibbetts, 'Early Muslim traders in South-East Asia', *JMBRAS* 30, pt. 1 (1957), pp. 1–45; G. R. Tibbetts, *A Study of the Arabic Text Containing Material on South-East Asia* (Leiden and London, 1979); David Whitehouse and Andrew Williamson, 'Sasanian maritime trade', *Iran* 11 (1973), pp. 29–43. Of particular interest in the present context is also Julian Reade (ed.), *The Indian Ocean in Antiquity* (London and New York, 1996), a proceedings volume of a conference conducted at the British Museum from 4–8 July 1988 containing several articles related to the activities of pre-Islamic Iran in the region.

2. Riazul Islam, *Indo-Persian Relations. A Study of the Political and Diplomatic Relations between the Mughal Empire and Iran* (Tehran, 1970). See, however, also Patricia Risso, *Merchants & Faith: Muslim Commerce and Culture in the Indian Ocean* (Boulder, CO, 1995); Sinnappah Arasaratnam, *Maritime India in the Seventeenth Century* (Delhi, 1994); K. N. Chaudhuri, *Trade and Civilisation in the Indian Ocean. An Economic History from the Rise of Islam to 1750* (Cambridge, 1986, reprint), Ashin Das Gupta, 'Indian merchants and the trade in the Indian Ocean, c. 1500–1750', in T. Raychaudhuri and I. Habib (eds), *The Cambridge Economic History of India. Vol. I: c. 1250–c. 1750* (Cambridge: Cambridge University Press, 1982), pp. 407–33; Ashin Das Gupta, 'Introduction II: The story', in A. Das Gupta and M. N. Pearson (eds), *India and the Indian Ocean, 1500–1800* (Delhi, 1987), pp. 25–45; Ashin Das Gupta, 'The maritime merchant, c. 1500–1800', *Proceedings of the Indian History Congress, Presidential Address to the Medieval Section, 35th Session 1974, Jadavpur University Calcutta* (Delhi, 1974), pp. 1–15.

3. See 'Bibliography'.

4. Useful for a general introduction is Roger M. Savory, *Iran under the Safavids* (New York and Melbourne, 1980). See also my 'The reputed issue of the "ethnic origin" of Iran's Safavid dynasty (907–1145/1501–1722): Reflections on selected prevailing views', *Journal of the Pakistan Historical Society* 49/2 (2001), pp. 5–19.

5. David K. Wyatt, 'A Persian mission to Siam in the reign of King Narai', in David K. Wyatt (ed.), *Studies in Thai History. Collected Articles* (Chiang Mai: Silkworm Press, 1999, 2nd reprint), p. 89, review article of {Mohammad Rabi'} Ibn Muhammad Ibrahim, *The Ship of Sulayman*, trans. John O'Kane (New York, 1972), first published in *Journal of the Siam Society* 62/1 (January, 1974), pp. 151–7.

6. Ibn Muhammad Ibrahim, *The Ship of Sulayman*, trans. John O'Kane (New York, 1972) (henceforth *Ship of Sulayman*, trans. O'Kane).

7. Mohammad Rabi' b. Mohammad Ebrahim, *Safine-ye Solaymani*, British Museum manuscript BM Or. 6942, described in G. M. Meredith-Owens, *Handlist of Persian Manuscripts, 1895–1966* (London, 1968), pp. 48–9.

8. See Jean Aubin, '*The Ship of Sulaiman*, translated from the Persian by John O'Kane (London, 1972)' (review article) *Studia Iranica* 2/2 (1973), p. 286; Wyatt, 'A Persian mission to Siam in the reign of King Narai'. From the perspective of Thai studies, certain criticism in this regard was also reiterated to me in personal communications by Professor B. J. Terwiel. Apparently, there exists also a recent Thai translation of the *Safine*, to which I had no access at the time of writing.

9. I should like to mention that I am planning to prepare an apparatus of annotations on those terms and features which involve Iranian studies.

10. Apparently, in the Kitabkhane-ye Malek, see Aubin, '*The Ship of Sulaiman*, translated from the Persian by John O'Kane (London: Routledge and Kegan Paul, 1972) (review article)', p. 286.

11. Mohammad Rabi' b. Mohammad Ebrahim, *Safine-ye Solaymani. Safarname-ye safir-e Iran be Siyam, 1094–1098, naveshte-ye Mohammad Rabi' b. Mohammad Ebrahim*, ed. 'Abbas Faruqi (Tehran, 2536 shahanshahi [1977]). I am first indebted to my friend Professor Houchang E. Chehabi of Boston University for sending me a photocopy of the 1999 edition, and finally to Professor Mehdi Mohaghegh of Tehran University for sending me a printed copy. I am planning to prepare a review.

12. The following summary is based on O'Kane's translation.

13. *Ship of Sulayman*, trans. O'Kane, pp. 15–16.

14. Ibid., p. 17.

15. Ibid.

16. Ibid.
17. Ebn Mohammad Ebrahim's work contains numerous references to technical matters and offices of the Safavid administrative system: on the *tofangchis* see my *Mirza Rafi'a's Dastur al-Muluk: A Manual of Later Safavid Administration. Annotated English Translation, Commentary on the Offices and Services, and Facsimile of the Unique Persian Manuscript* (Kuala Lumpur, 2002), indices (henceforth Marcinkowski, *Mirza Rafi'a's Dastur al-Muluk*). See also on the *Dastor ol-Moluk* my 'Mirza Rafi'a's *Dastur al-Muluk* a prime source on administration, society and culture in late Safavid Iran', *Zeitschrift der deutschen morgenländischen Gesellschaft* vol. 153, no. 2, 2003, pp. 281-310.
18. *Ship of Sulayman*, trans. O'Kane, pp. 17-19.
19. Ibid., p. 19.
20. Ibid., p. 20.
21. Ibid., pp. 20-1.
22. Ibid., p. 25.
23. Ibid., p. 27.
24. Ibid., p. 29.
25. Ibid.
26. Ibid., p. 30.
27. Ibid., p. 32. We shall refer below to some aspects of the activities of Iranians in the region.
28. Ibid., p. 35.
29. Ibid., p. 36. We shall return briefly below to this issue, when addressing Safavid activities in the region.
30. Ibid., p. 36.
31. Ibid., p. 41.
32. Ibid., p. 43.
33. Ibid., pp. 43-4.
34. On him more later.
35. *Ship of Sulayman*, trans. O'Kane, p. 46.
36. I shall return to the term *Shahr-e Nav* further below.
37. *Ship of Sulayman*, trans. O'Kane, p. 47.
38. Ibid., p. 48.
39. Ibid., p. 49.
40. Ibid.
41. Ibid., p. 50.
42. Ibid.
43. Ibid., p. 50.
44. Anthony Reid, *Southeast Asia in the Age of Commerce, 1450-1680. Volume Two: Expansion and Crisis* (New Haven, CT and London, 1993), p. 191.
45. *Ship of Sulayman*, trans. O'Kane, p. 51.
46. Ibid., p. 55, also pp. 56-60.
47. On this subject see Marcinkowski, Christoph, *From Isfahan to Ayutthaya: Contacts between Iran and Siam in the 17th Century* (Singapore: Pustaka Nasional, 2005).
48. *Ship of Sulayman*, trans. O'Kane, p. 56.
49. Ibid., p. 57.
50. See Marcinkowski, *Mirza Rafi'a's Dastur al-Muluk*, index.
51. Ibid.
52. *Ship of Sulayman*, trans. O'Kane, p. 58.
53. Ibid., pp. 50-9. For a (controversial) reappraisal of Phaulkon see George A. Sioris, *Phaulkon, the Greek Counsellor at the Court of Siam: An Appraisal* (Bangkok, 1998).
54. *Ship of Sulayman*, trans. O'Kane, p. 66.
55. Ibid., pp. 61-5.
56. Ibid., pp. 66-74.

57. Ibid., p. 74.
58. Ibid.
59. Ibid., p. 75.
60. Ibid. and p. 77.
61. Ibid., pp. 77–8. See also Guy Tachard, *A Relation of the Voyage to Siam, Performed by Six Jesuits, Sent by the French King, to the Indies and China, in the Year, 1685* (Bangkok, 1999, first published in 1688, 3rd reprint), pp. 214–15. For further information on *ta'ziye* in Iran and elsewhere see also Peter J. Chelkowski, ed., *Ta'ziyeh. Ritual and Drama in Iran* (New York, 1979).
62. Mohammad had no surviving son; perhaps referring to his cousin and son-in-law 'Ali, the first Shi'ite Emam, most probably, however, to 'Ali's sons Hasan and Hosayn.
63. Tachard, *A Relation of the Voyage to Siam*, pp. 214–15. Ebn Mohammad Ebrahim, who was in Siam about the same time mentioned *ta'ziyyah* as being performed by the Iranians resident at the Siamese capital Ayutthaya (*The Ship of Sulayman*, trans. John O'Kane, pp. 77–8 and 95).
64. *Ship of Sulayman*, trans. O'Kane, pp. 76–7.
65. Ibid., p. 86.
66. Ibid., pp. 87–8.
67. Ibid., p. 88.
68. Ibid., pp. 80–94.
69. Ibid., pp. 94–5.
70. Ibid., p. 99.
71. Ibid., p. 100.
72. Ibid., pp. 96–106 and 111.
73. Ibid., pp. 111–21.
74. Ibid., pp. 121–7.
75. Ibid., pp. 128–36.
76. Ibid., 140–9.
77. Ibid., pp. 136–8.
78. Ibid., pp. 138–40.
79. Ibid., pp. 149–55.
80. Ibid., pp. 155–6.
81. Ibid., pp. 149–55.
82. Ibid., pp. 156–7.
83. Ibid., p. 159ff.
84. Ibid., pp. 168–73.
85. Ibid., p. 174ff.
86. Ibid., p. 174.
87. Ibid., pp. 174–5.
88. Ibid., p. 174ff.
89. Ibid., pp. 181 and 182ff.
90. Ibid., p. 185ff.
91. Ibid., p. 186.
92. Ibid.
93. Ibid., p. 187.
94. Ibid., pp. 193–8.
95. Ibid., pp. 198–203.
96. Ibid., p. 215ff.
97. Ibid., p. 218.
98. Ibid., p. 219.
99. Ibid.
100. Ibid., p. 220ff.
101. Ibid., p. 225.

102. Ibid., p. 226ff.
103. Ibid., p. 229.
104. Ibid., p. 229ff.
105. Ibid., p. 230ff.
106. Ibid., p. 231.
107. Ibid., p. 233.
108. H. K. Sherwani, *History of the Qutb Shahi Dynasty* (New Delhi, 1974), p. 650. See furthermore R. M. Eaton, 'Kutb Shahis', *Encyclopedia of Islam*, New Edition (henceforth *EI2*), vol. 5 (1986), pp. 549–50; J. Burton-Page, 'Haydarabad', *EI²*, vol. 3 (1986), pp. 318–23; H. K. Sherwani, 'Golkonda', *EI2*, vol. 2 (1983), pp. 1118–19; H. K. Sherwani, 'Dakhan', *EI²*, vol. 2 (1983), p. 99; Carl W. Ernst, 'Deccan: I. Political and literary history', *Encyclopedia Iranica* (henceforth *Enc.Iran.*), vol. 7 (1994), pp. 181–5. Of relevance is also the fascinating (unfortunately so far almost neglected) study by T. N. Devare, *A Short History of Persian Literature at the Bahmani, the Adilshahi and the Qutbshahi Courts (Deccan)* (Poona, 1961).
109. *Ship of Sulayman*, trans. O'Kane, p. 236ff. See also Muhammad Baqir, 'Bijapur', *Enc.Iran.*, vol. 4 (1989), pp. 253–4; R. M. Eaton, "Adelshahis', *Enc.Iran.*, vol. 1 (1985), pp. 452–6; P. Hardy, "Adil Shahs', *EI2*, vol. 1 (1986), p. 199.
110. *Ship of Sulayman*, trans. O'Kane, 236.
111. Ibid., pp. 239–40.
112. See, for instance, Reid, *Southeast Asia in the Age of Commerce*, p. 190.
113. Steve Van Beek, *The Chao Phya. River in Transition* (Kuala Lumpur, 1995), p. 29.
114. For more details on him refer to Syed Muhammad Naguib al-Attas, *The Mysticism of Hamzah Fansuri* (Kuala Lumpur, 1970), p. 5; Syed Muhammad Naguib al-Attas, 'New light on the life of Hamzah Fansuri', *JMBRAS* 40, pt. 1 (July, 1967), pp. 42–51; Syed Muhammad Naguib al-Attas, *Concluding Postscript to the Origin of the Malay Sha'ir* (Kuala Lumpur, 1971); G. W. J. Drewes and Lode Brakel, eds, *The Poems of Hamzah Fansuri* (Dordrecht, 1986).
115. Abdul Rahman Haji Ismail, ed., *Sejarah Melayu. The Malay Annals. MS. Raffles No. 18. New Romanized Edition* (Kuala Lumpur, 1998), p. 110ff. The English translation of this Malay reference is to be found in C. C. Brown (trans.), 'The Malay annals', *JMBRAS* 25, pt. 2–3 (1952), p. 45ff. A date of composition of the earliest draft of the *Sejarah Melayu* between 1511 and 1535 was already advocated by Sir R. O. Winstedt, ed., 'The Malay annals or Sejarah Melayu. The earliest recension from MS. No. 18 of the Raffles collection, in the Library of the Royal Asiatic Society, London', *JMBRAS* 16, pt. 3 (Dec. 1938), p. 27 (Winstedt's introduction).
116. For this assertion see, for instance, al-Attas, *The Mysticism of Hamzah Fansuri*, p. 3 n. 2.
117. G. R. Tibbetts, *Arab Navigation in the Indian Ocean before the Coming of the Portuguese* (London, 1981), p. 488.
118. Transliterated as such by the translator O'Kane, see *The Ship of Sulayman*, trans. John O'Kane, p. 42ff.
119. For instance, in my 'The Iranian-Siamese Connection: An Iranian Community in the Thai Kingdom of Ayutthaya', *Iranian Studies*, vol. 35, nos. 1–3 (2002), pp. 23–46.
120. Van Beek, *The Chao Phya*, p. 29. See also Sumet Jumsai, *Naga: Cultural Origins in Siam and the West Pacific* (Singapore, 1988), p. 161.
121. Apparently, this headline was added by the translator O'Kane.
122. *Ship of Sulayman*, trans. John O'Kane, p. 88. On the supposed 'genesis' of the Thai people Ebn Mohammad Ebrahim has, however, only the following to offer: 'The Iranians and the Franks [i.e. the Europeans] call the natives of Shahr Nav, Siamese, but the natives themselves trace their stock back to Tai, whom they hold to be one of their devils and genii [sic!].' (ibid.).
123. Engelbert Kaempfer, *A Description of the Kingdom of Siam 1690* (Bangkok, 1998, reprint), p. 49.
124. Van Beek, *The Chao Phya*, pp. 54–6.
125. See also 'Ali-Akbar Dehkhoda, *Loghatname-ye Dehkhoda*, 50 vols (Tehran, 1330 AH solar/1951), vol. 47, p. 280, col. 1, entry 'nav'.

126. Engelbert Kaempfer, *Am Hofe des persischen Großkönigs (1684-85). Das erste Buch der Amoenitates Exoticae*, German introduction and translation by Walther Hinz (Leipzig, 1940), p. 135.
127. Charnvit Kasetsiri, *The Rise of Ayutthaya: A History of Siam in the Fourteenth and Fifteenth Centuries* (Kuala Lumpur, 1976), and Charnvit Kasetsiri, 'Origins of a capital and seaport: The early settlement of Ayutthaya and its East Asian trade', in Kennon Breazeale (ed.), *From Japan to Arabia: Ayutthaya's Maritime Relations with Asia* (Bangkok, 1999), pp. 55-79.
128. David K. Wyatt, *Thailand. A Short History* (Chiang Mai, 1999, reprint), pp. 61-74, and David K. Wyatt, 'Ayutthaya, 1409-24: Internal politics and international relations', in Kennon Breazeale (ed.), *From Japan to Arabia: Ayutthaya's Maritime Relations with Asia*, pp. 80-8.
129. Van Beek, *The Chao Phya*, p. 32.
130. Ibid., pp. 28-9.
131. *Ship of Sulayman*, trans. John O'Kane, p. 94.
132. J. Kennedy, *History of Malaya* (Kuala Lumpur, 1970), pp. 20-7.
133. Sunait Chutintaranond, 'Mergui and Tenasserim as leading port cities in the context of autonomous history', in Kennon Breazeale (ed.), *From Japan to Arabia: Ayutthaya's Maritime Relations with Asia*, pp. 104-18.
134. See John F. Richards, *The Mughal Empire* (Cambridge, 1996 [The New Cambridge History of India, I, 5], reprint), p. 7.
135. Ibid., p. 7 (map).
136. See C. E. Bosworth, *The New Islamic Dynasties. A Chronological and Genealogical Manual* (Edinburgh, 1996), pp. 319-21, which contains a useful bibliography.
137. For a comprehensive survey refer to Sherwani, *History of the Qutb Shahi Dynasty* which, however, does not have much to say about the religious beliefs of the Qutb Shahi kings and the role played by Twelver Shi'ites/Iranians in society and culture. See also Vladimir Minorsky, 'The Qara-Qoyunlu and the Qutb-Shahs (Turmenica, 10)', *Bulletin of the School of Oriental and African Studies* (henceforth *BSOAS*) 18/1 (1955), pp. 50-73.
138. Studies on the history of the Twelvers in southern India include Omar Khalidi, 'The Shi'is of the Deccan: A historical outline', *Al-Tawhid* 9/2 (November 1991-January 1992), pp. 163-75 (with an excellent bibliography); John Norman Hollister, *The Shi'a of India* (New Delhi, 1979), pp. 101-25; and Sayyid Athar Abbas Rizvi, *A Socio-Intellectual History of the Isna Ashari Shi'is in India*, 2 vols (Canberra, 1986), vol. 1, pp. 247-341.
139. A remarkable, but so far also almost neglected study on Persian literature under the southern Indian Muslim rulers is Devare's *A Short History of Persian Literature*.
140. For instance, Sanjay Subrahmanyam, 'Iranians abroad: Intra-Asian elite migration and early modern state formation', *The Journal of Asian Studies* 51/2 (1992), pp. 340-63. Of interest in this regard are also Jean Calmard, 'Les marchands iraniens', in Denys Lombard and Jean Aubin (eds), *Marchands et hommes d'affaires asiatiques dans l'Océan Indien et la Mer de Chine 13e-20e siècles* (Paris, 1988), pp. 91-107; Michel Aghassian and Kéram Kévonian, 'Le commerce arménien dans l'Océan Indien aux 17e-18e siècles', in ibid., pp. 155-81; Jean Aubin, 'Marchands de Mer Rouge et du Golfe Persique au tournant des 15e et 16e siècles', in ibid., pp. 83-90.
141. Shah Manzur Alam, 'Masulipatam: A metropolitan port in the seventeenth century', *Islamic Culture* 33/3 (1959), pp. 169-87. For the developments during the following century see Sinnappah Arasaratnam, 'The Coromandel-Southeast Asia trade 1650-1740: Challenges and responses of a commercial system', *Journal of Asian History* 18/2 (1984), pp. 113-35, and Sinnappah Arasaratnam, 'The Chulia Muslim merchants in Southeast Asia 1650-1800', *Moyen Orient et Océan Indien* 4 (1987), pp. 126-43. See also Reid, *Southeast Asia in the Age of Commerce*, p. 147.
142. Alam, 'Masulipatam', p. 177. See also Kennon Breazeale, 'Thai maritime trade and the ministry responsible', in Kennon Breazeale (ed.), *From Japan to Arabia: Ayutthaya's Maritime Relations with Asia*, p. 41, which refers to 'trade representatives' of Siam residing in Golconda, and vice versa.
143. See my *From Isfahan to Ayutthaya: Contacts between Iran and Siam in the 17th Century* (Bangkok, 2003), which contains further bibliographical information.

144. Subrahmanyam, 'Iranians abroad', p. 348.
145. Ronald W. Ferrier, 'Trade from the mid-14th century to the end of the Safavid period', in Peter Jackson and Laurence Lockhart (eds), *The Cambridge History of Iran, Volume 6: The Timurid and Safavid Periods* (Cambridge, 1986), p. 423. See for a survey of the general framework of seventeenth-century Safavid trade also Rudi Matthee, *Trade in Safavid Iran: Silk for Silver, 1600-1730* (Cambridge, 1999), an extended version of his 'Politics and trade in late Safavid Iran: Commercial crisis and government reaction under Shah Solayman (1666-1694)' (Ph.D. dissertation, University of California at Los Angeles, 1991).
146. Nagazumi Yoko, 'Ayutthaya and Japan: Embassies and trade in the seventeenth century', in Kennon Breazeale (ed.), *From Japan to Arabia: Ayutthaya's Maritime Relations with Asia*, pp. 89-103; Hiromu Nagashima, 'Persian Muslim merchants in Thailand and their activities in the 17th century: Especially on their visits to Japan', *Nagasaki Prefectural University Review* 30/3 (30 January 1997), pp. 387-99 (thanks are due to Professor Terwiel, Hamburg, who sent me a copy of the last-mentioned article).
147. Breazeale, 'Thai maritime trade and the ministry responsible', pp. 1-54.
148. Ibid., p. 5.
149. Kaempfer, *A Description of the Kingdom of Siam 1690*, p. 39.
150. Chevalier Alexandre de Chaumont, 'Relation of the embassy to Siam 1685', in Michael Smithies (ed., trans.), *The Chevalier de Chaumont and the Abbé de Choisy: Aspects of the Embassy to Siam 1685* (Chiang Mai, 1997), p. 111.
151. Breazeale, 'Thai maritime trade and the ministry responsible', p. 5.
152. This and the following based on Wyatt, *Thailand. A Short History*, p. 108. See also Wyatt, 'Family politics in seventeenth- and eighteenth-century Siam', in Wyatt (ed.), *Studies in Thai History. Collected Articles* (Chiang Mai, 1999, 2nd reprint), p. 96 (stemma).
153. Wyatt, 'Family politics in seventeenth- and eighteenth-century Siam', p. 96.
154. Alam, 'Masulipatam', p. 178.
155. *Records of the Relations between Siam and Foreign Countries in the Seventeenth Century. Copied from Papers Preserved at the India Office*, 5 vols (Bangkok, 1915-17), vol. 2, pp. 92-8.
156. E. W. Hutchinson, *1688 Revolution in Siam. The Memoir of Father de Bèze* (Hong Kong and Bangkok, 1990), p. 11 n. 2, pp. 127-8).
157. Père Raphaël Du Mans, *Estat de la Perse en 1660*, ed. Charles Schefer (Paris, 1890), p. 339 (appendix).
158. Engelbert Kaempfer, *Am Hofe des persischen Großkönigs*, pp. 99 and 212-13.
159. Ibid., p. 212.
160. *Ship of Sulayman*, trans. John O'Kane, pp. 20, 104 and 105. See on him also Jean Aubin, 'Les Persans au Siam sous le regne de Narai (1656-1688)', *Mare Luso-Indicum* 4 (1980), pp. 121-2 (thanks are again due to Professor Terwiel who sent me a copy of the last-mentioned article).
161. Thus contrary to the view of Breazeale, 'Thai maritime trade and the ministry responsible', p. 39. For further evidence see *Ship of Sulayman*, trans. John O'Kane, p. 20.
162. Subrahmanyam, 'Iranians abroad'; Aubin, 'Les Persans au Siam.'
163. See, for instance, François Caron and Joost Schouten, *A True Description of the Mighty Kingdoms of Japan and Siam. A Facsimile of the 1671 London Edition in a Contemporary Translation from the Dutch by Roger Manley* (Bangkok, 1986), p. 134.
164. *Ship of Sulayman*, trans. John O'Kane, p. 94.
165. Subrahmanyam, 'Iranians abroad', p. 349. On the quotation referred to 'Abd al-Razzaq Gilani see *Ship of Sulayman*, trans. John O'Kane, 97, on Aqa Mohammad Astarabadi see ibid., pp. 55, 59, 98, 100.
166. Subrahmanyam, 'Iranians abroad', p. 349.
167. As elaborated in my 'Twelver Shi'ite scholarship and Buyid domination. A Glance on the life and times of Ibn Babawayh al-Shaykh al-Saduq (d. 381/991)', *Islamic Culture* 76/1 (January 2002), pp. 69-99.
168. Reid, *Southeast Asia in the Age of Commerce*, pp. 190-1.

169. Apart from the already cited works by Sherwani, Rizvi, Khalidi and Hollister, refer also to Devare, *A Short History of Persian Literature*. The precarious situation of the Golconda kingdom during that time was also noticed by Ebn Mohammad Ebrahim, see *Ship of Sulayman*, trans. John O'Kane, pp. 234–40.
170. See n. 61, *supra*.
171. Ibid.
172. Kaempfer, *Am Hofe des persischen*, p. 135. See also Aubin, 'Les Persans au Siam', p. 106.
173. Breazeale, 'Thai maritime trade and the ministry responsible', p. 11.
174. The conference was conducted on 15 May 1994. For the proceedings volume see Cultural Center of the Islamic Republic of Iran (Bangkok), ed., *Sheikh Ahmad Qomi and the History of Siam* (Bangkok, 1995/2538 Buddhist Era). Of relevance are the following contributions therein: Oudaya Bhanuwongse, 'Speech', pp. 206–7; Srisak Vallipodom, 'The roles of Sheikh Ahmad Qomi in the court of Ayutthaya', pp. 208–14; Pensri Karnjanomai, 'The Muslims' role in the time of Ayutthaya and the cultural transference', pp. 221–4; Pluplung Kongchana, 'The Persians in Ayutthaya', pp. 233–41, P. Ahmadchula 'Sheikh Ahmad Qomi', pp. 246–52; Pluplung Kongchana, 'The historical development of the Persian community in Ayutthaya', pp. 253–69; Pitya Bunnag, 'Some facts regarding the Bunnag family', pp. 272–84. See also Omar Farouk, 'Shaykh Ahmad: Muslims in the kingdom of Ayutthaya', *JEBAT Journal of the History Department Universiti Kebangsaan Malaysia* 10 (1980–1), pp. 206–14, cf. Imtiyaz Yusuf, 'Islam and democracy in Thailand: Reforming the office of *Chularajmontri/Shaykh al-Islam*', *Journal of Islamic Studies* 9/2 (July 1998), p. 284 n. 32.
175. Private communication.
176. Additional remarks in square brackets are by the present author.
177. Wyatt, 'Family politics in seventeenth- and eighteenth-century Siam', p. 96 (stemma).
178. For examples see ibid., p. 98 n. 2, and p. 99 n. 5. For further sources see also Srisak Vallipodom, 'The roles of Sheikh Ahmad Qomi in the court of Ayutthaya', pp. 213–14.
179. For some interesting observations in this regard see Pitya Bunnag, 'Some facts regarding the Bunnag family', pp. 280–1.
180. See my 'Iranians, *Shaykh al-Islams* and *Chularajmontris*: Genesis and development of an institution and its introduction to Siam', *Journal of Asian History*, vol. 37 (2003), pp. 59–76, and my 'A brief demarcation of the office of *Shaykh al-Islam* based on the two late Safavid administrative manuals *Dastur al-Muluk* and *Tadhkirat al-Muluk*' *Islamic Culture* 74/4 (2000), pp. 19–51.
181. Pluplung Kongchana, 'The historical development of the Persian community in Ayutthaya', p. 265.
182. Wyatt, 'Family politics in seventeenth- and eighteenth-century Siam', pp. 96–105, and Wyatt, 'Family politics in nineteenth-century Thailand', in Wyatt (ed.), *Studies in Thai History. Collected Articles* (Chiang Mai, 1999), pp. 106–30, stemma of the Bunnag family on p. 115. Both of Wyatt's articles contain also rich references and discussions of relevant Thai sources. See also Kukrit Pramoj, *Khwampenma khong Itsalam nai prathet Thai* [*The Origin of Islam in Thailand*] (Bangkok, B.E. 2514) (in Thai).
183. See previous note.
184. An English abstract of the speech that he gave on that occasion is to be found in, *Sheikh Ahmad Qomi and the History of Siam*, pp. 193–4. However, I could not establish what effect Thailand's latest general elections of early 2001 had in this regard.
185. Yusuf, 'Islam and democracy in Thailand', pp. 284–5.
186. Wyatt, 'A Persian mission to Siam in the reign of King Narai', p. 95.

Bibliography

Abdul Rahman Haji Ismail (ed.), *Sejarah Melayu. The Malay Annals. MS. Raffles No. 18. New Romanized Edition* (Kuala Lumpur, 1998).

Aghassian, Michel and Kéram Kévonian, 'Le commerce arménien dans l'Océan Indien aux 17e-18e siècles', in Denys Lombard and Jean Aubin (eds), *Marchands et hommes d'affaires asiatiques dans l'Océan Indien et la Mer de Chine 13e-20e siècles* (Paris, 1988), pp. 155-81.

Alam, Shah Manzur, 'Masulipatam: A metropolitan port in the seventeenth century', *Islamic Culture* 33/3 (1959), pp. 169-87.

Arasaratnam, Sinnappah, 'The Coromandel-Southeast Asia Trade 1650-1740: Challenges and responses of a commercial system', *Journal of Asian History* 18/2 (1984), pp. 113-35.

Arasaratnam, Sinnappah, *Maritme India in the Seventeenth Century* (Delhi, 1994).

al-Attas, Syed Muhammad Naguib, *Concluding Postscript to the Origin of the Malay Sha'ir* (Kuala Lumpur, 1971).

al-Attas, Syed Muhammad Naguib, 'New light on the life of Hamzah Fansuri', *Journal of the Malaysian Branch of the Royal Asiatic Society* 40, pt. 1 (July 1967), pp. 42-51.

al-Attas, Syed Muhammad Naguib, *The Mysticism of Hamzah Fansuri* (Kuala Lumpur, 1970).

Aubin, Jean, 'Marchands de Mer Rouge et du Golfe Persique au tournant des 15e et 16e siècles', in Denys Lombard and Jean Aubin (eds), *Marchands et hommes d'affaires asiatiques dans l'Océan Indien et la Mer de Chine 13e-20e siècles* (Paris, 1988), pp. 83-90.

Aubin, Jean, 'Les Persans au Siam sous le regne de Narai (1656-1688)', *Mare Luso-Indicum* 4 (1980), pp. 95-126.

Aubin, Jean, '*The Ship of Sulaiman*, translated from the Persian by John O'Kane (London: Routledge and Kegan Paul, 1972)', review article, *Studia Iranica* 2/2 (1973), p. 286.

Baqir, Muhammad, 'Bijapur', *Encyclopaedia Iranica*, vol. 4 (1989), pp. 253-4.

Bosworth, Clifford Edmund, *The New Islamic Dynasties. A Chronological and Genealogical Manual* (Edinburgh, 1996).

Breazeale, Kennon (ed.), *From Japan to Arabia: Ayutthaya's Maritime Relations with Asia* (Bangkok, 1999).

Breazeale, Kennon, 'Thai maritime trade and the ministry responsible', in Breazeale, Kennon (ed.), *From Japan to Arabia: Ayutthaya's Maritime Relations with Asia* (Bangkok, 1999), pp. 1-54.

Brown, C. C. (trans.), 'The Malay annals', *Journal of the Malayan Branch of the Royal Asiatic Society* 25, pt. 2-3 (1952), pp. 5-276.

Burton-Page, J., 'Haydarabad', *Encyclopaedia of Islam* (new edition), vol. 3 (1986), pp. 318-23.

Calmard, Jean, 'Les marchands iraniens', in Denys Lombard and Jean Aubin (eds), *Marchands et hommes d'affaires asiatiques dans l'Océan Indien et la Mer de Chine 13e-20e siècles* (Paris, 1988), pp. 91-107.

Caron, François and Joost Schouten, *A True Description of the Mighty Kingdoms of Japan and Siam. A Facsimile of the 1671 London Edition in a Contemporary Translation from the Dutch by Roger Manley* (Bangkok, 1986).

Charnvit Kasetsiri, 'Origins of a capital and seaport: The early settlement of Ayutthaya and its East Asian Trade', in Kennon Breazeale (ed.), *From Japan to Arabia: Ayutthaya's Maritime Relations with Asia* (Bangkok, 1999), pp. 55-79.

Charnvit Kasetsiri, *The Rise of Ayutthaya: A History of Siam in the Fourteenth and Fifteenth Centuries* (Kuala Lumpur, 1976).

Chaudhuri, K. N., *Trade and Civilisation in the Indian Ocean. An Economic History from the Rise of Islam to 1750* (Cambridge, 1986).

Chaumont, Chevalier Alexandre de, 'Relation of the embassy to Siam 1685', in Michael Smithies (ed., trans.), *The Chevalier de Chaumont and the Abbé de Choisy: Aspects of the Embassy to Siam 1685* (Chiang Mai, 1997), pp. 21-149.

Chelkowski, Peter J. (ed.), *Ta'ziyeh. Ritual and Drama in Iran* (New York, 1979).

Colless, B. E., 'Persian merchants and missionaries in medieval Malaya,' *Journal of the Malaysian Branch of the Royal Asiatic Society* 42, pt. 2 (1969), pp. 10-47.

Colless, B. E., 'The traders of the Pearl. The mercantile and missionary activities of Persian and Armenian Christians in South East-Asia', *Abr Nahrain* 9 (1969-70), pp. 17-38; *Abr Nahrain* 10 (1970-1), pp. 102-21; *Abr Nahrain* 11 (1970), pp. 1-21; *Abr Nahrain* 13 (1972-3), pp. 113-35; *Abr Nahrain* 14 (1973-4), pp. 1-16; *Abr Nahrain* 15 (1974-5), pp. 6-17; *Abr Nahrain* 18 (1978-9), pp. 1-18.

Cultural Center of the Islamic Republic of Iran (Bangkok) (ed.), *Sheikh Ahmad Qomi and the History of Siam* (Bangkok, 1995/2538 Buddhist Era).

Cushman, Richard D. (trans.), *The Royal Chronicles of Ayutthaya*, ed. by David K. Wyatt (Bangkok, 2000).

Das Gupta, Ashin, 'Indian merchants and the trade in the Indian Ocean, c. 1500–1750', in T. Raychaudhuri and I. Habib (eds), *The Cambridge Economic History of India. Vol. I: c. 1250–c. 1750* (Cambridge, 1982), pp. 407–33.

Das Gupta, Ashin, 'Introduction II: The story', in A. Das Gupta and M. N. Pearson (eds), *India and the Indian Ocean, 1500–1800* (Delhi, 1987), pp. 25–45.

Das Gupta, Ashin, 'The maritime merchant, c. 1500–1800', *Proceedings of the Indian History Congress, Presidential Address to the Medieval Section, 35th Session 1974, Jadavpur University Calcutta* (Delhi, 1974), pp. 1–15.

Das Gupta, Ashin and M. N. Pearson (eds), *India and the Indian Ocean, 1500–1800* (Delhi, 1987).

Dehkhoda, 'Ali-Akbar, *Loghatname-ye Dehkhoda*, 50 vols, vol. 47 (Tehran, 1330 AH solar/1951), p. 280, col. 1, entry '*nav*'.

Devare, T. N., *A Short History of Persian Literature at the Bahmani, the Adilshahi and the Qutbshahi Courts (Deccan)* (Poona, 1961).

Drewes, G. W. J. and Lode Brakel (eds), *The Poems of Hamzah Fansuri* (Dordrecht, 1986).

Du Mans, Père Raphaël, *Estat de la Perse en 1660*, ed. Charles Schefer (Paris, 1890).

Eaton, R. M., "Adelshahis' *Encyclopaedia Iranica*, vol. 1 (1985), pp. 452–6.

Eaton, R. M., 'Kutb Shahis', *Encyclopaedia of Islam* (new edition), vol. 5 (1986), pp. 549–50.

Ernst, Carl W., 'Deccan: I. Political and literary history', *Encyclopedia Iranica*, vol. 7 (1994), pp. 181–5.

Farouk, Omar, 'Shaykh Ahmad: Muslims in the kingdom of Ayutthaya', *JEBAT Journal of the History Department Universiti Kebangsaan Malaysia* 10 (1980–1), pp. 206–14.

Ferrier, Ronald W., 'Trade from the mid-14th century to the end of the Safavid period', in Peter Jackson and Laurence Lockhart (eds) *The Cambridge History of Iran, Volume 6: The Timurid and Safavid Periods* (Cambridge, 1986), pp. 412–91.

Hardy, P., "Adil Shahs' *Encyclopaedia of Islam* (new edition), vol. 1 (1986), p. 199.

Hiromu Nagashima, 'Persian Muslim merchants in Thailand and their activities in the 17th century: Especially on their visits to Japan', *Nagasaki Prefectural University Review* 30/3 (January 30, 1997), pp. 387–99.

Hollister, John Norman, *The Shi'a of India* (New Delhi, 1979).

Hutchinson, E. W., *1688 Revolution in Siam. The Memoir of Father de Bèze* (Hong Kong and Bangkok, 1990, 2nd impression).

Ibn Muhammad Ibrahim, *The Ship of Sulayman*, trans. John O'Kane (New York, 1972).

Islam, Riazul, *Indo-Persian Relations. A Study of the Political and Diplomatic Relations between the Mughal Empire and Iran* (Tehran, 1970).

Kaempfer, Engelbert, *Am Hofe des persischen Großkönigs (1684–85). Das erste Buch der Amoenitates Exoticae*, German introduction and translation by Walther Hinz (Leipzig, 1940).

Kaempfer, Engelbert, *A Description of the Kingdom of Siam 1690* (Bangkok, 1998).

Kennedy, J., *History of Malaya* (Kuala Lumpur, 1970).

Khalidi, Omar, 'The Shi'is of the Deccan: A historical outline', *Al-Tawhid* 9/2 (November 1991–January 1992), pp. 163–75.

Kukrit Pramoj, *Khwampenma khong Itsalam nai prathet Thai* [*The Origin of Islam in Thailand*] (Bangkok, B.E. 2514) [in Thai].

Marcinkowski, Christoph, 'A brief demarcation of the office of *Shaykh al-Islam* based on the two late Safavid administrative manuals *Dastur al-Muluk* and *Tadhkirat al-Muluk*' *Islamic Culture* 74/4 (2000), pp. 19–51.

Marcinkowski, Christoph, *From Isfahan to Ayutthaya: Contacts between Iran and Siam in the 17th Century* (Bangkok, 2003).

Marcinkowski, Christoph, 'Ittiphon dan sasana lae wattanatham khong Iran nai prethet Siam lae khong dindaen rim fhang thale Asia tawan-auk chiangtai nai thassana wisai dan prawatsat, kham wingwon hai mi withikan chai wicha tang-tang ruamkam' ['Persian religious and cultural influences in Siam/ Thailand and maritime Southeast Asia in historical perspective: A plea for a concerted interdisciplinary approach'] *San Islam* [*The Message of Islam*] (Bangkok, Thailand), vol. 1, no. 2 (June–August 2002), pp. 50–61 (in Thai).

Marcinkowski, Christoph, 'Mirza Rafi', 'Persian religious and cultural influences in Siam/Thailand and maritime Southeast Asia in historical perspective: A plea for a concerted interdisciplinary approach', *Journal of the Siam Society* 88, pt. 1–2 (2000), pp. 186–94 (paper presented at the *International Conference on the Southeast Asian Religious Mosaic in the Third Millennium* (1–4 February 2001), Mahidol University International College (MUIC), Salaya Campus, Nakhon Pathom, Thailand).

Marcinkowski, Christoph, 'The reputed issue of the 'ethnic origin' of Iran's Safavid dynasty (907–1145/1501–1722): Reflections on selected prevailing views', *Journal of the Pakistan Historical Society* 49/2 (2001), pp. 5–19.

Marcinkowski, Christoph, 'Twelver Shi'ite scholarship and Buyid domination. A glance on the life and times of Ibn Babawayh al-Shaykh al-Saduq (d. 381/991) *Islamic Culture* 76/1 (January 2002), pp. 69–99.

Marcinkowski, Christoph, *Mirza Rafi'a's Dastur al-Muluk: A Manual of Later Safavid Administration. Annotated English Translation, Commentary on the Offices and Services, and Facsimile of the Unique Persian Manuscript* (Kuala Lumpur, 2002).

Marcinkowski, Christoph, 'Bridging the ocean: Some aspects of the Iranian cultural presence in Southeast Asia with emphasis on the Siamese kingdom of Ayutthaya', *Al-Shajarah. Journal of the International Institute of Islamic Thought and Civilization* 7/1 (2002), pp. 27–56 (paper presented at the *35th Annual Meeting of the Middle East Studies Association of North America (MESA)*, San Francisco, CA (17–20 November 2001)).

Marcinkowski, Christoph, 'Iranians, *Shaykh al-Islams* and *Chularajmontris:* Genesis and development of an institution and its introduction to Siam', *Journal of Asian History* 37/2 (2003), pp. 59–76 (paper presented at the *8th International Thai Studies Conference*, Nakhon Phanom, Thailand (8–12 January 2002), organized by Ramkhamhaeng University, Bangkok).

Marcinkowski, Christoph, 'Holier than thou: Buddhism and the Thai people in Ebn Mohammad Ebrahim's 17th-century travel account *Safine-ye Solaymani*' *ZDMG* 156/2 (2006) (paper presented at the *Fifth European Conference of Iranian Studies*, Ravenna, Italy, 6–11 October 2003, organized by Societas Iranologica Europaea (SIE)).

Marcinkowski, Christoph, 'The Iranian-Siamese connection: An Iranian community in the Thai kingdom of Ayutthaya' *Iranian Studies* 35/1–3 (2002) pp. 26–43 (two versions of this paper had been presented at the *Second Australian National Thai Studies Conference, Royal Melbourne Institute of Technology (RMIT)*, Melbourne, Victoria, Australia (12–13 July 2001), and at the *4th Biennial Conference of the Society for Iranian Studies*, Bethesda, MD (24–26 May 2002), respectively).

Marcinkowski, Christoph, 'Research on the Safavid-Siamese relations: A reappraisal of the current state of affairs' (paper presented at the *International Round Table Conference on the Safavids*, 5–6 July 2003, Bamberg, Germany).

Matthee, Rudi, *Trade in Safavid Iran: Silk for Silver, 1600–1730* (Cambridge: Cambridge University Press, 1999), an extended version of his 'Politics and trade in late Safavid Iran: Commercial crisis and government reaction under Shah Solayman (1666–1694)' (Ph.D. dissertation, University of California at Los Angeles, 1991).

Meredith-Owens, G. M., *Handlist of Persian Manuscripts, 1895–1966* (London, 1968).

Minorsky, Vladimir, 'The Qara-Qoyunlu and the Qutb-Shahs (Turmenica, 10)', *Bulletin of the School of Oriental and African Studies* 18/1 (1955), pp. 50–73.

Mohammad Rabi' (b. Mohammad Ebrahim), *Safine-ye Solaymani*, British Museum manuscript BM Or. 6942.

Mohammad Rabi' (b. Mohammad Ebrahim), *Safine-ye Solaymani. Safarname-ye safir-e Iran be Siyam, 1094–1098, naveshte-ye Mohammad Rabi' b. Mohammad Ebrahim*, ed. 'Abbas Faruqi (Tehran, 2536 *shahanshahi* [1977]).

Nagazumi Yoko, 'Ayutthaya and Japan: Embassies and trade in the seventeenth century', in Kennon Breazeale (ed.), *From Japan to Arabia: Ayutthaya's Maritime Relations with Asia* (Bangkok, 1999), pp. 89–103.
Oudaya Bhanuwongse, 'Speech' in Cultural Center of the Islamic Republic of Iran (Bangkok) (ed.), *Sheikh Ahmad Qomi and the History of Siam* (Bangkok, 1995/2538 Buddhist Era), pp. 206–7.
P. Ahmadchula, 'Sheikh Ahmad Qomi' in Cultural Center of the Islamic Republic of Iran (Bangkok) (ed.), *Sheikh Ahmad Qomi and the History of Siam* (Bangkok, 1995/2538 Buddhist Era), pp. 246–52.
Pensri Karnjanomai, 'The Muslims' role in the time of Ayutthaya and the cultural transference' in Cultural Center of the Islamic Republic of Iran (Bangkok) (ed.), *Sheikh Ahmad Qomi and the History of Siam* (Bangkok, 1995/2538 Buddhist Era), pp. 221–4.
Pitya Bunnag, 'Some facts regarding the Bunnag family', in Cultural Center of the Islamic Republic of Iran (Bangkok) (ed.), *Sheikh Ahmad Qomi and the History of Siam* (Bangkok, 1995/2538 Buddhist Era), pp. 272–84.
Pluplung Kongchana, 'The historical development of the Persian community in Ayutthaya' in Cultural Center of the Islamic Republic of Iran (Bangkok) (ed.), *Sheikh Ahmad Qomi and the History of Siam* (Bangkok, 1995/2538 Buddhist Era), pp. 253–69.
Pluplung Kongchana, 'The Persians in Ayutthaya' in Cultural Center of the Islamic Republic of Iran (Bangkok) (ed.), *Sheikh Ahmad Qomi and the History of Siam* (Bangkok, 1995/2538 Buddhist Era), pp. 233–41.
Reade, Julian (ed.), *The Indian Ocean in Antiquity* (London and New York, 1996).
Records of the Relations between Siam and Foreign Countries in the Seventeenth Century. Copied from Papers Preserved at the India Office, 5 vols (Bangkok, 1915–17).
Reid, Anthony, *Southeast Asia in the Age of Commerce, 1450–1680. Volume Two: Expansion and Crisis* (New Haven, CT and London, 1993).
Richards, John F., *The Mughal Empire (The New Cambridge History of India, 1/5)* (Cambridge, 1996).
Risso, Patricia, *Merchants & Faith: Muslim Commerce and Culture in the Indian Ocean* (Boulder, CO, 1995).
Rizvi, Sayyid Athar Abbas, *A Socio-Intellectual History of the Isna Ashari Shi'is in India*, 2 vols (Canberra, 1986).
Savory, Roger M., *Iran under the Safavids* (New York and Melbourne, 1980).
Sherwani, H. K., 'Dakhan', *Encyclopaedia of Islam* (new edition), vol. 2 (1983), p. 99.
Sherwani, H. K., 'Golkonda', *Encyclopaedia of Islam* (new edition), vol. 2 (1983), pp. 1118–19.
Sherwani, H. K., *History of the Qutb Shahi Dynasty* (New Delhi, 1974).
Sioris, George A., *Phaulkon, the Greek Counsellor at the Court of Siam: An Appraisal* (Bangkok, 1998).
Srisak Vallipodom, 'The roles of Sheikh Ahmad Qomi in the court of Ayutthaya' in Cultural Center of the Islamic Republic of Iran (Bangkok) (ed.), *Sheikh Ahmad Qomi and the History of Siam*, pp. 208–14.
Subrahmanyam, Sanjay, 'Iranians abroad: Intra-Asian elite migration and early modern state formation', *The Journal of Asian Studies* 51/2 (1992), pp. 340–63.
Sumet Jumsai, *Naga: Cultural Origins in Siam and the West Pacific* (Singapore, 1988).
Sunait Chutintaranond, 'Mergui and Tenasserim as leading port cities in the context of autonomous history', in Kennon Breazeale (ed.), *From Japan to Arabia: Ayutthaya's Maritime Relations with Asia*, pp. 104–18.
Tachard, Guy, *A Relation of the Voyage to Siam, Performed by Six Jesuits, Sent by the French King, to the Indies and China, in the Year, 1685* (Bangkok, 1999).
Tibbetts, G. R., 'Early Muslim traders in South-East Asia', *Journal of the Malaysian Branch of the Royal Asiatic Society* 30, pt. 1 (1957), pp. 1–45.
Tibbetts, G. R., 'Pre-Islamic Arabia and South-East Asia', *Journal of the Malaysian Branch on the Royal Asiatic Society* 29, pt. 3 (1955), pp. 182–208.
Tibbetts, G. R., *A Study of the Arabic Text Containing Material on South-East Asia* (Leiden and London, 1979).
Tibbetts, G. R., *Arab Navigation in the Indian Ocean Before the Coming of the Portuguese* (London, 1981).
Van Beek, Steve, *The Chao Phya. River in Transition* (Kuala Lumpur, 1995).
Whitehouse, David and Andrew Williamson, 'Sasanian maritime trade', *Iran* 11 (1973), pp. 29–43.

Winstedt, Sir R. O. (ed.), 'The Malay annals or Sejarah Melayu. The earliest recension from MS. No. 18 of the Raffles collection, in the Library of the Royal Asiatic Society, London', *Journal of the Malayan Branch of the Royal Asiatic Society* 16, pt. 3 (December 1938), pp. 1-226.

Wyatt, David K., 'A Persian mission to Siam in the reign of King Narai', in Wyatt, David K., *Studies in Thai History. Collected Articles* (Chiang Mai, 1999, 2nd reprint), pp. 89-95, review article of [Muhammad Rabi'] b. Muhammad Ibrahim, *The Ship of Sulayman*, trans. John O'Kane (New York, 1972), first published in *Journal of the Siam Society* 62/1 (January 1974), pp. 151-7.

Wyatt, David K., 'Ayutthaya, 1409-24: Internal politics and international relations', in Kennon Breazeale (ed.), *From Japan to Arabia: Ayutthaya's Maritime Relations with Asia* (Bangkok, 1999), pp. 80-8.

Wyatt, David K., 'Family politics in nineteenth-century Thailand', in Wyatt, David K. (ed.), *Studies in Thai History. Collected Articles* (Chiang Mai, 1999), pp. 106-30.

Wyatt, David K., 'Family politics in seventeenth- and eighteenth-century Siam', in Wyatt, David K. (ed.), *Studies in Thai History. Collected Articles* (Chiang Mai, 1999), pp. 97-105.

Wyatt, David K., *Thailand. A Short History* (Chiang Mai, 1999, reprint).

Yusuf, Imtiyaz, 'Islam and democracy in Thailand: Reforming the office of *Chularajmontri/Shaykh al-Islam*', *Journal of Islamic Studies* 9/2 (July 1998), pp. 277-98.

25

The Safavid Potter at the Crossroad of Styles

Yolande Crowe

Recent publications such as *The Sea Route from Europe to Asia* by Harry Holcroft (2000), or *Lords of the East* by Joan Sutton (1981), a cycle of conferences such as 'India, Land and Empire' in Lisbon (2002) and even the 2002 exhibition on 'Trading Places: The East India Company and Asia' at the British Library, neglect aspects of the trade that took place on the northern shores of the Gulf in the seventeenth and early eighteenth centuries. Admittedly it was of less importance than the spice trade and other commercial exchanges in ports of India, south-east and far-eastern Asia, but this is not a sound enough reason for neglecting the supplies and demands of Persia in particular. Even international conferences dealing with the ceramic trade pursued by the East India companies, especially the Dutch VOC (Vereenigde Oost-indische Companie) and the English East India Company, have omitted to draw attention to the part played by Persia and the Persian potter in the history of world ceramics. Although occasionally the Cape has been mentioned, it is as if there was neither ceramic production nor port of call along the sea route between far-eastern Asia, India and Europe.

And yet the Persian contribution was well documented by Volker as recently as 1954 and three years later by Lane.[1] In his pioneering work Volker presented a list of the transhipments of high-fired wares from the Far East to Asian trading ports including Bandar 'Abbas; furthermore, he recorded the quantities and approximate shapes of the ceramics. Surprisingly, in one very short chapter entitled 'A Persian interlude', he reports the important fact that while the Chinese imperial kilns of Jingdezhen were closed, for a short time the VOC attempted to replace the missing Chinese production with similar wares produced in Persia. According to Volker's analysis of the Dutch *dagh-registers,* this period would have started in 1652 and lasted until official production was resumed in the Chinese kilns of Jingdezhen in 1683. It is likely that the Dutch factors, while gathering special goat wool called *khos* in the region of Kirman, realized that the area also produced glazed ceramics, most of which were inspired by Chinese export porcelain, especially blue and white wares.[2]

When in 1957 Arthur Lane published his *Later Islamic Pottery* he set aside two chapters to discuss Safavid ceramics and in the index gathered a number of significant quotations from narratives by contemporary European travellers. This was the first attempt at a classification of late Persian ceramics since up to that time most researchers had concentrated on the earlier periods. No further work of this importance was attempted until the *catalogue raisonné* of Safavid blue and white ceramics in the Victoria and Albert Museum. The Museum has a comprehensive collection of at least a thousand Persian ceramics assembled by Richard Murdoch Smith during the 1870s and 1880s.

Arthur Lane proposed a classification of post-Timurid ceramics according to the colours used on different shapes. This method meant that, rather than gathering similar shapes together, ceramics were placed in groups painted with blue, red and even green shades, as well as monochrome. As a result the overall picture was rather confusing. Since most of the collection consists of blue and white wares, a study of shapes seemed to be a more suitable method of classification. All through the Safavid dynasty shapes obviously evolved according to the requirements, not only of local buyers but also of European and far-eastern fashions.

In the first place it should be emphasized that the long-lasting influence of Chinese, so-called, *Kraak* porcelain on Persian blue and white material, with few dated pieces from 1615 until 1641, continued well after the fall of the Ming dynasty in 1643, although the production of *Kraak* porcelain in China would have dwindled by that time. With only about ten dated pieces for the second half of the seventeenth century it was at first difficult to catalogue most of the later Safavid production, which showed a number of new patterns, to the effect that the picture remained confusing. In the *catalogue raisonné* a manageable classification has been suggested for Safavid blue and white ceramics in the Victoria and Albert Museum, and in particular for the period covering the two last Safavid reigns, that of Shah Solayman (1666–94) and that of Shah Soltan Hosayn (1694–1722).

During this period of the Safavid dynasty new shapes and motifs appeared, which do not relate immediately to the earlier repertoire though *Kraak* panels were still used, albeit in a simplified manner. It is during this period that the influence of European shapes became increasingly apparent. For practical reasons it has been necessary to limit the choice of examples to blue and white pieces of the late seventeenth and early eighteenth centuries taken from the Museum collection; a few shapes and two special motifs have been selected for further discussion.

We know that earlier the VOC would have sent out wooden shapes to be copied in China. Then in turn some of these shapes appear to have been copied by the Persian potter; for example, the *klapmutz* or Dutch porringer imitated in *Kraak* wares. Of the shapes selected for discussion below from later Persian wares, the posset pot, the eggcup, the candlestick, the small jug and small shoes, all were first devised in western Europe and presumably shipped out to Asia for copying in order to fulfil the requirements of international trade, which demanded the reproduction of such intriguing shapes for Asian taste.

When a new European shape for a pourer arrived on the market (Figure 25.1), the Persian potter appears to have immediately responded with three handles instead of the original two. The example from the Victoria and Albert Museum (Figure 25.2 and 25.3) is painted in blue and white, and other similar Persian pieces are decorated in lustre on a blue glaze. One example of the latter belongs to the British Museum and another to the David Collection in Copenhagen. Both are signed by *Hatem*.[3] An English Delft example from the J. P. Kassebaum collection came through Sotheby's sale rooms in 1991 (Figure 25.4). It has a flat base, a double-spouted, puzzle pouring system, and is casually painted with the arms of the Merchants' Taylors Company, including the date of 1674. A more sophisticated shape dated 1700, also casually painted, is illustrated in van Dam's catalogue of Dutch dated Delftware.[4] This pot stands on three feet and the date is inscribed inside the base ring. The lid has been lost. One cannot help thinking that the Persian potter faced with an example of the double-spouted English pot had decided to replace the second spout with an extra handle for the sake of balance. He could of course have produced a

Figure 25.1 Posset pot, h. 16 cm, w. 23 cm, English 2002-65

Figure 25.2 Posset pot, h. 14.8 cm, V&A 882-1876

Figure 25.3 Posset pot, h. 14.8 cm, V&A 882-1876

Figure 25.4 Posset pot, h. 14 cm, English

tricked container but probably did not see the use for it. Interestingly the Persian painting is more elegant than the decoration on the European models. The scroll decoration of flattened flowers and buds on long stalks, both on lid and body, reproduces a pattern similar to that seen on Chinese bowls early in the reign of the Qing emperor Kangxi (1662–1722). It also includes a similar band of dense panel patterning around its neck. As to the design of the Ariana pot, it echoes Transitional patterns (Figure 25.1) whereas that of the English pot keeps to the vocabulary of heraldry. At the crossroad of styles the posset pot *à la Persane* draws on Europe for its shape but on China for its decoration. And in both these aspects, the Persian product is more elegantly shaped and painted, with the additional use of fine black lines to sharpen the design.

The second group of shapes consists of eggcups, candlesticks and small jugs, all alien to the Persian way of life. There are two eggcups in the Victoria and Albert Museum collection, 5.5 cm high and 10 cm wide, with saucer and body in one piece (Figures 25.5 and 25.6). One has lobed rims and bodies with vegetal motifs, the other straight rims and reserve-painted geometric patterns. A candlestick, 8 cm high, has also been made in one piece with a zigzag band painted inside the saucer rim (Figure 25.7). The casual painting of all three pieces contrasts vividly with the graceful decoration of the posset pot.

As for the small jug, its eight-faceted walls and slanted rolled rim suggests a metal shape, perhaps based on an octagonal bottle shape listed in a VOC document.[5] The slightly recessed base is also octagonal. A blue and white example from the Godman collection now in the British Museum is painted with panels of buds and criss-

Figure 25.5   Eggcup, h. 5.6cm, V&A 605-1889

Figure 25.6   Eggcup, h. 5.5cm, V&A 1143-1883

Figure 25.7 Candlestick, h. 6.3cm, V&A 2472-1876

crossed lozenges, and is dated 1109/1697. In the Victoria and Albert Museum the average height of its four examples is 16 cm and the faceted walls may be decorated with single panels filled with hook-shaped leaves, reciprocal ruffled leaves or luscious flowers. Other decorations take up the space of two panels with either reserve-painted pairs of birds or daisy-like flowers amidst leaves. One example has no separate panels and includes a faceless robed figure with a striped bird on either side (Figure 25.8). Here again the brushwork, although professional, has been hastily executed without the use of fine black lines.

The third group consists of small objects in the shape of a woman's shoe or slipper. They number eight in the Victoria and Albert Museum (Figure 25.9). Their length varies from 7 cm to 14 cm and they are, in a similar manner to the small jugs, reserve-painted with overall designs of leaves, panels of leaves or geometric designs. Arthur Lane in his *French faïence*[6] suggests wittily that they were used for drinking champagne and he illustrates three examples, two of which relate to the production of Nevers in the seventeenth century; one of these shoes has a rather high heel and pointed toe. A more sophisticated English Delft pair with a back, 12 cm long, once in the F. L. Dickson collection, displays the date 1695 painted at the top of the tongue.[7] Similar shapes were also produced in Delft but the earlier examples appear to have originated in Nevers. The two pairs in the Museum of Art of the Rhode Island School of Design, either French or Dutch, about 13 cm long, come closer to the Persian slipper with an open heel, a small pattern on top of the heel and decorated panels reaching to the pointed toe[8] (Figure 25.10). One pair has a bracketed top

Figure 25.8 Jug, h. 15.2cm, V&A 639-1889

Figure 25.9 Shoes, V&A 1067b-1876, 2476b-1876, 1067c-1876, 442-1874, 443-1874

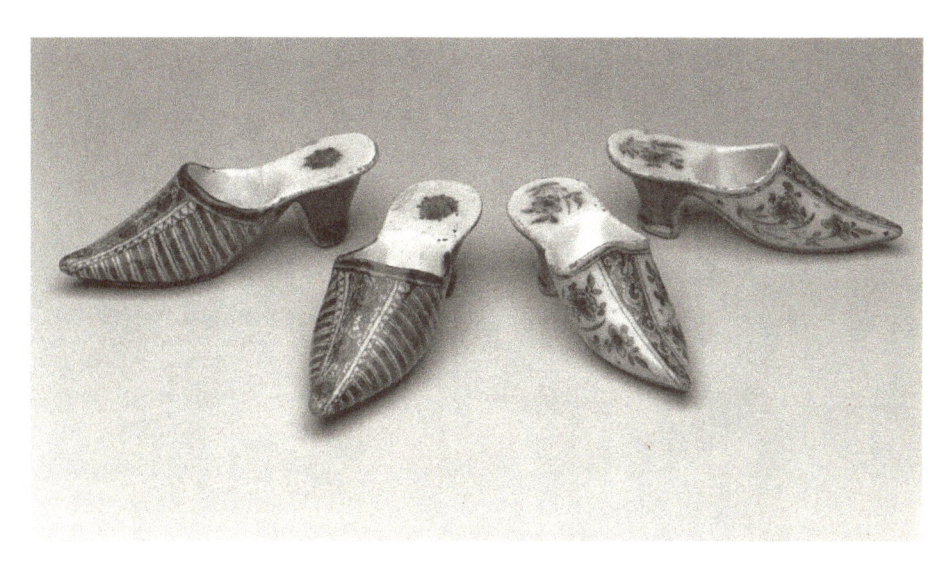

Figure 25.10 Two pairs of European shoes, l. 13 cm, 78 046.ab, 78 046.22ab

rim similar to the Persian one. Chinese shoes are also known to have been made in different materials, porcelain, cloisonné and tin, but their style is truly Chinese and it is obvious that they belong to the eighteenth century, replicating local tradition in women's footwear. So the original idea is more likely to be European and the shape may have been used as a trinket, perhaps to be included in a wedding basket. The meaning is not yet clear.

Making a choice among designs from late Safavid blue and white ceramics is a difficult task, yet two special designs stand out which recall well-known Kangxi patterns from the turn of the century: those are aster flowers and cone shapes represented worldwide in public collections of Chinese export porcelain. Their imitations, with an occasional addition of an Armenian monogram, look rather intriguing in a Persian context yet may help to make the dating more precise.

The first design concerns the so-called aster motif. The Chinese aster design appears as a wheel-shape repeat on large and small export dishes; it also repeats attractively on the body of bowls and small pots. Such a regular pattern would obviously appeal to, and satisfy, the Persian sense of geometry. A number of well-preserved Safavid bowls and dishes with a similar aster decoration were found among the finds of the British excavations of Qandahar in 1974 and 1975[9] (Figure 25.11). At

Figure 25.11 Bowl, w. 18.8 cm, h. 8.8 cm, G200 Pl. 240 a,b, Qandahar excavations

the time these finds were puzzling and thus began a search for such decoration among late Safavid ceramics from before 1738, when the whole site was totally destroyed by Nadir Shah. This quest led to the Victoria and Albert Museum where one dish, 22.5 cm wide, has a very similar type of decoration with the addition of a central Armenian monogram (Figure 25.12). As far as is known, no such writing had appeared on earlier ceramics, so that the deciphering of the owner's name could help to date the dish.

This first monogram with the aster pattern may be read as *nazaret*. In 1975 Kurdian[10] published the dish as well as two other blue and white ceramics with a different monogram to be discussed later. He related *nazaret* to one specific person, *Nazar*, the *kalantar* of New Julfa who died in 1636. Unfortunately the 1630s are far too early in time to justify the presence of a Qangxi design around this monogram. The Ming dynasty only collapsed in 1643. In any case, Nazar was a common name among the Julfa Armenians, making the link with a specific individual unreliable, especially given that the form of the name is *nazaret* rather than *nazar,* and Nazaret also was used as a personal name.

On the other hand if *nazaret* can be understood as a family name rather than that of a specific person, *nazaret* could be referring to one of several merchant families who had settled in Russia between the time of the first Armenian trade agreements

Figure 25.12 Aster dish, w. 22.5 cm, V&A 2715-1876

in Moscow of 1667, renewed in 1673, and the fall of the Safavid dynasty; this would then be the *Nazaret'eank* family.[11]

A third possibility is that the inscription relates to a church or monastery to which the plate was donated. Holy Nazareth (*Surb Nazaret*) is a common name for Armenian churches, and there was one of this name in New Julfa in Isfahan.

Obviously the Chinese, and subsequent Persian, aster designs could not have been devised before regular production at the Chinese imperial factories of Jingdezhen was resumed in 1683. Similar painted dishes have gone through the sale rooms in recent years suggesting the production of a complete dinner service decorated with the same monogram.

European coats of arms had been reproduced by Chinese workshops, not always correctly, since the mid-sixteenth century on single bowls, jars and vases, for the use of Portuguese governors and the Jesuit community in China. Yet the same coat of arms was not repeated on a series of vessels, which suggests that they did not belong to dinner services. The Armenian aster service could then be one of the first *Perse de commande*, even before the eighteenth century standard *Chine de commande* for the European market. Therefore the *nazaret* aster dish may have been produced within a time frame of about 30 years, between the late 1680s and the fall of Isfahan to the Afghans in 1722.

A second Armenian monogram could help to narrow this time span as it appears with the second motif in the shape of a cone. In a similar manner to the original Chinese cone, the Persian counterpart is filled with small scrolls and the outline

Figure 25.13 Pot, h. 11.5 cm, V&A 1248-1876

is marked precisely with dots. Four of these cones have been applied to the body of a pot, perhaps a water sprinkler with a broken neck, 11.5 cm high (Figure 25.13). This monogram has been painted upside down between two of the cones, possibly because it was easier to paint that way round. A similar fragment of a pot, but without a monogram, came up for sale at Christie's on 10 October 1999. It was attributed to Kutahya. Four cones also decorate the body of a ewer almost 23 cm high (Figures 25.14 and 25.15). The same monogram has been painted the right way up on the cup shape of the neck. The shape of the ewer, and in particular its everted neck with a vertical band under its flattened rim, recalls the shape of the Iznik ewer in the British Museum dated 1510 and signed in Armenian script by Abraham of Kutahya.[12] Michael Rogers has suggested a European prototype for this type of shape and 200 years later the contour of the ewer has acquired a more attractive silhouette.

This monogram appears for the third time on a dish 21 cm wide (Figure 25.16) but on this occasion with an incised band of 12 lappets instead of blue painted cones. As the same monogram is painted on three different shapes, this suggests once more the notion of a dinner service. In his article, Kurdian also published the above pot and dish and read the name of *Sarfraz,* a name which he suggested corresponded to that of the son of *kalantar Nazar* who died in 1656.[13] Again the date is too early to account for the appearance of the cone pattern on Persian wares and an alternate reading could be that of the name of *Safraz*. If so, this could be *Safraz,* the second of four sons of Khwaja Minas's second marriage. Minas was, like the representative of the *Nazaret'eank* family, one of the 23 leaders of the Armenian community in New Julfa who signed in 1671 the confirmation of the Russian trade agreement of 1667. And this agreement led, in 1689 with a renewal in 1711, to a trade monopoly of the Armenians on Russian soil at the expense of other Oriental merchants.

According to Edmund Herzig the eldest son of Minas, Kahnan, should have inherited the leadership of the family at the death of his father in 1701, but he made off with more than his fair share from his father's will, so that Safraz became the head of the family, which meant the head of the family firm. Such a position implied being responsible for a very large trading concern, which was manned by all the male members of a joint family system.[14] Although the economic situation of Persia had been at a very low ebb since the 1670s, the Armenian merchant community, through its expertise, had managed to keep control of its international network of purchases and credit facilities. No doubt through the growing trade to India and to Europe through Russia the house of Minas was able to survive beyond the siege and the surrender of Isfahan in 1722 to the Afghans by the last effective Safavid ruler Shah Soltan Hosayn. *Safraz* died the same year as the defeated ruler in 1727. The survival of a few pieces from a dinner service with his monogram points to his social standing in his community; it would have been produced in the early part of the eighteenth century and most likely before the Afghan onslaught. A span of less than 20 years may thus be allowed for the manufacturing of *Paron Safraz*'s service.[15]

Figure 25.14 Ewer, h. 22.7 cm, V&A C.185-1977

Figure 25.15 Ewer, h. 22.7 cm, detail of neck and monogram

Figure 25.16 Dish, w. 23.1 cm, V&A 2714-1876

A number of letters dated from 1706 to 1714 between Catholicos Alexander in Etchmiatsin, elected to the Holy See in 1705, and *Paron Safraz* and his brothers have survived. One of them, written in 1707 to Safraz by the Catholicos, acknowledges 'the arrival of a large donation of ceramics by Safraz to the Holy See'. The Catholicos reports that he has distributed 'the ceramics to his monks and other clergy visiting the Holy See, giving to each a cup, a saucer (*nalbaki*) and a mug (*tas*)'.[16] These gifts were only a small part of the regular and generous donations offered by the merchants of New Julfa to the Holy See. Catholicos Alexander had served earlier in New Julfa and had been unanimously voted to the See of Etchmiatsin. Such gifts of ceramics surely indicate that the production of Persian ceramics must have been specially appreciated in the region of Yerevan, where presumably such vessels could not be produced. There are at least three other examples of Armenian monograms which remain to be analysed. One of them was presented by Dr A. Jamkotchian at the sixth International Congress of Turkish Art in Istanbul in 1991[17] (Figure 25.17). It was placed in the centre of the well of a bowl with a surrounding pattern similar to that on bowls excavated in Qandahar.

The different locations of kiln sites that produced such ceramics still remain an open question. It should be remembered that the Armenian diocese of New Julfa covered a vast territory with a large number of villages where a variety of trades could have included Armenian workers.[18] Recently Lisa Golombek has drawn

Figure 25.17 Bowl from Erivan

attention to the town of Shah Reza some 60 kilometres south of Isfahan, as a possible centre of ceramic production.[19] Whatever the answer, European shapes were reproduced, far-eastern patterns were used as decorations, and asters and cones, both Qangxi motifs, were not only adopted by the Persian potter but also became favourite patterns with European workshops such as Wedgwood as late as 1876. Cones and asters of late Safavid production are often mistaken for Kutahya decoration, though they also appear on early eighteenth century blue and white Kutahya pieces. This is a useful indication which shows that patterns travelled not only by sea with the East India companies but also by land across the Anatolian plateau to the Mediterranean shores of the Ottoman Empire. These patterns followed the trade route of the silk bales exported from Persia to Aleppo by Armenian merchants at the expense of the East India companies.

Notes

1. T. Volker, *Porcelain and the Dutch East India Company, as Recorded in the Dagh-Registers of the Batavia Castle, Those of Hirado and Deshima and Other Contemporary Papers 1602–1682* (Leiden, 1954). A. Lane, *Later Islamic Pottery* (London, 1957).

2. Y. Crowe, Thèmes et variations du style Transition dans la céramique persane du XVIIe siècle, in *La porcelaine chinoise de Transition et ses influences sur la céramique japonaise, proche-orientale et européenne*, Musée Ariana (Genève, 1997).
3. Lane, *Later Islamic Pottery*, pl. 85b; Folsach K. von, *Islamic Art in the David Collection* (Copenhagen, 1990), no. 175.
4. Sotheby's London 1 October 1991 no. 13. Illustrated in L. L. Lipski and Archer M., *Dated English Deftware* (London, 1984), no. 903; Dam J. D. van, *Dated Dutch Delftware* (Zwolle, 1991), no. 21.
5. C. J. A. Jörg, *Porcelain and the Dutch China Trade* (The Hague, 1982), p. 95.
6. A. Lane, *French Faïence* (London, 1948), pl. 96 b, c, d.
7. Sotheby's (London, 10 October 1991), no. 10.
8. I am grateful for Deborah Del Gais's help at the RISD Museum of Art in Providence, RI, USA.
9. Y. Crowe, 'Glazed ceramics', *Excavations at Kandahar 1974 and 1975*, BAR international series 641 (Oxford, 1996), pp. 313–64.
10. H. Kurdian, 'A note on Persian blue and white wares with Armenian monograms in the Victoria and Albert Museum', *Journal of the Royal Asiatic Society* (1975), pp. 54–6.
11. K. Kevonian, 'Marchands arméniens au XVIIe siècle', *Cahiers du monde russe et soviétique* 16 (1975), pp. 199–244, note 141, pp. 238–9.
12. Lane, *Later Islamic Pottery*, pl. 24a.
13. Kurdian, 'A note on Persian blue and white wares'.
14. Edmund Herzig, 'The family firm in the commercial organisation of the Julfa Armenians', *Etudes Safavides* (Paris-Tehran, 1993), pp. 287–304.
15. This conclusion makes the dating slightly later to that suggested in Y. Crowe, *Persia and China: Safavid Blue and White Ceramics in the Victoria and Albert Museum* (London, 2002), p. 205.
16. The quotation is taken from a personal letter sent by Vazken Ghougassian.
17. Institute of Archaeology and ethnography, Erevan, Republic of Armenia. Further pieces were reproduced in the publication of the excavations at New Nissa. See M. E. Masson, pp. 7–72 fig. 52; M. I. Vyasmitina, pp. 147–158. Archaeological work on the site of New Nyssa in 1947, *Trudi IUzhno-Turkmenistanskoi arkheologicheskoi kompleksnoi* II (1951).
18. V. S. Ghougassian, *The Emergence of the Armenian Diocese of New Julfa in the Seventeenth Century* (Atlanta, GA, 1998).
19. L. Golombek, Mason R. B. and Proctor P., 'Safavid potters' marks and the question of provenance', *Iran* 39 (2001), pp. 207–36.

26

European Religious Iconography in Safavid Iran: Decoration and Patronage of *Meydani* Betʻghehem (Bethlehem of the Maydan)

Amy S. Landau[1]

Sometime in the late seventeenth century, the Safavid ruler Shah Solayman (1666–94) and the renowned Armenian theologian and artist Yovhannes Mrkʻuz (1642–1716) are recorded to have engaged in a lengthy debate inside the elaborately decorated All Saviour's Cathedral in New Julfa. Among the subjects they discussed were the cathedral's paintings, specifically, their suitability and function in a place of worship. The eighteenth-century historian Khachʻatur Jughayetsʻi recounted this exchange in *Patmutʼiwn Parsitsʻ* (*History of the Persians*):

> Occasionally, the Emperor, King Solayman, with a great entourage, would visit the splendid monastery of All Saviour for diversion. [On one occasion] he entered the Church and ordered that the holy Gospel be read. [Yovhannes] went up to the holy altar and read 'Think not' (Matt. 5:17), and expounded its meaning to the King (...) The King then asked many questions about the gilded and coloured images that were painted in the house of the Lord our God, about the divinity of Christ and the nature of the Trinity (...) He inquired: 'Why do you paint images in houses of prayer where it is not appropriate?' The blessed one, Yovhannes, answered: 'The paintings have many reasons and significations. Shall I give an account of them according to the Intellect, that is natural reasoning, or according to Scripture?' 'First speak according to the Intellect' – said the King – 'and, if I am pleased, according to Scripture.'[2]

According to the argument of Yovhannes, image and form are necessary as it is through them that people who cannot read and thus do not know the sacred writings may come to understand and contemplate God: through things visible we are able to comprehend the invisible.³ After the shah had been sufficiently pleased with this argument, Yovhannes proceeded to offer an explanation based on the Scripture:

> God commanded Moses, the first prophet, to set up two cherubs and to place them above the ark, whence God would speak. Further, when Solomon built the Temple, he similarly furnished it with cherubs. Our Lord Christ fashioned His image, which was not made by human hands, on a handkerchief and sent it to the king of the Armenians, Abgar. And thus in ancient times and today there is no prohibition of images; rather, it is idolatry that is prohibited.⁴

The shah's attention to the paintings of the cathedral and the Christian theologian's apology reflect renewed sensitivities to the use of religious images. In his argumentation Yovhannes Mrk'uz, a prominent member of New Julfa's ecclesiastical community, who had actively defended the Armenian faith both in print and in public disputation,⁵ brings out the didactic function of the paintings and justifies their use by following closely patristic and medieval Armenian tradition.⁶ In 1666, when Solayman (Shah Safi II) acceded to the throne, the murals of All Saviour's Cathedral had only recently been painted.⁷ They were part of a broader initiative in New Julfa dating approximately to the second half of the seventeenth century, when wall paintings characterized by a European style and iconography adorned Armenian churches.⁸ The Muslim reaction to the cathedral's novel decoration is described by Jean Chardin, the French Huguenot who travelled in Iran during the 1660s and 1670s: '… les Mahometens viennent à cette Eglise, comme à un Théatre, pour se divertir de la vue de ces peintures; Il leur en faut ouvrir les portes à toute heure.'⁹ [The Muslims come to this church as if to a theatre, to amuse themselves by looking at the paintings; it is necessary to open the door for them at all hours.] The Apostolic Armenians themselves were unaccustomed to such highly ornate churches: as Sirarpie Der Nersessian has pointed out, although the Armenians were not iconoclasts, they were inclined to a subtle interior décor for their churches.¹⁰ Within that tradition, the elaborate decoration in New Julfa was atypical, although certainly not unique.¹¹

What were the reasons for adopting a novel style to decorate churches in New Julfa? How did artists and patrons translate European material and what sources did they draw upon?¹² I would like to address briefly these interrelated questions by focusing on *Meydani* Bet'ghehem (Bethlehem of the Maydan), commonly known as Surb Bet'ghehem (Holy Bethlehem), located in Mets Meydan (Great Maydan), not far from the cathedral where the debate between Shah Solayman and Yovhannes Mrk'uz took place.¹³ I have chosen to concentrate on the Bethlehem Church for three reasons. First, the decoration of the Bethlehem Church, which may be attributed to the late 1630s–1650s, seems to provide the earliest extant example of Europeanized wall paintings in New Julfa's religious spaces. On a broader level, I believe that the Bethlehem murals constitute one of the earliest exercises in a painterly Europeanized mode by local painters (Persian, Armenian or Georgian artists) in Safavid Iran.¹⁴

Second, the Bethlehem Church is well documented by inscriptions that provide information not only on dating, but also on patronage and the artists who supervised its decoration. Finally, a European source closely associated with missionary visual culture can be identified as the model for the murals in the assembly area (*Zhoghovaran*). Through an initial investigation of the Bethlehem Church I hope to demonstrate the importance of this building for our understanding of seventeenth-century Safavid painting and its relationship to foreign stimuli. Generally, it has been assumed that Safavid painters did not integrate European techniques, such as atmospheric and linear perspective and chiaroscuro, until the final third of the seventeenth century.[15] The evidence from the Bethlehem Church, however, allows us to trace the fruitful artistic encounter between Iran and the European artistic tradition to an earlier period.

The Bethlehem Church was founded in 1077/1628–9 by *Khvaje* (Armenian *Khoja*) Petros Velijanian, one of the wealthiest merchants of New Julfa.[16] Its interior consists of gilded and painted stucco, tiled dadoes and wall paintings (Figure 26.1).[17] The murals are painted in distinct styles; while the sanctuary is decorated in a

Figure 26.1 Panoramic view of Bethlehem Church

Figure 26.2   Christ Pantocrator

variety of modes, the west end and assembly area are enveloped by European-style depictions. Paintings of Old Testament prophets, New Testament saints, and Christ Pantocrator (Figure 26.2), all located in the apse, were executed in an Armenian manuscript style that has been compared with that of Vaspurakan.[18] Close to these paintings in a 'traditional' mode are European-inspired images of the martyrdoms of St George and St Minas and the Massacre of the Innocents. On the chancel walls, two murals, namely the Adoration of the Magi and the Baptism of Christ (Figure 26.3), are executed in what has been described as a hybrid mode that combines elements of Safavid miniature painting with the Armenian manuscript style.[19] Entering the building one finds European-style murals of, for example, heaven, hell, the martyrdom of St Gregory the Illuminator (Figure 26.4) and images of St Sarkis, St Theodore, St Mercurius, all three on horseback. The distinctively large assembly area is dedicated to narratives related to the New Testament, illustrated with European style and iconography.

The church inscriptions document the building's history. The foundation date of 1077/1628–9 and the names of Petros Velijanian and his family are inscribed throughout the church.[20] Armenian artists are named in an inscription in the central niche of the apse above the Westernized depiction of The Serpent of Bronze: 'The paintings were drawn by Minas [and] Martiros. The floral decoration was drawn by Astuacatur'.[21] Unfortunately, this inscription does not offer a date and

Figure 26.3 Baptism of Christ

thus we cannot place the Westernized murals more precisely in the history of the building.[22] A nineteenth-century inscription over the west door states that the church, which was founded in 1628, took 20 years to complete.[23] An inscription dated 1084/1635 and located in the assembly area between the European-style paintings of the Ascension of Christ and the Pentecost supports an ongoing stage of decoration.[24] This suggestion is supported further by a *terminus post quem* of 1646 for the frieze of paintings of St Gregory the Illuminator's martyrdom in the west end of the church (see Figure 26.4). The models for this frieze were engravings brought back from Europe to Persia in 1646 by Yovhannes Jughayets'i, a student at All Saviour's Monastery, who had been sent to Italy by the bishop of New Julfa to master the art of printing.[25] On the basis of the nineteenth-century inscription supported by the 1084/1635 inscription and the *terminus post quem* of 1646 for a Westernized frieze of murals, we may accept that the execution of the decorative scheme of the church lasted approximately two decades and that it was completed by ca. 1650.[26]

There is indeed evidence for Armenian artists working in a Europeanized mode in Iran during the first half of the century. The Minas mentioned in the inscription of the apse has been identified with the artist of that name discussed by Arak'el

Figure 26.4 Martyrdom of St Gregory the Illuminator

Dawrizhets'i in *Girk Patmut'eants'*.[27] According to the seventeenth-century historian, Minas was trained in Aleppo by a European master-painter. Afterwards he returned to Iran, where, during the reign of Shah Safi (1629–42), he painted murals in the houses of the Safavid elite.[28] His contemporaries referred to him as 'the painter of European paintings' and apparently he trained and supervised other artists.[29] Minas and a group of artists, whom he may have supervised, executed the murals of the Bethlehem Church sometime between the mid-1630s and the 1650s. I would like to underline the importance of this dating for artistic developments in New Julfa in particular and for Safavid art in general.

The evidence from the Bethlehem Church is crucial for our understanding of Westernization in the Safavid arts. As mentioned earlier, scholars have tended to date the encounter between Iran and the European painterly tradition to the 1660s and later. Contrary to this view, the Bethlehem murals, which reflect the integration of Western perspective, chiaroscuro and modulation of form, indicate that a fruitful exchange defined by the study of Western painterly techniques on behalf of local painters took place even earlier. The date of the murals in the Bethlehem Church serves to underline the important role played by Armenian artists and patrons in the development of the European-style at the Safavid court, as well as the interrelation of the Armenian and Persian interest in European culture in Safavid Iran.[30] In the context of seventeenth-century court painting the earliest suggestion of the merging of the Persian and European traditions is found in the Chehel Sutun built by 'Abbas II and located in the palace precinct in Isfahan.[31] In the Chehel Sutun audience hall murals, Western devices, such as gradation of colour as well as linear and atmospheric perspective, are used to depict the Safavid shahs hosting their eastern neighbours.[32] Sussan Babaie, based on primary sources and architectural surveys, has shown that these murals were contemporary with the completion of the building (1647).[33] If one were only to consider the evidence from the court, such an early dating for the European-style Chehel Sutun murals might seem unlikely; although at least as early as the first decades of the seventeenth century Safavid notables (a'yan) would commission European painters and order Western paintings from abroad and Persian artists would copy European print sources,[34] there is no evidence to argue that, in the first half of the century, Persian court artists were assimilating Western painterly techniques for indigenous expression.[35] In view of the evidence from Bethlehem Church, however, we know that there were local artists in New Julfa who were integrating such techniques during the first half of the seventeenth century, strengthening the hypothesis that Armenian artists and patrons contributed to the development of the Occidental mode at the Safavid court.

The Bethlehem murals that date between the late 1630s and the 1650s are also important for our understanding of artistic developments in New Julfa, as they constitute the earliest attestation of a Westernized style employed in New Julfa's religious spaces: paintings in this mode in, for example, All Saviour's Cathedral, St Minas and St Mary's Church date to the 1660s. Against the background of the surviving churches in New Julfa, the iconographic scheme of the Bethlehem Church is somewhat unusual. Here, I shall concentrate on the assembly area. Two rows of paintings of New Testament themes wrap around this space; paintings in the upper level are framed in large square panels and those below in smaller rectangular ones. These murals are based on an identifiable source whose circulation and adaptation in Safavid Iran has yet to be studied. So far, attention has been focused on the oeuvre of the Dutch woodcut engraver Christoffel van Sichem II (b. 1577, Basel; d. 1658, Amsterdam) as an important source for church decoration in New Julfa.[36] A great part of van Sichem's oeuvre was based on well-known northern European artists, including Dürer, Lucas van Leyden, Henri Goltzius and the Wierix brothers, whose compositions he would only slightly alter and identify as his own by adding his monogram.[37] Van Sichem's works were used to illustrate a number of books, often of a religious subject matter, including the *Biblia Sacra* printed by Pieter Iacobsz Paets (Amsterdam, 1646; reprinted 1657).[38] The Armenian printing house that was

Figure 26.5 Deposition scene by Christoffel van Sichem

established in Amsterdam in the late 1650s acquired van Sichem's woodcuts,[39] and used them extensively in its publications, most notably in the Armenian Bible printed by Oskan Erevants'i in Amsterdam, 1666–1668.[40]

Were van Sichem's compositions used as models for the New Testament scenes in the assembly area of the Bethlehem Church? Let us compare van Sichem's version of the Deposition (Figure 26.5) with the mural of the same subject in the Bethlehem Church (Figure 26.6).[41] Though a quick glance might lead us to believe that van Sichem's woodcut could lie behind the wall painting, on closer inspection we notice

Figure 26.6 Deposition scene in the Bethlehem Church

significant iconographic differences. First, in the mural, on the left-hand side of the composition, the man on the ladder wears a European hat; in the print, however, the man in the same position has a handkerchief tied around his head and wears a large hoop earring.[42] Second, in the mural, on the ladder opposite, the soldier wears headgear; in the print, however, the soldier's head is uncovered. Finally, in the Bethlehem wall painting, on the lower left-hand side of the composition, the man carrying a vessel is clearly visible; in the print, he is hidden.

I would like to suggest that for the inspiration of the Deposition scene at the Bethlehem Church we should not look at van Sichem, but rather at his prototype. Many of the Dutch artist's New Testament woodcuts that appear in, for example, *Der zielen lusthof* (1629), *'t Schat der Zielen* (1648), *Biblia Sacra* (1646 and 1657) and *Goddelycke wenschen* (1651) derive from the engravings in *Evangelicae historiae imagines* (Antwerp, 1593), and *Adnotationes et meditationes in Evangelia* (Antwerp, 1594) by the Jesuit priest Jerome Nadal.[43] Nadal's Bible (the *Imagines* and the *Adnotationes*) contained works by Jan and Adriaen Collaert and the Wierix brothers and was among the most important collections of European religious iconography in the late sixteenth and seventeenth century. We can trace the origin of the headgear and the foreground figure holding the vessel in the Bethlehem mural to the Deposition by Hieronymous Wierix (Figure 26.7) (both elements are absent from van Sichem's print). There is also exact correspondence in iconographic details between the Temptation in the Bethlehem Church (Figure 26.8) and the Temptation by Hieronymous Wierix in *Imagines* (Figure 26.9): the pelican stands on top of the rocks in both (van Sichem's print contains no pelican, but a goat (Figure 26.10)).[44] Another good example is provided by The Storm at Sea in the Bethlehem Church, where the mural (Figure 26.11) mirrors Adriaen Collaert's engraving (Figure 26.12). In contrast, van Sichem's version has variants: for example, in one of his illustrations for the *Biblia Sacra*,[45] Peter is beardless, and in his woodcut used for the *Oskan Bible* of 1666, the positioning of the boat and its passengers has been altered radically.[46] On the basis of these comparisons, I would like to suggest that New Julfa artists were drawing upon the *Imagines*, or, alternatively, upon compositions more faithful to the *Imagines* than van Sichem's versions had been. To be sure, not all of the scenes of Nadal's Bible are found in the Bethlehem Church. Those, however, that are attested there, with a few exceptions, correspond closely to the ones of the same subject matter in the *Imagines*.[47]

Whether the *Imagines*, which were printed several times during the sixteenth and seventeenth centuries and were circulated in Europe, the New World, South Asia and the Far East,[48] were accessible in New Julfa as a complete set or as loose leaves is an open question. The precise means by which they might have reached Safavid Iran also remain a mystery. They proved very influential outside Europe, where artists trained in a two-dimensional style would copy them in order to learn how to render three-dimensional effects such as the plasticity of form. Considering that the Bethlehem Church murals are an early instance of European style and iconography in Safavid Persia, we may appreciate the role of the *Imagines* during the nascent stage

Figure 26.7 Deposition scene by Hieronymous Wierix

in the development of the arts in the first half of the seventeenth-century in New Julfa, where most Armenian artists, trained as manuscript painters, were not well acquainted with the European tradition.

I would like to suggest two possible avenues through which the *Imagines* (or a set of compositions closely based on them) might have reached seventeenth-century

Figure 26.8 Temptation scene in the Bethlehem Church

Persia.⁴⁹ First, Yovhannes Jughayetsʻi, who, as mentioned earlier, had returned from Italy with engravings of the martyrdom of St Gregory the Illuminator, might have brought back depictions of the Gospel narrative as well. Yovhannes intended to print the Armenian Bible upon his return to New Julfa and could have made use of such scenes for his project.⁵⁰ Alternatively, the *Imagines* could have reached Asia through Catholic missionaries.⁵¹ The *Imagines*, which narrated the life of Christ in diagrammatic terms, served as a mnemonic device for Christian

Figure 26.9 Temptation scene by Hieronymous Wierix

instruction.⁵² Out of all the Catholic missionaries, the Jesuits placed special emphasis on the universal language of images. They underlined the role of art not only as an aid for meditation among the literate, but also as a means through which to communicate Christian doctrine to the uneducated as well as to those with whom they did not share a language. Although the Jesuits were only allowed to obtain a licence to establish a mission in Isfahan in 1647 and were only fully established in New Julfa after the middle of the century,⁵³ Armenians from

Figure 26.10 Temptation scene by Christoffel van Sichem

Figure 26.11 Storm at sea in the Bethlehem Church

New Julfa, who profited from their international network, would have had occasion for interaction with the Jesuits earlier in Poland, Mughal India and China, for example.

We may recall the dialogue between Shah Solayman and Yovhannes Mrk'uz quoted at the opening of this chapter where the Armenian theologian argues that pictures are important for the masses who cannot read and do not know Scripture. As we have seen, the Jesuit approach to images is comparable to that of Yovhannes: both the Apostolic Armenians and the Jesuits had educational philosophies that recognized art as an effective means of guidance and instruction. For their part, the Armenian merchants, who underwrote the expenses for churches and copies of Holy Scripture richly decorated with images, would not have been unaware of the didactic value of art. These compatible outlooks would have facilitated the adaptation of the *Imagines* whose rich narrative cycle would conveniently fill the exceptionally large assembly area of the Bethlehem Church.

The above considerations are interrelated with issues of prestige for the Velijanian family. Petros Velijanian would have commissioned a Europeanized style and iconography that had captivated the imagination of the Armenian notables (*metsametsk'*)[54] in order to draw attention to the church and to present himself and his family as devout and affluent patrons.[55] Seeing that the Europeanized wall paintings of the Bethlehem Church date to the period between the late 1630s to the 1650s, the Velijanian family may very well have played a central role in facilitating the adoption of a novel painterly idiom based on the European tradition, not only for New Julfa's religious spaces, but also for Safavid art in general.

Figure 26.12 Storm at sea by Adriaen Collaert

The nineteenth-century historian Ter Yovhaneants' records the oral tradition concerning the motivation that lay behind Petros Velijanian's founding of the Bethlehem Church. In Holy Week, Petros could not enter St Mary's Church, located adjacent to where the Bethlehem Church came to stand. According to some, this happened because the patron of St Mary's Church forbade Petros to enter in order to incite him to build another church in the suburb. According to others, this happened because St Mary's was too crowded with the faithful. Therefore, according to both traditions, Petros decided to build a massive and gloriously decorated church of his own in the *Great Maydan*.[56] The accounts imply that a new church of greater capacity than that of St Mary's was needed to accommodate the large number of New Julfa's faithful: here, we may reflect upon the distinctly large assembly area of the Bethlehem Church enriched with scenes of the New Testament based on European religious iconography. Irrespective of the historicity of these traditions, one thing is clear: the lavishly decorated Bethlehem Church, which occupies a special place in the history of exchange between Iran and the European artistic tradition in the late Safavid period, captured the imagination of the Armenian community of New Julfa and seems to have had an impact far beyond the Armenian suburb, most notably at the Safavid court.

Notes

1. I am grateful to Robert Thomson, Sussan Babaie, Julian Raby, Theo van Lint, Edmund Herzig, and Willem Floor for their invaluable comments and suggestions. I also wish to thank the participants in the conference, especially Kathryn Babayan, Ina Baghdiantz McCabe, Robert Hillenbrand and Tim Stanley, for their valuable suggestions. Of course, any errors of fact or interpretation remain my own.
2. Khach'atur Jughayets'i, *Patmut'iwn Parsits'* (Vałarsapat, 1905), pp. 155–6. I wish to thank Professor Robert Thomson for help with this translation. Khach'atur Jughayets'i, the eighteenth-century author, noted that the questions and answers voiced by the Persian king and the Armenian theologian were written down and collected in a book. The text was written in Armenian on one side of the page and in Persian on the other. Khach'atur added that 'this book is in our midst up to the present day', see ibid., p. 156. For the theological works of Yovhannes Mrk'uz, see Raymond H. Kévorkian, *Catalogue des 'Incunables' arméniens (1511/1695), ou Chronique de l'imprimerie arménienne* (Geneva, 1986), pp. 122–4, and Kevork B. Bardakjian, *Reference Guide to Modern Armenian Literature (1500-1920)* (Detroit, MI, 2000), pp. 567–8. A bilingual text in Persian and Armenian, with a modern Armenian translation of one of his theological works is given in G.M. Nalbandyan, *Hovhannes Vardapet Mrk'uz Jughayec'i. Ełdzali K'ristosi Orenkě* (Erevan, 1998); a recent study of his work is H.Ł. Mirzoyan, *Hovhannes Mrk'uz Jughayec'i* (Erevan, 2001).
3. Khach'atur Jughayets'i, *Patmut'iwn Parsits'*, p. 158.
4. Ibid., p. 158.
5. For his anti-Catholic polemics, see Kévorkian, *Catalogue des 'Incunables'*, pp. 122–4. Concerning his debates with Muslim intellectuals, Khach'atur Jughayets'i relates: 'he [Yovhannes] never ceased speaking with them or writing to them, by which means he promulgated the truth of our religion and softened their hard hearts that had been inclined against us', see *Patmut'iwn Parsits'*, p. 205. For a concise overview of Yovhannes's contributions, see Vazken S. Ghougassian, *The Emergence of the Armenian Diocese of New Julfa in the Seventeenth Century* (Atlanta, 1998), and bibliography therein.
6. For the use of images among the Armenians and earlier apologetics, see Sirarpie Der Nersessian, 'Image worship in Armenia and its opponents', *Armenian Quarterly* 1 (1946), pp. 67–81 (reprinted in her *Études byzantines et arméniennes* (Louvain, 1973) vol. 1, pp. 405–15), and Sirarpie Der Nersessian, 'Une Apologie des images du septième siècle', *Byzantion* 17 (1944–45), pp. 58–87 (reprinted in her *Études*

byzantines et arméniennes ibid., vol. 1, pp. 379–403). See also Thomas F. Mathews, 'Vrt'anes K'ert'oł and the Early Theology of Images', *Revue des Études Arméniennes*, vol. 31 (2007-2009), pp. 101–6.

7. The murals of the cathedral are attributable to ca. 1660s. According to Minasian, 'Khoja Awetik ew Amenap'rkich' Vank'i tachari Nkarazardumĕ', *Hask* (January 1971), pp. 20–3, the precise date of the decoration is unclear. The construction of the church started in 1655 and was completed in 1664. For discussions of this building and the dating of its construction, see, for example [N.B. discrepancies therein], John Carswell, *New Julfa: The Armenian Churches and Other Buildings* (Oxford, 1968), pp. 30–4; Armen Hakhnazarian and Vahan Mehrabian, *Nor Djulfa* (Documents of Armenian Architecture, no. 21) (Venice, 1992), pp. 22–35 and 104–6; L. G. Minasian, *Nor Jughayi Ekeghets'inerĕ...* (New Julfa, 1992), pp. 49–55; and Ter Yovhaneants', *Patmut'iwn Nor Jughayu or yAspahan* (New Julfa, 1880), vol. II, pp. 1–15.

8. The Europeanized wall paintings in All Saviour's Cathedral and the churches of St Mary and St Minas, for example, date to the second half of the century. In St Mary's there is a dated inscription (1666) mentioning the painter Apov, see Ter Yovhaneants', *Patmut'iwn*, vol. II, p. 192. For the dates of St Minas, see Carswell, *New Julfa*, p. 55, and Ter Yovhaneants', *Patmut'iwn*, vol. II, pp. 211–17.

9. Jean Chardin, *Voyages du Chevalier Chardin, en Perse, et autres lieux de l'Orient...* (Amsterdam, 1735) vol. 2, p. 106; quoted and discussed in Ina Baghdiantz McCabe, *The Shah's Silk for Europe's Silver. The Eurasian Trade of the Julfa Armenians in Safavid Iran and India (1530-1750)* (Atlanta, 1999), pp. 175–7.

10. Der Nersessian points out that the Armenians, who did not wish to be associated with Chalcedonian Christians, were suspicious of excessive forms of decoration and image-worship; see her 'Image worship', pp. 405–15.

11. There are indeed other examples of elaborate interior decoration in Armenian churches, such as the murals in the church of the Holy Cross at Aght'amar (915–921), see Sirarpie Der Nersessian, *Aght'amar: Church of the Holy Cross* (Cambridge, MA, 1965).

12. We may begin to investigate these questions now that preliminary surveys of New Julfa's art and architecture have been made available and the suburb's historical landscape has been systematically studied. Recent historical and art-historical studies of New Julfa include the following: McCabe, *The Shah's Silk*; Ghougassian, *The Emergence of the Armenian Diocese*; Edmund Herzig, 'The Armenian merchants of New Julfa, Isfahan: A study in premodern Asian trade', D.Phil. thesis (Oxford University, 1991); Shushanik L. Khach'ikyan, *Nor Jughayi hay vacharakanut'yunĕ ev nra arevtratntesakan kaperĕ Rusastani het XVII-XVIII darerum* (Erevan, 1988); Carswell, *New Julfa*; Hakhnazarian and Mehrabian, *Nor Djulfa*; Karapet Karapetian, *Isfahan, New Julfa: The Houses of the Armenians* (Rome, 1974); Sirarpie Der Nersessian and Arpag Mekhitarian, *Armenian Miniatures from Isfahan* (Brussels, 1986); L. G. Minasian, *Nor Jughayi Ekeghets'inerĕ* (New Julfa, 1992); Eleanor Sims, 'Late Safavid painting: The Chehel Sutun, the Armenian houses, the oil paintings', *Akten des.VII Internationalen Kongresses für Iranische Kunst und Archäologie, München, 7.-10. September, 1976* (Berlin, 1979), pp. 408–18. And now the excellent works by Sebouh David Aslanian: *From the Indian Ocean to the Mediterranean: The Global Trade Networks of Armenian Merchants from New Julfa* (Berkeley, 2011); '"The Salt in a Merchant's Letter": The Culture of Julfan Correspondence in the Indian Ocean and Mediterranean', *Journal of World History*, vol. 19, no. 2 (2008), pp. 127–88; 'The Circulation of Men and Credit: The Role of the Commenda and the Family Firm in Julfan Society', *The Journal of the Social and Economic History of the Orient*, vol. 50, no. 2 (2007),pp. 124–71; and 'Social Capital, "Trust" and the Role of Networks in Julfan Trade: Informal and Semi-formal Institutions at Work', *Journal of Global History* vol. 1, no. 3 (2006), pp. 383–402.

13. The nineteenth-century historian Ter Yovhaneants' refers to this building as *Meydani Bet'ghehem* in *Patmut'iwn*, see vol. II, p. 173. Henceforth I shall be referring to this building as the Bethlehem Church. The present study reflects an initial investigation based on published sources. I hope to visit the building anew and to work towards a detailed study of it in the near future.

14. By painterly Europeanized mode I mean the visual idiom that reflects the interweaving of such Western painterly techniques as atmospheric perspective, cast shadows and modelling of forms on the part of Safavid artists.

15. See, for example, Basil Gray, 'The arts of the Safavid period', in Peter J. Jackson and Lawrence Lockhart (eds), *The Cambridge History of Iran. The Timurid and Safavid Periods* (Cambridge, 1986), pp. 877–912; Eleanor Sims and Ernest Grube, 'Wall paintings in the seventeenth-century monuments of Isfahan', *Studies on Isfahan* (*Iranian Studies* 7), ed. Renata Holod (Boston, MA, 1974), pp. 511–42; and Sims, '*Late Safavid painting.*'
16. The Bethlehem Church has been discussed in the following studies: John Carswell, *New Julfa*, pp. 50–1; Ghougassian, *The Emergence of the Armenian Diocese*, especially pp. 178–9; Hakhnazarian and Mehrabian, *Nor Djulfa*, pp. 44–51; Edmund Herzig, 'The Armenian merchants of New Julfa, Isfahan', p. 76; L. G. Minasian, *Nor Jughayi Ekeghets'inerě*, pp. 72–90; Ter Yovhaneants', *Patmut'iwn*, vol. II, pp. 173–9. The building is richly documented in Rev. Hamazasb (Hacob) Arakelian's *A Pictorial Guidebook to St. Bethlehem Church of New Julfa, Isfahan* (Tehran, 1999). Concerning this last work, the reader should be aware of a few inconsistencies between the Armenian, Persian and English texts.
17. This decorative scheme is analogous to that found in other churches of New Julfa, see John Carswell, *New Julfa*. There are striking similarities between the decoration in the Bethlehem Church and that of the 'Aleppo-Zimmer' in the Museum für Islamische Kunst in Berlin, see Julia Gonnella, *Ein christlich-orientalisches Wohnhaus des 17. Jahrhunderts aus Aleppo (Syrien): das 'Aleppo-Zimmer' im Museum für Islamische Kunst, Staatliche Museum zu Berlin-Preussischer Kulturbesitz* (Berlin, 1996). I wish to thank Dr Julian Raby for pointing out these similarities and directing me to this work.
18. See Hakhnazarian and Mehrabian, *Nor Djulfa*, p. 45.
19. Their background elements (e.g. high horizon, streaked sky and trees) immediately recall early- to mid-seventeenth-century Safavid manuscript painting, such as illustrations of a copy of the *Shahnameh*, Windsor Castle, MS A/6 Holmes, dated 1648. A study of this manuscript by Robinson, Basil W. and Eleanor Sims, *The Windsor Shahnama of 1648* (London: Azimuth Editions for the Roxburghe Club, 2007). For a full discussion of the artists who employed this style, see Massumeh Farhad, 'Safavid single page painting, 1629–1666' (doctoral dissertation) (Harvard University, 1987). In recent research, Massumeh Farhad has proposed that this style derives from the workshops of Mashhad, see Sussan Babaie, Kathryn Babayan, Ina Baghdiantz McCabe and Massumeh Farhad, *Slaves of the Shah: New Elites of Safavid Iran* (London and New York, 2004). Features of the Bethlehem paintings seem to have been repainted in the nineteenth century when the building was restored in 1870 and 1899.
20. For example, the inscription in the half dome of the apse, underneath Christ Pantocrator, gives the date 1077; for the Armenian text, see Ter Yovhaneants', *Patmut'iwn*, vol. II, p. 174; for an English translation of this inscription, see Hakhnazarian and Mehrabian, *Nor Djulfa*, p. 104.
21. For translations of this inscription, see, for example, Ghougassian, *The Emergence of the Armenian Diocese*, p. 183; Hakhnazarian and Mehrabian, *Nor Djulfa*, p. 104; and Rev. Hamazasb (Hacob) Arakelian, *A Pictorial Guidebook*, p. 82. There is a discrepancy as to whether the names should be read 'Minas Martiros' (i.e. one person), or 'Minas [and] Martiros.' Minas is discussed below and Astuatsatur has been identified as the painter of that same name who moved from New Julfa to the court of Tsar Aleksei Mikhailovich. In the late 1660s Astuatsatur was in Russia, where he worked under the name Bogdan Saltanov and executed Europeanized works for the Tsar. For a monograph on this painter, see M. Ghazaryan and V. Oskanyan *Bogdan Salt'anov* (Erevan, 1986). It is curious that Ter Yovhaneants' does not document this important inscription. It is possible that the inscription was not legible before the 1899 renovation (the history of Ter Yovhaneants' was published in 1880).
22. According to L. G. Minasian, 'Ostad Minas, naqqash-e mashhur-e Julfa', *Honar va Mardom* 179 (1356/1977), pp. 28–30, esp. p. 30, the last part of the inscription is damaged and the date no longer legible.
23. Twenty years may be an approximation that corresponds with the date of the death of Petros in 1098/1649. This suggestion is supported by the inscription's phrasing: 'in the course of twenty years it was completed by *Khvaje* Petros Velijanian'. For the date of the patron's death inscribed on his gravestone, see Ter Yovhaneants', *Patmut'iwn*, vol. II, p. 179; and for a translation of the nineteenth-

century inscription, see Hakhnazarian and Mehrabian, *Nor Djulfa*, pp. 103–4 [N.B. misprint of 1625 for 1628]. In Rev. Hamazasb (Hacob) Arakelian's *A Pictorial Guidebook*, p. 17, the English and Persian descriptions mention the eastern entrance; it is only the Armenian description that correctly mentions the western entrance.
24. For the inscription, see Ter Yovhaneants', *Patmut'iwn*, vol. II, pp. 174–5.
25. Archbishop Goriun Babian is about to publish a detailed discussion of these engravings and their use in All Saviour's Cathedral and the Bethlehem Church. I wish to thank him for generously sending me prints from the seventeenth-century engravings that have survived. For Yovhannes's activities in Italy, see Kévorkian, *Catalogue des 'Incunables'*, pp. 32–4, and Vrej Nersessian, *Catalogue of Early Armenian Books, 1512-1850* (London, 1980), pp. 23–4. As will be suggested below, Yovhannes, whose return falls within the period of the decoration of the Bethlehem Church, may have inspired additional adaptations of Western religious iconography.
26. To the best of my knowledge there is only one other later Safavid inscription (dated 1160/1710–11). This inscription, however, pertains only to the stone bema along whose edge it runs, see Ter Yovhaneants', *Patmut'iwn*, vol. II, p. 174, and L. G. Minasian, *Nor Jughayi Ekeghets'inerě*, pp. 75–7.
27. For Minas, see Arak'el Davrizhets'i, *Girk' Patmut'eants'*, ed. L. A. Khanlaryan (Erevan, 1990), pp. 324–6; for a Persian translation of the relevant Armenian passage, see L. Minasian, 'Ostad Minas, Naqqash-e mashhur-e Julfa'; for accounts based on Arak'el, see Mohammad 'Ali Karimzade Tabrizi, *Ahval va asar-e naqqashan-e qadimi-ye Iran*, vol. 3 (London, 1991), pp. 1355–7, and Ghougassian, *The Emergence of the Armenian Diocese*, p. 182. In Amy S. Landau, *Farangi-sazi at Isfahan: The Court Painter Muhammad Zaman, the Armenians of New Julfa and Shah Sulayman (1666-1694)* (Oxford, 2009), I discuss its relevance in the context of Safavid interest in 'life-like' representation. For an English translation of Arak'el's work see: George A. Bournoutian (Introduction and Annotated Translation from Critical text) *Arak'el of Tabriz: Book of History (Arak'el Dawrizhets'i, Girk' patmuteants')* (Costa Mesa, 2010).
28. Arak'el relates that Minas painted pictures in the house of *Khvaje* Sarfraz. Shah Safi visited that house and remarked on the 'life-likeness' of the murals, see Arak'el Dawrizhets'i, *Girk' Patmut'eants'*, p. 324.
29. This is based on information provided by the documents published by Minasian, 'Mi k'ani grawor pastat'ghter ZE dari nkarich' Minasits'', *Bazmavep* 13 (1982), pp. 190–3. One of these documents indicates that Minas offered tuition to an artist referred to as Master Riza.
30. I document the Armenian contribution to the development of Europeanization in Safavid court arts in my doctoral dissertation. Amy S. Landau, *Farangi-sazi at Isfahan: The Court Painter Muhammad Zaman, the Armenians of New Julfa and Shah Sulayman (1666-1694)* (Oxford, 2009).
31. For a comprehensive study of the Chehel Sutun, see Sussan Babaie, 'Shah 'Abbas II, the conquest of Qandahar, the Chihil Sutun, and its wall paintings', *Muqarnas* 11 (1994), pp. 125–42, and *Palaces at Isfahan. Continuity and Change, 1590-1666* (doctoral dissertation) (New York University, 1994). See also Sussan Babaie, *Isfahan and its Palaces: Statecraft, Shi'ism and the Architecture of Conviviality in Early Modern Iran* (Edinburgh, 2008). In many respects the Bethlehem Church is comparable to the Chehel Sutun. Though a discussion of their similarities is beyond the scope of the present chapter, it may be pointed out that, like the Bethlehem Church, the Chehel Sutun is decorated with both 'traditional' and Westernized wall paintings.
32. For an analysis of the subjects depicted in the Chehel Sutun, see Babaie, 'Shah 'Abbas II', pp. 125–42.
33. Ibid.
34. For Dutch artists in Iran, see Willem Floor, 'Dutch painters in Iran during the first half of the 17th century', *Persica* 8 (1979), pp. 145–61, and Amy S. Landau, 'From Poet to Painter: Allegory and Metaphor in a Seventeenth-Century Persian Painting by Muhammad Zaman, Master of Farangi-Sazi', *Muqarnas* vol. 28 (2011), pp. 101–31. For an early example of a Safavid artist copying a Western print source, see Gauvin A. Bailey, 'In the manner of the Frankish masters: A Safavid drawing and its Flemish inspiration', *Oriental Art* XL.4 (1994/95), pp. 29–34; for an even earlier instance, see Julian Raby, 'Samson and Siyah Qalam', *Islamic Art* I (1981), pp. 160–3.

35. The lack of evidence in the first half of the century is in dramatic contrast with abundant evidence of the use of Western painterly techniques by court painters during the reign of Shah Sulayman (1664–94).
36. To the best of my knowledge, T. S. R. Boase was the first to compare All Saviour's murals with compositions by Christoffel van Sichem illustrating the Armenian Bible of 1666 (–1668), see his 'A seventeenth-century typological cycle of paintings in the Armenian Cathedral at Julfa', *Journal of the Warburg and Courtauld Institutes* 13 (1950), pp. 323-7. O. Meinardus, 'The Last Judgement in the Armenian churches of New Julfa', *Oriens Christianus* 55 (1971), pp. 182–94 suggested that van Sichem was the source for the Last Judgement scene in St Minas and possibly in All Saviour's Cathedral.
37. For the artists van Sichem copied, see M. Funck, *Le livre belge à gravures: guide de l'amateur de livres illustrés imprimés en Belgique avant le XVIIIe siècle* (Paris, 1925), p. 394, and Marie Mauquoy-Hendrickx, *Les estampes des Wierix*, vols I–III (Brussels, 1978–83); for discussions of van Sichem's oeuvre, see F. W. H. Hollstein, *Dutch and Flemish Etchings, Engravings and Woodcuts (ca 1450-1700)*, vol. 27, pp. 39–53. In the van Sichem family there were four woodcut artists named Christoffel, see H. Lehmann-Haupt, 'Christoffel van Sichem, a family of Dutch 17th-century woodcut-artists', *Gutenberg-Jahrbuch*, pp. 274–306, and H. F. Wijnman, 'De Van Sichem-puzzle', *Oud Holland* 46 (1929), pp. 233–44.
38. This work is often referred to as the 'van Sichem Bible', see Funck, *Le livre belge à gravures*, p. 394, and Lehmann-Haupt, 'Christoffel van Sichem', p. 290.
39. Kévorkian, *Catalogue des 'Incunables'*, p. 6.
40. For the extensive use of van Sichem's compositions at the Oskanian press, see Nersessian, *Catalogue of Early Armenian Books*, p. 28; for Armenian printing in Amsterdam, see, for example, Ina Baghdiantz McCabe, 'Merchant capital and knowledge: The financing of early printing presses by the Eurasian silk trade of New Julfa', *Treasures of Heaven: Armenian Art, Religion, and Society*, Pierpont Morgan Library (New York, 1998), pp. 59–71; Kévorkian, *Catalogue des 'Incunables'*, pp. 39–66; and Nersessian, *Catalogue of Early Armenian Books*, pp. 24–9. Willem Floor, who has carried out extensive research on the Dutch East India Company in Persia, has noted the dispatch of a certain painter, Barend van Sichem, to Iran by the company's governor-general. For Barend van Sichem and possible links with Christoffel, see Floor, 'Dutch painters in Iran', pp. 145–61. Whether van Sichem's compositions influenced paintings in other churches of New Julfa remains an open question.
41. Although the iconography is clearly that of the Deposition, the Armenian inscription reads 'the Crucifixion of Christ' (followed by Arakelian, *A Pictorial Guidebook*, p. 42).
42. See *Biblia Sacra... verciert met veele schoone figueren (gesneden door Christoffel van Sichem)* (Amsterdam, 1657), pp. 65, 99, 166; *Goddelycke wenschen verlicht met sinnebeelden en vierige uytsprake der Out-vaders* (Amsterdam, 1651), p. 357.
43. For the editions of these two works, see Carlos Somervogel S. J., *Bibliothèque de la Compagnie de Jésus* (Louvain, 1960), vol. 5, pp. 1517–1520. Marie Mauquoy-Hendrickx, *Les estampes des Wierix*, vol. III (Brussels, 1982), pp. 491-6, esp. p. 491, points out that the *Bible de Natalis* is the title widely used by scholars for both the *Evangelicae* and Nadal's own work *Adnotationes*; the two works were often bound together. Gauvin Bailey has made a passing reference to the influence of Nadal's compositions on the murals of All Saviour's Cathedral; see his *Counter Reformation Symbolism and Allegory in Mughal Painting* (doctoral dissertation) (Harvard University, 1996), p. 188, n. 20. After the presentation of this paper at the conference and the submission of it for publication, Sayeh Laporte-Eftekharian published her 'Diffusion et exploitation des gravures religieuses dans la Perse safavide: l'exemple de la Nouvelle Djoulfa' in *Annales d'Histoire de l'Art et d'Archéologie: Publication annuelle de la Section d'Histoire de l'Art et d'Archéologie de l'Université Libre de Bruxelles*, vol. XXV (2003), pp. 51-70, where she too comes to the conclusion that the sources for these paintings were not van Sichem, but rather van Sichem's sources.
44. See *Biblia Sacra*, p. 11; *Goddelycke wenschen*, p. 112; 'Oskan Bible' (Amsterdam, 1666), p. 505.
45. See *Biblia Sacra*, p. 21; cf. also *Bybels Lusthof, ofte twee hondert en veertig, zoo historien als leeringen des Bybels... met de Schriftuurplaatsen daar toe dienende. Gesneeden door... Christoffel van Sichem. En verrykt met vaerfen [sic] door B. Blens* (Amsterdam, 1754), p. 27.

46. See 'Oskan Bible', p. 478. This version also appears in *Biblia Sacra*, p. 131, illustrating the Gospel of St Luke.
47. The scenes of the Annunciation and the Assumption of Mary in the assembly area of the Bethlehem Church do not resemble the corresponding compositions in the *Imagines*. In general, the Armenian artists deviated from their source in certain compositional details.
48. For the transmission and reception of the *Imagines* in the East, see Gauvin A. Bailey, *Art on the Jesuit Missions in Asia and Latin America, 1542-1773* (Toronto, 1999); Gauvin A. Bailey, 'The Truth-Showing Mirror: Jesuit catechism and the arts of Mughal India', in *The Jesuits: Cultures, Sciences, and the Arts 1540-1773*, eds. John W. O'Malley, et al. (Toronto, 1999), pp. 380–401; and Samuel Y. Edgerton, *The Heritage of Giotto's Geometry. Art and Science on the Eve of the Scientific Revolution* (Ithaca, NY and London, 1991), p. 257.
49. These engravings and works based upon them were reprinted and widely circulated during the seventeenth century. According to Mauquoy-Hendrickx, *Les estampes des Wierix*, pp. 494–5, the plates which were originally made for Nadal's Bible were later used in other works, as, for example, in Bartolomeo Ricci's *Consideratami sopra tutta la Vita de NS Giesu Christo* (Rome, 1607) (other editions followed); the same plates were used in the Latin translation of Ricci's work, published in 1609 and 1610.
50. See Nersessian, *Catalogue of Early Armenian Books*, p. 24.
51. For the establishment and activities of missionaries in Safavid Persia, see Francis Richard 'Catholicisme et Islam chiite au "Grand Siècle". Autour de quelques documents concernant les missions catholiques en Perse au XVIIème siècle', *Euntes Docete* 33/3 (1980).
52. The legibility of these compositions was achieved through illusionistic techniques, such as perspective, chiaroscuro and modelling; see Edgerton, *The Heritage of Giotto's Geometry*, p. 256.
53. The Jesuit father, François Rigordi obtained permission to establish a mission in Isfahan in 1647; in 1653, the Jesuits obtained permission from the shah to establish two additional houses, one in New Julfa and another one in Shiraz, see Richard, 'Catholicisme et Islam', pp. 380–1. Although the Jesuits met with much resistance in the Armenian suburb, there is important evidence of intellectual exchange between the Armenians and the Jesuits in Iran during the seventeenth and eighteenth centuries.
54. Arak'el Dawrizhets'i, *Girk Patmut'eants'*, i and *Girk Patmut'eants'* ip. 324, relates that when Minas returned from Aleppo, where he was trained by a European painter, he was employed to decorate houses of Armenian notables.
55. Ina Baghdiantz McCabe, *The Shah's Silk*, pp. 171–2, suggests that in the 1630s a rivalry broke out in New Julfa concerning the position of *kalantar*. If, as Baghdiantz McCabe has proposed, Polos Velijanian, a co-founder of the Bethlehem Church together with his father Petros (see the interior inscription documented by Ter Yovhaneants', *Patmut'iwn*, vol. II, pp. 173–4), was indeed involved in that rivalry, the adoption of a Westernized style in the decoration of the Bethlehem Church might be seen in light of the Velijanian family's political ambitions. I hope to address this possibility in the future.
56. *Patmut'iwn*, vol. II, pp. 177–8.

27

Borrowed Terminology and Shared Techniques in New Julfa Armenian Commercial Documents

Edmund Herzig

Seventeenth- and eighteenth-century Julfa Armenian commercial and financial documents provide a wealth of evidence about the commercial practice of the Julfa Armenian merchants. Both the language of the documents – a unique dialect of Armenian – and comparison with the practice of other merchant communities of South and West Asia and the Mediterranean suggest a high degree of correspondence between the practice and terminology of the Julfa Armenians and that of merchants from communities belonging to very different cultural traditions, such as Muslim Persians and Hindu Multanis and Bengalis. Much of the Julfans' commercial law, for instance, appears to have been based on Islamic *shari'a* law, and much of their accounting and financial terminology is apparently Indian in origin. The Armenians were as quick as any of their contemporaries to take advantage of anything that could give them commercial advantage, adopting European shipping and navigation with enthusiasm, experimenting with new commodities and exploring unfamiliar markets.

The same documents tell us also that the Armenian merchants had business dealings with a wide variety of non-Armenian traders, producers, service-providers and consumers. This was almost inevitable given the nature of their business, which can be characterized as long-distance trade in both primary commodities and manufactures. Julfa merchants sometimes bought direct from the peasant or artisan producers and carried the goods all the way to the retail markets where they were sold to consumers. In other cases they dealt with only a part of the process, buying from and selling to other merchants. These business contacts must have provided the channel by which the Armenians became aware of the language and practices of other communities (and vice versa). We may presume that one of the principal reasons for convergence in language, practice and norms was that it facilitated such cross-cultural business relationships, providing competitive advantage to merchants who could most easily have dealings with members of other communities.

In some areas of their social and cultural life also – areas only tangentially, if at all, connected with trade – the Julfans were receptive to foreign influences. Their dress, their homes (even to a large extent their churches) and their cuisine (at least the banquets, of which descriptions have come down to us) show a strong imprint of the Safavid style of contemporary Persian culture. Julfa Armenians in Europe were often mistaken for, and reckoned as, Persians; and, starting in the seventeenth century and continuing into the eighteenth, they showed a growing interest in the culture and ideas of western Europe.

Yet, despite the cosmopolitanism of their business jargon and practice and their receptiveness to outside influences in certain aspects of their social and cultural life, the Julfa Armenians, like many other merchant communities, jealously guarded their particular sociocultural identity and maintained a high degree of social segregation. If they were promiscuous in their business relationships, they were anything but in their social relations, showing a strong tendency to 'keep it in the family' when it came to choice of marriage partners and close business associates. For the best part of a century they successfully guarded the exclusively Christian character of their suburb (located in the mostly Muslim capital of the Safavid Empire). Even other Armenians, we are told, could not readily become fully accepted members of the Julfa community. Their letters, books of advice for merchants and the comments of European travellers, all testify to the closed and tight-knit character of Julfan society.

If they readily adopted and adapted Persian dress, design and cuisine, there were other aspects of contemporary Persian society they rejected or ignored. Persian poetry, philosophy and theology, all prominent aspects of Safavid cultural life, elicited little or no response from the Julfans, except in the form of religious polemic *against* Islam.

In some respects then the Julfa Armenians were highly receptive to external influence, while in others they were strongly resistant to it. In its conclusion, this chapter offers some tentative ideas towards an explanation of this paradox, but a thorough exploration of the mechanisms, motivations and limits of cross-cultural exchange among the Julfa Armenians is beyond its ambitions, though that would make an interesting case study. Here the focus will be specifically on exchange in the field of commercial practice, sketching the nature of the Julfa Armenians' contacts with other merchant communities, giving some salient examples of Julfan borrowing in terminology and practice and considering their relevance for understanding the place of Safavid Iran in the early modern trading world.

That the Armenians had close and numerous economic ties with merchants of other communities is not in doubt. Among those communities we might expect Muslim Persians – members of the majority Safavid ethno-religious community – to predominate, and surviving documents do indeed attest to commercial relations between Christian Armenian and Muslim Persian merchants. In 1731, for instance, an Armenian merchant, Manuk-Agha Lazarean, entered into a *commenda* partnership with a Muslim named Hajji Ibrahim. Manuk-Agha was the active partner and contributed 300 tumans while Hajji Ibrahim invested 900 tumans, making this a very substantial contract.[1] Whether through the chance survival of a non-representative sample of documents, or because the available sources are yet to be fully explored, or because such relationships were in fact relatively rare, commercial relations with Muslim Persians were less common than might be expected, given the fact that the Julfans lived and had the centre of their trading network in the Safavid capital.

There are also frequent references in the sources, both Armenian and European, to Armenian-European commercial ties. In the early seventeenth century, for example, the Dutch East India Company (VOC) agent Visnich was accused by colleagues of having business connections with several Julfa Armenians active in the Aleppo trade, in breach of company rules. There are many other examples of private commercial deals between Armenians and English and Dutch East India Company factors.[2] Both Tavernier and Chardin – merchants whose fame today rests on their travelogues of the second half of the seventeenth century – had commercial links with Julfa Armenians.[3] Chardin had close connections with the Ghalandarean family and was involved in their proposed cooperation with the English East India Company. In 1691 he wrote a bill for £50,000 on Agha-Piri Ghalandarean in Surat.[4]

In Marseille in 1629 a Catholic Armenian, formerly resident in Venice, entered a partnership with one of the principal local silk importers and together they secured a royal letter patent from Louis XIII (confirmed by Louis XIV in 1645) to act as sole brokers for Armenian and Persian merchants in Marseille.[5] There is also a record of a commercial agreement between some Armenian silk merchants and a Dutch Levant firm, while the first Armenian merchants in Amsterdam used the services of a Jewish broker and translator.[6] It is more surprising to find an Englishman, Thomas Brain, appointed as the Julfa Armenians' broker in Moscow following their 1667 agreement with Tsar Alexei Mikhailovich.[7]

In India the Julfans formed commercial relationships with merchants belonging to a wide range of other communities. Armenian merchants in Madras, for example, frequently traded in partnership with Coromandel Muslims and Hindus.[8] Financial dealings between the Julfa Armenians and Indian merchant or banking communities seem to have been especially common. The documentary sources provide numerous examples of loans and bills involving both Armenians and non-Armenians. While the Julfans were themselves no strangers to currency dealing, credit transactions and complex accounting, they made extensive use of Hindu (Multani or *banya*) bankers who enjoyed an international reputation for financial expertise and were working as bankers throughout the Safavid Empire as far afield as the Caspian. Hovhannes Ter-Davt'yan – a late seventeenth-century merchant whose accountbook has been published – opened accounts with local Hindu bankers in all the major north-west Indian towns he visited, depositing his funds with them, arranging cash transfers through them and using them like a current account to draw cash when required, while collecting interest at the same time. When he moved on to a new location he settled the account and arranged for his funds to be transferred to his next destination. The British Library Lansdowne Manuscripts contain a number of bills of exchange (*hundis*) for transfers between towns in Bengal arranged by Indian bankers for Armenian merchants in the mid-eighteenth century.[9] The use of Indian bankers was not restricted to Armenians in India; in Isfahan too Julfa families might keep an account with one of the many resident Indian banking firms.[10] Armenians also borrowed from the Multanis. Zakʻaria Aguletsʻi – a late seventeenth-century Armenian (though not a Julfan) merchant whose diary has survived – describes how he became heavily indebted because of liabilities arising from his brother's death and was forced to borrow 300 tumans from Multanis in Tabriz, mortgaging his land as security.[11]

The Julfans themselves often lent money to non-Armenians. This seems to have been considered a branch of normal commercial activity rather than a specialized profession. In the early seventeenth century they were described by Pietro Della Valle as bankers to Shah ʻAbbas I and they lent considerable sums to the VOC in Iran, also borrowing from it on occasion.[12] In the late eighteenth century two Armenian merchants of Bengal loaned money to the French Compagnie des Indes in Basra.[13] Hovhannes Ter-Davtʻyan lent to Europeans in India and a number of surviving bills record financial transactions with Europeans.

As the Indians were used by the Julfans for their expertise in finance, so the Europeans were relied on for shipping. This was true in the Mediterranean – where the Dutch Levant vessels frequently transported Armenian merchants and their goods to Livorno and Amsterdam – in the Indian Ocean and Persian Gulf, and on the last leg of the Russian route from Iran to Europe, from Archangel or the Baltic ports to Amsterdam.[14] By the second half of the seventeenth century there were some Armenian merchants who had themselves become shipping magnates, owning ships built to European design and captained and crewed in part by Europeans.

From the above it is clear that, even though a seventeenth-century Armenian merchants' handbook recommends merchants, as far as possible, to rely on family members and fellow Armenians as agents and partners, the demands of international trade required them to develop extensive commercial and financial relations with members of other communities. Often such relations were one-off or short-term in nature, but sometimes they were dense, complex and long-term. Such relations formed the conduit for the exchange not only of goods and services between merchants, but also of terminology and techniques. They provided, moreover, a strong incentive for convergence among the commercial practices of the various parties and indeed for the sharing of best practice among them. The efficient management of such relationships demanded a high level of compatibility between the Armenian and non-Armenian parties. Many such relationships were governed by written contracts and those contracts must have been comprehensible and acceptable to merchants belonging to diverse communities; terminology must have been shared and understood in similar ways by both parties.

The clearest statement of the convergence of Julfa Armenian commercial practice with that of Muslim Persian merchants is found in the Astrakhan Lawbook, an eighteenth-century codification of Julfan law, whose authors explain that:

> ...the rule of trade which we have written in this book is found particularly among the Armenians who dwell in the kingdom of the Persians, and not the Armenians who are under the rule of the Turks. And the reason for this is that the Armenians living in each province of the Persians and the Turks follow their civil laws, customs and conditions. Now, everyone knows that the Turkish merchants are extremely artless and have no rule or laws in trade, but the Persian merchants have very prudent and excellent commercial rules and laws. And our people follow their customs and conditions, so those living in Turkey are artless and without rules and laws, but those living in Persia have rules and laws of trade, which we also follow.[15]

Investigation into surviving documents reveals just how much the contractual forms and terminology of the Julfa Armenians had in common with those of other merchant communities. This can best be illustrated by considering a number of specific types of contract.

One of the commonest types of partnership contract employed by the Julfa Armenians was the *commenda* or sleeping partnership. In her study of Julfa Armenian trade, Khach'ikyan draws attention to the close resemblance of the Armenian *commenda* to the medieval Italian version, and suggests that the form may have been adopted by the Armenians in the Middle Ages through their trading contacts with the Italians in Cilician Armenia.[16] The similarities between Mediterranean and Armenian *commendas* are certainly strong,[17] but the European version was not the only one from which the Armenian could have developed, and was itself probably based on earlier Byzantine and Islamic models.[18] In fact, Islamic contracts from Fatimid Egypt and from Ottoman Aleppo are closer to the Armenian *commenda* than are European contracts.[19] The Islamic *commenda*, generally termed *mudharaba*, is similar in most essentials to the European, but while the latter was essentially an instrument of maritime trade, and limited in most cases to a single voyage (in the case of the equivalent form for overland trade – the *societas terrae* – to a fixed period of one, two or three years),[20] the Islamic *commenda*, like the Armenian, was generally open-ended and might last for many years.[21] Linguistic evidence also suggests a link between the Islamic and Armenian forms, since the Arabic/Persian term occurs sometimes in the Julfa documents as *muzarbay* or *muzarabat'*, while the term *commenda* is not encountered. It seems more likely, therefore, that the Julfa Armenian *commenda* was adopted from the commercial practice of the Persian merchants rather than from Europeans.

If the *commenda* partnership reveals close similarities between Armenian partnership contracts and those of Italy, the Muslim Middle East and of Byzantium, Armenian financial instruments also suggest common ground with merchant communities from the Indian Ocean.

The Astrakhan Lawbook uses the word *barat'* (Arabic-Persian *barat*) in its section devoted to bills of exchange. Very few surviving bills of exchange, however, use this term.[22] By far the commonest term for bill of exchange in the actual documents is *avak'* (also *awak'*), derived from the Hindi *avak*, which in the Indian context is usually described as a bottomry or *respondentia* contract.[23] The Julfans used *avak'* in the latter sense (see below), and often to refer to ordinary bills of exchange, when it usually appears with one or both of the descriptives *zmei* (derivation and meaning obscure), and *bijuk'am*, unsecured (Persian or Hindi *bi* 'without', and Hindi *jokhim* or *jokham*, 'security' or 'insurance'). Other terms are also encountered, bills circulating between Indian cities, usually drawn through the service of local Hindu merchants, *sarrafs* or *dallals* are called *hendvi* (or *hendwi*) from the Hindi term *hundi*, meaning bill of exchange. The *hundis* in the British Library Lansdowne collection all come from Bengal in the 1740s, but the account-book of Hovhannes Ter-Davt'yan contains frequent references to his use of *hundis* in north-west India in the 1680s. One bill of exchange drawn in Isfahan on Venice or Livorno describes itself as a *bijuk'am kampi* (from Italian *[lettera di] cambio*), a combination of Indian and Italian elements in an Armenian document reveals in two words the cosmopolitan character of Julfan trade and commercial practice.[24] There is no significant difference between these variously named bills; all correspond closely to types listed as *barat'* in the Astrakhan Lawbook and contain most of the same clauses in roughly the same order. Apart from the differences in nomenclature these are all, more or less, similar types of bill of exchange, suggesting the convergence of financial instruments of Mediterranean, Middle Eastern and Indian origin.

The Julfa Armenians also employed the type of exchange contract usually termed sea or maritime exchange, or *respondentia* in the European context. In the Julfans' Persian Gulf and Indian Ocean trade these, like the bill of exchange, were called *avak'*, but were distinguished as *juk'ami* (secured), *ek' gushi* ('one way', 'outward' – the derivation of *gushi* is obscure, though the sense of the term is clear from context), and *do gushi* ('two way', 'return').[25] Khach'ikyan has discovered examples of similar contracts for the Caspian trade, where they were known as *eolborji* (from Turkish *yol borj*, 'way loan').[26] The principal difference between such contracts and the ordinary bill of exchange was that, while the latter was repayable regardless of circumstances (Persian *bi 'ozr*, 'without excuse'), in the *respondentia* contract the loan was secured against a specified item in the cargo of a ship (referred to in the Armenian documents as the *juk'am*, 'security', or *putikat* – a term whose derivation remains obscure), and was repayable at a specified period after that item was unloaded at its destination. If the ship was wrecked, or the security lost through piracy or other cause, the bill did not have to be repaid and the loss was borne by the creditor.[27] *Respondentia* contracts operated as a form of insurance and allowed merchants to take out a commercial loan without bearing the full risk if the venture failed through circumstances beyond their control. That contracts of this type were used in both the Mediterranean and Indian Ocean trades in the seventeenth and eighteenth centuries is well known.[28]

The facility with which the Julfa merchants adopted the local name for such contracts, while keeping the form and clauses of the agreement essentially the same, offers strong evidence that the several varieties of *respondentia* contract encountered between the Mediterranean and the Bay of Bengal all fitted into a more or less consistent system of commercial contract law.

From the above it is evident that Julfa Armenian merchants entered into a wide range of sometimes complex and long-lasting relationships with merchants belonging to a wide range of other communities, among them Persian, Turkish and Indian Muslims; Italian, French, Dutch, English, Greek and Russian Christians; and Hindus. It is also evident that the commercial practice, norms and terminology of the Armenians had much in common with those of the other merchants with whom they traded. Judging by the frequency of Persian (and Arabic) terminology in the Julfa Armenian documents, the Muslim Persian community of the Safavid Empire was most important in this respect and Perso-Islamic commercial practice and norms appear to have been the main basis for those of the Julfans. There was also, however, a great deal of common ground with communities from the Indian Ocean to the Mediterranean. Further comparative research is required to clarify the extent of borrowing and sharing between the long-distance merchants of the era.

Even on the basis of the few examples presented here, however, it is clear that there was a good deal of exchange among geographically remote and culturally distinct merchant communities. That exchange allowed, or perhaps required, them to develop compatible ways of mobilizing human and financial resources for commerce in the social, economic and cultural space of their era. Thus we encounter the phenomenon of Christian Armenians borrowing directly from Islamic law and Indian finance without any evidence of qualms that this posed a threat to their values or identity, when we know that in most respects they maintained a marked and sometimes hostile distance from Muslim and Hindu communities and showed little receptivity towards the intellectual culture of non-Christian communities.

The Armenian merchants, it seems, were able to select and adopt forms and norms of Muslim Persian commercial law and practice while rejecting the underlying value system and beliefs of Islamic religion and culture. If selectivity favoured cross-cultural transmission, so also did the ready availability of channels of communication among long-distance merchant communities, whose daily business was commercial transmission and who were brought into frequent contact through the exchange of goods and services. We may also suppose that the Julfa merchants were receptive to foreign cultural elements – techniques, terms, norms – which facilitated trade and increased their competitive advantage, at least insofar as these could be dissociated from other more threatening elements that might erode or dilute the Armenians' distinct social and cultural identity. The world of commerce, in which particular trading and financial functions and collaborations among merchants were frequently repeated, was a context that tended to reinforce specialized cross-cultural exchange and convergence of norms and practices among different trading groups and communities.

For present purposes, however, perhaps the most interesting and significant conclusion to be drawn concerns the cosmopolitanism of the merchants of Safavid Iran. The borrowed terminology and shared techniques recorded in the Julfa Armenian commercial documents tell us that, at least as far as long-distance trade is concerned, the Safavid world was integrated into a wider trading world whose principal axis ran from the Mediterranean to the Indian Ocean.

Notes

1. Shushannik Khach'ikyan, *Nor Jughayi hay vacharakanut'yune ev nra arevtratntesakan kapere Rusastani het XVII-XVIII darerum* (Yerevan, 1988), p. 128.
2. Hendrik Dunlop, ed., *Bronnen tot de geschiedenis der Oostindische Compagnie in Perszië, 1611-1638* (The Hague, 1930), p. 297; Ronald Ferrier, 'The agreement of the East India Company with the Armenian nation, 22nd June 1688', *Revue des Etudes Arméniennes*, new series, vii (1970), p. 436.
3. On Tavernier's Armenian connections see Robert Gulbenkian, 'Philippe de Zagly, marchand arménien de Julfa, et l'établissement du commerce persan en Courlande en 1696', *Revue des Etudes Arméniennes*, new series, vii (1970), pp. 361–426.
4. Ferrier, 'The agreement', p. 436.
5. C.-D. Tékéian, 'Marseille, la Provence, et les Arméniens', *Mémoires de l'Institut Historique de Provence*, vol. 6 (1929), pp. 22–4. On relations between Julfa Armenians and the French in the Safavid period, see also Ina Baghdiantz McCabe, *The Shah's Silk for Europe's Silver: The Eurasian Trade of the Julfa Armenian Merchants in Safavid Iran and India, 1530-1750* (Atlanta, 1999).
6. A. Sarukhan, *Hollandan ew Hayere XVI-XIX darerum* (Vienna, 1926), pp. 49–51.
7. V. A. Parsamyan et al., eds, *Armyano-russkie otnosheniya v XVII veke* (Yerevan, 1953), pp. 58–62.
8. Sinnapah Arasaratnam, *Merchants, Companies and Commerce on the Coromandel Coast 1650-1740* (Delhi, 1986), p. 158.
9. British Library, *Lansdowne Manuscripts*, 1047 and 1048. An example is given in Edmund Herzig, *The Armenian Merchants of New Julfa*, D.Phil. thesis (Oxford, 1991), Part 3, Document 18.
10. See the settlement document cited in note 9 above.
11. Zak'aria Aguletsʻi, *Oragrut'yune* (Yerevan, 1938), p. 100.
12. Rudolph P. Matthee, *The Politics of Trade in Safavid Iran* (Cambridge, 1999), p. 87; M. A. P. Meilink-Roelofsz, 'The earliest relations between Persia and the Netherlands', *Persica*, vi (1977), p. 31.
13. Archives Nationales, Paris, *Séries colonies*, F2b 10.
14. Sarukhan, *Hollandan ew hayere*, passim; Jean Chardin, *Voyages de Chardin…*, ed. L. Langlès, 10 vols and atlas (Paris, 1811), i, p. 10; P. Masson, *Histoire du commerce français dans le Levant au XVIIe siècle* (Paris, 1896), p. 127; Ferrier, 'The Armenians and the East India Company in Persia in the seventeenth and early eighteenth century', *Economic History Review*, second series, xxvi/1 (1973), p. 45; F. Martin, *Mémoires de F.M. fondateur de Pondichery 1665-1696*, ed. A. Martineau, 3 vols (Paris, 1931-4), ii, p. 189.
15. F. G. Poghosyan, ed., *Datastanagirkʻ Astrakhani hayotsʻ* (Yerevan, 1967), p. 7.
16. Khach'ikyan, *Nor Jughayi hay vacharakanut'yune*, pp. 121–2.
17. Robert, Lopez and Irving Raymond, *Medieval Trade in the Mediterranean World* (New York, 1955), pp. 174–84, gives examples of typical European *commenda* contracts.
18. Ibid., p. 174.
19. Abraham Udovitch, *Partnership and Profit in Medieval Islam* (Princeton, NJ, 1970), pp. 170–3, 194–5; S. D. Goitein, *A Mediterranean Society*, 5 vols (Berkeley and Los Angeles, 1967-88), i, pp. 169–72; Bruce Masters, *The Origins of Western Economic Dominance in the Middle East: Mercantilism and the Islamic Economy in Aleppo, 1600-1700* (New York, 1988), pp. 50–3.
20. Lopez and Raymond, *Medieval Trade*, pp. 174–5, 185–6, 188–9.

21. Udovitch, *Partnership and Profit*, pp. 199, 246–8.
22. Examples of bills various kinds are given in Herzig, *Armenian Merchants*, pp. 336–60.
23. H. H. Wilson, *Glossary of Judicial and Revenue Terms and of Useful Words Occurring in Official Documents Relating to the Administration of the Government of British India* (Calcutta, 1940), p. 62; Tapan Raychaudhuri and Irfan Habib (eds), *The Cambridge Economic History of India*, vol. 1 (Cambridge, 1982), p. 347.
24. Venice, Archivio di Stato, *Documenti armeni*, document dated 25 Shbat' 111 (Azaria calendar).
25. For examples, see Herzig, *Armenian Merchants*, pp. 361–77.
26. Khachik'yan, *Nor Jughayi hay vacharakannut'yune*, p. 167.
27. For the European *respondentia* contract see, Lopez and Raymond, *Medieval Trade*, pp. 168–173; Raymond de Roover, *Money, Banking and Credit in Medieval Bruges* (Cambridge, 1948), p. 50.
28. *Cambridge Economic History of India*, i, p. 347; Arasaratnam, *Merchants*, pp. 278–81; *Histoire du Commerce de Marseille*, 5 vols (Marseille, 1949–57), iv, p. 588; v, p. 125.

Part V

The Caucasus: The Internal Frontier?

28

On the History of the Political Relations of Safavid Iran and Georgia: King Luarsab II and His Captivity in Iran

Grigol Beradze

I have presented the highly complicated political relations of Safavid Iran and Georgia in a separate article written in co-authorship with K. Kutsia and published in the proceedings of the International Symposium *Caucasia between the Ottoman Empire and Iran 1555-1914,* held in 1997 in Heidelberg.[1] Hence, here I shall not touch upon the general aspects of this theme but shall pass directly on to the specific topic of the present chapter. In this chapter I will draw the reader's attention to some concrete but significant episodes in the biography of Luarsab II (1606–15), king of Kartli (Eastern Georgia) – one of the most distinguished and tragic political figures in the history of seventeenth-century Georgia. The chapter consists of two parts: the first part deals with Luarsab II's captivity in Iran and the second discusses his seal with a Persian inscription.

The tragedy of King Luarsab II began in 1614 when the Eastern-Georgian kingdoms of Kakheti and Kartli were invaded and fully occupied by the military forces of Shah 'Abbas I (1587–1629).[2] Resorting to various tricks, the Safavid shah tried for the course of many months to lure the rebellious Luarsab II from Imereti (Western Georgia) where he had taken refuge, together with his ally and companion-in-arms, King Teimuraz I (1606–48) of Kakheti. In October 1614, King Luarsab II, in an effort to save his kingdom from the terrible ordeals that befell Kakheti, surrendered and presented himself to Shah 'Abbas I who took him into captivity in Iran – as it turned out, forever. In the eighth year of his captivity, Luarsab II was martyred in Iran, and the Georgian Church canonized him.

It is noteworthy that Persian historical sources say almost nothing about Luarsab II's long captivity in Iran and say nothing at all about his tragic end.

According to Persian chronicles, after Shah 'Abbas I succeeded in luring Luarsab to visit him in his camp near Gori, with negotiations, threats, sly ruses and promises he took the Georgian king with him from Gori to Tbilisi. Eskandar Bayg Monshi reports that Luarsab, accompanied to the royal camp by the shah's dignitary Ya'qub Khan Bayg Qaramanlu, presented himself to the shah on 13 Ramazan 1023 (17 October 1614).[3]

From the subsequent narration by the same author, we learn that Luarsab was received with great honour by the Safavid shah; but during a march along the road to Gori, he fled by night from the royal camp. Mohammad Reza Fidavi (alias Saru Khvaje), who had been placed in charge of Luarsab, went in pursuit, seized him in the vicinity of the camp, and brought him back to his quarters early in the morning.[4] Shah 'Abbas I, in the words of his court historian, considered it inexpedient 'to let the game that had got into the snare to slip away'.[5] He refused to allow Luarsab to stay in his own country and, passing through the hunting-grounds of Qarabagh, brought him to Gilan and then to Mazandaran.

On 4 Safar 1024 (5 March 1615) Shah 'Abbas I arrived in Farahabad.[6] In 1025 (1616) Shah 'Abbas I sent Luarsab from Farahabad to Astarabad, with instructions to the local governor to keep him in custody until the shah returned from his next Georgian campaign.[7] This is the last record in the Persian sources about the captive king of Kartli, available to me.[8] Nothing else is said in these sources about the subsequent fate of King Luarsab II, they are diffidently silent about it.

In contrast to the Persian chronicles, testimony of the last years of Luarsab's life in Iran has survived in Georgian, Armenian and European written sources.[9] Where we learn that Shah 'Abbas I, with many kind words, gifts and threats, offered the captive Luarsab II to renounce Christianity and embrace the Muslim faith. However, each time he received a decisive rebuff from the young Christian king of Kartli. The captive king was soon deported from Astarabad to Shiraz and was then incarcerated in a prison-fortress.[10] Notwithstanding his energetic endeavours, the Safavid shah failed to crush the staunch and refractory spirit of Luarsab II. The latter firmly withstood all terrible ordeals and torments, refusing – at the cost of his own life – to renounce Christianity. In 1622, by order of the shah, the recalcitrant Georgian king was done away with in his prison-fortress.

It should be noted that almost all Georgian sources point out that the fortress in which the captive King Luarsab II was incarcerated and then murdered was called Gulab, and that it was located in or near Shiraz. The anonymous Georgian chronicle, known as the *Paris Chronicle* (composed in the 1730s), is the only written source to report that the prison-fortress of Gulab was situated in Kolgalu, 'a rigorous, rocky and torrid place'.[11] This information is geographically more correct. The fact is that the form Kolgalu, mentioned in the *Paris Chronicle*, is none other than a distorted spelling of the well-known Iranian place name Kuhgilu.[12] As we learn from Persian geographical and historical writings of late medieval and modern times, the fortress of Gulab was one of the strong and famous

Iranian prison-fortresses situated in the mountainous province of Kuhgilu (Kuhgiluye).[13]

The Georgian sources, as well as the Italian traveller Pietro Della Valle (1586–1652),[14] point out that King Luarsab II was strangled with a bowstring in the Iranian fortress where he was imprisoned.[15]

Other versions of Luarsab's violent death are also recorded. The seventeenth-century French historian Claude Malingre notes in his essay *De Catherine roine de Géorgie et des princes géorgiens mis à mort par commendement de Cha-Abbas, roi de Perse* (first published in 1635 in Paris) that the captive Georgian King Luarsab (in the French text: Aloüassa Can) was poisoned on Shah 'Abbas I's order.[16] The same story is indicated by the German authors Andreas Gryphius (1616–64) and Eberhard Werner Happel (1647–90).[17]

In this connection, special mention should be made of a highly interesting piece of evidence, recorded in the *Book of Histories* by the seventeenth-century Armenian monk and historian Arakel Davrizhetsi (d. 1670). He points out that envoys from the Russian Tsar begged Shah 'Abbas I to release the captive Luarsab II and to return him to his domains in Georgia. The shah hypocritically promised the Russians to carry out this request. However, he had resolved to rid himself for good of the recalcitrant Georgian king, ordering a dignitary attached to Luarsab to finish him off. In obedience to the royal command, the dignitary went to Shiraz and, seizing an opportunity when fishing cut Luarsab's head off with a sudden stroke of a sabre from behind.[18] Further, the Armenian author reports that the severed head was brought to Shah 'Abbas I. 'And the Shah, seeing the head and understanding that it was Luarsab's, in his hard-heartedness fell into anger and irritation against the head, defaming and abusing it, he contemptuously kicked and rolled it up and down. Spending many hours in such an irritated state of mind with the head, the Shah then took it by the ear and threw it away. The head rolled down, for the place was inclined.'[19] Concluding this lurid story, Arakel Davrizhetsi writes: 'Such was the end of the life of Luarsab the King of Tbilisi. This is how the insidious Shah Abbas destroyed him, seizing his country by force.'[20]

Arakel Davrizhetsi's narration of the futile attempts by the Russian diplomats to help the captive Georgian king has something in common with the information contained in the widely known travel book by the Frenchman Jean Chardin (1643–1713), though some of his details differ from the Armenian's. Chardin also reports that Luarsab II was murdered (drowned) in prison at Shiraz in spite of an attempted Russian intervention on his behalf. This is what he writes in this connection:

> Le grand-duc de Moscovie avoit été longtemps sollicité par les princes géorgiens, partisans de Luarzab, d'intercéder pour lui auprès d'Abas. Il envoya une grande ambassade, uniquement pour ce sujet. Le roi de Perse, qui avoit un esprit et une activité incroyable, donna ordre au gouverneur de Chamaki, ville

sur la mer Caspienne, par où les ambassadeurs de Moscovie entrent en Perse, de découvrir si cet ambassadeur ne venoit que pour les affaires de Luarzab, et si le Moscovite prenoit tant d'intérêt en cette affaire, qu'il y eût quelque rupture à appréhender. On lui manda que l'ambassadeur ne venoit effectivement que pour cela; que c'étoit un grand seigneur, et que ses instructions étoient fort pressantes. Abas, qui ne vouloit nullement ni donner la liberté au prince géorgien, ni la refuser au grand-duc de Moscovie, écrivit au gouverneur de Chiras de se défaire de Luarzab, captif, d'une manière que sa mort parût un simple accident. Cela fut exécuté, et la nouvelle en fut apportée à Abas deux jours avant l'arrivée de l'ambassadeur de Moscovie. Le roi se la fit donner en public, et en fit fort le surpris et le fâché. *Ah! mon Dieu*, dit-il, *c'est dommage; et comment est-il mort? Sire*, répondit le courrier, *il étoit allé à la pêche, et en jetant le rets, il est tombé dans l'étang et s'est noyé. Je veux*, dit le roi, *qu'on fasse mourir tous ses gardes, pour n'avoir pas eu plus de soin de lui.* L'ambassadeur de Moscovie eut audience; après le festin, et qu'on l'eut bien fait boire, le roi le fit approcher de sa personne, et lui dit: *Eh bien, M. l'ambassadeur, que désire le roi des Russes, mon frère?* L'ambassadeur se mit á exposer sa commission; mais dès qu'il eut lâché le nom de Luarzab, *je crois*, répondit le roi, *que vous savez le malheur qui est arrivé á ce pauvre prince. J'en ai un extrême regret. Plût à Dieu qu'il ne fût pas mort, je ferois de tout mon cœur ce que désire votre maître.*[21]

[The Georgian princes, partisans of Luarsab, had long sought the Grand Duke of Muscovy's intercession with 'Abbas on his behalf. [The Grand Duke] sent a large embassy for this purpose alone. The king of Persia, who had extraordinarily high spirits and incredible energy, ordered the governor of Shamakhi, a city on the Caspian Sea where the ambassadors from Muscovy entered Persia, to discover whether the ambassador was coming for the Luarsab case, and whether the Muscovite was taking so much interest in it that damage [to relations] should be anticipated. He learnt that the ambassador was coming essentially only for that, that he was a great lord, and that his instructions were very pressing. 'Abbas, who did not wish either to release the Georgian prince or to refuse [the request] of the Grand Duke of Muscovy, wrote to the governor of Shiraz to get rid of the captive Luarsab in such a way that his death seemed accidental. This [order] was executed, and the news reached 'Abbas two days before the arrival of the ambassador of Muscovy. The king had the news be given to him in public, and made a show of being very surprised and angry. 'Ah! my God', he said, 'that is a pity; and how did he die?' 'Sire', replied the messenger, 'he had gone fishing, and casting the net he fell into the pond and drowned'. 'I wish', said the king, 'that all the guards be put to death for not having taken more care of him'. The ambassador of Muscovy had an audience after the feast, when he had had plenty to drink. The king brought him close to his person, and said, 'Well, ambassador, what does the King of the Russians, my brother, desire?' The ambassador began to explain his mission, but no sooner had he dropped the name Luarsab, than the king replied, 'I think that you know about the calamity that has befallen this poor prince. I regret it deeply. Would to God he was not dead. With all my heart I would have performed that which your master desires'.]

As already noted, the martyred King Luarsab II of Kartli was canonized and was numbered among the Saints of the Georgian Church. The liturgical feast of his martyr's death is, according to the Georgian church calendar, marked on 4 July (21 June Old Style).[22] This day (21 June) was fixed in the Georgian church calendar after the calendar reform carried out by Anton I Bagrationi (1720–88), the Catholicos-Patriarch of Georgia (1744–55, 1764–88). Before his reform, Luarsab II's martyrdom was usually liturgically feasted on 20 March.

* * *

In the next part of the chapter, I shall deal with the personal seal of King Luarsab II, which, as will be shown below, furnishes some additional traits to the historical portrait of this tragic figure.

The original of Luarsab's seal (the seal-matrix) has unfortunately not come down to us. It is known to us only through its impressions (the seal-stamps) preserved on some Georgian documents of the early seventeenth century. The collections of Georgian historical documents at the Kekelidze Institute of Manuscripts (Georgian Academy of Sciences) and the Central State Historical Archives of Georgia contain up to 30 royal letters patent, charters and decrees of diverse character, issued by Luarsab II in 1606–15.[23] The majority of these documents bear the personal signature of Luarsab II in Georgian script, while some of them bear – along with the Georgian signature of the king – impressions of his seal with a legend in Arabic letters.[24] Incidentally, these are the only impressions of King Luarsab II's seal, the impressions of which are attached to his documents. It is unknown whether he had another seal with a Georgian inscription. We only know that his father, King Giorgi X (1600–5) of Kartli, had a small quadrangular seal with a simple Georgian inscription 'Giorgi', impressions of which are preserved on some royal charters.[25]

King Luarsab II's seal that interests us has been referred to several times in the scholarly literature although it has not yet been studied.

The presence of impressions of this seal on some documents of Luarsab II was first noted by M. Brosset in 1854.[26] Later, the same seal was mentioned (without a detailed description) by E. Taqaishvili and A. Bakradze.[27] Recently, photographic copies of the originals of two royal charters, bearing Luarsab's Georgian signature and impressions of his seal, were published (without a description of the seal) in the book on the history of the Georgian princely family of Tarkhan-Mouravi,[28] the descendants of Luarsab's brother-in-law, the Great Mouravi Giorgi Saakadze (d. 1629). Both of these charters are addressed to Giorgi Saakadze, the first of them was issued by Luarsab II on 12 July 1608, and the second one on 24 October 1609.

The seal of Luarsab II, like the majority of Georgian royal seals of that period, is relatively small. The dimensions of this seal, according to the impressions, are

Figure 28.1 The seal of Luarsab II

25 mm × 19 mm (see Figure 28.1). In outline the seal resembles, to a certain extent, the so-called almond-shape type, although its outward circumference is not smooth but scalloped, pointed at its four dome-shaped extremities.

The shape of the seal is followed by a single-line rim (only fragments of this line are visible in the impressions preserved on the documents). The field of the seal is engraved with an inscription in Arabic letters. The inscription is executed in the cursive script and contains the name of the owner of the seal, introduced by the simple religious formula 'His [that is, God's] servant' – a well-known expression of submission to God, traditional to the Arabic-lettering seals of medieval and modern times. In the right corner of the seal (for the viewer), there are four engraved figures indicating the date in Muslim chronology.

The text of the inscription reads downwards as: 'abduhu Lavarsab ben Gorgi Khan 1014' ('His servant Lavarsab son of Gorgi Khan, 1014').

Thus, the name of the owner of the seal is rendered in extended form in this legend, indicating both Luarsab's name (spelt *Lavarsab*) and the name of his father Giorgi (spelt *Korki / Gorgi*), as well as their common Iranian title *khan*.

The lunar Hijra year, engraved on the seal (1014), converted to the Common Era, corresponds to the period 19 May 1605–8 May 1606. What date is this?

As is known from Georgian and other sources, following the sudden death of Luarsab's father on 7 November 1605,[29] the Georgian nobility addressed Shah 'Abbas I with a petition to confirm the young Prince Luarsab as the new king of Kartli. The Safavid shah gave his assent to this and in early 1606 Prince Luarsab, aged 14 at the time, was proclaimed king of Kartli.[30] Therefore, the date indicated on the seal coincides with the year of Luarsab II's accession and it may be surmised that the seal was made in the very first year of his reign.

In analysing the seal of Luarsab II special attention should be devoted to its outward form and the content of its legend.

From the viewpoint of shape, Luarsab II's seal differs from all other Eastern-Georgian royal seals known at present. The overwhelming majority of the extant Eastern-Georgian royal seals of the period under discussion are rectangular; there were also oval, pear-shaped and round seals, as well as round (or nearly round) seals adorned with a small superstructure (a fig-shaped dome or cap). As is known, all the above forms of seals were characteristic of the Near- and Middle-Eastern sphragistics of the period in question, and especially that of Safavid Iran. In this connection, special mention should be made of almond-shaped royal seals, which were fairly widespread in Western Georgia (in the kingdom of Imereti) in the seventeenth and the first third of the eighteenth century. In contrast to the Eastern-Georgian royal seals characterized by their Iran-influenced outward forms, the almond-shaped royal seals of Western-Georgian provenance undoubtedly indicate the influence of Ottoman sphragistic traditions.[31]

Thus, proceeding from the comparative analysis, one may conclude that, although the seal of Luarsab II is not purely almond-shaped, its outward form is typologically still more similar to the Turkish-influenced Western-Georgian royal seals than to the Iran-influenced and Iran-orientated seals of the Eastern-Georgian kings.

Besides the above interesting feature, Luarsab II's seal is characterized by another noticeable peculiarity connected with the legend of the seal.

As to the language of the legend, linguistically it must be defined as mixed Persian-Arabic. However, proceeding from the general historical context, as well as from some textual details and the graphic appearance of the letters executed in the *nasta'liq* script (that is, in the key calligraphic script of the so-called Persophonie),[32] the given legend may also be perceived and regarded as semiotically Persian.

That the seal under discussion is furnished with a Persian legend is no exception. Beginning with the early sixteenth century, most of the kings of Kartli, along with (and parallel to) their properly Georgian monolingual seals (that is seals with Georgian inscriptions alone), also had seals with legends done only in Arabic letters. As to language, such legends are predominantly Persian (purely Persian or mixed Persian-Arabic), but occasionally there also occur only Arabic inscriptions. Besides the above types of monolingual seals, historical documents of the sixteenth to eighteenth centuries have preserved impressions of Georgian royal seals with bilingual legends, in which inscriptions in Arabic letters (predominantly in the Persian language) are engraved alongside their Georgian legend.[33] Such an intricate linguistic situation in Georgian sphragistics is logically inscribed in the overall political and sociocultural context of the period in question, characterized by the political dependence of Eastern Georgia on Safavid Iran (occasionally this dependence weakened considerably; however, at times it became almost complete) and by the strengthened Iranian cultural influence in this region, especially on the local royal houses and feudal aristocracy.

As to the kings of Kartli proper, historical documents have preserved the impressions of monolingual Persian seals of David X (1505–25), Simon I (1556–69, 1578–1600), Luarsab II (1606–15), Simon II (1619–30), Rostom (1632–58), Vakhtang V Shahnavaz (1658–76), Giorgi XI (1676–88, 1703–9), and so on.

However, familiarization with the inscription of the seal of Luarsab II brings to our attention a very noticeable feature that distinguishes it from the extant seals (impressions) of other kings of Kartli. In particular, as a rule, the Persian-language seals of other kings of Kartli carry a special phrase-formula of vassalage, pointing to the servile submission of these kings to the Safavid shah as the supreme sovereign. By way of illustration, I shall adduce some concrete examples dating to the periods both before King Luarsab II and after his reign (that is before 1606 and after 1615).

Thus, for example, the round seal of King Simon I, grandfather of Luarsab II, is furnished with a monolingual Persian inscription, the translation of which reads as follows: 'Allah, who has no equal, knows that Semiyun (Simon) is a slave of the Shah from the bottom of his heart, 993 (1585)'.[34]

Two Persian-language oval seals of King Simon II bear the following inscriptions: 'Shah 'Abbas's slave Semiyun', and 'Slave of the Shah of the Truth, Semiyun, 1028 (1619)'.[35]

The Persian-language legends on the seals of subsequent kings of Kartli are formulated in an approximately equal spirit of loyalty and submission to the Safavids.[36]

It is noteworthy that pro-Safavid political formulas of submission and vassalage occur also on a number of royal seals of the kings of Kartli with Georgian legends. For example, the Georgian inscription on the seal of King Rostom reads: 'Ch[rist]. Being the dust of the Shah's feet, King Rostom endorses'.[37] The monolingual Georgian seal of King Vakhtang V Shahnavaz is furnished with the following inscription: 'Ch[rist]. By God's will [and with] Shah Abbas's permission, King Shahnavaz endorses'.[38] The monolingual Georgian legend on the seal of King Erekle I Nazaralikhan (1688–1703) reads: 'Ch[rist]. Being the slave of the blissful Shah, King Nazaralikhan endorses'.[39]

Significant to our present discussion is the fact that the legend of King Luarsab II's seal generally does not contain any such specific formula or phrase of servile submission to the Iranian shah, sharply differing thereby from the other Persian-language (as well as Georgian-language) seals of the Kartlian kings of the Safavid age. This peculiarity of the seal of Luarsab II is, of course, only one concrete sphragistic nuance but, I believe, a fairly noteworthy one.

In view of the rather unusual outward form of Luarsab's seal and the content of its legend, this seal may be interpreted as a double-natured sphragistic relic: on the one hand, it is of a fairly loyal and conformist nature, for the seal's inscription is drawn up in a Persian manner, with the Iranian title of the owner of the seal and the date in Muslim chronology; on the other hand, the seal is, to a certain extent, dissident, inasmuch as its shape is dissimilar to the Iran-orientated forms of Eastern-Georgian royal seals and – which is particularly interesting – the text of its legend does not contain a direct indication of unconditional political subordination to the Safavid shah.

As noted above, the seal under discussion dates from the first year of Luarsab II's reign. For the time being it is quite difficult to say whether the 14-year-old Luarsab, immediately after ascending the throne of Kartli, personally (or on somebody's advice) refused to include the political formula of submission to the shah in the legend of his seal, or whether the absence of such a formula on his seal was conditioned by some other circumstance. Leaving open this question, I shall restrict myself to stating another important point. Namely, I shall draw the reader's special attention to the fact that the non-Safavid shaped seal with its dissident legend, drawn up in 1606, was never altered by its owner, and it was this dissident seal that King Luarsab II attached – along with his Georgian personal signature – to the royal letters patent and charters of almost all subsequent years of his reign.

It is unknown whether Luarsab II had his dissident seal with him when he was taken to Iran by the Safavid shah. Among the extant Georgian documents of this king, there is one charter issued by him in 1615, that is in the first year of his captivity when he was already in Gilan (or in Mazandaran), but was not yet incarcerated. However, this royal charter of 1615 is not sealed and only bears Luarsab's personal signature.[40]

The seal of King Luarsab II, characterized by the absence of the special political formula of submission of its owner to the Safavid shah as the supreme sovereign and overlord, turned out – as fate had willed it – to be highly symbolic from a historical perspective. It proved to be a peculiar sphragistic overture to the subsequent political destiny of the young Georgian king, who dared to rebel against Shah 'Abbas I and, notwithstanding a long captivity, refused to bow to the mighty Safavid shah, sacrificed himself, and accepted a martyr's death in Iran.

An attempt has been made above to recall in brief the tragic story of Luarsab II and to discuss his dissident seal. The story of this Georgian king is only one concrete episode in the voluminous chronicle of Safavid-Georgian political relations, many pages of which are adorned with numerous other such tragic episodes and stories.

However, it would be wrong to end this chapter on such a minor key. It should be borne in mind that the history of Irano-Georgian relations in the Safavid age contains not only wars and bloody invasions. Despite dramatic and tragic political collisions, the traditional cultural relations of the Iranian and Georgian peoples, which were rooted in antiquity, developed fruitfully in the sixteenth to eighteenth centuries, holding an important place in the regional system of cross-cultural contacts and intellectual exchange. Therefore, allow me to close my chapter by way of an epilogue with the words of the Georgian historian Ivane Javakhishvili (1876–1940): 'Poetry and culture created a unity of spiritual life between Georgians and Iranians, developing love instead of enmity. The Persian Islamic culture was not alien to the Georgians – they always had a profound respect for the literature, scholarship and art of their political antagonists.'[41]

Notes

1. Grigol Beradze and Kutsia, Karlo, 'Towards the interrelations of Iran and Georgia in the 16th–18th centuries', in R. Motika and M. Ursinus (eds), *Caucasia between the Ottoman Empire and Iran 1555–1914* (Wiesbaden, 2000), pp. 121–31.

2. For details on this, see Grigol Beradze and Smirnova, Lydia, *Materialy po istorii irano-gruzinskikh vzaimootnoshenii v nachale XVII veka* (Tbilisi, 1988), pp. 14–22, 39–47, 62–106.
3. Eskandar Bayg Monshi, *Tarikh-e 'Alamara-ye 'Abbasi*, ed. by Muhammad Isma'il Rezvani, vol. II (Tehran, 1998), p. 1448; cf. Malik Shah-Hosayn Sistani, *Ehya al-moluk*, ed. by Manuchehr Sotude (Tehran, 1965), p. 504; Beradze, Smirnova, *Materialy po istorii*, pp. 21–2, 45, 98–102. According to another contemporary Persian author, Fazli b. Zayn al-'Abedin Khuzani Esfahani, Luarsab was received in audience on 15 Ramazan 1023 (19 October 1614), and this event was feasted with a special magnificence by the shah; see fo. 332b of the unique manuscript of the third volume of Fazli Khuzani Esfahani's *Afzal al-tavarikh*, discovered a few years ago by Dr Charles Melville in the library of Christ's College, Cambridge. I am very grateful to Dr Hirotake Maeda for his help in acquiring photographic copies of some necessary folios of this Cambridge manuscript.
4. Eskandar Bayg Monshi, *Tarikh-e 'Alamara-ye 'Abbasi*, vol. II, p. 1448; *History of Shah 'Abbas the Great by Eskander Beg Monshi*, trans. Roger M. Savory, vol. II (Boulder, CO, 1978), pp. 1091–2; Sayyid Hasan Astarabadi, *Az Shaykh Safi ta Shah Safi az Tarikh-e Soltani*, ed. Ehsan Eshraqi (Tehran, 1985), p. 205.
5. Eskandar Bayg Monshi, *Tarikh-e 'Alamara-ye 'Abbasi*, vol. II, p. 1448.
6. Ibid., p. 1450.
7. Ibid., p. 1480; *History of Shah 'Abbas the Great*, vol. II, p. 1113.
8. It is highly surprising that in such an important contemporary Safavid chronicle as Mirza Bayg Jonabadi's *Rawzat al-Safaviye*, completed in 1036 (1626–7), which contains a fairly detailed account of Shah 'Abbas I's punitive expeditions to Georgia in 1614 and 1616, King Luarsab II of Kartli is not mentioned at all, in contrast to King Teimuraz I of Kakheti, whose name is repeatedly mentioned in the text; see Mirza Bayg Junabadi, *Rawzat al-Safaviye*, ed. Gholam-Reza Tabataba'i Majd (Tehran, 1999), pp. 842–56, 889–90.
9. Certain information about Luarsab's captivity in Iran is found in some contemporary Russian sources as well. In particular, the captive Georgian king is repeatedly mentioned in the reports of Ivan Brekhov, Mikhail Tikhanov, Grigorii Shakhmatov and other Russian envoys. However, all these reports belong to the initial period of Luarsab's captivity, the latest of them dated to 1616; see: N. I. Veselovskii, ed., *Pamyatniki diplomaticheskikh i torgovykh snoshenii Moskovskoi Rusi s Persiei*, vol. II (St. Petersburg, 1892), pp. 292, 342, and vol. III (St. Petersburg, 1898), p. 131; Petr P. Bushev, *Istoriya posol'stv i diplomaticheskikh otnoshenii russkogo i iranskogo gosudarstv v 1613-1621 gg.* (Moscow, 1987), pp. 56, 87; Nodar Nakashidze, *Gruzino-russkie politicheskie otnosheniya v pervoi polovine XVII veka* (Tbilisi, 1968), pp. 65–6; Tamar Tivadze, 'Materialy po vneshnepoliticheskoi istorii Gruzii pervoi poloviny XVII veka soderzhashchiesya v arkhivnom fonde Snosheniya Rossii s Persiei', *Kartuli samepo-samtavroebis sagareo politikis istoriidan*, vol. II (Tbilisi, 1973), pp. 130, 141.
10. On this, see Pietro Della Valle, *Viaggi di Pietro Della Valle il Pellegrino*, ed. Mario Schipano, vol. II (Brighton, 1843), p. 154; Pietro Della Valle, 'Informatione della Georgia', in Zhordania, Givi and Gamezardashvili, Zurab (eds), *Rimsko-katolicheskaya missiya i Gruziya*, vol. I (Tbilisi, 1994), pp. 359, 621; *Parsadan Gorgijanidzis istoria*, ed. Sargis Kakabadze (Tbilisi, 1926), pp. 22–3; Tedo Zhordania, *Kronikebi da skhva masala Sakartvelos istoriisa da mtserlobisa*, vol. II (Tiflis, 1897), p. 444; Beri Egnatashvili, 'Akhali Kartlis tskhovreba, pirveli teksti', *Kartlis tskhovreba*, ed. Simon Qaukhchishvili, vol. II (Tbilisi, 1959), pp. 397, 399; Vakhushti Batonishvili, 'Aghtsera sameposa Sakartvelosa', *Kartlis tskhovreba*, ed. Simon Qaukhchishvili, vol. IV (Tbilisi, 1973), p. 427.
11. *Tskhovreba Sakartveloisa (Parizis kronika)*, ed. Giuli Alasania (Tbilisi, 1980), p. 84; cf. *Chronique géorgienne*, traduite par M. Brosset (Paris, 1831), p. 55; *Parizhskaya khronika*, trans. Giuli Alasania (Tbilisi, 1991), p. 57.
12. It should be noted that the identity of Kolgalu and Kuhgilu was not understood by the editors and researchers of the *Paris Chronicle*. Concerning the Kolgalu mentioned in the Georgian text, M. Brosset remarked that this geographical point 'n'est pas sur les cartes' (see *Chronique géorgienne*, p. 156). In the subsequent publications of the *Paris Chronicle* the geographical name we are concerned with has been not discussed at all.

13. On the fortress of Gulab in Kuhgilu see, for example, Shehab al-Din Hafez-e Abru, 'Abd-Allah Khwafi, *Joghrafiya-ye Hafez-e Abru*, ed. Sadeq Sajjadi, vol. II (Tehran, 1999), pp. 296, 304; Mohammad Mofid Yazdi, *Mokhtasar-e Mofid*, ed. S. Najmabadi, vol. I (Wiesbaden, 1989), pp. 331, 343; Hajj Mirza Hasan Hosayni Fasa'i, *Farsname-ye Naseri*, ed. Mansur Rastegar Fasa'i, vol. I (Tehran, 1999), pp. 770, 796, and vol. II (Tehran, 1999), pp. 1495–6, 1631; Mohammad-Ma'sum, *Kholasat al-siyar: tarikh-e ruzgar-e Shah Safi-ye Safavi*, ed. Iraj Afshar (Tehran, 1989), p. 310; Shamlu, Valiqoli b. Da'udqoli, *Qesas al-khaqani*, ed. Sayyed Hasan Sadat Naseri, vol. I (Tehran, 1992), p. 282.
14. Della Valle, 'Informatione della Georgia', pp. 359, 621; cf. Pietro Della Valle, *Delle Conditioni di Abbas Re di Persia* (Venice, 1628), pp. 51, 91; Bartolomeo Ferro, *Istoria della Missioni de Chierici Regolari Teatini*, vol. I (Rome, 1704), p. 57; Tamaz Natroshvili, *Moqvasi shoreuli Romidan* (Tbilisi, 1995), pp. 54–5.
15. *Tskhovreba Sakartveloisa (Parizis kronika)*, p. 85; Zhordania, *Kronikebi da skhva masala*, vol. II, pp. 444–5; Egnatashvili, 'Akhali Kartlis tskhovreba', p. 399; Vakhushti, 'Aghtsera sameposa Sakartvelosa', p. 427; E. Gabidzashvili, ed., *Dzveli kartuli agiograpiuli literaturis dzeglebi*, vol. IV (Tbilisi, 1958), p. 437; E. Gabidzashvili and M. Kavtaria, eds, *Dzveli kartuli agiograpiuli literaturis dzeglebi*, vol. V (Tbilisi, 1989), pp. 24, 44–5; D. Chubinov, ed., *Kartuli kristomatia*, vol. I (St. Petersburg, 1846), pp. 341, 343–4; cf. *Parsadan Gorgijanidzis istoria*, p. 23.
16. Claude Malingre, *Histoires tragiques de nostre temps* (Paris, 1635), p. 48; I. Tabaghua, ed., *Sakartvelos urtiertoba Evropisa da Amerikis kveqnebtan*, vol. III (Tbilisi, 1996), pp. 135, 154; Roberto Gulbenkian, 'Relation véritable du glorieux martyre de la Reine Kétévan de Géorgie', *Bedi Kartlisa/Revue de kartvelologie XL* (Paris, 1982), p. 70, no. 90; Tamaz Natroshvili, *Tseli erti da atasi* (Tbilisi, 1988), p. 257.
17. Andreas Gryphius, *Catharina von Georgien oder bewehrete Beständigkeit*, ed. Willi Flemming (Halle, 1951), pp. 25, 27, 31; cf. Andreas Gryphius, *Ketevan kartveli anu gautekheli simtkitse*, trans. Akaki Gelovani (Tbilisi, 1975), pp. 86–7, 152; Shota Revishvili, 'Hapeli da Sakartvelo', *Tsiskari* 1 (Tbilisi, 1973), pp. 147, 149; Shota Revishvili, *Germanul-kartuli etiudebi* (Tbilisi, 1977), pp. 101, 127, 129–30.
18. Arakel Davrizhetsi, *Kniga istorii*, trans. L. A. Khanlaryan (Moscow, 1973), pp. 132–3.
19. Ibid., p. 133.
20. Ibid., p. 133; *Collection d'historiens arméniens*, traduits par M. Brosset, vol. I (St. Petersburg, 1874), p. 338.
21. Jean Chardin, *Voyages du chevalier Chardin en Perse et autres lieux de l'Orient*, nouvelle édition par L. Langles, vol. II (Paris, 1811), pp. 60–1.
22. *Sakartvelos eklesiis kalendari 2002* (Tbilisi, 2001), p. 62.
23. On this, see D. Kldiashvili et al. (eds), *Pirta anotirebuli leksikoni XI–XVII ss. kartuli istoriuli sabutebis mikhedvit*, vol. I (Tbilisi, 1991), pp. 329–32.
24. See, for example, documents Hd-1942, Hd-2009, Hd-2283, Hd-13052, Hd-13179, Hd-14700, Sd-61, Sd-524, Sd-555 preserved at the Kekelidze Institute of Manuscripts, Tbilisi.
25. Ana Bakradze, *Masalebi kartuli spragistikis istoriisatvis*, vol. I (Tbilisi, 1978), p. 37, Pl. I, Fig. 27.
26. Marie Brosset, *Histoire de la Géorgie depuis l'antiquité jusqu'au XIXe siècle, IIe Partie, Histoire moderne, IIe Livraison* (St. Petersburg, 1857), pp. 443, 479.
27. Ekvtime Taqaishvili, *Sakartvelos sidzveleni*, vol. II (Tiflis, 1909), pp. 27, 158; Bakradze, *Masalebi kartuli spragistikis istoriisatvis*, vol. I, p. 16.
28. Giorgi D. Tarkhan-Mouravi and Tarkhan-Mouravi, David I., *Opyt istorii knyazheskogo roda Tarkhan-Mouravi (v kontekste fragmentov istorii Gruzii)*, vol. I (Tbilisi, 2002), Figs 45, 47.
29. The sources contain several versions of King Giorgi X's death. According to one of them, he was poisoned on the secret order of Shah 'Abbas I; see Davrizhetsi, *Kniga istorii*, pp. 104, 107; Zhordania, *Kronikebi da skhva masala*, vol. II, p. 433; David Bagrationi, *Istoriya Gruzii*, ed. A. A Rogava (Tbilisi, 1971), p. 144.
30. It should be noted that the earliest document in which Luarsab II is referred to as the king is a royal charter dated to 24 March 1606. As we learn from the text, this charter was issued jointly by three persons: Queen Nestan-Darejan (Luarsab's grandmother), Queen Tamar (Luarsab's mother), and the young King Luarsab II. On this document, kept at the Kekelidze Institute of Manuscripts

with the call number Hd-2091, see Odisheli, Jumber, 'Aghmosavlet Sakartvelos politikuri istoriisatvis (XIV–XVII ss.)', in N. Shoshiashvili (ed.), *XIV–XVIII saukuneebis ramdenime kartuli istoriuli dokumenti* (Tbilisi, 1964), p. 96.
31. Bakradze, *Masalebi kartuli spragistikis istoriisatvis*, vol. I, p. 12; Beradze, 'Towards the interrelations', p. 129.
32. Bert G. Fragner, *Die 'Persophonie': Regionalität, Identität und Sprachkontakt in der Geschichte Asiens* (Halle/Berlin, 1999), p. 103.
33. For more details on this, see: Bakradze, *Masalebi kartuli spragistikis istoriisatvis*, vol. I, pp. 12–16; Grigol Beradze, *Georgian Seals of the 17th–18th Centuries with Bilingual and Multilingual Inscriptions* (Moscow, 1986); Grigol Beradze, 'A Georgian seal with a trilingual inscription (late seventeenth century)', *Third European Conference of Iranian Studies*, Abstracts (Cambridge, 1995), pp. 3–5; Nugzar Dundua, 'Pechati gruzinskikh tsareii XVI–XVIII vv. s arabograficheskimi nadpisyami', *Vostochnoe istoricheskoe istochnikovedenie i spetsial'nye istoricheskie distsipliny*, vol. 3 (Moscow, 1995), pp. 267–79; Beradze, 'Towards the interrelations', pp. 129–31.
34. Dundua, 'Pechati gruzinskikh tsarei',p. 268, Pl. I, Fig. 1.
35. iIbid., pp. 268, 270, Pl. I, Figs 2, 3.
36. iIbid., pp. 270–5; Makar Khubua, *Sakartvelos muzeumis sparsuli pirmanebi da hokmebi* (Tbilisi, 1949), pp. 06, 22, 26, 64, 84, 114, 144, 147; Vladimer Puturidze, *Kartul-sparsuli istoriuli sabutebi* (Tbilisi, 1955), pp. 87, 341, 345, 403, 426.
37. The above-mentioned seal of King Rostom, characterized by M. Brosset as 'la sceau moitié musulman, moitié chretien', is round in shape with a fig-shaped superstructure (an imitation of the Safavid royal seals of the same form). The Georgian legend occupies almost the whole of the seal's field. Along with the Georgian legend, under the very dome of the seal, there is an inscription in Arabic letters: 'Allah', see: Brosset, *Histoire de la Géorgie*, II/2, pp. 443, 483; Bakradze, *Masalebi kartuli spragistikis istoriisatvis*, vol. I, p. 44, Pl. V, Fig. 3; Beradze, *Georgian Seals of the 17th–18th Centuries*, pp. 4–5, Fig. 1.
38. Bakradze, *Masalebi kartuli spragistikis istoriisatvis*, vol. I, p. 46, Pl. V, Fig. 22.
39. Ibid., vol. I, p. 44, Pl. V, Fig. 25.
40. The authentic manuscript of this charter is kept at the Kekelidze Institute of Manuscripts with the call number Ad-1410. The same Institute also possesses the manuscript of another charter of Luarsab II dating to 1615 (document Sd-600). However, the manuscript represents only a later copy of the royal charter, the original of which has unfortunately not come down to us. On the above charters of Luarsab II, see Valerian Gabashvili, *Kartuli peodaluri tsqobileba XVI–XVII saukuneebshi* (Tbilisi, 1958), p. 356; Odisheli, 'Aghmosavlet Sakartvelos politikuri istoriisatvis', p. 97.
41. Ivane Javakhishvili, *Kartveli eris istoria*, vol. II (Tbilisi, 1965), p. 306.

29

Exploitation of the Frontier: The Caucasus Policy of Shah 'Abbas I

Hirotake Maeda

Introduction: The royal gholams of Shah 'Abbas

The reign of Shah 'Abbas I is regarded as the height of the Safavid dynasty. Mastering crises both at home and abroad, the shah strongly encouraged trade and industry and the country enjoyed great prosperity. These advances were due to his successful state reform.[1] Savory suggests that 'the administration of the Safavid state was reorganized on entirely new bases by Shah 'Abbas I'.[2] Particular mention should be made of the shift in the state elite – that is, the introduction of the new political-military elites. The Caucasians in the service of Safavid shahs are considered to have played an essential role in the reorganization and centralization of state power.[3]

The Caucasians consisted of the royal *gholams* (*gholaman-e khasse-ye sharife*). Going under a variety of different names and titles, such as *gholams*, *mamluks* and *kapıkulus*, the activities of these elements could be observed in many Muslim dynasties during the long history of the Islamic Middle East. The political system of slave soldiers functioned as one of the most important recruitment mechanisms for political-military elites. The royal *gholams* of Safavid Iran are an example of this unique system. Though Shah Tahmasp I began this policy of elite recruitment and his successors, such as Prince Hamza, continued it, it was Shah 'Abbas I who particularly favoured these new elements and gave them a solid base in the newly restructured state organization.[4]

Influences of the slave soldiers' paradigm

The Safavid slave soldiers are usually assumed to have been recruited among war captives or their offspring who were brought to Iran during successive military campaigns in the Caucasus.[5] This view is reinforced by the slave soldiers paradigm, which denies any ties with original family and stresses the newcomers' absolute obedience to Islam and their new rulers. Recently, scholars such as Herzig, Matthee and Baghdiantz MaCabe have shed a clear light on the role of Armenians in the Safavid political economy.[6] Baghdiantz's idea of the Julfa Armenians as Royal Bankers and their similarity to the *gholam* elite is truly acute, though she adheres to the old theory of the slave soldier paradigm. Matthee simply refers to *gholams* in the Glossary of his book as follows '*Gholam*: Slave: the term for the Georgians, Circassians, and Armenians who after being captured were made to convert to Islam and were trained for military and administrative positions in the Safavid state'.[7] Following the traditional slave soldiers paradigm, which stresses their slave status, Baghdiantz wrote that 'it is difficult to determine, as we speak of the Armenian origins of a general or high administrator brought up since childhood in the harem, how clearly these origins were remembered, or if indeed they were. The objective was to dissolve all ethnic, tribal or religious ties to any existing group, to erase their previous identity, and to make the *gholam* entirely dependent on the shah's goodwill'.[8]

If this was indeed the theoretical aim of a *gholam's* upbringing, the real situation does not always seem so simple. The present author has already attested that some powerful *gholam* dynasties were from Georgian noble families. We were able to trace the origins of specific individuals and, through research on Georgian written sources such as chronicles and documents (including Persian-Georgian bilingual documents), found that their original families were flourishing at home in Georgia, even during the Safavid age.[9] Thus, it cannot be concluded that the new Safavid elite recruited in the Caucasus always had their local identities erased. The retention of their original identity contradicts the slave soldier paradigm. This fact calls for a major re-evaluation of that phenomenon.

The Caucasus: A place of transformation

In the Caucasus,[10] where these new elites were recruited, we observed many socio-political, economic and religious issues arising from the relationship between the Safavid dynasty and the surrounding world, such as its rivalry with the Ottomans, conflict with local rulers, tensions between the Christian population and Muslim powers, the recruitment of converted elites, scorched-earth policies, forced migrations, the state silk monopoly and so on. Situated on the border between 'the house of Islam' and 'the house of war', the Caucasus was the frontier for the Safavid shahs.

During the reign of Shah 'Abbas and his successor, Shah Safi, new state institutions seem to have been established. The tension between the Safavids and the Ottomans over the Caucasus also lessened to some extent after the treaty of Zuhab in 1639. However, the infiltration of Caucasians into Safavid elite society and the interrelationship between the Safavid government and indigenous Caucasians during 'Abbas's reign have not been investigated thoroughly. To begin with, at the time of the shah's accession to the throne, most of north-west Iran and the Caucasus was under the control of the Ottomans. So, at the same time that Caucasians were being raised to positions of authority at the Safavid court, Shah 'Abbas was busy with the reconquest of these territories. There is surely a connection between his use of Caucasian *gholams* and his frontier policy.

What were the features of this Caucasian frontier? When examining Shah 'Abbas's policy towards the Caucasus, we must take the geoethnical condition of the region into consideration. An important feature of Caucasian society was its multi-ethnic character. For example, the population of Chokhur-e Sa'd and Qarabagh included many Armenians and Muslim peasants. Shirvan had only been incorporated into the empire half a century before and its population consisted mainly of Sunnis. Georgia preserved its own social hierarchy and Christian character. The North Caucasian principalities were virtually independent of any neighbouring countries.[11] This unique composition of Caucasian society did not allow Safavid authority to penetrate it easily. In addition, the whole Caucasus was conquered by the Ottomans before and just after 'Abbas's accession to the throne. The basis of Safavid authority was not as strong as that of local princes and even some of the *qezelbash* tribes betrayed them and swore loyalty to the Ottomans. So 'Abbas needed not only to recover territory but also to re-establish effective Safavid authority in the region.

Discovery of volume III of the Afzal al-Tavarikh

To research this specific area, there have been few sources available until recently, apart from Eskandar Bayg Monshi's chronicle. However, in the 1990s, a new Persian chronicle was discovered by Charles Melville in the library of Christ College, Cambridge. It was volume III of the *Afzal al-Tavarikh*. This is the most interesting volume of the work, since it concerns the reign of Shah 'Abbas, which was contemporary with the lifetime of the author.[12] For information on the activities of the Caucasians in connection with Safavid authority, this new source is particularly valuable. Fazli Isfahani, the author of the chronicle, had a rich cultural background and bureaucratic experience and leaves a vivid account of the reign of Shah 'Abbas.

Fazli started his career as a *mostawfi* (finance/revenue officer) of the Barda administration in 1608. He then succeeded his brother as *vazir* of that province. After the revolt of Teimuraz (Tahmurath Khan) of Georgian Kakheti,[13] Shah 'Abbas gave the territory to Paikar Soltan *hakem* of Barda and Fazli worked as *vazir* of both Barda and Kakheti until the general uprising in Georgia in 1625. So Fazli was directly in charge of Safavid policy towards the Caucasus. His history contains much bibliographical information on state and provincial elites, including the newly ascendant Caucasians, whom Eskandar Bayg Monshi barely mentions in his chronicle. Fazli's description goes a long way to compensating for the previous lack of information.[14]

In this chapter, using the information given by this newly found source, the dynamics of politics during the process of conquering the Caucasus and the rise of the Caucasians at the Safavid court will be shown in detail. The result will much enrich our knowledge and understanding of the slave soldier or foreign elite paradigm in the Safavid context.

Caucasians and the Caucasus in 'Abbas's early reign

In the 1580s, because of internal instability, the Safavid authority took no effective action against the Ottoman invasion. Thus, the whole Caucasus and most of north-west Iran was lost during the early part of 'Abbas's reign. By the terms of the treaty of Istanbul in 1590, only Ardabil and its surrounding territories remained under Safavid control. Even the capital of the region, Tabriz, was conceded to the Ottomans.[15] However, Shah 'Abbas paid much attention to northwest Iran and the Caucasus even before he started his campaign to regain these territories in 1603. According to Fazli's chronicle, 'Abbas himself visited remnant parts of north-west Iran at least four times to investigate the situation. He paid a visit to the Ardabil shrine in three successive years in 1591, 1592 and 1593 and again in 1596.[16] In this last year he dispatched Mehtar Salman, who disguised himself as a merchant, to acquire rifles and Ottoman and European (*Rum o Frank*) goods from the Ottomans.[17] During these visits, the shah 'completely grasped the situation in Azerbaijan'.

Local Caucasian rulers also kept in contact with the Safavid court in the complex international situation. Between 1594 and 1595 Shah 'Abbas received messengers from the 'kings (*padshahan*) of the Crimea (*Tatar*), the Qipchaq Steppe (*dasht-e Qipchaq*), Russia (*Urus*), Circassia (*Cherkes*), Daghestan (*Lezgi*) and the commander (*farmanfarma*) of Astrakhan (*Haji Tarkhan bayn-e Qipchaq*)'. Envoys from Alexander II of Kakheti, Simon I of Kartli and Manuchehr of Samtskhe arrived at the Safavid court between 1596 and 1597 with many gifts, including slave boys and girls. They were entertained by Prince Kustandil/Constantine, the son of Alexander II, who had been brought up in the Safavid court.[18]

Atabek, the son of Manuchehr of Samtskhe, was later given the governorship of Khalkhal in Azerbaijan when he fled to the Safavid court.[19] During the same period, Prince Bagrat of Kartli, nephew of King Simon I, served 'Abbas and was given a fiefdom in Iran.[20] Bagrat later ascended the throne of Kartli (Bagrat VII 1616–19). After his death, his son Simon II became the king of Kartli and Bagrat's half-brother Khosrow was given Bagrat's land in Iran. Shah 'Abbas tried to exercise influence over Georgian princes by giving them fiefdoms inside the Safavid domain.

According to the chief court astrologer, Jalal Monajjem, at around the same time 'Abbas requested a daughter from the Amilakhori family, one of the most influential noble families in the kingdom of Kartli in Georgia. With the assistance of Prince Bagrat of Kartli, Farhad Khan Qaramanlu arranged the match.[21] This act shows that 'Abbas was keen to maintain the relationship not only with Georgian royal families but also directly with local Georgian nobles.

Two Georgian darughes of Isfahan

In parallel to these policies, 'Abbas made use of Georgians who were already serving the Safavid court. In 'Abbas's early reign, two Georgians are recorded as being appointed *darughe* (mayor) of Isfahan. This information emerged after the discovery of Fazli's chronicle. The first was Bijan beg, a royal *gholam* from the Saakadze clan of Kartli[22] (his eldest son and successor as royal *gholam*, Rostam, later became famous as the *sepahsalar* and *beglarbegi* of Azerbaijan in the reign of Shah Safi[23]). Bijan's appointment is very significant as he was recorded in Georgian sources as the *sakhltukhtsesi* (lord chamberlain) of the future king of Kartli, the above-mentioned Prince Bagrat (VII), who himself took refuge in the Safavid court at that time.[24] As Bijan was said to have fled to the Safavids in the company of a Georgian prince (recorded as 'a son of Davit X', probably Bagrat or Khosrow),[25] he must have been one of the highest-ranking Georgian court officials in terms of the Georgian internal hierarchy.

The second Georgian serving the Safavid court as *darughe* of Isfahan was Kustandil Mirza, or Prince Constantine of the kingdom of Kakheti. His previous career and the date of his appointment are also worth mentioning. Fazli first referred to Kustandil as *darughe* of the then capital of the empire, Qazvin, in 1593–4. The appointment would have been a strong response to the Russian demand to return the prince to his native Kakheti. In general, the post of *darughe* was a one-year appointment but Kustandil managed to hold the post until he became *darughe* of Isfahan in 1602–3. The appointment of a Georgian prince to the new capital should be regarded as a significant political gesture as this happened just before the war against the Ottomans.[26]

The examples of Bijan and Kustandil, one a Kartlian prince's court official and one a Kakhetian prince, show Shah 'Abbas's interest in them as political tools. Indeed, Kustandil's appointment shows that the practice of appointing Georgian princes to the post of *darughe* of the capital dates back some 30 years earlier than previous studies have suggested.[27] We know little about Prince Kustandil's activities before 'Abbas sent him back to Kakheti. Other than calling him a father-killer, Eskandar Bayg Monshi provides minimum information about him. However, a comparison of both sources suggests that Eskandar Bayg Monshi deliberately overlooked the role played by the Caucasians. According to Fazli's description, Shah 'Abbas recognized Kustandil as an important hostage and political tool. The tradition of giving a Georgian prince a key position in the imperial administration (as mayor of the capital) started with the appointment of Kustandil and must be understood in the context of the political situation in the Caucasus and the shah's ambitions to regain the territories ceded to the Ottomans.

A second example of a high-ranking Georgian gholam

By following the personal career of Kustandil, a clear picture of 'Abbas's intentions emerges. Shah 'Abbas used this pro-Safavid faction of Georgians during his operation to recover north-west Iran and the Caucasus. When he started the campaign in

1603, Shah 'Abbas I immediately sent Prince Kustandil to summon his father King Alexander II of Kakheti and he sent Tahmasp Qoli, a prince of the Mirimanidze clan, a Kartlian noble family, to King Giorgi X of Kartli.[28]

Tahmasp Qoli was originally from an ethnic Armenian noble family in Kartli, which became known as the Melikov (Melikishvili) family in the nineteenth century. Fazli attributes three different *nisbas* to the representative of this family such as *Gorji* (Georgian), *Armani* (Armenian) and *Kartili* (the Kartlian).[29] During 'Abbas's military operations, Tahmasp Qoli was in charge of the deportation of Julfa Armenians.[30] It is of note that his nephew and successor as royal *gholam*, Mirman Bayg (who was later called Safi Qoli Khan and was given the post of the *beglarbegi* of Hamadan and Baghdad, and *qurchibashi* of Najaf) was first mentioned as *darughe* of New Julfa in Isfahan in 1619, some fifteen years after his uncle deported the Julfan Armenians.[31] If 'Abbas had intended to erase the ethnic and national ties of the Caucasian *gholams*, he would presumably have kept them apart from other Caucasians. Contrary to this presupposition, the Safavid shahs never entirely cut these ties, but rather tried to make use of the ethnic and national affinities between Caucasians for their own political ends.

We can confirm these features of the royal *gholams* with Fazli's following accounts. When King Teimuraz of Kakheti arrived at the Safavid court, the converted Georgian princes welcomed him with 'gholams and servants of the Shah who were Georgians'.[32] On his way to his summer residence in Sahand near Tabriz, Shah 'Abbas learnt that King Teimuraz and King Luarsab were approaching. He dispatched Allahverdi Khan to welcome them. Allahverdi was also ordered to prepare a big banquet in Sarcheshme. Shah 'Abbas ordered them to be entertained with a 'Georgian' entertainment (*sohbat-e Gorjiyane*). 'Georgians of old and new' were ordered to attend the banquet and Georgians sang and danced in their own fashion. Fazli describes the mixture of two different cultures: 'the pure wine of Shiraz and the precious one from Georgia were gathered together at a banquet'.[33] The following year, when the two kings approached Tabriz, 'Abbas ordered Prince Bagrat (of the Kartlian royal family) and Prince 'Isa (of the Kakhetian royal family) and Atabek Khan (lord of Meskheti) to welcome Teimuraz and Luarsab with *gholams* of noble origin ('*gholaman-e tavat o aznavar*').[34]

All these descriptions strongly suggest that the Caucasians (especially the Georgians) in the service of the Safavid shahs were not alienated from their native land, or at least had some opportunities to recognize their identity. They demonstrate the dual character of Georgians in the Safavid court as both members of the Safavid political elite and as representatives of Georgian immigrant society, and contradict the idea that they were simply imported slaves.

'Abbas's Georgian campaigns: Reorganization of the regional order

Close examination of Fazli's description of the shah's expedition to Georgia makes 'Abbas's ideas about his Caucasian subjects clearer. The tension between the Safavid shah and the Georgian kings was raised substantially when Luarsab II, king of Kartli, invited Mohammad Khan Qazaqlar to Tbilisi and then killed him.[35] Teimuraz I, king of Kakheti, also refused the shah's invitation to the Safavid court. The political situation in Kartli worsened when one of the leading *aznaurs* (nobles), Giorgi Saakadze (also known as Mourav Bayg in Persian sources), left Luarsab and fled to the Safavid court.[36] This caused an immediate deterioration in the relationship between 'Abbas and the Georgian kings. In 1613 'Abbas decided to punish them with force. His campaign against the Georgian kingdoms caused serious ethno-demographic changes in the region and surrounding territories.[37]

Traditionally, this expedition has been considered as the direct cause for filling Persia with Caucasian slaves.[38] Indeed, Eskandar Bayg Monshi writes that more than 100,000 Georgians became war captives. Fazli's statement reinforced this idea, estimating that 118,000 persons were recorded as war captives, of which 10,500 were enrolled into the shah's service.[39] Thus, it was one of the major reasons why so many Caucasians lived in Safavid society. Yet we should keep in mind that, according to another account by Fazli, treacherous Kakhetians who were captured had their legs cut off and thrown away behind the Ordobazar.[40] So we cannot conclude that all of the captives were directly hired to be royal *gholams*. We should make a close inspection of 'Abbas's plans for regional reorganization.

The first measure taken by Shah 'Abbas to reorganize the region was to increase the presence of the *qezelbash*. The earlier Safavid shahs settled *qezelbash* tribes along two rivers, the Aras and the Kura. Shah 'Abbas continued this policy, making loyal *qezelbash* chiefs emigrate with their fellows. He fortified the castles against the Ottoman threat and garrisoned them with Iranian infantry from Iraq-e ajam equipped with firearms. As political elites, Shah 'Abbas never placed full confidence in the *qezelbash* amirs. However, the *qezelbash* continued to be deployed as mobilized military units which could be easily relocated to govern local societies. To control the *qezelbash* 'Abbas frequently reorganized and resettled various *qezelbash* tribes in the Caucasus. For example, the Moqaddam tribe, originally consisting of only 70 families and a subsidiary tribe of the Otoziki in Qarabagh, increased to 10,000 families during 'Abbas's reign and was given Urumiye as their fiefdom after the annihilation of a Kurdish tribe.[41] 500 Ottoman war captives, mainly soldiers from Sivas and Divri, who became Shahsevans, were given land near Erisbar and Aran.[42]

The assimilation of the local elite: Marriage as a political instrument

Shah 'Abbas not only conquered territory and settled his people in new regions, however. He also strengthened the Safavid position in the Caucasus and bound the local elite more closely with the Safavids by using political marriages. Before Shah 'Abbas's accession to the throne, marriage between Safavid shahs and Georgian kings had already been established. Shah 'Abbas continued this practice. At the start of his campaign to bring the Caucasus back into the hands of the Safavids in 1603, 'Abbas requested a daughter of King Giorgi X of Kartli and a daughter of Prince Davit of Kakheti, sister of the future King Teimuraz I for his harem. Daughters of Georgian noble families, such as the Amilakhori and Eristavi, regularly entered his harem. This policy was also pursued in the neighbouring principalities of the northern Caucasus. As a result, the Caucasians came to be linked directly to the Safavid court as members of the royal household.[43]

It was not only the royal harem that witnessed political alliances of this kind. Prince Kustandil of Kakheti was given a daughter of Mohammad Khan Torkman while his father King Alexander was present at the Safavid court to take part in the siege of Erevan in 1604.[44] The Torkman tribe, who traditionally held the governorship of Tabriz, had their base in Azerbaijan. This was part of a careful plan to integrate Georgians into the Safavid elite circle and make Georgia a secure base on the border with the Ottoman Empire. Kustandil was sent to Kakheti with his brother-in-law Bektash and his fellow Torkman tribesmen. According to Fazli, Bektash's mother was a daughter of King Alexander, so he was not only the son-in-law but also cousin of Kustandil. Shah 'Abbas I intended to make the Georgian royal house and *qezelbash* amirs relatives and to incorporate them into Safavid elite society. Kustandil killed Alexander II and Prince Giorgi and temporarily controlled Kakheti but the Georgians soon revolted and Kustandil was killed as a result. Shah 'Abbas had not yet conquered Shirvan and Qarabagh, but recognized the legitimacy of the Christian Teimuraz's kingship at the time.

Ten years later, when the shah himself led a punitive expedition to Georgia, Bektash was officially appointed as the first *qezelbash* governor of Kakheti.[45] Around the same period the governorship of Shakki in Shirvan was entrusted to Mohammad Hossayn Khan, who was a descendant of the Shirvan shah. At the time he was head of the Zulqadr tribe in Iraq and Azerbaijan because his mother was from that tribe.[46] At the same time, occupied Kartli was temporally entrusted to Ali Qoli Bayg and his brother Emamqoli Bayg. Their father, Behbud Aqa, was a *gholam* of Tohmaq Khan Ostajlu, former general governor Erevan.[47] According to Fazli, Behbud was from a Kartlian noble family (*tavad*) and converted to Islam while in the service of Tohmaq Khan. The two brothers were ordered to change the system of tax collection. These policies naturally caused demographic changes in the Caucasus. But the shah's more important aim was to increase ties and integrate the local elite into sharing Safavid political culture, and finally to incorporate the territory and the people permanently into the Safavid domain.

Of course, these policies were pursued to some extent in other frontier provinces as well as in the Caucasus. As we see, the situation in Kurdestan strongly influenced events in the Caucasus in connection with Ottoman actions. For example, the revolt of Davit Ganjeri in Kakheti and the revolt in Kurdistan started simultaneously in response to Ottoman military action against the Safavids.[48] 'Abbas's effort to integrate local hereditary princes into Safavid elite society is observed not only in Georgia and Shirvan but also in Lorestan, Kurdistan and Arabestan.

Shah 'Abbas gave his daughter Shah Baygom to Sayyed Naser, the son of Sayyed Mobarek of the Musha'sha dynasty and entrusted him with the governorship of Save in central Iran.[49] These policies later developed into what is called the *vali* institution described in *Tadhkirat al-Muluk*. So, if a similar policy was followed in other parts of the empire, what were the unique features of the shah's Caucasus policy?

Forced migration and 'emigrant' society

Two examples of forced migrations during 'Abbas's military expedition in the Caucasus in 1613–15 give us a hint to the answer. Many populations in the Caucasus were deported to central Iran and the coast of the Caspian Sea during Shah 'Abbas's reign. For example, 5,000 Muslim families and 1,200 Jewish families were exiled to Mazandaran as a result of the revolt in Shirvan. The population of Nakhchevan was also exiled.[50]

The two forced migrations in 1613–15 show 'Abbas's political intentions and strong grasp of Caucasian affairs. Kakheti, a rich and prosperous land ruled by the hostile Teimuraz, was the main target of 'Abbas's military campaign. 'Abbas conducted a reorganization of the provinces which modified the ethno-demographic makeup. While introducing *qezelbash* nomads headed by Bektash Bayg Torkman (whose parents were an influential *qezelbash* amir and a daughter of King Alexander of Kakheti), 'Abbas deported the Jews from Zagam to Farrokhabad.

According to Fazli, settlement in Mazandaran goes back to the early part of 'Abbas's reign. When Farhad Khan Qaramanlu was given the governorship of Mazandaran, he ordered Mir Hashem Shirvani and his fellow Shirvan people to go there. They fled to Qezelagaj, the base of the Qaramanlu in Azerbaijan after the Ottoman occupation but they could not work there as the land could not produce silk. The village of Takhun was developed and later named Farrokhabad. This episode shows that Mazandaran was exploited for economic purposes from early in 'Abbas's reign. Called Bazari (meaning 'bazaar') in Georgian sources, Zagam was the economic capital of Kakheti. The Jewish leader Khoja Lale Zar ebn Ya'qub later played an important role in the silk trade as Matthee has pointed out.

At the same time, the Circassians who 'came from the Alborz mountains and Qipchaq Steppe to live in Georgia' were ordered to migrate. Every Qasiq and Qabari (?) of the Circassians, headed by their leader Shalva, was deported to Isfahan. After the shah's return, their presence near the border (*sarhad*) was not desirable, for they were brave warriors. So they were ordered to go to Fars to be the retainers of Emamqoli Khan.[51] Shalva's group might have been the ancestors of Circassians living on the Isfahan-Shiraz route, who were described by many European travellers throughout the seventeenth century.[52] Fazli mentions elsewhere that the descendants of these groups produced many royal servants.

This clearly demonstrates the transportation of the economic and military human resources of the Kakhetian kingdom to a territory and sphere that the Safavid court could easily control. It is important to point out that this aimed not only to weaken the Kakheti kingdom but also to balance the newly deported peoples; that is, Jews counterbalanced the Armenians, Circassians the Georgians. 'Abbas clearly recognized the national character of these people. So the traditional slave soldier paradigm fails to work here. The infiltration of Caucasians into Safavid society was not that of individual slaves without any ties. Each social or ethnic group was transplanted to new soil as a collectivity while keeping its own characteristics. 'Abbas tried to introduce minorities into his domain as members of the extended royal household. He tried to combine different elements and counterbalance them. The multinational character of the Caucasians was quite useful to his aim.

Yet the marker of the collective identity, or the social cleavage, was not necessarily 'national' in modern sense. Abbas made use of the characteristics of not only different ethnic groups but also different social classes. Regarding the deported Georgians of Kakheti, Fazli tells us that if they were from the noble (*tavad* and *aznaur*) and military (*sepahi*) classes, they were enrolled among the shah's servants (*bandegan-e shahi*). If they were 'klakhi (or *glakhi*)' and farmers (*ra'iyat*), they would be given farmland in Farakhabad.[53] The use of the word '*glakhi*', which corresponds to the Georgian word *glekhi,* meaning 'free farmer' is itself very rare in Persian sources. As mentioned above, Fazli worked as *vazir* of Kakheti and Barda; his description indicates the deep local knowledge possessed by high-ranking Safavid officials.[54] Understanding these characteristics of the Georgian context, 'Abbas tried to use them in the creation and expansion of his new household, through his deliberate policy of dividing power among the different groups.

In addition, 'Abbas recruited royal *gholams* from among loyal Armenian headmen.[55] In some cases, the Safavid authorities took children by force.

Mohammad Taher Bayg Nasiri, a nephew of the former grand vazir Hatem Bayg, was enrolled as a Sayyed attendant and was ordered to go to the Armenian-populated parts of Azerbaijan and select children of both sexes to work in the service of the shah, bringing them to the imperial presence.

From this description, the recruitment of the Caucasians was regarded as a policy towards the *zemmis* (non-Muslim population). However, there is also the example of Mohammad Bayg, son of a former *kalantar* of Ganje, Malek Mahmud Jan, who was pardoned and subsequently enrolled as a royal *gholam* after his father's revolt. If we follow this description, Safavid royal *gholams* were not always recruited from among converted Caucasians.[56] The first priority was the transformation of local nobles into state elites. The institution of the royal *gholams* functioned as a channel to connect the local Caucasian elites directly with the royal court, at the same time, it helped to govern local populations by turning them into direct subjects of the Safavid dynasty. In other words, 'Abbas hoped to extend the royal household and consolidate his power. Providing state elites as well as state subjects, the policy towards the Caucasus fulfilled his two main aims for centralization.

After the conquest: The rise of gholams of Kartlian noble origin

These policies caused strong opposition in the region. During the general revolt in 1615, Bektash of Kakheti, Mohammad Hossayn of Shakki and Ali Qoli of Kartli were all slain on the spot.[57] Yet Shah ʿAbbas managed to suppress the revolt and Kartli was entrusted to Bagrat Khan. He had spent most of his life in the Safavid court and was Muslim by origin. Moreover, he was related to the Qazaqlar tribe governing the Lori-Pambak region. Shah ʿAbbas gave the governorship of Kakheti to Peykar Khan Ikirmidort, governor of Barda, and also gave him a sister of King Luarsab II of Kartli. At the same time, a sister of King Teimuraz of Kakheti was given to Mohammad Qoli Khan Qajar, governor of Qarabagh.

It is interesting that the role of *gholams* of Kartlian noble origin substantially increased after the expedition to Georgia. It seems that ʿAbbas hoped to calm the political situation in Georgia by elevating these elements. We see here ʿAbbas's deliberate policy to exploit the differences among the Caucasians to counterbalance each other and neutralize threats.

ʿAbbas's intention was to emphasize the differences among Georgians, in this case, Kartlians and Kakhetians. Eskandar Bayg Monshi and Fazli repeatedly mention the faithful attitude of the Kartlians in comparison to the treacherous nature of the Kakhetians.[58] After Prince Kustandil's murder and Prince Isa's dismissal,[59] ʿAbbas could find no suitable candidate to rule Kakheti among the hostage Kakhetian converted princes. On the other hand, Prince Bagrat, who was born a Muslim, ascended the throne of Kartli in 1616. In 1619–20 Mirman Mirimanidze, who was then a *yuzbashi* (officer) of the *gholam* corps, was appointed *darughe* of Julfa in Isfahan and the following year received the governorship of Hamadan and was promoted to the rank of Khan.[60] Otar Bayg, a royal *gholam* from the Baratashvili-Orbelishvili or Orbeliani clan, worked as the *darughe* of New Julfa sometime later.[61] He then acquired the governorship of Qandahar in Shah ʿAbbas II's time and his family continued to flourish until Nadir Shah's time. His original family, the Baratashvili-Orbeliani, was the largest noble family in Kartli. It seems no mere coincidence that the Mirimanidze and Baratashvili clans both ruled the Somkhit-Sabaratiano province of southern Kartli where Safavid authority had long been established.[62]

After the expedition to Georgia, the tradition of appointing Georgian princes to the post of *darughe* of the capital was renewed. The post was given to Khosrow Mirza, illegitimate brother of Bagrat VII of Kartli, who later became *vali* (king) of Kartli himself.[63] Rostam, son of Bijan Bayg the former *darughe* of Isfahan and a lord chamberlain of Bagrat VII, of the Saakadze clan, was selected as a *yasavol-e sohbat* after the conquest of Qandahar. A little later he was sent to Azerbaijan to supervise the army. Rostam became *sepahsalar* (commander-in-chief) and viceroy of Azerbaijan in Shah Safi's reign.[64] The specific rise of the *gholams* of Kartlian noble origin was partly due to the fact that the new king of Kartli, Simon II son of Bagrat VII, was only a child and there would have been an urgent need to strengthen his position. In Georgian Kartli, local nobles established their absolute right over their subjects and kings had little means to intervene. The rise of the Kartlian *gholams* would have been beneficial to both sides (Georgian nobles and the Safavid authority) and shows another dimension of the connection between Safavid elite recruitment policy and Caucasian politics.

Elites in transition: The sons-in-law of Emamqoli Khan

So, were the origins and socio-political characteristics of the Caucasian *gholams* preserved once they had entered royal service? Fazli provides very significant information on this point. In 1622 Shah 'Abbas gave several daughters of Emamqoli Khan, *beglarbegi* of Fars, in marriage to the royal *gholams* of Georgian noble origin.[65]

Thereafter Emamqoli Khan was given a robe of honour and returned to Shiraz. The governorship of Dawraq was given to his son, Safi Qoli, who was also promoted to the rank of soltan. The daughters of Emamqoli Khan were 22 in number and some of them had been given to the shah's *gholams* by order of the shah before. On this occasion, some other daughters were also given to *gholams*. Gifts for the bridegrooms were given to those *gholams* who came from Georgian noble families (*az a'yan-e Gorjestan*) and each of them was given a fief and salary according to his condition.[66]

Among these sons-in-law of Emamqoli Khan, we find Abd al-Gaffar Amilakhori, Aliqoli Saakadze (younger brother of Rostam Khan *sepahsalar*), Nawruz Tulashvili (appointed as governor of Barda when his wife's uncle Davud, son of Allahverdi, became beglarbegi of Qarabagh) and Davud Gorji (who became governor of Dashtestan in Shah 'Abbas II's time).

The following two points are deduced from this information. First, the ties between the *gholams* of Georgian origin were growing stronger with 'Abbas's active encouragement. The second point shows, however, an opposing tendency. Emamqoli and his father Allahverdi came from the lower rank of Kartlian nobles (possibly Undiladze[67]) and the strict Georgian social hierarchy meant that marriage between them and higher-ranking families, such as the Amilakhori, could never have taken place in Georgia. As they accepted Islam and lived in the Safavid society, their identity underwent a certain change. It shows the transformation of Georgian noble society under Safavid rules. In other words, all these facts should not be understood in the framework of a national understanding or the simple wholesale transplantation of the Caucasian society. 'Abbas carefully diverted and counterbalanced its power. Marriage itself served as a strong instrument to merge the transitional elite.

Isfahan and Farrokhabad: The hearts of the empire

In 1619 Shah 'Abbas ordered some 40,000 immigrant Georgian and Armenian families in Farahabad to conduct the Epiphany ceremony (*khaja shushan*). This was arranged as a New Year event to entertain the Mughal ambassador, and the shah himself was in attendance. The appointment of Qarchaqai Khan to the governorship of Tabriz happened the following day.[68] Roemer suggests the religious generosity of Shah 'Abbas as the motive. Yet we should probably regard all these actions as political. As Herzig rightly pointed out, Shah 'Abbas was the only Safavid shah who forced Armenians to convert to Islam. From Fazli's account we get the impression that the Christian performances were consciously prepared to celebrate the converted Armenian, from Erevan's promotion to the highest military rank. 'Abbas looked to recognize both converted and non-converted from the same nationality, in this case, Armenian. He showed his favour towards his Caucasian subjects, yet at the same time, made distinctions among them and emphasized his tremendous generosity towards his faithful converted Caucasian servant.

Around the same time the shah's favourite concubine, Tamar, a daughter of Faramarz Amilakhori, donated 30,000 tomans for the construction of an all-weather paved causeway to Farrokhabad.[69] She dedicated it to God as an offering for 'Abbas's health. Her brother, Abd al-Gaffar Amilakhori, was brought up at the shah's court and later became a leading pro-Safavid Georgian converted noble. The imperial harem functioned as a hothouse for the Caucasian political elites of the Safavid dynasty. In this connection we can recall that the mayor of the capital of the empire, Isfahan, was a converted prince from the kingdom of Kartli in Georgia, Prince Khosrow.

The two largest construction projects during 'Abbas's reign were entrusted to Allahverdi Khan and Emamqoli Khan, a father and a son who, between them, worked as *beglarbegi* of Fars for over 30 years. These were the construction of the Si-o-se-pol (the Thirty-three [arches] Allahverdi Khan) bridge over the Zayande-rud and the blasting operations to link the head waters of the Karun and Zayande-rud rivers.[70] Both projects were intended to secure and augment the water supply to 'Abbas's new capital, Isfahan.

Thus, the new residence in Mazandaran was populated by deported Caucasians and the new capital was governed by the Caucasian prince. There was a leading Caucasian woman in the imperial haram in that new capital and the construction of its most ambitious infrastructure was entrusted to Caucasian officials who governed the richest provinces of the empire. Allahverdi Khan and Emamqoli Khan were top-ranking royal courtiers; however, below them there were numerous military commanders, bureaucrats, workers of the imperial workshops, women of the harem, and village farmers, including those who worked in silk production – all of them of Caucasian origin. Caucasians living in Safavid society formed a minority elite, originating in a foreign land but occupying the heartland of the empire's power system because, spread across Isfahan, Shiraz and Farrokhabad, they represent the core of the royal household.

The wedding of Simon II and the shah's granddaughter

In 1624 Shah 'Abbas decided to marry his granddaughter to the Georgian king of Kartli, Simon II.[71] The bride's parents were Isa Khan Shaykhaband Qorchibashi and 'Abbas's beloved daughter Fateme Soltan Begom. From the moment of their arrival at the Safavid court the Caucasians had become household members in that they became the wives, brothers-in-law and domestic servants of the shahs. This was the first time, however, that a member of the shah's household was given in marriage to a Caucasian and left the royal household to live in the Caucasus. This marriage symbolized the extension of 'Abbas's Caucasian household and a reorientation towards their native land.

This event gives us an insight into how 'Abbas handled the complexity of ethnic, national, social and cultural tensions. 'Abbas appointed Qarchaqai Khan *sepahsalar*, a royal *gholam* of Armenian origin from Erevan to be *lala* and Khanzade Khanom, sister of late Bagrat VII to *dada*, a combination of a member of the new Caucasian elite of (originally) low rank with a Caucasian from a royal background. One of Emamqoli Khan's daughters, who was married to Abd al-Gaffar (Anduqapar in Georgian sources) Amilakhori – one of the most powerful Kartlian nobles – was a companion to the bride. We may recall that this couple (the wife from the minor Georgian aristocracy and the husband from one of the noblest Georgian families) had themselves been married by the arrangement of the shah.[72]

A big banquet was held near Tbilisi.[73] In the first term, Qarchaqai Khan ordered Yusof Khan, a royal *gholam* of the same Armenian origin and a childhood friend, now *beglarbegi* of Shirvan, to host the banquet. In the second term, Mohammadqoli Khan Qajar *beglarbegi* of Ganja ordered Peykar Khan Ikirmidort *beglarbegi* of Kakheti to host it. They both represented the now localized *qezelbash* amirs in Qarabagh and Kakheti (they had both been given a Bagratid princess in marriage by Shah 'Abbas). According to Fazli, the Qajars in Erisbar and the Ikrmiderts in Barda were in conflict with each other over Qarabagh.[74] Shah 'Abbas gave a Kartlian princess to a lesser Ikrmidert leader, Peykar, and a Kakhetian princess to the distinguished Qajar Mohammadqoli, when the governorship of Kakheti was entrusted to Peykar. This shows how 'Abbas tried to foster rivalries even among the *qezelbash* tribes in the Caucasus.[75]

In the third term, Mourav Bayg ordered Abd al-Gaffar Amilakhori and Sohrab (or Zurab) Araghvis Eristavi to entertain the guests. Mourav Bayg, Giorgi Saakadze, represented one of the newly ascendant *aznauri* families in Georgia. He succeeded in catching 'Abbas's attention and was appointed *vakil* of Simon II.[76] Abd al-Gaffar Amilakhori was a typical member of the new Georgian converted elite brought up in the shah's court. He took one of the daughters of Emamqoli Khan as his wife.

Zurab Eristavi represented the local Georgian *tavads*. Here we see a humble *aznaur* giving orders to two great nobles as a result of the authority given him by the shah. 'Abbas was clearly conscious of their collective identity, and carefully handled the individual's identity as well. While counterbalancing them with one other, 'Abbas was trying to create a new social order in the Caucasus – externally, at the Safavid court – and internally, in order to extend the royal household. Armenian *gholams*, Qarabagh *qezelbash* and Georgian *tavad-aznaurs* were comrades and, at the same time, rivals. Their path of advancement to power was reliant on the shah's goodwill.

Conclusion: The Caucasus – the 'true frontier'

Shah 'Abbas tried to extend the members of the royal household through recruitment in the Caucasus. This policy was not, however, simply a matter of acquiring large numbers of slaves for the formation of a slave soldier corps. 'Abbas hired Caucasians *en masse* to make up various levels of the royal household. The infiltration of the Caucasians into the Safavid domain continued throughout 'Abbas's reign by various channels such as war captives, annual tribute, defection, hostage, marriage, deportation and so on. They were subordinate nations who became members of the Safavid royal household at the same time. Among them, converted loyal Caucasians were organized as a state elite, the royal *gholams*.

The fact that royal *gholams* were often in charge of the execution of the deportation or administration of the newly deported Caucasians demonstrates that Shah 'Abbas I intended to integrate each deported Caucasian group into the Safavid royal household under the leadership of newly converted elites. Deported farmers from Kakheti, Ganja, Shirvan, Nakhichevan cultivated the royal land to produce silk in Mazandaran. Selected merchants from the Caucasus traded that silk. Caucasians were working in the royal workshops and entering the harem to benefit the Safavid state and adorn royal life. The Caucasus was a suitable arena in which to recruit them, since the Safavid shahs could exploit the local situation in the context of protecting subordinate peoples.

These movements were connected with reforms aimed at state centralization by way of the extension and reinforcement of the royal household; that is, the *khasse* policy. In that process the shah's household organization became more official and his personal servants obtained state power. While the sources do not acknowledge the borrowing, it seems obvious that Ottoman imperial policy towards the Balkans and the Caucasus substantially influenced Safavid practice.

In contrast to other examples of slave elites, 'Abbas recognized the importance of the social networks and individual status of the Caucasians and deliberately preserved, or rather renewed and modified, their ethnic and national ties. In the light of this, the old slave soldier paradigm should be revised to take account of specific concrete examples to be understood in their own historical context.

In 1625 Giorgi Saakadze revolted just after the marriage of Simon II and 'Abbas's granddaughter. He liberated Eastern Georgia and temporarily occupied Qarabagh. In response to the crisis, Shah 'Abbas negotiated with Teimuraz of Kakehti who had revolted against him ten years before and had been in exile since. Through the mediation of Emamqoli Khan and his brother Davud, 'Abbas permitted Teimuraz to return to power and even gave his son a part of Kartli. This event clearly shows that 'Abbas's policy towards the Caucasus had as a principal objective the division of power among the ruling elites: the *qezelbash* and the Caucasians at court, and the *qezelbash* nomads and the local nobles in the Caucasus. In this regard, the diverse origins of the Caucasian subjects and the preservation of their distinct identities were in some way useful in avoiding the concentration of royal *gholam* power.

We have paid considerable attention to Georgia's situation on the border between Islamic and non-Islamic worlds. As a frontier, the nearest foreign land, Georgia, was frequently in direct relations with Muslim powers. As Petrushevskii states, in the Caucasus it was only in Georgia that the term *toyul-e mawrusi* (permanent *toyul*) was used. The existence of indigenous state structures and local military elites characterized Georgian society. Serving as military elites in the Safavid court, they were simultaneously slave soldiers and possessed of a distinct tribal or national background.

Because of geopolitical factors, Georgians became prominent in the Safavid court as the foreign elite with the most marked national character. This tendency became clearer during the latter half of 'Abbas' reign when relations between the Safavid court and local Georgians were very strained.[77]

The activities of the converted elites were influenced by the local political climate of the Caucasus, and affected it in return. So it is essential to analyse the phenomenon of the Caucasian infiltration into the Safavid domain in parallel with the sociopolitical situation in the Caucasus. This phenomenon exemplifies the complexity of Safavid external and internal policies for it was partly a frontier policy, but also strongly affected the Safavid state's internal political map.

All this evidence suggests that Georgian noble society, by accepting conversion and some social changes, took root in the heartland of Safavid political society. As it relied on the shah's careful handling of the complicated power balance inside the Caucasians, it suffered severe casualties whenever that balance was broken.

The old slave soldier paradigm was simplistic in regarding slave soldiers as possessing no other identity. However, the Safavid foreign elite actually moved between the two different cultures. We see two faces in the Safavid *gholams*, as Safavid courtier elites and as representatives of the Caucasian emigrant society. This dual identity was experienced by various minority elites in various societies, not only in the history of Iran or the Middle East. Study of the example of the Caucasians in the Safavid dynasty enriches our understanding of the slave soldier paradigm of Islamic society and, more generally, of the history of political elites in the pre-modern world.

Notes

1. Hans R. Roemer, 'The Safavid period', in Peter Jackson and Laurence Lockhart (eds), *The Cambridge History of Iran*, vol. 6 (Cambridge, 1986), pp. 262-78.
2. Roger M. Savory, 'The Safavid administrative system', in Peter Jackson and Laurence Lockhart (eds), *The Cambridge History of Iran*, vol. 6 (Cambridge, 1986), pp. 356-7.
3. Savory recognizes them as a sort of 'third force'. 'Safawids i-Dynastic, political and military history', *The Encyclopaedia of Islam*, New Edition, vol. VIII (Leiden, 1995), p. 765.
4. Hirotake Maeda, 'Hamza Mirza and the *Caucasian Elements* at the Safavid Court: A Path toward the Reforms of Shah 'Abbas I', *Orientalisti*, I (Tbilisi, 2001), pp. 155-71.
5. C. E. Bosworth, 'Ghulam. ii-Persia', *The Encyclopaedia of Islam*, New Edition, vol. II (Leiden-London, 1965), pp. 1081-4.
6. Edmund M. Herzig, 'The Armenian merchants of New Julfa, Isfahan: A study in pre-modern Asian trade', Ph.D. thesis submitted to the Faculty of Oriental Studies, University of Oxford, 1991; Rudolph P. Matthee, *The Politics of Trade in Safavid Iran: Silk for Silver, 1600-1730* (Cambridge, 1999); Ina Baghdiantz McCabe, *The Shah's Silk for Europe's Silver: The Eurasian Trade of the Julfa Armenians in Safavid Iran and India (1530-1750)* (Atlanta, 1999).
7. Matthee, *The Politics of Trade*, p. 248.
8. Baghdiantz McCabe, *The Shah's Silk*, p. 40.
9. Hirotake Maeda, 'On the ethno-social background of the four *Gholam* families from Georgia in Safavid Iran', *Studia Iranica*, 32/2 (2003), pp. 243-78. This article is the extended version of a Japanese paper by the same author, '*Gholam* of the Safavid dynasty: The case of Georgian origin', *Toyo Gakuhou* 81-3 (1999), pp. 1-32, vi-vii (in Japanese, with a summary in English).
10. No reference was made to the word 'Caucasus' in Persian original sources during this period. Yet the region north of the Aras River stood out for its multi-ethnic character. This area included the administrative provinces situated south-east of the Caucasus such as Shirvan, Chokhur-e Sa'ad, Qarabagh, the Georgian kingdoms of Kartli and Kakheti as well as northern Caucasian tribal principalities.
11. Such reference was made to indigenous rulers as 'rulers of Georgia, the Alborz mountain area and the khans of the Qipchaq Steppe'. Fazli, *Afzal III*, fo. 300b (... *hokkam-e Gorjestanat o kuh-e Alborz o khavanin-e dasht-e Qipchaq*). The Caucasian Mountains are here described as the Alborz mountain area (*kuh-e Alborz*: Fazli, *Afzal III*, fos. 258a, 414a).
12. Fazli Khuzani al-Esfahani, *Afzal al-tavarikh*, University of Cambridge, Ms.Dd.5.6. The chronicle was wrongly catalogued, referred to as an old manuscript of Eskandar Bayg Monshi's *Tarikh-e alam-ara-ye 'Abbasi*. See: Charles Melville, 'A lost source for the reign of Shah 'Abbas: The *Afzal al-tawarikh* of Fazli Khuzani Isfahani', *Iranian Studies* 31/ii (1998), pp. 263-5.
13. Kakheti and the Kartli are two kingdoms of Eastern Georgia which accepted Safavid suzerainty during this period.
14. On Fazli's life see Mellville's article, in addition to the article of M. Haneda who conducted a close inspection of the first and second volume of Fazli's above-mentioned work. Charles Melville, 'New light on the reign of Shah 'Abbas: vol. III of the Afzal al-Tavarikh', in Andrew J. Newman, ed., *Society and Culture in the Early Modern East: Studies on Iran in the Safavid Period* (Leiden: Brill, 2003), pp. 63-96. Masashi Haneda, 'La Famille Fuzani d'Isfahan', *Studia Iranica* 18 (1989), pp. 77-92. For example, his reference to the names of the northern Caucasian leaders will substantially fill gaps in our knowledge: Fazli, *Afzal III*, fos. 259a-b.
15. On the Ottoman conquest of its eastern frontier, see Bekir Kütükoğlu, *Osmanlı-Iran Siyasi Münasebetleri (1578-1612)* (Istanbul, 1993) and M. Fehrettin Kizroğlu, *Osmanlılar'in Kafkas-Elleri'ni Fethi (1451-1590)* (Ankara, 1993).
16. Fazli, *Afzal III*, fos. 49a, 56a, 64a, 95b.
17. Ibid., fo. 101a.
18. Ibid., fos. 84b-85a, 102a, 110b.

19. Instead of Atabek, who was just a child, his mother managed the land tenure. Ibid., fos. 242b, 244a.
20. Prince Bagrat was an heir of King Davit X (Dautkhan) who became the first converted ruler of Kartli. Jalal al-Din describes Bagrat's participation in the Safavid war against Uzbek during this period. Jalal al-Din Monajjem, *Tarikh-e 'Abbasi*, ed. Sayfullah Vahidniya (Tehran, 1366), p. 173.
21. Ibid., p. 156.
22. Fazli, *Afzal III*, fos. 40a, 133a, 453b.
23. Vladimir Puturidze, 'Iranis spasalari Rostom-khan Saakadze', *Kavkasiis khalkhta istoriis sakitkhebi* (Tbilisi, 1966), pp. 288–93.
24. Anonymous, *Ts'khovreba Sak'art'veloisa (Parizis k'ronika)*, ed. G. Alasania (Tbilisi, 1980), p. 92; Tedo Zhordania, *K'ronikebi da skhva masala Sak'art'velos istoriisa da mtserlobisa, shekrebili, k'ronologiurad datsqobili da akhsnili T' Dzordanias mier*, II (Tbilisi, 1897), p. 463.
25. Bijan, *No title (Tarikh-e Rostam Khan)*, British Library, MS. Add. 7655, 7a.
26. W. E. D. Allen, ed., *Russian Embassies to the Georgian Kings* (1589–1605) 2 vols (Cambridge, 1970), pp.79–81. Fazli, *Afzal III*, fos. 77b, 95a, 132a (*darughe-ye hamesale-ye qazvin*), 149b (When the shah arrived at Isfahan, Kustandil who had then become the permanent (*be geid-e hamesale*) *darughe* of Isfahan welcomed him). It should be noted that Isfahan was a centre of the royal *gholams'* activity even before 'Abbas's reign, see Maeda, 'Hamza Mirza and the *Caucasian Elements*', p. 159.
27. Karlo Kutsia has already discussed the Georgian *darughe* (*tarugha* in Georgian) of Isfahan in detail, but the first Georgian *darughe* was long considered to be Prince Khosrow who later became king of Kartli (Rostom or Rostam Khan). Karlo Kutsia, 'Ispahanis kartveli trughebi (1618–1722)', *Makhlobeli Aghmosavletis istoriis sakitkhebi* II (Tbilisi, 1972), pp. 93–103. cf. Willem Floor, *Safavid Government Institutions* (Costa Mesa, 2001), p. 118.
28. Fazli, *Afzal III*, fos. 156b–157a.
29. Ibid., fos. 409b, 417b, 552b. Also see Maeda 'On the ethno-social background', pp. 253–7.
30. Fazli, *Afzal III*, fo. 170a; Edmund Herzig, 'The deportation of the Armenians in 1604–1605 and Europe's myth of Shah 'Abbas I', in Charles Melville (ed.), *Persian and Islamic Studies in Honour of P.W.Avery* (Cambridge, 1990), pp. 59–71.
31. Fazli, *Afzal III*, fos. 409b, 468a.
32. Ibid., fo. 243b.
33. Ibid., fo. 269a.
34. Ibid., fo. 284b.
35. Ibid., fos. 307b–308a.
36. Ibid., fo. 311b.
37. Ibid., fos. 315a, 320b.
38. Anonymous, *Tadhkirat al-muluk*, ed. and trans. V. Minorsky (London, 1943), p. 18; Kathryn Babayan, 'The waning of the Qizilbash: The spiritual and the temporal in seventeenth century Iran', Ph.D. thesis (New York University, 1993), p. 42.
39. Fazli, *Afzal III*, fo. 359b.
40. Ibid., fos. 359b, 379b.
41. Ibid., fos. 239a, 267b.
42. Ibid., fo. 387b; Richard Tapper, 'Shahsevan in Safavid Persia', *Bulletin of the School of Oriental and African Studies*, 37 no. 2 (1974), pp. 321–54.
43. Fazli, *Afzal III*, fo. 169a etc.
44. Ibid., fo. 165a.
45. Ibid., fo. 325a. According to Ahmad Qomi, Bektash's father married a daughter of Iese, younger half brother of Alexander (not a daughter of Alexander). Qazi Ahmad Qomi, *Kholasat al-tavarikh*, ed. Ehsan Eshraqi, 2 vols. (Tehran, 1359–63), p. 709.
46. Ibid., fos. 325a, 327b–328a, 339b.
47. Ibid., fo. 328a.
48. Ibid., fo. 341a.
49. Ibid., fo. 311a.

50. Ibid., fos. 326b, 352b. On the 'Abbas' forced migration policy, see Hirotake Maeda, 'The Forced Migrations and Reorganisation of the Regional Order in the Caucasus by Safavid Iran: Preconditions and Developments Described by Fazli Khuzani', in Ieda Osamu and Uyama Tomohiko (eds.), *Reconstruction and Interaction of Slavic Eurasia and Its Neighboring Worlds* (Sapporo, 2006), pp. 237-73.
51. Ibid., fos. 323a-b. The word Qabari(?) recalled the Kabardians of the Circassian people though details are unknown. See explanation on the Circassians of the time: W. E. D. Allen, ed., *Russian Embassies to the Georgian Kings (1589-1605)* 2 vols (Cambridge, 1970), pp. 23-9, 270-85. Allen, ed., *Russian Embassies*, pp. 23-9, 270-85.
52. P. Oberling, 'Georgians and Circassians in Iran', *Studia Caucasica* 1 (1963), pp. 127-43.
53. Fazli, *Afzal III*, fos. 413b-414a. 'Abbas ordered to give city population the houses and farmers lands. Ibid., fos. 353b-354a.
54. Among Georgians, who were deported, only the so-called Fereidan Georgians (Pereidneli Gurjebi) survived to keep their language and national identity. cf. Guram Sherashenidze, *P'ereidneli Gurjebi* (Tbilisi, 1979); Fridrik Thordarson, 'Georgia ii Language Contact: Shahrestan of Faridan', *Encyclopaedia Iranica*, vol. X (New York, 2001), pp. 94-5.
55. Fazli, *Afzal III*, fo. 195b.
56. Ibid., fo. 302a. See my discussion on the household of Allahverdi Khan: Hirotake Maeda, 'The Household of Allahverdi Khan: An Example of Patronage Network in Safavid Iran', in Florence Hellot-Bellier and Iréne Natchkebia (eds.), *Géorgie et sa capitale Tbilissi entre Perse et Europe* (Paris-Tbilissi, 2009), pp. 149-70.
57. Ibid., fos. 342a, 348a, 349b.
58. Prince Bagrat repeatedly expressed the faithful attitude of Kartlian kings towards the Safavids. Ibid., fos. 316b, 322a.
59. His appointment ibid., fo. 327b.
60. Ibid., fos. 409b, 417b.
61. Ibid., fo. 482b.
62. See Maeda, 'On the ethno-social background'.
63. Fazli, *Afzal III*, fo. 416b.
64. Ibid., fo. 479b.
65. Ibid., fo. 409b.
66. Ibid., fo. 409b.
67. See his origin, Maeda, 'On the ethno-social background', pp. 262-6; idem, 'The Household of Allahverdi Khan'.
68. Fazli, *Afzal III*, fo. 405a.
69. Ibid., fo. 483a. Her name is described as tumar (roll, volume). Eskandar Bayg Monshi, *Tarikh-e Alamara-ye 'Abbasi*, Iraj Afshar ed., 2 vols. (Tehran, 1350), pp. 850, 990; Matthee, *The Politics of Trade*, pp. 75-6.
70. R. Savory, 'Allahverdi Khan', *Encyclopaedia Iranica*, vol. I (1998), p. 394.
71. At this time Simon was 16 years old. Fazli, *Afzal III*, fos. 495a.
72. According to Fazli, 'Abd al-Gaffar was 22-years-old when he married. It is not certain, however, whether this happened in 1622 as cited above. Fazli, *Afzal III*, fo. 495a.
73. Ibid., fo. 498a.
74. Ibid., fo. 372a.
75. Ibid., fos. 413b-414a. On the tribal confederation in Qarabagh, see George A. Bournoutian, *A History of Qarabagh: An Annotated Translation of Mirza Jamal Javanshir Qarabaghi's Tarikh-e Qarabagh* (Costa Mesa, 1994).
76. Fazli, *Afzal III*, fo. 408a.
77. Indeed, there existed a clear boundary between serving the Safavid shah and remaining a member of Georgian landed nobility. See Hirotake Maeda, 'Parsadan Gorgijanidze's Exile in Shushtar: A Biographical Episode of a Georgian Official in the Service of the Safavids', *Journal of Persianate Studies* vol. 1 no. 2 (2008), pp. 218-29 and my upcoming article in print, 'Slave Elites Who Returned Home: Georgian Vali-king Rostom and the Safavid Household Empire', *Memoirs of the Research Department of the Toyo Bunko* vol. 69 (2012).

30

Iranian-Georgian Relations during the Reign of Rostom (1633–58)

Nana Gelashvili

The formation of the Safavid state (1501–1722) in Iran led to a new era in Iranian-Georgian relations that lasted for many centuries. This change of relations came about because of certain specific features of the historical situation not only in Iran and Georgia, but also in the entire Middle East. From this point of view, special attention should be paid to the early thirties of the seventeenth century when relations between Iran and Georgia entered a new phase, revealing new political, economic and cultural characteristics. At the time Iran was under Shah Safi I (1629–42), who kept a policy of compromise with Georgia, similar to that of his grandfather Shah Abbas I (1587–1629). It meant leaving the country's socio-economic system unchanged, and maintaining the Bagrationi in power as the rulers of Georgia, holding the title of *vali* (viceroy), after their conversion to Islam.[1]

This new form of relation found its clearest expression during the reign of Rostom, also known as Khosrow Mirza, Bagrationi in Eastern Georgia (king of Kartli in 1633-58, king of Kartli and Kakheti in 1648–56). This chapter covers the cardinal moments in political relations between Iran and Georgia during these decades. It is based on information derived from a comprehensive exploration of the historical sources, which brought some matters to light for the first time.

Though various aspects of King Rostom's reign have already been studied, his personality and activity have not previously been treated objectively and directly. Some scholars assess his activity positively, others negatively. The period of Rostom's reign is so full of significant, sometimes contradictory, events and developments that the material describing it is far from being sufficient for scientific research. This makes the subject interesting. Even a simple glance over this period obviously testifies that the Muslim Georgian prince succeeded in performing his functions both in Iran as well as on the throne of Georgia, while being engaged in political warfare for a long time.

Here we are briefly concerned with Rostom's promotion in Iran. As is known, he was the son of Daud Khan and the nephew of the king of Kartli, Simon I. Rostom was brought up in Iran and consequently he was Muslim. His promotion at the royal court was contributed to by Giorgi Saakadze (the 'Georgian *mouravi*'): in 1618 he was appointed as *darughe* of Isfahan, later he held the post of commander-in-chief of the shah's guards – *qullaragasi*. Rostom reached the height of his power after the death of Shah Abbas, when he played a role in averting the danger to the Safavid court of a possible dynastic succession contest and in conformity with Shah Abbas's will played a decisive role in the enthronement of the shah's grandson Sam Mirza who, on his accession to the throne, adopted the regnal title of Shah Safi. Georgian sources provide ample evidence on these matters: the works of Beri Egnatashvili, Parsadan Gorgijanidze, Vakhushti Bagrationi (Batonishvili), the so-called *Paris Chronicle*; as do the Persian chronicles: Eskandar Beg's *Zayl*, Mohammad Ma'sum's *Kholasat al-siyar*, Mohammad Yusof's *Khold-e Barin*, and Mir Timur Mar'ashi's *Tarikh-e khandan-e Mar'ashi-ye Mazandaran*. The evidence from Persian sources is particularly important since they often record authentic and valuable information unrecorded in the Georgian sources. The evidence provided by European missionaries and travellers is also not devoid of interest.

According to Parsadan Gorgijanidze, after the accession of Shah Safi, Khosrow Mirza enjoyed immense prestige and authority.[2] Analogous evidence occurs in the accounts of Eskandar Eskandar Beg Monshi and Mir Timur Mar'ashi.[3] Vakhushti Bagrationi states, in addition, that the grateful young shah called Khosrow Mirza 'father'.[4] *A Chronicle of the Carmelites* informs us that one of the persons closest to the new shah was the *darughe* of Isfahan, Khosrow Mirza.[5] The success of Khosrow Mirza in Iran aroused the increasing discontent of the Undiladze – another very influential Georgian family. Thus, shortly after the death of Shah Abbas, two opposing Georgian groups were singled out: Khosrow Mirza with his supporters backed by Shah Safi; and the supporters of the Undiladze, headed by brothers Emamqoli Khan and Daud Khan. The most decisive consideration in this connection was the fact that further strengthening of the Undiladze family, who had been promoted at the court of his grandfather, no longer suited Shah Safi's interests. Besides, they were noted for their special sympathy for King Teimuraz – in 1626 Daud Khan helped King Teimuraz reascend to the throne of Kartli and Kakheti when Shah Safi had intended to make his faithful Khosrow Mirza, the crown prince, king of Kartli. In short Daud Khan was removed from state affairs and being frustrated, together with King Teimuraz, he rose in rebellion against Shah Safi in Ganje-Qarabagh in 1632. The details of this rebellion are widely known in historiography.[6] But as the above-mentioned revolt paved the way for and accelerated Rostom's enthronement in Kartli, we shall point out this fact.

Eskandar Beg Monshi, as well as the Italian missionaries Archangello Lamberti and Don Pietro Avitabile, state that the chief aim of the rebels was to make king of Kartli the son of Shah Abbas, who had been brought up by Emamqoli Khan, beglerbeg of Fars and was known as his foster son.[7] This would have enabled Teimuraz to consolidate his position on the throne. But events took a different course and the rebellion was put down by the shah's troops, led by *sepahsalar* Rostom Khan

Saakadze.⁸ In the aftermath Teimuraz lost his throne and found asylum in Imereti, while Daud Khan was forced into exile in the Ottoman Empire. The furious Shah Safi completely annihilated Daud Khan's remaining relatives, beginning with his innocent brother Emamqoli Khan.

With regard to the date of Rostom's enthronement, Mohammad Ma'sum informs us that Shah Safi issued a decree about it in Rabi al-sani, 1041 (November 1632).⁹ According to Georgian sources (Beri Egnatashvili, Vakhushti Bagrationi), Shah Safi named Khosrow Mirza Rostom and made him king of Kartli.¹⁰ Eskandar Beg specifies the following events: Rostom left Isfahan on 1 December (18 Jomadi al-avval). Due to awful weather and snow, he had to move slowly, taking rests from time to time.¹¹ It is clear that under such conditions, he might have reached Georgia either by the end of the same year or at the beginning of 1633. This is attested to by the data of Don Pietro Avitabile, stating that the last ravages of Ganje-Qarabagh by Teimuraz and Daud Khan took place on Christmas Eve.¹²

Soon after ascending the throne in Tbilisi, Rostom focused his attention on repairing fortresses and the deployment of *qizilbash* garrisons in them, as well as consolidating the government. To achieve this, the officials of Teimuraz were replaced by his trustworthy men. It is worth noting that before Rostom, Bagrat Khan and Simon Khan (kings of Kartli) had also held the title of *vali*, but in official documents of the Iranian shahs they are referred to as 'sons', while Rostom is referred to as a 'brother'.¹³ This obviously points to the fact that he was recognized as equal to the shah and enjoyed full rights. According to Beri Egnatashvili and Vakhushti Bagrationi, the shah granted lands to King Rostom not only in Georgia, but also beyond its borders, namely in Iran. Besides, he was given financial support.¹⁴ In return Rostom was bound to provide the shah with gifts, young girls and boys, and to render military aid. The *vali* was deprived of the right to establish foreign relations without the permission of the shah. The Safavid government reciprocated by refraining from attacking Christianity in Eastern Georgia and leaving the royal dynasty of the Bagrationi inviolable. This Safavid policy of compromise in Georgia opened the door to *qizilbash* influence: a number of Persian terms entered administrative nomenclature, replacing Georgian ones, though the offices themselves remained essentially unchanged; for example, *nazer, qullaragas, divanbeg, sardar, qorchibash*.¹⁵

Implementing a delicate and balanced policy, Rostom ruled the country with great care. By the time of his arrival in Kartli, he had already gained vital experience (he was about 70 years old then). Thanks to his high authority, Rostom remained *darughe* of Isfahan even after becoming king of Kartli, and continued to be so for the rest of his life. Only he was responsible for appointing his *na'ib* (deputy) there, while the shah approved his Georgian candidate readily, provided that the person appointed adopted Islam.¹⁶

First, Rostom firmly supported the shah's interests, without forgetting the adversity of his people and native land. On the one hand he laboured to revive Christian churches by launching building campaigns, on the other hand it was under Rostom's rule, that *qizilbash* traditions and posts were widely spread in Georgia. Beri Egnatashvili and Vakhushti Bagrationi inform us about it. Though, at the same time the latter stresses that Rostom did not abolish Georgian traditions either.[17] The French traveller Jean Chardin, who visited Georgia in 1672, also notes that Georgians followed Persian customs. He is quite right in suggesting the factors which influenced this process: some Georgian nobles were Islamized to be promoted as state officials, while others encouraged their ladies to become ladies at court.[18] Since many Georgian princes, kings and noblemen used to spend time in Iran, it is not surprising that Persian traditions spread throughout Georgia. Thus, this phenomenon should not be ascribed only to Rostom, since it had begun to be manifest prior to his reign. Against this background the increasing influence of Persian elements is quite apparent in Georgian culture from the sixteenth century and throughout the seventeenth century. It is particularly reflected in painting, architecture and literature. It is noteworthy that a great number of books were translated from Persian into Georgian, including the Qur'an, the *Rostomiani* (*Shahname*), the *Visramiani* and so on.

Rostom had to rule under the most wretched conditions: the deposed Teimuraz, supported by some noblemen, incessantly competed with him. In order to consolidate power in his hands, it was necessary to establish contacts with neighbouring kingdoms and principalities. No less important was the issue of the crown prince. Rostom was a childless widower and therefore needed a wife and offspring. Eventually it was decided to marry him to Mariam, the sister of Levan II Dadiani – the most powerful governor in Western Georgia Odishi (Mingrelia). This marriage would have provided Rostom with an alliance against Teimuraz and Giorgi III – king of Imereti. Being a faithful vassal, he naturally consulted Shah Safi about the decision. The latter approved his choice, as this marriage seemed to suit the interests of Iran by creating favourable conditions for the consolidation of power in the hands of persons loyal to the Safavid dynasty. In addition, it was deemed to set the scene for joint war against Imereti and, in case of a military campaign against the Ottoman Empire, the alliance with the Dadiani (who might potentially become vassals of Iran) would be of major significance.

Despite some divergences, the account of the marriage in Georgian sources (Beri Egnatashvili, Parsadan Gorgijanidze, Vakhushti Bagrationi)[19] is broadly similar to that in Persian sources (Mohammad Yusuf, Mohammad Ma'sum), stressing the decisive role played by Shah Safi. From then on, the government of Iran granted the Dadiani a salary of 1,000 *tumans* annually, in his turn the latter used to send ambassadors to Iran.[20] In connection with the above-mentioned fact, the brief information provided by the Italian missionary Don Juseppe Judichi Milanian (he visited Levan Dadiani in Mingrelia then),[21] as well as that of seventeenth-century Ottoman historians Mustafa Naima and Katib Chelebi, are of a certain interest. They make it clear that the Ottoman sultan was greatly worried about the news of Rostom's marriage. He regarded it as the demonstration of a hostile political act and carried out urgent measures to strengthen bordering regions.[22]

Thus, the marriage alliance of the Rostom and Dadiani families entailed considerable changes both in the internal political life of Georgia and in the international situation of the entire Middle East. Shifts in the political orientation of the king-governors, as well as in the internal balance of power in Georgia, were undoubtedly closely related to analogous processes in the relationship with Iran, Ottoman Turkey, Russia and West European countries. For instance, temporary peace between Rostom and Teimuraz in its turn conditioned significant changes in relations between Teimuraz and Shah Safi. But, prior to that, Teimuraz and the king of Imereti, Giorgi had attempted (unsuccessfully) to destroy Rostom's marriage. Under these circumstances Teimuraz found no way out other than to seek reconciliation with Rostom. Having apologized, he promised Rostom to send his daughter Tinatin to the shah. The delighted Rostom informed Shah Safi. Iran was then facing a grave political situation: the Ottoman Sultan Murad IV (1623–40) launched military operations against Transcaucasia, thus providing a stimulus to Iranian-Ottoman war. Under such conditions reconciliation with Teimuraz seemed to be timely and attractive in many respects. From Parsadan Gorgijanidze's report we learn that Rostom sent Teimuraz's daughter to Iran accompanied by Kakhetian nobles and a dowry, and that in return the shah confirmed Teimuraz as the king of Kakheti again. He married Tinatin, but not long after she was suffocated on his order.[23] Analogous evidence occurs in the account of the French traveller Jean Baptiste Tavernier.[24] Adam Olearius, Don Pietro Avitabile as well as Mohammad Yusuf and Mohammad Ma'sum describe the sending of Tinatin to Shah Safi, but do not mention her tragic death.[25] The account provided by the Russian ambassadors, E. Mishetski and I. Klucharev, who conducted negotiations with Teimuraz in Kakheti during 1641 to 1643, is different. According to them, Tinatin was murdered by Shah Abbas II.[26] The analysis of the above-mentioned evidence and the contemporaneity of the information given leads us to suppose that Tinatin might have arrived in Iran in autumn 1635–December 1637 and that she was murdered during the reign of Shah Safi. As mentioned earlier, Teimuraz reconciled with Rostom temporarily, but further difficulties emerged later. By then Iran was already ruled by Shah Abbas II (1642–66), who confirmed Rostom as the king of Kakheti too.

Considering Rostom's multi-faceted activities, it is important to deal with his attitude towards religion. Most remarkable here is the fact that, after his marriage to Mariam, there was clear and considerable progress in the development of Georgian culture and the Christian faith. Queen Mariam was renowned for her intense piety. The simple fact that their wedding ceremony was held according to Christian rites is in itself very telling. Don Pietro Avitabile, who attended this ritual, informs us that in conformity with the queen's request, Rostom had been baptized before the wedding ceremony. He repeatedly stresses that in spite of being Muslim, Rostom used to cross himself in the presence of his spouse, he liked to attend the liturgy and listen to church bells, and he protected Catholic missionaries working in Kartli as well.[27]

It is also noteworthy that Rostom's royal seal was adorned with a Christian cross. This sheds further light on Rostom's inner, genuine attitude towards Christianity, while in general he showed equal attention towards Orthodoxy, Catholicism and Gregorianism, and supported all of them materially as well. The above-mentioned Georgian and European sources unanimously attest this. However, we should not forget either that Rostom, being a personal protégé and henchman of Shah Safi, was predominantly a defender of Iran's interests in Georgia. Owing to this factor, his support for Christianity, or for national Georgian interests, was achieved with great care and tact. We would be wrong, moreover, to believe that every step taken by the king in this field was prompted only by affection towards the above-mentioned religions. First of all this was closely connected with his political goals and is, therefore, not surprising at all: being a far-sighted and vigilant politician, his religious activities satisfied the requirements of state policy. In order not to irritate alien eyes watching him, he could not and probably did not desire to reveal obviously his genuine attitude towards Christianity. There were many such observers in Georgia sent by the Shah – as, for instance, *vazir, mostawfi, monshi*. On the other hand Shah Safi greatly respected and trusted Rostom, sometimes even ignoring some inconvenient facts. This concession was considered as one of the components of the compromise policy carried out towards Georgia. At the same time the shah spared no efforts to win the favour of the Georgian noblemen. History provides ample evidence to illustrate this.

With regard to Rostom's attitude towards Islam, we can briefly state the following: if we follow the information in the sources, we can see that the Muslim faith was not firmly rooted in Georgia. The area of its active functioning was limited to the *qizilbash* garrisons deployed in the Tbilisi and Gori fortresses. Islamization chiefly applied to the upper stratum of society and, except in a few urgent cases, it was never forcibly imposed. Besides, adoption of this faith was a temporary and formal step for some Georgian nobles. It should be stressed that the population of the country fought against Islamization furiously, trying every possible way to avoid it.[28]

By the 1650s the growth of the political power and prestige of the unified Kartli-Kakheti kingdom, wielded under this astute and sensible king, as well as the revival of this region, were no longer desirable for Shah Abbas II. For this reason in 1656 Rostom was deprived of Kakheti and a *qizilbash* khan was appointed there instead. The Islamized Vakhtang V Shah Navaz (1658–75), a representative of the Bagrationi side branch (Mukhranbatoni), replaced the aged Rostom in Kartli. He was appointed as a *janeshin* (deputy) of Rostom. The latter died in 1658 and according to Georgian sources, he was transferred for burial in Qum in Iran.[29]

In connection with the above-mentioned facts, it is noteworthy to cite the viewpoint of David Marshall Lang, who stresses that Rostom was a leading figure and one of the accomplished kings of this late period of the Georgian monarchy. To conduct relations with the shah, the country needed a ruler of exactly this kind. The political flexibility exercised by him allowed the wounds of his country to heal.[30]

Thus, under the circumstances of the Safavids' compromise policy with reference to East Georgia, by following a moderate and balanced course, Rostom managed to preserve the state system of hereditary rule, the socio-economic structure in the country and, most importantly, the Christian faith.

Notes

1. Eskandar Beg Monshi, *Zayl-e Tarikh-e 'Alamara-ye 'Abbasi (Tsnobebi Sakartvelos shesakheb)*, ed. and trans. Nana Gelashvili (Tbilisi, 1981), p. 10.
2. *Parsadan Gorgijanidzis istoria*, ed. Sargis Kakabadze (Tbilisi, 1926), p. 238.
3. Eskandar Beg Monshi, *Zayl-e Tarikh-e 'Alamara-ye 'Abbasi* p. 64; *Tarikh-e khandan-e Marashi-ye Mazandaran, Ta'lif-e Mir Timur Mar'ashi*, ed. Manuchehr Setude (Tehran, 1977), pp. 370-2.
4. Vakhushti Bagrationi, 'Aghtsera sameposa Sakartvelosa', *Kartlis tskhovreba*, vol. IV, ed. Simon Qaukhchishvili (Tbilisi, 1973), p. 441.
5. *A Chronicle of the Carmelites in Persia and the Papal Mission of the XVII and XVIII cc.* vol. I (London, 1939), p. 279.
6. Gelashvili Nana, 'Daud Khanis da Teimuraz I-is ajankeba Eskander Beg Monshi's "Zeilis" mikhedvit', in *Matsne*, Series of history, archaeology, ethnography and art history, No. 2 (Tbilisi, 1977), pp. 103-11; Gelashvili Nana, 'Sakartvelo da Irani XVII saukunis 30-ian tslebshi', in *Kartuli diplomatia, tselits-deuli*, no. 3 (Tbilisi, 1996), pp. 187-208.
7. *Eskandar Beg, Zayl*, p. 31; Nasrollah Falsafi, *Zendegani-ye Shah 'Abbas-e Avval*, vol. I (Tehran, 1371).
8. See: Giorgio Rota, 'Three less known Persian sources of the seventeenth century', *Orientalist* I (Tbilisi, 2001), pp. 190-4.
9. Mohammad Ma'sum, *Kholasat al-siyar*, Institute of Oriental Studies of St. Petersburg, microfilm No. 27, fo. 73a-73b.
10. Beri Egnatashvili, 'Akhali Kartlis tskhovreba', *Kartlis tskhovreba*, vol. II, ed. Simon Qaukhchishvili (Tbilisi, 1959), p. 416; Vakhushti, Bagrationi *Aghtsera sameposa Sakartvelosa*, (History of Georgia) (Tiflis, 1745), p. 584.
11. Eskandar Beg, *Zayl*, p. 58.
12. *Avitabile Don Pietro, Tsnobebi Sakartveloze, XVII saukune*, ed. and trans. Bezhan Giorgadze (Tbilisi, 1977), p. 25.
13. Puturidze Vladimer, *Sparsuli istoriuli sabutebi Sakartvelos tsignsatsavebshi*, vol. I, no. 1 (Tbilisi, 1961), p. 48.
14. Egnatashvili, 'Akhali Kartlis tskhovreba', p. 110; Vakhushti Bagrationi, 'Aghtsera sameposa Sakartvelosa', p. 438.
15. Valerian Gabashvili, *Kartuli peodaluri tskobileba XVI-XVII saukuneebshi* (Tbilisi, 1958), p. 270.
16. Karlo Kutsia, 'Ispahanis Kartveli tarughebi', *Makhlobeli aghmosavletis istoriis sakitkhebi*, vol. II (Tbilisi, 1972), pp. 96-8.
17. Vakhushti Bagrationi, 'Aghtsera sameposa Sakartvelosa', p. 439.
18. *Jean Chardenis mogzauroba Sparsetsa da aghmosavletis skhva kveknebshi*, ed. and trans. Mzia Mgaloblishvili (Tbilisi, 1975), pp. 85-8.
19. Gorgijanidze, Parsadan, *Istoriia Gruzii*, trans. R.K. Kiknadze and V.S. Puturidze (Tbilisi: Metsniereba, 1990), p. 242; Egnatashvili, 'Akhali Kartlis tskhovreba', p. 420; Vakhushti Bagrationi, 'Aghtsera same-posa Sakartvelosa', p. 441.
20. Mohammad Yusuf, *Khold-e barin*, ed. Sohayli Khvansari (Tehran, 1317), p. 159; Ma'sum, *Kholasat al-siyar*, fo. 80a-80b.
21. *Don Juzeppe Judichi Milaneli, Tserilebi Sakartveloze, XVII saukune*, ed. and trans. Bezhan Giorgadze (Tbilisi, 1964), p. 34.
22. Shengelia Nodar, *Mustafa Naimas tsnobebi Sakartvelosa da Kavkasiis shesakheb* (Tbilisi, 1979), p. 190; Alasania Giuli, *Katib Chelebis tsnobebi Sakartvelosa da Kavkasiis shesakheb* (Tbilisi, 1978), p. 236.
23. Gorgijanidze, *Istoria*, p. 244.

24. Jean Batist Tavernier, *Beschreibung der Sechs Reisen in Turkey, Persien und Indien* (Genf, 1681), p. 56.
25. Adam Olearius, *Veremehrte neue Beschreibung der Muskowitischen und Persischen Reise* (Schleswig, 1656), p. 561; Don Pietro Avitabile, 'Tsnobebi Sakartveloze', pp. 14–28.
26. *Posolstvo knyaza E. Myshetskogo i I. Kluchareva v Kakhetiyu v 1640-1643 godakh*, ed. Mikhail Polievktov (Tbilisi, 1928), p. 176.
27. Avitabile, 'Tsnobebi Sakartveloze', pp. 20–8.
28. Gulkan Zhorzholiani, *Sakartvelo XVII saukunis 30-50-ian tslebshi* (Tbilisi, 1987), p. 61.
29. Egnatashvili, 'Akhali Kartlis tskhovreba', p. 435; Gorgijanidze, *Istoria*, p. 269.
30. David Marshall Lang, *The Last Years of the Georgian Monarchy (1658-1832)* (New York, 1957), p. 13.

Index

'Abbas I, Shah, 3, 5, 6, 21–6, 81, 85, 150, 192–3, 309, 491
    Caucasus policy of, 12, 471–89
    Christianity and, 310
    diplomacy by, 152–4
    embassy of Silva y Figueroa to, 161–80
    image of, 116–20
    in literature, 349
    Mughals and, 103–30
    Sistan and, 142–4
    victory at Sufiyan by, 91–101
Abd al-Gaffar Amilakhori, 484–5
'Abdi Bayg, 358
'Abdollah Khan II, 132, 141
'Abdullah Khan, 103
Abreu, don Miguel de, 185, 187–91
absolutist centralism, 27
account-book, of Sarhad, 285–90
Acem *tüccari*, 7–8, 246–8
Acosta, Francisco de, 181, 193, 194–7
Afghans, 27, 86, 87, 106, 319, 418, 419
Afshars, 132–3
Afzal al-Tavarikh, 12, 473–4
Agra, 105
Ahmadnagar, 114–15, 120, 122
Akbar, Jalal-al-Din Muhammad, 5, 103, 106, 108, 120, 121
'Ala' al-Dawle, 53–7, 68, 74n7
Alevîs religious movement, 19, 21
Alexandrine, Cardinal, 183–4, 185
'Ali Bali, 151, 154
All Saviour's Cathedral, 425–6
Allahverdi Khan, 483
Almeida, Francisco de, 105
dell'Altissimo, Cristofano, 347
Alvand, Prince, 17
Amasya, treaty of, 21, 82, 84–5
Amin Bayg, 151
Amir Hajji Mohammad, 135
Amir Sayf, 52
Amir Timur, 105
Amman, Jost, 297–300
Amsterdam
    Armenian merchants in, 8, 259–83
    Stock Exchange, 270–1
Anatolia, 18, 19, 21

Anatolian Muslim traders, 239–40
ancient texts, 329–41
anti-Catholic decrees, 376–7
Aq Qoyunlu, 17–19, 21, 24, 51–4
Armenian Church, 260–2, 268–9, 377
Armenian merchants, 7–8
    in Amsterdam, 259–83
    bookkeeping practices, 272
    commercial activities of, 285–90
    commercial terminology of, 447–55
    decline of, in Amsterdam, 279
    habits of, 272–3
    motivations of, for arrival in Amsterdam, 265–6
    residential pattern of, 266–8
    social life of, 258
    trading networks of, 273
Armenians, 2, 193, 197
    Catholic missionaries and, 10, 371–8
    Gregorian, 10, 11, 371
    Julfa, 447–55
    Swedish and, 256–7
Asad Bayg Qazvini, 121–5, 150, 152
aster motif, 416–18
Astrakhan Lawbook, 451–2
Augustinians, 10, 195–7, 365–9
Austria, 91–2
Ayutthaya, Siam, 387–8
Azerbaijan, 17–19, 51, 86, 322, 342n10, 474

Badi-al-zaman Mirza, 24
Baghdad, 57, 81, 153, 154
Bagrat, Prince, 475
balance of power, 5, 17–29
Baltic Sea, 8
Bandar Abbas, 4
Baqi Mohammad Khan, 138–9
Baron, Robert, 349–50
Bayezid II, Sultan, 53, 64–5
Bayg, Dangiz, 367
Bembo, Ambrogio, 317
Berze, Gaspar, 182
Bethlehem of the Maydan, 426–46
Bicudo, Matías, 181, 184, 186, 187, 190, 197
Bijapur, 110–11, 123, 126
border lords, 240–2

Borgia, Don Juan, 186
Borgia, Francis, 181, 183–5, 186, 197
British colonialism, 27
Budaq, Shah, 53
bullion, 38, 39, 40
Burhan Nizam Shah, 107–11
Bursa, 34
Bursa silk industry, 243–4
business jargon, 447–55
Butler, Samuel, 354

Cairo, 51, 56, 57
    envoys to, 58–64
Calvinists, 184, 317, 320–1
Cape of Good Hope, 42
capitals, 25
Capuchins, 315
caravansaries, 212
caravan trade, 2, 209–35
Carmelites, 196–7, 315, 368
cartography, 293–308, 327–8
Cartwright, William, 350–1
Caspian Sea, 8–9, 293, 303–4, 328
Catholic Church, 7, 181–203
Catholic missionaries, 10, 193, 310–11, 314–15, 321, 371–8
Catholic religious orders, 2
    see also Augustinians; Jesuits
Caucasus, 2, 11–13, 41, 86, 471–89
Central Asia, 2
ceramics, 34, 407–24
Chalderan, Battle of, 19, 20, 54, 66, 67, 73, 81, 105
chancellery documents, 25–6
Chardin, Jean, 314, 315, 357, 426, 460–1
Charles V, King, 181, 309, 310
Chinese porcelain, 407–8
Christian art, 13, 425–46
Christianity, 12, 194, 195, 309–10
Christian missionaries, see Catholic missionaries
churches, decoration of, 11, 425–46
Cingalazade Sinan Pasha, 93–100
Clement VIII, Pope, 181, 193–7, 367
clockmakers, 320–1
coinage, 25, 240
Collaert, Adriaen, 440
Colombe, Philippe, 319–20
colonialism, 27
Colonna, Marco Antonio, 184–5
commerce, 3–4, 7–8, 11, 22, 31–47
    account-book of Sarhad and, 285–90
    documents, 447–55

    see also trade
commercial terminology, 447–55
commodities, 3–4, 31–4, 40
Constantinople, 18, 73n4, 185, 321
contracts, 451–3
copper, 240, 247
Cordero, Alonso, 193
Counter-Reformation, 320
Coutre, Jacques de, 121
Creswell, Joseph, 194
Crusius, Philip, 254–5
Cruz, Redento de la, 368
cultural exchange, 2, 4, 8–11
    missionaries and, 314–15
cultural identity, 23, 28
custom duties, 212, 245–6, 248

Damascus, 54, 67, 72–3
    envoys to, 58–64
dar-al-saltanes, 24–5
Davrizhetsi, Arakel, 460
Day, John, 349
Deccan, 2, 5, 105, 106–15, 120–5, 126
Denham, Sir John, 349–50
Deshayes de Courmenin, Louis, 310
Din Mohammad Khan, 139, 142
diplomacy, 4–5
    with Holy See, 181–203
    nation-state, 87
    with Ottomans, 81–9
    with Spain, 6–7, 161–80, 181–203
    with Venice, 6, 149–60
    see also foreign relations
documents, 359–60
    chancellery, 25–6
    commercial, 447–55
Don Sebastian, King, 182
du Mans, Raphaël, 314, 321
Dutch, contacts between Armenians and, 263–5
Dutch East India Company, 39, 126, 263–5, 407

East India French Royal Company, 318–19
Ebn Mohammad Ebrahim, 379–94
Ebussuud Efendi, 83
economy, 3–4, 31–47
Egypt, 56, 71, 72, 186
Elizabeth I, Queen, 327
Emamqoli Khan, 482–4, 486
embassy trade, 41
Emperor of Iran, 3
English East India Company, 407
English literature, 9, 347–55

Eskandar Bayg Monshi, 358–9
Esmail I, Shah, 3, 4, 17, 19–21, 26, 27, 81, 131, 150, 309
   alliances of, 181–2
   envoys of, in Damascus and Cairo, 58–64
   portrait of, 347
   relations with Malmuks, 51–79
   Selim I and, 65–6
   Sistan and, 131–2
Estado da Índia, 105, 107, 120, 126–7
de l'Estoile, Isaac Boutlet, 316, 317, 321
de l'Estoile, Louis-Guilherme, 316–17
de l'Estoile, Alexandre, 318–19, 321
de l'Estoile, family, 316–19, 321, 323
Eurocentrism, 2
Europe
   alliances with, 18, 19
   contacts with, 1–3, 4, 9–10, 22, 27, 358–9, 447–54
   in Persian historiography, 9–10, 357–63
   trade with, 42
   see also specific countries
European travellers, 313–15
exchange contracts, 452–3
exoticism, 9, 347–55
exports, 34, 39

Fabre, Jean-Baptiste, 312
Fabritius, Ludvig, 8, 255–7
Farang, 357–63
Farangestan, 357–63
Farangi, 357–63
Farrokhabad, 483–4
Fayzi Fayyazi, 111–20, 127
fermans, 25–6
Feynes, Henry de, 321–2
fifteenth century, 17–19
Firishta, 108, 109–10
forced migration, 479–81
foreign relations, 2, 4–5
   Georgia, 459–70
   Ottoman Empire, 81–9
   Venice, 149–60
   see also diplomacy
France
   relations with, 310–11
   trade with, 312
François I, King, 310
Freire, Fulgencio, 186
French community, 9, 309–26

French East India Company, 311–12, 318–19
French literature, 9, 347–55

Galdor, Johannes di Jacob, 274–9
Gama, Francisco da, Count of Vidigueria, 103–5, 120, 193
Gama, Luís da, 126–7, 162, 164, 171
Ganj 'Ali Khan, 142–3
Gastaldi, Giacomo, 327–8
Geneva, 320
Genoa, 18
geography, 327–41
geopolitics, in sixteenth and seventeenth centuries, 17–29
Georgian-Iranian relations, 12–13, 459–70, 471–86, 491–8
Georgians, 2, 11–12
Germany, 181
Ghazan-Khan, 17
gholams, 12–13, 471–3, 475–6, 481–2
Gioerida, Ferdinando, 151
Goa, 6, 103, 105–7, 110, 125, 126, 161–3, 175–7
gold, 4, 39, 40
Golkonda, 110
Gouvea, Antonio de, 197, 214, 367–8
Great Northern War, 8, 257
Greaves, John, 307
Gregorian Armenians, 10, 11, 371
Gregory XIII, Pope, 181, 187–91
Grotius, 87
Gujarat, 106, 107, 109
Gunpowder Empires, 3, 22, 23, 26–8
Gustav II Adolf, King, 254

hajj, 84–5, 107
halting stations, on Qandahar-Isfahan route, 215–29
Henri IV, King, 310
Herat, 24, 25
Hidden Imam, 21
historiography, 357–63
Hodgson, Marshall, 3, 22
Holy Bethlehem Church, 11, 426–46
Holy League, 183, 186–7
Holy See, 181–203
Homann, Johann Baptist, 306
Hormuz, 107, 126, 182, 310
   Augustinian mission on, 10, 365–9
   Portuguese control of, 4–6, 37–8, 365–9
Hosayn 'Ali Bayg, 367
Huguenots, 9, 320
Humayun, 106
Hungary, 91

Husain Khan, 118
Ibrahim 'Adel Shah II, 110, 120–1, 123–4
iconography, religious, 425–46
identity game, 3, 23, 24
Il-Khanid dynasty, 3, 17
In Coena Domini, 182
India
    Maleks in, 140–1
    Mughal Empire, 5, 21, 23, 27, 103–30
    Portuguese in, 103–30
    trade with, 4, 7, 22, 32, 36–9, 207–9
Indian Ocean, 2, 22, 35, 207, 379–401
infernal triangle, 5, 103–30
infidels, 82
inter-imperial rivalry, 3
international trade, 3
    see also trade
intra-Asian trade, 2
Iran
    as nation-state, 82
    see also Persia
Iranian history, approaches to, 1–2
Iranian identity, 1, 3, 23, 24, 28
Iranzamin, 3, 18
iron, 240, 247
Isfahan, 3, 7, 17, 25, 86, 315, 483–4
    route between Qandahar and, 207–35
Isfahani, Fazli, 12
Islam, conversions to, 13, 491
Islamic Revolution (1979), 2
Isma'il, Shah, *see* Esmail, Shah
Italian city-states, 87
    see also Venice

Jahangir, Emperor, 126
Jahanshah, 17
Javier, Francisco, 182
Jenkinson, Anthony, 327, 348
Jesuits, 7, 11, 107, 181–203, 315, 437, 439
Jews, 2, 182, 479
Johnson, Samuel, 348

Kakheti, 13, 496
    see also Georgian-Iranian relations
Karbala, 84, 85
Karim Khan Zand, 28
Kartli, 12–13, 475, 477, 496
    see also Georgian-Iranian relations
Khan-e Khanan, 112, 116, 120–3, 125, 136
Khayr al-Din Pasha, 70
Khodabande, Muhammad, 191–2
Khorasan, 18, 24, 131, 132–4, 142
Khosrow Mirza, *see* Rostom, King

Khurasan, 64
Khvaje Mohammad, 150
Kirman wool, 34
Kraak porcelain, 408
Kurdish lords, 240–2
Kurds, 95, 97
Kustandil Mirza, 475–6

La Boullaye, *see* Le Gouz, François
Labrosse, Joseph, 315
land trade, *see* overland trade
Lane, Arthur, 408, 413
language, 23–4, 28, 447–55
Lascari, Costantino, 150
Law, John, 312
law of nations, 87
Le Gouz, François, 322
Lemaire de Belges, Jean, 347–8
Levant, 4, 39–40, 310
literature
    English, 347–55
    French, 347–55
    Persia in, 9, 347–55
    travel, 313–15, 321–2, 328–41, 379–94
Louis XIV, King, 311, 314, 322, 375
Luarsab II, King of Kartli, 11–12, 459–70, 477
luxury goods, 240–4

Maduny, Ceide, 182
Malek Hamze, 143, 145
Malek Jalal al-Din, 133–44
Malek Mahmud ebn-e Malek Haydar, 132–4
Malek Mahmud ebn-e Nezam al-Din Yahya, 131–2
Malek Mohammad, 139–40
Malek Shah Hosayn, 137–8, 140, 141, 143
Malek Zarif, 133–4
Maleks, 131–45
Mamluks, 4
    fall of, 66–73
    Ottomans and, 51–4, 66–73
    political relations with, 51–79
Mansur-e Bakhshi, Shah, 131–2
Manzikert/Malazgirt, Battle of, 18
map making, 8–9, 293
maps of Persia, 293–308, 327–8
maritime trade, 2, 4, 22–3, 31–2, 35, 37–8, 42, 43, 210–12
marriage, political, 477–9
Mas'ud Mirza Zell-al-Soltan, 28
Matthee, Rudi, 360
Maximilian II, Emperor, 182
Mazandaran, 479, 483–4

Mecca, 84
Medina, 84
Mehmet II, Sultan, 53
Mehrabanid Maleks, 131–45
Melo, Nicolás de, 193, 366
Meneses, Alejo de, 367
mental isolation, 3
Mercator, Gerhard, 328
merchants, 3–4, 7–8, 11, 43
   Armenian, in Amsterdam, 259–83
   Dutch, in Middle East, 263–5
   New Julfa, 285–90, 374, 447–55
metals, 240
military, 5
   decline of Ottoman, 91–101
   Safavid, 117
military slavery, 26
minorities, internal, 2
Miranda, Diego de, 194
Mir Jamal-al-Din Husain Inju Shirazi, 121–5
missionaries
   Catholic, 10, 193, 309, 310–11, 314–15, 321, 371–8
   French, 319–20
   Jesuit, 107
Mohammad-e Mofid, 24
Mohammad Rabi', 360–1, 380
monetary system, 25
Mongols, 3, 17
monks, 315
Moraes, Simón de, 365–6
Mourav Bayg, 484
Mughal Empire, 2–5, 21, 23, 27, 144–5
   expansion of, 106–8
   Portuguese and, 106–15
   relations with, 103–30
Muhammad Khan, 55
Murad, Sultan, 55
Murat III, 191–2
Murtaza Nizam Shah, 108, 110
Muscovite State, 253–4
Muslim societies, cultural exchange with, 2

Nadal, Jerome, 11, 434
Nader Shah, 28
Nader Shah Afshar, 17
Nader-Qolu, 17
Najaf, 84, 85
Narva, Sweden, 8, 256–7
nationalist approach, 1
nation-state diplomacy, 87
natural law, 87
Netherlands
   trade with, 8
   see also Amsterdam
New Julfa, 11, 425–6, 437
New Julfa merchants, 285–90, 374, 447–55
Nóbrega, Miguel de, 186
non-Muslims, attitudes toward, 2
Nova Delineatio Persiae et Confiniorum, 293–308

Olearius, Adam, 8–9, 293–308
Orientalism, 2
Ortelius, Abraham, 328
Ottoman Empire, 2, 3, 4, 18, 51, 149, 181
   Battle of Sufiyan and, 91–101
   decline of, 27
   French community in, 9
   Mamluks and, 51–4, 66–73
   military decline of, 91–101
   opposition to, 181–2
   Qezelbash and, 65–6
   relations with, 4–5, 21–2, 81–9
   trade with, 7–8, 237–51
   wars with, 5
overland trade, 35, 37, 207–35

padshah-e Iran, 17, 21
painting, 11, 430–41
Papal-Spanish-Persian relations, 7
partnership contracts, 451
Paul V, Pope, 191
peace agreements, Ottoman-Safavid, 84–7
Peace of Zohab, 156
Pepys, Samuel, 351
Persepolis, 7
Persia, 6, 7
   in English and French literature, 9, 347–55
   maps of, 293–308, 327–8
   see also Iran; Safavid Empire
Persian Gulf, 2, 4, 22, 23, 38, 126, 208
Persian language, 23–4, 28
Persons, Robert, 194
Philip II, King, 182, 183, 185, 187, 188–9, 192
Philip III, King, 161, 196, 367, 368
Picquet, François, 311
pilgrimage sites, 84, 85
Pius V, Pope, 7, 181, 183–7
Poland, 18
political conversions, 13
political geography, 17–18
political identity, 23
political marriages, 477–9
Pontchartrain, Jerome de, 312
porcelain, 34, 407–8
Portugal, 182

Portuguese, 22, 103-4, 105-30
  on Hormuz, 4-6, 37-8, 365-9
  Mughals and, 106-15
  relations with, 310
  trade and the, 207-8
Posset pots, 409-11
pottery, 10-11, 407-24
power balance, 2-3, 5, 17-29
Ptolemy, 305

Qal'e-ye Fath, 134, 137, 139-41
Qandahar, 4, 7, 18, 37, 136, 141, 143
Qandahar-Isfahan route, 207-35
Qansu al-Ghuri, 54, 56-9, 66-73
Qara Qoyunlu, 17-18, 51
Qazvin, 25
Qezelbash, 20, 21, 24, 26, 27, 55, 65-6, 72, 83
qezelbash tribes, 12, 477, 479

raw silk, 242-4
Red Sea trade, 4
regional balance of power, 3, 4
religion
  Christianity, 7, 195, 309-10
  hostilities over, 83-4
  impact of Shi'ism, 3
  importance of, 2
  Safavid, 19
  Shi'ism, 1-3, 20, 309-10, 1954
  state, 1
  Sunni, 19, 20, 309
  Twelver Shi'ism, 1, 3, 4, 19-21, 23, 309-10
religious iconography, 11, 425-46
Renaissance, 313
Richelieu, Cardinal, 310
road protection, 209-10
road security, 211
Rostam-al-hokama, Mohammad Hashem, 28
Rostam Mirza, 132-4
Rostom, King, 12-13, 491-8
Rota, Giovanni, 347
Rousseau, Isaac, 317-18
Rousseau, Jacob, 317-18
Rousseau, Jean-François-Xavier, 318
Rousseau, Jean-Jacques, 317-18
Rousseau, Joseph, 318
royal documents, 25-6
royal domains, 26-7
royal fermans, 25-6
royal *gholams*, 471-3, 475-6, 481-2
royal seals, 26
Rumlu, Hasan, 358

Russia, 2, 10, 86, 460
  trade with, 4, 8, 40-2, 253-8

Safavid Empire, 1
  balance of power and, 2-3, 17-29
  contacts with Siam, 388-93
  decline of, 27
  eastern borders of, 6
  economy of, 3-4, 31-47
  end of, 17, 28
  in English and French literature, 347-55
  establishment of, 54-5
  foreign relations of, 2-6, 81-9, 149-60
  French in, 9, 309-26
  geography, 327-41
  geopolitics in sixteenth and seventeenth centuries, 17-29
  historiography, 357-63
  maps of, 293-308, 327-8
  studies of, 2
Safavid frontiers, 2
Safavid religious movement, 19
Safi I, Shah, 12-13, 143, 491
Sahid, Anne-Marie, 318
Santa Ana, Diego de, 367
Sanudo, Marin, 150
Sarhad, Godge, 272, 273-4
Saruqaplan, 55
Sasanian Empire, 17
Savar, Shah, 53
Schipano, Mario, 329
seals, 26
Sebastian, King, 185-6
sectarian hatred, 83
Selim I, Sultan, 53, 238
  attack on Iran by, 66-73
  coming to power of, 64-6
Selim II, Sultan, 183
seventeenth century, 22, 27
Shahjahan, 126
Shahom Qorchi Sepahsalar, 132
Shakespeare, William, 348
Shaybak Khan, 59
Shaybani Khan Uzbak, Mohammad, 58
Shaybani Uzbeks, 2, 3, 4
Sherley, Antonio, 194-7, 309, 348-9, 367
Sherley, Robert, 348-9, 368
Shi'i Arab clerics, 2
Shi'ism, 1-3, 19, 20, 54, 309-10
The Ship of Solayman, 10, 379-401
Siam, 379-94
siege warfare, 5, 92-3

silk trade, 2, 7-8, 31-5, 40-2, 237-8, 242-4, 263-5
Silva, García de, 368
Silva y Figueroa, Don García de, 6-7, 161-80
silver, 4, 39, 240, 247
Simon II, King, 484-5
Sistan, 6, 131-48
    Uzbeks in, 134-9
Sixtus V, Pope, 191-3
slavery, 26
slave soldiers, 12, 26, 471-3, 477, 486
smuggling, 240, 241
Society of Jesus, *see* Jesuits
Solayman I, Shah, 151, 425
Soltan Hosayn, Shah, 17, 152
South Asia, economic links with, 4, 36
Spain
    diplomatic exchange with, 6-7, 161-80, 181-203
    relations with, 310
specie exports, 39
spices, 32
state provinces, 26
state religion, 1
St Petersburg, Russia, 8
Sufiyan, Battle of, 5, 91-101
sugar, 32, 38-9
Sulayman, Shah, 311
sulphur, 182
Sunnis, 2, 19, 20, 309
Sweden, 8, 253-8
Syria, 69-70, 71

Tabas, 7
Tabriz, 17-18, 24-5, 54
Tachard, Guy, 384
Tahmasb I, Shah, 6, 21, 131-2, 347
Tahmasb II, Shah, 17
Tahmasb-Qoli, 17, 476
Tarqun, 140-1
Taymurbay Hindi, 63, 64
Tehran, 25
Teimuraz I, King, 459, 477
textiles, 32, 33, 37, 38, 40, 41, 242-4
Thailand, 379-94
Thévenot, Jean de, 313
Tiepolo, Giovanni, 151
Timurids, 24, 51, 131
Tnegri Berdi Ughlan, 136-8
Trachtenbuch (Weigel and Amman), 297-300
trade
    caravan, 2, 209-35
    ceramics, 407-24

    with Dutch, 8
    embassy, 41
    with Europe, 42
    with France, 312
    with India, 7, 32, 36-9, 207-9
    international, 3
    intra-Asian, 2
    with Levant, 39-40
    luxury goods, 240-4
    maritime, 2, 22-3, 31-2, 35, 37-8, 42, 43, 210-12
    maritime trade, 4
    with Ottomans, 7-8, 237-51
    overland, 35, 37, 207-35
    Persian Gulf, 4
    Red Sea, 4
    routes, 4, 7, 8, 22, 31, 35, 37, 207-35
    with Russia, 4, 8, 40-2, 253-8
    scope of, 32-6
    silk, 7-8, 31-5, 40-2, 237-8, 242-4, 263-5
    with Sweden, 8, 253-8
    transit, 34-5, 42-3
transit trade, 34-5, 42-3
Transoxiana, 18, 22
travel
    by Europeans, 313-15
    Qandahar-Isfahan route, 207-35
travel literature, 313-15, 321-2, 328-41, 379-401
Turkish language, 23-4
Türkmens, 18-19
Turkomans, 51, 52
Turks, 181, 191-3
Twelfth Night (Shakespeare), 348
Twelve Imams, 20
Twelver Shi'ism, 1, 3, 4, 19-21, 23, 309-10

Uzbak Khan, 60-2
Uzbeks, 6, 22, 131-48
Uzun Hasan, 17, 18, 51-2, 72

Valle, Pietro della, 9, 327-45, 368, 460
van Sichem, Christoffel, 11, 431-4, 438
Vecchietti, Giovanni Battista, 190-1, 194
Velijanian, Petros, 439
Venetian-Safavid relations, 6, 149-60, 309
Venice, 6, 18, 149-60
Vermehrte Newe Beschreibun der Muscowitischen und Persischen Reyse (Olearius), 293, 297
Vidigueria, *see* Gama, Francisco da, Count of Vidigueria
Vienna, 18
Visnich, Hybert, 263-4
Voltaire, 353

warfare, 5, 92–3
War of Candia, 151, 156
War of the Holy League, 152, 156
War of Morea, 152
watch makers, 320–1
Weigel, Hans, 297–300
West
   contacts with, 3, 4, 27
   Iranian understanding of the, 357–63
   links with, 19
   see also Europe
Western Asia, 2
Wierix, Hieronymous, 34–5
wool, 34

world economy, 3, 31–47
world power, shifts in, 1–2

Yakan Khan Afshar, 132
Ya'qub, Sultan, 52
Ya'qub Khan, 118–19
Yishbak Khan, 52, 58
Yovhannes Mrk'uz, 425–6, 439

Zahir-al-Din Muhammad Babur, 105–6
Zamindavar, 136
Zoroastrians, 2
Zuhab, treaty of, 5, 81–2, 85–8, 248
Zu'l-Qadrs, 4, 52–5